W9-BJI-704

THE NEW AMERICAN COMMENTARY

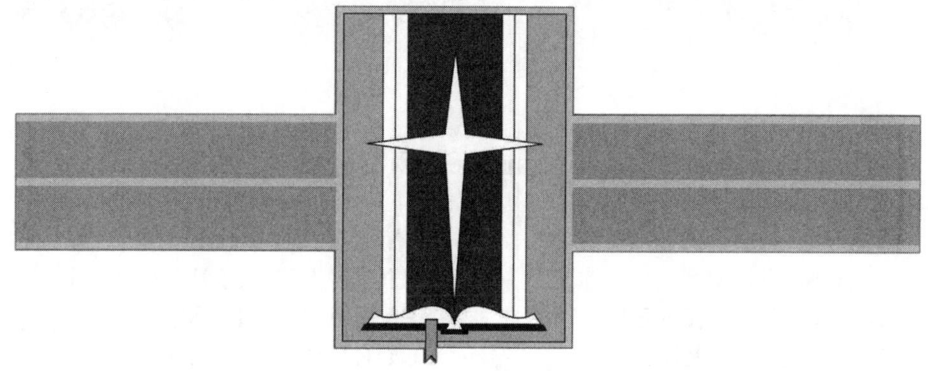

An Exegetical and Theological Exposition of Holy Scripture

THE NEW AMERICAN COMMENTARY

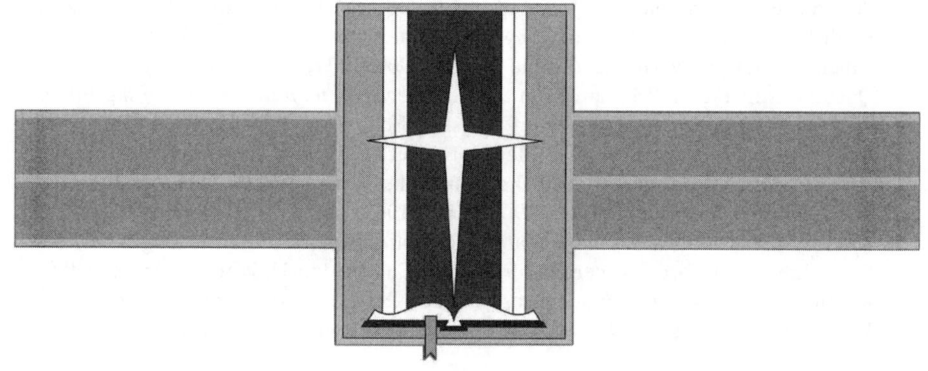

Volume
1A

GENESIS 1–11:26

Kenneth A. Mathews

Nashville, Tennessee

ISBN 978-0-8054-0101-1
Dewey Decimal Classification: 222.11
Subject Heading: BIBLE. O.T. GENESIS 1–11 \ CREATION
Library of Congress Catalog Number: 95–42762
Printed in the United States of America
16 15 14 13 12 11   16 15 14 13 12 11 10

Library of Congress Cataloging-in-Publication Data

Mathews, K. A.
Genesis 1–11 / Kenneth A. Mathews.
p. cm. — (The new American commentary ; v. 1A)
Includes bibliographical references and indexes.
ISBN 0–8054–0101–6 (HB)
1. Bible. O.T. Genesis—Commentaries. I. Bible. O.T. Genesis. English. New International. 1995. II. Title. III. Series.
BS1235.3.M37 1995
222'.11077—dc20

To Dea Grayce

Gift from God

וַיְבִאֶהָ אֶל־הָאָדָם (Gen 2:22)

Editors' Preface

God's Word does not change. God's world, however, changes in every generation. These changes, in addition to new findings by scholars and a new variety of challenges to the gospel message, call for the church in each generation to interpret and apply God's Word for God's people. Thus, THE NEW AMERICAN COMMENTARY is introduced to bridge the twentieth and twenty-first centuries. This new series has been designed primarily to enable pastors, teachers, and students to read the Bible with clarity and proclaim it with power.

In one sense THE NEW AMERICAN COMMENTARY is not new, for it represents the continuation of a heritage rich in biblical and theological exposition. The title of this forty-volume set points to the continuity of this series with an important commentary project published at the end of the nineteenth century called AN AMERICAN COMMENTARY, edited by Alvah Hovey. The older series included, among other significant contributions, the outstanding volume on Matthew by John A. Broadus, from whom the publisher of the new series, Broadman Press, partly derives its name. The former series was authored and edited by scholars committed to the infallibility of Scripture, making it a solid foundation for the present project. In line with this heritage, all NAC authors affirm the divine inspiration, inerrancy, complete truthfulness, and full authority of the Bible. The perspective of the NAC is unapologetically confessional and rooted in the evangelical tradition.

Since a commentary is a fundamental tool for the expositor or teacher who seeks to interpret and apply Scripture in the church or classroom, the NAC focuses on communicating the theological structure and content of each biblical book. The writers seek to illuminate both the historical meaning and contemporary significance of Holy Scripture.

In its attempt to make a unique contribution to the Christian community, the NAC focuses on two concerns. First, the commentary emphasizes how each section of a book fits together so that the reader becomes aware of the theological unity of each book and of Scripture as a whole. The writers, however, remain aware of the Bible's inherently rich variety. Second, the NAC is produced with the conviction that the Bible primarily belongs to the church. We believe that scholarship and the academy provide an indispensable foundation for biblical understanding and the service of Christ, but the editors and authors of this series have attempted to communicate the findings of their research in a manner that will build up the whole body of Christ. Thus, the commentary concentrates on theological exegesis while providing practical, applicable exposition.

THE NEW AMERICAN COMMENTARY's theological focus enables the reader to see the parts as well as the whole of Scripture. The biblical books vary in content, context, literary type, and style. In addition to this rich variety, the editors and authors recognize that the doctrinal emphasis and use of the biblical books differs in various places, contexts, and cultures among God's people. These factors, as well as other concerns, have led the editors to give freedom to the writers to wrestle with the issues raised by the scholarly community surrounding each book and to determine the appropriate shape and length of the introductory materials. Moreover, each writer has developed the structure of the commentary in a way best suited for expounding the basic structure and the meaning of the biblical books for our day. Generally, discussions relating to contemporary scholarship and technical points of grammar and syntax appear in the footnotes and not in the text of the commentary. This format allows pastors and interested laypersons, scholars and teachers, and serious college and seminary students to profit from the commentary at various levels. This approach has been employed because we believe that all Christians have the privilege and responsibility to read and seek to understand the Bible for themselves.

Consistent with the desire to produce a readable, up-to-date commentary, the editors selected the *New International Version* as the standard translation for the commentary series. The selection was made primarily because of the NIV's faithfulness to the original languages and its beautiful and readable style. The authors, however, have been given the liberty to differ at places from the NIV as they develop their own translations from the Greek and Hebrew texts.

The NAC reflects the vision and leadership of those who provide oversight for Broadman Press, who in 1987 called for a new commentary series that would evidence a commitment to the inerrancy of Scripture and a faithfulness to the classic Christian tradition. While the commentary adopts an "American" name, it should be noted some writers represent countries outside the United States, giving the commentary an international perspective. The diverse group of writers includes scholars, teachers, and administrators from almost twenty different colleges and seminaries, as well as pastors, missionaries, and a layperson.

The editors and writers hope that THE NEW AMERICAN COMMEN-

TARY will be helpful and instructive for pastors and teachers, scholars and students, for men and women in the churches who study and teach God's Word in various settings. We trust that for editors, authors, and readers alike, the commentary will be used to build up the church, encourage obedience, and bring renewal to God's people. Above all, we pray that the NAC will bring glory and honor to our Lord who has graciously redeemed us and faithfully revealed himself to us in his Holy Word.

SOLI DEO GLORIA
The Editors

Author's Preface

On Christmas Eve 1968, astronaut Frank Borman from the *Apollo 8* spacecraft, orbiting the moon, read a message for the people of the earth: "In the beginning, God created the heavens and the earth." Twenty-five years later, Borman reminisced, "I had an enormous feeling that there had to be a power greater than any of us. That there was a God, that there was indeed a beginning and that maybe even our choosing to read from Genesis wasn't a haphazard thing. Maybe it had been ordained in some way." The president of the Czech Republic, Vaclav Havel, in his remarks on receiving the Liberty Medal in Philadelphia at Independence Hall, July 4, 1994, commented: "Politicians at international forums may reiterate a thousand times that the basis of the new world order must be universal respect for human rights, but it will mean nothing as long as this imperative does not derive from the respect of the miracle of being, the miracle of the universe, the miracle of nature, the miracle of our existence. . . . The Declaration of Independence, adopted 218 years ago in this building, states that the Creator gave man the right to liberty. It seems man can realize that liberty only if he does not forget the one who endowed him with it."

My generation has witnessed both the quintessential achievement of human knowledge and the collapse of the tyrannical Soviet empire which had subjugated millions in Western Asia and Eastern Europe for seventy years. My goal has been to present a commentary on Moses' First Book which offers insights but also incites the church to proclaim the Bible's first words to such a world. Whether we are encircling the vast heavens or entangled in terrestrial turmoil, we as persons created in the "image of God" long to experience a right relationship with our Maker. Genesis presents the first word about our Creator, who has revealed himself to us and entreats us to know him. In the study of Genesis I have learned anew both how inconsequential humanity is in God's expansive universe and yet the immense value that he has placed on each individual human life. It has been said that we will know when civilization has come to an end when half of the world's population sits in front of the television watching the other half starve to death. In a world increasingly made up of affluent technocrats and desperate autocrats, Genesis is God's first word concerning his gracious and faithful purpose to bless all men and women. Although unseen satellites bring into our homes the global village, humanity remains intent on division along race and religious lines. Genesis is another first word that tells us we are all of one human family and that we can experience peace with and respect for all persons when we honor the dignity of "humanness." But Genesis also has a first word that tells us we are sinners and have spoiled the good world, pointing us toward another Word, the full and last Word, who alone achieves for those who trust him the blessing that humanity was created to enjoy. May the words of this volume honor the first words and be acceptable to the last Word.

Genesis and controversy are synonyms in ecclesiastical circles. One person observed, "Genesis 1–11 is a mine field." Those who have negotiated its fields without the aid of a mine detector have come away dismembered. What has helped me in traversing textual, exegetical, and theological challenges has been the long tradition of evangelical Christian interpretation to which I am indebted. A layperson remarked to me after learning of my writing this commentary on Genesis, "Don't we already have one of those?" Both in antiquity and as recently as this past year we have an abundance of evangelical commentators whose labors have clarified the issues and on a sound exegetical basis have treated reverently the text as Scripture. My own studies in Genesis resulted in agreement with the evangelical conclusions that have undergirded the march of the Christian church for these two millennia. Genesis requires the reader, if we are to agree with the author's perspective, to take the early chapters of Genesis as recounting historical events, telling of the Lord God's creation of the universe by his omnipotent word, the unique creation of individual Adam and Eve, the event of the garden's fall, and the dire consequences of the sin that showed itself wantonly in the generation of Noah and among his descendants at Babel. What the later apostles, the Early Fathers, and the sixteenth-century Reformers amplified and clarified in the early chapters of Genesis was not a misunderstanding of early Genesis but a recognition of the organic unity of Genesis and the unfolding revelation of canonical Scripture.

I am indebted to many in the writing and production of this volume. Especially do I offer thanksgiving to my wife and confidant, Dea G. Mathews, for her unwavering encouragement. A special word of appreciation is for E. Ray Clendenen, general editor of the NAC, whose labors resulted in helpful additions and whose friendship made the journey an easier road. The professional assistance by Broadman & Holman's manuscript editors, Linda L. Scott, Marc A. Jolley, and Trina Fulton, ably refined the manuscript's language and the book's appearance. Also I am grateful for the useful comments by my OT editorial colleagues of the NAC, L. Russ Bush, Duane A. Garrett, and Larry L. Walker. Still others who contributed recommendations were Frank Thielman, friend and colleague at Beeson Divinity School, and Kirk Spencer, former colleague at Criswell College. My students who assisted were Robert Hutto, Anthony Chute, and Jeffrey Mooney. I thank the cheerful and capable staff of the Davis Library, Samford University, particularly Jana M. Hamil, in obtaining resources. Also I acknowledge Timothy George, friend and dean of Beeson Divinity School, who remained a loyal advocate during the tenure of this project.

—Kenneth A. Mathews

Abbreviations

Bible Books

Gen	Isa	Luke
Exod	Jer	John
Lev	Lam	Acts
Num	Ezek	Rom
Deut	Dan	1, 2 Cor
Josh	Hos	Gal
Judg	Joel	Eph
Ruth	Amos	Phil
1, 2 Sam	Obad	Col
1, 2 Kgs	Jonah	1, 2 Thess
1, 2 Chr	Mic	1, 2 Tim
Ezra	Nah	Titus
Neh	Hab	Phlm
Esth	Zeph	Heb
Job	Hag	Jas
Ps (pl. Pss)	Zech	1, 2 Pet
Prov	Mal	1, 2, 3 John
Eccl	Matt	Jude
Song	Mark	Rev

Apocrypha

Add Esth	*The Additions to the Book of Esther*
Bar	*Baruch*
Bel	*Bel and the Dragon*
1,2 Esdr	*1, 2 Esdras*
4 Ezra	*4 Ezra*
Jdt	*Judith*
Ep Jer	*Epistle of Jeremiah*
1,2,3,4 Mac	*1, 2, 3, 4 Maccabees*
Pr Azar	*Prayer of Azariah and the Song of the Three Jews*
Pr Man	*Prayer of Manasseh*
Sir	*Sirach, Ecclesiasticus*
Sus	*Susanna*
Tob	*Tobit*
Wis	*The Wisdom of Solomon*

Commonly Used Sources

AB	Anchor Bible
ABD	*Anchor Bible Dictionary,* ed. D. N Freedman
AEL	M. Lichtheim, *Ancient Egyptian Literature*
Ag.Ap.	*Against Apion,* Josephus
AJSL	*American Journal of Semitic Languages and Literature*
Akk.	Akkadian
AnBib	Analecta Biblica
ANET	*Ancient Near Eastern Texts,* ed. J. B. Pritchard
Ant.	*Antiquities of the Jews, Josephus*
AOAT	Alter Orient und Altes Testament
AOS	American Oriental Society
AS	Assyriological Studies
AUSS	*Andrews University Seminary Studies*
AV	Authorized Version
BA	*Biblical Archaeologist*
BAGD	W. Bauer, W. F. Arndt, F. W. Gingrich, and F. W. Danker, *Greek-English Lexicon of the New Testament*
BARev	*Biblical Archaeology Review*
BASOR	*Bulletin of the American Schools of Oriental Research*
BDB	F. Brown, S. R. Driver, and C. A. Briggs, *Hebrew and English Lexicon of the Old Testament*
BHS	*Biblia hebraica stuttgartensia*
Bib	*Biblica*
BibOr	Biblica et orientalia
BibRev	*Bible Review*
BJRL	*Bulletin of the Johns Rylands University Library*
BJS	Brown Judaic Studies
BSac	*Bibliotheca Sacra*
b. Sanh.	Babylonian Talmud, *Sanhedrin*
b. Hag.	Babylonian Talmud, *Hagiga*
BSC	Bible Student Commentary
BST	Bible Speaks Today
BT	*The Bible Translator*
BZ	*Biblische Zeitschrift*
BZAW	Beihefte zur ZAW
CBQ	*Catholic Biblical Quarterly*
CBQMS	Catholic Biblical Quarterly Monograph Series
CD	Cairo *Damascus Document*
CGTC	Cambridge Greek Testament Commentaries
Comm.	J. Calvin, *Commentary on the First Book of Moses Called Genesis,* trans., rev. J. King
CSR	*Christian Scholar's Review*
CT	*Christianity Today*
CurTM	*Currents in Theology and Mission*
DSS	Dead Sea Scrolls
EBC	Expositor's Bible Commentary
Ebib	Etudes bibliques
EE	*Enuma Elish*

EGT — *The Expositor's Greek Testament*
EV(s) — English Version(s)
EvQ — *Evangelical Quarterly*
EvT — *Evangelische Theologie*
ExpTim — *Expository Times*
FOTL — Forms of Old Testament Literature
Gen. Rab. — *Genesis Rabbah,* ed. J. Neusner
Gk. — Greek
GKC — *Gesenius's Hebrew Grammar,* ed. E. Kautzsch, trans. A. E. Cowley
GNB — Good News Bible
GTJ — *Grace Theological Journal*
HAR — *Hebrew Annual Review*
HBD — *Harper's Bible Dictionary,* ed. P. Achtemeier
HBT — *Horizons in Biblical Theology*
HS — *Hebrew Studies*
HSM — Harvard Semitic Monographs
HTR — *Harvard Theological Review*
HUCA — *Hebrew Union College Annual*
IBC — Interpretation: A Bible Commentary for Teaching and Preaching
IBS — *Irish Biblical Studies*
ICC — International Critical Commentary
IDB — *Interpreter's Dictionary of the Bible,* ed. G. A. Buttrick, et al.
IDBSup — Supplementary volume to *IDB*
IBHS — B. K. Waltke and M. O'Connor, *Introduction to Biblical Hebrew Syntax*
IEJ — *Israel Exploration Journal*
Int — *Interpretation*
IOS — *Israel Oriental Society*
ISBE — *International Standard Bible Encyclopedia,* rev. ed., G. W. Bromiley
ITC — International Theological Commentary
ITQ — *Irish Theological Quarterly*
JAAR — *Journal of the American Academy of Religion*
JAARSup — *Journal of the American Academy of Religion,* Supplement
JANES — *Journal of Ancient Near Eastern Society*
JAOS — *Journal of the American Oriental Society*
JBL — *Journal of Biblical Literature*
JBR — *Journal of Bible and Religion*
JCS — *Journal of Cuneiform Studies*
JETS — *Journal of the Evangelical Theological Society*
JJS — *Journal of Jewish Studies*
JNES — *Journal of Near Eastern Studies*
JNSL — *Journal of Northwest Semitic Languages*
JPOS — *Journal of Palestine Oriental Society*
JRT — *Journal of Religious Thought*
JSOR — *Journal of the Society for Oriental Research*
JSOT — *Journal for the Study of the Old Testament*

JSOTSup	JSOT—Supplement Series
JSS	*Journal of Semitic Studies*
JTS	*Journal of Theological Studies*
JTT	*Journal of Translation and Textlinguistics*
Jub.	*Jubilees*
KB	L. Koehler and W. Baumgartner, *Lexicon in Veteris Testamenti libros*
KB^3	L. Koehler and W. Baumgartner, *The Hebrew and Aramaic Lexicon of the Old Testament,* trans. M. E. J. Richardson
KD	*Kerygma und Dogma*
LSJ	Liddell-Scott-Jones, *Greek-English Lexicon*
LW	*Luther's Works. Lectures on Genesis,* ed. J. Pelikan and D. Poellot, trans. G. Schick
LXX	Septuagint
MT	Masoretic Text
NAB	New American Bible
NASB	New American Standard Bible
NAC	New American Commentary
NB	*Nebuchadrezzar and Babylon,* D. J. Wiseman
NBD	*New Bible Dictionary,* ed. J. D. Douglas
NEB	New English Bible
NIB	The New Interpreter's Bible
NICNT	New International Commentary on the New Testament
NICOT	New International Commentary on the Old Testament
NJB	New Jerusalem Bible
NJPS	New Jewish Publication Society Version
NRSV	New Revised Standard Version
NRT	*La nouvelle revue the´ologique*
NTT	Norsk Teologisk Tidsskrift
OBO	Orbis biblicus et orientalis
Or	*Orientalia*
OTL	Old Testament Library
OTP	*The Old Testament Pseudepigrapha,* ed. J. H. Charlesworth
OTS	*Oudtestamentische Studiën*
PEQ	*Palestine Exploration Quarterly*
POTT	*Peoples of Old Testament Times,* ed. D. J. Wiseman
PTMS	Pittsburgh Theological Monograph Series
PTR	*Princeton Theological Review*
Pss. Sol.	*Psalms of Solomon*
RA	*Revue d'assyriologie et d'archéologie orientale*
RB	*Revue biblique*
REB	Revised English Bible
ResQ	*Restoration Quarterly*
RTR	*Reformed Theological Review*
SANE	Sources from the Ancient Near East
SBLDS	Society of Biblical Literature Dissertation Series
SBLMS	Society of Biblical Literature Monograph Series
SBLSP	Society of Biblical Literature Seminar Papers

SBT	Studies in Biblical Theology
Sib. Or.	*Sibylline Oracles*
SJT	*Scottish Journal of Theology*
SJLA	Studies in Judaism in Late Antiquity
SLJT	*Saint Luke's Journal of Theology*
SOTI	*A Survey of Old Testament Introduction,* G. L. Archer
SP	Samaritan Pentateuch
ST	*Studia theologica*
Syr.	Syriac
TD	*Theology Digest*
TDNT	*Theological Dictionary of the New Testament,* ed. G. Kittel and G. Friedrich
TDOT	*Theological Dictionary of the Old Testament,* ed. G. J. Botterweck and H. Ringgren
Tg(s).	Targum(s)
Tg. Onq.	*Targum Onkelos,* ed. B. Grossfield
Tg. Neof	*Targum Neofiti 1,* ed. M. McNamara
Tg. Ps.-J.	*Targum Pseudo-Jonathan,* ed. M. Mahler
T.Levi	*Testament of Levi*
TNTC	Tyndale New Testament Commentaries
TOTC	Tyndale Old Testament Commentaries
T.Rub	*Testament of Reuben*
TS	*Theological Studies*
TWOT	*Theological Wordbook of the Old Testament*
TynBul	*Tyndale Bulletin*
UF	*Ugarit-Forschungen*
Ug.	Ugaritic
UT	C. H. Gordon, *Ugaritic Textbook*
Vg	Vulgate
VT	*Vetus Testamentum*
VTSup	Vetus Testamentum, Supplements
WBC	Word Biblical Commentaries
WTJ	*Westminster Theological Journal*
YES	Yale Egyptian Studies
ZAW	*Zeitschrift für die alttestamentliche Wissenschaft*
1 Clem.	*1 Clement*
1QapGen	Genesis Apocryphon from Qumran Cave 1
2 Apoc.Bar	Apocalypse of Baruch, Syriac
4QDeut[q]	Deuteronomy text from fourth cave, Qumran

Contents

Genesis 1:1–11:26

INTRODUCTION OUTLINE

1. Commenting on Genesis
2. Literary Genesis
   (1) Structure
   (2) Contents
   (3) Conclusion
3. Genesis and Canon
   (1) Title
   (2) Genesis and Pentateuch
      Interdependence of the Pentateuch
      Structure of the Pentateuch
      Theme of the Pentateuch
   (3) Genesis and the Mosaic Community
   (4) Genesis and the Christian Proclamation
4. Theology of Genesis
   (1) Patriarchal Promises
      Blessing
      Seed
      Land
   (2) God and His World
   (3) Human Life
   (4) Sin
   (5) Civilization
   (6) Covenant
5. Interpreting Genesis
   (1) Innerbiblical
   (2) Jewish Interpretation
   (3) Christian Interpretation
   (4) Pentateuchal Criticism
      Source
      Form and Tradition History
      Revisionist Trends
      Traditional
      Literary Readings
      Canon

INTRODUCTION

Genesis stands second to none in its importance for proclaiming "the whole will of God" (Acts 20:27). It presents the literary and theological underpinning of the whole canonical Scriptures. If we possessed a Bible without Genesis, we would have a "house of cards" without foundation or mortar. We cannot insure the continuing fruit of our spiritual heritage if we do not give place to its roots. The first verse declares the metaphysical assumption, that is, a present transcendent Creator-God, that acts as the philosophical cornerstone of the entire biblical revelation. Just as we have no gospel without the cross, we would have no salvation story without the sacred events of Moses' first book. Although this is transparent for the ancestral account with its emphasis on the call of Abraham as the recipient of divine blessing (12:1–3), it is also true for the primeval history of chaps. 1–11. Israel's faith in God as Creator, not just Redeemer, provided "an all-embracing framework, as the fundamental, all-underlying premise for any talk about God, the world, Israel, and the individual."[1]

Our Christian proclamation of hope has antecedents in the theological soil of three divine programmatic expectations first heard in Genesis: (1) God will bless the human family with procreation and dominion (1:26–28); (2) he will achieve victory over mankind's enemy (3:15); and (3) he will bring about both through the offspring of Abraham (12:1–3)—namely, the one man Jesus Christ. Although in Genesis we discover the embryonic stages of God's historical-eschatological plan for all humanity, it is left to the unfolding revelation of God to nurture and clarify the outworking of that divine agenda by means of historic

[1] R. Rendtorff, *Canon and Theology,* trans. and ed. M. Kohl (Minneapolis: Fortress, 1993 [1991]), 107–8.

Israel and its Greater Son, Jesus of Nazareth, our Living Lord.

This Book of Beginnings gives at the start what we come to know and see confirmed through the complete collection of Holy Writ. What is said about God, human nature, the world, and salvation-history in the succeeding library of biblical books is already in microcosm in the Book of Creation and Blessing. Those books clarify, specify, and explicate; but there is "nothing new under the sun" of the precursory light of Genesis. Can we possibly understand Law and Gospel without their Genesis? Do we have Matthew and Luke's historical Gospel without the Genesis genealogies? Does not Paul's Galatians and Romans rely on Adam and Abraham? And can we still see the future Eden in John's Apocalypse without the imagery of Genesis's idyllic past?[2] It is not too much to say that as there is no community without its first parents, there is no Christian world and worldview without its "Genesis."

It is imperative in our day of pluralism to impart to the parishioner a gospel that has a coherent center that accommodates the whole of life's issues that men and women seek to have answered. This gospel is not a potpourri of disparate ideas but a unified revelation in history, interpreted by the sacred Scriptures. It has its pinnacle in the cross and resurrection of our Savior, who alone holds all things together in his one Person (Col 1:16–17). Creator and creatures, the now and the not-yet, life and death, Eden lost and Eden regained, virtues and vices, family kinship and the community of nations—all these and more are the theological substance of the Book of First Things. In the language of Genesis, let us "covenant" together to proclaim these things of the past so that we now at the end of our century and with the view to the next might encourage our brethren to endure in faith and hope (Rom 15:4).

1. Commenting on Genesis

The scholarly literature concerning Genesis could be appropriately named "Legion." No attempt will be made here to untangle every historical-critical problem that can be found in Genesis 1–11. Rather, a middle course will be taken to confront the exegetical-theological concerns that have made Genesis such a delectable feast for commentators and critics alike. The focus is a literary-theological exposition of the text that draws on its compositional features with the aim of detecting what is highlighted by the text itself. Biblical exposition is that which permits the text—both its contents and its shape—to dictate the meaning. The intention of a biblical composition is rarely stated; rather it is to be inferred. Thus we must depend on the grammatical and narrative structure as signposts. Only through the window of the text can we discern the intent of the ancient writer.

---

[2] See, e.g., the chart "Restoration of Edenic Ideals," in L. E. Cooper, *Ezekiel,* NAC (Nashville: Broadman & Holman, 1994), 349.

From a study of the extant shape of the text, we propose to derive its theological contribution to canonical revelation, expressing it in its own terms and not in the philosophical categories of systematics. Furthermore, we will not be distracted by incessant attention to actual or putative literary sources as commentaries on Genesis often do. We will mention these briefly, for it is necessary to do so where the sources impact theological concerns, but even there they are not fully treated.

We are satisfied that Genesis in its present, final form is a cohesive unit that shows thoughtful order and a self-consistent theology. This, we believe, can be demonstrated. Essentially, there is one mind that has shaped the book, whom we believe to have been Moses. Therefore we are comfortable speaking of that mind as "author," though most likely some compiling of sources was involved. So we will speak of an "author/compiler." We welcome the new attention given by biblical scholars to the canonical form of the text, and we hope that our remarks will contribute to the church's apprehension of the holistic message of Genesis.

Our goals then will be to describe the literary and theological contours of the composition in light of the book's macrostructure. Since we are well aware that Genesis is not an autonomous work but is introductory to the "book" of Moses (i.e., the Pentateuch), we also invite the larger canonical setting of the Torah to inform us concerning the meaning of Genesis and how its message functioned in the Mosaic community. Also since ours is a Christian understanding of Genesis, we address how the passage speaks to the Christian community as we are guided by New Testament interpretation. Thus we will set each passage in the theological contexts of succeeding stages of interpretive meaning: (1) Genesis and Israel's Torah and (2) Genesis and the Christian canon.

This Introduction intends to orient the reader to special matters necessary for the commentary discussion. Since our commentary centers on literary-theological concerns, the Introduction speaks to the literary and theological features of Genesis as a literary creation of sacred Writ. Commentary on Genesis has a three thousand-year history, but we can only highlight a few of the most productive eras as we review how Genesis has been read in the past. Also because Genesis is a product of antiquity, we will consider its ancient context where it fits most naturally and without which it cannot be rightly understood. Simply put, it is methodologically superior to start with Genesis in the historical-cultural context of its original audience (though we dare not leave it there) before we relate it to our contemporary context. There are also the inescapable problems that arise when reading the creation account against the background of modern science. If we are to formulate a Christian worldview that is inclusive, we must give attention to it. This calls for a discussion of the Books of Scripture and Nature.

2. Literary Genesis

The literary makeup of Genesis is analogous to the architectural features of a stained-glass window adorning an edifice. At a distance the viewer sees the window holistically and recognizes the identity of the scene or person depicted in the representation; but as the glass collage is approached, it reveals the intricate design of the juxtaposed pieces—differing in shape, size, and color—whose lines, unnoticed from afar, become obvious to the eye. Genesis is a complex literary composition with symmetrical unity but a diversity of genres (e.g., narrative, genealogy, and lyric poetry).[3] These literary pieces, some previously written and some original compositions by the author, have been brought together by the author/compiler, who did not always blend them to our satisfaction. Yet together they form an unmistakably coherent, unified story line.

The Joseph story (chaps. 37–50), for example, possesses a different rhetorical style from the preceding patriarchal narratives and can be read as an independent, self-standing discourse. Yet it has been integrated into the structure of the whole by means of the book's framing device (NIV "account," *tôlĕdōt,* 37:2) so that it makes a vital contribution to the book's overarching theme. These chapters show how the Jacob family fared after the patriarch's return to Canaan and how God preserved the family and thus the promise, placing the Jacob clan of "seventy souls" (AV, Gen 46:27; Exod 1:5) in Egypt. Also we can consider within the Joseph narrative the embedded Judah and Tamar account (chap. 38), which appears at first reading to be foreign to the narrative flow of a consecutive plot line. Its placement shows that the compiler was not opposed to such disjunctures in fastening his materials. There has been a joining of two literary elements: the Joseph story proper (chaps. 37; 39–48) and the wider narrative of Jacob and the family (chaps. 38; 49–50).[4] Yet it is not a mere adding

---

[3] In accord with H. Gunkel's form criticism and its heir, tradition history, it is commonplace to carve Genesis into numerous small, literary pieces, designate their genre (e.g., heroic sagas and sundry "reports"), imagine their setting of composition, and trace their oral history to their reduction to writing. See, e.g., G. W. Coats, *Genesis: With an Introduction to Narrative Literature,* FOTL 1 (Grand Rapids: Eerdmans, 1984). This method has been seriously challenged, and the form categories assigned to the individual units have been found to be anachronistic or meaningless. See B. K. Waltke, "Oral Tradition," in *A Tribute to Gleason Archer,* ed. W. Kaiser and R. Youngblood (Chicago: Moody, 1986), 17–34; R. N. Whybray, *The Making of the Pentateuch: A Methodological Study,* JSOTSup 53 (Sheffield: JSOT, 1987) 133–219; and D. Garrett, *Rethinking Genesis: The Sources and Authorship of the First Book of the Pentateuch* (Grand Rapids: Baker, 1991), 35–50.

[4] See R. E. Longacre, whose study recognizes the two strands (*Joseph, A Story of Divine Providence: A Text Theoretical and Textlinguistic Analysis of Genesis 37 and 39–48* [Winona Lake: Eisenbrauns, 1989], 22). Longacre attributes the inclusion of the Judah-Tamar story by the author in part to the building of suspense in the plot line, "to leave his reader dangling for a while—even as the whole family was left in total ignorance of what happened to Joseph for some thirteen years" (p. 26).

of another story regarding a son of Jacob.[5] Rather it advances the book's thematic concern for the spiritual succession of the promises within the Joseph pericope. Chapter 38 involves the motif of barrenness (though here due to the fault of the men, not the woman), which echoes the recurring trauma of a missing heir in the Abraham clan (Abraham-Sarah, Isaac-Rebecca, Jacob-Rachel). The Judah-Tamar story concludes with another echo of the past, the birth struggle of twins, reminding the reader of the birth of Esau and Jacob (chap. 25). This sibling rivalry pattern occurs when Zerah, whose hand first emerged from Tamar's womb, is supplanted by his twin, Perez. This brings to the fore the recurring issue of patriarchal succession. Reuben, Jacob's eldest son, and Simeon and Levi, next in line, had disqualified themselves to succeed Jacob by their treacherous actions against their father (34:18–31; 35:22).

Whereas Joseph's dreams in chap. 37 appeared to designate him as the successor to Jacob, chap. 38 hints by virtue of the odd birth of Judah's twins, Perez and Zerah, that the lineage of Judah-Perez would carry forth the Jacob tradition. This is confirmed in the blessing of Jacob upon Judah (49:8–12), which possesses allusions to the Judah-Tamar account.[6] Judah therefore would prove after all to be the preeminent son of the Jacob household. Moreover, Judah's sordid deeds in the story contribute to the book's developing picture of the sons' moral deficiencies, jeopardizing their spiritual heritage. The Egypt sojourn arrests this decline in part, for their Egyptian hosts segregated the Hebrews (43:32), which encouraged them to value the spiritual heritage of their father Abraham. When the Judah-Tamar account is seen in such light, it is not extraneous to the purpose of the Joseph narrative. What the Western reader therefore may perceive as incongruous did not bother the procedure of the biblical author, who let his sources stand with their "rough edges," resulting in a richer and more complex literary texture.

(1) Structure

We should not be surprised that a complex of genealogies and stories as we find in Genesis would give itself to varying structural analyses, though there are some general lines of agreement among scholars. It is agreed that the content of chaps. 1–11 distinguishes it from the patriarchal stories found in chaps. 12–50, though there is dispute about where exactly the so-called "Primeval History" ends. Also within the early chapters we can discern four accounts that are found with sundry genealogies: creation, human life in and outside the garden (Adam/Eve; Cain/Abel), Noah's flood, and the Tower of Babel. Among the

---

[5] So C. Westermann, *Genesis 37–50: A Commentary,* trans. J. Scullion (Minneapolis: Augsburg, 1986 [1982]), 49.

[6] See J. Goldin, "The Youngest Son or Where Does Genesis 38 Belong?" *JBL* 96 (1977): 27–44, and Garrett's argument for the unity of the Joseph narrative, *Rethinking Genesis,* 173–77.

patriarchal accounts are three narrative collections: the Abraham, Jacob, and Joseph stories. The absence of a distinctive Isaac collection is due to his marginal role as a transition figure, overshadowed by both father (Abraham) and son (Jacob). Also all are agreed that the *tōlĕdōt* (NIV "account," AV "generations") superscriptions and the genealogies are critical to the broader structural outline of the book.

At the surface level the prominent literary device in the book is the genealogical rubric, "this is the account of" (AV, "these are the generations [*tōlĕdōt*] of"). Its occurrences in Genesis point to possible pre-Genesis sources (e.g., 5:1) but also provide a clue for the significance of genealogy for the macrostructure of the book.[7] Rather than the usual Hebrew term for "generation" *(dôr),* the word *tōlĕdōt* ("begettings") is used, from the verb *yālad* ("to bear, beget"). It is commonly used to introduce a list of descendants or a tribal genealogy, both in and outside Genesis.[8] Often the *tōlĕdōt* reference includes a brief biographical or historical description (e.g., Noah, 6:9). Such notes are well attested for genealogies and king lists in the ancient Near East, as in the Sumerian King List. However, the *tōlĕdōt* phrases at 2:4 and 37:2 are followed immediately by extensive narrative. In attempting to resolve this difficulty, translations suggest that *tōlĕdōt* in the catchphrase is broader in use than "generation," meaning narrative "account" (2:4; 37:2) or "story of the family" (NRSV, 37:2). It is likely, however, that 2:4 is an imitation of the *tōlĕdōt* language found in Genesis. Its purpose is to show a succession in creation, narrowing attention on the "earth" in chap. 2 (see commentary). Genesis 37:2 can be explained as the formal *tōlĕdōt* heading for Jacob's genealogy, which follows the Joseph narrative at 46:8–27. The placement of Jacob's genealogy after the Joseph corpus was expedient since the Joseph episode would explain how Joseph's sons were born in Egypt, outside Canaan (46:26–27).[9] The detached *tōlĕdōt* at 37:2 then demarcated the Joseph story as it had marked the previous patriarchal cycles (11:27; 25:19), giving a symmetry to the *tōlĕdōt* use in the patriarchal narratives.

If we follow the *tōlĕdōt* phrases as providing the book's infrastructure, they divide the book into twelve sections, the *tōlĕdōt* formula introducing all but the first:

Section I	Creation of Heaven and Earth (1:1–2:3)
Section II	The *Toledot* of Earth's Family (2:4–4:26)
Section III	The *Toledot* of Adam's Line (5:1–6:8)
Section IV	The *Toledot* of Noah (6:9–9:29)

[7] 2:4; 5:1; 6:9; 10:1; 11:10,27; 25:12,19; 36:1,9; 37:2. Beyond this stereotypical phrase in Genesis, the word תּוֹלְדוֹת occurs in Gen 10:32 and 25:13. Outside Genesis, וְאֵלֶּה תּוֹלְדוֹת "these are the generations of" occurs in Num 3:1 and Ruth 4:18; cp. also 1 Chr 1:29.

[8] E.g., Gen 5:1; 10:1; 11:10; 11:27; 25:19; 36:1,9; Exod 6:16; Num 1:20; 3:1; 1 Chr 1:29; 5:7.

[9] So Garrett, *Rethinking Genesis,* 100.

Section V	The *Toledot* of Noah's Sons: Shem, Ham, and Japheth (10:1–11:9)
Section VI	The *Toledot* of Shem (11:10–26)
Section VII	The *Toledot* of Terah: Abraham (11:27–25:11)
Section VIII	The *Toledot* of Ishmael (25:12–18)
Section IX	The *Toledot* of Isaac: Jacob (25:19–35:29)
Section X	The *Toledot* of Esau and Family (36:1–8)
Section XI	The *Toledot* of Esau (36:9–37:1)
Section XII	The *Toledot* of Jacob: Joseph (37:2–50:26)

The significance of the *tōlĕdōt* phrase for the structure of Genesis and its possible pre-Genesis sources has no consensus. A number of problems are created by the appearance of the *tōlĕdōt* phrase that have not been satisfactorily answered.[10] At times the superscription appears to relate more to the preceding material (e.g., Adam, 5:1); at other times the person named is the subject of the section (e.g., Noah, 6:9); and still at other places the superscription names the father of the descendant who is the subject of the subsequent material (e.g., Terah, 11:27). Its placement does not always seem to be at the most reasoned junctures. What has been segregated by the rubric at points cuts across what seems to belong together (e.g., Esau's genealogy twice, 36:1 and 36:9), and what would appear to belong to separate sections are found under the same heading, such as the narrative conclusion (6:1–8) to the Sethite genealogy (5:1–32). Also the contents of the *tōlĕdōt* sections vary considerably in length and character. For example, some comprise primarily genealogy (e.g., 5:1; 11:10) and others narrative (2:4; 37:2). Coupled with this is whether the *tōlĕdōt* headings indicate pre-Genesis written sources of family records (e.g., "written account," 5:1a) constituting genealogy or narrative or both genealogy and narrative. If taken as a series of written family records, do we have in Genesis the register/story in its entirety or only in part? Moreover, there is even some dispute about whether the formula introduces a new section or concludes the former material.

Distinct patterns appear among the *tōlĕdōt* sections, although the sections are not perfectly symmetrical. The three patriarchal collections—Abraham, Jacob, and Joseph—intersperse genealogy:[11]

Toledot of Shem (11:10–26)
    Abraham narratives (*tōlĕdōt* of Terah) (11:27–25:11)
Toledot of Ishmael (25:12–18)
    Jacob narratives (*tōlĕdōt* of Isaac) (25:19–35:29)

[10] Among recent attempts is the proposal of T. D. Andersen ("Genealogical Prominence and the Structure of Genesis," in *Biblical Hebrew and Discourse Linguistics,* ed. R. Bergen [Dallas: Summer Institute of Linguistics, 1994], 242–66), who suggests a consistent internal structure for the story *tōlĕdōt* sections (i.e., heavens and earth, Noah, Terah, Isaac, and Jacob); but the exceptions to his proposed pattern are many and not always easily explained.

[11] Noted in G. Wenham, *Genesis 1–15,* WBC (Waco: Word, 1987), 248.

Toledot of Esau (36:1–8; 36:9–37:1)
Joseph narratives (*tōlĕdōt* of Jacob) (37:2–50:26)

To achieve this arrangement, however, the puzzling repetition of the *tōlĕdōt* phrase for Esau at 36:1 and 36:9 must be ignored, collapsing the two as one piece. When we add early Genesis, treated as one block, we have a fourfold arrangement intersected by genealogy:

1. Creation and Early Mankind (1:1–11:9)
   Genealogy of Shem (11:10–26)
2. Abraham's story (11:27–25:11)
   Genealogy of Ishmael (25:12–18)
3. Jacob's story (25:19–35:29)
   Genealogy of Esau (36:1–8; 36:9–37:1)
4. Joseph's story (37:2–50:26)

This arrangement must also collapse the Esau genealogies and obviously disregard the *tōlĕdōt* catchphrase as a separate heading for the genealogies at 5:1–32 and 10:1–32. Another alternative is a grouping of five units for both the early history and the patriarchal narratives:[12]

Heaven and Earth (1:1–4:26)	Terah (Abraham) (11:27–25:11)
Adam (5:1–6:8)	Ishmael (25:12–18)
Noah (6:9–9:29)	Isaac (Jacob) (25:19–35:29)
Noah's Sons (10:1–11:9)	Esau-Edom (36:1–37:1)
Shem (11:10–26)	Jacob (Joseph) (37:2–50:26)

This follows generally the recurring *tōlĕdōt* pattern, though also collapsing the Esau lists, and also has the advantage of recognizing the Noah and Jacob accounts as the central episodes in each half. The overriding difficulty, however, is that it must ignore the *tōlĕdōt* phrase at 2:4, which distinguishes between the creation and garden narratives.

Scholars have recognized a similarity, at least to some degree, in the contents of Genesis 1–11 and the Babylonian myth of origins, *Atrahasis*. I. Kikawada and A. Quinn proposed by thematic and structural parallels between chaps. 1–11 and the Babylonian myth that they reflect an ancient literary convention.[13] The myth tells of the creation of mankind and of their surviving three divine threats, the second containing a double threat and the third a flood. It concludes on a compromise agreed among the gods that imposed limits on human population growth but assured its preservation. The broad outline then possesses three movements: Creation, Threats, Resolution. The early chapters of Genesis were viewed similarly by Kikawada and Quinn, but there

[12] So J. Blenkinsopp, *The Pentateuch: An Introduction to the First Five Books of the Bible* (New York: Doubleday, 1992).

[13] I. Kikawada and A. Quinn, *Before Abraham Was: A Provocative Challenge to the Documentary Hypothesis* (Nashville: Abingdon, 1987), 36–53.

the three threats concern the promissory blessing, the second also having a double threat, and the third, Noah's flood: (1) Adam's Sin, (2a) Cain and Abel, (2b) Lamech's taunt, and (3) flood. The Genesis counterpart to the Resolution is 10:1–11:32, including Abraham's departure from Ur. Kikawada and Quinn's arrangement of chaps. 1–11 also accounted for the genealogies, with the result that they intersect the narrative as we saw earlier:[14]

A Creation (1:1–2:3)
  Genealogy=Heaven and Earth (2:4)
B Adam and Eve (2:5–3:24)
  Genealogy=Eve's Sons (4:1–2)
C Cain and Abel (4:3–16)
  Genealogy=Cain's Line (4:17–22)
C′ Lamech's Taunt (4:23–24; 4:25–26?)
  Genealogy=Adam/Seth (5:1–32)
D Noah's Flood (6:1–9:29)
  Genealogy=Nation Table (10:1–32)
E Dispersion (11:1–9)
  Genealogy=Shem's Line (11:10–26)

What immediately strikes us is that the *tōlĕdōt* catchphrase does not occur at 4:1–2 and 4:17 for the genealogies of Eve's son and Cain's line. There is an attempt to accommodate the *tōlĕdōt* markers, but it is not altogether successful. D. Garrett in his *Rethinking Genesis* improved on Kikawada and Quinn's analysis, proposing that the Creation-Threat-Resolution structure of chaps. 1–11 served as a guide for the whole of Genesis, with the threats concerning the preservation of the Abrahamic offspring:[15]

Prologue	Primeval History	1:1–11:26
Transition	Genealogy	11:27–32
Threat	Abrahamic Cycle	12:1–25:11
Transition	Genealogy	25:12–18
Threat	Jacob Cycle	25:19–35:22b
Transition	Genealogy	35:22c–36:43
Threat	Joseph Cycle	37:1–46:7
Transition	Genealogy	46:8–27
Resolution	Settlement in Egypt	46:28–50:26

What is attractive about the work of Kikawada-Quinn is the attempt to relate Genesis to an attested ancient Near Eastern form concerning origins *(Atrahasis)* as opposed to the theoretical form and tradition history reconstructions commonly attempted. The proposal by Garrett is helpful since it tries to work

[14] Ibid., 60. We have supplied the Scripture references in part from their earlier plot outline at pp. 47–48.

[15] Garrett, *Rethinking Genesis,* 123.

with the most obvious redactional element in the book *(tōlĕdōt)*. But there is reason to question whether almost any story would not involve the idea of threat and final resolution, especially one including a flood.[16] Kikawada and Quinn find the similar model in a Zoroastrian tale and apply it to several other stories in the Bible, such as David and Bathsheba, Exodus 1–2, and Matthew 1–3, which follow the same plot of Genesis 1–11.

Another recent attempt at finding the structural key to Genesis is G. Rendsburg's *The Redaction of Genesis.* Rendsburg appeals to redactional structuring, such as parallel and chiastic structures. The patriarchal cycles—Abraham, Jacob, and Joseph—are chiastic, and the primeval history is parallel in structure. Although some value is found in his treatment of the patriarchal cycles,[17] Rendsburg does not offer a comprehensive structure for the whole of Genesis.[18] His analysis of chaps. 1–11 depends on J. Sasson's earlier work, which finds two parallel sequences of five episodes, each covering ten generations: (I) Creation to the Nephilim (1:1–6:8) and (II) Flood to the Genealogy of Shem (6:9–11:26). Below is Rendsburg's display, which we set in parallel columns:

A Creation, God's Words to Adam (1:1–3:24)	A´ Flood, God's Words to Noah (6:9–9:17)
B Adam's Sons (4:1–16)	B´ Noah's Sons (9:18–29)
C Technical Development of Mankind (4:17–26)	C´ Ethnic Development of Mankind (10:1–32)
D Ten Generations from Adam to Noah (5:1–32)	E´ Downfall: Tower of Babel (11:1–9)
E Downfall: The Nephilim (6:1–8)	D´Ten Generations from Noah to Terah (11:10–26)

One can complain that the panels do not match perfectly (D and E´ and E and D´), but that is not detrimental since the genealogy of 11:10–26 functions in the larger structure as a bridge between the tower episode (11:1–9) and the emergence of Abraham (11:27–25:11), who is God's answer to the dispersion experienced by the nations. The primary pitfall is that the analysis does not give sufficient weight to the *tōlĕdōt* device, which is the most noticeable redactional feature in the compositional makeup of the primeval history.

We have chosen to stick to the simpler course by resorting to the book's redactional device *(tōlĕdōt),* setting out sections as we find them marked in the text. It is best to take the *tōlĕdōt* references as evidence of pre-Genesis sources that have been appropriated and modified according to the compositional interests of Genesis. We saw earlier that the author/compiler was not slavish in his use of the catchphrase. At 2:4 it is the creation of the author,

[16] See P. K. McCarter, "A New Challenge to the Documentary Hypothesis. Have Modern Scholars Failed to Appreciate the Overall Structure of Genesis 1–11?" *BibRev* 4 (1988): 34–39.

[17] Rendsburg recognizes, e.g., the unity of the patriarchal accounts. See G. W. Coats, "Redactional Unity in Genesis 37–50," *JBL* (1974): 15–21, and M. Fishbane, "Composition and Structure in the Jacob Cycle (Gen. 25:19–35:22)," *JJS* 26 (1975): 15–38, rev. in Fishbane, *Text and Texture* (New York: Schocken, 1979), 40–62.

[18] See the critique in Garrett, *Rethinking Genesis,* 115–21.

imitating the superscription found for a listed genealogy or a family record. Genesis 5:1–2 adds a narrative supplement, a foreword to the formal genealogical listing (5:3–32), which intentionally echoes the earlier creation narrative with significant variations (see commentary). The completion of the last paragraph in Seth's genealogy regarding Noah's family (5:32) is postponed by the intervening flood story and completed at 9:28–29. The relationship of chaps. 5 and 11, which possess similar patterns, is uncertain; they may be of two different sources or one (written) source that has been modified at chap. 11. These well illustrate the elasticity found for the use of the *tōlĕdōt* phrase in Genesis. What follows the catchphrase in the extant Genesis then is not necessarily the material of the original source.[19] Thus we cannot possibly reconstruct the pre-Genesis sources with confidence as to their origins and contents.

Because of such flexibility in the use of the *tōlĕdōt* phrase, there is some dispute about how it functions in the extant text. Most agree that the refrain introduces the contents of the following section, either involving genealogy and/or narrative. But, conversely, P. J. Wiseman and others have argued that the *tōlĕdōt* phrase is part of a concluding sentence, referring to what has preceded.[20] External evidence produced for this is the cuneiform practice of ending a clay tablet with a colophon that named the scribe or owner of the tablet, gave its date, and entitled the tablet.

Following R. K. Harrison's version, the original sources of Genesis were eleven clay tablets constituting what is found in the extant chaps. 1–36. These tablets were more or less gathered end to end by the compiler (Moses), who supplied the final story of Joseph, perhaps from an oral source (chaps. 37–50).[21] Selective internal evidence from biblical Genesis can support this reconstruction,[22] but the proposal is not compelling for the whole and cuts across the obvious sense of the term *tōlĕdōt,* which focuses attention on what is born or

[19] So Garrett, ibid., 97–100, 102–3.

[20] P. J. Wiseman, *New Discoveries in Babylonia about Genesis* (London: Marshall, 1936), reissued in D. J. Wiseman, ed., *Ancient Records and the Structure of Genesis* (Nashville: Nelson, 1985); also see R. K. Harrison, *Introduction to the Old Testament* (Grand Rapids: Eerdmans, 1969). A modified version is in D. S. DeWitt, "The Generations of Genesis," *EvQ* 48 (1976): 196–211, whose revision has improved the theory and answers some objections to this reconstruction.

[21] DeWitt, "The Generations of Genesis," contends for ten tablets, the obverse side possessing the "decisive history" and the reverse side (on some tablets) containing a genealogy; thus the *tōlĕdōt* refers to the preceding history and the subsequent genealogy.

[22] E.g., sometimes the principal information concerning the person named in the colophon precedes (e.g., Adam, 5:1; also 25:19; 37:2), and in most instances a reference to descendants occurs before the colophon; sometimes תּוֹלְדוֹת appears better rendered "account" (NIV) or "story" (e.g., NRSV at 37:2) since only 10:1 and 11:10 preface a genealogical table without an intervening narrative; and the reference to "book" (סֵפֶר 5:1; cf. the LXX's "the book [βιβλος] of the origins of the heavens and earth," 2:4a) indicates a written record.

produced, that is, what follows.[23] Also the person named in the colophon is in fact the first name of the following genealogical record (5:1–3; 10:1–2; 11:10; 25:12–13; 36:1–2), which decidedly points the reader to what follows.

We are helped in understanding how the *tōlĕdōt* formula functions by its occurrences outside Genesis, in Num 3:1 and Ruth 4:18 (cp. 1 Chr 1:29). Numbers 3:1a introduces the lineage of Aaron's descendants: "This is the account of the family of Aaron and Moses." Its role in Numbers appears to be the same as found in Genesis: it narrows focus on the elect, heads a genealogy, and looks forward to progeny (see section "Genesis and Canon").[24] The preceding segment concerns the census of Israel (Num 1–2), listing all the tribes, except the Levitical group, which Moses is specifically commanded to omit from the count (1:49). Although there is mention of Moses and Aaron in the preceding narrative, they are not principal to the subject matter, and there is no reference to their heritage. The *tōlĕdōt* reference identifies especially what follows, the four sons of Aaron's household (Num 3:2). Yet there is no comparable record for Moses' clan, which suggests that the inclusion of "Moses" in the heading anticipates his prominent role in the narratives to follow. The Ruth example, "this . . . is the family line of Perez," is transparently behaving as an introduction to the subsequent genealogy, consisting of ten names from Perez to David (4:18–22). It is unlikely that it is a colophon since "Perez" is only mentioned before the colophon and cannot possibly be the subject or author of the preceding story. This argument is important for understanding Genesis since David's genealogical scheme is similar to the Genesis style of genealogy (5:1–32; 10:11–26).[25] The Ruth example indicates that the *tōlĕdōt* reference is a hinge verse that points to an element in the previous section (i.e., Perez) but focuses attention on the subsequent material (i.e., Perez-David). It back-references and ties together two units by forming a bridge. In the case of Ruth's account, it binds the narrative and the genealogy; the name "Perez" in the formula reaches back to the narrative where "Perez" appears to be cited incidentally (4:12) and ties the patriarchal heritage of Perez directly to King David (4:18–22).

In the same way the *tōlĕdōt* phrase in Genesis serves as a linking device that ties together the former and the following units by echoing from the preceding material a person's name or literary motif and at the same time anticipating the

---

[23] See M. H. Woudstra, "The *Toledot* of the Book of Genesis and Their Redemptive-Historical Significance," in *Calvin Theological Journal* 5 (1970): 184–89, esp. 187, and the critique by V. Hamilton, *The Book of Genesis Chapters 1–17,* NICOT (Grand Rapids: Eerdmans, 1990), 9. There is no clear parallel between the use of תּוֹלְדוֹת in Genesis and the cuneiform practice since there is no scribe named or date.

[24] See D. T. Olson, *The Death of the Old and the Birth of the New: The Framework of the Book of Numbers and the Pentateuch,* BJS 71 (Chico, Cal.: Scholars Press, 1985), 83–125.

[25] E. F. Campbell, *Ruth: A New Translation with Introduction, Notes, and Commentary,* AB (Garden City: Doubleday, 1975), 170, 172.

focal subject of the next. The catchphrase is a device binding sections, functioning like a hinge that swings back, recalling the information in the prior section, and also swings forward by suggesting the topic in the section it introduces. The formula as the framework for the Genesis collection is the book's strategy for declaring its organic unity—from the creation of the universe to the election of Israel's historical precursors. By this overarching pattern the composition's framework is historical genealogy, tying creation and human history in continuum. The superscription then has a unifying effect.

Also the *tōlĕdōt* rubric collaborates with Genesis's recurring use of genealogy to achieve a restricting effect. Within the flow of human history, from the universal to the particular, the genealogies indicate God is separating out by selection a righteous lineage by whom he chooses to bless the world of nations (cp. 5:1 and 10:1; 11:10). Related to this is the theme of promissory "blessing" that links the creation with human history. The blessing of procreation for humanity (1:28) is repeated for the second Adam (Noah, 9:1,7) and is (partially) realized in the genealogical tables of chaps. 5 (Adam/Seth) and 10 (Noah's sons), indicating how the promissory blessing unfolds through succeeding generations (see commentary at 5:1b–3).[26] This is most obvious in comparing the twice-told lineage of Shem (10:21–31; 11:10–26), where the two lines run parallel until the naming of Joktan and Peleg, after which the lineage parts. A formal difference between the two genealogies is chap. 10's segmented style (Joktan), where all descendants are named, and chap. 11's linear style (Peleg), as also found in chap. 5 (Seth), which names only one offspring per generation. Joktan's nonelect line is traced in chap. 10, but Peleg's descendants are detailed in chap. 11, ending in the birth of Father Abraham (11:26). The "blessing" for Abraham (12:1–3) found in the succeeding Terah *tōlĕdōt* (11:27–25:11) shows that the blessing applies to the one family of Abraham (not Nahor or Haran), the precursors of national Israel.

Like the genealogical records of early Genesis, the patriarchal narratives exhibit the (partial) realization of the promise by citing genealogy, including the rejected sons (e.g., Ishmael, 25:12–18; Esau, 36:1–43). This inclusiveness corresponds to citing in early Genesis the rejected lines of Cain and Ham-Canaan, whose families prosper (4:17–24; 10:15–19) but whose antics disqualify them. Presenting even the nonelect offspring fathering nations testifies to the certainty and the extent of the promise for the patriarchal chosen. In early Genesis the genealogies of the selected sons, Seth and Shem in chaps. 5 and 11, share in a distinctive genealogical pattern that distinguishes them from their counterparts (Cain; Ham and Japheth). This genealogical highlighting, however, does not occur for the patriarchs; there are no extensive multigenerational presentations for the elect Abraham, Isaac, and Jacob, for such rosters

---

[26] C. Westermann, *Creation,* trans. J. Scullion (Philadelphia: Fortress, 1974), 24.

would eclipse the narrative tension of succession found in the accounts. It is left to the narratives to tell of the rejected and selected descendants. For the most part the strategy of the book gives the genealogy of the nonelect line before the elect line is found (except Jacob precedes Esau, 35:22–26), indicating that once the nonelect family is noted, it can be set aside for the more judicious treatment of the appointed lineage.

(2) Contents

With our understanding of the *tōlĕdōt* as a hinge device, we offer below a summary of the catchphrase and contents of the book.

1:1–2:3 The opening section does not have the introductory formula. Since this first section has no prior material, there is no requirement for a binding device.

2:4a "This is the account *[tōlĕdōt]* of the heavens and the earth when they were created."

2:4–4:26 The *tōlĕdōt* phrase at 2:4a is the first part of a chiastic structure formed with 2:4b. Although many divide the verse (as NIV), as a chiasmus the verse is best taken as a structural unity (see commentary). The *tōlĕdōt* half-verse (2:4a) back-references the preceding creation narrative by its echo of the language in 1:1 ("heavens," "earth," "created"). The latter half of the chiasmus at 2:4b, however, inverts the merism ("the heavens and the earth") to "earth and heaven," narrowing attention in the succeeding account of human life to "earth." This section exceeds the creation narrative of 1:1–2:3 and presents a complementary view of creation by emphasizing the origin of mankind and their immediate environment (garden of Eden). The repetition of the starting point of creation in 2:4 is to establish the context for understanding the ensuing story of human sin and its devastating consequences on the human family and environs. Chapter 2 clarifies the place of humanity in its creation on "earth." (1) The welfare of the earth's vegetation is dependent upon and related to the human condition (1:11–13; 2:5–6). Humanity exercises a mastery over the environment—the vegetative and the animal worlds (1:28–30; 2:15,19). (2) Human life is a special creation that enjoys communion with the Creator but also is intimately related to the physical environment as creature (1:26–28; 2:7,15). (3) Also human life, which comprises two distinct sexes, is distinguished further by their respective roles played in the created order (1:26–27; 2:18–24). The woman is fully human, corresponding to the man, and her creation out of the man indicates that there is one connectional human family.

By virtue of these relationships established in chap. 2, potential conflict is created. The prospects for confrontation are: (1) human life opposed by the environment, (2) human life opposing God, and (3) the male and the female as opponents. Chapters 3–4 play out these conflicts and show how these relationships, which are universal to the human condition, have been altered.

Without warning chap. 3 introduces an unexpected character, the serpent, a lecherous animal that misspeaks God and lures the first couple into gaining a deadly wisdom by asserting independence. The serpent, the woman's chief adversary, succeeds in creating adversarial roles between mankind and God, who imposes curses on the serpent and the ground (3:14,17) and also predicts the conflict that will ensue in the human family (3:15). Man no longer has mastery over the animal or plant worlds; the murder of Abel by brother Cain shows human life has no mastery over itself (4:3–16). The human predicament is exacerbated by the development of civilization within the descendants of Cain (4:17–24), but there is hope yet through Seth, the new Abel, and the worship of God (4:25–26).

5:1a "This is the written account of Adam's line *[tōlĕdōt]*."

5:1–6:8 Unlike the giving of Cain's lineage (4:17), the Sethite lineage is directly related to the name "Adam." This second occurrence of the formula binds the foregoing garden account with a formal genealogical record tracing the Adamic line down to the new protagonist Noah. "Adam" in the superscription (5:1a) echoes the account of individual man's creation and life (2:7), and the narrative elaboration (5:1b–2) references generic "Adam" ("man," 1:26–28). Thus the genealogy is another telling of human creation and succession but from the perspective of progressive human procreation. (1) Individual "Adam" (5:1a) is reminiscent of chaps. 2–4 in which humankind is created and cared for by God, marred by sinful disobedience, but preserved by the grace of God. (2) The term *tōlĕdōt* of Adam announces the following genealogy, which sketches briskly what became of this first family over many centuries. It shows human life procreating and dying, evidence of both God's continued promissory blessing (3:20) and the tragic realization of divine judgment (3:17–19) as found in the refrain "and he died." This section ends with a narrative afterword (6:1–8). The opposing lines of Cain and Abel/Seth, now represented by the lineages of Cain (chap. 4) and Seth (chap. 5), come to a temporary respite through marriage (6:1–2). Like the conclusion of the former section with the marriages of Cain, which produce a murderous seed (Lamech), the fruit of the "daughters of men" (Cainites) and the "sons of God" (Sethites) results in the disaster of unprecedented violence among increasingly populous human society. Nevertheless, there remains hope through God's favor on righteous Noah (6:8).

6:9a "This is the account *[tōlĕdōt]* of Noah."

6:9–9:29 By this simple catchphrase "Noah" reaches back to creation via the genealogy of Adam (5:1–32) since it ends with reference to Noah's family (5:29–32). Although God has condemned the earth for its wickedness (6:7), Noah's name *(nōʾaḥ)*, a play on the word "comfort" *(nāḥam;* 5:29), sounds hope for this degenerative race. "Noah" in the heading, therefore, anticipates his story of deliverance and his role as the new Adam (9:1,7). The final verse of the section (9:29) tells of Noah's age at death and thereby completes the stylized genealogy of chap. 5, which was left open-ended where according to pattern the age at death follows the patriarch's age as father (5:32). The conclusion of Noah's place in the genealogy is delayed since the significance of Noah's story required an intervening narrative expansion. The flood narrative therefore is embedded within Adam's table of descendants; by design the composition considers Noah to be the second Adam, who fathers the human race anew.

10:1 "This is the account *[tōlĕdōt]* of Shem, Ham and Japheth, Noah's sons, who themselves had sons after the flood."

10:2–11:9 The triad "Shem, Ham and Japheth" (cf. 5:32; 6:10; 10:1; 1 Chr 1:4) links the account to 5:32, where Noah's sons are first named, giving a sense of proximity to the first Adam. In the flood narrative the close relationship of Noah and his sons is kept in view. Their experience is their father's experience. The sons escape the wrath of God's floodwaters but not altogether the wrath of their drunken father (9:24). The formulaic trilogy connects the curse and blessing that Noah utters upon his progeny (9:26–27) and the Table of Nations that eventuates (10:1–32; also 11:10–26). Noah's sons then are the tie looping together the world before the flood and the world "after the flood" (10:1). Adam had sons who were the progenitors of mounting sin that ultimately led to worldwide human destruction (6:1–8); the second Adam (Noah) also fathered sons who were the progenitors of renewed sin, which ultimately led to geographical dispersion (11:1–9). As the Adamic line possessed hope for future humanity in the figure of Noah for a new beginning ("comfort," 5:29), there is a veiled hope for the dispersed nations by the genealogical names "Eber" and "Peleg" (10:21,25), who are the ancestors of the Hebrew Abraham.

11:10a "This is the account *[tōlĕdōt]* of Shem."

11:10–26 The name "Shem" not only recalls the genealogies of the three sons (10:1–32) but, more importantly, ties the present section with the tower of Babel at the close of the previous unit (11:1–9). The Hebrew words "Shem" *(šēm)* and "name" *(šēm)* sound alike and call to mind the debacle of the tower episode; the tower was erected by his descendants to make a "name" for themselves (11:4). The genealogy of Shem is given twice, before and after the Babel incident, but with significant differences. The first listing occurs in the context of all Noah's sons (chap. 10), whereas the second stands alone following the Babel account. Also the first genealogy tracks Shem's descent through Eber's (the father of the Hebrews) second son, Joktan (10:26), while only mentioning "Peleg" *(peleg)* for the play on the meaning of his name ("division"; 10:25).[27] The second record of Shem in 11:10–26, however, mimics the linear pattern of Seth's genealogy in chap. 5 by following the descent exclusively through one son—namely, Peleg. This establishes the selective connection of Shem-Peleg-

[27] Heb. פֶּלֶג is a play on נִפְלְגָה ("was divided").

Abram. The significance of the name "Peleg" is uncertain (see commentary), but as a wordplay it may indicate the dispersion at Babel or that the descendants named through Peleg have been "divided" out as the chosen lineage. Casting the Shem genealogy in the same schematic pattern as that of Adam-Noah (chap. 5) distinguishes the Shem lineage from that of his brothers. Both genealogies close in the same way, with Shem occurring as the first of Noah's three sons and Abram listed as the first of Terah's three sons (see 11:26 note). Together Adam and Shem's genealogies elevate the chosen offspring: Seth (not Cain), Shem (not Ham, Japheth), and Abram (not Nahor, Haran).

11:27a "This is the account *[tōlědōt]* of Terah."

11:27–25:11 "Terah" links the present section with the foregoing list of Shem's descendants; "Terah" is the last lineal descendant named (11:26). The name also anticipates the "Abram" account since he is listed first among Terah's sons (11:26). It has long been observed that the name in the *tōlědōt* formula for the patriarchs does not correspond to the major figure of the section it introduces; rather, it is the father of the focal character: Terah for Abraham (11:27), Isaac for Jacob (25:19), and Jacob for Joseph (37:2). One would expect, following this arrangement, to find "the *tōlědōt* of Abraham" as a heading for Isaac's story; but there is no extensive narrative for Isaac, whose role is limited in the patriarchal account. Of course, there is no narrative interest in the succeeding patriarch for the rejected lines of Ishmael and Esau. Why the father is named in the superscription may be related to that person's role as grandfather to two or more descending lines (Adam, Noah, Japheth, Ham, Shem, Terah, Isaac, Esau, Seir, and Jacob).[28] This permits the tension of the chosen versus rejected lines to be more fully explored.

Up to this point Genesis has followed the general pattern of referring to an individual and listing descendant(s) or clans (except 2:4). The notice of the father's death ("and he died") occurs in chap. 5 (cp. 9:29) and is imitated by 11:32, "Terah lived 205 years, and he died in Haran." This echo of chap. 5's genealogy is drawing together the converging lines of exclusive lineal descent: from Adam to Noah's son, Shem, and from Shem to Terah's son, Abram. Citing "Terah" casts Abraham under his father, who is his link to the postdiluvian era of Shem. Abraham then stands in the text as part of the stream of the Babel problem (11:1–9). "Terah" serves as the transitional figure in the genealogical thought of the text. By using genealogies, the text creates a sense of nearness between the eras. There is no disjuncture between Babel and the patriarchs; the juxtaposition of "Terah" and the Abraham story interprets Abraham's call as God's answer to the problem of the Babel dispersion. This is further indicated by the theme of "name" in the subsequent promissory blessing, "I will bless

---

[28] Andersen, "Genealogical Prominence," 253. Other double-line grandfathers whose names do not occur in a superscription are Eber, Abraham, Nahor, and Joseph.

you; I will make your name great" (12:2), which builds on the "Shem—name" (*šēm*) word play of the Babel account.

25:12 "This is the account *[tōlĕdōt]* of Abraham's son Ishmael, whom Sarah's maidservant, Hagar the Egyptian, bore to Abraham."

25:12–18 The death of Abraham (25:7–11) is followed by the genealogies of his sons Ishmael and Isaac (25:19). In the case of Ishmael a formal listing of his descendants is given, whereas for Isaac the "genealogy" is a narration of Esau and Jacob's birth. This same arrangement occurs with Isaac and his sons: the notice of his death and burial (35:28–29) followed by the lengthy recounting of Esau's descendants (36:1–43) and the "genealogy" of Jacob, which details the story of Joseph's dreams (37:2ff.). This tactic distinguishes the excluded sons since this is opposite the practice of the earlier accounts, where the designated offspring Seth and Shem have such an elaborate genealogical tabling (5:1–32; 11:10–26). As we indicated, the narrative tension created in the patriarchal stories would be diminished if such a schematic genealogy were given for each patriarch. If an extended genealogy were given for Abraham, for instance, the question of chosen seed and the concomitant motif of customary primogeniture that make up each succeeding patriarchal account would not be as effective for the storytelling effect intended.

Since the tension created in the account by the rivalry between Sarah and Hagar has been put to rest, the text safely relates the outcome of Ishmael. The practice of the book is to include the genealogical records of the nonelect (e.g., Cain, Ham, Nahor, the sons of Abraham by Keturah, and Esau). However, the point of including the Ishmael genealogy is not just for completeness; the interest of the text is not tidiness. The identification of Ishmael as "Abraham's son" ties this section with the foregoing account, which told of Abraham's *two* sons, Ishmael and Isaac. The formula expands by referring to "Hagar," indicating that Ishmael did not have the same elevated status as the chosen son Isaac through whom the promises will be perpetuated. Despite his maternal origins, Ishmael's fortunes are fertile because of his father, Abraham. Ishmael's genealogy demonstrates the fulfilling of God's promise to Abraham to become a father of "many nations" (17:5,20; cf. the announcement to Hagar first, 16:10). "Ishmael" also anticipates the ensuing list of the twelve tribal leaders who descended from him and settled in the Arabian desert areas: "He will be the father of twelve rulers, and I will make him into a great nation" (17:20b). Since God gives attention to realizing his promises for the lesser son, the prospects for the appointed ones are secured.

25:19a "This is the account *[tōlĕdōt]* of Abraham's son Isaac."

25:19–35:29 The *tōlĕdōt* formula links this section with the genealogy of Ishmael by the addition "Abraham's son." The previous *tōlĕdōt* includes "Hagar's son," but the introduction of Isaac has no reference to his maternal descent. The silence points up (by implication) that this son came by Sarah, sealing Isaac's credentials as the legitimate claimant for the promises. As discussed earlier, the *tōlĕdōt* formula is not so concerned with the individual named as it is with his family. In this case the name of "Isaac" anticipates the events of the third generation, Jacob and Esau, which revives the fraternal tensions concerning who will inherit the patriarchal blessing. The genealogy for Jacob is limited to the naming of his twelve sons; it does not follow the narrowing pattern of Seth and Shem, which lists the one offspring of each descendant (35:23–26). We have said that the giving of this kind of genealogy, beginning with Abraham, would diminish the tension created by the narrative where the sons of each patriarch struggle for ascendancy. The inclusive naming of Jacob's twelve sons can be attributed to the parallel twelve tribes of Esau's descendants.

36:1 "This is the account *[tōlĕdōt]* of Esau (that is Edom)."

36:1–8 The name "Esau" bridges the former section, which depicts the disputed blessing between Jacob and Esau; its denouement is the favored Jacob residing in Canaan (35:27) and Esau living outside the land in Seir (33:16–20). Attendant to this conflict over inheritance in the Jacob-Esau cycle is the anxiety over Jacob's possession of the land. Though he has Isaac's blessing, he escapes to Haran for his life, where he resides in Laban's house. The Bethel episodes explain that God has secured the land for Jacob (cp. 28:13; 35:1,7). By the superscription's geographical reference, "Edom," the land issue as resolved in the preceding narrative is reinforced, and also "Edom" anticipates Esau's final residence at Seir (36:8), relinquishing the promised Canaan to Jacob (36:6b–8).

36:9 "This is the account *[tōlĕdōt]* of Esau the father of the Edomites in the hill country of Seir."

36:9–37:1 A second *tōlĕdōt* occurs for Esau. The formula is not an exact repetition, however; this second genealogy gives the specific lineage of the Edomites, listing their royal heads. Whereas the first *tōlĕdōt* of Esau focuses on the land, the second *tōlĕdōt* is concerned with the Edomite chieftains and kings who owed their origins to Esau (cf. 36:43b). As with the Ishmael genealogy (25:12–18), the promise to Abraham of fathering many nations is partially fulfilled through the lineage of Esau. The editorial addition, "These were the kings who reigned in Edom before there was any Israelite king" (36:31), draws the parallel that is implied by the inclusion of Esau's royal progeny. Both Jacob and Esau sired rival kingdoms. "Seir" back-references the first Esau genealogy where "Seir" closes out the passage (36:8). The prominence given in the formula to the "country of Seir" contrasts with Jacob, who remained in Canaan "where his father had stayed" (37:1).

37:2 "This is the account *[tōlĕdōt]* of Jacob."

37:2–50:26 The last occurrence of the formula ties the Joseph cycle to the preceding Jacob narratives. In both the Jacob and Joseph accounts, the issue of dispersion dominates. As with the practice of naming the patriarch to introduce the account of his progeny, the name "Jacob" evokes an anticipation of what becomes of his twelve sons. In the previous section the geographical setting of Jacob in Canaan (37:1) has been an important indicator in showing his rightful place as heir in the Jacob-Esau dispute; in the last section of the book the dispersion of Joseph to Egypt and Jacob's subsequent move outside the land revives the former tension. The theme of sibling rivalry continues in Jacob's household. His return to share in the land of his father is shortened by a new threat to his life; like the first occasion, he escapes Canaan in order to preserve his life. The sons take refuge with their father under Joseph in Egypt. The book closes with Jacob's sons in Egypt, where they ultimately die as did their brother Joseph. Genesis ends with Joseph dead "in Egypt" (50:26), but not before his brothers promised by oath to return him to the land of his fathers when God again would show favor to Israel's household (50:24–25).

(3) Conclusion

The artifice of the *tōlĕdōt* structure results in a unified composition made up of diverse kinds of materials that have been set in a wider literary framework. It is the foremost feature marking structure and functions as a hinge by linking the preceding material and the subsequent section. It concerns primarily what becomes of the patriarch's family named in the superscription. The genealogies are the strongest indicator that written sources were employed in the writing of the book, but Genesis has not preserved them in their entirety. The recurring formulaic *tōlĕdōt* device shows that the composition was arranged to join the historical moorings of Israel with the beginnings of the cosmos. In this way the composition forms an Adam-Noah-Abraham continuum that loops the patriarchal promissory blessings with the God of cosmos and all human history. The text does not welcome a different reading for Genesis 1–11 as myth versus the patriarchal narratives. Contemporary categories used by scholars to differentiate early Genesis, such as primeval myth, tales, saga, and historicizing myth, are at odds with the author's perspective and product.

3. Genesis and Canon

(1) Title

The English title "Genesis" is derived from Jerome's Vulgate, *Liber Genesis*. This Latin name followed the Greek (Septuagint) title, which probably was taken from Gen 2:4a where a form (genitive plural) of *genesis* ("source, birth, generation") renders Hebrew *tōlĕdōt*. This title reflects the content of the book whose macrostructure is marked by the recurring *tōlĕdōt* formula. On the other hand, the Hebrew title *bĕrēšît,* "in the beginning," conforms to the custom of entitling a composition in the Pentateuch by its opening word(s). That the

Hebrew name also reflects the content of Genesis as a book of beginnings is therefore coincidental. Rabbinic sources expanded the title to *sēper bĕrēšît* ("The Book of Bereshith") and *sēper hā-yāšār* ("The Book of the Upright"), the latter referring to the lives of the patriarchs that dominate the narrative of the book.

(2) Genesis and Pentateuch

Genesis is the first book of the Hebrew canon and introduces the first division, known as the "Torah" ("Law"). This division is the first of the traditional tripartite Hebrew arrangement: the Law, the Prophets, and the Writings (cf. Matt 5:17; Luke 24:44). The Torah consists of the first five books of the collection, Genesis through Deuteronomy, but it was not originally viewed as five distinctive works.[29] Rather, the Torah was one book. The singular "Book of Moses," "book of the law," or simply "book," is attested in exilic and postexilic times (e.g., 2 Chr 25:4; 34:14; 35:12; Ezra 6:18; Neh 8:3,5; 13:1) and in Mark's Gospel (12:26). In the second century B.C. the preface to *Ecclesiasticus* (Ben Sirah) refers to the "Law and the Prophets and the others that followed them," indicating that the Torah was one book. The traditional rabbinic expression "the five-fifths of the Law" is first found later in the Talmudic period (*b. Sanh.* 44a; *b. Hag.* 14a), but it reflects a much older recognition of the five parts.[30]

When the division into five books occurred is uncertain, though it clearly antedated the time of Christ. Both Josephus (*Ag. Ap.* 1.8) and Philo (*On Abraham* 1.1) in the first century A.D. spoke of the five books of Moses. The Damascus Document (CD VII.15), by referring to the "books of the law," also suggests the fivefold arrangement of the Pentateuch.[31] Textual evidence from the Greek tradition comes from the late uncial codices, but the Letter of Aristeas speaks of the "scrolls" and the "books" in reference to the law. The division occurred no later than the mid-third century B.C. The Greek *hē pentateuchos biblos,* meaning "the book of the five (parts)" or "five books," probably was a translation of the Jewish expression "five-fifths of the Law." The term *pentateuchos* is attested in the second century A.D. and later was rendered by the Latin *pentateuchus,* from which English "Pentateuch" derives. Although it is commonplace to explain the dividing of the Pentateuch by the pragmatic advantage of smaller scrolls for easier handling, J. Blenkinsopp notes that other arrangements (such as four and six) were conceivable, and the

[29] See O. Eissfeldt, *The Old Testament: An Introduction,* trans. P. R. Ackroyd (New York: Harper & Row, 1965), 155–56; J. Sailhamer, *The Pentateuch as Narrative* (Grand Rapids: Zondervan, 1992), 1–2; Blenkinsopp, *The Pentateuch,* 43–45.

[30] Cp. *b. Kid* 33a, "two-fifths of the book of Psalms," a reference to two books of the five in which Psalms may be divided.

[31] Cp. the comparable "books of the prophets" (CD VII.17).

division into *five* units creates a central book, Leviticus.[32] This central book has its sole attention on the Sinai cult, which we will see is focal in the compilation of the Pentateuch, where preeminent space is given to the Sinai events.

INTERDEPENDENCE OF THE PENTATEUCH. The literary structure of the Pentateuch discloses a compilation of literary blocks that form a cohesive unity.[33] The coming together of the diverse components of the Pentateuch, including narratives, law collections, poetry, genealogies and lists, and sundry other embedded sources, has left its signs of irregular juxtaposition in the text. Yet the overall pentateuchal arrangement witnesses to a literary configuration that shows a reasoned plan of organization. The "Five Books," as received in the Hebrew canon, are in fact one story—from creation (Gen 1:1) to the death of Moses (Deut 34). These five works may be read as independent books, but they have an interdependence that cuts across the traditional fivefold division. The center books of Exodus, Leviticus, and Numbers are the most interdependent; together they tell of the migration of Israel from Egypt to the plains of Moab and the transition from the exodus generation to that of the conquest. Genesis and Deuteronomy come closest to being independent works, but by themselves each lacks a satisfactory denouement, each looking beyond itself to the next epoch events.

The unity of the Pentateuch is evidenced most clearly by the *narrative framework* that focuses on the Sinai revelation in terms of space allocation, giving attention to Exodus–Deuteronomy. The core of Exodus–Deuteronomy is the Sinaitic covenant and the cultic regulations designed to order the life of the newly formed community as the people of God (Exod 19:1–Num 10:10). This block is sandwiched between Exodus 1–18, which is preparatory for the giving of the covenant-law, and Num 10:11–Deut 34:12, which relates the experiences of God's people living under it. Deuteronomy presents a reinterpretation of the Exodus covenant in light of Israel's history in the desert and in anticipation of the new generation's residence in Canaan. By geographical itinerary Exodus–Deuteronomy follows this arrangement:

Exodus 1–18	Egypt to Sinai
Exod 19:1–Num 10:10	At Sinai and the Covenant-Law
Num 10:11–Deut 34:12	Departure from Sinai to Moab

Since the contents of Genesis antedate the Sinai event, its role—though crucial for understanding the whole—is subsidiary to the chief narrative interest. Genesis 12–50 introduces the Sinai account by telling of Israel's precursors, particularly tracing the transmission of the promissory blessings. Chapters 1–11 provide a preamble to the whole by setting Israel's birth at Sinai in the con-

[32] Blenkinsopp, *Pentateuch,* 46–47, and "Pentateuch," NIB (Nashville: Abingdon, 1994), 307.

[33] This discussion reflects the author's "Preaching in the Pentateuch," in *Handbook of Contemporary Preaching,* ed. M. Duduit (Nashville: Broadman, 1992), 257–79.

text of cosmic history. As the new community prepared to engage the hostile environs of Canaan, chaps. 1–11 provided an introduction and orientation to Israel's neighbors—especially as given in the Table of Nations (chap. 10).

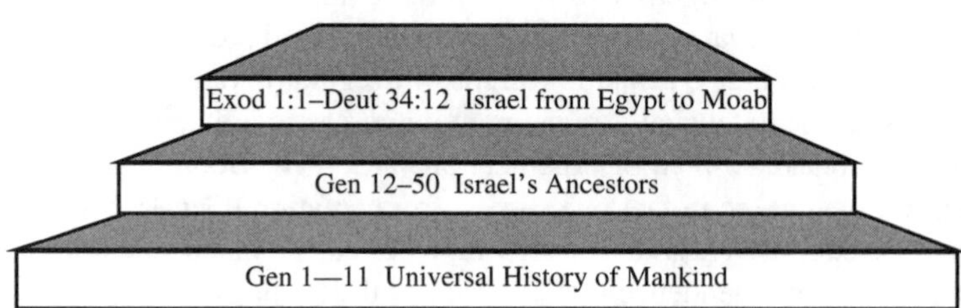

The unity of the Pentateuch is also indicated by a focal character—the prophet *Moses*.[34] The birth (Exod 2) and death (Deut 34) of Israel's mediator bracket the compilation of Exodus–Deuteronomy, forming a literary inclusio. These four books are given to the hundred and twenty years of Moses' life, while Genesis spans millennia with its expansive Genesis 1–11. There is no single person who captivates the attention of Genesis as does Moses in Exodus–Deuteronomy. The main persons of Genesis may be interpreted as preparatory for the role of Moses. Moses is like Adam, for he meets with God "face to face" (Exod 33:11); like Noah, for he too is delivered by an "ark" coated with pitch, and he faithfully carries out God's specifications in building the tabernacle (Exod 2:3; 40:16); like Abraham, for he likewise is divinely appointed to dwell in Canaan, "a land flowing with milk and honey" (Exod 3:6,8); and like Jacob, for he offers a final blessing upon future generations (Deut 33). We do not have "biographies" in the Pentateuch, but in terms of central figures to the unfolding narrative of the Pentateuch, we have the following hierarchy of narrative attention:

[34] R. P. Knierim in "The Composition of the Pentateuch," *SBL 1985 Seminar Papers*, ed. D. Lull (Atlanta: Scholars Press, 1985), 393–415, goes so far as to argue that the Pentateuch is the biography of Moses. He concludes that Genesis is preparatory for Moses, who cannot be properly interpreted in isolation from the universal history of Genesis. Conversely, Genesis's first humanity must be understood in terms of Moses' role (p. 414). Sailhamer (*The Pentateuch as Narrative*, 65–66) rather views the Pentateuch as a series of biographies in which the lives of the patriarchs before the law are set against the biography of Moses under the law.

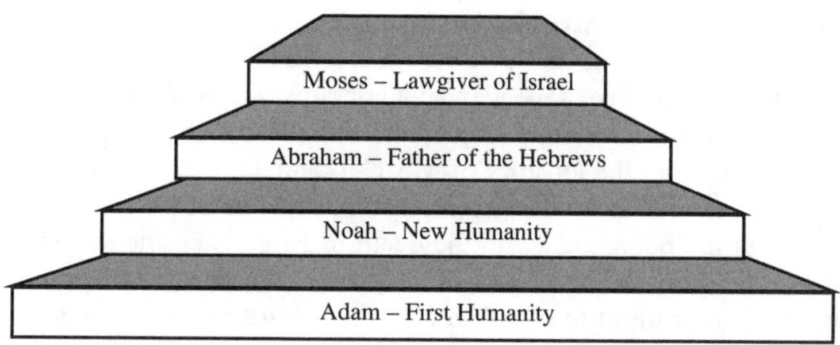

Beyond the narrative framework and the person of Moses are evidences of literary interdependence by means of *back-referencing* where the books come together, showing the five books are to be read as one. Genesis anticipates the central concern of Exodus when Joseph's final words announce the return of Jacob's seed, "to the land he [God] promised on oath to Abraham, Isaac, and Jacob" (50:24; cp. Exod 6:3–8). The final verse of Genesis refers to the death and embalming of Joseph and ends with "Egypt" (50:26). The prologue of Exodus (1:1–7) back-references the ending of Genesis by recalling Joseph's death again and describing the circumstances of Jacob's offspring in Egypt. It does so by including a genealogical listing of the sons of Jacob who migrated to Egypt, the favorite structural device of the Genesis composer. As we will note, it is significant that the cessation of one generation (i.e., Joseph's generation) and the inauguration of a new is at the juncture of Genesis and Exodus, for this is a thematic interest in Exodus–Deuteronomy, which portrays the succession of Moses' generation by Joshua's new wilderness generation. Even the language of Israel's numerical growth echoes creation (1:22,28), Noah's new creation (8:17; 9:1,7), and patriarchal promise (e.g., 17:6,20; 28:3): "the Israelites were fruitful and multiplied greatly and became exceedingly numerous, so that the land was filled with them" (Exod 1:7).

Although the people have not yet moved from their encampment at Sinai, Exodus concludes with this proleptic comment on Israel's movements recorded in Numbers: "The cloud of the LORD was over the tabernacle by day, and fire was in the cloud by night, in the sight of all the house of Israel during all their travels" (Exod 40:38). Leviticus is sandwiched between Exodus and Numbers. It begins with Moses meeting the Lord at the "Tent of Meeting" (Lev 1:1) and it concludes with Israel still on "Mount Sinai" (Lev 27:34). Numbers continues the narrative with Moses still consulting the Lord at the "Tent" in the "Desert of Sinai" (Num 1:1), but the ensuing travels of Israel as recounted in Numbers puts the people "on the plains of Moab" by the book's end (Num 36:13). Exodus and Numbers form roughly a balanced pair in length with the events of Exodus presupposed by Numbers. For instance, the striking of the rock by Moses (Num 20:11) can only be understood if it is known that he was commanded to do so in Exod 17:5–7.[35]

Deuteronomy stands as the least dependent work of the five books. It too, however, shows contextual dependence; it contains Moses' final word to Israel in one day (1:3) from the same locale where the Book of Numbers closes—"east of the Jordan in the territory of Moab" (Deut 1:5). The opening section (chaps. 1–4) back-references the sojourn from Sinai to Moab as described in Numbers, and the book ends with the death of Moses and the succession of Joshua as anticipated in Num 27:12–23. Again we find that both Numbers and Deuteronomy are careful to establish the proper transition in leadership from the old generation to the succeeding one. The personal address of Moses (Deut 5–26) presents a theologically reflective restatement of the Sinaitic covenant as portrayed in Exodus. Chapters 27–34 consist of final warnings about Israel's prospective life in Canaan, a blessing, and the epilogue regarding the death of Moses. Moses is buried in "Moab," and as the Pentateuch volume closes, Israel is still encamped in the plains of Moab without a homeland.

STRUCTURE OF THE PENTATEUCH. The narrative plot, as we have said, distinguishes Exodus–Deuteronomy from the Book of Genesis by virtue of their attention to the formation of Israel and God's provision for the life of that people. We already have found that internally there is ample evidence of a narrative overlap among the five books, usually achieved by back-referencing the locale of the people (e.g., Sinai). There are additional internal signs that large narrative blocks have been stitched together. J. Sailhamer has identified three major literary "seams" in the Pentateuch where narrative blocks have been connected, indicating a fusion of units.[36] The first seam joins Genesis and Exodus–Deuteronomy at a juncture we would expect, given the earlier analysis of the narrative plot. The three "seams" are the poetic blessing of Jacob (Gen 49), the poetic oracles of Balaam (Num 23–24), and Moses' song and blessing (Deut 32–33). The rhetorical pattern at each of the three junctures consists of three recurring elements: an extensive narrative block, a poetic speech, and an epilogue. The narrative block Genesis 1–48 is followed with Jacob's blessing (Gen 49:1–27) and concluded with the epilogue of chap. 50. The Exodus and Sinai-wilderness narratives each conclude with poetic discourses (Exod 15; Num 23–24). Last, the whole of the Pentateuch is concluded with the poetic song and blessing of Moses (Deut 32–33) and completed with the epilogue of Deuteronomy 34.

Common language and motifs at each of the three major junctures, where

[35] For further discussion see Y. T. Radday, "Chiasmus in Hebrew Biblical Narrative" in *Chiasmus in Antiquity,* ed. J. W. Welch (Hildesheim: Gerstenberg, 1981), 84–86.

[36] Sailhamer, "Genesis," EBC (Grand Rapids: Zondervan, 1990), 6–8, and *The Pentateuch as Narrative,* 35–37.

the narrative and poetic speech occur, show a "homogeneous compositional stratum." At each point the central character (i.e., Jacob, Balaam, Moses) calls his audience together and declares his intention to speak of future events in "days to come." This expression, "days to come" *(bĕʾaḥărît hayyāmîm),* introduces the poetic speech to follow (Gen 49:1; Num 24:14; Deut 31:29). The occurrence of this phrase at only one other place (Deut 4:30) in the whole of the Pentateuch (where it too occurs at a connective seam) indicates that the composition of the Pentateuch reflects a strategy to shape the final work into one book. The theological implications of this analysis will concern us later. Here our point is that within the Pentateuch, though possessing diversity and disjunctures, there is a unifying strategy for the entire work.

This analysis is complemented by the study of D. T. Olson, who proposes that the *tōlĕdōt* formula that is integral to the arrangement of Genesis (occurring eleven times[37]) is also structurally significant for the whole of the Pentateuch.[38] It occurs once more in the Pentateuch at Num 3:1, "This is the account of the family of Aaron and Moses."[39] This would give twelve occasions of the formula, corresponding in number to Israel's tribes. According to Olson's reconstruction, the compiler of Numbers wants to demonstrate the generational hope in the new descendants who supplant the old exodus generation. What is critical to Olson's thesis is the threefold function of the *tōlĕdōt* formula in Genesis: (1) it has a narrowing function where it brings into sharp relief the elect line of promise; (2) it introduces the subject matter of the subsequent block of narrative (or genealogical list); and (3) it looks forward to future progeny. In the case of the *tōlĕdōt* superscription at Num 3:1, we find that chaps. 1–2 report the census numbers of the twelve tribes and locate each one's position with respect to the tent of meeting. Chapter 3's superscription introduces the restricted genealogy of Aaron's sons, which has the narrowing effect of distinguishing the elect priesthood of Aaron. This explains why Numbers 3–4 presents a Levitical census after that of Israel's general census. As the census lists at chaps. 1 and 26 show the perpetuation of the twelve tribes of Jacob, the Levitical census at chaps. 3–4 and 26 shows the same for the tribe of Levi. The former *tōlĕdōt* of Jacob (Gen 37:2) concerns the twelve sons, now Israel's tribes, and the Aaron *tōlĕdōt* spotlights the Levitical tribe. The appearance of "Moses" in the superscription, though Moses' genealogical listing is not presented, is appropriate since the following narrative of Numbers concerns him as the central figure. Also the reference to Moses looks ahead to the new leadership that will take Israel into Canaan.

As we saw in Sailhamer's analysis with the recurring reference to the future

---

[37] Gen 2:4; 5:1; 6:9; 10:1; 11:10; 11:27; 25:12; 25:19; 36:1; 36:9; 37:2.

[38] D. T. Olson, *The Death of the Old and the Birth of the New: The Framework of the Book of Numbers and the Pentateuch,* BJS 71 (Chico, Cal.: Scholars Press, 1985), 83–125.

[39] Also Ruth 4:18; cp. the similar 1 Chr 1:29.

by "days to come" *(bĕʾaḥărît hayyāmîm),* the theme of Numbers concerns the future conquest generation as the narrative describes the passing of the dying exodus generation.[40] Deuteronomy fits therefore as the epilogue to the generational framework of Genesis-Numbers, giving Moses' word of forewarning to the new generation about to receive its forefathers' inheritance lost through disobedience. So as Numbers is occupied with the death of the old generation, Deuteronomy also attends to the death of the former era by the death of Moses, who closes out the old generation, opening the way for the conquest generation to enter Canaan.

THEME OF THE PENTATEUCH. Since we have recognized the essential homogeneity of Genesis and the remaining books of the Pentateuch, we must consider the unifying theme of the work. We have said that the core of the Pentateuch is the Sinai revelation, but this does not account for the development of the Pentateuch as a whole. D. J. A. Clines has shown that the theme, that is, the idea that explains the unity and structural development of the Pentateuch, is the not-yet realized promise of blessing for the patriarchs.[41] The promissory blessing to Abraham in Gen 12:1–3 expresses the thematic material of the Pentateuch: (1) promise of *descendants,* (2) promise of *relationship* with God, and (3) the promise of *land* (see "Theology of Genesis" on p. 54). This "blessing" is repeated in varied forms for Abraham (15:4–5,9–21; 17:4–7,19–20; 18:18; 22:17), Isaac (26:3–4), and Jacob (28:13–14; 32:29). Genesis 12–50 features the promise of *descendants,* and although the tension of a son born to Sarah is resolved, the book closes with a mere "seventy" persons descended through Jacob. Moreover, they are in "Egypt," not Canaan (46:27), living under the protective custody of Egypt's royal house.

Exodus and Leviticus emphasize the promise of *relationship* with God, which is cast in the form of the patriarchal blessing: "I will take you as my own people, and I will be your God . . . and I will bring you to the land I swore with uplifted hand to give to Abraham, to Isaac and Jacob" (Exod 6:7–8). Leviticus elaborates on this relationship by establishing the cultic regulations required to preserve this communion (Lev 26:46). Although the relationship is sealed by covenant ("I am the LORD your God," 20:7), the people remain at Sinai as Exodus concludes. Nevertheless, its closing anticipates a departure for Canaan (40:38). Leviticus also begins and ends with Israel remaining at the "door of the Tabernacle" at Sinai (1:1; 27:34). Though there is no movement toward Canaan, the book depicts the animated life of Israel's

[40] E.g., the disobedient generation (14:20–37), the second census noting that none of the exodus generation had survived (26:63–65), the death of the first generation's leadership (Miriam, 20:1; Aaron, 20:22–28), and the provision of Joshua as Moses' successor (27:12–23). See Olson, *The Death of the Old,* 90–97.

[41] D. J. A. Clines, *The Theme of the Pentateuch,* JSOTSup 10 (Sheffield: University of Sheffield Press, 1978).

cultic institutions, looking to the future.[42]

Numbers begins with Israel still encamped in the shadow of Sinai; its attention is given to the *land* promise as preparations are underway for departure to Canaan (Num 1:1–10:11). Although the book opens in Israel's second year, it closes thirty-eight years later, and the people have progressed only as far as the banks of the Jordan (1:1; 10:11). Their efforts to obtain the land were thwarted by unbelief (chaps. 13–14), and the remainder of the account tells of Israel's vagabond existence in the desert. Nevertheless, the land remained its hope and goal (chap. 20); a foretaste of their inheritance is enjoyed by the dispossession of Amorite kings in Transjordan (chaps. 22–24). After overcoming additional setbacks, the people finally arrive on the plains of Moab (33:48), anticipating the realization of the promises, and there they remain. But the narrative of Numbers also recounts the transition in the *descendants* of the promise, closing out the old generation, now dead and buried, save Moses himself, as the Lord had said at Kadesh (e.g., 14:29–35).[43] This leaves the new generation poised to receive Moses' final testament and then occupy the land.

The final work of Deuteronomy continues the emphasis on the *land* element of the promises: "In the land the LORD your God is giving you to possess as your inheritance, he will richly bless you" (15:4; also 3:2,18,20; 4:1; 12:1). It is described as a land "flowing with milk and honey" which was promised to the "fathers" (6:3; 11:9; 26:5,15; 27:3). The last words of Moses reiterate the promise: "This is the land I promised on oath to Abraham, Isaac and Jacob when I said, 'I will give it to your descendants'" (34:4). The promises of descendants (1:8) and covenant relationship (e.g., 26:18) are not neglected. The forewarning of covenant disloyalty sobers the enthusiasm of entering Canaan (chap. 29). Indeed, Deuteronomy concludes with Israel's heroic leader obtaining not one handful of sacred soil; he has but one look at the elusive land still awaiting the people (chap. 34). Prematurely, he dies and is buried outside the land as divine recompense for his disobedience. D. T. Olson has argued that the motif of Moses' death is crucial to the theme of Deuteronomy.[44] Reference to Moses' death is prominent in the chapter preparing the way for new leadership under Joshua (31:2,14,16,27,29). Moses' death is necessary for the closing out of the old generation, enabling the new to go forward; except for the faithful spies Joshua and Caleb, he alone remains of that disobedient generation.

The Pentateuch concludes, like each of its books, looking beyond itself to

---

[42] See J. R. Porter, *Leviticus* (Cambridge: Cambridge University Press, 1976), 7, quoted in Clines, *Theme,* 51; also J. Milgrom, "Leviticus," IDBSup, 541, quoted in B. S. Childs, *Introduction to the Old Testament* (Philadelphia: Fortress, 1979), 129.

[43] So Olson, *The Death of the Old,* 186–91.

[44] E.g., 1:37; 3:23–27; 4:21–22; 18:15–19; 33:1; 34:4–7. See Olson, *Deuteronomy and the Death of Moses: A Theological Reading* (Minneapolis: Fortress, 1994).

the fulfillment of the promissory blessing. The collection as it stands is open-ended, without a satisfactory resolution. Why was the Book of Joshua excluded so as to form a Pentateuch, although it is not until Joshua's conquest narratives that Israel enjoys the land? Much scholarly debate has swirled around this problem for the traditional Jewish canon of five books.[45] Although this question remains unanswered by scholars, the fivefold arrangement is widely regarded as an artificial product of the postexilic period, probably formed by Ezra, because of the sociopolitical demands of the times. Since the Jews of the diaspora, such as those living in Babylon, had no part in the land, the conquest narrative as the realization of the patriarchal promise was problematic. By defining the normative expression of the Jewish faith as that which was found in the Pentateuch, the land promise was not required for Jews outside Palestine to lay claim to their religious heritage.[46]

It is more convincing, however, that the imposing figure of Moses himself explains the canonical gathering of the Pentateuch as a distinctive unit. Since Moses was paradigmatic for the mediatorial role of prophet (Deut 18:15–22; 34:10), irrespective of the land, for he died outside the land, the laws he revealed were consequently normative for future generations whether or not in the land (cf. Deut 31:11–13,19–22,26).[47] The Pentateuch shows that prophetic activity is derived from Moses (Num 11:25).[48] From the outset, whatever one believes the contents of the expression "Book of the Law" (Josh 1:8) may be, it was authoritative as the Word of God because it was given by "my servant Moses" (Josh 1:7). Rabbinic tradition followed suit, reflecting the long-held opinion that Genesis–Deuteronomy was by Moses and was authoritative for the regulating of the Jewish community. This is consistent with the eschatological perspective of the Pentateuch; it is ever looking forward to future generations, where appropriation of the promissory blessings can be reexperienced. Whenever the practice in the nation drifted alarmingly from the Mosaic pattern, reformation inevitably followed. The eighth-century prophets (Amos, Hosea, Isaiah, and Micah) and their later counterparts (Jeremiah, Ezekiel), as well as the scribe Ezra and even the heterodox "Covenanters" of Qumran—all called Israel back to the authentic faith of Moses. The same was true of Jesus (cf. Matt 8:4; 19:7–8; 23:2; Mark 7:10; 12:26; Luke 16:29,31; 24:44; John 5:45–46; 7:19).

The survival of Israel as a nation was not necessary for its religion to con-

---

[45] E.g., G. von Rad, "The Form-Critical Problem of the Hexateuch," in *The Problem of the Hexateuch and Other Essays,* trans. E. Dicken (1938; reprint, New York: McGraw-Hill, 1966), 1–78; M. Noth, *The Deuteronomistic History* (1943; reprint, Sheffield: JSOT, 1981).

[46] E.g., J. A. Sanders, *Torah and Canon* (Philadelphia: Fortress, 1972), 44–53.

[47] Childs discusses this in part in his redefinition of Mosaic authorship as merely a theological function (*Introduction,* 133–34).

[48] T. W. Mann, *The Book of the Torah* (Atlanta: John Knox, 1988), 157.

tinue into the exile. The promissory blessing of God's people, therefore, transcended the requirement of a geopolitical state. It was in the desert, not Canaan, that they first knew their God. The Pentateuch therefore spoke a relevant message to those in and outside the land. Although the Pentateuch ends without conclusion, it still reflects the accomplishment of the immediate goal—the creation of a people ruled by God. Thus the Pentateuch's ending resounds its opening. God has created humanity to exercise dominion in the world under the beneficence of God (Gen 1:28), and Israel too was formed to rule in the land under the theocratic umbrella of Sinai's revelation.[49]

Now we must backtrack to the inauguration of the Pentateuch and explain how Genesis 1–11 functions thematically. By virtue of Abraham's relationship to God, his descendants can be a vehicle of blessing (or curse) for all the families of the earth. This universal aspect of the promissory blessing reflects God's intention to "bless" humanity from the dawning of human life (1:28; cf. "blessing" also at 1:22; 2:3). The realization of that blessing is postponed (though not completely) by human disobedience; the ensuing generations depict an encroaching evil. Yet God resolves to perpetuate the hope of blessing through the Adamic line of Seth (5:1–3) and Noah (9:1,7). Nevertheless, the motif of "curse" runs parallel through the episodic events of Genesis 1–11: God curses the serpent (3:15), the soil from which man was made (3:17), Cain for murder (4:11), and the earth for the wickedness of society (8:21). Finally, Noah curses Canaan (9:25). As though countering this fivefold cursing, the patriarchal promises (Gen 12:1–3) contain a fivefold repetition of "blessing."[50]

This thematic linkage between the preamble (Gen 1–11) and the not-yet realized blessings of the patriarchs (Gen 12–Deut 34) binds the whole. Our theme must be expanded to include the not-yet realized promissory blessing of *humanity,* which is partially fulfilled through the historical descendants of the Mesopotamian Abraham, father of the Hebrews.

(3) Genesis and the Mosaic Community

Since the Mosaic community was defined by the formative events of Sinai, how do the events of Sinai and the desert narration bear on the telling of Genesis? We have found that the Pentateuch in structure (cf. "days to come" and *tōlĕdōt*) and theme (not-yet realized blessings) looks beyond itself to the eschatological realization of the promissory blessings (see "Structure of the Pentateuch," p. 46). Genesis also must be viewed as a component of this eschatological perspective. This suggests that Genesis is read as an interpretation of the past with an eye on Israel's future. It should not be surprising then to discover in the Genesis narratives precursory images that have their parallel in the

[49] Ibid., 161.

[50] G. Wenham, *Genesis 1–15,* WBC (Waco: Word, 1987), li.

experiences of Israel. Genesis was cast so that the Mosaic community could draw the inferential analogies between the distant past and their present experiences.

We find this well-illustrated in the language of Genesis and in patriarchal events. First, the vocabulary and imagery found in the Mosaic economy describe a pre-Mosaic event. The garden description of Genesis 2–3 has striking parallels with the symbolism and language of the later tabernacle.[51] Eden is distinguished by pure gold and onyx (2:12). Both materials were commonly used in the adornment of the tabernacle (Exod 25:3–7) and the holy vestments of the high priest (Exod 25:11,17; 25:24; 25:31; 26:6,29; 28:4–5; 30:1–6). In particular the clasps of the sacred ephod are two onyx stones, each inscribed with the names of Israel's tribes (28:9–11; 1 Chr 29:2). The "resin" of 2:12 (or "bdellium") is among the aromatic fragrances used at the altar especially blended for the occasion of the Lord's presence at the tabernacle (Exod 30:34–38).

The language of the man's work (*ʿābad* and *šāmar*) in 2:15 is found in the description of priestly duties; the tandem of terms occurs only here and in detailing the responsibilities of the Levites (Num 3:7–8; 8:26; 18:5–6). The clothing of the man and woman in garments (*yalbiš* and *kotnôt,* 3:21) is analogous in description to the use of the priestly garments (Exod 28:39,41; 29:8; 40:14; Lev 8:13). The "cherubim" (3:24) oversee the ark (Exod 25:18–22) and decorate the walls of the tabernacle (Exod 26:31). The cherubim are "placed" *(yaškēn)* on the "east side" of the garden to guard its entrance. The term "placed" ("dwell"), from *škn,* is commonly used of God's presence in Israel's camp (Exod 25:8; 29:45–46; Num 5:3), and the word *miškān*, "tabernacle" or "dwelling," is a noun derivative. The significance of the location of the garden to the east (2:8,14) and the cherubim "at the east side of the garden of Eden" (3:24) parallels the direction of the tabernacle, whose entrance faced east (Exod 27:13; 38:13).

Second, patriarchal episodes prefigured events in the life of Israel, thus connecting the experiences of Moses' community with those of its fathers. We find this, for example, in the route of Abraham into Canaan by way of Shechem, Ai/Bethel, and the Negev (Gen 12:1–9), which is repeated by Jacob upon his return from Haran (Gen 33:18–20; 35:14–15,27); both patriarchs build altars of worship at Shechem and Bethel. The pattern of traversing these three regions is repeated in the conquest narratives of Joshua: Ai/Bethel (Josh 7:2; 8:9), Shechem, where an altar is built (Josh 8:30), and south of Ai/Bethel toward the Negev (Josh 10) and then north of Shechem (Josh 11). Again the

[51] E.g., Wenham, "Sanctuary Symbolism in the Garden of Eden Story," in *Proceedings of the Ninth World Congress of Jewish Studies. Division A. The Period of the Bible* (Jerusalem: World Congress of Jewish Studies, 1986), 19–25; and his *Genesis 1–15,* which notes many tabernacle echoes (esp. 65, 86).

narrative of Abraham's sojourn in Egypt (Gen 12:10–20) is shaped remarkably like the account of Israel's experience in Egypt, from Jacob's descent to the exodus events (Gen 41–Exod 12).[52] Jewish tradition explicitly connects 12:12–20 with the history of Israel: "You find that whatever is written in regard to our father, Abraham, is written also with regard to his children" (*Gen. Rab.* 40.6). The language of Abraham's faith (Gen 15:6; 22:1,12) is found again in Exod 20:2,20, where the Ten Commandments are revealed to Israel, showing that Abraham's faith is a precursor to Israel's obedience to the covenant-law.[53] Thus the lives of the patriarchs by divine sovereignty prefigure as a shadow the life of Abraham's descendants, Israel.

(4) Genesis and the Christian Proclamation

Since the Pentateuch is "prophetic," both as Moses' proclamation and in its eschatological perspective, it readily speaks to the Christian community, which proclaims that the not-yet-realized promises of blessing are being filled up in Jesus Christ and his church. The Pentateuch looks to the revelation of Christ and the formation of his new community in two significant ways. First, it looks for the coming of the eschatological Second Moses, whom Moses announced as his successor (Deut 18:15,18–19). Both Jesus and the apostles interpreted him as the realization of Moses' forecast (John 1:21,25,45; 5:46; 6:14; 7:40; Acts 3:22–26; 7:37). Moses is typological of Christ.

Second, the Mosaic community was typological of the church. The Pentateuch must look to the Christian community to witness the realization of God's blessing on the human family through Abraham's seed. The promise of progeny, says the apostle Paul, is realized by all those in Christ who are the offspring of Abraham's faith (Rom 4:11,16–21; Gal 3:29). This progeny is made up of all nations, and thus the promise of blessing is enjoyed by Gentile and Jew alike (Gal 3:6–9). Finally, the inheritance of a promised land, which Abraham longed to enter, is found in the heavenly Jerusalem (Heb 11:8–10 with Gen 12:7; 13:15). Thus the eschatological character of Genesis as the foundation to the Pentateuch encourages the Christian community to see itself as the fulfillment ("filling up") of the ancient community, a continuum of God's people. Christian proclamation requires therefore a gospel moored in the Hebrew Torah, for the apostles did not neglect the Jewish parentage of the church's birth. The theological "Bethlehem" of the church is inseparably wedded to the promissory blessing of the fathers and the nativity of Abraham's descendants as a nation.

---

[52] U. Cassuto, *A Commentary on the Book of Genesis. Part II. From Noah to Abraham,* trans. I. Abrahams (Jerusalem: Magnes, 1964), 303–6 and 334–37.

[53] See R. W. L. Moberly, *The Old Testament of the Old Testament: Patriarchal Narratives and Mosaic Yahwism* (Minneapolis: Fortress, 1992), 144–45.

For the New Testament church, persons and events in early Genesis served as paradigms for Christian theology and ministry. Adam points to the "last Adam" (Rom 5:12–21; 1 Cor 15:21–22,35–49), and Adam and Eve are instructive for proper order in worship (1 Cor 11:1–16; 1 Tim 2:13–15). Noah's flood and his subsequent deliverance speak to the rite of Christian baptism and the eschatological conflagration of the Second Advent (1 Pet 3:20; 2 Pet 2:5). But more than symbols and shadows as particulars, early Genesis in its entirety concerns all peoples. It is universal in scope as is the church and therefore addresses the antecedent history shared by all people groups in every age. Genesis 1–11 transcends the historical contingencies of Hebrew people and institutions. Its interests are as broad as cosmic history and the vicissitudes of Everyman.

4. Theology of Genesis

Although the focus of this volume is on the theology of Genesis 1–11, it cannot be discussed independently of chaps. 12–50 as though the two exist autonomously. We do not have two theologies but one unified message regarding God as beneficent Creator and Savior whose election of Abraham, Isaac, and Jacob is the nuclear fulfilling of divine intention for the worldwide human family first announced at creation (1:28). The genealogical schema (i.e., *tōlĕdōt*) of the book that dominates the structure of the whole has set the primeval narratives as the preamble to Israel's history, thus understanding these first events as part and parcel of Israel's national history (see "Literary Genesis" on p. 25).[54] This puts the particularistic past of Israel in a cosmic setting and shows thereby that its history of salvation pertains to all humanity. In considering the theology of Genesis, therefore, we must give proper weight to its literary character. Its extant literary shape is our only access to Genesis's theology. So we face the challenge of deriving the theological contribution of Genesis 1–11 from the shape and contents of Genesis as a composition made up of diverse literary genres and sources. The literary theme of Genesis will serve as our first entry point into the theological substratum of the composition.

(1) Patriarchal Promises

When we consider the narrative story line of Genesis, the pivotal episode is the election of Abraham (12:1–3), which turns the narrative interest from the universal setting of the human family, viewed as essentially one people before the tower event, to the singular family of Terah's son, Abraham. In particular, the patriarchal promises first found in 12:1–3 are diligently pursued by the author as they occur repeatedly in the Abrahamic narrative chain (e.g., 12:7;

[54] See Westermann, *Genesis 1–11: A Commentary* (Minneapolis: Augsburg, 1984), 64–67.

13:15–17; 15:7–21; 17:4–8; 22:16–18), again for Isaac (26:2–4) and Jacob (28:13–14; 35:9–12), and in the Joseph narrative as well (46:1–4). The narrowing technique of genealogy in early Genesis and, second, narrative duration sharpen the focus on the uninterrupted line from Adam to the central figure Noah, constituting ten generations, and from Noah to Abraham, who is the goal, also constituting ten generations. Conversely in later Genesis narrative duration and, second, genealogy highlight the three character interests of Abraham, Jacob, and Joseph. Abraham, as has been said elsewhere, is the funnel whereby the universal promises find their realization in the salvation-history of Abraham's Israel.

BLESSING. Genesis 12:1–3 possesses the three elements which as intertwined into one entity make up the book's thematic-theological core and also provide the unifying center for the book's parts: the divine promises of *blessing, seed,* and *land* for Abraham and his successors.[55] It is the last of three programmatic statements given in Genesis that establish the divine agenda whereby we measure the progress of the divine purpose in the book (also 1:26–28; 3:15). Genesis 12:1–3 establishes that by the Abrahamic lineage the nations (all humanity) will enter into the blessing envisioned for all peoples created in the "image of God" (1:26–27; 5:1b–2). Blessing for "all peoples on earth" (12:3) is reiterated at the dawning of the postdiluvian era (9:1,7) when the creation charge is reissued for Noah and his sons as the progenitors of the nations (9:18–19; 10:1–32). This universal perspective in 10:1–11:9 is the ideological preamble as well as the geopolitical setting for the emergence of Terah's seed, Abraham (11:10–26). God in effect appoints a new people, not named in the extensive Table of Nations (10:1–32) and yet also in continuum with the world of nations by virtue of Terah's descent from Shem. The debacle at the Tower of Babel (11:1–9) explains both the existence of the diverse nations and the redemptive necessity of an Abram, whose later name "Abraham" reflects his status as the "father of many nations" (17:5–6,16).

Primarily the literary thread uniting the promises for humanity and those of Israel's fathers is the unbroken genealogical line from Adam to Abraham (5:1–32; 11:10–26). This also concerns the historical continuum that yokes creation and the antediluvian world with that of the patriarchs. As we find in 5:1–2, the blessing for all humanity in 1:26–28 is presupposed in the recounting of the Adamic line and is heard anew for the Noahic family (9:1,7). Actually, the central figure in the genealogical scheme is Noah, listed tenth in the twenty generations spanning Adam and Abraham, who bridges the old world of creation and the world of the subsequent patriarchs. His *tōlĕdōt* story (6:8–9:29) is set at the

[55] See Clines, *The Theme of the Pentateuch*, JSOTSup (Sheffield: University of Sheffield Press, 1978); T. W. Mann, "'All the Families of the Earth': The Theological Unity of Genesis," *Int* 45 (1991): 34–53.

midpoint of the primeval history and occupies the preeminent attention of the early corpus. Both Adam and Noah, who father three sons, are matched by Terah's three sons, the first of whom named is Father Abraham (11:26).

But the very notion of election and the explicit language of "curse" in the patriarchal promises (12:3) require the explanation provided in early Genesis—human sin and its consequences, curse and death (3:14–19). "Curse" is a repeated motif, first uttered against the offending serpent, who was instrumental in the woman's transgression (3:14), and second, against the "ground" from which man was taken (3:17) and to which he was to return (3:18–19). "Curse" occurs thrice more: against Cain (4:11), the earth again (8:21), and against Canaan, although this time by a human imprecation (9:25). Although the postdiluvian sacrifice of Noah alleviated the punishment of curse against the ground for societal wickedness (6:5–7,11–12; 8:21), the Edenic curse against the "ground" remained, and thus the primeval history must look forward to another, namely, Abraham, by whom the blessing can be realized.

As we noted already, our author's favorite structural device of genealogy provides the linkage for the carrying out of the death sentence upon disobedient humanity. Genesis 5 shows at one and the same time the blessing of procreation in the Adamic family and, conversely, the consequence of human sin by the refrain "and then he died." This twofold reality is rehearsed at the Noahic midpoint in the postdiluvian era. There we find a proliferation of offspring, i.e., the "nations" (9:1, 18–19; 10:1–32), but continuing evidence, despite the purge of the watery abyss, that creation is still afoul requiring new safeguards to preserve human life (9:2–6). Moreover, the first utterance of human "curse" is Noah's against his own offspring (i.e., Canaan, 9:25), which we learn from the Table of Nations (10:15–19) pertains to one of the nations which Abraham's family will ultimately dispossess (15:18–21). Those peoples outside the Abrahamic line who threaten its integrity (even unwittingly) are subject to the plagues and death of curse (12:17; 20:3).

Human death has its explication also in the earlier garden *tōlĕdōt* (2:4–4:26), which tells of human freedom to obey the Lord's command (2:17). But Adam and Eve's ill-fated choice (3:1–6) results in expulsion and denial to the "tree of life" (3:22), which otherwise secured the divine blessing. Nevertheless, God is also free to achieve the promissory blessing despite human disobedience, and he secures for the fallen couple both garments of atonement (3:21) and a promissory hope in the "seed" of the woman (3:15), who is the "mother of all the living" (3:20).

SEED. This brings before us yet another element of the theological fulcrum in 12:1–3, namely, the promise of "seed," a prominent motif in later Genesis (e.g., 12:7; 13:15–16; 17:7; 22:17; 26:3–4; 28:4; 48:4). This lexical item joins the motif of "blessing and curse" to constitute the book's preoccupation with *inherited* blessing. Alienation and separation within the patriarchal family is commonplace (i.e., Lot, Ishmael, Esau), though even the rejected enjoy the shared blessing of Abraham by propagating nations (17:20–21; 21:18; 36:6–8). Yet those nations (i.e., Ammonites and Moabites, Ishmaelites, and Edomites) are excluded from the full blessing since they remain outside the land of promise. This feature of patriarchal history has its antecedents in chaps. 1–11, where we find the same alienation among early human life (i.e., Cain, Canaan, Babel).[56] It is no surprise that the genealogical tables are pressed into service as the bridge for the "seed" element between the earlier and later narratives. This is a natural vehicle for the "seed" theme in light of its prominent metaphorical sense in Genesis, meaning "offspring."[57] However, its first appearance is literal, occurring in the creation account (1:11–12,29),[58] which establishes at the outset that the "seed," whether of creation or patriarch, has a proper place as appointed by the sovereign Creator-Lord.

"Seed" has its first metaphorical sense in 3:15, where the antipathy between an evil "seed" and the "seed" of the woman is the second programmatic statement in Genesis. This dual lineage of serpent's family versus the woman's family has its history evidenced throughout the whole of human and patriarchal narratives as they reveal the approved line of descent versus the outcast—as early as Cain and as late as Esau. The remarkable parallel in genealogical structure in 5:3–32 and 11:10–26 distinguishes their heritage as the elect lineage (Seth-Shem-Abram), bridging the antediluvian and postdiluvian eras as constituting the one tree of lineal blessing. Genealogical records for the excluded "seed" also are found, but the excluded family tree is usually presented first and passed over so as to pave the way for the appointed line that supersedes in the narrative sources: Cain precedes Seth (4:17–24; 5:3–32), Japheth and Ham precede Shem (10:2–20; 10:21–31; 11:10–26), Nahor precedes Abraham (22:20–24; 25:1–4), and Ishmael precedes Isaac (25:12–18; 25:19–20). This pattern is altered with the Jacob-Esau rivalry, where the record of Esau's Edomite offspring (36:1–43) follows Jacob's twelve-son genealogy (35:22b–26). But after dispensing with Esau's family, the narrative interest is sustained on the twelve sons, particularly Joseph, in the remainder of the book (chaps. 36–50).

In the history of early humanity, the "seed" and sibling-rivalry theme is first found in the murder of Abel by brother Cain (4:1–16). Yet the birth of Seth provides another "seed" to Eve in place of murdered Abel (4:25), establishing a new line of descent (4:25–26). The parallel but separate lines of Cainites and Sethites (4:17–26; 5:1–32) intermarry, coinciding with the last days of the wicked antediluvian age (6:5–7), leaving the aftermath recalled in the Noah

[56] Mann, "All the Families of the Earth," 350–51.

[57] See T. D. Alexander, "From Adam to Judah: The Significance of the Family Tree," *EvQ* 61 (1989): 5–19.

[58] Also in the Joseph narrative, 47:19,23–24.

tōlĕdōt (6:8–9:29). Although not as well represented, "seed" occurs twice in the flood narrative, a slight echo of the antediluvian past (7:3; 9:9), but the vineyard debacle (9:20–27) resounds the earlier division in the Adamic family by the rejected Ham-Canaan clan that is envisioned as subservient to the Shemite-Japhethite tent (9:24–27). The Ham-Canaanite dishonor is anticipated at 9:18 even before the sordid incident that leads to Ham's rejection, implying that emerging from the ark Ham was already to be distinguished from his brothers. The Table of Nations spells this out in listing the descendants of the three brothers as people groups of which the Hamite tree includes later Israel's notorious enemies (e.g., Egyptians, Canaanites, Mesopotamians).

LAND. We have yet to consider the third element in the promissory triad—the land/earth *(hāʾāreṣ)*—which prominently figures in the patriarchal stories, particularly the tension in the Jacob and Joseph narratives in which these patriarchs are estranged from Canaan (e.g., 12:5–7; 15:8; 26:1–3; 28:13; 35:12; 48:3–4; 50:24). The "land" component is alluded to in chaps. 1–11 as shown by the early attention to the "earth"/"land" in creation's six days (1:1–2:3) and the garden *tōlĕdōt* (2:4–4:26). The "earth" is first described as an uninhabitable wasteland (1:2) that is specially prepared on the third day of creation for the sustaining of life (1:9–12), after which it is the "earth" of blessing (1:26–30). Moreover, the Lord plants a garden (2:8–9) in the barren land (2:5–6) for the man made of the "ground" (2:7), and fruit of the ground becomes his source of sustenance (2:15–16). But it is the man's crime that results in divine curse against the "ground" (3:17), leading to Adam's new toil; and it is the blood-stained soil of innocent Abel that results in harsher penalty for Adam's son, Cain, who is expelled from the land (4:11–12).

This theme of earth/land is particularly dense in the central episode of the primeval history, which details the increasing violence in the "earth" by violent mankind (6:5–13) and the subsequent purging by the flood waters (chaps. 7–8).[59] This violence is the habit of antediluvian man and results in the destruction of the "earth" (6:17) and its inhabitants (e.g., 7:4; 7:21). Particularly, the flood episode demonstrates the inherent creaturehood of humanity and the interdependence of man and beast as well as humanity's connection to the earth as both source and domain. Human sin brought on the fierce recompense of the Lord's anger against all terrestrial life over which humanity presided (1:28).

Beyond the divine outrage, however, the "earth" receives God's persistent favor as shown by his re-creation of the new earth from the midst of the waters (8:7,11–14) and by the reissuing of the creation command to replenish the earth (9:1,7), assuring of a new beginning for the postdiluvian world. And in that new world is born Abraham, who will bring renewal to all the peoples now

[59] Noted among others by Kikawada, "The Shape of Genesis 11:1–9," in *Rhetorical Criticism: Essays in Honor of James Muilenburg,* PTMS 1 (Pittsburgh: Pickwick, 1974), 31.

scattered upon the "earth" (11:4,8–9; cp. 10:25,32). The land/earth language, "over the face of the whole earth" (11:4,9), in the Babel account echoes creation's charge to mankind (1:28–29), suggesting that the outcome of the dispersal at Babel in fact aided fearful man in fulfilling the divine charge to subdue the earth. In the aftermath of this dispersal arises the Terah clan whose member Abraham will bring blessing to those families of the earth (12:3).

While this promissory triad of blessing, seed, and land is the thematic cord binding the Book of Genesis, we find that the counterthemes of fratricide, violence, uncreation, and expulsion are the literary-theological foil for the promissory blessing. Man's constitution as "living being" is reversed by returning Adam to the dust (3:19). Reversal of creation's second and third days at the flood shows the waters drowning the earth in judgment (6:9–7:24). Adam and Eve are expelled from Eden (3:24), Cain is exiled from the "LORD's presence" (4:16), and the Babelites are scattered (11:9), all oriented toward the "east," indicating the loss of blessing. But remarkably in each instance the grace of God supersedes earth's wasteland or the just deserts of the sinner. The barren earth takes on resplendent glory, disobedient Adam finds survival outside Eden, ignoble Cain receives his protective "mark," Noah is "remembered" and the doomed earth is replenished by the ark's inhabitants, and finally the Babelites' folly is matched by the birth of Terah's son. Without Abraham the primeval history ends on the despairing note of exile. The primeval history therefore looks ahead to the divine call of Abraham to answer the sin and punishment that has recurred in the human family. God must make a new nation, the Hebrews, to achieve his blessing for humanity.

Israel's story is also the nations' story, for Abraham emerged from the world of nations and is the linchpin in the course of world history. But the patriarchal narratives show that the hope of redemption resides only with the Caller, not with Abraham, for his spiritual heritage experiences a slow but sure deterioration. This is prototypical of later Israel, whose apostasy resulted in expulsion from Canaan, landing Abraham's descendants back in Babylon. Consequently, Israel's historical vicissitudes of sin-punishment-restoration recycle the primeval history's call for a savior. The Old Testament is also ever looking forward to the divine realization of the primeval blessing. For the apostolic tradition the cosmic promise is realized in the spiritual headship of Jesus Christ and achieved in history. His death-resurrection accomplishes the eternal blessing of life in the church made up of the Jewish and Gentile nations (Rom 4:16–17; Gal 3:6–8,16).

Having established that thematically the theology of early Genesis is found related to the patriarchal stories, we can ask how the particular episodes of chaps. 1–11 contribute to the theme and theology of the book. There is dispute about what is the overarching plan for the joining of these early accounts: creation, Adam and Eve, Cain and Abel, the flood, and the tower. It probably is too simple to adhere to one theme, such as spread-of-sin/spread-of-grace or human hubris transgressing its inherent limits. Any one pattern is found reductionistic, unable to account for all the contents satisfactorily, especially when we include with the narratives the place of the genealogies and the linking materials.[60] What we find in chaps. 1–11 is the divine initiation of blessing, which is compromised by human sin followed by gracious preservation of the promise: blessing-sin-grace. This is matched by the patriarchal stories, where the patriarchs receive the promise but fail the Lord; and though meriting no special favor, they are restored by divine prerogative. We find, for example, that the sin (or threat) is human hubris in Eden and the tower or human murder and violence in Cain-Abel and the flood. The restoration may be the provision of life despite Eden's sin or re-creation following the un-creation of the earth.

What we learn from the episodes of early Genesis collectively is that the Lord is good and that human sin does not ultimately derail his beneficent plan for his good world.[61] But also, God is not indifferent to human sin; he always punishes sinners and always in relation to a concrete infraction. In other words, the Lord is not capricious and can be counted on to act justly and effectively with human culprits. Yet we must mitigate this last observation since the Lord does not act as a robot in each case; his response varies in nature and intensity. We are puzzled at times how he can act so benevolently (Cain) in some cases and in others so vehemently (e.g., the flood). Moreover, we find that human beings are especially related to God and also have weighty obligations as a consequence of his special endowment. Man and woman are responsible for their actions, and while there is always an accountability, the outcome of forgiveness and preservation follows. The grace of God in Genesis always supersedes the sin regardless of its kind or degree.

(2) God and His World

God is Maker of all that exists, including time and space, and he shapes the life of his world to achieve his ends for the earth and its inhabitants. The Creator transcends his physical creation. He is neither equivalent to the material world and its processes nor subservient to them. The material world is not an extension of his Being (not divine), and the world is not living ontological

[60] See the primary proposals reviewed in Clines, "Theme in Genesis 1–11," *CBQ* 38 (1976): 483–507, reprinted in *I Studied Inscriptions from before the Flood: Ancient Near Eastern, Literary, and Linguistic Approaches to Genesis 1–11* (Winona Lake: Eisenbrauns, 1994), 285–309. Also for the proposal of hubris see J. Sasson, "The 'Tower of Babel' as a Clue to the Redactional Structuring of the Primeval History [Gen. 1–11:9]," in *The Bible World: Essays in Honor of Cyrus H. Gordon* (New York: Ktav, 1980), 211–19. For the idea of threat, based on the *Atrahasis* parallel, see Kikawada and Quinn, *Before Abraham Was,* 62–69.

[61] See the observations of Clines, "Theme of Genesis 1–11," and F. Mauldin, "Story Patterns: How It Says and What It Says," *SLJT* 30 (1987): 125–40.

Being. His world is a "good" world, and it testifies to his glory, power, and majesty as Creator. Also the Lord has a relationship with his material creation by superintendence and involvement. He has dressed the earth so that it might be the hospitable home for his personal imprint on creation, namely, human life. He also is One who has moral demands and calls those made in his image to accountability for their choices. But he is not shackled by their choices, for he is free to act benevolently by preserving his creation despite human waywardness and sets about to deliver them, even making a safe haven for the most recalcitrant. He is irrevocably committed to the preservation of his "earth" and its inhabitants, including the lower creatures (e.g., 9:1–17). Thus we have a Sovereign Lord who purposes that the earth enter into his bounty, yet without diminishing the integrity of human choice and culpability.

(3) Human Life

God has made human life distinct from all other material life by virtue of mankind's creation "in the image of God." Human life has been set in authority over the terrestrial earth to exercise responsible governance. It is the *imago Dei* that defines the human. Humanity is unique and uniquely represents God. Mankind is creature, not divine, but made alive by the divine inbreathing. Although all life is valuable, human life is sacred and requires the severest penalty if violated. Since all human life is created in the image of God, there is no person or class of humans lesser than others. The human family is of one kind, all descendants of the same mother (3:20), and therefore are of the same kinship. There also is diversity within the human family according to gender differentiation and geopolitical ethnic groups. Mankind is also sexual, male and female, and has the endowed power to propagate. God created humanity as community, husband and wife, living in coordinated harmony. Human beings as created persons in community enjoy a relationship with God and with one another. Thus human beings are persons, individually and collectively, who worship God as Creator through obedience and offerings of repentance and thanksgiving.

(4) Sin

Evil is extraneous to God's "good" creation; it did not originate with God nor man. The origins of evil remain a mystery. Human beings are sinners making sinful choices and imagining sinful thoughts. The human condition of selfish autonomy and moral degeneracy had its origin as event in the sinful choice of Adam. Sin did not always exist but came into the world at a specific point in human history, impacting all human choice and environment. Sin results in divine punishment, including defeat, painful labor, and death. God, however, is not bound by sin and mitigates the punishment by divine mercy. Sin does not obliterate the *imago Dei,* making a sinner a nonperson, but sin diminishes humanity's glory. Ultimately, human life will have victory over sin and evil.

(5) Civilization

The arts and sciences are the invention and discovery of human knowledge and are not divine in origin or nature. Human progress is granted and favored by God, but when appropriated in isolation from or in opposition to God, it is wicked folly. The state is a social instrument for achieving orderly life among people groups, but it is not divine and has no *absolute* authority over human beings.

(6) Covenant

The importance of "covenant" *(bĕrît)* for the patriarchal narratives is found in the formal covenant declarations made by God in 15:18 in the context of Abraham's faith in the Lord and in 17:2–27, where the sign of the covenant (circumcision) is explained. In the Abrahamic case the covenant forms a unique relationship between the Lord and the patriarch to which God commits himself for all future generations of the Abrahamic family. It is similar in type to a royal grant, established between patron deity and king as in the Davidic covenant (2 Sam 7).

The Noahic "covenant" is like Abraham's in that it presupposes the righteousness of the recipient, Noah (cp. 6:8; 15:6); and it possesses a sign, the rainbow (9:13–14,16). As with the royal grant, the covenant pertains to Noah as an individual, but it also is given for subsequent generations. Another common feature between the two is the absence of stipulations. Noah and Abraham are the recipients of this gracious favor without regard to human contribution or obligation.[62] What distinguishes the Noahic from the patriarchal one and for that matter all others recounted in the Old Testament is its truly universal perspective. It is God's commitment to the whole of humanity and all terrestrial creation—including the surviving animal population. It is not a covenant related to election (Abraham, David) nor salvation (Sinai). It is, however, a covenant pledge that insures there will be a future world where election and salvation for Israel can occur.[63] Since the flood was divine retribution for humanity's wickedness (6:5–7,11–13), the recognition that man would not change in his essential corruption was answered, not by severer penalties but by the promise that another catastrophe of this sort would never be experienced again (8:21–22). The covenant with Noah (9:8–17) assures by sustaining

[62] For an argument, however, that there are conditional aspects even in the covenants with Noah and Abraham, see B. K. Waltke, "The Phenomenon of Conditionality within Unconditional Covenants," in *Israel's Apostasy and Restoration,* ed. A. Gileadi (Grand Rapids: Baker, 1988), 126–27, 128–30.

[63] See Rendtorff, *Canon and Theology,* 126–29.

human existence that the renewed charge of blessing to postdiluvian humanity (9:1,7) can take place. God therefore has committed himself to the world in such a way as to insure the birth and prosperity of humanity in its volatile environment with the purpose of ultimately redeeming mankind despite its deplorable wickedness.

5. Interpreting Genesis

The history of interpreting Genesis is a microcosm of the various critical schools that have dominated biblical studies in the post-Enlightenment era. Genesis has always been a fascinating sample text for scholars in applying experimental methods of biblical research. Yet the history of interpretation did not begin with the rise of source criticism in the eighteenth century with H. B. Witter and J. Astruc. There is a common prejudice on the part of modern interpreters to view modernity's readings as the only way of entering the passage. Genesis was a source of theological reflection since earliest times as attested in the Pentateuchal materials themselves.

Until the modern critical period there was a consensus that the Pentateuch was a unified, coherent work that came substantially from the pen of Moses, though there were diverse hermeneutical systems employed, including Jewish midrash and Jewish and Christian allegorical and literal readings. Some quarters pondered if Moses were the author at every point, such as the medieval Jewish commentator Ibn Ezra (1092–1167), and most commentators recognized that Moses made use of sources in some sense, especially in the writing of Genesis. But with the rise of historical-critical methods, the centuries-long agreement of an essentially homogeneous Pentateuch was displaced for many by the new paradigm of a composite text that was constructed by many hands across many centuries.

In the case of Genesis its compositional history was attributed to three putative interwoven documents (J, E, and P) that could be excavated from the extant text by employing literary and historical criteria. Once extricated, the sources could supposedly be delineated as to contents and theology, and dated within a half century with reasonable assurance. By the end of the nineteenth century this "source" approach dominated all Old Testament scholarship with few exceptions, and it has reigned supreme with only some modifications (albeit important ones) until the last two decades. Now, however, Pentateuchal studies are at a crossroads because the old model that had been presupposed as the starting point of scholarly inquiry has eroded. Yet there is no certain replacement on the horizon, and while some scholars have sung a dirge for the source and tradition-history model, it is premature because it remains staunchly defended. We will return to this after considering how Genesis was read from earliest antiquity.

(1) Innerbiblical

Innerbiblical or innertextual interpretations are reapplications or reinterpretations of Scripture in a new context.[64] Moses' sermon in Deuteronomy 4, for example, shows how Genesis 1 functioned as a basis for the prohibition against idolatry. Moses anticipates the new dilemma of Canaanite idolatry that awaits Israel upon its entry into the land. The language and order of creation (Gen 1:14–27) occur in Deut 4:16b–19a, though there Moses inverted the creation order (from man to sun and moon). Also common to innerbiblical interpretation is the typological function of persons and events in Genesis that correspond to later events in Israel's history. These typologies grant an unsuspected unity between former events and the present antitype as perceived by the biblical author. For example, Hosea 12:2–6[3–7] and Jer 9:3–5 make use of Jacob's biography, his devious character and deeds, as typological of national Israel's sin. This kind of correspondence is practiced in the New Testament, particularly by Paul, as he appeals to patriarchal characters and their stories as historical prototypes (e.g., Rom 9:6–13; Gal 4:21–31).

(2) Jewish Interpretation

Postbiblical interpretation of Genesis among the Jews is reflected by the apocrypha (e.g., *Ecclesiasticus*), pseudepigrapha (e.g., *Jubilees*), ancient versions (e.g., LXX and targums), Alexandrian Jews (Philo), Qumran (e.g., *Genesis Apocryphon*), and rabbinic literature (e.g., *Genesis Rabbah*). Such diversity is indicative of the variety of exegetical methods practiced by the Jews. Additionally, the great medieval commentators, such as the eminent biblical scholar Rashi (1040–1105), contributed to the life of Jewish interpretation. The common systems of Jewish interpretation were *peshat* and *midrash.*[65] The former system was interpretation based on the historical context of the passage and the normal grammatical meaning of the Hebrew, whereas *midrash* interpreted Scripture without regard for either the historical meaning or the normal sense of the Hebrew language. In *midrash* the biblical text contained a multiplicity of "hidden" meanings that lay beneath the literal sense, and each minute detail had the potential for significant meaning. *Midrash* includes *halakah,* which has to do with the practice of religious law, and *haggadah,* which are illustrative anecdotes, Jewish legends, and folklore.

The rabbinic period created a plethora of ways to view the text; the rabbis produced diverse ways of learning and commenting on the text, such as talmud, midrash, *sifra,* and homilies. Representative of rabbinic interpretation is the targumic versions and the rabbinic literature of the Talmud and Midrash.

---

[64] See M. Fishbane, *Biblical Interpretation in Ancient Israel* (Oxford: Clarendon, 1985).

[65] See R. Kasher, "The Interpretation of Scripture in Rabbinic Literature," *Mikra,* ed. M. Mulder and H. Sysling (Assen: Van Gorcum/Philadelphia: Fortress, 1988), 547–94.

The Aramaic targums were verse-by-verse translations of the Hebrew Bible, ranging from the more literal rendering to the imaginative, including targums Onkelos, Pseudo-Jonathan, and Neofiti. Onkelos (fourth century A.D.) is more literal in its renderings than other targums, but it too contains interpretive expansions. For example, Gen 2:7 reads, "Now the Lord God created Adam as dust from the earth and breathed into the nostrils of his face the breath of life and it became in Adam a spirit uttering speech." The interpretive clarification "uttering speech" incorporates the rabbinic opinion that man exhibits his superiority to the animal world (both of which are called "living beings") by the human ability of speech. Onkelos is typical of the targumic tradition, which avoids anthropomorphisms and emphasizes the transcendence of God.[66]

The first systematic commentary on Genesis among the rabbis was the midrash *Genesis Rabbah.* It was unified as a composite of resources after the establishment of Judaism in the late fourth century A.D. and therefore reflects the authoritative voice of formal rabbinic Judaism on Genesis. Its method is midrash, where the commentary on a verse of Scripture is derived from a rabbinic sage. The rabbis explained the hidden, underlying meanings of the text. The past held the hidden meanings for their future. In their day the antithesis to Judaism was Rome, and they read the patriarchal stories in this light. They interpreted the opponents of the promised lineage, such as Ishmael and Esau, as Rome, which was now a Christian empire.[67]

The biblical commentary form was perpetuated in the Middle Ages and incorporated both the plain sense and the midrashic tradition of the talmudic period. Rashi of French Jewry (1040–1105) was the most influential Jewish expositor of his era; he produced an impressive commentary on the Torah, particularly on Genesis. Exposition during this age placed greater emphasis on the literal meaning of Scripture *(peshat)* as a result of the labors of the massoretes, who produced a fixed "accurate" Hebrew text (A.D. 500–1000), and the Karaites, who deserted the rabbinic tradition of interpretation (eighth century). Rashi gave first attention to the plain meaning of the text, but he also appealed to midrashic interpretations and Jewish legends in those places where the *peshat* did not adequately explain the sense of the text or solve problems created by the literal level. His liberal use of the rabbinic homily and *haggadah* inhibits its use among modern exegetes, but Rashi's comments on the literal meaning are still helpful as a result of his philological and grammatical insights.[68]

---

[66] B. Grossfeld, ed. and trans., *The Targum Onqelos to Genesis,* Aramaic Bible 6 (Wilmington: Michael Glazier, 1988), 44–46; J. Bowker, *The Targums and Rabbinic Literature: An Introduction to Jewish Interpretations of Scripture* (Cambridge: Cambridge University Press, 1969).

[67] J. Neusner, *Genesis Rabbah: The Judaic Commentary to the Book of Genesis, A New American Translation,* BJS 104, 3 vols. (Atlanta: Scholars Press, 1985), 1.ix–xvi.

[68] C. Pearl, *Rashi* (New York: Grove, 1988), and *Rashi: Commentaries on the Pentateuch* (New York: Viking, 1970).

(3) *Christian Interpretation*

Among the apostolic fathers, the champion of the Alexandrian school of allegorical interpretation was Origen (A.D. 185–254). Although the Alexandrian school is remembered for its allegorical approach, it did not avoid the historical meaning of the text. In Origen's homily on Genesis, for instance, he defended the literal understanding of Noah's ark against Apelles, a second-century Gnostic, who denied the authority of Moses' writings on the basis of the implausibility of the ark's size for accommodating the number of animals in the world (*Gn. Hom.* 2.2). But Origen was never satisfied with the historical alone; there were the "allegorical" and "moral" levels of the text that remained to be explored. Clearly the historical was secondary to the allegorical; he comments that the flood narrative did not speak of the places on the ark for the excrement of the animals since such a topic would not fit a "spiritual meaning" (*Gn. Hom.* 2.1). The ark's three-tiered construction indicated to Origen that the narrative held three levels of meaning: the historical, allegorical, and moral (*Gn. Hom.* 2.6). An example of his allegorical reading is the equation of the ark with the church. Christ (=Noah) has prepared heavenly chambers (=ark's "nests"; cf. Isa 26:20) for the church. Like the "nests" on different decks, the chambers are different for each Christian who comes to the Lord in "his own order" (cf. 1 Cor 15:23; *Gn. Hom.* 2.3).

The Antiochene school of interpretation focused on the historical level of the text. Its proponents rejected the arbitrary assignment of hidden meanings about Christ and the church to dubious Old Testament passages as the allegorists did. The literalists recognized the fuller sense of Scripture, but they built their hermeneutical approach on the model of the apostolic tradition of interpretation. The premier exponent of historical interpretation was John Chrysostom (A.D. 354–407), pastor at Antioch and later archbishop of Constantinople. He is remembered as the most prodigious homilist in the Eastern church. Among his homilies were sixty-seven on Genesis and a second group of nine sermons.[69] Unlike the allegorists of his era, he understood the flood story literally, refuting the allegorists' practice of assigning foreign meanings to the details of the ark. He was not, however, naive about the difficulties of the text. He anticipated questions about the "clean" and "unclean" animals before the food laws of Moses and the different number of unclean ("two by two") and clean ("seven by seven") animals. For the former issue he explained that natural intuition teaches the proper distinction. For the latter question he explained that the "pair" is the preferred number in Scripture and the "sevens" provided additional animals for Noah's sacrifice to God upon disembarking from the ark (*Homily* 24.16–17).

---

[69] See R. C. Hill, trans., *Saint John Chrysostom: Homilies on Genesis 1–17,* The Fathers of the Church 74 (Washington: Catholic University Press, 1985), 1–19.

Augustine, the bishop of Hippo (A.D. 354–430), penned three commentaries on Genesis, including one left incomplete, and discussed Genesis extensively in his *Confessions* and *The City of God*. He authored twelve books devoted to a detailed study of Genesis 1–3, drawing on contemporary scientific discussion and philosophy, entitled *The Literal Meaning of Genesis*. By "literal" Augustine had in mind what the author intended to convey, that is, what actually happened in the past. By "allegorical" he meant what the events foreshadow in the future.[70] With special attention to the Genesis narratives, his *City of God* describes the birth and progress of the two realms or "cities," the heavenly and the earthly, which are revealed through the Old and New Testaments. Augustine defended the real, material meaning of the text (e.g., *City* 14.22), but he also saw in the literal a symbolic value. The ark in the floodwaters, for example, is the City of God riding as an alien in the world. The detailed construction of the ark "symbolizes some aspect of the church" (*City* 15.26).

From the time of Augustine to the Reformers, allegory reigned supreme. Thomas Aquinas, the most influential theologian of the church, helped free theology from the traditional system of allegorical interpretation.[71] He insisted on the primacy of the literal and held that it was sufficient for doing theology. He affirmed a literal garden of Eden, for example, declaring that "the things which are said of Paradise in scripture are set forth by means of an historical narrative. Now in everything which scripture thus sets forth, the truth (of the story) must be taken as a foundation and upon it spiritual expositions are to be built."[72] Although Aquinas believed that the literal was the intention of the author, the potential for multiple meanings of the allegorical system was proper too in his view since the text was also authored by God.

The Reformers and Humanists as well turned to the hermeneutics of literal readings, although these "literal" readings took into account figures of speech, symbols, and types. Martin Luther used a "moderate form of allegory" in his interpretation of the Old Testament.[73] In his lectures on Genesis, the last given by the Reformer (1535–1545), he sought a literal interpretation. Regarding the ark, his literal understanding led him to comment on the disposal of the "manure" of the animals; yet he considered the popular allegorical interpretation of the ark as the church (e.g., Augustine) harmless and useful except in debates.[74] For Luther the literal meaning also possessed a typological refer-

---

[70] For Augustine's hermeneutic see J. H. Taylor, trans., ed., *St. Augustine: The Literal Meaning of Genesis,* Ancient Christian Writers 41 (New York: Newman Press, 1982), 7–12, 253–54.

[71] See R. Grant and D. Tracy, *A Short History of the Interpretation of the Bible,* 2d ed. (Philadelphia: Fortress, 1984), 83–91.

[72] Quoted in Grant and Tracy, *A Short History of the Interpretation of the Bible,* 90.

[73] H. Bornkamm, *Luther and the Old Testament,* trans. E. and R. Gritsch (Philadelphia: Fortress, 1969 [1948]), 87–120.

[74] *LW,* 67–68.

ence to Christ and the church. For example, the covenant with Noah (6:18) is interpreted as a promise of Christ. Luther's *Genesis* shows mature theological reflection, and many consider it second only to his famous lectures on Galatians.[75]

The quintessential expositor of the Reformation was John Calvin, who lectured on Genesis in 1550 and completed a commentary on the book in 1554, well after the completion of his New Testament commentaries.[76] Calvin distanced himself from the multiple meanings of the former period though he admitted the efficacy of occasional allegory.[77] He did not appeal to allegory to escape difficulties, and he admitted, for instance, the difficulties of the size and shape of Noah's ark (Gen 6:15); but he rebuffed Origen's and Augustine's allegories of the human body or the church. The literal reading is the "more profitable." Yet Calvin, because of the unity of the Testaments, could comfortably relate the literal meaning of the Old to the theological truth found in the New. This method of *anagogy,* as he called it, is a transference from one literal meaning to another. At Gen 3:15 he remarked: "We must now make a transition from the serpent to the author of this mischief himself; and that not only in the way of comparison, for there truly is a literal *anagogy;* because God has not so vented his anger upon the outward instrument as to spare the devil with whom lay the blame."[78] Calvin's *Genesis* draws many moral lessons from his study and also attacks heresies. Against the Anabaptists, he saw in God's covenant with Noah (9:9) evidence for infant baptism. The covenant with Noah includes future generations not yet born, and so he reasoned that since the Noahic covenant includes infants, the covenant of God includes the infants of households.

(4) Pentateuchal Criticism

Although there were precursors who questioned the traditional interpretation of Genesis and the Pentateuch as a unified corpus, the eighteenth century saw the emergence of studies that would ultimately serve as the basis for the modern (as opposed to the traditional) understanding of the compositional history of Genesis. Apparent problems in the Pentateuch had long been recognized, but not systematically and freely addressed. The intuition of scholars about how texts should be composed and interpreted forced them to account for what they perceived as inconsistencies and ambiguities in the Pentateuch.[79]

The founders of the new method sought to establish religion on a firmer "sci-

[75] M. Brecht, *Martin Luther: The Preservation of the Church 1532–1546,* trans. J. Schaaf (Minneapolis: Fortress, 1993 [1987]), 134–41.

[76] For discussion of Calvin's hermeneutic of the OT, see T. H. L. Parker, *Calvin's Old Testament Commentaries* (Edinburgh: T & T Clark, 1986).

[77] Cf. Gen 27:27, where he applauds the allegory of Ambrose.

[78] Calvin, *Comm.,* 168.

[79] See J. Barton, *Reading the Old Testament* (Philadelphia: Westminster, 1984), 22–27.

entific" basis. They hoped to recover the real heart of the Old Testament religion, believing that this recovery would help modern man appreciate the biblical message unencumbered by the scholasticism of the church. This optimism is evidenced by the remarks of W. R. Smith, who penned the Preface to the English edition of J. Wellhausen's *Prolegomena to the History of Ancient Israel:* "The history of Israel is part of the history of the faith by which we live, the New Testament cannot be rightly understood without understanding the Old, and the main reason why so many parts of the Old Testament are practically a sealed book even to thoughtful people is simply that they have not the historical key to the interpretation of that wonderful literature."[80] Although the new method was met with stiff opposition by traditional Jewish and Christian interpreters, by the end of the nineteenth century the historical-critical school had won the day in Europe and had made significant inroads in the American mainline denominations.

At this place in our discussion we might ask what difference it makes to the interpreter how one views the compositional character and history of Genesis (or Pentateuch). R. E. Clements comments on the rabbinic practice of ascribing biblical literature to prominent figures: "It is a matter of significance that the Pentateuch is ascribed to Moses, whereas it hardly matters at all to the understanding of the books of 1 and 2 Samuel that they have been ascribed to Samuel's authorship, at least up to the point of his death."[81] Authorship is important for the exegesis of the Pentateuch; for as the rabbinic community recognized, so much of the Pentateuch was anchored in Moses' personal experiences, and thus it attributed the core to Moses himself. But this is not the case for Genesis, it would seem, since it antedates Moses' experience. Yet a trend among recent commentators is to find, as did the rabbis, that Genesis is not an isolated literary work, serving only as a prologue to Exodus–Deuteronomy. Rather, the recounting of Genesis has been shaped by the Mosaic experience. We cannot interpret Genesis fully unless we recognize its place under the looming shadow of Sinai (see "Genesis and the Mosaic Community," p. 51).

First, the question of authorship impacts the issue of the historical value of the pentateuchal witness. The consequence of historical-critical reconstructions has eventuated for most modern interpreters to be at best skeptical and at worst nihilistic when evaluating the historicity of the patriarchs.[82] Defense of

[80] W. R. Smith, "Preface," in J. Wellhausen, *Prolegomena to the History of Israel* (New York: Meridian, 1957 [1888]), vii.

[81] R. E. Clements, "Solomon and the Origins of Wisdom in Israel," in *Perspectives in Religious Studies* 15 (1988): 23.

[82] T. L. Thompson, *The Historicity of the Patriarchal Narrative: The Quest for the Historical Abraham* (Berlin: de Gruyter, 1974); J. van Seters, *Abraham in History and Tradition* (New Haven: Yale University Press, 1975); R. B. Coote and D. R. Ord, *The Bible's First History: From Eden to the Court of David with the Yahwist* (Philadelphia: Fortress, 1989); G. Mendenhall, "The Nature and Purpose of the Abraham Narratives," *Ancient Israelite Religion* (Philadelphia: Fortress, 1987), 337–57.

the general reliability of the patriarchal narratives was led by W. F. Albright, whose American school of archaeology had argued that the patriarchs were real persons living in the second millennium. A. Alt's German school of thought was much more reserved in finding much historical certainty in the stories of Israel's fathers. The optimism found, for example, in J. Bright's *History of Israel* (3d. ed., 1981)[83] has come upon hard times with the current undermining of the archaeological evidence for a second millennium date. Also the supposed source Yahwist (called "J" for the German spelling "Jahwist"), once widely accepted by critics as coming from the time of the monarchy, has been dated later, removing it all the more from patriarchal times. R. Rendtorff recognizes the interplay between the revisionists' postexilic dating and Israelite history when he observes, "The late dating of texts is an indication of the loss of confidence in their historical credibility."[84] Is there a correspondence between what Genesis affirms and "how it really was"?[85] The resounding no to this question presently among critics is deafening.

Second, the question of composition influences whether it is feasible to do a biblical theology.[86] Does Genesis have a coherent theology based on a literary unity, or does it consist of competing theological traditions, reflecting different viewpoints from many eras? Which theology imbedded in Genesis is normative? Wherein lies the Word of God? The historicism of the previous century had averted the task of doing biblical theology other than as a purely descriptive or comparative religions approach. The attempt to recover the Reformation heritage of preaching the Bible to hear the Word of God led to the Biblical Theology Movement,[87] but it stumbled when no satisfactory "sci-

---

[83] Also R. de Vaux, *The Early History of Israel*, trans. D. Smith (Philadelphia: Westminster, 1978). Contrast this with J. M. Miller and J. H. Hayes, whose history of Israel begins with the Book of Judges, considering Genesis–Joshua unreliable for reconstructing history (*A History of Ancient Israel and Judah*) [Philadelphia: Westminster, 1986]). Also J. A. Soggin's history, which begins with the monarchy: "Of the period before the formation of the state we therefore know little (if anything), so that it would seem impossible to verify the validity of the biblical thesis according to which 'Israel' will have gone through a relatively long period, up to the end of the second millennium" (*An Introduction to the History of Israel and Judah,* rev. ed., trans. J. Bowden [Valley Forge: Trinity Press International, 1993], 33).

[84] R. Rendtorff, "The Paradigm Is Changing: Hopes—and Fears," *Biblical Interpretation* 1 (1992).

[85] This is the now-famous description by L. von Ranke of the historian's task; see the discussion of B. Halpern, *The First Historians: The Hebrew Bible and History* (San Francisco: Harper & Row, 1984), 19.

[86] See H. G. Reventlow, *Problems of Biblical Theology in the Twentieth Century,* trans. J. Bowden (Philadelphia: Fortress, 1986).

[87] E.g., H. W. Wolff, "The Kerygma of the Yahwist," originally in *EvT* 24 (1964): 73–97, trans. W. Benware and reissued in W. Brueggemann and Wolff, *The Vitality of Old Testament Traditions,* 2d ed. (Atlanta: John Knox, 1982), 41–66.

entific" basis could be found for doing theology. Despite the renewed efforts of the canon criticism movement at staking a claim to biblical theology (see "Canon" in this section of the Introduction), the question remains how to integrate historical-critical advances and a holistic biblical theology. In other words, what role does history have in doing theology?

SOURCE. The pinnacle achievement in the triumph of the historical-critical method was the appearance of J. Wellhausen's *Prolegomena to the History of Israel* in 1878.[88] Within a mere decade of its publication, Wellhausen's reconstruction of Israel's religious history captured the academic chairs of all British and European Old Testament scholarship, propagated by A. Kuenen of Holland and W. R. Smith and S. R. Driver of Britain.[89]

Foundational to Wellhausen's reconstruction was his earlier literary-source analysis of the Hexateuch, which was indebted to a century of labor by the pioneers of the method, such as J. G. Eichhorn, W. M. L. de Wette, and J. F. L. George.[90] In particular Wellhausen's teacher at Göttingen, H. Ewald, made use of the new scientific methods in his *History of Israel* (1843), which was the first attempt of its kind at such a comprehensive history.[91] Wellhausen's achievement was his ability to integrate the literary studies of his predecessors with his own insights into a systematic and cohesive picture of Israel's religious life and institutions.

---

[88] The work was first published as *Geschichte Israels* (Berlin: Reimer) and intended as the first of two volumes. The 1883 second edition therefore renamed it *Prolegomena zur Geschichte Israels;* the 1885 English edition included the preface of W. R. Smith, the most articulate champion of Wellhausen in England (Edinburgh: Adam & Charles Black), which has been reprinted, *Prolegomena to the History of Ancient Israel* (New York: Meridian, 1957).

[89] See R. E. Clements, "The Study of the Old Testament," in *Nineteenth Century Religious Thought in the West,* 3 vols., ed. N. Smart et al. (Cambridge: Cambridge University Press, 1985), 3.129.

[90] Wellhausen published a series of articles, "Die Composition des Hexateuchs," in *Jahrbücher für deutsche Theologie* in 1876–77, which were reissued as *Die Composition des Hexateuchs und der hebräische Bücher des Alten Testaments,* 3d ed. (Berlin: Reimer, 1899).

[91] H. Ewald, *The History of Israel I–VI,* trans. R. Martineau (London: Longmans, Green, and Co., 1869–1883). See J. Rogerson, *Old Testament Criticism in the Nineteenth Century, England and Germany* (London: SPCK, 1984), 93, and R. E. Clements, *One Hundred Years of Old Testament Interpretation* (Philadelphia: Westminster, 1976), 7. There are many accounts of the history of Pentateuchal criticism; see additionally O. Eissfeldt, *The Old Testament: An Introduction,* 3d ed. (Oxford: Clarendon, 1966 [1934]); R. E. Friedman, *Who Wrote the Bible?* (New York: Harper & Row, 1987); and J. Blenkinsopp, *The Pentateuch: An Introduction to the First Five Books of the Bible* (New York: Doubleday, 1992).

Wellhausen's now-famous document arrangement of "J, E, D, and P" is a disservice to the complicated analysis of the sources that he envisioned. For each document Wellhausen saw a complex literary past. He approached the material as a Hexateuch that traced the story of beginnings to the conquest. Setting aside Deuteronomy, he saw the remaining books as a composite of the "Jehovistic history-book" (=JE), which was a composite of the J(ehovistic) and E(lohistic) sources redacted during monarchic times (ca. 850 and 750 respectively) and later redacted to the seventh-century D source. The Priestly work (P) had a historical framework running parallel with that of JE from creation to the conquest. Actually, Wellhausen interpreted the Priestly Code as composite as well: at the core was the Book of the Four Covenants (=Q), which experienced later revisions (=RQ). The Jehovistic and Priestly works were finally interwoven in the postexilic era, forming the extant text (ca. 450 B.C.).

Though literary criticism was his method, Wellhausen's purpose was to write a religious history of Israel's sacred institutions on a "scientific" basis. For him to do this meant a painfully detailed look at the sources by which he could evaluate their testimony. What Wellhausen's *Prolegomena* achieved was an altogether new way of looking at the history of Israel's religious life. He proposed that the Mosaic theocracy was the beginning of late Judaism, a postexilic innovation, and not the history of ancient Israel. Wellhausen assumed that the sources were witnesses to the stages of Israel's religious life at the time of their writing, not the period they proposed to describe. JE, therefore, could not be dependably used for reconstructing the life of the patriarchs since they were projections from the era of the monarchy, but it could witness to the state of Israel's religious life during the ninth-eighth centuries. D therefore witnessed to the seventh-century religion of Josiah's times; and P, to the postexilic period. Wellhausen assumed an evolving character of Israelite religion, from the simple and spontaneous features of premonarchic religion (as reflected in Judges and Samuel) to the legislative and ritualistic of the priestly. For Wellhausen the prophets were the pinnacle of Israel's religious expression. Although some have contended that Wellhausen was not impacted by Hegel's developmentalism, most admit that Vatke, to whom Wellhausen admits his indebtedness in the *Prolegomena,* was at least influenced by Hegel.[92] The significant difference, however, between Wellhausen's reconstruction and developmentalism is that the late priestly religion was detrimental rather than a superior religious expression.

FORM AND TRADITION HISTORY. Although the source analysis of the nineteenth century underwent significant revision, it remains the working framework for most contemporary pentateuchal studies. At the beginning of the twentieth century, the critical model we outlined above was first modified, though perhaps unwittingly, by the form-critical work of H. Gunkel (1852–1932), who published

[92] Rogerson, *Old Testament Criticism,* 70–71.

his groundbreaking work *Schöpfung und Chaos (Creation and Chaos)* in 1895 and later his commentary on Genesis (1901). Essentially, Gunkel took note of the many ancient Near Eastern literary recoveries from the archaeological endeavors during his era that provided a comparative basis in the Levant for understanding Israel's religious institutions. He applied a rigorous literary criticism to the Hebrew Bible. But unlike his predecessors, he concentrated on the smaller literary units he believed were behind the documents of Wellhausen, classifying them according to literary form *(Gattungen)* and genre and reconstructing the formative settings *(Sitz im Leben)* that produced the preliterary traditions. These smaller narratives and law collections at one time existed independently, and they were composed and transmitted orally, thus serving as an older witness to the ancient Israelite settings. J. Blenkinsopp summarizes the change in focus that occurred as a result: "The weight was therefore shifted from large-scale documents (J and E) to smaller units, from texts to traditions, and from individual authors to the anonymous products of a preliterary society."[93] Influenced by Scandinavian folklore models, Gunkel read Genesis's narratives as family *sagen,* which were Israel's way of transmitting its earliest origins.

Building on this approach were the most influential voices of the twentieth century, Gerhard von Rad and Martin Noth. It was the Gunkel-von Rad-Noth formulation of Old Testament religion and history that forged the consensus that served critical scholars from the 1940s to recent times.[94] Like Gunkel they worked within the old Wellhausen model, but their interests were in the transmission of the preliterary traditions that Gunkel's methods sought to elucidate. They wanted to answer how these numerous smaller units were brought together by the disparate groups that constituted Israel; thus these traditio-historical critics were more interested in streams of tradition than authors. Von Rad's "Form Critical Problem of the Hexateuch" (1938) sets out his interpretive agenda: he believed that the key was found not in a Pentateuch but the Hexateuch, Genesis to Joshua, which as one long narrative gave the official theological history of Israel from creation and land promise of the patriarchs to its realization in the conquest.[95] The central tradition comprised the exodus to conquest narratives, which were an expansion based on Israel's earliest confessional statement, Deut 26:5b–9 (cp. also Deut 6:20–24; Josh 24:2b–13). Strikingly, von Rad, by the omission of Sinai in the earliest credo, segregated the Sinai narrative as an originally separate tradition from the exodus–conquest narratives. It was the able "Yahwist" of the monarchic period who fused together these disparate traditions and added the stories of the patriarchs and Genesis 1–11 to produce the Hexateuch. The appli-

[93] Blenkinsopp, *The Pentateuch,* 15.

[94] See D. Knight, "The Pentateuch," in *The Hebrew Bible and Its Modern Interpreters,* ed. D. Knight and G. Tucker (Philadelphia: Fortress/Chico, Cal.: Scholars Press, 1985), 263–96.

[95] G. von Rad, "The Form-Critical Problem of the Hexateuch," in *The Problem of the Hexateuch and Other Essays,* trans. E. Dicken (New York: McGraw-Hill, 1966 [1938]), 1–78.

cation of von Rad's method can be found in his theological commentary on *Genesis,* which is dominated by his attention to the theological shaping given by the "Yahwist." By this understanding of the Yahwist's role, however, it is apparent that we do not have Wellhausen's "J" document.

Noth's work in *A History of Pentateuchal Traditions* (1948) and *History of Israel* (1950)[96] took a different approach by excavating from the Pentateuch five original themes around which the Pentateuch was formulated: (1) the patriarchs, (2) exodus tradition, (3) wilderness tradition, (4) Sinai, and (5) guidance into cultivable land. The merger of these once-independent themes was accomplished by the cultic function of Israel's tribal league during the settlement of Canaan. On this basis Noth reconstructed the history of Israel, believing Moses was original to only one tradition and who was later added to the others. For Noth the patriarchs might have been historical individuals, but nothing more could be known of them. More important, some observed that the work of form and tradition-history criticisms was a significant departure from the Wellhausen model of documents, but still the old devotion to a chronologically linear series of literary documents held sway.[97]

REVISIONIST TRENDS. But dissatisfaction had set in early on, for discerning the original oral units from a written exemplar, as Gunkel's form criticism required, was not assured, and the traditio-historical reconstructions appeared arbitrary. Also the mechanism, whether von Rad's "Yahwist" or Noth's amphictyony, for forming the final tradition collapsed. As a consequence there was a parting from the classical interpretation of pentateuchal studies by a new emphasis on the final form of the biblical text. The clarion call was sounded by James Muilenberg in his presidential address to the Society of Biblical Studies in 1968, entitled "Form Criticism and Beyond."[98] Deemed "rhetorical criticism," this method concerned the rhetorical-literary features of the text without special attention to the preliterary stages of the Pentateuch. This shift to the synchronic description of the text diverged from the diachronic questions that had dominated biblical scholarship for centuries. A whole army of literary approaches has become popular and is a continuing trend (see "Literary Readings," p. 81).

Although there were dissenting voices among critical scholars earlier,[99] a

---

[96] M. Noth, *A History of Pentateuchal Traditions* (Englewood Cliffs: Prentice-Hall, 1972 [1948]), and *The History of Israel,* 2d ed. (New York: Harper & Row, 1960 [1950]).

[97] See the critique found in Rendtorff, *The Problem of the Process of Transmission in the Pentateuch,* JSOTSup 89, trans. J. J. Scullion (Sheffield: JSOT, 1990 [1977]).

[98] J. Muilenburg, "Form Criticism and Beyond," *JBL* 88 (1969): 1–18.

[99] E.g., the Scandinavian school, I. Engnell, "The Pentateuch," in *A Rigid Scrutiny: Critical Essays on the Old Testament,* trans. J. Willis (Nashville: Vanderbilt University Press, 1969 [1962]), 50–67; and F. V. Winnett, "Reexamining the Foundations," *JBL* 84 (1965): 1–19. Also opponents were the conservative scholars, such as the early W. H. Green, *The Higher Criticism of the Pentateuch* (New York: Scribner, 1895), and especially U. Cassuto, *The Documentary Hypothesis and the Composition of the Pentateuch* (Jerusalem: Magnes, 1961 [1941]).

wave of new assertions that set the old theory reeling occurred in the mid-1970s in a series of monographs.[100] Among the new proposals for pentateuchal origins are diverse methodologies and remarkable differences in conclusions, but for our purposes we will present the primary features in a nutshell.[101] Recent trends (1) have redefined the character of J from a literary strand to either an author or redaction and expanded J's role in the final stage(s) of pentateuchal composition, dating it to the exilic period; (2) have squeezed the already-shrinking E source; (3) have conferred broader involvement on the deuteronomic school of editors in Genesis–Numbers; and (4) have continued to dispute P's extent, whether a continuous narrative source or a redactional framework that housed the JE materials, as well as debating whether P is exilic/postexilic (as usually assumed) or preexilic.

With more and more of the formerly designated J and E passages assigned to deuteronomic origins (e.g., Exod 3–4; 19–34), it has become increasingly popular to deny a place in the preexilic period for a continuous narrative, tracing Israel's history from creation to the conquest. This is of course the most serious rejection of the old Gunkel-von Rad-Noth consensus that assumed continuous narrative histories coming from the Solomonic era. Rather, the earliest period for the formation of a continuous narrative has been reassigned to the sixth century. This narrative is attributed to either a deuteronomic redaction (e.g., Schmid, Rendtorff) or to the "Yahwist" author/historian (e.g., van Seters, Whybray), followed by some P editorial work. Now the Pentateuch is seen as made up of massive "larger units" (Rendtorff) or "traditional complex-chain narratives" (Thompson) that were originally self-contained, having a developmental history of their own with no cross-pollination among them. At the final stage in the exilic period these blocks were linked together with slight additions by a P editor (Rendtorff) or set with additional materials within the *tōlĕdōt* framework (Thompson). It is for such reasons that Rendtorff has declared, "I believe that the traditional Documentary Hypothesis has come to an end."[102]

---

[100] Especially the following studies, which have proposed diverse alternatives, though none is likely to succeed the Gunkel-von Rad-Noth consensus: J. van Seters, *Abraham in History and Tradition* (New Haven: Yale University Press, 1975); H. H. Schmid, *Der sogenannte Jahwist. Beobachtungen und Fragen zur Pentateuchforschung* (Zurich: Theologischer Verlag, 1976); Rendtorff, *The Problem of the Process of Transmission in the Pentateuch,* JSOTSup 89, trans. J. J. Scullion (Sheffield: JSOT, 1990 [1977]). More recently, e.g., see T. L. Thompson, *The Origin Tradition of Ancient Israel. I. The Literary Formation of Genesis and Exodus 1–23,* JSOTSup 55 (Sheffield: JSOT, 1987), and R. N. Whybray, *The Making of the Pentateuch: A Methodological Study,* JSOTSup 53 (Sheffield: JSOT, 1987).

[101] See Knight, "The Pentateuch," 263–96; D. J. McCarthy, "Twenty-Five Years of Pentateuchal Study," in *The Biblical Heritage in Modern Catholic Scholarship,* ed. J. Collins and J. Crossan (Wilmington: Michael Glazier, 1986), 34–57; J. De Vries, "A Review of Recent Research in the Tradition History of the Pentateuch," SBLSP 26 (Atlanta: Scholars Press, 1987), 459–502; J. S. Kselman, "The Book of Genesis: A Decade of Scholarly Research," *Int* 45 (1991): 380–92.

[102] Rendtorff, "The Paradigm Is Changing," 11.

There is a propensity now among revisionists to view the Pentateuch as a single literary work that may or may not have been the culmination of developing literary sources. Whybray goes so far as to posit that the first edition of the Pentateuch was the final form created by a single historian, "a controlling genius," in the sixth century.[103] Of course, there remain strong proponents for the former consensus,[104] and recently studies have given renewed credence to the source (Wellhausen) and tradition-history (Noth) reconstructions.[105]

TRADITIONAL. What does this unsettling state in pentateuchal studies mean for traditional evangelical scholars? Those who adhere to the precritical understanding of the Pentateuch as a unified whole, possessing a Mosaic core, can take no solace from the doomsayers who have declared the former consensus disintegrating. The revisionists have not won a new consensus (though their influence is pervasive); if anything, they distance the written witnesses all the more from the events of the Late Bronze Age, creating the odd circumstance of a biblical text that is now deemed useless for constructing Israel's ancestral origins, history, and religious institutions. It is striking to find a new work arguing that Genesis had its origins in the Davidic-Solomonic period.[106] Yet for the traditionalist's camp, which has been shut out of the debate for two centuries, it may be its most propitious moment to contend for a viable alternative in the topsy-turvy environment of pentateuchal studies that has arisen. A recent voice is that of D. Garrett's *Rethinking Genesis,* suggesting a four-stage development of Genesis whose major redaction is attributed to Moses. He posits that the early Genesis accounts were perpetuated among the Israelites by the tribal Levites. These accounts were then taken up and given shape by Moses.[107] Helpful also have been the arguments of G. Wenham, though without reference to Mosaic authorship, that the P framework of Genesis 1–11 dates best to the second millennium B.C.[108]

Resistance to speculation about preliterary sources used in Genesis has been

---

[103] Whybray, *The Making of the Pentateuch,* 235.

[104] E.g., De Vries, "A Review of Recent Research in the Tradition History of the Pentateuch"; G. W. Coats, *Genesis: With an Introduction to Narrative Literature,* FOTL 1 (Grand Rapids: Eerdmans, 1983); J. A. Emerton, "An Examination of Some Attempts to Defend the Unity of the Flood Narrative in Genesis, Part I," *VT* 37 (1987): 401–20, and "Part II," *VT* 38 (1988): 1–21; E. W. Nicholson, "The Pentateuch in Recent Research: A Time for Caution," *Congress Volume, Leuven, 1989,* ed. J. Emerton (Leiden: Brill, 1991), 10–21; S. McEvenue, *Interpreting the Pentateuch* (Collegeville, Minn.: Liturgical Press/Michael Glazier, 1990); A. F. Campbell and M. A. O'Brien, *Sources of the Pentateuch: Text, Introductions, Annotations* (Minneapolis: Augsburg, 1993).

[105] E.g., S. Boorer, *The Promise of the Land as Oath: A Key to the Formation of the Pentateuch,* BZAW 205 (Berlin: Walter de Gruyter, 1992).

[106] E.g., Rendsburg, *The Redaction of Genesis* (Winona Lake: Eisenbrauns, 1986), which places it in the monarchy, but not on the basis of the Documentary Hypothesis.

[107] Garrett, *Rethinking Genesis,* 91–106, 191–232.

[108] Wenham, *Genesis 1–15,* xxxvii–xlv.

common among conservatives, however, who generally focus on the final form of the text without much ado regarding its pretextual operations. Since Genesis and the Pentateuch are anonymous, we cannot prove Mosaic authorship as a whole, especially for Genesis, which describes events that antedate the time of the lawgiver. Nevertheless, it is defensible from both internal and external evidence that the Pentateuch is Mosaic. What continues as the strongest testimony for Genesis (and the Pentateuch) as the product of one author/compiler is its essential unity governed by a discernible overarching plan (see "Structure of the Pentateuch," p. 46). This does not eliminate the possibility of source and tradition-history reconstructions, but it casts suspicion on such hypothetical constructions when a simpler formulation suits the evidence and is consistent with long-standing testimony among the rabbis and apostles.[109] Newer literary methods (discussed later) have brought a renewed appreciation for the unity of smaller units. When applied to the larger units of Genesis, indeed to the Pentateuch as a whole, it seems likely that a single inventive mind accessed an array of ancient sources, such as genealogies and written narratives, in the authoring of Genesis.

With current trends emphasizing a primary redaction of larger narrative units (whether deuteronomic or "J"), newer pentateuchal studies are in some respects conducive to the traditional proposal of a single author/compiler for Genesis. The recognition of the larger narrative cycles in Genesis (e.g., Joseph, chaps. 37–50) and the Pentateuch (e.g., Exod 1–15) urge a simpler explanation for their compilation than the source reconstruction. And the growing recognition of deuteronomic language and theology in Genesis–Numbers can be accommodated by the thesis of a single author, who in assembling the whole utilized deuteronomic language and theology in Genesis–Numbers as preparatory for the consummating conclusion of the Pentateuch. It is now widely acknowledged that Genesis was written with Israel's religious law and institutions established at Sinai in mind. Significant elements of what we find in both Genesis 1–11 and 12–50 are prototypical of later Israel. We are not surprised that a Mosaic work penned in light of Israel's experience at Sinai and wilderness would be evidenced at places throughout the composition, including Genesis.

What remains is whether dating the narrative corpus of the Pentateuch to the exile as emphasized in recent studies is convincing. Similarities between the literary character of the Pentateuch and the Greek historical works, such as Herodotus's *Histories,* has fueled sixth-century speculation for its date. More

[109] This is well illustrated by the dispute on the compositional character of Gen 6–9 found in the debate between Wenham ("The Coherence of the Flood Narrative," *VT* 28 [1978]: 336–48, and "Method in Pentateuchal Source Criticism," *VT* 41 [1991]: 84–109) and the source critic Emerton ("An Examination of Some Attempts to Defend the Unity of the Flood Narrative in Genesis, Parts I and II").

often the argument is put forward that the meager references to the patriarchal figures in preexilic biblical sources indicate a later period for the composition of Genesis. This also has been the standard critical approach to explaining the legal materials (P) that are routinely dated to the exilic/postexilic periods. Additionally, it is contended that the religious and social needs of the Jews in the Persian period best explain a completed Pentateuch and Deuteronomistic History (Deut–Kings). During this period the Jews required an authoritative body for accomplishing the renewal of Jewish identity and cultic activity that the Persian authorities expected (e.g., Blenkinsopp). The conclusion of the Pentateuch in which Moses (Deut 34:10–12) is regarded the paragon of prophetic revelation establishes the wilderness era as the normative expression of the Hebrew faith-tradition. Moreover, the absence of the conquest would serve the political necessities of the times with Judah under the authority of the Persian Empire.

But the arguments fielded here are not compelling. Too many significant differences between Greek historiography and the narrative of the Pentateuch exist to conclude that they come from the same era of historiographic development.[110] The argument that the preexilic prophets rarely refer to the lives of the patriarchs is based on silence, which is a tricky business when used as a support for establishing a thesis. It is not effective in proving or disproving the existence of a composition concerning the patriarchs but can only be employed in arguing that the preexilic prophets did not know about the lives of the patriarchs. Yet when we consider that the exilic community readily accepted the patriarchal story, it is dubious that the ancestors' tradition would have been new to them. It is most difficult to accept that the Hebrew people did not have a written tradition of their ancestral heritage until the exilic period, as some have contended today.

It is better to explain the paucity of patriarchal references as the result of the different setting and interests of the prophets. Theirs was a call back to the Mosaic faith when Israel was formed as a nation; thus the ancestral stories that antedated the Sinai-wilderness-conquest narratives were not central to their purpose.[111] We can add here that the diminished role of Moses in early Israel, according to the new trends, conflicts with the prominence given him in the formation of the Pentateuch by these same critics. Last, the exilic/postexilic period as the setting for the final stage(s) of the Pentateuch is unsatisfactory. As we have shown earlier, the literary and thematic shape of the Pentateuch is eschatological, looking ahead to the realization of the ancestral promises in

---

[110] Consider the cautions in Garrett, *Rethinking Genesis,* 57–64, and Blenkinsopp, *The Pentateuch,* 37–42.

[111] So argued by Garrett, *Rethinking Genesis,* 64–66; also see Cassuto, "The Prophet Hosea and the Books of the Pentateuch," in *Biblical and Oriental Studies,* vol. 1, trans. I. Abrahams (Jerusalem: Magnes Press, 1973), 79–100.

Canaan. A postexilic perspective cannot explain this feature of the Pentateuch since its interest in the patriarchal stories and Israel's national history would have been looking backward, not forward.[112] Such doubts cast upon the newer dating recommends a rejection of the later period as the setting for the Pentateuch's compilation.

Several lines of internal evidence, while unable to prove traditional Mosaic authorship, indicate the concurrence of a second millennium date, such as the antiquity of Deuteronomy's literary structure having similarity to international treaty formulas of the Late Bronze Age.[113] The argument for an early setting of the Pentateuch's composition has been well rehearsed elsewhere in detail.[114] The names of persons and places in the Pentateuch are consistent with onomastica (ancient records of names), and social customs practiced in the Pentateuch are attested in second-millennium sources. The names of the coalition of kings in Genesis 14 and the political circumstances accord well with what we know of this early period. The author was an eyewitness of the events in Exodus–Deuteronomy and was well acquainted with Egyptian language and geography. Egyptian loanwords from the second millennium are found in Hebrew. Also Exodus–Deuteronomy testifies to Moses as authoring diverse materials and genre, involving a battle memorial (Exod 17:14), a travel journal (Num 33:2), legal collections (Exod 24:4–8; Deut 31:9), and a poetic hymn (Deut 31:22).[115] Apparently these materials and others were perpetuated and revered as authoritative within the near time of Moses' own life (e.g., Josh 1:7–8 with Exod 20:5). The ascription to Moses of a written legal corpus ("book of the law") was thus accepted early (e.g., Josh 8:31; 23:6; 2 Kgs 14:6) and found widespread in the postexilic period (e.g., 2 Chr 34:14; Neh 8:1) as well as accepted among the Jews (e.g., *Sir.*, Josephus, Philo, Talmud) and by Jesus and the early church

---

[112] Also noted by Garrett, *Rethinking Genesis,* 233–37.

[113] E.g., M. G. Kline, *Treaty of the Great King* (Grand Rapids: Eerdmans, 1963); P. C. Craigie, *Deuteronomy,* NICOT (Grand Rapids: Eerdmans, 1976); E. Merrill, *Deuteronomy,* NAC (Nashville: Broadman & Holman, 1994).

[114] E.g., P. J. Wiseman, *New Discoveries in Babylonia about Genesis* (London: Marshall, 1936), reissued in P. J. Wiseman and D. J. Wiseman, *Ancient Records and the Structure of Genesis* (Nashville: Nelson, 1985[1936]); G. C. Aalders, *A Short Introduction to the Pentateuch* (London: Tyndale, 1949); G. Archer, *A Survey of Old Testament Introduction,* rev. ed. (Chicago: Moody, 1985 [1974]); R. K. Harrison, *Introduction to the Old Testament* (Grand Rapids: Eerdmans, 1969); K. A. Kitchen, *Ancient Orient and Old Testament* (Chicago: InterVarsity, 1966); O. T. Allis, *The Five Books of Moses,* 2d ed. (Philadelphia: Presbyterian and Reformed, 1949 [1943]); and E. J. Young, *An Introduction to the Old Testament,* rev. ed. (Grand Rapids: Eerdmans, 1964 [1949]). Among Jewish scholars see Cassuto, *The Documentary Hypothesis and the Composition of the Pentateuch,* trans. I. Abrahams (Jerusalem: Magnes/Hebrew University, 1983 [1941]; M. H. Segal, *The Pentateuch: Its Composition and Authorship* (Jerusalem: Magnes, 1967); B. Jacob, *Das erste Buch der Tora: Genesis übersetzt und erklärt* (Berlin: Schocken, 1934).

[115] See G. C. Aalders, *Genesis,* BSC, vol. 1, trans. W. Heynen (Grand Rapids: Regency Reference/Zondervan, 1981), 20–25.

(e.g., John 1:45; Luke 20:28; Acts 3:22). This does not demonstrate that the whole of the Pentateuch is exclusively from Moses' hand, but it shows that the Five Books are essentially Mosaic, possessing legal writings and extensive first person accounts. Slight editorial additions and some revisions may be found in the Pentateuch also (cf. Josh 24:26),[116] but this is not to be confused with the source and tradition-history proposals of the Gunkel-von Rad-Noth sort.

When we consider the authorship of Genesis, the structure and contents of chaps. 1–11 point to a second-millennium origin when compared to the Babylonian *Atrahasis* (ca. 1600 B.C.). Although one would be unwise to suppose that the Hebrew author was dependent on this Babylonian tradition, it presents a significant piece of testimony that the contents of Genesis 1–11 are more consistent with an early date than with a late one.[117]

When considering the patriarchal accounts of chaps. 12–50, the controversial dating of the patriarchal materials must be faced head-on. Among conventional source and tradition-history critics, chaps. 12–50 consisted of J and E materials brought together with the P source. J was assumed a work of the monarchy, though it possessed much earlier traditions. But now, whether viewed as a redactor or author, the so-called J materials have been reassigned by the revisionists to the exilic/postexilic era. What we find for chaps. 12–50 is that the *tōlĕdōt* structure of chaps. 1–11 continues as the foremost structural feature in the present arrangement of the patriarchal accounts, though, of course, the hypothetical "JE" (or just "J") stories dominate. There is no compelling reason to depart from the pattern evidenced by chaps. 1–11, where the structure shows an early provenience that was supplemented by additions. In the case of chaps. 12–50, networks of patriarchal accounts have been assembled, perhaps even the Joseph cycle of one cloth, and are set within the *tōlĕdōt* plan of the whole. Despite recurring objections, these patriarchal accounts have been found to fit best in the second-millennium context. Taken together this would point to a second-millennium dating for both structure and supplements that constitute the composition of Genesis.

---

[116] E.g., Gen 14:14; 36:31; Exod 11:3; 16:35; Num 12:3; 22:1; Deut 2:10–12; 34:5–12. Conservative scholars acknowledge there are some non-Mosaic sections in the Pentateuch; there is disagreement as to their extent (see R. Dillard and T. Longman, *An Introduction to the Old Testament* (Grand Rapids: Zondervan, 1994), 38–48. E.g., the third-person sections (referring to Moses) are also attributed to the lawgiver (e.g., Archer, *A Survey of Old Testament Introduction,* 83, n. 1) or to a later author who set the first-person Mosaic sections in a narrative framework referring to Moses in the third person (e.g., Aalders *Genesis,* 28).

[117] So argued in Wenham, *Genesis 1–15,* xli. Blenkinsopp, for example, acknowledges this similarity between P's structure and *Atrahasis*, but his insistence on the exilic dating of P forces him to assign chaps. 1–11 to the Persian period (*The Pentateuch,* 93–94). The evidence would point the opposite direction, however, showing that the structure and content of the so-called P work reflect early provenience. In turn this skeletal structure appears to be filled out by later additions, which also Blenkinsopp admits, by the so-called "J" passages (p. 78).

Although one can argue that the Genesis accounts were not reduced to writing until much later, this view is an entrenched holdover from the long-held assumption that lying behind the written sources is a prolonged oral history. This notion of an extensive period of tradent activity of solely oral nature has been abandoned by many critical scholars as untenable or at least unprovable. It is evident elsewhere in the Levant that peoples were busily recounting and recording their ancestral origins. That the early Hebrews did too and that Moses, the prominent contributor to Israel's formative period and to Exodus–Deuteronomy, should be the Genesis compiler agrees with what we know of this early period.

LITERARY READINGS. Recently a new wave of synchronic literary approaches has begun to rival the diachronic methods.[118] In biblical studies historical questions dominate both evangelical interpretation (grammatical-historical) and the historical-critical methods (source, form, and tradition-history). But the new literary approaches are not interested in diachronic questions, at least not primarily. Their focal study is synchronic, that is, the final form of the text without reference to how or by whom the text came together. Synchronic studies had their greatest impetus in the 1940s and 1950s movement known as the New Criticism, which perceived the text as an autonomous entity, like an artistic artifact (e.g., a sculpture).[119] The New Criticism took an ahistorical stance toward the text, a position that significantly departed from traditional literary criticism.

Contemporary literary approaches to the Bible draw on a myriad of literary-critical theories and other disciplines, such as anthropology, psychology, linguistics, and political theory. Among the new literary readings is the once-influential movement of Structuralism that emerged in secular literary circles during the 1960s. *Structuralism* does not refer to an organizational plan at the surface level, such as an outline. It is a philosophy of reality that may be applied to any entity that is a "system," such as language and literature. Literary structuralism is indebted to the structural linguistics of F. de Saussure, whose theory envisioned language as *systems* of signification. He differentiated between language as a system *(langue)* and language as a speech act *(parole)*. *Langue* is the structural network of language that is intuitively imposed on a speaker. *Parole* is the specific expression of language, as found in a particular discourse. The structuralist seeks primarily to discover the underlying or "deep" structure that governs specific language acts. Structural exegesis seeks to show how the universals of lan-

---

[118] For this discussion see the author's "Literary Criticism of the Old Testament," in *Foundations for Biblical Interpretation,* ed. D. S. Dockery et al. (Nashville: Broadman & Holman, 1994), 205–31.

[119] W. K. Wimsatt and M. C. Beardsley, "The Intentional Fallacy," in *The Verbal Icon: Studies in the Meaning of the Poetry* (Lexington: University of Kentucky, 1954 [reprint]). Also W. K. Wimsatt and C. Brooks, *Literary Criticism: A Short History* (New York: Knopf, 1957).

guage take part in the meaning of a specific text.[120] Structural narratology, which has had the greatest impact on biblical studies, defines the components and processes of narrative as a system.[121] Representative of this movement are the theorists V. Propp, C. Lévi-Strauss, and A. J. Greimas.[122] Structural reading of Old Testament texts was pioneered by French structuralists, particularly R. Barthes, whose analysis of Jacob's struggle with the angel (Gen 32:23–32) has become a parade illustration of structural readings applied to biblical texts.[123]

Composition criticism focuses on formal literary features of the text as clues of the narrator's message. R. Alter defines this kind of literary analysis as a study of the "artful use of language . . . the kind of disciplined attention, in other words, which through a whole spectrum of critical approaches has illuminated, for example, the poetry of Dante, the plays of Shakespeare, the novels of Tolstoy."[124] Such literary interpretations have often been applied to the narratives of Genesis.[125] Exemplary of this has been the early work of J. P.

---

[120] See D. Patte, "One Text. Several Structures," *Semeia* 18 (1980): 3–24; R. Polzin, *Biblical Structuralism: Method and Subjectivity in the Study of Ancient Texts, Semeia Supplements* (Philadelphia: Fortress/Missoula: Scholars Press, 1977), 5; S. A. Geller, "Through Windows and Mirrors into the Bible. History, Literature, and Language in the Study of Text," in *A Sense of Text: The Art of Language in the Study of Biblical Literature* (Winona Lake: Eisenbrauns for Dropsie College, 1983), 28.

[121] A helpful analysis of the leading theoreticians and biblical applications is D. C. Greenwood, *Structuralism and the Biblical Text* (Berlin: Mouton, 1985). See also R. C. Culley, "Exploring New Directions," in *The Hebrew Bible and Its Modern Interpreters,* ed. D. Knight and G. Tucker (Philadelphia: Fortress/Chico, Cal.: Scholars Press, 1985), 175–77; the articles in VTSup 22 (1972) and *Int* 28 (1974).

[122] Originally published in 1928 (Russian), Propp's work was translated in 1958 and revised in this second edition: *Morphology of the Folktale,* rev., ed. L. A. Wagner (Austin: University of Texas Press, 1968). Also see C. Lévi-Strauss, "The Structural Study of Myth," in *Structural Anthropology,* trans. C. Jacobson and B. G. Schoepf (New York: Basic, 1963), 206–31; A. J. Greimas, *Structural Semantics: An Attempt at a Method,* trans. D. McDowell et al. (Lincoln: University of Nebraska Press, 1984). Greimas's model has been described by J. Calloud, *Structural Analysis of Narrative,* trans. D. Patte (Philadelphia: Fortress/Missoula: Scholars Press, 1976).

[123] R. Barthes, "The Struggle with the Angel: Textual Analysis of Genesis 32:23–32," in *Structural Analysis and Biblical Exegesis,* ed. R. Barthes et al., trans. A. M. Johnson (Pittsburgh: Pickwick, 1974), 21–33. See also, e.g., E. Leach, *Genesis as Myth and Other Essays* (London: Jonathan Cape, 1969); Leach and D. A. Aycock, *Structuralist Interpretations of Biblical Myth* (Cambridge: Cambridge University Press, 1983); "Genesis 2 and 3: Kaleidoscopic Structural Readings," *Semeia* 18 (1980); "Classical Hebrew Narrative," *Semeia* 3 (1975); and "Perspectives on Old Testament Narrative," *Semeia* 15 (1979).

[124] R. Alter, *The Art of Biblical Narrative* (New York: Basic, 1981), 12–13.

[125] E.g., K. R. R. Gros Louis, et al., eds., *Literary Interpretations of Biblical Narratives, Volume I* (Nashville: Abingdon, 1974), and Gros Louis and Ackerman, eds., ibid., *Volume II* (1982); R. Alter and F. Kermode, eds., *The Literary Guide to the Bible* (Cambridge: Harvard University Press, 1987); and A. Preminger and E. L. Greenstein, *The Hebrew Bible in Literary Criticism* (New York: Ungar, 1986); D. M. Gunn and D. N. Fewell, *Narrative in the Hebrew Bible* (Oxford: Oxford University Press, 1993).

Fokkelman and more recently H. C. White's study in the function of narrative discourse in Genesis.[126]

During the 1960s to 1970s, discourse analysis of conversation (oral text) and written text was developed,[127] but it has had less influence among biblical scholars. As a subfield of textlinguistics it gives attention to the "grammar" of discourse above the word and phrase levels. Discourse typologies were identified, each with its own constituent "grammar" of composition, including, for example hortatory, narrative (story), and exposition. R. E. Longacre is best known in biblical studies for applying discourse analysis to Genesis, as found in his study of the Joseph cycle and the flood narrative.[128] The profile of a discourse can be traced by recognizing certain junctures where particular grammatical-lexical features at the surface level mark its stages of growth, such as shifts in verbal tense, incidence of repetition, change in participants, and dialogue length. The macrostructure has a structural *peak*(s) that is indicated by the surface markers, where a "zone of turbulence" occurs. When the *peak*(s) is plotted with the story's event line, the contour of the discourse's rise and fall of tension(s) can be drawn.

More popular has been reader-response criticism, which focuses on meaning in terms of the reader's experience. For the reader-response critic, reading the Bible "as literature is to retrieve it from the museum, to relate it to the life of contemporary readers."[129] Meaningful knowledge is discovered when the reader's social experience impacts the text so as to make it meaningful to that person. Since the interpretive process includes the reader's own worldview as well as that presupposed by the text, the text becomes infinite in its potentialities for meaning. P. Ricoeur's hermeneutics acknowledges that the text had a meaning for author and original audience, but once that was experienced, the sense of the text lies beyond it and resides in us as readers "in front of" the text.[130] Marxist, feminist, materialist, and liberation readings are among socio-

---

[126] J. P. Fokkelman, *Narrative Art in Genesis: Specimens of Stylistic and Structural Analysis,* 2d ed. (Sheffield: JSOT, 1991 [1975]), and H. C. White, *Narration and Discourse in the Book of Genesis* (Cambridge: Cambridge University Press, 1991).

[127] E.g., K. L. Pike, *Language in Relation to a Unified Theory of Human Behavior,* reprint (The Hague: Mouton, 1964); T. A. van Dijk, *Some Aspects of Text Grammars* (The Hague: Mouton, 1972); R. A. de Beaugrande and W. Dressler, *Introduction to Text Linguistics* (London: Longman, 1981); R. E. Longacre, *The Grammar of Discourse* (New York: Plenum, 1983).

[128] For an overview of Longacre's method, see his *Joseph: A Story of Divine Providence: A Text Theoretical and Textlinguistic Analysis of Genesis 37 and 39–48* (Winona Lake: Eisenbrauns, 1989). Also see his "Verb Ranking and the Constituency Structure of Discourse," in *Journal of the Linguistic Association of the Southwest* 4 (1982): 177–202, and "Discourse Peak as Zone of Turbulence," in *Beyond the Sentence,* ed. J. Wirth (Ann Arbor: Karona, 1985), 81–92.

[129] E. McKnight, *Post-Modern Use of the Bible: The Emergence of Reader-Oriented Criticism* (Nashville: Abingdon, 1988), 123.

[130] P. Ricoeur, *Essays on Biblical Interpretation,* ed. L. S. Mudge (Philadelphia: Fortress, 1980).

logical approaches to the Bible. Exemplary of ideological readings is feminist criticism that reads a biblical account through the lens of gender.[131] E. Schüssler Fiorenza explains the shift from androcentric readings to a feminist hermeneutic: "A feminist critical interpretation of the Bible cannot take as its point of departure the normative authority of the biblical archetype, but must begin with women's experience in their struggle for liberation."[132]

Deconstructionism, also known as "poststructuralism," has become an important force in literary criticism since the 1980s, but it has had little influence on biblical studies. This movement had its inception in the philosophy of J. Derrida (*De la grammatologie* in 1967), whose extreme skepticism about the possibility of meaning has challenged the traditional understanding of how meaning is achieved in communication.[133] When applied to literary analysis, deconstructionists explain how the text subverts or deconstructs itself. J. Culler comments: "To deconstruct a discourse is to show how it undermines the philosophy it asserts, or the hierarchical oppositions on which it relies, by identifying in the text the rhetorical operations that produce the supposed ground of argument, the key concept or promise."[134] The text then is metaphor or pun. P. D. Miscall has read Genesis 12 and 1 Samuel 16–22 from a deconstructionist perspective. His "close reading" of the text exposes what he believes are the ambiguities, ambivalences, and gaps of the narrative.[135] The indeterminateness of the text prevents a definitive reading and a coherent one; there can be no historical or theological or ideological meaning.

CANON. Canon criticism has received a more sympathetic hearing from biblical scholars, for while it shares in some features of the literary approaches, it can be distinguished from literary studies by its interest in history. Its most vocal proponents have been the biblical scholars B. S. Childs and J. Sanders.[136] Childs argued that the proper beginning point for criticism is the final form of the canon, which functions as the normative expression of reli-

---

[131] E.g., P. Trible, *Texts of Terror: Literary Feminist Reading of Biblical Narratives* (Philadelphia: Fortress, 1984), and A. Bach, ed., *The Pleasure of Her Text: Feminist Readings of Biblical and Historical Texts* (Philadelphia: Trinity Press International, 1990). A recent illustration of a psychoanalytical reading of Genesis is the work of I. N. Rashkow, *The Phallacy of Genesis: A Feminist-Psychoanalytical Approach* (Louisville: Westminster/John Knox, 1993).

[132] E. Schüssler Fiorenza, *Bread not Stone: The Challenge of Feminist Biblical Interpretation* (Boston: Beacon, 1984), 13.

[133] See V. B. Leitch, *Deconstructive Criticism: An Advanced Introduction* (New York: Columbia University Press, 1983), and R. Selden, *A Reader's Guide to Contemporary Literary Theory* (Lexington: University Press of Kentucky, 1985), 84–89.

[134] J. Culler, *On Deconstruction: Theory and Criticism after Structuralism* (London: Routledge & Kegan, Paul, 1982), 86.

[135] P. D. Miscall, *The Workings of Old Testament Narrative* (Philadelphia: Fortress, 1983); also his *1 Samuel: A Literary Reading* (Bloomington: Indiana University Press, 1986).

[136] B. S. Childs, *Biblical Theology in Crisis* (Philadelphia: Fortress, 1970), and J. Sanders, *Torah and Canon* (Philadelphia: Fortress, 1972).

gious faith by the believing communities of Judaism and Christianity. The proper stance of the critic toward the Bible, contends Childs, is a person of faith within the community who views the text as "Scripture."[137] Approaching the text as "Scripture" gives the text its referential orientation in the roots of historic Israel, whereas synchronic studies view the Bible as nonreferential. Nevertheless, Childs speaks of canonical context in the sense of its literary context, not its historical.

Sanders agrees that historical criticism effectively cuts the Bible off from the very communities that revered it.[138] Sanders, however, views his "canonical criticism" (not "canon criticism") as the natural extension of the historical-critical methods. For him the proper canonical context includes the precanonical stages in its historical development. Historical tools, therefore, are needed to isolate the various stages of canonical development, tracing the function of those traditions that finally reside in the extant canon.

CONCLUSIONS. Although modernity has focused on the preliterary stages of Genesis, the rich precritical history of interpretation found that the canonical shape of the book was edifying for synagogue and church. On the horizon the attention to the holistic nature of the biblical text will persist, but the old atomizing methods (with revisions) are still very much alive and remain standard in most universities and many mainline denominational seminaries. Occupation with the prehistory of the text, however, led to consequences unforeseen by their progenitors—a faith-tradition without a historical basis. Evangelical scholars have found that those literary approaches that contribute to establishing the priority of the extant form of the text and emphasize its rhetorical unity are most fruitful to biblical interpretation for the church, since the canonical text is the one certain form which has survived and has been found authoritative.[139] But any literary method whose philosophical assumptions drive a wedge between history and the referential value of the text for knowing reality undercuts the assumption of the Bible itself. Biblical revelation is grounded in historical events which have been interpreted by the sole authoritative voice of the text.

---

[137] B. S. Childs, *Introduction to the Old Testament as Scripture* (Philadelphia: Fortress, 1979). Also his *Biblical Theology of the Old and New Testaments: Theological Reflection on the Christian Bible* (Minneapolis: Fortress, 1993).

[138] See his review of Childs in "Canonical Context and Canonical Criticism," *Horizons in Biblical Theology* 2 (1980): 173–97; reprinted in *From Sacred Story to Sacred Text* (Philadelphia: Fortress, 1987), 153–74.

[139] For an assessment of the literary approaches from an evangelical perspective, see T. Longman, *Literary Approaches to Biblical Interpretation* (Grand Rapids: Zondervan/Academie, 1987), 47–64, and C. Walhout and L. Ryken, eds., *Contemporary Literary Theory: A Christian Appraisal* (Grand Rapids: Eerdmans, 1991); also for a traditional historical-critical scholar's critique, see Geller, "Through Windows and Mirrors," 3–40.

6. Genesis 1–11 and Ancient Literature

"Parallelomania" was the entitled address delivered by Samuel Sandmel to the annual meeting of the Society of Biblical Literature in 1961.[140] It focused on the excesses in New Testament studies where literary parallels and influences, such as Palestinian and Hellenistic Jewish literature, exercised inordinate influence in interpretation. However, cautions that Sandmel noted transfer as sober warnings for our subject as well. When it comes to the primeval history and ancient Near Eastern literature, there has been much "parallelomania."[141] As with Sandmel's address thirty-five years ago, a disclaimer is required. The point is not that ancient Near Eastern literatures and languages have no bearing, only that the common practice of the comparative method has often made ancient literature the interpretive template for the biblical account of beginnings. This is done at times for the slightest reason and often without due regard to the contextual function of either the biblical account or the alleged nonbiblical parallel. We would reject the extremes of either overplaying the value of the comparative materials or of flatly ignoring them.

Sandmel recommends several considerations in weighing the value of extrabiblical sources. First, the basis for judgment must reside in the details of the specific application where a parallel is considered, not merely an abstract statement. Parallels, even where they are exact, do not guarantee a significant meaning for interpretation. Many parallels are not important in the study of beginnings because they arise due to common subject matter and reflect common language. We are not surprised, for example, in considering the subject of a great flood, that ancient myths and the Bible share certain descriptive elements. In both the survivor built a craft to escape the waters and equipped it with the necessary elements that would found the new postflood world (i.e., a menagerie of animals). Some parallels therefore are significant for interpretation, and others are not. In determining possible dependence, too often the differences between the Hebrew account and the myths are minimized while the agreements are exaggerated.

Second, numerous and even sometimes quite striking alleged agreements do not guarantee that the nonbiblical text is a true parallel that can serve as a window for interpreting the Hebrew passage. The many similarities between the Babylonian flood story *Gilgamesh* and Genesis in themselves do not mean the myth and the biblical author must have shared the same interpretation of the

---

[140] S. Sandmel, "Parallelomania," *JBL* 81 (1962): 1–13.

[141] E.g., R. A. Simkins argues that the differences between Genesis and the pagan myths must be viewed in the context of their similarities. By a cross-cultural model of origins, Simkins flattens out the distinctives and argues that there is a "cultural continuity" between Israel and its neighbors. They essentially held the same view of reality (*Creator and Creation* [Peabody, Mass.: Hendrickson, 1994], 88–91).

flood. Thus, to paraphrase Sandmel, what value is there in pointing out hypothetical parallels? Additionally, in Old Testament studies we have the slippery business of explaining how the variant stories came to have similarities: who is borrowing from whom? Hebrew from the pagan cultures? Or the pagan cultures from the Hebrews? This latter option usually is deemed unlikely since the pagan myths antedate the Hebrew composition. A third and more profitable option is that the diverse perspectives arise from an antecedent tradition. The proposal, however, is not of a common text or an original story or a cultural continuum, but rather a common universal memory.

Third, many alleged parallels result from extracting a superficial similarity without due regard for the context of the pagan or biblical text. *Gilgamesh,* for example, is not primarily a flood story. Rather it tells of Gilgamesh's search for the secret of immortality. The flood, while taking up many lines, is only incidental to this overarching interest. It is a story within the story, in which Utnapishtim, the Babylonian "Noah," explains to Gilgamesh how his achieving immortality was a special case and will be of no help to Gilgamesh. Noah's flood, on the other hand, is central to early Genesis and has nothing to do with the search for or acquisition of immortality. Some argue that the intermarriage of the "sons of God" and the "daughters of men" in 6:1–4 was the illicit attempt by mortals to obtain divinity and that the flood was God's response. But this is only arrived at by starting with the mythological materials; the Noahic passage says nothing of such a search, and it is not so clear that the "sons of God" are in fact divine beings.

Yet another layer of contextual duplicity exists among scholars. This is the practice of reconstructing the historical and compositional context of the biblical passage. Rather than reading Genesis 1–11 as the preamble to Moses' second-millennium Torah, the typical reconstruction sets the accounts of the primeval history in later, diverse settings, such as the court of David and the exilic community of the sixth century B.C. And of course there is always the historical setting of the putative redactor who put all this together. For example, Gen 1:1–2:4a is attributed to the Priestly writer in the exilic period when the Jewish exiles faced the imposing threat of pagan idolatry as they were situated in Babylon. The best way to head this off was supposedly a cosmogony that appealed to Mesopotamian stories for achieving the task. There can be little question that Genesis 1 does that very thing—oppose pagan idolatry—but would it not be better methodologically to see how it functioned in the Mosaic community where indeed it did operate for that purpose (cf. Deut 4:15–20)?

Although caution is required, there is a legitimate place for considering the witness of ancient Near Eastern recoveries. It is not found so much in the counting or discounting of parallels but in the general ideological climate in which the biblical materials are found. G. Wenham expresses this best in considering the striking similarities between *Gilgamesh* and the biblical flood: "This is not to say that the writer of Genesis had ever heard or read the Gilgamesh epic: these ideas were just part of the intellectual furniture of that time in the Near East, just as most people today have a fair idea of Darwin's *Origin of the Species* though they have never read it."[142]

The advantage for the biblical scholar in studying ancient myths is the broad sweep of how ancient peoples conceived of cosmogony and the origins of civilization. Against this backdrop the innovation of the Hebrew thinker, in dependence on divine revelation, becomes clear to the modern reader. The radical thinking of the biblical author compared to his counterparts, the prime example being the absence of a female deity or consort for Yahweh, shows that the Hebrew did not rely on ancient thinking to speak to origins. Other assumptions by the biblical author mark Genesis as distinctive: Israelite monotheism, the autonomy of God from creation and creation processes, the consistent moral factor that pervades early Genesis, and the insistence on the historicity of the events placed as they are under the *tōlĕdōt* ("generations") rubric.

There is no myth comparable to the literary composition of Genesis 1–11. There are pieces, but close examination shows that the biblical handling of even those subjects is so uniquely sculpted that it is hard to justify a true parallel. The closest continuous compositional example to Genesis 1–9 is the Babylonian *Atrahasis* (ca. 1600 B.C.), which consists of the framework creation-flood. T. Jacobsen has also appealed to Sumerian tradition as a parallel by splicing together several disparate texts so as to create his "Eridu Genesis," entailing creation, the Sumerian King List (cp. Gen 5), and the Sumerian flood story.[143] It is too much to claim, however, that the ancient Near East possessed a literary "convention" or "model" of events that was followed by our biblical writer.[144] There is found in ancient literature in a general way a framework that traces creation, founders of early civilization, and the flood.[145] But there is no genuine equal in Mesopotamian traditions with the

[142] Wenham, "The Perplexing Pentateuch," *Vox Evangelica* 17 (1987): 12.

[143] T. Jacobsen, "The Eridu Genesis," *JBL* 100 (1981): 513–29.

[144] Jacobsen argues that the Sumerian tradition was the model for the P(riestly) writer: "The Mesopotamian materials will have served as models rather than having been directly borrowed from" (ibid., 529). Others argue that the Yahwist (J) shows closer dependence on Babylonian *Atrahasis* than P. See W. M. Clark, "The Flood and the Structure of the Pre-patriarchal History," *ZAW* 83 (1971): 184–210, esp. 187–88; C. Sinclair, "A Near-Eastern Prototype for the Primeval History," in *Tradition as Openness to the Future: Essays in Honor of Willis W. Fisher,* ed. F. O. Francis and R. P. Wallace (Lanham: University Press of America, 1984), 5–31; P. D. Miller, "Eridu, Dunnu, and Babel: A Study in Comparative Mythology," *HAR* 9 (1985): 227–51, esp. 233–34.

[145] E.g., K. A. Kitchen contends that Mesopotamian (Sumerian, Akkadian) and West Semitic (Gen 1–11) traditions, while independent, show a common tradition of early events (*The Bible and Its World* [Downers Grove: IVP, 1978 [1977], 30–36). Sumerian (King List; flood story), though here creation must be supplied, Akkadian (*Atrahasis*), and West Semitic literature (Gen 1–11) evidence a common theme: creation-crisis-continuance of man.

garden scene of human sin, and the concluding episode of Babel's tower stands without parallel.[146] On this latter point, some conclude for this reason that the primeval history ends formally with 9:29,[147] but this hardly does justice to the anticipation of the world's nations found in 9:1,18–19 and to the critical linkage between Noah and Abraham for the author that is found in the genealogies of chaps. 10–11. The tower episode explains the rise of the nations and the necessity of Abraham for resolving the tension found at Shinar (11:1–9). A. R. Millard concludes regarding *Atrahasis* and Genesis: "All who suspect or suggest borrowing by the Hebrews are compelled to admit large-scale revision, alteration, and re-interpretation in a fashion which cannot be substantiated for any other composition from the Ancient Near East or in any other Hebrew writing. If there was borrowing then it can have extended only as far as the 'historical' framework, and not included intention or interpretation."[148]

As commentators have commonly noted, biblical Genesis shows a rejection of pagan ideas. Viewed as a "polemic," the biblical description of ancient events takes on remarkably different meaning. Instead of a borrowing or a historicizing of ancient myth, it is fairer to say that Genesis comes closer to a repudiation of pagan ideas about origins, mankind, civilization, and the flood. It is doubtful that the biblical writer intentionally set out to attack pagan notions, as the word "polemic" has come to mean. If polemic is found in early Genesis, the clearest example would be the Hebrew parody in Gen 11:1–9 on Gentile empire building, the episode absent in the pagan framework. Rather than true polemic, however, in general the Genesis accounts are inferentially undermining the philosophical basis for pagan myth. There are undertones of refutation in Genesis 1–11, but they are not disputations.

---

[146] The idea of rebellion is found by some to lie behind the noisy sounds of the human populace, desiring to become more than the servants of the gods, which provokes Enlil to rid himself of the tumult by plague, droughts, and finally flood. See R. Oden, "Divine Aspirations in *Atraḫasis* and in Genesis 1–11," *ZAW* 93 (1981): 197–216. But the noise is explicitly said to be disturbing the god's sleep; the issue is the overpopulation of humanity, and the epic shows the resolution by establishing means for population control. See A. D. Kilmer, "The Mesopotamian Concept of Overpopulation and Its Solution as Reflected in the Mythology," *Or* 41 (1972): 160–77, and the arguments of W. L. Moran, "Some Considerations of Form and Interpretation in *Atra-ḫasis*," in *Language, Literature, and History: Philological and Historical Studies Presented to Erica Reiner,* AOS 67, ed. F. Rochberg-Halton (New Haven: AOS, 1987), 245–55. Even if one supposes that human rebellion is behind the noisy populace, there the semblance to the garden ends; the biblical couple are not in bondage to God, and they have no complaint.

[147] E.g., Clark, "The Flood and the Structure of the Prepatriarchal History," 209–10.

[148] A. R. Millard, "A New Babylonian 'Genesis' Story," *TynBul* 18 (1967): 12–18.

The primary areas that Genesis and myth address are (1) creation and mankind, (2) Eden, (3) the long-lived patriarchs, and (4) the flood.[149]

(1) Creation and Mankind

EGYPT. In Egyptian literature creation is not treated in one text, nor is there an authoritative account, though underlying this diversity is one consistent viewpoint.[150] The text of the Memphite Theology is the longest sustained creation myth, but other significant creation remarks are found dispersed among numerous early and late texts. For the ancient Egyptian the universe consisted of beings, not things. There are no impersonal forces, only the will and actions of the gods. Creation is a process of the unfolding of undifferentiated matter, the primeval Monad; thus Egyptian creation is more developmental than causal. Atum of Heliopolis, the creator-god, is the single source from which all emanates. The primeval hillock spontaneously emerges from the waters (Nun), and it is there that the creator-god is self-realized. In Genesis the role of primeval waters (1:2) is highlighted, but there they are attributed to God's creation (1:1). The "Spirit of God" superintends the waters, preparing the earth for the creation word. But Atum actualizes himself as the primal seed (egg) floating upon the waters:

> I am the one who made me.
> It was as I wished, according to my heart, that I built myself.[151]

The lesser gods have a genealogical relationship to Atum. From Atum by means of sneezing, spitting, or masturbating come the primal elements of atmosphere, Shu and Tefnut, followed by their offspring the earth (Geb) and the sky (Nut). "Magic" is the operative power that enables the idea or concept of creation to be realized through command. In the Coffin texts and the text of the Memphite Theology, the deity Ptah (speech) is the intellectual principle, the thought and word, that achieves the development of the forces that arise from the primeval Monad.[152]

---

[149] For helpful resources see J. B. Pritchard, ed., *Ancient Near Eastern Texts (ANET);* W. Beyerlin, ed., *Near Eastern Religious Texts Relating to the Old Testament,* OTL, trans. J. Bowden (Philadelphia: Westminster, 1978); and J. H. Walton, *Ancient Israelite Literature in Its Cultural Context* (Grand Rapids: Zondervan, 1989).

[150] For this discussion and translations, see J. P. Allen, *Genesis in Egypt: The Philosophy of Ancient Egyptian Creation Accounts,* YES 2 (New Haven: Yale University Press, 1988). Also for translations of relevant texts see J. A. Wilson, "Creation and Myths of Origins," *ANET,* 3–10; W. K. Simpson, ed., *The Literature of Ancient Egypt: An Anthology of Stories, Instructions, and Poetry,* trans. R. O. Faulkner et al. (New Haven: Yale University Press, 1973). M. Lichtheim, *Ancient Egyptian Literature,* 3 vols. (Berkeley: University of California Press, 1980).

[151] See Allen, *Genesis in Egypt,* 13.

[152] Ibid., 42–45.

Through the heart and through the tongue something developed into Atum's image.
And great and important is Ptah,
who gave life to all the gods and their *kas* as well
through this heart and this tongue
through which Horus and Thoth both became Ptah.

Magic is the means by which the creator's *fiats* produce the universe from the Monad. Here the relationship to Genesis, creation by the transcendent word, differs since it is by the power of "Magic" that Ptah's word is realized.

Also the Egyptian view saw Ptah as the single source of creation; he was the preexistent matter, the primeval waters, from which all came. J. D. Currid concludes that Memphite Theology has creation *ex nihilo,* as in the Genesis account, since the primeval waters (the god Nun) are equaled with Ptah and all came from Ptah.[153] But in the Genesis account the Creator is not the source as Ptah is of material life, for God transcends all that exists. J. P. Allen questions whether Egyptian cosmology has *creatio ex nihilo* since the creator's "heart" and "tongue" produced the elements of the world by acting upon the primordial Monad, namely, Atum.[154] In Theban theology the Ultimate Cause is Amun. All material and intellectual principles derive from him. Although Amun is depicted as a transcendent creator, the difference with biblical creation is that Amun is viewed as both the source and the realization of the gods: "*Gods* are many; *deity* is one."[155]

As for the creation of mankind, there are diverse accounts in Egyptian literature, but a recurring conception is the making of man from clay. This has similarities to Gen 2:7, where man is made with the "dust" of the earth. The Hymn to Khnum depicts the deity at the potter's wheel forming man, and Hekat the goddess gives the clay figure the breath of life in its nostrils.[156] The Instruction of Amenemope reads, "Man is clay and straw, and God is his potter."[157] In the Instruction for Merikare the deity Re made man: "He placed the breath of life in their nostrils. They who have issued from his body are his images."[158] In Egyptian sources, unlike the Bible, there is little interest in the creation of the woman.

MESOPOTAMIA. Since the recoveries in the nineteenth century of the Babylonian creation myth *Enuma Elish* and the flood story *Epic of Gilgamesh,* Mesopotamian studies have inordinately influenced scholarship's understand-

[153] See J. D. Currid, "An Examination of the Egyptian Background of the Genesis Cosmogony," *BZ* (1991): 18–40, esp. 28–29.

[154] Allen, *Genesis in Egypt,* 36–38, 58–59.

[155] Ibid., 62.

[156] See J. K. Hoffmeier, "Some Thoughts on Genesis 1 and 2 and Egyptian Cosmology," *JANES* 15 (1983): 39–49.

[157] Simpson, *The Literature of Ancient Egypt,* 262.

[158] *ANET,* 417.

ing of Genesis 1–11.[159] The old opinion of "pan-Babylonia," that is, the assumption that the ideas of Babylonian religious myth permeated Near Eastern cultures, has left its legacy.[160] Pan-Babylonianism assumed that Mesopotamian ideas migrated to the west, where they were taken up by the Hebrews and were the source of Israel's ideas and institutions. This assumption that all ideas traveled from Mesopotamia has been found untenable.[161] Nevertheless, there remains the widespread opinion that Hebrew culture depended on the cultural perceptions of the Mesopotamians.

Mesopotamia's *Enuma Elish* is known from extant texts recovered from the first millennium B.C., but all are agreed that it is much older, reaching into the second millennium, though it cannot be dated precisely. The story comprises several elements: *theogony*, explaining the origins of the gods born to the inert waters Apsu and Tiamat; *theomachy,* in which the lesser gods threatened by Apsu kill him, raising the revenge of Tiamat; and *monarchy*, describing the rise of Marduk as permanent ruler of the gods.[162] Tiamat's murderous intentions against the children born to her are countered in the assembly of the gods by appealing to young Marduk, who volunteered to combat the watery goddess. The reward for his task is his elevation as king of the gods and ultimately the building of Babylon by the deities and of its temple for his permanent royal citadel and center of administration. As the victorious king, Marduk created the cosmos and formed mankind for the benefit of the gods. Their response was to recognize his monarchy as permanent. Mesopotamia's creation epic was shaped to justify the political ascendancy of Babylon and its chief deity Marduk by setting their origins and character of their rule in the mythic, eternal present. Thus it explained Mesopotamia's city-state system ruled under the hegemony of Babylon's king and gave divine authority for the political monarchy of the state.

Enuma Elish depicts the creation of the sky and earth as the consequence of

---

[159] For helpful surveys of Mesopotamian studies and the Bible, see R. S. Hess, "One Hundred Fifty Years of Comparative Studies on Genesis 1–11: An Overview," and D. T. Tsumura, "Genesis and Ancient Near Eastern Stories of Creation and Flood: An Introduction," in *I Studied Inscriptions from before the Flood: Ancient Near Eastern, Literary, and Linguistic Approaches to Genesis 1–11,* ed. Hess and Tsumura (Winona Lake: Eisenbrauns, 1994), 3–26, 27–57. This volume includes reprints of many important studies on early Genesis and the comparative method.

[160] See H. B. Huffmon, "*Babel und Bibel:* The Encounter Between Babylon and the Bible," in *Backgrounds for the Bible,* ed. M. P. O'Connor and D. N. Freedman (Winona Lake: Eisenbrauns, 1987), 125–36.

[161] W. G. Lambert, "A New Look at the Babylonian Background of Genesis," *JTS* 16 (1965): 289. A. W. Sjöberg, "Eve and the Chameleon," in *In the Shelter of Elyon: Essays on Ancient Palestinian Life and Literature in Honor of G. A. Ahlström,* JSOTSup 31, ed. W. B. Barrick and J. R. Spencer (Sheffield: JSOT, 1984), 199–215, comments: "It is amazing that there still is a tendency of theologians to carry around a lot of pan-Babylonianism in their scientific luggage" (p. 218).

[162] See Jacobsen, *The Treasures of Darkness: A History of Mesopotamian Religion* (New Haven: Yale University Press, 1976), 167–91.

the monumental battle between Marduk and the primeval waters Tiamat.[163] After killing the evil Tiamat, the champion god slices her body lengthwise and forms the sky and earth from her carcass:

> He [Marduk] divided the monstrous shape [Tiamat] and created marvels
> (from it).
> He sliced her in half like a fish for drying:
> Half of her he put up to roof the sky,
> Drew a bolt across and made a guard hold it.
> Her waters he arranged so that they could not escape.

This idea that creation's inception involved primeval waters (i.e., Tiamat) is shared by Genesis (i.e., "deep," *tĕhôm*), and the horizontal differentiation in the cosmic sky and earth has similarity to the division of the waters below and above (1:6–8). The attention of ancient cosmogony is on the generation of the gods and how the present order and cultural institutions came into existence. Mesopotamian telling was more theogonic (i.e., the origins of the gods) than cosmogonic. Moreover, "creation" is depicted not as the creating of matter but as the organizing of preexistent matter into the ordered universe.

This Mesopotamian battle motif as the means of creation (where the elements of chaos are overcome by the creation-god) often appears in ancient cosmogonies, and it is widely held that cosmogonic conflict was the original motif behind Genesis 1. M. K. Wakeman studied cosmogonic myths from the ancient Near East, including Indian, Hittite, Mesopotamian, and Greek examples. The underlying "myth" they hold in common was the defeat of the "monster," that is, the repressive power, which is subsumed and sometimes utilized by the Liberator to achieve right order in the world and society. "The basic meaning of 'god killed the dragon' is that time proceeds, bringing fulfillment as it brings death; water flows rather than floods, the sun rises as surely as it sets, sons become fathers as they engender sons. What makes Indra, Marduk, Zeus, Horus, Baal, etc. heroes is their ability to provide order in which this free yet regulated movement is assured."[164] It has been typical of scholarship since H. Gunkel's *Schöfung und Chaos* (1895) to interpret Genesis 1's subjugation of the "deep" and division of the "waters" as a remnant of the battle motif between Marduk and watery Tiamat, which was taken up by the Hebrew author and demythologized.[165] But scholars have come to recognize that the association

---

[163] For translations and discussion see A. Heidel, *The Babylonian Genesis: The Story of Creation,* 2d ed. (Chicago: University of Chicago Press, 1963); E. A. Speiser, "The Creation Epic," *ANET,* 60–72; S. Dalley, *Myths from Mesopotamia: Creation, the Flood, Gilgamesh, and Others* (Oxford: Oxford University Press, 1991).

[164] M. K. Wakeman, *God's Battle with the Monster: A Study in Biblical Imagery* (Leiden: Brill, 1973), 39–40.

[165] E.g., B. W. Anderson, *Creation Versus Chaos: The Reinterpretation of Mythical Symbolism in the Bible* (1967; reprint, Philadelphia: Fortress, 1987).

of Hebrew *tĕhôm* ("deep," 1:2) with Tiamat is superficial, and there is nothing Babylonian about the Genesis account of creation.[166]

Some scholars associate Hebrew creation with the divine conflict in Canaanite backgrounds where Baal defeats Yam (Sea) and the sea monsters (e.g., Leviathan), especially in light of Psalm 104. Thus the Hebrew account at 1:2,6–10 is thought to be an appropriation of Canaanite mythology that was later historicized as an account acceptable to orthodox Yahwism.[167] But there is no assurance of a linkage for two reasons. (1) There is no consensus that the Baal-Yam cycle is a creation myth at all. The epithet "Creator" is reserved for El and Athirat, not Baal; his role is not to organize the cosmos but rather to preserve it by giving it life.[168] (2) There is question about whether there is a "chaos" in 1:2 as most have supposed for a century now.[169] If there is a mythological element in Genesis's creation, it is best taken as a repudiation of myth, not an adaptation.

The creation of mankind in Mesopotamian myths involves the blood of slain deities and sometimes the mixture of clay material. *Enuma Elish* tells how the deity Kingu, leader of the Tiamat armies, was slain and from his blood was made mankind, whose purpose was to relieve the lesser gods of their toil.[170] In the *Atrahasis* epic the lesser gods revolted against their duties of canal digging, and the higher gods called upon the mother-goddess, Nintu, to create mankind. Upon Enki's direction the deity Geshtu-e (or Wê-ila) is slaughtered, and from his blood and flesh mixed with clay was formed a clay figure. The lesser gods spat upon the clay.

> From his [Geshtu-e] flesh and his blood
> Let Nintu [mother-goddess] mix clay,
> that the god and man may be thoroughly mixed together in the clay.[171]

Later, after Nintu's incantation, she pinches off fourteen pieces, constituting seven males and seven females. *Atrahasis* has human beings made up of both

[166] Lambert, "A New Look at the Babylonian Background of Genesis," 295.

[167] E.g., J. Day, *God's Conflict with the Dragon and the Sea: Echoes of a Canaanite Myth in the Old Testament* (Cambridge: Cambridge University Press, 1985).

[168] See M. S. Smith, "Interpreting the Baal Cycle," *UF* 18 (1986): 319–20; D. T. Tsumura, *The Earth and the Waters in Genesis 1 and 2,* JSOTSup 83 (Sheffield: JSOT, 1989), 50–65. For Baal myth as cosmogonic see L. R. Fisher, "Creation at Ugarit and in the Old Testament," *VT* 15 (1965): 313–24; F. M. Cross, *Canaanite Myth and Hebrew Epic* (Cambridge, Mass.: Harvard University Press, 1973); R. J. Clifford, "Cosmogonies in the Ugaritic Texts and in the Bible," *Or* 53 (1984): 183–201; J. Grønbæk, "Baal's Battle with Yam—A Canaanite Creation Fight," *JSOT* 33 (1985): 27–44; and Day, *God's Conflict with the Dragon and the Sea,* 7–17.

[169] See, e.g., Tsumura, *The Earth and the Waters in Genesis 1 and 2,* 17–43.

[170] *ANET,* 74.

[171] W. G. Lambert and A. R. Millard, *Atraḫasîs: The Babylonian Story of the Flood* (Oxford: Clarendon, 1969), 59; also W. Moran, "The Creation of Man in Atrahasis I 192–248," *BASOR* 200 (1970): 48–56.

material and divine elements, here the blood of a deity. Sumerian *Enki and Ninmah* depicts mankind created of clay, also for the purpose of relieving the gods from their hard duties. It involves a bizarre and disastrous twist where the rival gods in a drunken orgy make humans with all manner of defects, the chief being a crippled human.[172] In Gen 2:7 the first man is made of "dust" and endued with life by the divine inbreathing. But there the analogy ends, for mankind is not created to meet the needs of deity, but God's actions serve the needs of the man and woman by providing the idyllic Eden.

(2) Eden

Parallels for Adam and the paradise of Eden also have been proposed in comparative studies. *Adapa* is a second-millennium B.C. Akkadian tale about how the priest and "sage" *(apkallū)* Adapa lost his opportunity at immortality.[173] In Babylonian tradition there lived before the flood seven *apkallū* who brought the civilized arts and sciences to mankind. Adapa was the patron sage of the first city, Eridu. The god of wisdom, Ea, granted Adapa wisdom, but not eternal life. In the tale Adapa angers Anu, god of heaven, by breaking the "South Wind's wing" and is required to stand before Anu in heaven to give an account for his actions. Ea advises Adapa to approach the citadel but to refuse food and drink, for they are the food of death. He follows wise Ea's instructions perfectly, but conversely the food offered him by Anu guarantees eternal life:

> They [gods] fetched him [Adapa] the bread of (eternal) life, but he would not eat.
> They fetched him the water of (eternal) life, but he would not drink. . . .
>
> Anu watched him and laughed at him.
> "Come, Adapa, why didn't you eat? Why didn't you drink?
> Didn't you want to be immortal? Alas for downtrodden people!"
> "(But) Ea my lord told me: 'You mustn't eat! You mustn't drink!'
> Take him and send him back to his earth."[174]

At this point the tablet is missing the end of the story. How to interpret Ea's actions is not clear, and the outcome of Adapa is unknown. This theme of immortality missed by man is found also in *Gilgamesh,* where the central figure obtains the secret of immortality but also loses it by a cruel twist of fate. Gilgamesh is told by the flood hero Utnapishtim of a plant in the sea that when eaten will rejuvenate his life. He obtains the plant, but before he eats it he washes himself in a pool. Unfortunately, the fragrance of the plant he has set aside draws a snake that slithers away with it. The Eden narrative has been

[172] See S. N. Kramer and J. Maier, *Myths of Enki, the Crafty God* (New York: Oxford University Press, 1989), 13–14, 31–37.

[173] For translations see Dalley, *Myths from Mesopotamia,* and Speiser, "Adapa," *ANET,* 101–3.

[174] Dalley, *Myths from Mesopotamia,* 187.

interpreted likewise as a tale explaining why mankind cannot obtain the status of divinity and circumvent death.[175] Detailed similarities and differences between Adapa and biblical Adam have been delineated at length, leaving no certainty that the two have a common origin, whether Mesopotamian or West Semitic.[176]

What these stories share, including *Gilgamesh,* is the same concern over human mortality. This is not surprising and argues only that ancient cultures approached the same question but offered perceptions of man's mortality that were radically different from the Bible. The pagan myths depict human immortality as missed by divine duplicity (i.e., Ea or Anu) or by happenstance (i.e., snake). Ironically both Adapa and Gilgamesh missed immortality as a consequence of obeying their instructions, but the Bible recounts that Adamic mortality came as a result of disobedience. Biblical Eden is fundamentally at odds with the pagan perception since it describes what Adam had initially but lost because of sin.[177]

Also it has been proposed that Sumerian culture had its own "Eden," found especially in the myth *Enki and Ninhursag,* a story of paradisiacal abode in the city Dilmun, a Mesopotamian name for Bahrain.[178] The land Dilmun is described as "holy," "pure," and "bright," characterized by perfect peace and the absence of wild animals and human disease:

> The land Dilmun is holy, the land Dilmun is pure,
> the land Dilmun is pure, the land Dilmun is bright.
>
> . . . .
>
> In Dilmun the raven screaks no croaking sounds, . . .
> The lion kills not,
> the wolf snatches not the lamb.
>
> . . . .
>
> The sick-eyed says not, "I am sick-eyed."
>
> . . . .
>
> Its old woman does not say, "I am an old woman."[179]

Coupled with this is the epic *Enmerkar and the Lord of Aratta,* which begins by describing a time when there is one people and one language and "no

---

[175] E.g., J. Barr, *The Garden of Eden and the Hope of Immortality* (Minneapolis: Fortress, 1993), and A. S. Kapelrud, "You Shall Surely Die," in *History and Traditions of Early Israel,* ed. A. Lemaire and B. Otzen (Leiden: Brill, 1993), 50–61.

[176] See N. Andreasen, "Adam and Adapa: Two Anthropological Characters," *AUSS* 19 (1981): 179–94.

[177] Ibid., 191.

[178] Note Kramer's title, "Enki and Ninhursag: A Paradise Myth," in *ANET,* 37–41; also his revised translation, "Enki and Ninhursag: A Sumerian Paradise Myth," in Kramer and Maier, *Myths of Enki, the Crafty God,* 22–30.

[179] Kramer and Maier, *Myths of Enki, the Crafty God,* 23.

snake," "no wild dog," "no fear" and "no terror." It has been interpreted as Sumer's view of the "Golden Past."[180] But this interpretation of Sumerian myth has been disputed by scholars who deny that Sumerian culture envisioned such an idyllic past.[181] B. Alster agrees that on the face of it such mythical representations suggest a perfect paradise, but setting such passages in the wider corpus of Sumerian myth shows that the Sumerians viewed the beginnings of life before civilization as a period of crude barbarism. Civilization is the ideal in Sumerian thought, which had its origins in the emergence of kingship.[182] Thus the world described in *Enki and Ninhursag* is a world without human existence, and there is no fresh water for life, for Enki must provide Dilmun with water. Also *Enmerkar and the Lord of Aratta* describes a period when there was no kingship; rather, it looks toward the future when kingship will bring all peoples under one hegemony. Sumerians viewed civilization as progress, whereas the Bible presents it as precipitated by human disobedience.

(3) Long-lived Patriarchs

Sumerian tradition shares with Genesis the memory that antediluvian peoples had exceptionally long life spans. The Sumerian King List summarizes the political history of ancient Sumer and Akkad. It lists ruling cities and their kings from the inception of kingship before the flood to the reign of the famous Hammurapi of Babylon (eighteenth century B.C.).[183] As in the Bible, where the flood is between the genealogies of the patriarchs (chaps. 5 and 11), reference to the flood divides the Sumerian list into kings before and after the flood:

> The Flood swept thereover.
> After the flood had swept thereover,
> when the kingship was lowered from heaven
> the kingship was in Kish.[184]

---

[180] "Something like the mythical Golden Age—an age when human beings lived at peace in nature and with one another—is linked in the story with what looks like a version of the Tower of Babel" (Kramer and Maier, *Myths of Enki, the Crafty God,* 88–89).

[181] B. Alster, *Dilmun: New Studies in the Early Archaeology and History of Bahrain,* ed. D. Potts (Berlin: Dietrich Reimer, 1983), 39–74, esp. 52–60; also B. F. Batto, "Paradise Reconsidered," in *The Biblical Canon in Comparative Perspectives,* ed. K. L. Younger et al. (Lewiston, N.Y.: Edwin Mellen, 1991), 33–66.

[182] So argues Jacobsen, "The Eridu Genesis," 513–29.

[183] For the standard critical edition see Jacobsen, *The Sumerian King List,* AS 11 (Chicago: University of Chicago Press, 1939). For additional fragments published see the publications in R. R. Wilson, *Genealogy and History in the Biblical World* (New Haven: Yale University Press, 1977), 73–74. For translations of the antediluvian section also see A. L. Oppenheimer, "The Sumerian King List," in *ANET,* 265–66, and H. Schmökel, "Mesopotamian Texts," in *Near Eastern Religious Texts Relating to the Old Testament,* 87–88.

[184] Jacobsen, *Sumerian King List,* 71.

The list of the antediluvian kings probably was a secondary addition, designed to trace Mesopotamian kingship back to its mythical beginnings and show that united Mesopotamia had always been under a single city's reign.[185] The reigns of the antediluvian kings are fantastically long, the longest being 72,000 years.[186] Noticeably there is a decline in the years of the reigns following the flood. This is well known from the Bible, which shows the same trend following the flood. The term "King List" is misleading, however, for its concern is not so much the ruling family as it is the city where the dynastic rule was founded. Kingship, which began at Eridu before the flood, is said to have been "lowered from heaven," and after the flood was "lowered" again to Kish.[187] Succeeding paragraphs trace the transition of kingship from city to city. The main body is a collection of local lists of rulers from Babylonia, made up of legendary material and chronicles. Biographical notes are integrated into the general framework, citing information about the ruler's origin (e.g., parentage and native city) and achievements (e.g., military).

Some of these same literary features are attested in Genesis 5, such as the listing of ten antediluvian persons, but the differences in Genesis and the Sumerian King List are too remarkable for one to be the source of the other.[188] Genesis names persons, not reigns, and its purpose is religious, not political. Genesis takes a dismal view of the past, whereas the King List idealized the past with the divine origins of kingship. Together the King List and the biblical witness attest to an ancient memory of a time before the flood when people lived much longer.

(4) Flood

There probably is no event better remembered by humanity than an ancient flood. Flood stories are found around the world and have been a source of special interest for the study of early Genesis.[189] Ancient memory viewed the

---

[185] Ibid., 55–68.

[186] There was no official list of the antediluvian kings, and their length of reigns varies also. For a listing among the diverse tablets recovered, see J. J. Finkelstein, "The Antediluvian Kings: A University of California Tablet," *JCS* 17 (1963): 39–51, esp. p. 46; also Wilson lists the antediluvian cities and kings but without regnal years (*Genealogy and History,* 79).

[187] *ANET,* 265.

[188] See T. C. Hartman, "Some Thoughts on the Sumerian King List and Genesis 5 and 11b," *JBL* 91 (1972): 25–32; Hess, "The Genealogies of Genesis 1–11 and Comparative Literature," *Bib* 70 (1989): 241–54; also G. F. Hasel, "The Genealogies of Gen 5 and 11 and Their Alleged Babylonian Background," *AUSS* 16 (1978): 361–74. Hartman shows Gen 5 and the Sumerian King List both reflect independently an old Amorite (West Semitic) genealogical pattern of using a ten-name genealogy. Thus he concludes that the similarities are superficial.

[189] B. Lang, "Non-Semitic Deluge Stories and the Book of Genesis: A Bibliographic and Critical Survey, *Anthropos* 80 (1985): 605–16, cites twenty-three studies from 1869–1981 of non-Semitic flood stories.

flood as the "archetype of human catastrophe."[190] For the biblical tradition the closer parallels are those recovered from the ancient Near East, deriving from Sumero-Akkadian culture. The Mesopotamian tradition is found in its most complete version in the eleventh tablet of the *Epic of Gilgamesh.* An earlier version of the same tradition is the *Atrahasis* story, and there is the similar but fragmentary Sumerian flood version. Also in the third century B.C. the Babylonian priest Berossus includes in his history a version of the Mesopotamian account. Among these stories are many points of contact but also significant differences, such as the names of the heroes, the context of the flood story, and the reason for the flood. Having already commented on how Genesis 1–9 resembles the comparable *Atrahasis,* only a summary of the salient points is necessary for the biblical flood alone with attention on the fuller *Gilgamesh.* The commentary will point out specific correspondences and contrasts with the Mesopotamian tales.

Although initially scholars thought Genesis was dependent on the Mesopotamian traditions, it is now agreed that the Hebrew account was independent and the versions together testify to a widely remembered corpus of events. Genesis and *Gilgamesh* contain a number of remarkable similarities. Both Noah and Utnapishtim, the Babylonian hero, are told of the impending flood by a sympathetic deity, specifics are given for constructing a vessel coated with pitch, animals are preserved on board, the "hatch" is closed, birds are dispatched, the ship lands on a mountain top, and the survivor offers up a sacrifice. As Noah is granted covenant blessing, Utnapishtim is the recipient of a divine dispensation, granting him immortality as his reward. Between these are numerous small divergencies, such as the difference in the size and shape of the vessel (a perfect cube of 120 cubits), the duration of the flood (six days), and the landing site (Mount Nisir); but the closest parallel is the description of the birds that are freed in *Gilgamesh* to find a "resting-place." Utnapishtim releases a dove that returns, a swallow that returns, and finally a raven that finds refuge. Noah's raven and dove serve the same purpose.

When the seventh day arrived,
I put out and released a dove.
The dove went; it came back,
For no perching place was visible to it, and it turned round.
I put out and released a swallow.
The swallow went; it came back,
For no perching place was visible to it, and it turned round.
I put out and released a raven.
The raven went and saw the waters receding.
And it ate, preened (?), lifted its tail and did not turn round.[191]

---

[190] Westermann, *Genesis 1–11,* 399.
[191] Dalley, *Myths from Mesopotamia,* 114.

Atrahasis comes closer to a complete tale of beginnings, though the narrative says little about creation, presuming the universe to be in order and the gods at work. As we found with *Enuma Elish,* the creation of mankind is designed to alleviate the gods' labors. It supplies the rationale for the flood; it was the angry response of Enlil against noisy mankind for disturbing his sleep:

The [land] was bellowing like a bull,
The god (Enlil) got disturbed with [their uproar].

[Enlil heard] their noise
[And addressed] the great gods,

"The noise of mankind [has become too intense for me],
[With their uproar] I am deprived of sleep."[192]

The flood, however, is only the last of four attempts to undo man; it is preceded by a plague and two droughts. In each case Enlil's efforts are foiled by the rival deity Enki, who informs his devotee Atrahasis how to avoid it. By means of a dream, the hero learns of the flood and sets about making a craft, probably involving his reed hut, and he rides out the storm to survive. In all three Mesopotamian accounts the survivor upon disembarking offers up a sacrifice to the gods. The gods realize the value of man, and Enlil is persuaded to cease any further destruction when the gods, including the mother-goddess Nintu, take steps (such as infertility) to limit population growth.

Various alternatives have already been mentioned to explain the similarities which the Mesopotamian stories share with the biblical account. W. G. Lambert reflects the popular interpretation: "The flood remains the clearest case of dependence of Genesis on Mesopotamian legend."[193] He is impressed by the evidence on two counts: (1) the remarkable report of the birds found in *Gilgamesh* and (2) the parallel between Genesis 5 and the Sumerian King List of lengthy life spans before the flood.

Differences in details, however—such as the duration of the flood, the disembarking site, and the occupants in the vessels—between the Hebrew and Mesopotamian traditions rule out the direct dependence theory. We would expect any story of flood and rescue to have a number of common properties, especially in its general story line. What distinguishes the biblical account from others is its theological underpinnings and the reason for the disaster. First, the Mesopotamian accounts are crude polytheistic tales that depict selfish, deceptive deities embroiled in a dispute. The pagan ideology of the stories is seen, for instance, in the postdiluvian sacrifice by Utnapishtim that serves as food for the hungry deities who have gone without animal offerings during the flood: "The gods smelled the sweet savor / The gods crowded like

---

[192] Lambert and Millard, *Atrahasis,* 67.

[193] Lambert, "The Babylonian Background of Genesis," 291.

flies about the sacrificer."[194]

Second, from *Atrahasis* we learn that the motivation for the flood was the explosion of human population, whose noisy habits had troubled Enlil's sleep. The flood was but the most severe of several attempts, including plague and drought (twice), to obliterate humanity. In *Gilgamesh* the reason for inflicting the inundation is not stated. The god Ea rebukes Enlil for his unfounded actions: "How couldst thou, unreasoning, bring on the deluge"?[195] Some have found in the following line evidence that it was due to human sin: "On the sinner impose his sin, / On the transgressor impose his transgression!" But here the remark suggests that Enlil has breached that principle by imposing the flood upon innocent humanity. Genesis, on the other hand, repeatedly attributes the flood to the wickedness of man and explains that the corruption of the earth has merited the response of a moral God. There is no flood story comparable to the moral stature of Genesis. For example, Ea forewarns Utnapishtim in order to betray his rival Enlil, but the biblical tradition shows Noah's deliverance is related to his distinctive moral character. Although it is true that the Mesopotamian flood heroes are devotees of the gods, the righteous character of the favored survivor does not receive the attention we find in Genesis.

Third, the consequence in the Mesopotamian stories is the immortality of the flood survivor, but in Genesis the survivor is altogether mortal, and the passage dismisses the mythic notion of a divine hero. What is important in Genesis is the fidelity of Noah to God's word and the continuation of the divine promise designed for all future generations. Comparing the Babylonian versions and Genesis, A. Heidel in his classic study concluded, "The skeleton is the same in both cases, but the flesh and blood and, above all, the animating spirit are different."[196] Although the flood stories share in a general framework, it is speculative to say any more than that the pagan stories and Genesis arise from a common memory of the ancient deluge. Here we have "two literary perspectives on a single actual event,"[197] not a shared cultural tradition.

7. Creation and Contemporary Interpretation

Many modern readers are troubled by the style of Genesis 1–11 in that it varies from contemporary ways of reporting human events. The times and happenings are not like anything we know; they occur in the distant past in almost surreal circumstances. Hermeneutically, it is incumbent upon us to understand the Genesis account of origins in the context of its own world (see "Genesis 1–

[194] *ANET,* 95.

[195] Ibid.

[196] A. Heidel, *The Gilgamesh Epic and Old Testament Parallels* (Chicago: University of Chicago Press, 1946), 268.

[197] Walton, *Ancient Israelite Literature,* 40.

11 and Ancient Literature" on p. 86), for it is against the backdrop of the ancient environment that its powerful and distinctive message can be heard most clearly. This is the track chosen here for the expositional comments, but the demands of the modern reader put questions to early Genesis that require the interpreter to address the complexities of interpreting the ancient witness in light of our modern "scientific" world. Such a subject requires a fuller deliberation than can be presented here; the reader will only be directed to the crucial interpretive problems and offered a cursory response.

The most challenging inquiry concerns what evolutionary biology says about the origins of life as opposed to the affirmation in Genesis that God directly created all that exists. Was human life created on purpose by a transcendent intelligence (God), an intelligent Being whom we can know and to whom we are accountable? Or are we the consequence of impersonal forces driven by time and chance without purpose or transcendent meaning?

(1) Creationism and Naturalism

Essentially, there are two models that have been proposed to explain the origins of life: biblical creationism and scientific naturalism.[198] "Creationism" is popularly ascribed to one particular view of creationism, known as scientific creationism, but it is not limited to this method of explanation. Creationism, in its widest sense, proposes that God is the ultimate cause for the universe and all its life-forms; human life is not an accident of nature but the result of God's creative activity. All that exists, creationism says, owes its ultimate origins to the all-powerful and all-wise God, who freely chose to create life with deliberate design and for an ultimate destiny.

Naturalism, on the other hand, is altogether different. Naturalism, sometimes called "atheistic naturalism" or "scientific naturalism," views the universe as an eternal, self-governed, self-generated universe. There is no allowance for a transcendent Being to explain its origins or governance. Philosophical naturalism denies the existence of God, while methodological naturalism, though not explicitly rejecting deity, excludes God in developing a theory of the universal process. Scientism limits its search for knowledge to only those processes that can be known from natural science. Scientific naturalism submits a system of compatible theories that attempt to account for all cosmic history, including the origins and development of life on earth. It draws from the cumulative evidence of cosmic chronology (the temporal development of space, galaxies and planets), terrestrial history, and chemical and biological evolution.

The most widely accepted theory of the late twentieth century is that the uni-

---

[198] I thank Mr. Kirk Spencer for his helpful suggestions in the preparation of this discussion.

verse resulted from the sudden appearance of a single particle out of an absolute vacuum (ca. 12–20 billion years ago). This particle, called a "singularity," consisted of all space, time, and matter crushed together. The particle experienced an explosion ("Big Bang") or, as some prefer, rapid development ("Big Bloom") that produced the hydrogen and helium gases necessary for the formation of stars in an expanding universe. Inside the superhot furnacelike interiors of these stars, the heavier elements were "cooked" and fused. Then as the stars one by one exploded, these chemical elements were spewed out into space as a cloud of gas and dust called a nebula. These nebular clouds then collapsed in on themselves and fragmented into smaller rotating clouds, which fostered planetary formations such as our solar system. The earth is thought to have formed in this way ca. 4.6 billion years ago. With the subsequent cooling of the earth's surface, its atmosphere and surface features were generated.

Natural processes are then invoked to explain the emergence of simple living cells from nonliving chemicals (biogenesis). The surface gases of the cooling earth (ca. 3.5 billion years ago) aided by external energy forces, such as solar radiation, are thought to have permitted the formation of various organic compounds. These chemical compounds in the setting of warm, shallow bodies of water—a prebiotic "soup"—experienced the necessary chemical concentrations for producing the first protocells. These living cells survived long enough to develop internal complexity and replicating power.

Biological or organic evolution, popularly called "macroevolution," seeks to explain how these first cells developed into the diversity of life we take for granted in our everyday experience. It proposes, given sufficient time, that random mutation (variation) in organisms and natural selection working together satisfactorily account for the changes in a line of ascent from the simple cell to the most complex life-form, the human being.

Traditionally, apart from biblical revelation, the strongest evidence for the existence of a Creator has been the immense complexities found in the universe and in living organisms that are best explained as the consequence of an intelligent Designer.[199] There has been, however, a long-standing assault on this line of argument by skeptics, charging that such a theoretical construct results in a nonscientific and nonrational conclusion. What is attributed to intelligent design, say the critics, is in fact only apparent design. Methodological naturalism operates along a continuum that permits only evidence that is itself the product of scientific inquiry based on naturalistic assumptions. By definition, then, any evidence that one might present for an intelligent Agent can only be explained as the result of natural processes—never as evidence for God. This supposition that only naturalistic explanations have merit and that all nonnatu-

---

[199] The following is indebted to the collected essays in J. P. Moreland, ed., *The Creation Hypothesis: Scientific Evidence for an Intelligent Designer* (Downers Grove: IVP, 1994).

ralistic explanations are nonscientific restricts science to a narrow inquiry that predetermines its outcomes. It can be shown that the postulation of any scientific theory must involve scientific and nonscientific presuppositions. Moreover, consistent methodological naturalism limits the inquiry that science itself intends to pursue.

This does not mean, however, that any theory that explains the origin of life should be deemed acceptable. For example, the notion of "parallel worlds" (realities coexisting in other dimensions) is bad scientific theory, yet we cannot by fiat declare it nonscience. In the same way, some theistic theories may be rebutted as bad science, but this does not in itself rule out as nonrational or nonscientific evidence that argues for a transcendent Mind.

The argument for a Creator based on what appears to be intelligent design contends that naturalistic explanations are not by themselves sufficient for resolving the riddles of origins and for explaining the varied and complex organizational principles for living systems as well as the behavior of inanimate matter. Alternatively, it proposes that the existence of an intelligent Agent best accounts for the evidence of an absolute beginning and of the purposeful development of the universe and life systems with all their diversity and complexity. Apologists for the argument from intelligent design distinguish their argument from apparent design and optimum design. What is meant by "intelligent design" is not an appeal to any pattern observed in nature—the pattern of the snowflake, for example, can be explained by inherent natural cause—but the "design" that points to an intelligence is extraneous to nature and therefore must be attributed to an external intelligence.

W. L. Bradley and C. B. Thaxton have illustrated the difference by likening these two kinds of design to two different experiences of a tourist traveling in the wilderness.[200] Along the way the tourist comes upon a number of striking rock formations, some of which resemble a human face. Upon closer examination, with the help of a guide, the tourist recognizes that the rock formation is the result of natural erosion; its correspondence to a face is merely apparent. However, our tourist also visits the famous Mount Rushmore with its carved faces of four American presidents. In this case he observes that the chiseled faces show that the chipping of the stone is not the consequence of erosion. This leads the intelligent observer to conclude on the basis of "uniform experience" that the faces are the result of intelligent design. If only intelligence produces these types of patterns in the present, such patterns found in the past (e.g., genetic code) would necessitate intelligence as the explanation, based upon the principle of uniformity (the foundation of historical science). If nonintelligent processes do not produce such patterns in the present, to insist that they did in the past is not only non-

---

[200] W. L. Bradley and C. B. Thaxton, "Information and the Origins of Life," in Moreland, *The Creation Hypothesis,* 203–4.

science but nonsense. It is intelligent design, observed in the universe and among terrestrial life systems, that points to an external Designer.

The lines of evidence that suggest an intelligent cause for life range from cosmic "coincidences" to peculiar human imponderables, such as human intelligence and human language systems. It is now widely acknowledged by physicists that the universe testifies to a beginning—not only a beginning for matter and energy but also for space and time. This means that time itself is a part of creation and not a transcendent property; thus theories relying on an infinitely old universe are increasingly thought to be untenable. Also proponents of intelligent design point out that recent developments in astronomy and its measuring techniques show that the parameters within our universe must have fixed values, falling within narrowly defined ranges, in order to generate and support life. This is exactly what would be expected from a Creator of staggering power and wisdom.[201] In other words, the cosmic universe, including life as we know it on this planet, is so finely tuned that it testifies to an ingenious design.

The nontheists J. D. Barrow and J. Silk raise the question of whether the structure of the universe evidences a "Grand Designer." While they resist necessarily concluding a cosmological Designer, they ably express the marvel of the special suitability of the universe for human life:

> In many respects, the universe is tailor-made for life. It is cool enough, old enough, and stable enough to evolve and sustain the biochemistry of life. The laws of nature allow atoms to exist, stars to manufacture carbon, and molecules to replicate—but just so. . . . Anyone looking at the modern findings about the universe faces a similar paradox. On the one hand, there is a striking symmetry underlying the universe, and were it not present, life could not exist. At the same time, we see that these symmetries are invariably only "almost symmetries," and the tiny violations of perfect symmetry that we observe are equally necessary for our existence. It is the minute deviation from complete uniformity in the universe that allows the existence of galaxies, planets, and people.[202]

P. Davies, a noted physicist and also a non-Christian, recognizes that life is not a purposeless accident. He concludes in *The Mind of God:* "I cannot believe that our existence in the universe is a mere quirk of fate, an accident of history, an incidental blip in the great cosmic drama. Our involvement is too intimate. . . . Through conscious beings the universe has generated self-awareness. This can be no trivial detail, no minor by-product of mindless, purposeless forces.

---

[201] See H. Ross, "Astronomical Evidences for a Personal, Transcendent God," in Moreland, *The Creation Hypothesis,* 141–72, who cites specific examples (pp. 160–69). Also P. Davies, *The Cosmic Blueprint: New Discoveries in Nature's Creative Ability to Order the Universe* (New York: Simon & Schuster, 1988).

[202] J. D. Barrow and J. Silk, *The Left Hand of Creation,* 2d ed. (New York: Oxford University Press, 1993), 227–28.

We are truly meant to be here."[203] The tyranny of naturalism is losing its grip.

Moreover, advances in our knowledge of biochemistry have shown that the essential building blocks for life, such as DNA and proteins, contain specific and complex information. Both the genetic code preserved in DNA and human thoughts perceived in language involve complex sequencing of information. DNA's information code directs chemical processes in the cell to construct the necessary building blocks and sequence of events we call life. It is not enough to have the biochemical environment for life; there must be a biochemical blueprint ordering the precise functions of the cell. DNA provides this informational system. Therefore proponents for intelligent design argue that in the same way experience tells us to look to an intelligent cause for the complexities required for communication systems, intelligent Cause best explains the origins of the earliest informational molecules.

The current creation-evolution debate shows no sign of abatement.[204] The insistence on methodological naturalism that forbids arguments of ultimate cause, such as intelligent design, results in a hypothesis that cannot accommodate all the evidence science has discovered. Even the theoretical reconstructions by science include nonnaturalistic suppositions and entities, such as fields and quarks, so that one might say that "naturalistic explanation is an oxymoron."[205] For the apologist of creationism, the defense of a particular theory of creationism may divert the discussion from the validity of general creationism to a particular view of biblical interpretation that requires more demonstration than is necessary for the immediate apologetic purpose. In the present argumentative environment it is best to stick to the simpler road and show how what we know from the "Book of nature" points rationally to the omnipotent and all-wise *Who*. Ultimately we can proclaim with the apostles that this Infinite One can be known through the Incarnate Son who "is before all things, and in him all things hold together" (Col 1:17).

(2) Problems in Interpretation

Disagreement swirls among those who hold to the creationist's premise,

---

[203] P. Davies, *The Mind of God* (New York: Simon & Schuster, 1992), 232.

[204] For further discussion see, e.g., R. Jastrow, *God and the Astronomers* (New York: Warner, 1980); F. Hoyle, *The Intelligent Universe* (New York: Holt, Rinehart & Winston, 1984); D. Ratzsch, *Philosophy of Science* (Downers Grove: IVP, 1986); M. Denton, *Evolution: A Theory in Crisis* (Bethesda, Md.: Adler & Adler, 1986); J. P. Moreland and K. Nielsen, *Does God Exist? The Great Debate* (Buffalo: Prometheus, 1990); Moreland and D. Chiochi, *Christian Perspectives on Being Human* (Grand Rapids: Baker, 1993); P. Johnson, *Darwin on Trial,* 2d ed. (Downers Grove: IVP, 1993); Ross, *The Creator and the Cosmos* (Colorado Springs: NavPress, 1993); K. P. Wise, "The Origins of Life's Major Groups," in Moreland, *The Creation Hypothesis,* 211–34.

[205] So W. A. Dembski; see his discussion in "Scientific Creationism and Intelligent Design," *Transactions* 2 (1994): 3.

not about *who?* but about *how?* and *how long?* and *when?*[206] So mammoth and complex is the discussion that we can only briefly refer to what we believe are the two central problems that underlie the diverse interpretations of biblical creation: (1) what is the proper relationship between Scripture and modern science? and (2) what is the literary genre of the Genesis description?

SCRIPTURE AND KNOWLEDGE. The first quandary is how knowledge obtained from Scripture and physical science should be properly related, or whether they can be related at all.[207] For those who draw a rigid distinction between the domains of science and religion, the Bible is recognized as the witness to ultimate causation, but its propositions cannot be subject to the empirical deliberation of science. Proper science concerns the study of physical properties and behavior, which are subject to empirical falsification.[208] Still others hold that metaphysical arguments have a proper place in science but only as "origin science" (versus "operational science"), which investigates unrepeated events on the basis of plausible, not falsifiable, reconstruction. When origins are pursued in this venue, philosophical presuppositions must be admitted—whether materialism or theism—and the reconstruction of origins must be judged as to its probability or improbability in light of the

[206] For the Restitution ("Gap") Theory, see A. C. Custance, *Without Form and Void* (Brockville, Canada: Custance, 1970). For Recent Creationism see H. Morris and J. Whitcomb, *The Genesis Flood* (Philadelphia: Presbyterian & Reformed, 1961); Morris, *Scientific Creationism* (San Diego: Creation-Life, 1974); D. Gish, *Evolution? The Fossils Say NO!* rev. ed. (San Diego: Creation-Life, 1979), and "Creation, Evolution and the Historical Evidence," *But Is It Science?* ed. M. Ruse (Buffalo: Prometheus, 1988). For Progressive Creationism see B. Ramm, *The Christian View of Science and Scripture* (Grand Rapids: Eerdmans, 1954); R. C. Newman and H. J. Eckelmann, *Genesis One and the Origin of the Earth* (Downers Grove: IVP, 1977); P. P. T. Pun, *Evolution: Nature & Scripture in Conflict?* (Grand Rapids: Eerdmans, 1982); W. Bradley and R. Olsen, "The Trustworthiness of Scripture in Areas Relating to Natural Science," in *Hermeneutics, Inerrancy, and the Bible,* ed. E. Radmacher and R. Preus (Grand Rapids: Academie, 1984), 285–317, and the "Responses" of G. Archer and H. Morris. For Theistic Evolution see H. J. Van Till, *The Fourth Day* (Grand Rapids: Eerdmans, 1986); Van Till et al., eds., *Portraits of Creation: Biblical and Scientific Perspectives on the World's Formation* (Grand Rapids: Eerdmans, 1990). For the Framework ("Literary") view see H. Blocher, *In the Beginning* (Leicester: IVP, 1984); C. Hyers, *The Meaning of Creation* (Atlanta: John Knox, 1984). For the Pictorial Day view P. J. Wiseman's *Creation Revealed in Six Days* (1948) was reissued in *Clues to Creation in Genesis,* ed. D. J. Wiseman (London: Marshall, Morgan & Scott, 1977).

[207] E.g., R. T. Wright identifies four models: (1) concordism, in which the Bible supplies some information that can be harmonized with science; (2) substitutionism, in which the Bible takes priority over modern science; (3) compartmentalism, in which science and Scripture are totally different realms of knowledge; and (4) complementarism, in which the Bible and science are complementary ways of viewing the universe (*Biology through the Eyes of Faith* [San Francisco: Harper & Row, 1989], 84–92).

[208] See H. J. Van Till, D. A. Young, and C. Menninga, *Science Held Hostage: What's Wrong with Creation Science AND Evolutionism?* (Downers Grove: IVP, 1988), 10–25.

evidence.[209] The appeal by creationists to the existence of God is not by itself the introduction of religion into science since "God" is not used in a religious sense as an object of worship by the creation scientist but rather in a theoretical sense as a necessary premise. Also operational science involves metaphysical concerns; the categories of "origin" and "operational" science cannot be neatly drawn.[210] The dichotomy between science and religion proposed by many is neither practically nor philosophically possible.

To prohibit dialogue between Scripture and science is to suggest that the Bible cannot say anything about the physical world. To compartmentalize knowledge is to run the risk of saying that Christianity is not inclusive of all truth and cannot address the whole person, whereas in fact, Christianity is a comprehensive worldview that integrates and explains how all truth, regardless of source, is God's truth. This is not to say, however, that the Bible comments on physical mechanisms in such a way that specific correlations with modern reconstruction can be made conclusively. Rather, scientific discovery adds to our sensibilities in the hermeneutics of a literal versus nonliteral interpretation. Because we have a knowledge of our universe that exceeds that of our predecessors, we are in a better position to recognize in the Bible phenomenological descriptions of our world (e.g., Ps 93:1b; Eccl 1:5).

When we consider the relationship between Scripture and science, we may look to the famed theologian of the last century, B. B. Warfield, who championed biblical authority while at the same time adhering to the new wave of evolution science.[211] As we have said, we think that evolutionary science is wrongheaded and that the purveyors of this science eventually will come to admit it, especially since rumblings of discontent are becoming louder. Although we think Warfield was wrong in joining the Christian Darwinian movement, the issue for him was not whether the "old faith" could stand up to science's new claims: "The only living question with regard to the doctrine of evolution is whether it is true."[212] Warfield was right to allow science to have its say, but he was no slave to a particular theory of origins. He recognized that evolution was subject to correction whereas Scripture was not—only human

---

[209] N. Geisler and J. Anderson, *Origin Science* (Grand Rapids: Baker, 1987). Also see C. B. Thaxton, W. Bradley, and R. Olsen, *The Mystery of Life's Origins: Reassessing Current Theories* (New York: Philosophical Library, 1984), 202–6.

[210] Argued by J. P. Moreland, *Christianity and the Nature of Science* (Grand Rapids: Baker, 1989). He also shows how the theory of falsification may mislead the investigator. As example, he appeals to Newton's laws of motion and gravitation, which failed to explain the irregularities in the motion of Uranus. This in itself could have falsified the theory, but adjustment in the theory (positing the existence of an unknown planet, which could explain the irregularities) was the proper response and was vindicated by the later discovery of Neptune (pp. 84–86).

[211] Noted by M. Noll, *The Scandal of the Evangelical Mind* (Grand Rapids: Eerdmans/Leicester: IVP, 1994), 208.

[212] Cited by Noll, ibid.

interpretation of Scripture could be revised, not the text itself.

HISTORY OR STORY. Now we must ask to what extent the Genesis description of creation and of Eden is literal or metaphorical. The heart of the matter lies in the literary intention of 1:1–2:3.[213] Is it history? parable? poetry? liturgy? hymn? vision? To determine genre on the basis of formal similarities is hazardous. History and nonhistory writing share in many of the same literary features. To judge straightforward prose as "history" and the more ornate as "literary artifice" is a false conclusion derived from modern assumptions.[214] The possession of metaphorical language does not necessarily rule out Genesis 1 as history writing.

When Genesis is compared with the mythopoetic language of pagan cosmogonies, it is radically different in literary genre since it is set in a historical framework of six successive days and is related to the historical framework of Genesis by the *tōlĕdōt* ("generations") pattern (2:4; 5:1; see "Literary Genesis" on p. 25).[215] At least for the author of Genesis, it was not mythical tale or mere parable. It is not, however, the same kind of history writing as Genesis 12–50, or even chaps. 3–4, and it is quite different from Samuel and Kings. Neither is it like the creation hymns found among the Psalms. And there is no evidence that Israel celebrated a New Year's festival drawing on the liturgy of creation. Moreover, it is difficult to accept it as parable since this genre usually is an illustration drawn from everyday experience. Vision is not a likely assessment since the Genesis text lacks the typical preamble normally introducing visions (cf. 15:1). Genesis 1:1–2:3, in fact, does not clearly fit a traditional literary category. Although it comes closest to "narrative," we must conclude that it is a unique piece of literature. This insight goes far in explaining why modern interpreters are groping for the key that unlocks its mysteries.

Many interpreters recognize the intentional literary symmetry of 1:1–2:3. For example, the passage possesses a parallelism between the six days in which

[213] For discussion of genre see T. Fretheim, "Were the Days of Creation Twenty-Four Hours Long? Yes," and for the "No" response see R. C. McClone, *The Genesis Debate: Persistent Questions about Creation and the Flood,* ed. R. Youngblood (Nashville: Nelson, 1986), 12–35; C. Pinnock, "Climbing out of a Swamp: The Evangelical Struggle to Understand the Creation Texts" *Int* 43 (1989): 143–55; B. K. Waltke, "The Literary Genre of Genesis, Chapter One," *Crux* 27 (1991): 2–10; J. H. Stek, "What Says the Scriptures?" in *Portraits of Creation,* 203–65.

[214] See M. Sternberg, *The Poetics of Biblical Narrative* (Bloomington: Indiana University Press, 1987), 23–35.

[215] For many Gen 1–3 is the mythological equivalent to the pagan myths of Israel's neighbors (see "Genesis 1–11 and Ancient Literature" on p. 86). Others, while accepting this, consider it a witness to ultimate truth. E.g., D. S. Russell upholds Scripture as unique revelation but finds it expressed in the mythological language of the ancients, whose thought forms were mythological (e.g., reflecting the battle motif of Enuma Elish and Baal-Yam; Russell, "Interpreting Scripture: Myth and Remythologizing," *ExpTim* 104 [1993]: 356–59). Thus modern interpreters must demythologize the biblical account to obtain its transcendent truth about God as Creator and hence remythologize its revelation in our contemporary, cultural symbols.

the creative acts of productivity in days one to three correspond to the works of populating in days four to six. Eight creation acts are distributed among six days, with days three and six balanced by two creation acts (see 1:1–2:3 introduction). The schema of six units plus one is a literary convention attested in the Bible and among peoples of the ancient Near East to emphasize the seventh member, the culminating event of the configuration (see 2:1–3 commentary). Creation shows a patterned hierarchy: from the inanimate to the animate and, within the animate, from vegetation to human life. This corresponds well with the world we know. Also all agree that Genesis 1 is theologically a preamble to the Pentateuch specifically relating creation to the pinnacle event of the Sinai revelation by the Fourth Commandment, honoring the seventh day (Exod 20:8–11).

Disagreements remain, however, in what we are to make of this elegant literary presentation. Is Genesis 1 solely a literary artifice, having exclusively religious significance?[216] Such symmetry does not preclude a historical telling of early Genesis. This only suggests at most that 1:1–2:3 may be topical in arrangement and dischronologized.[217] A strict chronological hermeneutic creates a world difficult for us to envision where vegetation (day three) flourishes before the existence of the sun (day four), and the concluding expression of days one to three, "there was evening and there was morning," presupposes a planetary situation that could not have existed without a sun (see discussion at 1:5). A topical arrangement does not sacrifice the historicity of the account and thus does not prohibit any harmonization with what we know of terrestrial history.

On the other hand, if we interpret early Genesis as theological parable or story, we have a theology of creation that is grounded neither in history nor the cosmos. It is unlikely that the community of Moses, which understood its God as the Lord of history, would have tolerated such a cosmology. The *tōlĕdōt* structure of Genesis requires us to read chap. 1 as relating real events that are presupposed by later Israel (Exod 20:8–11). If Genesis 1–3 is theological story without correspondence to reality, the creation account conveys no information

---

[216] Among those who consider chap. 1 a literary artifice, some hold to the historicity of Adam as an individual who at a real time and in a real place sinned against God (Blocher, *In the Beginning,* 154–90). Pinnock asserts that interpreting chaps. 1–3 as symbol does not negate the historicity of the "event" of creation and the fall into sin; nor does it condone the unbridled practice of existential hermeneutics as carried on by liberal theologians ("Climbing out of a Swamp," 143–55).

[217] The creation account has a schematic arrangement ("sevens") that has a literary history in antiquity and that, as a pattern, was experienced by Moses and his community (e.g., Exod 16:21–30; 24:16–18). It is not surprising then that just as other portions of Scripture follow a schematic arrangement, the creation week was told topically. E.g., the Table of Nations recounted in chap. 10 chronologically follows 11:1–9 but is placed before the Babel account for thematic reasons; also see the schematic genealogies in Ruth 4:18–22; Matt 1:1–17; Luke 3:23–38 (see chap. 5 commentary).

about creation except that it owes its existence to God. This undermines the very purpose of the preamble, which establishes a real linkage between creation and covenant history, for the latter clearly is rooted in history. B. Ramm's early criticism in 1954 of such a strict dichotomy between theology and science still holds true:

> The vice of the theory [religious-only] is that if this much concession is made to the view of science it will be difficult to maintain any theological validity for the record at all. . . . It may make an apparent peace with geology but usually such a peace ends with the irrelevancy of theology, so that the very disease the theory seeks to avoid is the one to which it succumbs and by which it is destroyed.[218]

Also if taken as theological story alone, the interpreter is at odds with the historical intentionality of Genesis. By virtue of its predisposition to employing genealogies, Genesis has treated Adam and Eve as real historical individuals. The word *ʾadām* serves two overlapping roles in Genesis: a generic figure ("man") representing universal humanity (1:26) and a historical individual ("Adam"; 5:1–3). Interpreting "Adam" as a symbolic figure alone flies in the face of the chronologies (chaps. 5 and 11) that link Adam as a person to Israel's father, Abraham.[219]

Thus we conclude that the creation narrative claims historicity. It should not be interpreted allegorically or treated solely as literature. It also conveys discursive information about reality, using schematic ornamentation. There is a general correspondence between Genesis's telling of the earth's origins and modern reconstructions, but the correlation of the details cannot be worked out satisfactorily.

---

[218] Ramm, *The Christian View of Science and Scripture,* 178–79.

[219] The NT recognizes this dual function as individual (e.g., Luke 3:38) and type (e.g., 1 Cor 15:20–50; Rom 5:12–21). It is clear that Jesus and the apostles understood Adam as a historical figure (e.g., Matt 19:4–6; Mark 10:6–9; 1 Cor 4:7–9; 2 Cor 6:15; Eph 5:31; 1 Tim 2:12–14; Jude 14) regardless of which role may have been emphasized. See B. Ramm, *Offense to Reason: A Theology of Sin* (San Francisco: Harper & Row, 1985), 62–75. The plausibility of Paul's soteriological argument in Rom 5:12–21, which contrasts the first and last Adam, though generic in emphasis, assumes the historicity of chaps. 2–5 and requires a real correspondence between the individuals Adam and Jesus. The consequences of revising human origins require further revisions of theological and historical affirmations in the NT. E.g., Paul's argument in 1 Cor 11:7–12 is based (esp. vv. 8–9) on the order of creation as presented in 2:18–24. For Paul's synthesis of chaps. 1 and 2 in his argument, see G. Fee, *The First Epistle to the Corinthians,* NICNT (Grand Rapids: Eerdmans, 1987), 515–17.

OUTLINE OF GENESIS 1:1–11:26

I. Creation of Heaven and Earth (1:1–2:3)
  1. Creator and Creation (1:1–2)
  2. Six Days of Creation (1:3–31)
  3. Seventh Day—Day of Consecration (2:1–3)

II. The Human Family in and outside the Garden (2:4–4:26)
  1. The Man and Woman in the Garden (2:4–25)
  2. The Man and Woman Expelled from the Garden (3:1–24)
  3. Adam and Eve's Family outside the Garden (4:1–26)

III. Adam's Family Line (5:1–6:8)
  1. Introduction: Creation and Blessing (5:1–2)
  2. "Image of God" from Adam to Noah (5:3–32)
  3. Conclusion: Procreation and Perversion (6:1–8)

IV. Noah and His Family (6:9–9:29)
  1. Righteous Noah (6:9–10)
  2. Corrupt World (6:11–12)
  3. Coming Judgment but the Ark of Promise (6:13–7:10)
  4. Waves of Judgment (7:11–24)
  5. God Remembered Noah (8:1a)
  6. Winds of Rescue (8:1b–5)
  7. Drying Earth (8:6–14)
  8. Exiting the Ark (8:15–19)
  9. Worship and the Word of Promise (8:20–22)
  10. Covenant with the New World (9:1–17)
  11. Noah's Sons and Future Blessing (9:18–29)

V. The Nations and the Tower of Babel (10:1–11:9)
  1. Table of Nations (10:1–32)
  2. Tower of Babel (11:1–9)

VI. Shem's Family Line (11:10–26)
  1. Shem "After the Flood" (11:10–11)
  2. Shem's Sons (11:12–26)

SECTION OUTLINE

I. CREATION OF HEAVEN AND EARTH (1:1–2:3)
   1. Creator and Creation (1:1–2)
      (1) In the Beginning (1:1)
      (2) Now the Earth (1:2)
   2. Six Days of Creation (1:3–31)
      (1) First Day of Creation (1:3–5)
      (2) Second Day of Creation (1:6–8)
      (3) Third Day of Creation (1:9–13)
      (4) Fourth Day of Creation (1:14–19)
      (5) Fifth Day of Creation (1:20–23)
      (6) Sixth Day of Creation (1:24–31)
   3. Seventh Day—Day of Consecration (2:1–3)

I. CREATION OF HEAVEN AND EARTH (1:1–2:3)

Creation's mystery and its Maker beckon us to know the One in whom "we live and move and have our being."[1] The opening section of Genesis introduces us to the Creator. He is the main character of the book, even all Scripture. The creation account is theocentric, not creature centered. Its purpose is to glorify the Creator by magnifying him through the majesty of the created order. The passage is doxological as well as didactic, hymnic as well as history. "God" is the *grammatical* subject of the first sentence (1:1) and continues as the *thematic* subject throughout the account. "And God said" is the recurring element that gives 1:1–2:3 cohesion as he is the primary actor. For this reason, one could use as the title of this first section the affirmation of the Apostles' Creed, "God the Father Almighty, Maker of Heaven and Earth."

LITERARY STRUCTURE. The literary contours of this first section are disputed among scholars. Some translations and many commentators have chosen to divide 2:4 so as to end the creation account in 1:1–2:4a, leaving the latter half to begin a second account of creation in 2:4b–3:24 (e.g., NRSV, REB, NJPS). This reconstruction is related to the proposal that Genesis contains two separate and independent creation stories having different origins and conflicting theological perspectives: 1:1–2:4a is credited to the so-called Priestly tradition (P), and 2:4b–3:24 to the supposed old epic tradition, the Yahwist (J). The recurring phrase "this is the account of" (traditionally, "these are the generations of [*tôlĕdôt*]") is considered the distinctive terminology of the P source in Genesis. Its appearance at 2:4a is assigned to the preceding narrative, for

[1] Epimenides, *Cretica*, quoted by Paul at the Areopagus, Athens (Acts 17:28).

otherwise a P statement introduces the J account of origins. Since the language of 2:4a has clear similarities with 1:1, it is contended that 2:4a is best taken as the précis of the previous narrative and forms a literary inclusio, marking out the beginning and end of the priestly story.

There are problems, however, that discourage dividing the verse in this way. First, the *tôlĕdôt* formula in 2:4a, if taken as a summary, would differ from its common use in Genesis where it uniformly refers to genealogy or narrative that follows, not precedes.[2] The *tôlĕdôt* rubric is best taken as a binding device or hinge verse (see Introduction) and always refers to what follows, though it does allude to the preceding so as to create a linkage between two sections. Second, the genealogy or narrative that is introduced by the *tôlĕdôt* usually concerns those who descended from the parent or family named in the *tôlĕdôt* rather than the head of the family himself. Again, 2:4a if taken with 1:1–2:3 would not conform to the common *tôlĕdôt* usage since that section tells of the origins of creation ("heavens and earth") and not what became of it. Third, the chiastic structure[3] of 2:4a and 2:4b argues for retaining the unity of the verse (see 2:4 discussion) as an introduction to what follows.

Moreover, 1:1–2:3 has been shown to be a symmetric, cohesive unit that makes 2:4a, if taken as its conclusion, an awkward appendage.[4] What matches 1:1 is not 2:4a but 2:1–3, where the seventh day serves as a satisfying denouement to the account's narrative progression. The key terms of 1:1—*bārā'*("created"), *'ĕlōhîm* ("God"), and *haššāmayim wĕ'ēt hā'āreṣ* ("the heavens and the earth")—are repeated in 2:1–3 but in reverse order, which recommends that 2:1–3 forms the inclusio ending to the first section without the unnecessary 2:4a.[5] The final three words of 2:3 (*bārā' 'ĕlōhîm la'ăśôt*, lit. "God created to do") also repeat the primary lexical and theological terms of chap. 1 so as to reflect its content. Also there is the striking similarity in the use of "seven" and its multiples in 1:1 and 2:1–3. As a whole 1:1–2:3 shows a proclivity to groups

[2] This incongruity is admitted by proponents of the view. Thus it has been suggested that 2:4a originally stood before 1:1 as a superscription to the first creation account. It was then moved to its present place by a later editorial hand (cf. S. R. Driver, *The Book of Genesis,* rev. [London: Methuen & Co., 1926], ii, 19.d). More recently, scholars have abandoned this notion and alternatively have considered 2:4a as a late addition to conform the creation story to the structure and theology of P, which sets creation and history in the framework of genealogy. See G. von Rad, *Genesis: A Commentary,* OTL, rev. ed.; trans. J. H. Marks (Philadelphia: Westminster, 1973), 63, 70, and C. Westermann, *Genesis 1–11: A Commentary,* trans. J. J. Scullion (Minneapolis: Augsburg, 1984), 81.

[3] This is the use of two series of elements, the second series repeating or reflecting the first in reverse order as in a mirror.

[4] E.g., see B. W. Anderson, "A Stylistic Study of the Priestly Creation Story," in *Canon and Authority,* ed. G. Coats and B. Long (Philadelphia: Fortress, 1977), 148–62, and G. Wenham, *Genesis 1–15,* WBC (Waco: Word, 1987), 5–6.

[5] Cf. M. Greenberg, *Ezekiel, 1–20,* AB (New York: Doubleday, 1983), 198.

of sevens, which would further suggest that 1:1–2:3 is an inclusive section.[6]

The arrangement of the passage consists of an introduction and seven paragraphs. The introduction identifies the Creator and creation (1:1–2); six paragraphs are carved up according to six creation days (1:3–31); and the final paragraph regards the climactic seventh day, the day of consecration (2:1–3). The presentation of each creation day follows a predictable order: (1) "God said," (2) command given, (3) the fact of creation, (4) God's evaluation, (5) the boundaries of the created element, and (6) the naming. This pattern is not slavish; there is variation within the account, but this does not distract from the impression of the general pattern, namely, that the creation is shaped by a supreme Overseer.

In v. 2 the condition of the earth as "a wasteland and empty" (the literal meaning of *tōhû wābōhû*)[7] provides the foil by which God directs his creation agenda. Since the earth *(ʾereṣ)* is lifeless, God sets about creating it inhabitable (i.e., no longer an unproductive wasteland) and inhabited (no longer empty) in six creation days, or two parallel sets of three days each.[8] Days three and six, which conclude each pair, are highlighted by the repetition of the divine word "And God said" (vv. 9,11,24,26) and the divine assessment "and it was good" (vv. 10,12,25,31).[9] There are eight acts of creation, one on each day except days three and six, when there are two. Day three commences a productive earth that provides vegetation for both animals and humans: "Let the land *[ʾereṣ]* produce vegetation" (v. 11); day six describes its first habitation: "Let the land *[ʾereṣ]* produce living creatures" (v. 24). Unlike vegetation and the animals, where the "land" *(ʾereṣ)* is God's intermediary, the second act of creation on day six (mankind) is achieved by God directly (vv. 26–27).

UNPRODUCTIVE BECOMES PRODUCTIVE	UNINHABITED BECOMES INHABITED
Day 1 Light and Darkness	Day 4 Luminaries

[6] "The structure of our section is based on a system of numerical harmony. Not only is the number *seven* fundamental to its main theme, but it also determines many of its details. . . . This numerical symmetry is, as it were, the golden thread that binds together all the parts of the section and serves as a convincing proof of its unity" (U. Cassuto, *A Commentary on the Book of Genesis. Vol. 1. From Adam to Noah, Genesis I–VI:8,* trans. I. Abrahams [Jerusalem: Magnes, 1961], 12.

[7] The NIV translates the rhyming couplet תֹהוּ וָבֹהוּ as "formless and empty" (see 1:2 discussion). Some render it as a hendiadys: "formless void" (NRSV, NJB), "formless wasteland" (NAB), or "vast waste" (REB).

[8] See D. T. Tsumura, *The Earth and the Waters in Genesis 1 and 2*, JSOTSup 83 (Sheffield: Sheffield Academic, 1989), 42. Alternatively, a common schematic pattern for the six days has attempted to show the six days as changing the "formless" and "empty" state of the earth (see Anderson, "A Stylistic Study of the Priestly Creation Story"). The first three days give form to the earth through three "separations," and the second three days resolve the problem of "emptiness," filling the restructured universe with heavenly bodies and life forms.

[9] See Wenham, *Genesis 1–15,* 6–7.

Day 2	Sky and Waters	Day 5	Fish and Fowl
Day 3	a. Land and Seas	Day 6	a. Beasts
	b. Vegetation		b. Human: male and female

This culminates in the seventh day, which has no matching member and is distinctive in many ways from the former six, distinguished as a day of rest and consecration.

Before we turn to the exposition, we will preview the primary theological affirmations of 1:1–2:3 and how the passage fits into the canonical shape of the whole Scripture. This introductory discussion is not a digression, for without a proper historical and theological orientation the power of the Genesis message is lost on the modern reader.

LORD OF CREATION AND HISTORY. The creation account, as the preamble to the Pentateuch, announces that the God of Israel, the covenant Deliverer of his people, is Creator of all that exists.[10] The opening verse is the theological presupposition of true biblical religion: the Lord of covenant and the God of creation are one and the same.[11] This story of beginnings introduces the thematic interests of Genesis as well as the whole Pentateuch; it tells of God's creation of "land" and his promise of "blessing" and "seed" (progeny).[12] These three motifs integrate the universal history (1:1–11:26) and the patriarchal accounts (11:27–50:26) under the overarching rubric of *tōledōt.* The Pentateuch is developed along the lines of these three motifs, and, for that matter, the continuing Primary History (Genesis–2 Kings) reflects the same concerns. It tells how Abraham's *seed* faltered in their faithfulness to God, forfeiting their *blessing*, and suffered expulsion from the *land* of their fathers. God's promissory blessings of land and seed had their inception at creation (1:10,22,28) and hence are universal promises bestowed upon all those created in the "image of God" (1:26–27). Genesis 1–11 shows how the universal blessing is realized only through a particular lineage, namely, through the progeny of Seth and his descendant Shem (chaps. 5; 11). Even more so, the genealogies narrow on the one man Abraham (11:26), who is deemed the recipient of divine blessing par excellence (12:1–3). Creation therefore entails the beneficent intentions of God, sets the course for their outworkings in human history, and prepares us for the ensuing account (2:4–11:26) of how God, despite recurring human disobedience, preserves his promises through the appointed seed of Abraham (11:27–50:26).

[10] See the discussion of C. Barth, *God with Us: A Theological Introduction to the Old Testament,* ed. G. W. Bromiley (Grand Rapids: Eerdmans, 1991), 9–11.

[11] Cf. Pss 74:12–17; 77:13–20[14–21]; 89:5–13[6–14]; 135:6–12; 136:5–22; Isa 42:5–6; Jer 10:12–16.

[12] See R. J. Clifford, "The Hebrew Scriptures and the Theology of Creation," *TS* 46 (1985): 522.

We have said that the telling of the creation account is framed so as to proclaim and demonstrate that Israel's God is the one and only true Creator Lord without rival. More than this, its depiction of God and his creation of the world resonates with what Israel had come to recognize in the words and deeds of their God, who formed them and ordered their life as a redeemed community at Sinai.

First, God is depicted as autonomous Master who has by his uncontested word commanded all things into existence and ordered their design and purpose. The spoken "word" is the preeminent motif of Genesis's affirmation concerning God as Creator.[13] Egypt's Memphite Theology has creation by the speech of the deity Ptah, but it is a magical utterance that energizes life, whereas in Hebrew cosmology divine decree is the transcendent word (see Introduction).[14] Creation by word stands in stark contrast to Mesopotamian cosmogony. In the mythopoetic stories of the ancient Near East, the ordered universe owed its existence to a cosmogonic struggle whereby "cosmos" resulted from the victorious clash of a hero deity overcoming a monster who restrains order.[15] The gods of creation were themselves the product of the generative primeval material.[16] The cosmogonic stories told little about creation itself but focused on theogony (origins of the gods).[17] The gods of creation were depicted primarily as re-ordering unruly primeval matter, not creating matter. Moreover, cosmogonic myths were sociological in function and goal, presenting a divine, cosmic explanation or pattern for the established social system.[18]

The ancients' understanding of origins was tied to their concept of the nat-

[13] "And God said" occurs ten times at 1:3,6,9,11,14,20,24,26,28, and 29. Cf. Pss 33:6,9; 148:5–6, where creation is attributed to the speech of God.

[14] N. H. Sarna, *Understanding Genesis* (New York: Schocken, 1970), 12; G. Hasel, "The Significance of the Cosmology in Genesis 1 in Relation to the Ancient Near Eastern Parallels," AUSS 10 (1972): 1–20; J. P. Allen, *Genesis in Egypt: The Philosophy of Ancient Egyptian Creation Accounts,* YES 2 (New Haven: Yale University Press, 1988), 36–38, 58–59.

[15] M. K. Wakeman, *God's Battle with the Monster: A Study in Biblical Imagery* (Leiden: Brill, 1973).

[16] In *Enuma Elish,* e.g., the gods are the offspring of the primeval waters Apsu and Tiamat. Among the diverse Egyptian cosmogonies, the creator-god Atum materializes by self-creation after the primeval hill emerges from the waters or he comes from the primeval waters Nun; in Memphite Theology, Atum comes from the thought and speech of the first principle Ptah (*ANET,* 3–4).

[17] E.g., in Egypt the creator-god produced the lesser deities through spitting them out of the mouth or through masturbation.

[18] E.g., the social structure of the Mesopotamian city-state system is reflected in the creation myths of Babylon (see T. Jacobsen, "Mesopotamia: The Cosmos as a State," in *The Intellectual Adventure of Man* [Chicago: University Press, 1946], 125–84). "Ancient cosmogonies were primarily interested in the emergence of society, organized with patron gods and worship systems, divinely appointed kings or leaders, kinship and marriage systems" (Clifford, "Cosmogonies in the Ugaritic Texts and in the Bible," *Or* 53 [1984]: 186–87).

ural world as alive and personal. They believed that nature was a divine "Thou," not an impersonal "It," and that natural phenomena were related to the activities of the gods. There was a mysterious correspondence between what happened in heaven and what occurred on earth.[19] For instance, procreation among the family, herd, and crop was dependent upon sexual relations among the deities. As a result, fertility deities were focal in the thinking of ancient religions. The existence and well-being of life were dependent in some way upon the activity and favor of the gods. The fertility deities among ancient Near Eastern peoples, no matter by what name, were responsible for the reproductive forces of the universe.[20]

Ancient myth reflects this ongoing pattern of struggle between the forces of plenty and those features of nature that threatened prosperity. The vehicle of literary myth expressed this understanding of the world's processes by describing the lives of the gods. Myth was not just entertaining fable; it conveyed a heavenly imitation of earth, like a cosmic mirror that reflected terrestrial, human experience.[21] Myth is like looking up into heaven and seeing ourselves masquerading as gods. Therefore the gods have the properties of everyday human experience and feelings—love and marriage, giving birth, fighting, and war. The gods were truly the creations of man! Ancient myth, then, tells of a threatening and unpredictable world where the gods operate, placing society at their mercy. Ancient religion celebrated the gods but also attempted to control them through cultic rituals.

Against this backdrop the Genesis account speaks volumes regarding the uniqueness of biblical revelation. Indeed, "revelation" was required to liberate antiquity from its superstitions and fear of the world that was viewed as a playground for capricious deities. "The God Israel worships is the lord of nature, but he is not the soul of nature."[22] Biblical religion has as its fundamental

---

[19] The Mesopotamian creation myth mirrors the seasonal threat of the environment with its rising Tigris-Euphrates river system and destructive rains: "The conflict between chaos and cosmos is only another aspect of the annual cycle of the universe, which causes nature to flower anew after being overthrown by the storms of winter" (S. Moscati, *The Face of the Ancient Orient* [Garden City: Doubleday, 1962], 79).

[20] E.g., although the primary motif of the Baal cycle is kingship, the fertility theme is apparent in the Canaanite Baal-Mot story and his relations with the consorts Athtart and Anat. Baal's capture in the netherworld by Mot spells disaster for the human world. El cries: "Baal's dead!—What becomes of the people? Dagon's Son!—What of the masses?" (*ANET,* 139). But once freed by Anat from Mot's clutches, Baal achieves life and fertility once again for the world, and El could say: "The heavens fat did rain,/The wadies flow with honey./So I knew/ That alive was Puissant Baal!/ Existent the Prince, Lord of Earth!" (*ANET,* 140).

[21] "Earthly existence, in short, is participation in heavenly existence" (W. Harrelson, "The Significance of Cosmology and the Ancient Near East," in *Translating and Understanding the Old Testament: Essays in Honor of Herbert Gordon May* [Nashville: Abingdon, 1970], 241).

[22] B. W. Anderson, *Creation Versus Chaos: The Reinterpretation of Mythical Symbolism in the Bible* (Philadelphia: Fortress, 1987), 32.

premise that God *is* and that he is Sovereign Lord above and over nature, not bound up in the process of creation nor a fertility participant in the cycle of life and death, plenty and famine.[23] There is no Hebrew theogony. God has no father. He has no consort. "The idea of creation by the word preserves first of all the most radical essential distinction between Creator and creature. Creation cannot be even remotely considered an emanation from God; it is not somehow an overflow or reflection of his being, i.e., of his divine nature, but rather is a product of his personal will."[24]

We have said that ancient myth commonly portrays creation in terms of conflict between forces in which the creator-gods subjugate their cosmic enemies and bring an ordered universe out of disarray. This underlying conception of order versus chaos is reflected in the Bible by the employment of word imagery, but there is far more here.[25] It is not just that God controls an uninhabitable earth (1:2); rather Hebrew cosmology declares that the existence of all things is due to God's own free, determined will.[26] This is stated explicitly in 1:1 and is implied throughout the account. The author was not a mimic who historicized a pagan version in order to satisfy a developed Yahwism. Although it is too strong to claim that the biblical account is a direct polemic, it is clear that the author had no use for pagan ideology and carefully distinguished biblical cosmology from pagan misconceptions.[27] The author chose the conven-

---

[23] "Although Yahweh is free to use the storm wind and associated meteorological phenomena in holy warfare, he stands over and separate from them (cf. Exodus 15), unlike the divine warriors Baal, Marduk, or Zeus" (L. Clapham, "Mythopoetic Antecedents of the Biblical World-View and Their Transformation in Early Israelite Thought," in *Magnalia Dei, The Mighty Acts of God: Essays on the Bible and Archaeology in Memory of G. Ernest Wright* [Garden City: Doubleday, 1976], 116).

[24] von Rad, *Genesis,* 51–52.

[25] These opponents of God are named Rahab (e.g., Pss 87:4; 89:10; Isa 30:7; 51:9: Job 9:13; 26:12), Leviathan (Job 3:8; 41:1 [40:25]; Pss 74:14; 104:26; Isa 27:1), sea-monsters or תַּנִּין (Job 7:12; Ps 74:13; Isa 27:1; 51:9; Ezek 29:3; 32:2). The poets and prophets do not speak of them as gods or cosmic forces but merely use their imagery to portray figuratively the physical forces that threaten life or the historical enemies of Israel (e.g., the Egyptians). As did the author of Gen 1, the prophets and poets rejected idolatry, and the prophets in particular despised such pagan notions of competing deities. Also, the "deep," "darkness," and the "creatures of the sea" (תַּנִּין) in the creation account are physical properties, not personified monsters (1:2,21).

[26] Attributing to the author of 1:1–2:3 the same conceptual framework as that of the battle motif found in Mesopotamia and Canaanite myths is commonplace. "To the priestly writer, God is in complete control of the universe. He brought it under his control in creation. . . . To him this was the thing of importance; this was all that needed to be known about creation. Philosophically we are forced to add a prior step: All this is true because God brought all things into existence *ex nihilo.* But theologically is his view inferior to ours? It is certainly not as impossible a view as some have tried to indicate" (W. R. Lane, "The Initiation of Creation," *VT* 13 [1963]: 73). We contend rather that while the passage at times uses the language of the ancient conceptual framework, it bursts the old framework by attributing to God everything that exists and by giving the events of creation a historical framework.

[27] See, e.g., G. Hasel, "The Polemic Nature of the Genesis Cosmology," *EvQ* 46 (1974): 81–102.

tional language of his times, but he was not a conventional thinker. In the biblical tradition the universe is *creatio ex nihilo* (see 1:1–2 discussion). Moreover, in distinction from pagan myth, which is always timeless and stands alone outside history, biblical creation inaugurates history ("In the beginning").[28] Creation is inseparably linked with the *tôlĕdôt* ("account") of human history (see 2:4 discussion).

Also God's authority is demonstrated by the efficacy of his spoken word. The pattern of creation includes with the mandate an executed response. God commanded, "Let there be light," and the text says, "there was light" (1:3). The recurring declaration "and it was so" (1:7,9,11,15,24) leaves no doubt about the mastery of the creative word. Moreover, God's authority is indicated by the act of naming the constituent parts of the created order (1:5,8,10). The three acts of naming are related to the three acts of separation: day and night (v. 5), skies (v. 8), and land from seas (v. 10). In the ancient world the naming of an entity signified and defined its existence.[29] By giving names to his creatures, God's word authenticates their existence and demonstrates his superiority.[30]

Second, the literary arrangement of the six days plus one (seven) depicts God as the authoritative Designer who invokes structure, boundaries, as well as gives life—all culminating in the sanctification of the day of rest. Also, the narrative has the repeated use of the number "seven" and multiples of seven, followed in frequency by the use of "three's" and "ten's."[31] The macrostructure of seven days is transparent, but also the first verse has seven words and the second verse fourteen words (7 x 2). The last section (2:1–3), concerning the seventh day, consists of thirty-five words (7 x 5) and possesses the expression "seventh day" three times. The days consist of two groups of three parallel, corresponding days, leaving the final seventh day without a match. God speaks ten times, with seven commands for creation and creatures and three

---

[28] See Anderson, *Creation Versus Chaos,* 11–42; J. Grønbæk, "Baal's Battle with Yam—A Canaanite Creation Fight," *JSOT* 33 (1985): 36.

[29] *Enuma Elish* begins, "When on high the heaven had not been named,/Firm ground below had not been called by name" (*ANET,* 60–61). In other words, the heavens and earth had no name because they had no existence; divine naming means bringing into existence. An Egyptian text describes the world before creation when nothing had yet come into being and "when no name had yet been named" (see W. Beyerlin, ed., *Near Eastern Religious Texts Relating to the Old Testament* [Philadelphia: Westminster, 1978], 7). But the naming of darkness as "night" (1:5) may not be intended to express the sense of existence, for "darkness" already existed before the first creative word (v. 2; so Cassuto, *Genesis,* 27).

[30] The custom of naming a person, child, or city expresses source, command, or leadership (e.g., Gen 2:19–20,23; 4:17; 5:2; 17:5; 32:28–29). Cf. particularly Ps 147:4 and Isa 40:26, where God names the stars.

[31] See Cassuto, *Genesis,* 12–15.

pronouncements concerning humanity.[32] The divine evaluation "it was good" occurs seven times ("very good," the seventh).[33] This numerical repetition speaks to the literary unity of the narrative and emphasizes the idea of perfection and completion in God's finished creation.

This schematic arrangement marks the harmony and symmetry of the created order; the Designer sets limits for the creation. The skies, land, and seas know their place. They hearken to their Master's dictum, not overreaching their imposed boundaries. Life forms, including vegetation, are instructed to reproduce within the restrictions of their own "kinds" (vv. 11–12,21,24). Neither God nor his world is capricious. He produces an orderly, predictable, and dependable world. Also, neither God nor man is threatened by rampaging waters, engulfing darkness, or teeming monsters; God sets the rhythm and course of nature, maintaining its tempo. Thus, the world is "good," and in its entirety it is "very good." The world is friendly, valued, and to be utilized without fear; here is "the good order of life"[34] that human life enjoys with the Creator.

Furthermore, the creation account, tied to the chronological *tôlĕdôt* scheme of Genesis, indicates that God as Creator has established history as his arena of revelation and action. In biblical cosmology creation is event, an inauguration of history that will culminate in the eschatological "day of the LORD."[35] Pagan cosmogonies commonly are concerned with rehearsing the eternal present,[36] but chronology is the controlling framework for the telling of origins in chaps. 1–11.

That Israel's concept of Yahweh acting in history has no correspondence

---

[32] The seven commands are jussives, and the latter three are expressed by different verbal forms; also, "and it was so" occurs seven times, and God names and blesses seven times (see B. K. Waltke, "The Literary Genre of Genesis, Chapter One," *Crux* 27 [1991]: 5; and H. Blocher, *In the Beginning: The Opening Chapters of Genesis,* trans. D. Preston [Leicester: IVP, 1984], 33).

[33] Cf. 1:4,10,12,18,21,25,31.

[34] W. Brueggemann, *Genesis,* IBC (Atlanta: John Knox, 1982), 30.

[35] E.g., Isa 24–27; 65; Amos 5:18–20; Rev 21.

[36] Sumerian tradition, however, incorporates the Sumerian King List to form a "mytho-historical" literary genre of origins (so T. Jacobsen, "The Eridu Genesis," *JBL* 100 [1981]: 520). Ancient historiographers tended to integrate history and myth since they viewed the world from a mythic framework and thus viewed past to present as a mythic continuum. So R. E. Averbeck, who notes that similar to Sumerian tradition, Gen 1–11 gives the ideological framework for Israel to view itself and its origins; he raises the question whether Gen 1 should thus be read as theological-literary rather than historical ("The Sumerian Historiographic Tradition and Its Implications for Genesis 1–11," in *Faith, Tradition, and History,* ed. A. R. Millard et al. [Winona Lake: Eisenbrauns, 1994], 79–102). But unlike the pagan worldview, Israel did not view itself within a mythological framework but rather a historical one, and thus the appropriation of myth or only a literary telling would be foreign to the Hebrew's viewpoint.

among pagan nations has been challenged.[37] Although it is true that the pagan deities intersect with historical events, bringing about national outcomes, this is not the same as the Israelite idea of God as Lord of history whose motivation is grounded in history and who has an encompassing plan for history. Pagan deities are motivated by mythical concerns and act in continuity with the mythic world, while biblical religion insists that Yahweh always transcends nature.[38]

If chaps. 1–2 are theological story, without correspondence to history, the creation account says nothing about cosmos or covenant-history, for both are intertwined in history.[39] In Sumerian and Babylonian traditions, creation is paired with the poetic hymns of praise for the gods and in some instances related to incantations and temple rituals.[40] Such myths were designed to invoke praise for the creator-god. Yet Genesis remains in a narrative arrangement, unlike the mythopoetic style of Mesopotamia. Though it shows some hymnic echoes, the presentation of 1:1–2:3 is cast in a historical framework, analogous to the human week, and not in the genre of descriptive praise. Genesis no doubt is implicitly calling Israel to praise its Creator, but it is in the Psalms where the explicit call to praise is heard (e.g., Pss 19; 104). This praise of God as Creator is tied to the historical deeds of God, who delivered Israel from its enemies (e.g., Ps 107:32–37; cf. also Isa 40–48).

For later Israel the affirmation concerning the life-giving word was central to their experience. Although God transcends the material world, he is only known in terms of his self-determined relationship to it. God is the autonomous "I AM WHO I AM," the self-existing One (Exod 3:14), but more importantly for Israel, God is the "I AM" who revealed himself to the Fathers and would deliver his people from Egypt's bondage (Exod 3:15). Thus, God is known primarily by his salvific acts in behalf of his people. Similarly, 1:1 indicates that God is known in terms of his relationship with the world. He is not defined or explained either in the cosmogonic thinking of the ancients or the philosophi-

---

[37] See B. Albrektson, *History and the Gods: An Essay on the Idea of Historical Events as Divine Manifestation in the Ancient Near East and Israel* (Lund: CWK Gleerup, 1967); R. Gnuse, *Heilsgeschichte as a Model for Biblical Theology: The Debate Concerning the Uniqueness and Significance of Israel's Worldview* (Lanham: University Press of America, 1989).

[38] See B. T. Arnold, "The Weidner Chronicle and the Idea of History in Israel and Mesopotamia," in *Faith, Tradition, and History,* ed. A. R. Millard et al. (Winona Lake: Eisenbrauns, 1994), 129–48.

[39] See R. H. Moye, "In the Beginning: Myth and History in Genesis and Exodus," *JBL* 109 (1990): 577–98. While we disagree with his pretextual analysis that the genealogies wed "myth" with "history" so as to have a historicizing function in the narrative, the line of his argument shows that the *extant* text integrates creation with the patriarchs as one forward-moving historical account.

[40] "Enuma Elish is first and foremost a hymn in honor of Marduk" (A. Heidel, *The Babylonian Genesis: The Story of Creation* [Chicago: University of Chicago Press, 1942], 3, also 49, 53, 55.

cal categories of moderns. He is met in history, and that history is told primarily by historical discourse.[41]

Also the Israelite's entire way of life was ordered by the words of God as spoken through the prophet Moses. The Ten Words and the covenant-law tradition were uttered by God in the hearing of Moses, either on the mountain or at the Tent of Meeting.[42] The commandments of God were not "idle words" but the source of life for the community (Deut 32:47). "For the man who obeys them will live by them" (Lev 18:5). These words secured order for the community and promised prosperity, but they also were the heartbeat of the obedient who came to faith—those whose hearts were circumcised (Deut 30:6,11–14).

The New Testament acknowledges that God is Creator and Redeemer, and he has revealed himself fully in his Son Jesus Christ. That same God who is known relationally as Creator and Covenant Lord is John's *Logos,* who has dared to become incarnate with us (John 1:14). The Word is known both by his relationship "with God" and also his relationship with all things as their source (John 1:1–3; Col 1:15–17). He who had no biography took on one so that he might redeem human history (Gal 4:4). He alone explains God to us (John 1:18), and only those rightly related to him by faith are born "children of God" (John 1:12). While the Christian community affirmed the Hebrew tradition concerning God as author of all things (e.g., Acts 4:24–30; Rom 11:36), it identified Christ as the incarnate Creator-Redeemer who has equal footing with God (John 1:3; Heb 1:2; Col 1:15–16; 1 Cor 8:6). More importantly, the creation finds its focus and culmination in Christ, who has subjected all things under his lordship through the cross and resurrection (Eph 1:9–10; Phil 2:6–11). Those who are in Christ are new creations (2 Cor 5:17; Gal 6:15), and he in his regal glory will usher in "a new heaven and a new earth" (Rev 21:1).

The apostolic tradition recognizes too that the promise of life in the law transcends the social operations of the community. For while the righteous lived in accordance with the law, it was by the word of faith, affirmed in this law, that established righteousness. Thus the gospel was available to whoever "confessed with their heart" the Lord Jesus (Rom 10:5–10). The Christian voice declares, drawing on creation language, that in the divine Word "was life, and that life was the light of men" (John 1:4). So it is that this creative Word that brought the worlds into existence is the same Word that creates Israel (e.g., Isa 43:15), orders Israel's life, and proclaims the gospel of faith whereby the believer is liberated from the darkness of sin.

RESPONSE OF GOD'S PEOPLE. In the creation account human life is explicitly charged with caring for the terrestrial world (1:28; cf. 2:15,20). The

[41] So G. Trenkler, "Creation," in *Encyclopedia of Biblical Theology,* ed. J. B. Bauer (New York: Crossroad, 1981), 147.

[42] E.g., Exod 20–24, esp. 24:12; Lev 1:1; Num 1:1. Also Moses' Deuteronomic legislation is attributed to divine initiative (e.g., Deut 26:16).

proper response of God's people is to subjugate the created order through procreation, responsible conservation, and exploration. At the command of God Israel subjugated the "good" land of Canaan. It was the gift of God, and as tenant Israel was required to act in holiness lest the land and its people suffer (Lev 25–26; Deut 28). But we know that sin's effects have meant not only death for man but also a tortured creation that languishes "subjected to futility," awaiting its liberation from decay (Gen 3:17–19; Rom 8:18–25). Just as humanity must be redeemed, so must the creation. This, Paul declared, will occur at the advent of Christ, who will redeem through the resurrection our mortal bodies and will transform creation. Hence, ultimately, this subjugation will be achieved through the last Adam, who will bring the heavens and the earth to their knees and release them finally from the bondage of sin's curse (Heb 2:5–9; Phil 2:10), at which time there will be "new heavens and a new earth" (Isa 65:17; 66:22; 2 Pet 3:10,13).

At present we who are the children of God enjoy our redemption by faith, yet we realize that our full inheritance is eschatological. Similarly we acknowledge that creation remains untamed and will not come into its full liberation until the "day of the LORD," although we strive toward the mastery of the present world through responsible stewardship enabled by human advancements in knowledge and technology. "The Christian will neither hold that at present 'all is for the best in the best of all possible worlds' nor write the world off as belonging to the devil."[43]

Israel's response to God as Creator was obedient trust and worship. We have said earlier that the God of Israel was understood by the Hebrews as autonomous Ruler who transcended nature and brought into being all that exists through his irreversible commands. The universe was systematically and progressively organized by the establishment of boundaries through separations and limits. By delegated authority the operations of divine rule were bestowed upon his supreme creation, human life. The universe inherently possesses a hierarchy of value and function. "Cosmic order depends upon maintaining clear demarcations among the elements of the universe. God maintains the division between light and dark, waters and dry land, world above from world below. People are to maintain the other divisions in the universe."[44] Hence, human life was distinguished from the divine above and the animals below. Through the Mosaic law the community honored divisions, distinctions, and hierarchy within human society itself. There were a host of "classifications" that pertained to sexual behavior, dietary laws, and the holy in cultic matters. For Israel to transgress the covenant-law that governed their lives meant unset-

---

[43] F. F. Bruce, "The Bible and the Environment," in *The Living and Active Word of God: Studies in Honor of Samuel J. Schultz* (Winona Lake: Eisenbrauns, 1983), 29.

[44] T. Frymer-Kensky, "Biblical Cosmology," in *Backgrounds for the Bible* (Winona Lake: Eisenbrauns, 1987), 236, esp. 236–39.

tling the cosmic order and bringing upon itself the response of God, whose weapons were the destabilizing forces of the environment, such as floods, drought, and pestilence. It was incumbent upon later Israel to honor the Lord as Creator-Redeemer through careful observance of the covenant-law.

Some have supposed that chap. 1 is a liturgical text, but there is no compelling evidence of such a creation ritual in Israel. Moreover, its polemical tenor opposing the myth-ritual practices of the ancient Near East obstruct a liturgical explanation for its composition. Rather, we must turn to the voice of the poets to discover how Israel integrated creation theology into the life of worship.[45] The psalmist implored all peoples to worship the Maker of heaven and earth (Ps 150:1–6), who has sustained the world through his mighty word and deeds (Pss 33:6–12; 103:19–22; 113:4–5; 145:10–13). For God has given order to the universe (104:1–9), and the heavens testify to his eternal glory (Ps 19:1–6[1–7]). Therefore all people must respond in obedience by moral uprightness (19:7–14[8–15]). God is found trustworthy in sustaining his creation; he provides for all creatures without fail (104:27–30). The psalmist inferred that since the heavens and the earth obey the utterance of the Lord, do men and women, his most excellent creative work, chance to disobey his moral precepts?

Creation theology was also an important source of speculation in the wisdom tradition of Israel. "Genesis 1:1 stands behind all biblical wisdom tradition,"[46] which considered critical the consequences of creation's order for human behavior (e.g., Prov 14:31; 17:5). The achievement of successful living was through conformity to the inherent order in the cosmos, but that way of life could only be grasped through the "fear of the LORD," who as Maker of heaven and earth alone possessed wisdom for living (Prov 8:22–31). This is especially true of Job's queries, where linkage between cosmic order and God's justice in human affairs is supposed.[47] God's response to Job was designed to show Job that he did not have the understanding required to run the moral order of human affairs any more than he had the power or wisdom to have designed the natural world (38:1–41:34). God alone understands the cosmos as its sole Maker and Designer, and he alone is qualified to keep in balance the tenuous aspects of the world—both its inanimate and animate

[45] The hymns commonly recognized as descriptive praises are Pss 8; 19:1–6; 29; 33; 104; 148; cf. also Pss 9; 24; 36; 74; 90; 93; 96–99; 139; 147; 149. The Hebrews were different from their neighbors in not celebrating creation annually in a New Year's festival. This absence of ritual-myth underscored how creation was viewed by Israel. It was understood as a one-time event that inaugurated history and as preamble to Israel's history (see G. J. Brooke, "Creation in the Biblical Tradition," *Zygon* 22 [1987]: 235).

[46] D. Garrett, *Proverbs, Ecclesiastes, Song of Songs,* NAC (Nashville: Broadman, 1993), 53.

[47] See F. I. Andersen, *Job: An Introduction and Commentary,* TOTC (Downers Grove: IVP, 1976), 287, and N. C. Habel, *The Book of Job,* OTL (Philadelphia: Westminster, 1985), 65–66.

properties. Hence, he alone can operate the moral order, and he accomplishes this not by a mechanical principle of retributive justice but according to his moral integrity.

From the prophets we hear the excelling witness that the Lord is both Judge and Savior. Divine judgment upon wicked Israel and the proud nations is grounded in God's role as Creator who imposes just deserts against the rebellious.[48] Isaiah's theology of comfort and restoration (chaps. 40–66) was anchored in God as Creator and only Lord. Because God is the Lord of all things, he is free to create for Israel a "new thing" (43:15,18–19; 45:21; 48:3,6–8). As Lord of the universe he alone determined the course of the nations (40:12–31), for the Gentile gods were mere idols who could not save (43:10–13; 44:6–20; 45:11–20). God created Israel (42:5; 43:1), and he will redeem his people, resulting in the transformation of the old into "new heavens and a new earth" (60:5–14; 62:6–9; 65:17–18).

1. Creator and Creation (1:1–2)

The Bible's first words announce how Israel's God can be known. He reveals himself in terms of the "when's" and "where's" of human life and history. Conceptually, this is how people orient themselves to their world. We locate ourselves in time in terms of our beginnings and endings. Our personal stories are also contoured by space. Thus as we see and identify ourselves by our finitude, so the Infinite One condescends by announcing his presence in the same terms—time and space. God is not merely an idea. He is Eternal Being whom we can know and experience personally. At the commencement of Scripture he invites us to learn of him. Yet the full manifestation of the Unknown One awaited the Incarnate Word, who as Son is the "exact representation of his being" (Heb 1:3).

(1) In the Beginning (1:1)

[1]In the beginning God created the heavens and the earth.

1:1 "In the beginning" *(bĕrēʾšît)* marks inauguration (see the excursus "Translating 1:1–2," p. 136), but it also anticipates the "end" of the universe and human history.[49] "Beginning" *(rēʾšît)* is often paired in the Old Testament with its antonym "end" *(ʾaḥărît)* indicating an inclusive period of time (e.g., Job 8:7; 42:12; Eccl 7:8; Isa 46:10). The occurrence of "beginning" *(rēʾšît)* in 1:1 suggests that it has been selected because of its association with "end"

[48] Cf. Jer 4:23–26; 31:22,35–37; Ezek 28:13–15; Amos 4:12–13; 5:5–9.

[49] For this discussion see Sailhamer, "Genesis," EBC (Grand Rapids: Zondervan, 1990), 20–23.

(*ʾaḥărît*).[50] If so, the author has at the outset shown that creation's "beginnings" were initiated with a future goal intended, an eschatological purpose. Thus the prophets and the apostles could speak of the end in terms of the beginnings, "new heavens and new earth" (Isa 65:17; Rev 21:1). At the commencement of the creation story the passage declares that God as Sovereign knows and controls the "end from the beginning" (Isa 46:10).

The majestic telling of earth's beginnings is accentuated by the exclusive use of *Elohim* ("God") in 1:1–2:3. It is not until 2:4b that the name *Yahweh* ("LORD") occurs and there in concert with *Elohim*. The Hebrew Bible has three names for "deity" or "god/God": *El, Eloah,* and *Elohim.*[51] The etymological relationship of these words, if any, is unclear. Of these, *Elohim* occurs by far the most often in the Bible (2,750x). As a plural in form it can refer to pagan deities, in which case it is translated "gods" (e.g., Exod 12:12; 20:3), or to the God of Israel. When used of the one God, it commonly occurs in the Hebrew with singular verbs as it is found here. Why the plural was also used of the one God of Israel is uncertain, though most ascribe it to the use of the Hebrew plural that indicates honor or majesty.[52] As a plural it is a literary convention that reflects special reverence.

Since its plurality does not designate more than one entity, its morphological shape does not necessarily refer to the plurality of the Godhead. It is unreasonable to burden this one word *Elohim* with a developed view of the Christian Trinity. It is fair to say, however, that the creation account (1:2,26–27) implies that there is a plurality within God (cf. 3:22; 11:7; 18:1ff.). But it is not until the era of the church that the Trinity is clearly articulated. New Testament tradition ascribes to Christ a role in creation (John 1:1–3; Col 1:15–17; Heb 1:2), but it is less clear about the role of the Spirit (see the discussion of the Spirit in v. 2).

The regular appearance of *Elohim* in 1:1–2:3 rather than *Yahweh* is due to the theological emphasis of the section. Creation extols God's transcendence and the power of his spoken word; thus *Elohim* is preferred, whereas *Yahweh* commonly is associated with the particular covenant agreement between God and Israel (Exod 3:15; 6:2–3).[53] The general name *Elohim* is appropriate for the creation account's universal framework and in effect repudiates the cos-

---

[50] In the Pentateuch the customary expressions for designating the first in a series of members are בַּתְּחִלָּה, which occurs in the Pentateuch four times, all in Genesis (13:3; 41:21; 43:18,20), and רִאשֹׁנָה, ten times, three of which are in Genesis (13:4; 28:19; 38:28). רֵאשִׁית occurs in Gen 10:10, but not used temporally.

[51] See H. Ringgren, "אֱלֹהִים, *ʾĕlōhîm*," *TDOT* 1.267–84.

[52] *IBHS* § 7.4.3b.

[53] The common expression "God of Israel" (אֱלֹהֵי־יִשְׂרָאֵל) distinguishes Israel as specially related to God by covenant, and the appellation *Elohim* is typically identified with *Yahweh* (e.g., Exod 6:7; Lev 26:13; Deut 26:17; 29:12).

mogonies of the pagan world, where the origins and biography of their "gods" are paramount. From the inception of Moses' "Five Books," polytheism and idolatry have no ideological or practical place among Israel (cf. Exod 20:1–6; Deut 4:12–24).

"Created" *(bārā')* is used in the Old Testament consistently in reference to a new activity. It forms a sound play with the previous "in the beginning," where the three initial letters are the same: *br'šyt br'*. It occurs in the creation account six times (1:1,21,27[3x]; 2:3; cf. also 2:4a).[54] The etymology of the term is disputed and is of little help, but its frequent appearance in the Old Testament enables us to define its meaning with some security.[55] The striking feature of the word is that its subject is always God.[56] It therefore conveys the idea of a special activity accomplished only by deity that results in newness or a renewing. Also *bārā'* always refers to the product created and does not refer to the material of which it is made. For these reasons commentators have traditionally interpreted the verb as a technical term for *creatio ex nihilo* ("creation out of nothing"). In doing so, it is often contrasted with the verb *'āśâ*, meaning "to make" or "do," which may have as its subject human activity (as well as divine). In particular *'āśâ* is used where "making" involves existing material.[57] As the argument goes, *'āśâ* can refer to human activity in which preexisting material is transformed, but *bārā'* is used exclusively of God's activity with no presence of preexisting material.

"Create," however, does not necessarily mean an altogether new thing. For example, Ps 51:10a[12a] reads, "Create *[bārā']* within me a new heart"; this line parallels "renew *[ḥādaš]* within me an upright spirit" (v. 10b), indicating here that "create" has the nuance of restoration.[58] David was asking for a transformation, not a new entity. Isaiah 57:19 speaks of God "creating praise on the lips of the mourners." The context of the passage involves restoration of his wayward people in which he will "heal" and "restore" ("repay," NRSV). The sense of *bārā'* in the context of Isaiah 57 indicates that God will renew again the lips of Israel's mourners where there once was praise.

More importantly, in the context of the creation account itself "create" and "make" are used interchangeably for the creation of human life (vv. 26–27; cp. 2:7; 5:1).[59] In the heading of the following *tôlĕdôt* section (2:4), "created" and

---

[54] Elsewhere it is found to reference God's creation of the cosmos (e.g., Isa 40:26,28; Amos 4:13), mankind (e.g., Deut 4:32; Ps 89:47[48]; Isa 45:12), and Israel (e.g., Isa 43:1).

[55] Of its forty-nine occurrences, it is found once as a nominal form (Num 16:30).

[56] I.e., in the *qal* stem.

[57] E.g., Gen 3:21, where God "made" tunics from skins for the first couple.

[58] Cf. the following terms that are also found in parallel with בָּרָא: עָשָׂה ("make," Isa 41:20); יָצַר ("form," Isa 43:1,7); כּוּן ("establish," Isa 45:18); יָסַד ("found," Ps 89:11[12]. See K.-H. Bernhardt, "בָּרָא, *br'*," *TDOT* 2.246–48.

[59] Also cf. Gen 1:1 with Exod 20:11 and Isa 41:20; 43:7; 45:7,12.

"made" occur in matching temporal clauses.[60] The term *ʿāśâ* at 2:3 is used to elucidate the meaning of *bārāʾ*: "which God created by *doing [ʿāśâ].*" By itself *ʿāśâ* occurs in 1:7,16,25, where it indicates God uniquely accomplished his creative task. If *bārāʾ* were a technical term among the Hebrews for *creatio ex nihilo,* in distinction from human endeavor, we would expect it to dominate the creation narrative. However, it is used sparingly in the account and is reserved for highlighting significant aspects of the creation where the blessing of procreation is bestowed on the first animate life (1:21–22) and supreme animate life (1:27–28). If the doctrine of *creatio ex nihilo* is expounded here, it must be from the tenor of the text and not from this single lexical term.[61] Elsewhere in the narrative it is apparent that God created *ex nihilo* (e.g., 1:3).

While we disagree that "create" is a technical term for fiat creation, it is clear that *bārāʾ,* with God exclusively as its subject, indicates special significance for God as autonomous Creator. The term maintains our focus on the thematic subject of God, who alone can accomplish creation. The declaration of v. 1 without any intimation of competing preexisting matter is so distinctive from its ancient counterparts that we must infer that all things have their ultimate origin in God as Creator.[62]

"Created" is found most often in Isaiah (twenty times in chaps. 40–66), where the prophet distinguishes Israel's God as Creator and true Lord of history. In the context of Babylon's religious practices of astrology and idolatry (e.g., Isa 40:26), Isaiah celebrated Yahweh as Creator who acts in history, creating Israel for himself (e.g., 42:5; 43:1,7,15) and accomplishing a "new thing" by delivering his people (43:15–19; 48:6–8). God then begins history at creation but continues to "create" history through his sovereign lordship among the nations.[63] Since God is Creator of all that exists, he is antecedent to it, distinct from it, while yet intimately involved with it. According to ancient Near Eastern lore, gods abounded in heaven, and deities were the forces of land and sea. The ancient myths did not adequately distinguish between the creator and the creature, but Israel declares that the universe is no more than a creature. In Israel's view there was no divine heaven or earth.[64] It was this view that freed the heavens and the earth from superstition and provided an ideological basis for the emergence of modern science.

The expression "the heavens and the earth" indicates the totality of the universe (see the excursus "Translating 1:1–2," p. 136).

---

[60] The parallel lines of 2:4 are obscured by the NIV's division; cp. AV, NASB.

[61] See Waltke, "The Creation Account in Genesis 1:1–3. Part IV," *BSac* 132 (1975): 335–37. T. E. McComiskey ("בָּרָא [*bara*']," *TWOT* 1.127) concludes that the verb does not inherently mean *creatio ex nihilo,* but it "lends itself to the idea of creation *ex nihilo.*"

[62] N. H. Sarna, בראשית *Genesis,* JPST (Philadelphia: Jewish Publication Society, 1989), 5.

[63] See Westermann, *Genesis 1–11,* 98–99.

[64] Noted by Barth, *God with Us,* 18–19.

(2) Now the Earth (1:2)

[2]Now the earth was formless and empty, darkness was over the surface of the deep, and the Spirit of God was hovering over the waters.

1:2 The "earth" is first described in its pristine state at the inception of creation before it is transformed into a suitable habitation for human life. Six creation "days" are described from the terrestrial perspective of a person observing the transformation. Also while *ʾereṣ,* "earth," stands opposite "heavens" in v. 1, together referring to the universe, in v. 2 *ʾereṣ* suggests by double entendre the "land" of Israel's habitation. The term *ʾereṣ* commonly means a territorial holding, designating "land." The recurring motifs of "land" and "blessing" introduced in 1:1–2:3 are thematic fixtures in the patriarchal narratives and the entire Pentateuch. For Israel the land was God's good gift that he prepared for his people to possess.[65] Creation prepared God's good "land/ earth," which was for man to enjoy (1:10,12,31) and for Israel to possess.

Three parallel clauses in v. 2 describe the conditions of the earth at its beginning:

"Now the earth was formless and empty *(tōhû wābōhû)"*
"darkness was over the surface of the deep *(tĕhôm)"*
"the Spirit of God was hovering over the waters *(mayim)"*

The rhyming couplet *tōhû wābōhû* (lit., "a wasteland and empty") was shown earlier to be the foil by which God apportions his labor for the six days of creation. Three days are given to making the "uninhabitable" earth productive, and three days concern filling the "uninhabited" earth with life. There is no consensus about the precise meaning of the terms nor how the two words are to be understood when they occur in tandem. Some have taken the two terms as a hendiadys, meaning "formless waste," while others treat them as a *farrago,* that is, two usually alliterative words that when taken together convey a different sense than when the two words appear independently. English equivalents such as "hodgepodge" and "mingled mass" have been suggested.[66]

Some have taken the phrase *tōhû wābōhû* as a negative emptiness, a dark abyss, like that of the Greek idea of primeval chaos (Hesiod, *Theogony* 116) or, alternatively, a disordered conglomerate, a kind of watery mass, which

---

[65] E.g., reference to the "land" of Canaan as "good" (cf. Exod 3:8; Num 14:7; Deut 1:25,35; 3:25; 4:21–22; 8:7,10; 9:6; 11:17; "good cities," 6:10) and "possession" of the "good" land (Deut 6:18; cf. also Gen 12:1; 15:7; 24:7; 28:13–14; 35:12; Deut 1:21; 3:20).

[66] For the former see J. Sasson, "Time . . . to Begin," *Shaʿarei Talmon: Studies in the Bible, Qumran, and the Ancient Near East Presented to Shemaryahu Talmon* (Winona Lake: Eisenbrauns, 1992), 188, and the latter, W. P. Brown, *Structure, Role, and Ideology in the Hebrew and Greek Texts of Genesis 1:1–2:3,* SBLDS 132 (Atlanta: Scholars Press, 1993), 75.

opposes creation.[67] The LXX's "unseen" and "unformed"[68] may have influenced the now-common understanding "chaos," an undifferentiated mass or vacuous nonentity.[69] We will find that *tōhû* and *bōhû* describe a "wasteland" and "empty" land. *Bōhû* is found only in *tōhû wābōhû,* occurring in 1:2 and in Jer 4:23; also the two terms are in parallel at Isa 34:11. The etymology of the word remains a mystery, and we are left with the meaning of *tōhû* to clarify the sense of the couplet.

Although the etymology is also unclear for *tōhû,*[70] it occurs sufficiently in the Old Testament (twenty times) to indicate its meaning. It refers to an unproductive, uninhabited land or has the sense of futility and nonexistence.[71] It is found once more in the Pentateuch, in the Song of Moses (Deut 32:10), where *tōhû* parallels "desert" *(midbār),* thus indicating a "desert-place." The same word "hover" *(rḥp)* that occurs in Gen 1:2 is in the following verse of the Song (32:11), where God is likened to an eagle that "hovers" over its young.[72] Since *rḥp* occurs in but one other place, there meaning "tremble,"[73] Deut 32:10–11 is probably a deliberate echo of Gen 1:2. Moses' Song is describing God's care and provision for his people during their desert sojourn, where apart from God they could not have survived (32:10–14). *Tōhû wābōhû* has the same sense in Genesis 1, characterizing the earth as uninhabitable and inhospitable to human life. Despite the threatening desert, God protects and matures Israel during its troubled times. Similarly, although the earth, as it stood, could not support terrestrial life, it was no threat to God, whose "Spirit" exercised dominion over it. God's purposes were not hindered by *tōhû*, for "he did not create it [earth] to be *tōhû* (i.e., desolate) but formed it to be inhabited" (Isa 45:18; cf. Job 26:7). Moreover, "hovering" *(rḥp)* has the nuance of motion. The movement of God's "Spirit" indicates that the creative forces for change commence with God's presence.[74]

[67] E.g., an "amorphous watery mass in which the elements of the future land and sea were commingled" (J. Skinner, *A Critical and Exegetical Commentary on Genesis*, ICC [2d ed.; Edinburgh: T & T Clark, 1910], 17).

[68] ἀόρατος καὶ ἀκατασκεύαστος.

[69] As noted by Sailhamer, "Genesis," 27.

[70] Some attempts have been made to relate it to Egyptian, but more likely is the connection of Ugaritic *thw,* meaning "desert." The combination תֹהוּ וָבֹהוּ has been associated with Ugaritic *tu-a-bi-[ú],* "to be unproductive," suggesting thereby an unproductive earth (see Tsumura, *The Earth and the Waters in Genesis 1 and 2,* 23–30).

[71] For the meaning "desert" see Deut 32:10; Job 6:18; 12:24=Ps 107:40; Isa 24:10; 34:11; 45:18–19; for "an empty place" see Job 26:7. It occurs in Isaiah, where the nations, their gods, and the idols' craftsmen are declared futile (Isa 29:21; 40:17,23; 41:29; 44:9; cf. also 1 Sam 12:21[2x]).

[72] The sense of "hover" appears for the verb in Ugaritic literature. C. H. Gordon (*UT,* 484) renders it "soar" (*1 Aqht* 32; 3 *Aqht* 20,21,31).

[73] This is in Jer 23:9, where it is *qal.* The other two uses are *piel.*

[74] "Hitherto all is static, lifeless, immobile. Motion, which is the essential element in change, originates with God's dynamic presence" (Sarna, *Genesis,* 7).

We have mentioned that Jer 4:23 has the only occasion other than 1:2, where the couplet *tōhû wābōhû* occurs. Its context is the prophet's description of Judah's demise at the hands of God's anger. Likewise, in Isa 34:11, where both terms appear (in parallel lines), the passage describes divine condemnation against Edom.[75] Jeremiah 4:23–26 clearly reflects the creation language of Genesis 1, and the prophecy has been commonly understood as a metaphorical "reversal" of creation that leads to primordial "chaos."[76] Thus Jeremiah announced that Judah would be "uncreated" as a consequence of God's judgment. Rather than a primordial "chaos," however, Jeremiah used the similar imagery of creation so as to announce that the "land" *(ʾereṣ)* of Judah will become a "desolate" place as was the "earth" *(ʾereṣ)* before its creation, that is, a land lifeless without the blessing of God. This is explicated in the following oracle (Jer 4:27–29), where the "whole land *(kol-hāʾāreṣ)* will be ruined." Similarly, Isa 34:11 describes "desolate" *(tōhû)* and "empty" *(bōhû)* Edom, which as a desert place becomes unfit for habitation and hence absent of life, except that of the desert fowl.[77] Moreover, the prophets' use of *tōhû wābōhû* does not require us to conclude that the earth in 1:2, as a first creation, is under God's judgment. Rather, Jeremiah drew on creation imagery to announce that God would dismantle the nation. Just as God made the earth habitable and alive, God had established Judah in the land alive and prosperous. But now God in his wrath would reduce Judah to barrenness by the expulsion of its people as when the earth at its inception had no light, no people, and no birds in the skies.

"Darkness" and the "deep" prevailed over the landscape. Much is made of the metaphorical significance of darkness, meaning "evil" (e.g., Isa 5:20); its imagery in the Old Testament often represents whatever jeopardizes life, and it also pertains to the realm of the dead.[78] Darkness, however, is treated as an actual entity in Genesis, not as a symbol for evil, and its existence is recognized by its naming (1:5). A common feature in ancient cosmogonies is that darkness preceded light, but in Hebrew tradition the darkness is not a primordial threat to God or a menacing evil, since God demonstrates his authority over it by naming it. Darkness is not necessarily negative since it is also associated with God (Ps 18:11[12]), and it is the Lord who made it as a part of his

[75] Similarly, תֹּהוּ is used figuratively in the context of God's judgment against the "city," symbolic for Babylon (Isa 24:10).

[76] E.g., W. McKane, *A Critical and Exegetical Commentary on Jeremiah,* ICC (Edinburgh: T & T Clark, 1986), 106. Tsumura (*The Earth and the Waters,* 36–40) argues otherwise. In our opinion the correlation between Gen 1 and Jer 4, whether or not they are type-antitype, does not necessitate that the idea of chaos is meant in Gen 1:2. The point is that Judah will experience exile, which means an expulsion from the land, leaving the land subject to the wild and thus as lifeless and unproductive as it was before God blessed Israel in the land. Here it corresponds to the lifeless "earth" at creation (1:2).

[77] Cp. EVs: "the measuring line of chaos" (NIV, REB) and "the plummet of chaos" (NRSV).

[78] E.g., Job 3:4–8; 10:21; 17:13; 1 Sam 2:9.

"good" creation: "I form the light and create darkness, I bring prosperity and create disaster" (Isa 45:7).[79] In Isaiah, creation's "light" and "darkness" are used metaphorically for "prosperity" and "disaster," indicating that he is Master over the historical fortunes of Judah. He alone has appointed Cyrus, and thereby he shows he has no rival (Isa 45:1–6).

"Over the surface of the deep" parallels "over the waters," which follows in the subsequent clause. The "deep" *(tĕhôm)* is best taken as part of the "earth" *(ʾereṣ)* and not as a distinctive entity.[80] On the second and third days these waters are eventually separated from the expanse and land masses when the waters are named "seas" (vv. 6–10). "Deep" may indicate simply "depth" (Ps 71:20) or subterranean waters (Gen 7:11; 8:2) or seas often found in parallel with "water/waters" *(yām/mayim).*[81] The "deep" (and "waters") often is portrayed as a threat to life and to the people of God.[82] Here, again, Genesis identifies the waters only for what they are, creations subject to the superintendence of God.

That the cosmos had its antecedents in primordial waters is known in Egyptian and Mesopotamian traditions as well. Babylonian *Enuma Elish* depicts the heavens and earth made from the carcass of the inert, watery Tiamat. The creator-god Atum in Egyptian cosmogony is on the primal hillock that emerges from the primordial sea. The earlier scholarly opinion that the biblical "deep" *(tĕhôm)* evidences a borrowing from Babylonian tradition where the primeval waters are personified as Tiamat has been shown wrong.[83] The Babylonian and Hebrew terms for "deep/ocean" are related to a common Semitic word, and therefore the Hebrew is not a derivative of Tiamat linguistically.[84] Furthermore, there is no place in the Old Testament where the "deep" is personified as it is with Tiamat in the Mesopotamian story. Also there is no justification for proposing a Canaanite influence in the telling of the Genesis account (see "Genesis 1–11 and Ancient Literature," p. 86). The similarity between Genesis and mythological cosmogonies lies in the prominent place that the "deep" plays. Yet the differences between them are monumental. Whereas Tiamat is a deity that rivals the creator-god Marduk, in Genesis the "deep" is not a threatening force at all, merely physical waters.[85] As for threatening waters, the Lord's battle against the waters is an important motif in the Psalms and Proph-

---

[79] The same language of 1:1–2, בָּרָא ("create") and חֹשֶׁךְ ("darkness"), occurs here.

[80] Tsumura suggests that אֶרֶץ and תְּהוֹם are a hyponymous word pair, in which the "deep" is a part of that referred to as the "earth" in v. 2 (*The Earth and the Waters,* 67–74).

[81] E.g., Pss 33:7; 104:6; Job 28:14; 38:16,30; Jonah 2:5[6]; Hab 3:10; it is substituted for "waters" at Ps 78:15 (cf. v. 20), which gives a poetic recounting of the incident at Meribah (Exod 17:6).

[82] E.g., Gen 7:11; 8:2; Exod 15:8; Amos 7:4, Jonah 2:5[6], Ps 107:26. It is also used of blessing, e.g., Gen 49:25; Deut 8:7; 33:13; Ps 78:15.

[83] See, e.g., Westermann, *Genesis 1–11,* 104–5.

[84] See Tsumura, *The Earth and the Waters,* 45–52.

[85] The poet invokes the waters to join in praising God (Ps 148:7; cf. Ps 77:17; Hab 3:10).

ets, but there is no "'battle of creation' in the true sense of the word."[86] In Genesis 1 there is no conflict motif as we find in the Baal-Yam or Baal-Mot myths. Among the later biblical writers, where the conflict theme is present, the raging waters pound their waves[87] yet are only waters circumscribed by the omnipotent rule of the Lord (Pss 33:7; 93:1–5).

The proper context for understanding the "deep" for its religious significance is the historical experiences of the Mosaic community where it confronted the waters. Yahweh, who had created the waters, employs them to achieve his salvific ends for his people. In the poetic account of Israel's deliverance, the Song of Moses declares that the "deep" drowned Pharaoh's armies at the Red Sea (Exod 15:5,8; cf. Ps 106:9; Isa 63:13). Isaiah directly linked the language of the primordial "Rahab" with God's deliverance of Israel by the drying up of the "great deep" (i.e., Red Sea, 51:9–10). In Genesis the "deep" of Noah's day assists the Lord in destroying what God himself had made (7:11; 8:2). The "deep" stands not only in the way of Israel's escape from Egypt (Exod 14:21–22) but also its entrance into Canaan (Josh 3:14–17); however, it too succumbs to its Creator. Later Ezek 26:19 echoes the primordial waters of v. 2 when the prophet announces Tyre's destruction by God, who will make it desolate, a city without habitation overwhelmed by the "deep" *(tĕhôm)*. Here the prophet ties it to the destructive forces of the waters (vv. 3–6), figurative for the nations, which will destroy this Mediterranean citadel of the Phoenician coast.

In Revelation the "new heavens and new earth" have no seawater (21:1), and the New Jerusalem experiences no night because of God's presence (21:25). By appealing to the imagery of Gen 1:2, John indicates that the eternal, blessed state will be God's completed new creation. He draws on the additional imagery of Isa 65:17 to show that the old earth and heaven have been supplanted by the new heavenly abode; the salvific work of God in the universe is declared complete.

Unlike the pagan stories, Israel knows of no chaos gods who trouble its Lord.[88] The primordial gods of pagan myths are no more than natural phenom-

---

[86] C. Kloos, *Yhwh's Combat with the Sea: A Canaanite Tradition in the Religion of Ancient Israel* (Leiden: Brill, 1986), 87. It is commonplace for scholars to attribute to Israel's poetic waters and the sea-monsters Leviathan and Rahab a Canaanite mythological background whose theology was later disregarded in Yahwistic orthodoxy. But even those who hold to this for Israel's poets deny that there ever was a cosmogonic battle myth in Israel. See Kloos, pp. 66–86, who also notes A. S. Kapelrud, "Baʿal, Schöpfung und Chaos," *UF* 11 (1979): 407–12.

[87] Pss 65:7[8]; 74:12–17; 77:11–20[12–21]; 89:9–10[10–11]; 93:3–4; 104:6–7; Isa 27:1; 51:9–10.

[88] F. M. Cross observes that creation myths include both theogonies, in which creation is achieved through sexual procreation among primal forces, and cosmogonies, where the theogonic gods ("olden gods") are defeated in warfare by young deities who afterward establish a created order and the institution of kingship ("The 'Olden Gods' in Ancient Near Eastern Creation Myth," in *Magnalia Dei, The Mighty Acts of God: Essays on the Bible and Archaeology in Memory of G. Ernest Wright* [Garden City: Doubleday, 1976], 329–38). Cross sees theogonic imagery in Gen 1:1–2 but rightly observes that in Genesis creation has "no element of cosmogonic conflict, no linkage to a cosmogony. God creates by fiat" (p. 335). Yet it prepares the way for the introduction of the Divine Warrior (Yahweh) who achieves for Israel its birth and salvation.

ena. The "Spirit *[rûaḥ]* of God was hovering" over the earth, that is, presiding over the earth and preparing it for the creative word to follow. The "Spirit" alone is moving, animated, while the elements of the lifeless earth remain static, passive, awaiting their command.

Rûaḥ may mean either "spirit" or "wind" in this passage. Traditionally it has been rendered as "Spirit," referring to the divine Spirit, but "wind" is a possible reading lexically and also fits the context of v. 2 (cf. 8:1).[89] Since the earth is described by natural phenomena, such as seawater, and "wind" corresponds well with a physical description, it follows that "wind" may be in view. If taken as wind, *ʾĕlōhîm* may be rendered as a superlative, "terrible" or "mighty,"[90] but this would leave the phrase without any religious significance. Though *ʾĕlōhîm* may occur as the superlative in the Old Testament (e.g., Gen 23:6; Jonah 3:3), its recurring use in Genesis 1 (thirty-five times) as the divine name would argue for taking it here also as "God."[91] The question concerns whether *rûaḥ* is personal, that is, God's Spirit, or an impersonal force working at God's direction. Job 33:4 is not helpful since it appears to be an allusion to 2:7, but Ps 104:30 resonates with a personal interpretation ("your Spirit," NIV).[92] Although Ps 104:30 does not refer to v. 2 specifically, rather to the six days of creation inclusively, it suggests that the psalmist affirmed the personal participation of God's Spirit in the transformation of the earth.

Yet the Mosaic community may have understood *rûaḥ* as having a double sense, "wind" as the prototype of the "Spirit" because of Israel's experience at the Red Sea, where God sent a mighty "wind" to part the waters and deliver Israel from the Egyptians (Exod 14:21; 15:10; cp. Exod 10:19; Num 11:31). Hence, for them, their God of salvation was equally at work in creation, where the "wind" of God (1:2) enveloped the mighty waters of the earth as he prepared to transform them. Also in the flood account the "wind" (*rûaḥ*) at God's direction blows across the "earth" *(ʾereṣ)* taming the floodwaters (8:1a), preparing for the return of the dry earth—creation anew. Whether it is understood as "wind" or "Spirit," the Hebrews could well appreciate the theology: God was sovereignly superintending the condition of the earth and preparing

---

[89] E.g., *Tgs. Onq.*, *Ps.-J.*; NRSV, "A wind from God swept over the face of the waters" (also NJB, NJPS).

[90] E.g., "mighty wind," NAB. The parallel expressions with עַל־פְּנֵי ("over") in vv. 2b and 2c suggest that רוּחַ אֱלֹהִים can be taken as a natural element as "darkness was *over* the face of the deep," so the "wind of God was hovering *over* the waters." However, the presence of the participle מְרַחֶפֶת ("was hovering") with רוּחַ אֱלֹהִים at v. 2c would argue against a purely natural understanding. See Brown, *Structure, Role, and Ideology*, 75.

[91] For superlative use see *IBHS* § 14.5b. D. W. Thomas contends that when אֱלֹהִים is used as a superlative in the OT, it always refers to someone or something that is brought into a relationship with God, and there is no unambiguous example in which the name is solely an "intensifying epithet" ("A Consideration of Some Unusual Ways of Expressing the Superlative in Hebrew," *VT* 3 [1953]: 209–24, esp. 215–19).

[92] The NIV at Ps 33:6 rightly renders "breath."

the way for his creative word.

This divine superintendence may be likened to an eagle "hovering" *(rāḥap)* over the earth. The same term is used of an eagle that expands its winged flight to protect its young (Deut 32:11; cf. *ʿûp*, Isa 31:5).[93] Earlier we commented on the similarity of 1:2 with the language in the Song of Moses, where the Lord is described as an "eagle" who is Israel's Protector in the wastelands of the desert (Deut 32:11–14). "By the secret efficacy of the Spirit"[94] the divine presence assures the abiding existence of the "earth," despite its impotent position and static condition, ready for the movement of God, who would make it fertile, blooming with beauty and life.

The theological significance of this was not lost on the ancient reader who recognized its polemical undertones regarding pagan cosmogonies. The poets and prophets recognized the theological implications of God's rule over the earth's primordial elements (e.g., Ps 89:9–11; Isa 27:1; 51:9–10). Whereas the hero god in the cosmogonic myths is threatened, the God of the Hebrews had no battle to rage for control and ownership of creation. He is depicted as Creator and sole "Proprietor" (e.g., Ps 24:1; Isa 66:1).[95] There is no reason to fear that deified forces, like escaped convicts, are racing around the universe playing havoc with nature and society. According to the biblical depiction of beginnings, the barren earth is made productive by the divine royal word which grants and insures productivity and life. This, theologically, speaks to any present or future threat to God's kingdom; by faith his people affirm their trust in his irrevocable rule.[96]

EXCURSUS: TRANSLATING 1:1–2

Martin Luther commented concerning 1:1, "The very simple meaning of what Moses says, therefore, is this: Everything that is, was created by God."[97] That it were only so "very simple"! If measured by the tangled web of scholarly debate, the meaning of the opening words of the Bible is anything but simple. The traditional opinion, reflected here by the Reformer, has an advantage over others by its straightforward, synchronic presentation; but we will discover that the matter is not plain. Both ancient and modern commentators disagree over the translation and sense of the very first word of the Bible, as well as almost every word of the opening two verses. One need go no further than a perusal of recent English versions to detect significant differences in the way the Bible's inaugural words have been understood.

VERSE 1. Since the issues are fundamentally syntactical, discussion must be primarily in those terms.Determining the preferred rendering of v. 1 rests with

[93] Here it is *piel;* in the *qal* stem, רָחַף has the meaning "shake" or "vibrate" at Jer 23:9.

[94] Calvin, *Comm.*, 74.

[95] Barth's term, *God with Us,* 18.

[96] Cf. von Rad, *Genesis,* 51.

[97] *LW* 1.7.

how the opening word "beginning" *(bĕrē᾽šît)* is understood in relation to the remainder of the verse. (1) One understanding results in an independent clause, as in the traditional translation: "In the beginning God created . . ." (AV, NKJV, NIV, NASB, REB, NJB). (2) The other view of *bĕrē᾽šît* makes v. 1 a temporal clause: "In the beginning *when* God created . . .," and the thought is completed in v. 2 or v. 3. The NRSV has v. 2 as the principal clause:[98]

> In the beginning when God created the heavens and the earth, [v. 1]
> the earth was a formless void and darkness covered the face of the deep, while a wind from God swept over the face of the waters [v. 2].

The NJPS shows the alternative (see also NAB), where v. 2 is parenthetical and v. 3 is the main clause of the sentence (vv. 1–3):

> "When God began to create the heaven and the earth—
> the earth being unformed and void, with darkness over the surface of the deep and a wind from God sweeping over the water—
> God said, "Let there be light."

Both alternatives to the traditional translation give a relative beginning to creation, permitting the possibility of preexisting matter, though not necessarily so, as we will see below. Support for reading v. 1 as temporal is found in the syntax of the clause,[99] the parallel language at 2:4b and 5:1b which commence with "when,"[100] and the similarity to the cosmogonic myths *Atrahasis* and *Enuma Elish,* which begin with a temporal clause.[101] *Enuma Elish* begins as follows:

---

[98] Contra RSV. The NEB also has v. 2 as the main clause, but the revision (REB) reads v. 1 as a principal statement. Early advocates of the temporal clause were the medieval Jewish commentators, Rashi (d. 1105) and Ibn Ezra (d. 1167). While Rashi took v. 3 as the main clause, Ibn Ezra differed by assigning it to v. 2. Of these Rashi's opinion, taking v. 2 as parenthetical, has had the greater following. The advantage of Ibn Ezra's rendering (as NRSV) is its simplicity of sequence, but the overwhelming difficulty is v. 2's beginning construction, which would be unlikely. Verse 2 has the order *wāw* + noun + verb: וְהָאָרֶץ הָיְתָה. The expected syntax for the principal clause is *wāw* + verb + subject: וַתְּהִי הָאָרֶץ.

[99] The absence of the definite article in בְּרֵאשִׁית (lit., "in beginning") recommends that the word has a construct relationship (dependent) with בָּרָא ("created"). "Beginning" (רֵאשִׁית) usually designates the head of a series and thus points to a relative beginning. Of the fifty-one occurrences of the noun רֵאשִׁית, it is said always to be in the construct. See P. Humbert, "Troise notes sur Genesis 1," in *Interpretationes ad Vetus Testamentum pertinentes S. Mowinckel septuagenario missae*, NTT 56 (Oslo: Forlaget land og Kirche, 1955), 85–96, cited in Westermann, *Genesis 1–11,* 95–98. The all-important exception to Humbert's analysis is Isa 46:10 (see below).

[100] Gen 2:4b–7 has the same pattern as 1:1–3 when 1:1 is understood as temporal:

Temporal heading	1:1	"In the beginning when . . ."
	2:4b	"When the LORD God made . . ."
Parenthetical	1:2	"the earth was formless and empty . . ."
	2:5–6	"and no shrub of the field had yet appeared . . ."
Main sentence	1:3	"then God said . . ."
	2:7	"then the LORD God formed . . ."

[101] See E. A. Speiser, *Genesis: A New Translation with Introduction and Commentary,* AB (Garden City: Doubleday, 1964), 12. Brown analyzes it differently: lines 1–2 and 7–8 are temporal, lines 3–6 are parenthetical, and line 9 is the main clause (*Structure, Role, and Ideology*, 67–68).

(1) When the heavens above had not been named,
(2) Firm ground below had not been called by name,
(3) Naught but primordial Apsu, their begetter,
(4) (And) Mammu-Tiamat, she who bore them all,
(5) Their waters commingling as a single body;
(6) No reed hut had been matted, no marsh land had appeared,
(7) When no gods whatever had been brought into being,
(8) Uncalled by name, their destinies undetermined—
(9) Then it was that the gods were formed within them.

Although the temporal rendering is syntactically possible, the arguments for its preference are not compelling; and the traditional rendering of a complete, independent sentence remains convincing. The traditional translation is syntactically defensible, and 2:4b and 5:1b as well as the Babylonian examples are not in fact the same as 1:1–3. Also the traditional reading has support from the ancient versions.[102] This cannot be taken as conclusive by itself since the versions may have misinterpreted the Hebrew, but it is evidence of an early interpretation of the verse. The syntactical arguments for taking v. 1 as an independent sentence are equally forceful,[103] which means that we cannot rely on the syntactical argument alone. In both 2:4b and 5:1b the temporal clause is explicitly marked by the Hebrew construction "in the day" *(bĕyôm),* which is absent in 1:1.[104] The older opinion that the opening temporal clause of the Babylonian creation myth, *Enuma Elish,* corresponds to vv. 1–3 has now been

---

[102] John 1:1 relies on the LXX, ἐν ἀρχῇ ἐποίησεν ὁ θεὸς τὸν οὐρανὸν καὶ τὴν γῆν.

[103] Some Greek transliterations and the Samaritan transliteration have the word vocalized with the definite article, indicating that at least some authorities read it as absolute (e.g., βαρησηθ and βαρησειθ; also some MSS of Aquila have the added article— ἐν τῳ κεφαλαίῳ; see J. W. Wevers, ed., *Genesis. Septuaginta* [Göttingen: Vandenhoeck & Ruprecht, 1974]). Samaritan reads *bārāšît* (see *BHS*). Again, while רֵאשִׁית ("beginning") commonly heads a temporal clause, the possibility of רֵאשִׁית indicating an absolute beginning is shown by Isa 46:10: מַגִּיד מֵרֵאשִׁית אַחֲרִית, which the NRSV renders "declaring the end from the beginning"; for רֵאשִׁית ("beginning") with its opposite אַחֲרִית ("end"), see Job 8:7; 42:12; Eccl 7:8. See W. Eichrodt ("In the Beginning: A Contribution to the Interpretation of the First Word of the Bible," in *Israel's Prophetic Heritage: Essays in Honor of James Muilenburg* [New York: Harper & Brothers, 1962], 1–10), who shows that the context of Isa 46:10 requires an absolute meaning for מֵרֵאשִׁית (contra Humbert). Some argue that the massoretic disjunctive accent *ṭipḥā'* with בְּרֵאשִׁית indicates that the massoretes read the phrase as independent (e.g., G. Hasel, "Recent Translations of Genesis 1:1: A Critical Look," *BT* 22 [1971]: 159). However, the *ṭipḥā'* is not decisive in determining the massoretic opinion since it can be shown that a disjunctive accent occurs with בְּרֵאשִׁית when the (construct) dependent relationship is certain (e.g., Jer 26:1; see, e.g., Brown, *Structure, Role, and Ideology,* 65; esp. Sailhamer, "Genesis," 22–23).

[104] Gen 2:4b (בְּיוֹם עֲשׂוֹת) and 5:1b (בְּיוֹם בְּרֹא) have the infinitive form of the verb, as opposed to the perfective form בָּרָא ("created") found in 1:1. At 1:1 we would expect the infinitive בְּרֹא to head a temporal clause as it does in 5:1b, though this too is not conclusive since the perfective verb is attested in such a dependent clause (e.g., Lev 14:46; Isa 29:1; Hos 1:2). V. Hamilton argues that the striking dissimilarity between the constructions at 1:1 and 2:4b/5:1b, if anything, should alert the reader to understand the syntax of 1:1 differently, not similarly (*The Book of Genesis Chapters 1–17,* NICOT [Grand Rapids: Eerdmans, 1990], 107).

revised.[105] Its beginning is closer to 2:4b–7 and next 1:2–3, though even there not precisely. Genesis 1:1 has no exact syntactical parallel among pagan cosmogonies.

Although we cannot rest our decision on a prior theological persuasion, it is proper to consider the tenor of the passage. Regardless of how one reads 1:1–3, there is no room in our author's cosmology for co-eternal matter with God when we consider the theology of the creation account in its totality. That ancient cosmogonies characteristically attributed the origins of the creator-god to some preexisting matter (usually primeval waters) makes the absence of such description in Genesis distinctive. Verse 1 declares that God exists outside time and space; all that exists is dependent on his independent will. We conclude that v. 1 is best taken as an absolute statement of God's creation.

VERSE 2. The question remains about how we are to understand the relationship of v. 1, as a completed sentence, to what follows in vv. 2–3. Three interpretations require our attention here: the "restitution" theory, the "title" view, and the traditional opinion.

Known popularly as the "gap" theory, the proponents of the "restitution" theory contend that v. 1 recounts an absolute beginning and describes a completed, pristine creation.[106] It differs from the traditional interpretation by understanding vv. 3–31 as describing a renewal of creation, that is, a restitution of the initial creation that became "chaos" as a consequence of a judgment of God described in v. 2. In effect, then, chap. 1 describes two creations. The verb in v. 2 is rendered "and then the earth *became* formless and empty" (italics added). Earth's elements in v. 2 are not neutral but negative, prohibiting life. Support for this is said to come from the description of the earth as chaos *(tōhû wābōhû)* in the Prophets, which entails the aftermath of divine judgment (Isa 34:11; Jer 4:23–26).[107] The judgment experienced by the universe is often attributed to Satan's rebellion and expulsion from heaven (Isa 14:9–14; Ezek 28:12–15). Thus there is an indeterminable time "gap" between vv. 1 and 2. Verses 3–31 portray the gracious intervention of God, who saves a remnant of the chaotic order.

The major obstacle to this viewpoint is the syntactical construction of v. 2, which does not introduce consecutive action but rather a disjunctive clause, distinguishing v. 2 as circumstantial.[108] While under different syntactical conditions the translation "became" is possible (e.g., Gen 3:20), it is unlikely in 1:2.[109] Moreover,

---

[105] See Westermann, *Genesis 1–11,* 96–97.

[106] G. H. Pember's *Earth's Earliest Ages* (1876) was one of the most influential works advocating this view. The "restitution" view has been popularized in this century by the notes of the *Scofield Reference Bible* (1909). See the defense by A. C. Custance, *Without Form and Void* (Brockville, Canada: Custance, 1970). For critique of this view see W. W. Fields, *Unformed and Unfilled: A Critique of the Gap Theory of Genesis 1:1, 2* (Winona Lake, Ind.: Light & Life, 1973), and Waltke, "The Creation Account in Genesis 1:1–3. Part II," *BSac* 132 (1975): 136–44.

[107] Cf. also Isa 24:1; 45:18.

[108] The word order is typically *wāw* disjunctive + nonverb (וְהָאָרֶץ) followed by the perfect form of the verb (הָיְתָה); thus, as the NIV, "Now the earth was . . ." (*IBHS* § 8.3b; 39.2.3).

[109] For sequential action וַתְּהִי הָאָרֶץ (*wāw* consecutive + verb) is customary.

there is no logical or philological necessity for interpreting the conditions of the earth described in v. 2 as the consequence of God's judgment (see 1:2 discussion).

We find that the crux in deciding between the remaining "title" and traditional views lies with how the phrase "heavens and the earth" is understood and with what weight is given to the phrase "in the beginning." The meaning of "created" *(bārā᾽),* whether or not a technical term for *creatio ex nihilo* ("creation out of nothing"), is not as decisive as has been commonly thought.

In the title view v. 1 is the summary heading of the whole account, announcing the subject matter, and 1:2–2:3 presents the details.[110] As a literary heading v. 1 stands outside the six-day scheme of creation. It tells generally of God's role as Creator and the object of his creation, namely, the well-formed and filled universe as we know it. Verse 2 details the state of the "earth" when the divine command "Let there be light" was first uttered (v. 3), but the chaotic elements of the precreated earth were under the superintendence of God's Spirit, who prepared the earth for the creative word. Verse 2 presents three circumstantial clauses that describe the "earth" at the time God first spoke "Let there be light" (v. 3).[111]

The most formidable argument for interpreting v. 1 as a summary is the phrase "the heavens and the earth," which uniformly means in Scripture the universe as a completed organization—the cosmos as we know it.[112] Verse 2 describes the earth in a negative state, a chaos of elements, which is opposed to creation (cf. Isa 34:11; Jer 4:23); therefore the well-ordered universe of v. 1 and the negative elements of the earth cannot have existed contemporaneously. If "heavens and earth" declares the existence of the well-ordered cosmos, how can it also be that the "earth" is disorganized and incomplete as portrayed in v. 2? Also "created" *(bārā᾽)* always designates a completed product; thus "created" in v. 1 summarizes the whole process described in vv. 3–31. Moreover, it does not mean *creatio ex nihilo* by itself; therefore the prologue's summary statement that God "created" the cosmos does not preclude that God used precreated matter (v. 2) in shaping the preexisting earth (vv. 3–31). Further, Scripture consistently attributes creation to the divine word (Ps 33:6,9; Heb 11:3), but no such divine command—"and God said"—introduces the description of the "earth" in v. 2. Finally, this arrangement of 1:1–3 has support from the parallel patterns in 2:4–7 and 3:1.[113]

Opponents to the title view commonly raise the question about the origins of the "darkness" and the watery chaos of the "earth" in v. 2. Some charge that the title view contradicts the traditional affirmation *creatio ex nihilo,* but this is not necessarily the case. The title view says the creation account proper starts with

---

[110] Among commentators who hold this view are H. Gunkel, S. R. Driver, Cassuto, von Rad, Westermann, and Hamilton. Also see the defense by Waltke, "The Creation Account in Genesis 1:1–3. Part III," 216–28.

[111] Some who hold this interpretation propose that v. 1 was a late scribal addition, but it is not a necessary consequence of this view. Verse 1 is best attributed to the original creation source, serving as a theological proclamation that the universe and all that is in it owes its origins to the will of an autonomous Creator.

[112] E.g., Gen 2:1,4; 14:19,22; Pss 8:6[7]; 121:2. For the following arguments see Waltke, "The Creation Account in Genesis 1:1–3. Part III," 216–28.

the existence of the "earth" in its uninhabitable state (v. 2) and that the narrative is silent about its origins. Earth's chaotic state is viewed as a "mystery."[114] As is the case with so much of the early chapters, Genesis does not speak on all matters pertaining to the subject. It is an unnecessary leap to conclude that the elements in v. 2 are autonomous, co-eternal with God and upon which he was in some way dependent for creation.[115] If anything, v. 2 shows that the "Spirit of God" reigns over the earth's components and it is they that are dependent upon God.[116] The idea of *creatio ex nihilo* is a proper theological inference derived from the whole fabric of the chapter.[117]

Although the title interpretation is defensible, more favorable is the traditional interpretation.[118] The title view fails to give sufficient weight to the initial

---

[113] Summary Heading

1:1 "In the beginning God created the heavens and the earth."
2:4 "This is the account of the heavens and the earth . . ."
(this functions also as the summary heading for 3:1)

Circumstantial Description (*wāw* disjunctive + noun + verb)

1:2 "Now the earth was without form and void . . ."
2:5–6 "Now no shrub of the field had yet appeared . . ."
3:1a "Now the serpent was more crafty . . ."

Main Clause (*wāw* consecutive + verb)

1:3 "Then God said . . ."
2:7 "Then the LORD God formed man . . ."
3:1b "Then he said . . ."

[114] "But what about the uncreated or unformed state, the darkness and the deep of Genesis 1:2? Here a great mystery is encountered, for the Bible never says that God brought these into existence by his word. . . . The biblicist faces a dilemma when considering the origins of those things which are contrary to God. A good God characterized by light could not, in consistency with His nature, create evil, disorder, and darkness. On the other hand, it cannot be eternally outside of Him for that would limit His sovereignty. The Bible resolves the problem not by explaining its origin but by assuring man that it was under the dominion of the Spirit of God" (Waltke, "The Creation Account of Gen 1:1–3. Part IV," 338–39).

[115] "Darkness" and watery chaos came from God as Creator, not from co-eternal matter, e.g., Isa 44:24; Jer 10:11–13; Ps 90:2; Col 1:17 (so Waltke, "The Literary Genre of Genesis, Chapter One," 4).

[116] "The first two verses simply do not reveal whether God created the list of 'elements' in 1:2, and they certainly do not claim a malevolent, autonomous chaos. Furthermore, a circumstantial beginning to cosmogony need not imply a contingent deity" (Brown, *Structure, Role, and Ideology,* 72).

[117] Elsewhere the Scriptures suggest *creatio ex nihilo* (e.g., Prov 8:22–26; John 1:1–3; Heb 11:3). The first explicit statement (early first century B.C.) of *creatio ex nihilo* is *2 Macc* 7:28: "I beg you, my child, to look at the heaven and earth and see everything that is in them, and recognize that God did not make them out of things that existed" (NRSV). Contrast the Hellenistic Jewish work *Wis* 11:17 from the same period: "For your all-powerful hand which created the world out of formless matter . . ." (NRSV).

[118] Among commentators who hold to the traditional view are the Reformers Luther and Calvin, C. F. Keil, F. Delitzsch, G. C. Aalders, H. Leupold, D. Kidner, and more recently Wenham and Sarna. For a defense of the traditional view see especially Hasel, "Recent Translations of Genesis 1:1," and M. F. Rooker, "Genesis 1:1–3: Creation or Re-Creation?" *BSac* 149 (1992): 316–23 (Part 1) and 411–27 (Part 2).

word of the account, "In the beginning." This brief description of the setting for creation in Genesis 1 appears to be absolute with respect to the heavens and the earth.[119] Since the "earth" commands the attention of the whole report in vv. 3–31, are we to believe that the account gives no word on the origins of its focal topic when it is the very subject of *origins* that drives the narrative? The opening two Hebrew words *br'šyt br'* ("in the beginning [he] created") have the same consonants and highlight the significance of "beginning" for understanding the passage. As a theological conception the startling absence of precreated matter distinguishes Israelite cosmogony from its rivals in the pagan Near East. The absolute sense of "beginning," the very first word of the Bible, awakens the reader to the exceptional Creator-God of Israel's faith.

Moreover, the simpler sentence structure proposed by the traditional view is consistent with what is found in 1:1–2:3.[120] Also the narrative describes a progression in creation. The creation of an incomplete "earth" in vv. 1–2 fits appropriately with the subsequent telling in days 1–6 where incomplete stages, such as the division of the waters, are apparent. The traditional view also has the advantage of being the oldest known since it is reflected in the LXX.

The primary obstacle to the traditional view is the phrase "the heavens and the earth" (v. 1). Again, this expression is taken as a merism, referring to the entire created order as a finished product, thus, "In the beginning God created the *cosmos*" (*Wis* 11:7). Although the phrase "heavens and earth" surely points to a finished universe where it is found elsewhere in the Old Testament, we cannot disregard the fundamental difference between those passages and the context presented in Genesis 1 before us, namely, that the expression may be used uniquely here since it concerns the exceptional event of creation itself. To insist on its meaning as a finished universe is to enslave the expression to its uses elsewhere and ignore the contextual requirements of Genesis 1. "Heavens and earth" here indicates the totality of the universe, not foremostly an organized, completed universe.[121] The term "earth" *('ereṣ)* in v. 1 used in concert with "heaven," thereby indicating the whole universe, distinguishes its meaning from "earth" *('ereṣ)* in v. 2, where it has its typical sense of terrestrial earth.[122] This recommends that the phrase "the heavens and the earth" differs from its common meaning found elsewhere.

---

[119] So Hasel ("Recent Translations of Genesis 1:1," 165): "It rather appears that the author of Gen. 1 wanted to convey more than to give in vs. 1 merely an introductory summary which expresses as Westermann and others hold that 'God is creator of heaven and earth.' If the writer of Gen. 1 had wanted to say merely this he would certainly not have needed to begin his sentence with *bᵉrē'šîṯ.*"

[120] The complex construction at 2:4–7 does not stand up as an exact parallel since 2:4 with its infinitival construction differs from 1:1. Hasel argues that 1:2 and 2:5 do not correspond as Westermann (and others) contend; 2:4 has the "not yet" formula, expressed negatively, while 1:2 states the condition of the earth positively ("Recent Translations of Genesis 1:1," 165). He does not include comment on 3:1, which also is stated positively.

[121] So Wenham, *Genesis 1–15,* 15.

[122] Some contend that the title view itself suffers from an inconsistency by proposing that God created the "earth" in v. 1 yet it already existed according to its understanding of v. 2. This misunderstands the title view, which sees no cause-effect relationship between vv. 1–2. For the proponents of the title view, they would argue indeed that the "earth" in vv. 1–2 have different meanings and are not synchronic—the former defined by the merism and the latter the preexistent chaos.

Moreover, proponents of the title view contend that v. 2 describes a chaotic earth whose elements oppose creation and are not harmonious with God's good creation (cf. Isa 45:18; Rev 21:1,25).[123] But this expects more of the passage than it says.[124] The description of the "earth" is best seen as neutral, if not positive; for elsewhere we learn that God is the Creator of "darkness" (Isa 45:7), and we recognize also that darkness ("evening") was a part of the created order the Lord named and deemed "good." As we showed at v. 2, the distinctive couplet *tōhû wābōhû* ("formless and empty") portrays an earth that is a sterile wasteland awaiting the creative word of God to make it habitable for human life. This is the point of the prophet's appeal to creation; "he did not create it [the land] to be empty *[tōhû]*" (Isa 45:18).[125] In his oracle Isaiah anticipated that the uninhabited Israel will once again know the return of the exilic captives, and, spiritually, the Gentiles who submit to the God of Israel will join Israel in its salvation (Isa 45:14–25). The passage speaks to the purposes of God, who as Creator will achieve his salvific ends for all peoples.[126] This is borne out by the term parallel to *tōhû* in v. 18, which shows purpose, "but formed it [the land] to be inhabited." Thus the prophet asserted that the Lord did not create the earth to remain *tōhû* but rather to become a residence for man. Finally, the three parallel clauses in v. 2's description of the "earth" include the "Spirit of God," who prepares the earth for the creative commands to follow. This suggests that the earth's elements are not portraying a negative picture but rather a neutral, sterile landscape created by God and subject to his protection.

By way of summary, then, vv. 1–2 describe the absolute beginnings, the initial stage in the creation of the "earth" that is brought to completion during the six days (vv. 3–31), climaxing in the consecration of the seventh day (2:1–3). Earth's beginning, we may surmise from the implications of the passage, was created *ex nihilo.* Since v. 1 clearly indicates that God created everything that we know as the universe, the "earth" (v. 2) had its origins ultimately in God.[127] Moreover, in the cre-

---

[123] E.g., Westermann comments on "darkness" in v. 2: "The sentence is not describing anything objective but presenting an aspect of the situation which is the opposite of creation. Darkness is not to be understood as a phenomenon of nature but rather as something sinister" (*Genesis 1–11,* 104). See also Waltke, "The Creation Account in Genesis 1:1–3. Part III," 220–21. Hamilton, though adhering to the title view, rightly questions the cogency of this line of argument: "Although Gen. 1 states that God created light (v. 3), it does not say that he created darkness. May we assume from this that darkness, unlike light, is not a part of God's creation, but is independent of it? Is day superior to night? Can we place spiritual meanings on physical phenomena?" (*Genesis 1–17,* 109).

[124] See E. J. Young, "The Interpretation of Genesis 1:2," *WTJ* 23 (1960–61): 151–78, esp. 157, 170, 171 n. 33; also Rooker, "Genesis 1:1–3 Part Two," 420–22.

[125] The NRSV renders it conventionally, "He did not create it a chaos," whereas the NIV has translated its contextual sense of purpose "to be empty."

[126] "Isaiah does not deny that the earth was once a *tohu;* his point is that the Lord did not create the earth to be a *tohu,* for an earth of *tohu* is one that cannot be inhabited, and has not fulfilled the purpose for which it was created" (Young, *The Book of Isaiah,* 3 vols. [Grand Rapids: Eerdmans, 1972], 3.211).

[127] Thus Young can say, "There is no explicit statement of the creation of the primeval material from which the universe we know was formed" (p. 143), yet he can conclude "Verse two describes the earth as it came from the hands of the Creator and as it existed at the time when God commanded the light to shine forth" ("The Relationship of the First Verse of Genesis One to Verses Two and Three," *WTJ* 21 [1959]: 146).

ation account the elements of v. 2 are not a hindrance or aid to God's creation of other elements *ex nihilo,* such as "light" (v. 3), the "expanse" (v. 6), and the celestial "lights" (v. 14).[128] The notion of *creatio ex nihilo* furthermore is reasonably derived from the passage when we consider the polemical undertones of chap. 1, which distances Israel's view of cosmogony from the ancient opinion that there once existed primordial forces that were the source of the creator-god. In biblical religion God has no antecedents, no companions, and no antagonists. As in the case with the subsequent creative events (vv. 3–31), the origin of the "earth" in vv. 1–2 can be attributed to divine fiat that is best reckoned with the first day.[129]

2. Six Days of Creation (1:3–31)

The six days of creation (vv. 3–31) are told from the perspective of one who is standing on the earth's surface observing the universe with the naked eye.[130] The account is geocentric in its telling. The arrangement of the six-day creation is regularly demarcated by the recurring phrase "there was evening and there was morning." The six sections routinely end with the same closure that numbers the creative day ("first day," etc.). Among the six days are eight creative acts, each introduced by the rubric "And God said." As noted earlier, the third and sixth days can boast of two creative acts, thus distinguishing their importance for the creation week. Also the fourth day has special significance since it contains the second longest description, next to day six. As we will see, the fourth day marks the beginning of movement, namely, the heavenly bodies. The pronouncement of "blessing," however, does not occur until the fifth day, when procreation is first assured for animate life. Yet it is in the sixth day that we reach the triumphant act of creation with mankind made in the "image of God" *(imago Dei).*

A parallel arrangement is found for the six days: the opening three days (1:3–13) change the barren earth (1:2) into a land that produces vegetation (1:11–13), and the final three days inundate the empty terrain with life above and below (1:14–31). There is a correspondence between the first group of three and the second group so as to form three coordinated pairs. Days one and four regard light and the light bearers; days two and five speak of the skies and waters that are filled with fowl and fish; and the third couple, days three and six, concern the productivity of the land that sprouts its flora for the sustenance of the created beast and human.

---

[128] See Sasson, "Time . . . to Begin," 189–90.

[129] Cf. *2 Esdr* 6:38: "I said, 'O Lord, you spoke at the beginning of creation, and said on the first day, "Let heaven and earth be made," and your word accomplished the work' " (NRSV). Also *b. Ḥag.* 12a, "Ten things were created on the first day . . ." (i.e., elements of 1:1–3).

[130] The most obvious evidence of this is the description of the earth's luminaries, which are viewed as light bearers for the earth (1:15–16).

(1) First Day of Creation (1:3–5)

[3]And God said, "Let there be light," and there was light. [4]God saw that the light was good, and he separated the light from the darkness. [5]God called the light "day," and the darkness he called "night." And there was evening, and there was morning—the first day.

1:3 The first step in remedying the dark earth was God's command to bring forth light. "The divine word shatters the primal cosmic silence and signals the birth of a new cosmic order."[131] This first of three separations effectively diminishes the enveloping darkness but leaves a remnant each "evening" of earth's primal darkness. G. von Rad suggests that this serves as a reminder of what the earth once was before the life-giving word of God; but each morning's new light, which again conquers our anxious nights, represents God's first creation.[132] The incessant "mornings" are evidence of God's loving-kindness and faithfulness (e.g., Gen 8:22; Ps 30:5; Lam 3:23).

The Hebrew community understood that God's creative word was the same authoritative word by which he brought about the affairs of human history and the nations. Just as the word created the universe, the word created the community of Israel. God created Israel as a nation among new environs, as God had called light into existence and curbed darkness. In the wilderness Israel enjoyed the cloud by day and the pillar of fire for "light" during its sojourn (Exod 13:21), and the tabernacle *menorah* with its perpetual light testified to the guidance of God's word and way for Israel (Exod 25:37; Lev 24:2). A derived authority of this creative word was extended to his spokesmen, the prophets, who declared the future by "thus says the LORD." Moses was the archetype for the prophet in the unfolding history of Israel (Deut 18:15–18). Because Moses spoke the word of God, the law of Moses became the creative and authoritative agent for the life of the community. He spoke with God "face to face," and the radiant glory of the Lord radiated from Moses' face (Exod 33:11; 34:29–35; cf. 2 Cor 3:7–18).

The source of creation's first "light" is not specifically stated. Since it is not tied to a luminating body such as the sun (vv. 15–16), the text implies that the "light" has its source in God himself (see 1:14 discussion). This is the thought of the poet who depicts the Creator wrapped in light as a garment (Ps 104:2) and the light witnessed by the prophet at the epiphany of the Lord (Hab 3:3b–4). The prophets and apocalyptists attributed to the coming "day of the LORD" terrestrial and cosmic transformations when the eschatological light will have its source in the Lord, not in the sun or moon.[133] Like the luminous cloud of God, witnessed by Israel in the wilderness and in the tabernacle (cf. Exod

[131] Sarna, *Genesis,* 7.

[132] von Rad, *Genesis,* 52–53.

[133] E.g., Isa 60:19–20; Joel 2:30–31 [3:3–4]; Zech 14:7; Rev 22:5. See H. G. May, "The Creation of Light in Genesis 1:3–5," *JBL* 58 (1939): 203–11.

24:15–18 w/40:38), this primal light indicated the divine presence.

This "light" on the first day then is indicative of the presence of God both at creation and among his people Israel, a light that both reveals and conceals the presence of God. The light at creation was the first word, the word that is indistinct from God's personal presence, and the light among his people is a revelation given by means of another intermediary, namely, Moses. Yet in contrast to the incompleteness of Moses, now the "true Light" has come who is that very same first "Word," not distinct from God, and who therefore alone can perfectly explain him (John 1:9–18).

The apostle Paul developed the theological significance of the creative light in 2 Cor 4:1–6, where he alluded to Gen 1:3. The New Testament interprets this light as the gospel of Christ. Paul paralleled God's creation of light that shines "out of darkness" (4:6) and the light that has revealed the glory of God in human hearts. This glory is in the "face of Christ," an expression that draws on the prototype of Moses (2 Cor 3:7–18). It also may allude to Paul's own Damascus experience (Acts 9:3) and perhaps the incident at the mount of transfiguration, where Jesus' face and clothing shone (Matt 17:2).

The intertwining of creation's light and the gospel with the motif of Moses' role is developed in John's Gospel (John 1:1–18), but there John gave prominence to the creative "Word." This Word is "life" and the "light of men" that shines to dispel the darkness of sin (1:4–5).[134] The role of Moses at the tabernacle, where the luminous glory of God's presence was manifested among his people, is contrasted at 1:14, where the Word has tabernacled among men and alone reveals the glory of God (the contrast between the Mosaic tradition and the new revelation in Jesus is made explicit in 1:17–18).

1:4 The divine evaluation that the light was "good" *(tôb)* indicates that God is Judge, as well as Landlord, who evaluates the consequences of his creative word (1:10,12,18,21,25,31). The meaning of *tôb* is quite fluid in the Old Testament as well as in Genesis, indicating for example that which is happy, beneficial, aesthetically beautiful, morally righteous, preferable, of superior quality, or of ultimate value.[135] Here "light" is declared "good" because it accomplishes its purpose of dispelling the "darkness" that had characterized the earth (v. 2). The division of light and darkness here is the first of three separations (1:6,9) that prepare the earth for life's possibilities.

There is no place in Hebrew thought for material being evil in itself. Whereas pagan cosmogonies depicted the primal matter as threatening, v. 31

---

[134] "The Prologue claims no more than the rest of the gospel, but sets first in a cosmological aspect what later will appear in a soteriological. The background of John's thought is here at its maximum width. Life and light are essential elements in the Old Testament creation narrative. . . . Old Testament teaching is summed up in Ps 36:10 [Eng 36:9] . . . a verse which has probably influenced John" (C. K. Barrett, *The Gospel according to St. John* [London: SPCK, 1955], 131).

[135] A. Bowling, "טוֹב (*tôb*)," *TWOT* 1.345–46.

confirms that all of God's created order is "very good." An ascetic lifestyle predicated upon the notion of an evil body or material world is inconsistent with the Old Testament's affirmation of the goodness of God's world, its bounty, and the joy it brings the heart (e.g., Ps 104:15; Eccl 3:12–13; Jer 31:10–14). It is thus an insult to the "Creator of heaven and earth" (Gen 14:19,22). Gnosticism taught that the material world was inherently evil.[136] But Paul opposed such heterodoxy at Ephesus by appealing to God's "good" creation as evidence that all foods were lawful (1 Tim 4:4; also Rom 14:14). Christian tradition recognizes that the material world is distorted by the aftermath of human sin, but it also affirms that it was not always so; the "earth" remains the salvific object of God's desires, and for the Christian it is subject to the eschatological dominion of the "new creation" entered by faith.

Also "good" as a double entendre indicates that God as Judge of the universe distinguishes between what is morally "good" and morally evil (e.g., the tree of "good and evil," 2:17; 3:5). There is in the biblical understanding of the universe an inherent moral factor that cannot be divorced from the proper order of things. The Lord revealed his moral expectations through the Sinaitic covenant. By compliance to divine norm, the Israelites prospered in personal and community life. To do otherwise meant death for the community. The Pentateuch, especially Deuteronomy, makes much of the "good land" the Lord has designated for Israel (e.g., Exod 3:8; Num 14:7; Deut 1:25,35; 4:22; 6:18; 8:7). Although the land is described as "good" in the sense of pleasant and beneficial, its continued fruition for Israel was dependent on their moral righteousness (Deut 11:17). Both the creative word and the covenant-forming word establish the norm for right response and behavior.

1:5 God showed his superiority over both the light and the darkness by naming them "day" and "night." The act of naming is an important feature in the creation account, indicating the existence ("being") of the element named and also God's authority over his creation. This divine prerogative of "naming" is extended to the first man, who names the animals and his companion "woman" (2:19,23; 3:20).

The description of each creative day regularly concludes with the refrain "there was evening, and there was morning." There is evidence that a day could be reckoned as beginning with the evening (Ps 55:17), or with the morning (e.g., Gen 19:33–34).[137] It may be that the sequence of "evening" fol-

[136] This Gnostic form of dualism was later championed by the third-century Manichaeans, who postulated that the world and man were created by evil powers that had entrapped the principle of Light. See W. A. Hoffecker, "Manichaeism," in *Evangelical Dictionary of Theology,* ed. W. A. Elwell (Grand Rapids: Baker, 1984), 683.

[137] Cassuto explains that the first "day" began with the creation of "light," which was followed by night—thus "there was evening"; and the appearance of the light again would explain the subsequent description "there was morning," constituting "one day" completed and the second day underway (*Genesis,* 28–29).

lowed by "morning" is only a formal pattern that mimicked the initial interchange of "darkness" followed by the appearance of "light" in vv. 2–3. If so, the refrain "evening" and "morning" is rhetorical, establishing the literary scheme of the creation week by distinguishing six units or "days."

The analogy between the creation week and the Hebrew work week is specifically drawn in the Fourth Commandment (Exod 20:10–11). By this the Hebrews tied their sacred calendar to the foundations of creation itself (Exod 23:12). By Israel's observance of the Sabbath, the people reexpressed that first harmony in God's "good" creation. This affirmed that the God of their community life and historic redemption was one and the same as the Creator of the universe and thus possessed universal sovereignty (see 2:1–3).

Each of the seven days is numbered and is indefinite, according to Hebrew idiom (lit., "a second day," "a third day," etc.).[138] The meaning of the creation "day" *(yôm)* has been variously interpreted.[139] There is much in the Bible regarding creation, but little is found regarding creation's "six days" (Exod 20:11; 31:17; Deut 5:12; cf. John 5:16–18; Heb 4:4). This contrasts with a greater fascination for the days on the part of both early interpreters (e.g., *Jub.* 2:1–33; 2 *Enoch* 28:1–33:2) and also moderns.

Early Jewish and Christian interpreters were troubled that it took God seven days to create the world, whereas modern interpreters are puzzled by the brevity of creation in light of geology's testimony to the age of the earth. The literal reading of "one day" (1:5) and "in the day" (2:4) suggested instantaneous creation to early interpreters, while the six days indicated progression. This tension was resolved by allegorists and literalists along different lines. Allegorists interpreted creation as simultaneous and the six days as metaphorical for perfection and order, not actual intervals of time and thus merely instructional for the human reader. Literal interpretations understood the creation days as literal days; all was created on the first day in terms of basic substance, and the following days gave form, or all was an initial conglomerate whose elements progressively were sorted out. For Luther the first day was the creation of the "crude and formless masses" that were sequentially ordered.[140] Calvin attributed the six literal days to God's accommodation to human understanding.[141]

The creation narrative sends ambiguous signals since on the one hand the

---

[138] According to *IBHS* § 15.2.1a, "the first day" is an appropriate translation for יוֹם אֶחָד, although the cardinal number "one" is substituted for the ordinal "first," a grammatical feature that is well attested and has no special significance (e.g., 2:11). G. L. Archer, Jr. suggests that the lack of a definite article means the numbered days "are well adapted to a sequential pattern, rather than to strictly delimited units of time" (*Encyclopedia of Bible Difficulties* [Grand Rapids: Zondervan, 1982], 61).

[139] See J. P. Lewis, "The Days of Creation: An Historical Survey of Interpretation," *JETS* 32 (1989): 433–55.

[140] *LW* 1.6.

[141] Calvin, *Comm.*, 78.

refrain "evening and morning" suggests a normal solar day, yet the sun was not created until the fourth day. Although understanding "day" as solar has the advantage of its simplicity, there are many indications that "day" in its customary sense may not be intended. The most obvious indication is the sun's absence for the first three "days." That "day" might not have its normal meaning here is not surprising since other Hebrew terms, such as "heaven" and "earth," also have varying meanings in the narrative (e.g., vv. 1,8). *Yôm* is a designation for the "daylight" of the first creative day, not a reference to a full solar day (v. 5), and it is used as a temporal expression for the *entire* creative period of six days in the *tôlĕdôt* section that follows, "in the *day* they were created" (2:4a; NIV "when").[142]

If we keep in mind the colloquial use of the language, "day" cannot have its common meaning before the sun is created. The very expression "evening and morning" demands the planetary arrangement of our solar system that does not come into existence until the fourth day.[143] On the other hand, "evening and morning" in a literal sense had figurative meaning for the Hebrew reader in Psalm 90, also attributed to Moses. God's "day" *(yôm)* is as a thousand years, but human life is like daylight *(yôm)* that passes by or as a nightwatch, and youth gives way to old age like "evening" overtakes "morning" (90:4–6). Also the seventh day does not have the concluding refrain "evening and morning," which suggests its continuation for some period and thus its nonliteral nature. Theological significance is attached to this feature by the writer to the Hebrews (2:1–3). As the climactic seventh day of the six-day series, it implies that all six days are nonliteral. The weight of the arguments favors a nonliteral "day," but definitive answers to the meaning of "day" and the duration of creation remain elusive.

(2) Second Day of Creation (1:6–8)

[6]And God said, "Let there be an expanse between the waters to separate water from water." [7]So God made the expanse and separated the water under the expanse from the water above it. And it was so. [8]God called the expanse "sky." And there was evening, and there was morning—the second day.

---

[142] Some argue that only יוֹם ("day") without a numerical qualifier is used figuratively in the OT. When "day" occurs in the singular, with a number, or in a numbered series, it always means either "solar day" or "daylight," never an undefined period of time. See T. Fretheim, "Were the Days of Creation Twenty-four Hours Long? Yes," in *The Genesis Debate,* ed. R. Youngblood (Nashville: Thomas Nelson, 1986), 12–35. Yet it is begging the question to argue on this basis since it assumes that the author could not use a numbered series to describe nonliteral days sequentially.

[143] Alternatively, some commentators argue that the sun, moon, and stars were created on the first day. The "light" of v. 3 consisted of diffused light from the sun and the planetary bodies that were hidden until the fourth day, which accounts for the "evening" and "morning" on days one through three (see 1:14–18). But this would mean that the fourth day is not a day of creation but a day of revelation of the planetary bodies, which does not fit the terminology of vv. 14,16—"Let there be lights" and "God made two great lights" (see more at 1:14).

1:6–7 The second separation of creation is the division in the waters. God formed an "expanse" to create a boundary, giving structure to the upper and lower waters (1:6–7). The "expanse" is the atmosphere that distinguishes the surface waters of the earth (i.e., "the waters below") from the atmospheric waters or clouds (i.e., "the waters above"). The Hebrew term *rāqîaʿ* ("expanse") may be used for something that is beaten out or spread out like a covering (e.g., Job 37:18; Ezek 1:22–26; 10:1). The stars are depicted as the brightness of the *rāqîaʿ*(Dan 12:3). The atmosphere then is depicted as a canopy or dome spread out over the earth.[144] There is no indication, however, that the author conceived of it as a solid mass, a "firmament" (AV) that supported a body of waters above it.[145] The "expanse" describes both the place in which the luminaries were set (vv. 14–15,17) and the sky where the birds are observed (v. 20). Thus Genesis' description of the "expanse" is phenomenological—to the observer on earth, the sun and stars appear to sit in the skies while at the same time birds glide through the atmosphere, piercing the skies.[146] In the Old Testament elsewhere there is evidence that the Hebrews understood that clouds produced rain and thus, from a phenomenological perspective, "water" can be described as belonging to the upper atmosphere.[147]

1:8 For the third time God named his creation; here the expanse is termed *šāmayim,* "sky," the same word rendered "heavens" in v. 1. The "expanse" is considered part of the "heavens," and the two occur together in the description "the expanse of the sky" (1:15,17,20). The "heavens" are the skies visible to the human eye, whereas God's abode is the heavens above, where his court convenes but cannot be seen.

The theological significance of God's creation of the skies is the clarification that God alone rules the powers of the heavens.[148] Divine rule of the skies was particularly important for Sumerian religion, which gave prominent place to the heavens in its pantheon of gods (cf. 1:14). It was Anu, the sky god, and Enlil, god of the atmosphere, who established and deposed the kings of the Sumerian city-states.[149] Baal in the Ugaritic pantheon is identified as the "Rider of the Clouds." He was the god of storm and rain (cf. 1 Kgs 18), but

---

[144] Cf. "dome" (NRSV, NAB, GNB) or "vault" (REB, NJB).

[145] The English term is derived from the Vg's *firmamentum.* Job 37:18, which describes skies without rain as a "bronze" expanse (cf. Deut 28:23), is figurative and does not support the common contention that the "expanse" was considered a bronze dome by the Hebrews.

[146] As B. Ramm explains, the Bible's "language about astronomy, botany, zoology, and geology is restricted to the vocabulary of popular observation. What can be seen through microscope or telescope is not commented on. Phenomenal language is true because all it claims is to be descriptive" (*Protestant Biblical Interpretation,* 3d ed. [Grand Rapids: Baker, 1970], 210).

[147] E.g., Deut 28:12; Judg 5:4; 1 Kgs 18:44–45; Eccl 11:3; Isa 5:6.

[148] See Barth, *God with Us,* 16–17.

[149] W. von Soden, *The Ancient Orient: An Introduction to the Study of the Ancient Near East,* trans. D. G. Schley (Grand Rapids: Eerdmans, 1994), 176.

Israel's faith declares that Yahweh is the source of heaven's powers (Ps 68:4). The passage therefore asserts that the heavens and their celestial inhabitants are merely instruments to serve God and his earthly creatures; they are not autonomous authorities.

(3) Third Day of Creation (1:9–13)

[9]And God said, "Let the water under the sky be gathered to one place, and let dry ground appear." And it was so. [10]God called the dry ground "land," and the gathered waters he called "seas." And God saw that it was good.

[11]Then God said, "Let the land produce vegetation: seed-bearing plants and trees on the land that bear fruit with seed in it, according to their various kinds." And it was so. [12]The land produced vegetation: plants bearing seed according to their kinds and trees bearing fruit with seed in it according to their kinds. And God saw that it was good. [13]And there was evening, and there was morning—the third day.

1:9–10 The third day concerns the surface of the earth: the waters are gathered into seas, thereby distinguishing the land masses (1:9–10), and the earth yields green vegetation (1:11–13). God's approval ("it was good") for the work of the second day was delayed until the third, when the final separation of the waters was achieved (1:10). This finishes the three "separations" of days one through three, which together differentiate the spheres of time and space where life exists.[150] The consequence of the three days is the productivity of the earth that yields its vegetation.

River systems were essential for the stability of the regions of the ancient Near East. Seasonal rains would reach flood stage, and then their departure would leave the land with drought and sometimes famine. Although the Nile and the Tigris-Euphrates river systems provided a more stable environment than Canaan, which was dependent solely on rainfall for its agricultural needs,[151] their seasonal inundations also could be devastating if too great. God's gathering and appointment of the waters show that they too are under his dominion. The seas are not independent forces to be feared and worshiped but creations that respond to the direct commands of God. He exerted authority as he named the dry ground "land" and the waters "seas," assigning them their place and function (1:10).

---

[150] The first separation concerns time (day and night), and the second and third are categories of vertical and horizontal space (expanse and land; see Westermann, *Genesis 1–11,* 119).

[151] The variation in climate alternates between a rainy season in the fall and winter months and a dry summer season. The rains commence in the autumn and are heaviest during December to March; the "latter rains" occur in April and May. Vegetation appears in early autumn, but after May the land suffers drought and the land dies. During the peak of the rainy season in December the rain comes in cloudbursts as opposed to steady rains. These rains cannot be absorbed, and they pool, causing flooding among the parched wadis.

1:11–13 Unlike the first two days of creation, the third day includes a second act of creation. After the appearance of the land masses, God creates vegetation upon the land. This is the climax of the first grouping of days, where for the first time the earth becomes productive. The presence of vegetation prepares the way for the life systems to follow by providing the diet for animal and human life (1:29–30). The arrangement of the six days differentiates between those creatures that have movement (even the sun and moon appear to move), which are created on days four through six, and those elements of creation that do not move, such as vegetation, which were created on days one through three. Vegetation may not have been considered "alive" in the way moderns think of it, since unlike animal or human life the term "living creature" is not used of it (cp. 1:20–21,24; 2:7).

Also for the first time God's creative decree is indirect (also 1:20,24). The land is commanded to produce vegetation (1:11). There is no hint of the pagan notion of Mother Earth. The land by itself, of course, does not produce vegetation; rather God enables the land to do so by his creative word. Whereas the ancients believed that vegetation and all reproducing processes were dependent upon the procreation of the gods, the Genesis account attributes vegetation to the inanimate soil. The sensual practices involved in fertility worship reflect the pagan misconception of life's origins and renewal. Procreation is the gift of God, deemed a divine "blessing" (1:22,28) that he graciously enables his creatures to enjoy (e.g., Gen 12:2; 22:17; 26:3–4; Deut 28:4; Ps 127:3).

The vegetation is of two kinds, expressed in general categories: (1) plants producing seed and (2) fruit trees whose fruit possess seeds. Here is the first occurrence of the term "seed" *(zeraʿ),* which takes on all-important thematic-theological significance in Genesis (e.g., 3:15; 9:9; 12:7). It most often has the metaphorical meaning "offspring" and speaks of the children of an individual or family (e.g., 4:25).[152] The motif of "seed" as family is joined by the recurring rubric *tôlĕdôt* ("generations") and points toward the elective promises of God for all Israel through Abraham's "seed" (e.g., 12:7; 15:5; 22:17–18). Here it is enough to observe that the "seed" of plants and fruit trees is inextricably associated with its "parent," an assumption that is consequential for understanding the outworking of God's covenant blessing for the appointed lineage.[153]

The vegetation, like the waters, is given prescribed boundaries: they reproduce "according to their various kinds." "Kind" *(min)* is used for broad categories of animals, birds, and fish (e.g., 1:21,24–25; 6:20; 7:14). Any attempt to correlate "kind" with a modern term, such as "species," is unwarranted,

---

[152] It is also used for birds (7:3). For its literal sense see 1:11–12,29; 47:19,23–24.

[153] T. D. Alexander, "Genealogies, Seed and the Compositional Unity of Genesis," *TynBul* 4 (1993): 260.

though the awareness of distinctive "kinds" is closer to a "scientific" description than is found in pagan cosmogonies.[154] Just as "separations" are integral to creation, so are distinctions among living beings as indicated by their "kinds." Creation and procreation according to "kind" indicates that God has established parameters for creation. But the term is never used of humanity, showing that we are a unique order of creation. Furthermore, ethnic distinctions are incidental to the commonality of the human family.

(4) Fourth Day of Creation (1:14–19)

[14]And God said, "Let there be lights in the expanse of the sky to separate the day from the night, and let them serve as signs to mark seasons and days and years, [15]and let them be lights in the expanse of the sky to give light on the earth." And it was so. [16]God made two great lights—the greater light to govern the day and the lesser light to govern the night. He also made the stars. [17]God set them in the expanse of the sky to give light on the earth, [18]to govern the day and the night, and to separate light from darkness. And God saw that it was good. [19]And there was evening, and there was morning—the fourth day.

1:14–15 The fourth day introduces the second group of three days that depict the filling of the universe with movement and life. On this day the luminaries are created and placed in the heavens, paralleling "light" decreed on the first day.[155] The importance of this day's events is indicated by the lengthy description, repetition, and place in the literary arrangement of the days. It is second only to the sixth day in detail, and it stands in the middle of the seven-day arrangement. The redundancy of the verse can be attributed to the inverted order that has been noticed in the passage: the commands of vv. 14–15 are fulfilled in their reverse order in vv. 17–18, and the creation of the sun and moon in v. 16 stands as the centerpiece.[156]

---

[154] Westermann, *Genesis 1–11,* 124.

[155] The expression "let there be" (v. 14) probably indicates a new creative act as it does in vv. 3 and 6; some think that the luminaries were created on the first day and are alluded to by the "light" of v. 3. However, there is no sense that they were once hidden and only now appear; contrast the language of the appearance of dry land in v. 9 (noted by M. G. Kline, "Because It Had Not Rained," *WTJ* 20 [1957–58]: 153). Others suggest that the first three days were served by a light source from God unrelated to the sun, and its duty was handed over to the sun and moon on the fourth day (e.g., Calvin, *Comm.,* 76; Cassuto, *Genesis,* 44).

[156] P. Beauchamp, *Création et séparation* (Paris: Desclée, 1969), 92–97, followed by Wenham, *Genesis 1–15,* 22. The construction is not precise, but it shows how the repetition and near complete inversion stress the roles of the celestial lights.

v. 14 לְהַבְדִּיל ("to separate")
  v. 15 לְהָאִיר ("to give light")
    v. 16a לְמֶמְשֶׁלֶת ("to govern")
    v. 16b לְמֶמְשֶׁלֶת ("to govern")
  v. 17 לְהָאִיר ("to give light")
v. 18 [לִמְשֹׁל ("to govern")]
לְהַבְדִּיל ("to separate")

The description of the celestial bodies is phenomenological (see on 1:6–7), presupposing a human view of the planets from the earth. The narrative stresses their function as servants, subordinate to the interests of the earth. They are to differentiate day and night and to distinguish the seasons, days, and years. This differs significantly from the superstitious belief within pagan religion that the earth's destiny is dictated by the course of the stars. Nevertheless, the celestial bodies have the honored role as "rulers," but their realm is carefully restricted to the skies, whereas on the sixth day human life is appointed to rule the terrestrial world. What appears to be at stake in the narrative is the answer to the ancient question about who "rules" the skies and the earth. Mesopotamian and Egyptian religions speak of their great cosmic gods of Heaven, Air, and Earth. The Sumerians have their Anu, Enlil, and Enki; the Babylonians have their trinity of stars, Sin, Shamash, and Ishtar; and Egypt has Nut, Shu, and Geb with the preeminent astral deity, the sun god Re.[157] Genesis declares otherwise: Israel's God rules the heavens and the earth. The ancients misinterpreted the prominence of the celestial bodies, which owed their existence and authority to the Unseen One.

1:16–18 The passage contradicts common pagan misconceptions. The usual Hebrew terms for "sun" *(šemeš)* and "moon" *(yārēaḥ, lĕbānâ)* are avoided; they are described as the "greater" and "lesser" lights (v. 16). Genesis shows that the sun and moon are not cosmic deities worthy of reverence; the stars are no more than light-bearing bodies that are subservient to the needs of the earth. The prophet Isaiah reflects this in his commentary on the incomparable excellence of the Lord (e.g., 40:25–26; 44:6–20).

The luminaries were a source of fascination for ancient peoples, who were dependent upon them for directing travel and for anticipating the seasons. In particular, Mesopotamian religion magnified the role of the stars. The moon deities of Mesopotamia are known from as early as the third millennium B.C., and they played an important role in cultic festivals into the first millennium B.C. Also West Semites paid homage to the moon; at Ugarit (1400–1200 B.C.) the moon deity was Yarik. The sun deity was of great importance to the Babylonians, who worshiped Shamash, and to the Egyptians, who paid homage to Re and Aton. The God of the Hebrews, however, had revealed to his people that the stars were no more than creations who were subject to his purposeful will. The passage also limits the importance of the stars. In the Babylonian cosmogony *Enuma Elish* the stars have a prominent role, but in the Genesis account the creation of the stars is treated almost as an aside, downplaying their role in God's sight. The Hebrew text simply adds afterward, as if a mere

[157] See E. R. Clendenen, "Religious Background of the Old Testament," in *Foundations for Biblical Interpretation,* ed. D. S. Dockery, K. A. Mathews, R. B. Sloan (Nashville: Broadman & Holman, 1994), 277–90.

afterthought—"and the stars" (1:16).

For the Hebrews, who sojourned from Egypt, their ancestors had seen the importance the Egyptians attached to the sun deity. Also the newly freed Hebrews, who knew of Abraham's sojourn from Ur, would have recognized the same idolatrous inclinations among his ancestors in Mesopotamia (Josh 24:2). The Mosaic community imposed the gravest penalty upon anyone worshiping celestial bodies (e.g., Deut 17:2–5). Moses recognized that one important implication of the creation account was the prohibition of idolatry.[158] Idolatry was perceived as a sin against God as Creator and Covenant Lord. In Deut 4:15–20 Moses draws on the language and imagery of chap. 1 (though in reverse order) and also refers to the Sinai revelation in prohibiting the representation of God as any living creature or heavenly body. Here is a stern warning for our times for any who would seek the stars in charting their lives.

The heavenly lights are regarded as "good" (1:18) because they fill the once-empty skies. While the darkness lingers as a daily reminder of how the earth once was before God's light-giving word, the stars of the night's skies attest to the beauty and magnanimity of God as Creator. The psalmist, after reflecting on the significance of the heavens, concluded that they attested to the weightiness of the Creator, Israel's God (Ps 19:1[2]). The stars send a constant and universal message that points the discerning viewer to the One who has set them in their place by his fingertips (Pss 8:3[4]; 19:2–4[3–5]). The proper response of the human observer is an admission of one's own smallness (Ps 8:4[5]) but also a recognition that human life is of incalculable worth to God as his special creation (Ps 8:5–6[6–7]; cp. Gen 1:26–28). For the author of the Epistle to the Hebrews, this inestimable potential of human life is only fully realized by the one true Man, even Jesus Christ (Heb 2:5–9).

(5) Fifth Day of Creation (1:20–23)

**20And God said, "Let the water teem with living creatures, and let birds fly
above the earth across the expanse of the sky." 21So God created the great creatures of the sea and every living and moving thing with which the water teems,
according to their kinds, and every winged bird according to its kind. And God
saw that it was good. 22God blessed them and said, "Be fruitful and increase in
number and fill the water in the seas, and let the birds increase on the earth."
23And there was evening, and there was morning—the fifth day.**

1:20–21 The fifth day concerns the filling of the waters and the skies. It parallels the second day and the creation of the "expanse" that separates the waters from the atmosphere (1:6–8). A distinctive feature of the fifth day is the first recorded "blessing" in the Bible. The fifth and sixth days that concern the

[158] See M. Fishbane, *Biblical Interpretation in Ancient Israel* (Oxford: University Press, 1985), 321–22.

creation of living things include God's benevolent enablement of all life forms to procreate. The creatures are classified according to their dwelling, whether sea or sky.[159]

God commands the waters to swarm with "living creatures" *(nepeš ḥayyâ)* and the birds to fill the atmosphere. The command to the waters is another indirect creative act (also 1:11,24). By this Genesis shows that the waters are not divine. The phrase *nepeš ḥayyâ* is the same expression used for animal (v. 24; 9:10,12,15) and human life (2:7; both at 9:16). All living creatures, including birds, are also said to possess *nepeš ḥayyâ* (v. 30). The traditional rendering of *nepeš* is "soul," generally regarded as the immaterial portion of a person, but here the context requires us to take the term as a generic word for "creature" ("living being," 2:7). The term "teem" *(šereṣ)* indicates the sense of abundance and movement that these creatures brought to the seas.[160]

"So God created" is the second of only four verses in which *bārā'* ("created") occurs in the narrative (1:1,27; 2:3; also 2:4a). It begins and ends the section, 1:1–2:3, and also is found at the two important junctures in creation: here, the creation of the first animate life,[161] and in 1:27, the creation of human life. These first living creatures included "the great creatures of the sea *[tannînim]*."[162] *Tannîn* in Ugaritic literature has been shown to be a generic term for the mythical chaos monster.[163] At Ugarit it was an alternate designation for Yam (Sea) and Lotan (= Leviathan), and in the Bible it describes Rahab (Isa 51:9) and Leviathan (Ps 74:14; Isa 27:1).

The poets and prophets used the imagery of *tannîn,* drawing on Canaanite mythological depiction, to describe God's sovereignty over the forces of nature (Ps 74:13–14; Isa 27:1) and his victory over the historical enemies of Israel (Jer 51:34; Isa 51:9). It is clear from the theology of the prophets that they were not imbibing the underlying polytheism of their neighbors but rather were using the mythopoetic materials only for allusion to express their

---

[159] Sarna, *Genesis,* 10.

[160] It may refer to any swarming thing, such as the frogs that plagued Egypt (Exod 8:3[7:28]). The term is used in the flood story of small land creatures (Gen 7:21; 8:17) but also of human life who are charged to "multiply" (שֶׁרֶץ) over the earth (Gen 9:7). The particular language of chap. 1 is found for the food laws of the Mosaic tradition. "Swarming" (שֶׁרֶץ) describes the movement of the aquatic and land creatures that are among those prohibited for consumption (e.g., Lev 5:2; 11:10,41–44), including insects (Deut 14:9). The same expression, "living creatures," also appears with "swarm" in Lev 11:10,46 (cf. Ezek 47:19). Evidence of God's blessing upon Israel in Egypt is its "swarming" growth ("multiplied greatly") despite its small beginnings with only seventy in Jacob's house (Exod 1:7).

[161] Ibid.

[162] The NIV translation "of the sea" is supplied from the context of the verse (cf. also Job 7:12; Ps 148:7). However, תַּנִּין refers to reptiles also and is translated "serpent" at Exod 7:9–10,12; Deut 32:33; and Ps 91:13.

[163] Wakeman, *God's Battle with the Monster,* 79. Translated "Dragon" in *ANET,* 137.

affirmation in the sovereignty of God.[164]

In the case of chap. 1, we have already seen how Hebrew thought differed remarkably from the ancient battle myth among the peoples of the Levant. The *tannîn,* so greatly feared, is depicted as no more than a sea creature. Though "great" in size to man's thinking, our passage shows that these creatures are numbered with the smallest of the sea in God's eyes. For all its fierce attributes, Leviathan in God's eyes is only a fish to be hooked or a pet for amusement (Job 41:1,10; Ps 104:26). The psalmist called upon these creatures to recognize with praise their Creator, the Lord (Ps 148:7).

The "living creatures," like the vegetation before (1:11–12), are created "according to their kinds" (1:21,24–25). Inherently, the created order possesses divinely imposed limitations that establish self-maintained and governed systematic categories. The Hebrews experienced limitations and prescriptions that governed their daily lives as part of the community of God. The great Architect of the universe does not permit the colors of his canvas to run together.

Later Hebrew custom differentiated between animals on the basis of their ceremonial "cleanness" or "uncleanness" with respect to their suitability for food and sacrifice (e.g., Lev 11:13–23; Deut 14:11–20). But God originally judged all creatures to be "good" because they contributed to his reversing the condition of the empty earth (Gen 1:2). Only after the introduction of sin will God require a differentiation between "good" and "not good," the "clean" and "unclean" in the created order (cf. 7:2,8; 8:20). Food restrictions were not primarily for hygienic purposes but to distinguish the people of God from their neighbors as a "holy" nation (Lev 11:44–45). The Christian community is exhorted to exercise the same discernment between righteous and sinful choices (e.g., Rom 6:19–23; Gal 5:16–26; Col 3:1–17; 1 Pet 1:13–16). Although food prohibitions served the ends of the Mosaic community, they became a hindrance to those who misunderstood the nature of righteousness in the kingdom of God (Matt 15:1–20 and parallels). This hampered the church's ministry among the Gentiles (e.g., Acts 10–11; 15) and ensnared some who maintained an ethnic distinction between Jew and Gentile (Eph 2:11–22) and who defined their righteousness in terms of regulations (Col 2:16–23).

1:22–23 Moreover, God "blessed" these creatures by enabling them to procreate, indicating again his superior position. This special endowment for living things comes only from God since his word alone brings life. This is the first occasion of a "blessing," and it is the theological keyword linking the history of the cosmos and of humanity (chaps. 1–11) with the promises to the

[164] See E. H. Merrill, "The Unfading Word: Isaiah and the Incomparability of Israel's God," in *The Church at the Dawn of the 21st Century*, ed. P. Patterson et al. (Dallas: Criswell Publications, 1989), 138-41.

patriarchs (chaps. 12–50; see Introduction).[165] Genesis shows that God has a blessing for all living creatures as a creation ordinance (1:22,28; cf. 5:2; 9:1), but the "blessing" for the nations will be realized only by those who bless Abraham and his seed (12:1–3; cf. Gal 3:6–9,16). It is commonplace in the Old Testament for divine "blessing" to favor the recipient with many descendants and material prosperity. A "blessing" presupposes a relationship between God and the persons blessed. Especially in the patriarchal narratives, God's blessing means proliferation and success (e.g., 12:2–3; 17:16; 22:17; 26:24; 39:5; 48:3–4).[166] Blessing by Israel's patriarchs calls for a fruitful progeny and understands that it is God who determines the outcome of the blessing (e.g., 28:1–3; 48:15–20). "Be fruitful and increase in number" *(pĕrû ûrĕbû)* in our verse is taken up again in 1:28 and repeated for Noah, the new Adam, in the flood account (9:1,7). The same expression is significant for the patriarchs, who receive God's promise of blessing as Israel's progenitors (28:3; 35:11; 47:27; 48:4). Israel enjoyed the reality of the promise as they multiplied in the womb of Egypt (Exod 1:7). Like the first two, the third imperative "fill" *(milʾû)* is reiterated in 1:28 and 9:1. All three contribute to the sense of life overflowing.

This blessing indicates that the creatures are in a favored position before the Lord. The only parallel to this in creation is 1:28, which reports God's blessing on human life, but there he speaks directly to the first humans (cf. 5:2; 9:1). Divine "blessing" occurs once more in this week but for a "day" (seventh day), though it presumes it is a "blessing" enjoyed by those who observe God's rest (2:3; cf. Exod 20:8–11). "Blessing" is found again in early Genesis but in its passive formulation, where Noah prayed, "Blessed *[bārûk]* be the LORD, the God of Shem." This is not actually a blessing of Shem, but Noah showed that the power to bless his favored descendant came only from God (see 9:26 discussion). Here at creation, by this simple dictum, God pro-

[165] ברך occurs in Genesis 8x in *qal,* 3x in *niphal,* 59x in *piel;* the noun בְּרָכָה occurs 16x, giving 88 occurrences of the root in Genesis, more than any other biblical book. See C. W. Mitchell, *The Meaning of BRK "To Bless" in the Old Testament,* SBLDS 95 (Atlanta: Scholars Press, 1987), Table 1, p. 184. Mitchell defines "blessing" as essentially a *statement* of favor toward the recipient(s) versus the *content* of the blessing, such as the power of fertility and dominion (pp. 165–67). God had already given the creatures power to reproduce by virtue of his creative word; thus the "blessing" is an expression of God's desire for them to do so, showing his favor toward them. The blessing, it is reasoned, does not enable fertility for Noah (9:1) and Jacob (35:9–12) as though they did not have it before; rather it urges their practice of procreation (pp. 62–65). Yet we think that since in the OT divine blessing is predominantly fertility and prosperity, it makes little difference if the blessing is merely statement or not since the power comes from the Lord ultimately. Both are in mind. It is best to understand "blessing" as a divine enablement at creation that is enjoyed by all as a creation ordinance for animal and people in general. Subsequently divine blessing (e.g., Noah or Jacob) is an assurance (i.e., statement) that this enablement will come to pass.

[166] See J. Scharbert, "ברך *brk;* בְּרָכָה *bᵉrākhāh,*" *TDOT* 2.279–308, esp. 284, 289, 294. Cf. also, e.g., Exod 20:24; Deut 1:11; 7:13; Ruth 2:4; 1 Chr 4:10; Isa 51:2; Pss 67:1,6[2,7]; 115:12–15.

vides these creatures with the security of a continued existence.[167] The animal world is valued by God and is placed under the caretaking of humans (1:26–28). The startling reversal of God's attitude toward his world of creatures by the flood exhibits the enormity of the world's corruption (6:17; 7:22–23). Nevertheless, his renewed covenant with the world includes these creatures who will again "be fruitful and increase in number" (8:17).

The fifth day was also deemed "good" since it reversed the empty earth. "Outside of God there is nothing to fear; even this creature *[tannîn]* is good in God's sight."[168]

(6) Sixth Day of Creation (1:24–31)

24And God said, "Let the land produce living creatures according to their kinds: livestock, creatures that move along the ground, and wild animals, each according to its kind." And it was so. 25God made the wild animals according to their kinds, the livestock according to their kinds, and all the creatures that move along the ground according to their kinds. And God saw that it was good.

26Then God said, "Let us make man in our image, in our likeness, and let them rule over the fish of the sea and the birds of the air, over the livestock, over all the earth, and over all the creatures that move along the ground."

27So God created man in his own image,
in the image of God he created him;
male and female he created them.

28God blessed them and said to them, "Be fruitful and increase in number; fill the earth and subdue it. Rule over the fish of the sea and the birds of the air and over every living creature that moves on the ground."

29Then God said, "I give you every seed-bearing plant on the face of the whole earth and every tree that has fruit with seed in it. They will be yours for food.
30And to all the beasts of the earth and all the birds of the air and all the creatures that move on the ground—everything that has the breath of life in it—I give every green plant for food." And it was so.

31God saw all that he had made, and it was very good. And there was evening, and there was morning—the sixth day.

The final day of the creation week is the most significant of the six. More space and detail are given to its creative events than to the previous five. As with the third day, there are two creative acts on the final day of the second grouping: land animals (vv. 24–25) and human life (vv. 26–28). Verses 29–30 concern the diet provided by God for the subsistence of created life. The concluding verse trumpets God's final evaluation that creation was "very good" (v. 31).

---

[167] So W. Eichrodt, *Theology of the Old Testament,* 2 vols., trans. J. Baker (Philadelphia: Westminster, 1967), 2.350, n. 1.

[168] von Rad, *Genesis,* 57.

1:24–25 The dry ground and vegetation were created on the third day (v. 9), and this sixth day corresponds to it by the creation of animal and man to populate the land and feed on its herbage (vv. 11,30). As with the creation of vegetation, the land mediates the command of God to produce land creatures ("Let the land produce living creatures"). Like the sea creatures in v. 20, these are identified as "living creatures" *(nepeš ḥayyâ)*. The animals are not explicitly said to be blessed, but we may assume that they too receive God's blessing since they are created on the same day as mankind (cf. 8:17). As with the fish and fowl (vv. 20–22), God set reproductive parameters ("according to their kinds") for these creatures. The major groupings are domesticated cattle, crawlers, and wild animals (v. 24). The text emphasizes that within the animal world there were limitations for each group (v. 25; see 1:21 discussion).

1:26 The crown of God's handiwork is human life. The narrative marks the prominence of this creative act in several ways: (1) the creation account shows an ascending order of significance with human life as the final, thus pinnacle, creative act; (2) of the creative acts, this is the only one preceded by divine deliberation ("Let us make" in v. 26); (3) this expression replaces the impersonal words spoken in the previous creation acts (e.g., "Let there be," "Let the earth");[169] (4) human life alone is created in the "image" of God and has the special assignment to rule over the created order (vv. 26–28); (5) the verb *bārāʾ* occurs three times in v. 27; (6) the event is given a longer description than previous ones; (7) in v. 27 the chiastic arrangement highlights the emphasis on "image"; and (8) unlike the animals, who are said to have come from the land in v. 24 (though v. 25 makes clear that God created them), mankind is referred to only as a direct creation of God.[170]

When we consider v. 26, we are faced with two interpretive dilemmas that have historically plagued ancient and modern commentators. First, what or who is the referent of the plural pronouns "let *us*" and "*our* image and *our* likeness"? Second, what is the significance of the terms "image" and "likeness" for understanding the unique place of human life in the divine scheme of creation? In what way can the author claim that mankind corresponds to God? The two issues are interrelated since in order to understand the "image" we must also hold before us the question of its Maker's identity.

Regarding the verb "make," we have already observed at 1:1 that the verbs "made" *(ʿāśâ)* and "created" *(bārāʾ)* are in parallel both structurally and semantically in 2:4a,b. Here the parallel between v. 26 ("Let us make") and v. 27 ("So God created") indicates that they are virtual synonyms. Neverthe-

---

[169] I. e., a cohortative of resolve is employed rather than another impersonal jussive. See Sarna, *Genesis*, 11.

[170] The absence of divine blessing upon the animals of the land also serves to distinguish the human family. The blessing of the sea creatures was no threat to man's honored role since the waters were lower in importance to the earth (so von Rad, *Genesis*, 57).

less, a significant difference here is that the verb "make" is grammatically plural. "Created" is highlighted in v. 27 by its repetition three times, and in v. 26 the plural form of the verb distinguishes "make." This is the first of four passages in the Old Testament where the plural is found in divine dialogue. Subsequently in Genesis the plural "like one of us" occurs in 3:22, and the plural verb "let us go down" is attested in 11:7. Finally, in Isaiah's vision of the heavenly throne the prophet hears the divine request, "And who will go for us?" (Isa 6:8).

Among commentators the plural reference is variously understood: (1) a remnant of polytheistic myth; (2) God's address to creation, "heavens and earth"; (3) a plural indicating divine honor and majesty; (4) self-deliberation; (5) divine address to a heavenly court of angels; and (6) divine dialogue within the Godhead.[171] It is unlikely when we consider the elevated theology of 1:1–2:3, that any polytheistic element would be tolerated by the author; therefore, the first option can be ruled out. The second option is flatly contradicted by v. 27, where God alone is identified as the Creator. The plural as used to show special reverence (honorific plural) is flawed since the point of the verse is the unique correspondence between God and man, not the majesty of God. The fourth viewpoint considers "Let us make" a plural of self-deliberation,[172] depicting God anthropomorphically as someone in contemplation. This is supported by the change to the singular ("*his* own image") in v. 27, which indicates that the figure of "deliberation" is completed.[173] In ancient myths divine deliberation prefaces the creation of humans.[174] Self-deliberation is attested in the Old Testament (e.g., Pss 42:5,11; 43:5), but there is no attestation that the plural form is used in this way.[175]

The fifth interpretation regarding a heavenly court of angels is more likely,

---

[171] For a review of the major positions, see D. J. A. Clines, "The Image of God in Man," *TynBul* 19 (1968): 53–103. The rabbis considered the eternal Torah (Prov 8:30) to be the source for God's consultation of creation; this is the backdrop for the further speculation about the creation of man. There was wide diversity of Jewish interpretation, including heavens and earth, angels, and self-deliberation. See J. Neusner's comments at *Gen. Rab.* 8.2–8 (*Genesis Rabbah: The Judaic Commentary to the Book of Genesis* [vol. 1; Atlanta: Scholars, 1985]). For yet another view, Speiser's (*Genesis*, 7) is the simplest: the plural is a mere matter of grammatical congruity without reference to meaning since *Elohim* is plural in form and is found as such at places, e.g., Gen 20:13.

[172] GKC § 124g, n.2.

[173] In addition to 1:26–27, the exchange between plural and singular occurs at Gen 11:7–8; 2 Sam 24:14; Isa 6:8. Gen 3:22, however, does not have this feature.

[174] In the Babylonian *Enuma Elish,* Marduk discusses the creation of human beings with Ea (*ANET,* 68), but the clearest parallel comes from an Assyrian text: "What are we to change, what are we to create?/O Annunaki, you great gods,/What are we to change, what are we to create?" Cited in Westermann, *Genesis 1–11,* 144, who takes this view.

[175] Hence, Cassuto (*Genesis,* 55) prefers a "plural of exhortation," as when "a person exhorts himself to do a given task he uses the plural," and points to the near parallel in 2 Sam 14:14.

though not sufficiently convincing.[176] Impressive evidence from the Old Testament and parallels from Mesopotamian and Canaanite mythology point to the idea of a heavenly court where plans are made and decisions rendered.[177] Furthermore, some argue that Psalm 8's commentary on the passage indicates that *ʾĕlōhîm* refers to angels.[178] A difficulty with this view is the inclusion of angels in the phrase "our image" in 1:26. In what sense is the human being created in the image of angels?[179] Appealing to 6:1–4 only begs the question since it is not clear that the "sons of God" are angels. The overriding problem with this view is that there has been no mention of an angelic court in chap. 1, and the text is clear that mankind is made in God's image ("his image," v. 27).[180] More important, the narrative has shown by its theological stance that God has no antecedent partner or source for creation. The sudden introduction of a heavenly court diminishes the force of the presentation. To answer this, some suggest that though he consulted with the heavenly court, God alone created man and hence he alone is the source of the "image." But such a resolution is odd since it undermines the very contention of the angel view, namely, that God consulted with the heavenly court when in fact the consultation had no appreciable meaning.

Finally, we consider the traditional contention that the plural refers to a divine plurality. The interpretation proposed by the Church Fathers and perpetuated by the Reformers was an intra-Trinity dialogue. However, this position can only be entertained as a possible "canonical" reading of the text since

---

[176] P. D. Miller argues that the correlation indicated by the plural is not just between human and God but between the human world and the divine world, i.e., supernatural beings (*Genesis 1–11: Studies in Structure and Theme,* JSOTSup 8 [Sheffield: University of Sheffield, 1978], 9–26). He sees the three passages where God uses the plural in chaps. 1–11 (1:26; 3:22; 11:7) as addressing the same issue of identifying the nature of the human and defining its relationship to the divine, e.g., where they may overlap (1:26–28; 3:22) and where humanity oversteps its boundaries (6:1; 11:7).

[177] Cf. Job 1:6–12; 2:1–6; 15:8; 38:7; 1 Kgs 22:19–28; Isa 6:1–8; Jer 23:18.

[178] Ps 8:5–6[6–7], a passage that clearly has 1:26–28 in mind, explains that man is created a "little lower than אֱלֹהִים." As in the rendering of the LXX translators (cf. Heb 2:6–8), אֱלֹהִים can be interpreted as "angels" ("heavenly beings"). But this rendering is itself disputed and so cannot be decisive for resolving 1:26. Ps 8:5[6] does not directly allude to the plural "Let us make" or "image" in 1:26; rather it speaks of v. 28, where mankind is charged with rule of the earth. The psalmist's focus was that human life is specially honored because of its preeminent role as caretaker over the terrestrial order. The writer to the Hebrews was simply seizing the rendering of the LXX's "angels" (ἀγγέλους) for אֱלֹהִים for his ongoing argument that Christ is superior to the angels.

[179] F. Delitzsch counters by pointing out that God does not concede to the angels a part in the creation any more than he does their participation in sending forth a divine messenger ([Isa 6:8] *A New Commentary on Genesis,* vol. 1, trans. S. Taylor [reprint, 1978; Edinburgh: T & T Clark, 1888], 99).

[180] von Rad explains that the abrupt appearance of the plural is designed to build suspense in the plot (*Genesis,* 59).

the first audience could not have understood it in the sense of a trinitarian reference. Although the Christian Trinity cannot be derived solely from the use of the plural, a plurality within the unity of the Godhead may be derived from the passage. This was the essential line of argument among the Reformers, who expanded this thought by appealing to the New Testament for corroboration.[181] Our passage describes the result of God's creative act by both plural and singular pronouns: the plural possessive "our image" in v. 26 and the singular pronoun "his image" in v. 27. Here the unity and plurality of God are in view. The plural indicates an intradivine conversation, a plurality in the Godhead, between God and his Spirit.[182] By its reference to "the Spirit of God" preparing the "earth" for the creative word (1:2), the narrative permits a coparticipant with God in creation. Moreover, Prov 8:30 speaks of the personified "Wisdom" as God's coparticipant in creation. The later poets and prophets attribute the source of life to the "Spirit" (e.g., Job 33:4; Ps 104:30; Ezek 37).

"Man" is the NIV rendering of *ʾādām,* which is used generically here for mankind, rather than individual "Adam." The inclusive meaning is transparently the correct understanding from the plural verb that follows, "let them rule," as well as the plural pronouns of vv. 27–28 (also 5:2). Specifically, v. 27 indicates *ʾādām* is created with sexual distinctions, "male and female." Thus by the term *ʾādām* all human life is said to be created in the "image" and "likeness" of God. The word *ʾādām* is theologically convenient since it can mean mankind yet can refer to an individual person (e.g., 2:5,7) or function as a proper name, "Adam" (at least by 5:1; see discussion at 2:7). The New Testament reflects this by referring to "Adam" as an individual (e.g., Luke 3:38; Rom 5:14) and also by acknowledging "Adam" as mankind (e.g., Rom 5:12–21; 1 Cor 15:22). In this latter case the apostle Paul focuses on the representative role of individual Adam, by whom all people have come under the sanction of death. Adam serves as the foil for Christ, the last Adam, who is at one time an individual (like Adam) but also a representative (like Adam) for the new humanity who enjoy life through the death and resurrection of Christ.

In Genesis the terms "image" *(ṣelem)* and "likeness" *(dĕmût)* occur in just three passages (1:26–27; 5:1,3; 9:6). Some contend that the theology of the "image of God" *(imago Dei)* had little significance among the Hebrews because of this paucity of references in the Old Testament. But this is fundamentally shortsighted, for 1:26–28 is the seedbed for understanding the promissory blessing of God for Israel's fathers and its realization in the life of the nation (see Introduction). We cannot look at 1:26–28 without viewing it

---

[181] *LW* 1.58; Calvin, *Comm.,* 92.

[182] Cf. "duality of Godhead" in Clines, "The Image of God in Man," 68–69, and "plurality of fullness" in D. Kidner, *Genesis,* TOTC (Chicago: InterVarsity, 1967), 52, and G. F. Hasel, "The Meaning of 'Let Us' in Gn 1:26," *AUSS* 13 (1975): 58–66.

through the prism of human sin, both in its beginning in the garden and its consequences for human life and humanity's relationship to creation. Theologically, it is essential for interpreting the Christian faith with its proclamation regarding human life, the universal sinfulness of mankind, and the sole resolution of sin through the incarnation, death, and resurrection of Christ.

Although Genesis tells who is created in the "image of God," both man and woman (1:27; 1 Cor 11:7; Jas 3:9), it does not describe the contents of the "image." The passage focuses on the consequence of that creative act, which is humanity's rule over the terrestrial world of life (1:28; Ps 8:6[7]). That lofty position merited the divine bestowal of "glory and honor" (Ps 8:5[6]) that one and at the same time acknowledged human creatureliness and yet honored mankind above all creatures as "human." Genesis 5:3 echoes 1:26 and indicates that the succession of the "image" and the blessing are realized through sonship. In the ancient Near East royal persons were considered the sons of the gods or representatives of the gods (cf. 2 Sam 7:13–16; Ps 2:7). Mankind is appointed as God's royal representatives (i.e., sonship) to rule the earth in his place. When sin marked the human family as disobedient children, however, they did not lose the "image" (9:6; 1 Cor 11:7; Jas 3:9); rather, the "glory" of sonship faded. In the New Testament these ideas of image, glory, and sonship are found closely related (e.g., 1 Cor 11:7; 2 Cor 3:18; 4:4,6; Heb 2:5–10). By the grace of the Creator the new humanity is created in the "image of Christ" (cp. 1 Cor 15:49) and through his perfect obedience achieves life and glory for believers as his adopted children (e.g., Rom 8:17,30; 9:23; 1 Cor 4:4,6; Col 3:9–10).

EXCURSUS: INTERPRETING THE "IMAGE OF GOD"

HISTORY. Historically, the issue of the "image of God" *(imago Dei)* has concerned two foci: the identity of the *imago Dei* and its relationship to human sin.[183] Theologians often consider the "image" within the broader questions of anthropology and soteriology. This often results in philosophical categories where the "image" is defined in terms of "being" (metaphysics) in the attempt to define the "human" and distinguish human from animal life. The principal thesis until this century had identified the "image" as the spiritual or immaterial properties of a person. Since the time of Irenaeus (ca. 185), a common view in the church was to differentiate between "image" *(ṣelem)* and "likeness" *(dĕmût)*. This may well have been influenced by the erroneous addition in the LXX where "and" *(kai)* was written between "image" and "likeness." It is thought that "image" refers to the ability to reason while "likeness" refers to a person's correspondence to God in spiritual attributes. As a consequence of human sin, the "likeness" has been lost but the "image," which distinguishes a person from the

[183] See G. A. Jónsson, *The Image of God: Genesis 1:26–28 in a Century of Old Testament Research,* Coniectanea Biblica OT Series, trans. L. Svendsen (Stockholm: Almqvist & Wiksell, 1988), and A. A. Hoekema, *Created in God's Image* (Grand Rapids: Eerdmans, 1986), 33–65.

animal order, persists unaltered. Augustine also attempted to explain the "image" in ontological terms by appealing to a trinitarian image, such as human memory, knowledge, and will (*The Trinity* X.4.17–19). This coincided with the common interpretation of the plural "Let us make" as a trinitarian reference. He emphasized that mankind was created perfect in the garden to do the good, but sin resulted in their incapacity to obey apart from God's enabling grace.

During the Middle Ages the bifurcation of "image" and "likeness" continued (e.g., Aquinas), but there was little textual evidence for this supposed distinction, and the view was abandoned by the Reformers. They nevertheless perpetuated the standard opinion that the *imago Dei* was spiritual, but they showed more willingness to understand the "image" in terms of human fellowship with God. The earlier Pelagian controversy (fourth century A.D.) was in part concerned with defining the "image." Pelagius had maintained that humans were created originally with a perfect free will and that they were free to choose obedience or disobedience. Adam's disobedience in the garden did not obviate that free will for mankind, and thus each person retains that freedom to believe apart from special grace. The Reformers following Augustine insisted that the "image," though perfect in humanity's original state, had been mortally wounded in the fall, which required the intervening grace of the Spirit for salvation.

Calvin's method dictated his results. He contended that only from the New Testament could the original meaning of the "image" in Genesis be discovered since in Christ that pristine "image" is restored in the Christian believer (Col 3:10; Eph 4:24). For him the "image" in Adam was "the perfection of our whole nature," which was "destroyed in us by the fall."[184] By "whole nature" Calvin meant foremostly knowledge, righteousness, and holiness, but he also admitted that the "image" included the human body: "Yet there was no part of man, not even the body itself, in which some sparks did not glow."[185] This pristine state, while lost, was not totally absent in fallen humanity; there remained "obscure lineaments of that image." It was the remnant of that original gift that continued to distinguish the human from creatures. Reformed theology has traditionally held that mankind was created in the image of God, which was perfect in knowledge and righteousness, suffered irreparable destruction in the fall, and is delivered only through Christ's death and resurrection, whereby the image is being progressively transformed in the believer (2 Cor 3:18) until its state of perfection at the resurrection (Rom 8:29; 1 Cor 15:49; Col 3:9–10).[186] Thus "the incarnate Son actualizes the perfection of the manhood which we have sinfully perverted."[187]

---

[184] Calvin, *Comm.,* 94–95.

[185] Calvin, *Institutes* 1.15.3.

[186] E.g., Calvin's *Institutes* 2.15.1–4. Luther spoke at length of the perfection that Adam enjoyed in the garden before the fall; his life was "wholly godly" and "without the fear of death." He also possessed perfections in physical ways that distinguished him from the lower orders: "I am fully convinced that before Adam's sin his eyes were so sharp and clear that they surpassed those of the lynx and eagle" (*LW* 1.64).

[187] P. E. Hughes, *The True Image: The Origins and Destiny of Man in Christ* (Grand Rapids: Eerdmans, 1989), 13.

Our century has witnessed the rise of rival viewpoints that have challenged the ascendancy of the old view that the "image" was primarily spiritual and ontological. Among them is the converse opinion that the *imago Dei* is chiefly physical form.[188] More influential, however, has been the view of Karl Barth, who interpreted human "image" not as "anything he is or does" but as the relationship or confrontational dialogue of "man to man."[189] Verse 27, "male and female he created them," is taken as explicative of the "image." Thus the "image" consists in the correspondence between the human ability to enter an "I-Thou" partnership on the human plane and the personal "intradivine" ("Let us") confrontation in the divine being. Human beings alone of all creatures can enter into partnership with God because a human can "stand in an I-Thou relationship." As man and woman, human life is not solitary, even as God is not. This existential reading of the "image" dwells on relationship, but the relationship is the consequence of the "image" rather than its contents. Not only is Barth's exegesis of 1:26–27 on shaky grounds, but Genesis's creation and fall are viewed as only paradigmatic of the human condition, not historical event (see 3:1–24 discussion).

During this latter half of our century the dominant interpretation, though not new (e.g., Chrysostom), has become the "functional" one, that the "image" is humanity's divinely ordained role to rule over the lower orders (1:26,28). Often related to this interpretation is the idea of "royal" administration: mankind is God's "image" representing him on earth as his royal vice-regent. This is connected, either vaguely or closely, with Mesopotamian and Egyptian sacral kingship, where the king was either perceived as divine himself or, once removed, the divinely elected representative of the god(s) before the people.

USE OF TERMS. "Image" and "likeness" occur in tandem only in 1:26 and 5:3, but the order of the words differs in 5:3.[190] The two terms are found essentially the same in use and are interchangeable. "Image" alone, for example, in v. 27 is adequate for the sense of v. 26, and "likeness" is sufficient by itself in 5:1. There is no special significance to their order since as we noted they have a transposed order in 5:3, a passage that certainly echoes v. 26. This would question the legitimacy of attributing to *dĕmût* a special feature in the tandem; some have recommended that it clarifies or heightens the meaning of *ṣelem*. Others have argued oppositely that it tempers the word "image" by assuring that mankind is not divine but only has a "likeness" (correspondence) to the divine.[191] The LXX translation distinguished between *ṣelem (eikōn)* and *dĕmût (homoiōsis)* at both 1:26 and 5:3, where the tandem of terms occur, but used the same term "image"

---

[188] E.g., H. Gunkel and more recently P. Humbert, *Etudes sur le récit du paradis et de la chute dans la Genèsis* (Mémoires de l'Université de Neuchatel 14, 1940). Von Rad, arguing for a holistic understanding of image, agrees: "The marvel of man's bodily appearance is not at all to be excepted from the realm of God's image" (*Genesis,* 58). Cassuto believes that originally the "image" was thought to be corporeal but later was understood as spiritual, made up of thought and conscience (*Genesis,* 56).

[189] K. Barth, *Church Dogmatics* III/Part One, ed. G. W. Bromiley and T. F. Torrance (Edinburgh: T & T Clark, 1958 [Eng. trans.]), 183–86. Also see Westermann, *Genesis 1–11,* 155–58.

[190] Ezek 23:14–15 has the order of 1:26.

[191] See discussion in Clines, "The Image of God in Man," 90–92.

(eikōn) for both Hebrew words at 1:27 *(ṣelem)* and 5:1 *(dĕmût),* indicating that the words have the same force. Further support for understanding the terms as interchangeable comes from a ninth-century statue recovered from Tell Fekheriyeh (ancient Sikan) in Syria that bears a bilingual text in Assyrian and Aramaic. As a pair *ṣelem* and *dĕmût* are used with the same meaning in reference to the statue.[192]

Furthermore, there is no special distinction to be made between the different Hebrew prepositions "in *[bĕ]* his image" and "according to *[kĕ]* his likeness," since the prepositions too are interchangeable at 5:3.[193] The possible significance of the prepositions, however, has been a source of debate. The preposition "in" *[bĕ]* is either expressing "in the manner of" (norm) or "as" (essence).[194] If the latter case, mankind is the image of God and not merely a copy of the "image." This use of *bĕ* is attested in the Old Testament; for example, "I appeared to Abraham, to Isaac and to Jacob as God Almighty" (Exod 6:3; cp. Exod 18:4).[195] Yet there is one place in the Pentateuch where a similar correspondence between heaven and earth as in 1:26 is described; the Mosaic tabernacle was made after the pattern *(bĕ)* of a heavenly original (Exod 25:40; cf. Heb 8:1–6; 10:1).[196] While not conclusive, it commends taking the preposition "in" similarly—thus both man and tabernacle are earthly icons of heavenly realities.

Both "image" and "likeness" are used of physical representations, where there is a correspondence between a physical statue or drawing and the person or thing it represents.[197] Most commentators have anatomized the individual person into material and spiritual properties, thus identifying the *imago Dei* as either physical or spiritual. This dichotomy, however, is at odds with Hebrew anthropology; as 2:7 bears out, a person is viewed as a unified whole. The whole person,

---

[192] A. R. Millard and P. Bordreuil, "A Statue from Syria with Assyrian and Aramaic Inscriptions," *BA* (1982): 135–41; D. Gropp and T. Lewis, "Notes on Some Problems in the Aramaic Text of the Hadd-Yithᶜi Bilingual," *BASOR* 259 (1985): 45–61. The inscription has the equivalent expressions "the statue *[dmwtʾ]* of Hadd-yithᶜi" and "the statue *[ṣlm]* of Hadd-yithᶜi."

[193] Cf. also 5:1, בִּדְמוּת. Whether man is the "image" per se or made "in" the image, the point of the prepositions is that God and humanity share sameness in some unspecified way. Note therefore the irony of the serpent's statement at 3:5.

[194] GKC § 19h-i.

[195] See Clines' extended argument for *beth essentiae* ("The Image of God in Man," 75–78).

[196] E.g., see J. Barr, "The Image of God in the Book of Genesis—A Study of Terminology," *BJRL* 51 (1968): 16–17, followed by Wenham, *Genesis 1–15,* 20, and Hamilton, *Genesis 1–17,* 137. Barr adds that usually *bĕ,* when used for the essence of a matter, concerns the properties of the subject, not the object of the verb. Here in 1:26 "image" clearly refers to the properties of mankind (object).

[197] צֶלֶם ("image") is used for idols (e.g., Num 33:52; 2 Kgs 11:18//2 Chr 23:17; Ezek 7:20; 16:17) and portraits (Ezek 23:14). Also it occurs metaphorically for the ephemeral character of humanity ("phantom," "fantasies"; Pss 39:6[7]; 73:20). דְּמוּת ("likeness") is usually thought to be used for the abstract idea of "representation," but it also occurs for idols (Isa 40:18), statues (2 Chr 4:3), sketches (2 Kgs 16:10), and portraits (Ezek 23:15). In Ezek 23:14–15 both terms refer interchangeably to portraits. In the Tell Fekheriyeh inscription both terms refer to the physical "statue." דְּמוּת is also used simply to indicate a correlation in appearance or nature between two things (e.g., Ps 58:4[5]; Ezek 1:10; 10:22; Dan 10:16).

even all human life collectively, is in mind in 1:26. Since Mosaic law prohibited any physical representation of God (Exod 20:1–2; Deut 4:16), it is commonly questioned that the physical form could be intended. Deuteronomy 4:16 may well echo 1:27, where it specifically prohibits making any idol in the form of "male or female," but neither Deut 4:16 nor the Sinai prohibition (Exod 20:1–2) has "image" or "likeness." We cannot on this basis rule out the physical dimension as constitutive of the "image." Of the words used for idols and statues in the Old Testament,[198] the term "image" *(ṣelem)* is less often associated with idol worship, though it does occur (e.g., Num 33:52), and therefore was not necessarily troubling to the reader. We may add that theophany usually involves a human form (e.g., Gen 18:1–2), and the prophets envision God in human form seated in his celestial throne room.[199] They do not say God is a human, for Ezekiel makes it certain that he saw a "figure like *[dĕmût]* that of a man" (Ezek 1:26).[200] Ezekiel's theophanic vision, with its recurring use of "likeness" *(dĕmût),* recalls Gen 1:26 and illustrates how "likeness" is associated with theophany in the Old Testament. "Image" and "likeness" then would have suggested that the presence of human life represented God, as did the tabernacle, not that man was divine. Moreover, that the "image" involved physical form does not mean that God is corporeal, for there is no warrant in the passage to look to human beings to reconstruct the properties of God.

RULERSHIP. Traditionally, commentators have said that the "image" must consist of noncorporeal features (cf. John 4:24), such as moral, intellectual, and personality characteristics that are shared with God.[201] Genesis, however, says nothing about the "image of God" as to its ontological content, and therefore to develop an anthropology rooted in this phrase is speculative.[202] Genesis 1:26–28 concerns itself primarily with the consequence of this special creation, the rule of

---

198 E.g., פֶּסֶל, מַסֵּכָה, and סֶמֶל; so Barr, "Image of God in Genesis," 11–26, esp. 20.

199 E.g., Isa 6:1; Ezek 1:25–28; Dan 7:9–14; cf. Amos 7:7.

200 So Clines, "The Image of God in Man," 70–71, who adds that Deut 4:12 and Isa 40:18 show that God has no form. In this we agree, but our point is *not* that God and humans share in possessing a form but rather that God condescended by expressing his presence in a visible form, and he did so in creating man as corporeal.

201 E.g., the Reformers. See recently R. W. Wilson and C. L. Blomberg, "The Image of God in Humanity: A Biblical-Psychological Perspective," *Themelios* 18 (1993): 8–15.

202 Thus Westermann (*Genesis 1–11,* 155–59), favoring Barth (*CD* III/1, p. 184), contends that "in our image" is descriptive of the process, not the product, of creation; the passage concerns the action God takes to create man, not the nature of human beings (metaphysics). But process is not the "image," for 5:3 shows that the "image" indicates product (so Wenham, *Genesis 1–15,* 31). Recently J. F. A. Sawyer has defined "image of God" contextually based on events in the garden narrative (chaps. 2–3), which he takes as a parallel account to the theological 1:26–28, explaining in story fashion how humans came to resemble God ("The Image of God, the Wisdom of Serpents and the Knowledge of Good and Evil," in *A Walk in the Garden,* JSOTSup 136, ed. P. Morris and D. Sawyer [Sheffield: JSOT, 1992], 64–73). Although Sawyer has rightly viewed the garden passage as a sequence to chap. 1's interest in mankind's creation, telling what became of the human family (see 2:4–25 discussion), the passage is broader and not bothered with an exposition of "image," which does not even occur (nor "likeness") in the garden account (but yet after the garden, in 5:3; 9:6).

human life over the terrestrial order, rather than defining the identity of the "image."[203] In the ancient Near East it was widely believed that kings represented the patron deities of their nations or city-states. Among the Mesopotamians and Canaanites, royal figures were considered "sons" adopted by the gods to function as vice-regents and intermediaries between deity and society. Egyptian society recognized pharaoh as divine who was Horus in life and Osiris in death. Some royal stelae describe the king as the "image" of god.[204] Rulers were responsible for the equilibrium between nature and society through securing the favor of the gods; also justice and the well-being of society were dependent upon the administration of the king's rule.[205] Royal imagery was used to describe the Hebrew king as the appointed "son" of Yahweh who ruled in his name (cf. 2 Sam 7:13–16; Pss 2; 72; 89).

The language of 1:26 reflects this idea of a royal figure representing God as his appointed ruler.[206] This appears also to be the understanding of Psalm 8, which focuses on human dominion, though without explicit mention of the "image" or "likeness." This is further indicated by the term "rule" *(rādâ)* in 1:26,28, which is used commonly of royal dominion.[207] Human jurisdiction over animate life in the skies, waters, and land corresponds to the "rule" *(māšal)* of the sun and moon over the inanimate sphere of creation.[208] Our passage declares that all people, not just kings, have the special status of royalty in the eyes of God.[209] It is striking that God consigns jurisdiction to one of his creatures, since the major tenet of 1:1–2:3

---

[203] Cp. *Sir* 17:2–3: "He [God] gave them [humans] a fixed number of days, but granted them authority over everything on the earth. He endowed them with strength like his own, and made them in his own image" (NRSV). The clause at v. 26b may be rendered explicitly as purpose, "so that they might rule." Most versions, however, translate the clause as coordinating ("and," e.g., NIV, NRSV). The volitional ("let us make") is followed by the imperfect form (or jussive) וְיִרְדּוּ, in which case it may be rendered either as a sequential purpose clause ("so that") or simply conjunctive ("and"). See GKC § 108d, 165a; also *IBHS* § 39.2.2, but it takes v. 26b as conjunctive (39.2.5b)

[204] E.g., Amon Re's speech to Pharaoh Amenophis II: "Thou art my beloved son, come forth from my limbs, my very own image, which I have put upon the earth. I have permitted thee to rule over the earth in peace" (cited in Westermann, *Genesis 1–11,* 153, following W. H. Schmidt).

[205] Cf. Clendenen, "Religious Background of the Old Testament," 289–90.

[206] In the Egyptian text *The Instruction for King Merikare* (twenty-second century B.C.), Re's creation of human beings is similar to 1:26–27 and 2:7: "He made the breath of life (for) their nostrils. They who have issued from his body are his images" (*ANET,* 417). See also Hoffmeier, "Thoughts on Genesis 1 and 2," 47, who adds that the articular form of the word "image" is frequently written with a hieroglyphic statue.

[207] E.g., 1 Kgs 4:24 [5:4]; Pss 8:5–6; 72:8; 110:2; Isa 14:2.

[208] Noted in J. M. Miller, "In the 'Image' and 'Likeness' of God," *JBL* 91 (1972): 290, n. 2.

[209] "Rulership" as the correspondence between God and man has been found offensive to feminist and environmental theologies, which contend that 1:26–28 projects a God who is a monarchical tyrant. But 1:26–28, which shows that all humans are made in the "image of God," actually liberates humanity from the bondage of oppressive class systems as in the ancient Near East, whose cosmogonies maintained the social system. The biblical tradition sets in motion those forces that will eventually undermine despotic structures of human misery (see J. R. Middleton, "The Liberating Image? Interpreting the *imago Dei* in Context," *CSR* 24 [1994]: 8–25).

is the sovereignty of God's creative word. It was this feature of creation that so astonished the psalmist; for him the Infinite One crowned human infancy with the glory of his rule (8:5–8[6–9]). The supreme value God places on human life is also reflected in 9:5–6. Whereas an animal may be wrongly brutalized, it is the taking of human life that merits the charge "murderer."[210]

SONSHIP. Elsewhere in Genesis we can infer more about the "image" of God that distinguishes human life. Genesis 5:1–3 clearly echoes 1:26–28 and demonstrates that the "likeness" *(dĕmût)* of God that stamped Adam was perpetuated by his offspring. Adam fathered a "son" in his own "likeness" and "image" (5:3), which showed that the Adamic family continued the *imago Dei* and also the divine blessing first received by Adam (5:3–31). This "image" is tied again to the blessing mankind enjoys through its power of procreation as "male and female" (5:2), but in 5:3 there is the explicit recognition of sonship. Although 5:3 speaks of a literal biological descent, the passage also shows that the divine "image" and the concomitant blessing of procreation are the inheritance of Seth too. The motif of sonship is also taken up in Luke's Gospel, where he appeals to Genesis 5 in reciting Jesus' genealogy and rightly infers that Adam is "the son of God" (3:38). Luke did not confuse the sense of sonship between God–Adam and Adam–Seth as the same; for the Evangelist the important factor is the continuity of humanity, which has its source in God, who created the first man, hence the "son of God" in its metaphorical sense. This is what we have in Genesis 5—a line of physical descent, that is, Seth has Adam's "likeness," which indicates that the human family perpetuates the *imago Dei.*

It is also evident from Genesis 5 that the "image" continues despite the sinful rebellion in the garden; this is further supported by 9:6, where in the postdiluvian world the sanctity of human life is safeguarded on the basis that humanity is a special creation of God, bearing the divine image. Human life, though fallen, is not any less human and retains the same dignity, guaranteeing all persons protection. What we observe in 5:3, however, is that the former emphasis in 1:26–28 on human dominion is absent. This leads us to suspect that something has gone awry, and this suspicion is confirmed in the Noahic covenant, where the postdiluvian world requires specific restrictions on "blood" and human life without reference to rule (9:4–7). While creation's hierarchy of human over beast remains intact, the forewarning against taking the life of a human, whether the culprit is beast or man (9:5), shows that the dominion of human over the animal order is precarious. Nevertheless, the commission of exercising dominion as God's promissory blessing is reissued (9:1,7), and there is no sense that the "image" has changed or diminished. The psalmist recognizes that the superiority of human life, noted by his "glory and honor," rests not in man's ontological features but in his commission as lord over the terrestrial world (Ps 8:5–8[6–9]). This "glory" *(kābôd)* bestowed exclusively upon human life, is distinguished in the Old Testament as the attribute of the Lord God.[211] It is creation's "glory," indicating

[210] So Sarna, *Genesis,* 12.

[211] G. von Rad, "εἰκών," *TDNT* 2.391: "This gives us a mysterious point of identity between God and man, for on the OT view כָּבוֹד belongs supremely to Yahweh."

mankind's appointment as the Lord's ruling sonship, that is diminished through sin. Humanity's future "glory" will be fully gained as adopted heirs through Christ his Son, who will "bring many sons to glory" (Heb 2:10).

NEW TESTAMENT. When we come to the idea of "image" in the New Testament, we see the same lines taken up. We discover as in Genesis that men and women, even as fallen sinners, are still considered the "image of God" (1 Cor 11:7; Jas 3:9). The existence of the "image" in its original state is the basis of Paul's argument in 1 Corinthians 11 and also James's appeal (Jas 3:9), though there he probably is alluding to Gen 9:6. Moreover, Jesus Christ is identified as the unique "image of God" in 2 Cor 4:4 and Col 1:15, but Paul does not allude here to 1:26–28, indicating that Adam and Christ bear the same "image." Second Corinthians 4:4–6 contributes to Paul's explanation of the glory of God (3:7–4:6) as revealed to Moses at Sinai (Exod 33:12–34:8). In both 2 Corinthians 4 and Colossians 1, Paul addresses the salvation that only Christ as the unique "image" of God can achieve in behalf of man. Christ's "image" in Paul's argument is distinctive from what might be said of Adam, for Jesus is the Uncreated One, the "image of the invisible God" (Col 1:15), the exact image of God's being (Heb 1:3).[212] Christ also took the "form" of a human being (Phil 2:7), and we know that Jesus' incarnation resulted in a formal correspondence with the first Adam by virtue of being human. Yet the point of this Pauline analogy is to demonstrate how Christ is unlike Adam (Rom 5:12–21; 1 Cor 15:21–22; cf. Rom 8:3). What awaits Christians is that they will "bear the likeness *[eikōn]* of the man of heaven," that is, they will enjoy the future life and resurrection of the Lord (1 Cor 15:49). This is the destiny God has determined for those who believe (Rom 8:29). Thus Paul's appeal to Jesus as "image of God" in 2 Cor 4:4 and Col 1:15 is not the created humanity of Gen 1:26–27; rather, it refers to Christ, who must be understood uniquely as one with God, who is a glorified humanity.[213] That the "image of Christ" is the Christian's destiny is certain, but not that it was Adam's starting point.

Also in the New Testament the association of "glory" and "image" is further pursued. We have just noted that the destiny of all believers in Christ is his "image," but also Paul concludes his triumphant exaltation of grace in Romans 8 with "those he justified, he also glorified" (Rom 8:30). Prominently elsewhere Paul closely links "image" and "glory" (1 Cor 11:7; 2 Cor 4:4,6; 2 Cor 3:18) as we also find it among rabbinic Judaism (e.g., *Wis* 7:25–26). This association is most likely derived from Psalm 8's commentary on Genesis 1. When the writer

---

[212] "Image" (εἰκών) is not merely a copy of the reality, as we moderns might assume, but rather εἰκών partakes of the reality itself (e.g., Heb 10:1). See H. Kleinknecht, "εἰκών," *TDNT* 2.389.

[213] See the argument of G. Bray, "The Significance of God's Image in Man," *TynBul* 42 (1991): 211–12: "We may therefore conclude that Paul's use of *eikōn tou Theou* [image of God] with reference to Christ is designed to emphasize His oneness with God, not His oneness with us" (p. 214). It is not the inherent image of Adam that is regained in salvation, for it was never lost; nor was man immortal and righteous in the garden, but rather the believer is destined for the new image of Christ and the glory of his Sonship as adopted heirs.

to the Hebrews (2:5–10) presents his Christological reading of Psalm 8, he connects with the united themes of "image-glory" yet one more motif—sonship (2:9–10). Paul recognizes this too in describing the privileged place of the Jews who by virtue of their "sonship" were recipients of the divine "glory" (Rom 9:4), a reference no doubt to the presence of God at Sinai (Exod 24:16–17). But the "glory" endowed at creation is for all men and women. Because of Christ's resurrection he has received the crown of "glory and honor," and by virtue of his death he will bring "many sons to glory." Peter likewise speaks of Christ as the valued Son who received "honor and glory from God the Father" (2 Pet 1:17) at the mount of transfiguration, where the disciples witnessed the "glory" of the kingdom to come (Matt 17:1–8). It is this "glory" for which redeemed humanity in Christ is destined who himself is the "glory" of God (John 1:14,18; 17:4).[214] From Genesis we have seen that the rule of mankind is not fully realized because of disobedience, which has meant the diminishing of that "glory," but Christ accomplished what sinful humanity could not achieve alone (Heb 2:9). The redeemed will share in Christ's "glory" as adopted heirs (Rom 8:17; 2 Thess 2:14; 1 Pet 5:1,4), for which humanity was intended before time (Rom 9:23; 1 Cor 2:7). Through the sanctifying Spirit, the Christian experiences this transformation presently "from glory to glory" as the redeemed reflect the glory of the Lord (2 Cor 3:18, NASB), but the transformation awaits its full reality in the believer's resurrection. Concomitant with the believer's participation in the divine "glory" is the believer's "new life," made in the "image of its Creator" (Col 3:9–10)[215] and like God in "righteousness" (Eph 4:24).[216]

1:27 Verse 27 amplifies on the idea of *imago Dei* introduced in v. 26. The construction of v. 27 is an embedded poem consisting of three lines, with lines one and two in chiastic arrangement (inverted repetition) and the last line an explication:

a So God created man *in his own image*
b *in the image of God* he created him
c male and female he created them

The inner elements of the chiastic lines identify the focus of the poetic verse: the divine image. The third colon specifies that *ʾādām* ("man"), created in the image of God, refers to both male and female human life. By the occur-

[214] See H. D. McDonald, who concludes that man was originally created for sonship but "sin is the condition wherein this sonship is not reflected" (*The Christian View of Man* [Westchester, Ill.: Crossway, 1981], 41). We conclude that it is the glory of human sonship as appointed ruler that is the consequence of the "image" that has diminished because of the fall.

[215] See C. F. D. Moule, who follows J. A. T. Robinson in recommending that Paul here meant the creation of the new humanity corporately whose present existence in the world is only gradually being recognized until its "full knowledge" by Christians and unbelievers (*The Epistles to the Colossians and to Philemon,* CGTC [Cambridge: Cambridge University Press, 1957], 119–20).

[216] Paul's allusion to Gen 1:26–27 is not to assert the reappearance of the first Adam in humanity at salvation but only that as God made the first Adam in his likeness he has made the new life of the believer in his image too, namely, Jesus Christ. See S. D. F. Salmon, *EGT* 3.344.

rence of "them," clearly referring to two distinct sexual persons, after the singular "him," the old misconception of an original androgynous (bisexual) man is unfounded (see 2:22 discussion). "Them" also is found in 1:28, where procreation is its primary interest, obviously assuming the sexual differentiation of two persons, male and female.

Hebrew terms for "male" *(zākār)* and "female" *(nĕqēbâ),* as opposed to man and woman, particularly express human sexuality (and animals; e.g., Gen 5:2; 6:19; 7:3,9,16). Absence of any reference to the sexual distinction in land animals is probably so as not to detract from the privileged role of human life whereby procreation contributes to humanity's dominion over the lower animals. Male and female human members are image-bearers who both are responsible for governing the world. Although the man and woman complete each other (see 2:18 discussion), making the full complement of "man" *(ʾādām),* it can be said that an individual alone bears the "image" (5:1–3; 9:5–6; Jas 3:9). Although male and female hold in common the same unique God-given status as image-bearers, there is an inherent distinction within the human family by virtue of their different sexual roles, and this implies that other distinctions are present. Genesis 2–3 explains the role differentiation suggested by this first reference to "male and female," while maintaining with chap. 1 the equal humanity of each sex. There is no contradiction, as some contend, between chap. 1's portrait of an egalitarian couple and chaps. 2–3, which distinguish the sexes in terms of leadership-followship. The idea of hierarchy as a creation ordinance is not absent in chap. 1; it is an integral feature of the structuring of the six-day progression and permits the explication found in chaps. 2–3. Both affirm that man and woman are equally human and share the same personal worth (see 2:18,23 discussion).

Reference to "male and female" is preparatory for understanding the nature of God's blessing in v. 28. This is only the second of three blessings in the creation account (1:22; 2:3). As with fish and fowl, the divine "blessing" involves procreation (see 1:22 discussion). This expression of blessing differs, however, since God speaks directly to human life ("to them"), which is another indication that mankind has a superior position. The blessing of procreation by animal and human life will fill the once-empty earth (1:2) and, as Genesis 5's genealogy shows, not even sin will deter God's blessing.

Being human means being a sexual person. Human sexuality and sexual bonding between husband and wife are deemed "very good" (1:31) by God and are to be honored as the divine ordinance for men and women (see 2:18–24 discussion).[217] There is no place in God's good order for unisexuality or for any diminishing or confusion of sexual identity. Human sexuality in Gene-

[217] See R. M. Davidson, "The Theology of Sexuality in the Beginning: Genesis 1–2," *AUSS* 26 (1988): 5–24.

sis is a blessed function in the creative purposes of God, and it is essential for carrying out God's mandate for humanity (cf. 9:1,7) and for the patriarchs in particular (e.g., 12:1–3; 26:24; 28:3–4). Whereas in the flood story there is reference to the sexuality of the animals (7:2–3), in the creation account there is no mention of their sexuality or procreation. This implies that human sexuality is of a different sort from animal procreation: human procreation is not intended merely as a mechanism for replication or the expression of human passion but is instrumental in experiencing covenant blessing. The union of man and woman as husband and wife is an inclusive oneness (see 2:18,23–24 discussion). Human life, unlike the lower orders, is not instructed specifically to reproduce "after its kind." This omission elevates the sexual experience and goal of the human family as distinctive. The text's silence also infers that mankind is only of one kind.[218] Since humanity is of one sort, the unity of the human race is prominently noted and, concomitantly, dismisses any notion that certain peoples are inherently superior or inferior.

The proper role of the sexes therefore is crucial to God's designs for human life and prosperity. In the later Mosaic tradition its activity is specifically regulated within certain bounds, which if unheeded will profane the holy community, requiring redress (e.g., Lev 18; 20). When human sexuality is distorted through neglect or abuse, the human family suffers as the image-bearers of God. This notion of blessing associated with reproduction is a constant in Israel, where children are seen as the providential favor of the Lord. The theme of filling and procreating continues as a significant motif in the patriarchal stories, where the blessing through Abraham's chosen seed is perceived as the fulfillment of this first command at creation (see Introduction). The tension in the patriarchal narrative will be the improbability of childbearing by Sarah (18:10–15; 21:1–7), but the intervention of God assures the realization of the blessing. Later, Israel too saw their number increase as God facilitated their proliferation in Egypt—much to the sorrow of Pharaoh—and as he cared for their multitude in the wilderness (Exod 1:7; Deut 1:11; 2:7). The Hebrew host emerged from the womb of Egypt, and its mandate to displace the nations was the favor of God's blessing for prosperity (e.g., Deut 7:12–15). The continuum in the Pentateuch is God's promised blessing, which reaches from the first parents at creation to the chosen seed of Abraham's family and is intended for all people groups. Yet it is only because of the one seed, "Christ," that this blessing can be shared now by all peoples who are the children of Abraham through faith (Gal 3:6–9,15–22).

1:28 The mandate to subjugate the world includes the major zoological groups: fish, bird, and land animals. The lists of the animals are only general classifications and vary in details within the account (1:26,28,30). This

[218] So Sarna, *Genesis,* 13.

appointment by God gave the human family privilege but also responsibility as "caretakers" (2:15). The Hebrew love for life and the sacredness of all life assumed a linkage between human righteousness and the welfare of the earth. In the agrarian economy of ancient Israel, this was best expressed in the care for its livestock: "A righteous man cares for the needs of his animal" (Prov 12:10a; also 27:23; Deut 25:4). Sin impacts the prosperity of the earth and its inhabitants. Genesis shows how human sin elicits God's curse upon the land (3:17), and the later wickedness of human society results in the destruction of the whole earth by flood, specifically these three zoological groups that have been placed under human care (7:21–23). Human life then bears this responsibility under God and is held accountable for the world God has created for humanity to govern, for "the earth he has given to man" (Ps 115:16b).

1:29–30 God is depicted as the beneficent Provider, who insures food for both man and animal life without fear of competition or threat for survival (cf. 9:2–5). Human life will enjoy both plant and tree for food (vv. 11–12), and the animal world may consume every green plant. In the Babylonian tradition man is created to alleviate the manual burden of the gods and provide food for their sustenance; men and women are mere slaves who survive at the whim of the deities. Biblical creation shows that God honors the human family by specifically addressing them ("you") as he gives them charge over the terrestrial world (v. 29). Moreover, "every" and "all" (vv. 29–30) emphasize the availability and generosity of God's provision. For this reason the specific dietary restriction of the "tree of the knowledge of good and evil," which is central to the garden episode (2:17), is not included in this description. God's dietary standards for mankind specifically include meat in the postdiluvian world (9:3). Dietary prescriptions become increasingly important in the Mosaic community (Lev 11; Deut 14), and dietary habits become a mark of fidelity to God and of one's "Jewishness" (e.g., Dan 1:8; Acts 10:12–14; Col 2:16).

1:31 God's summary evaluation of creation concludes the six days: "it was *very [mĕʾōd]* good." "All" that God had made was worthy of commendation. His highest acclaim is withheld until the completed creation because only after the six creation days has the lifeless earth been fully changed (1:2). Now the earth as a result of God's "Spirit" and animated word is well-ordered, complete, and abounding in life-forms under the watch care of royal humanity. If God had chosen to be mute, encroaching darkness, unrestricted waters, and the hollow sounds of the empty wastelands would be the earth's state, but God has transformed and filled the earth by a matchless wisdom (Ps 104:24; Prov 8:22–31). As the psalmist contemplated the wonders of God's world, he pledged obedience to the divine imperatives for his own life (104:34). In the same way, God's life-giving word spoken at Sinai revealed for Israel its directives for life and order. The poet captured again this connection of the "word" that gives life and the "word" of revelation that is a "light to the eyes" (Ps

19:8b[9b]). For Israel the specific appointment of Canaan's land *(ʾereṣ)* was God's good creation for them. This is best found in the mouths of the celebrated spies Joshua and Caleb, who declared that this "land is exceedingly *[mĕʾōd mĕʾōd]* good" (Num 14:7).

3. Seventh Day—Day of Consecration (2:1–3)

1Thus the heavens and the earth were completed in all their vast array.

2By the seventh day God had finished the work he had been doing; so on the seventh day he rested from all his work. 3And God blessed the seventh day and made it holy, because on it he rested from all the work of creating that he had done.

The climactic seventh day is remarkably different from the foregoing six days of creation. First, there is no introductory formula ("then God said") because his creative word is not required. Second, this day does not have the usual closing refrain "evening" and "morning" to indicate its termination. Theologically the absence of the refrain implies that creation was intended to enjoy a perpetual rest provided by God, although that rest was disrupted by human sin. Third, the seventh day is the only day of the week blessed and consecrated by God. Fourth, unlike the creation days, the number of the "seventh" day is repeated three times (twice more by the pronoun "it"). Fifth, the seventh day stands outside the paired days of creation, having no corresponding day in the foregoing creation week. The literary pattern of six plus one (6 + 1) is designed to highlight the seventh and culminating member in the seven-item arrangement.[219] This revered "seventh day" fueled the extensive theological reflection on sabbath rest found in Israel and the church.

2:1 The chapter break is usually deemed inappropriate since the description of the creation week continues until 2:3, but it may have been placed after the sixth day in recognition of the uniqueness of the seventh day. With language reminiscent of 1:1 ("the heavens and the earth"), the verse adds the phrase "in all their vast array" so as to pay tribute to the full transformation that included the populating of the once-empty earth. The NIV's "their vast array" is the rendering of the literal "their hosts" and refers to the sun, moon, and stars as in Deut 4:19 ("all the heavenly array") and also to the lively inhabitants of the earth that were made on days five and six.

2:2 Verses 2–3 contain four lines, the first three of which are parallel, each possessing seven words (in the Hebrew), with the midpoint of each line

---

[219] See e.g., Cassuto, *Genesis,* 12–13; Kline, "Because It Had Not Rained," 146–57; E. J. Young, *Studies in Genesis One* (Grand Rapids: Baker, 1964), 58; S. E. Lowenstamm, "The Seven Day Unit in Ugaritic Epic Literature," *IEJ* 15 (1965): 122–33; and F. R. McCurley, Jr., "'And After Six Days' (Mark 9:2): A Semitic Literary Device," *JBL* 93 (1974): 67–81.

having the same phrase, "the seventh day."[220] A literal translation displays the structure:

So God finished by *the seventh day* his work which he did,
and he rested on *the seventh day* from all his work which he did,
and God blessed *the seventh day* and sanctified it,
because on it he rested from all his work which God created to do.

This is one of the several ways the author highlighted the importance of the final day. In later Israel the "seventh" was displaced with the customary word "Sabbath," and its ritual observance became the preeminent sign of God's covenant with Israel (e.g., Exod 20:11; 31:17).

The AV's translation of v. 2a illustrates the ambiguity in the Hebrew, which permits divine "work" (i.e., creation) continuing into the seventh day: "And on the seventh day God ended his work which he had made" (also NRSV). To avoid this, ancient versions (LXX, SP, Syr) read, "On the *sixth* day God finished his work." Many English versions have remedied it by taking the verb as a pluperfect "had finished" and thereby clarifying that God had completed his creation *by* the seventh day, not on the seventh day (e.g., NIV, NASB). Since 2:1 declares that creation was completed before the seventh day is introduced (2:2), the passage indicates that no "work" occurred on the seventh day. Exodus 40:33b has the parallel expression, "And so Moses finished the work," which refers to Moses' previous work on the tabernacle before the endowment of the glory cloud. The parallel lines of 2:2 are synthetic, that is, should be read together: God completed his work by the seventh day (v. 2a), resulting in his rest (v. 2b).

Repetition of creation-sabbath language is found in the construction of the tabernacle: Moses "saw" all the work the people "had done," and he "blessed" them.[221] Linkage between creation-sabbath and Moses' tabernacle binds God's first work at creation with his newly directed work among Israel. The rare wording *rûaḥ ʾĕlōhîm* of 1:2 appears again in Exod 31:3, where Bezalel receives the "Spirit" for the purpose of constructing the tabernacle.[222] This tie between cosmic Creator and Israel's Redeemer who formed them at Sinai explains the special importance given to Sabbath observance by the Hebrew community (Exod 20:8–11; 31:14; 35:2). After the construction of the wilderness tabernacle, the Sabbath was deemed the sign of the covenant between God

---

[220] Noted by Cassuto, *Genesis,* 61.

[221] For parallel language see Exod 39:43a (Gen 1:31); 39:32a (2:1); 40:33 (2:2); and 39:43b (2:3a). The same conclusion is echoed at the end of the establishment of the sanctuary in Canaan and the division of the land in Josh 19:51 (suggested by J. Blenkinsopp, "The Structure of P," *CBQ* 38 [1976]: 275–76).

[222] See, e.g., M. Fishbane, *Text and Texture: Close Readings of Selected Biblical Texts* (New York: Schocken Books, 1979), 12.

and the nation (31:13,17). According to the tabernacle narrative (Exod 25–40), Israel's Sabbath and creation's rest meet in the holy place: the Creator who sanctified the seventh day because of "rest" (2:2–3) is the covenant Lord, who sanctifies his people and tabernacles among them (e.g., Exod 31:12–17).[223] As with man, made in the *imago Dei,* the earthly tabernacle also followed a "pattern" revealed by God to Moses at Sinai (Exod 25:9,40; cf. Heb 8:5). Worship then is related to the created order itself, which existed before the formation of Israel and its sanctuary at Sinai.[224] Worship is for all humanity—all those created in the "image of God." The observance of Israel's sacred custom of weekly and annual sabbaths was an expression of and attestation to God's presence as their Creator-Covenant Lord.

As with "seventh day," the same phrase "his work" (in the Hebrew) occurs three times in vv. 2–3 to emphasize that creation was God's work alone. Creation's "work" *(mĕlāʾkâ)* has its later human parallel in the construction of the tabernacle by skilled artisans who were inspired by the Lord (e.g., Exod 31:5; 35:29; 36:1–2). "Work" also has the meaning of common, human labor (e.g., Gen 39:11; 1 Chr 27:26). "When the name 'work' is given to God's six days' creation, human work is ennobled to the highest conceivable degree, as being the copy of his model."[225] The same repetition appears for the phrase "he had done,"[226] and the critical term "rested" *(šābat)* occurs twice in vv. 2–3. The repetition underscores that the end of his work was related to the completion of creation, not due to fatigue. There was simply nothing left to do; the created order was whole, requiring only the sustaining grace of God's superintendence. The verb "rested" means "the *cessation* of creative activity"; it has this same sense in its only other occurrence in Genesis, where God promises the postdiluvian world that the times and seasons "will never cease" (8:22). Elsewhere we find that God "rested" (*nûaḥ,* Exod 20:11; *napaš,* 31:17), but here the passage speaks of the absence of work—"he abstained" from work.[227] The derivative noun "Sabbath" *(šabbāt),* which is a transliteration (not translation) of the Hebrew word, does not actually occur in the creation account (though it is obviously alluded to by *šābat,* "ceased"), probably since the number "seventh day" is in keeping with the numerical format of the narrative.

---

[223] See H. N. Wallace, "Genesis 2:1–3—Creation and Sabbath," *Pacifica* 1 (1988): 235–50.

[224] Noted by J. Blenkinsopp, *The Pentateuch: An Introduction to the First Five Books of the Bible* (New York: Doubleday, 1992), 218.

[225] Delitzsch, *A New Commentary on Genesis,* 107.

[226] The NIV omits the second occasion of the clause, "which he had done," to avoid redundancy in English. The finale in 2:3b, "from all the work of creating that he had done," differs somewhat from the previous two by the verb "created" (בָּרָא) instead of "done" (עָשָׂה), but the infinitive "by doing, making" (לַעֲשׂוֹת) follows.

[227] Cassuto, *Genesis,* 63.

2:3 Of the creation week's days, this "seventh day" is uniquely "blessed" and "sanctified" by the Creator. The specific explanation in the text for the seventh day's special hallowedness is that God ceased from his work. God has already "blessed" the created order, enabling it to propagate (1:22,28); but here the dimension of time, the "seventh day," is said to be "blessed" of God. This "blessing" is explained by the subsequent act of consecration that is the first in the Bible. When God "sanctified" *(qādaš)* the day, he declared that the day was especially devoted to him. This was the charge in the Ten Words for later Israel—to observe the Sabbath by keeping it holy as a special possession of the Lord (Exod 20:8,11). The "seventh day" was subsequently called a holy Sabbath unto the Lord when no work was to be done by human or animal (e.g., Exod 31:15; 35:2). The prophets speak of the Lord's Sabbath as "my holy day" or "my sabbaths" (Isa 58:13; Ezek 22:8; cf. Neh 9:14). Consecration in the Old Testament meant designating or setting aside persons, places, and things that were regarded sacred by virtue of their relationship to or possession by the Lord, who is holy (e.g., firstborn, tabernacle, priests).[228]

In the Babylonian creation stories the gods are freed from their labors after the creation of humans, who were formed for the sole purpose of serving the deities' needs. God's sabbath, however, is not aversion to labor but the celebrative cessation of a completed work, whereby he expresses his mastery over time by sanctifying it. The observance of Sabbath was unique to ancient Israel.[229] Whereas in the Hebrew calendar (and those of other peoples) the days, months, and years were related to the solar and lunar cycles, the Sabbath is not tied to any celestial movement. "The Sabbath thus underlines the fundamental idea of Israelite monotheism: that God is wholly outside of nature."[230]

The Decalogue first directly ties Sabbath observance with the creation rest (Exod 20:8–11; cf. 31:17), furnishing the theological rationale for the Hebrew practice. Much of the decalogue terminology echoes Gen 2:1–3. "Sabbath" in the Fourth Commandment occurs as a synonym for "seventh"; in the direct allusion to Gen 2:3, "Sabbath" is substituted for "seventh": "Therefore the LORD blessed the Sabbath day and made it holy" (Exod 20:11b). The seventh day of creation as a consequence is viewed as God's "sabbath"; thus for the

---

[228] E.g., Exod 13:2; 19:10; 28:41; 40:9; Lev 8:10; 25:10.

[229] Mesopotamian culture also set aside special days; the fifteenth of each month, known as *shapattu*, was the day of the full moon (see G. F. Hasel, "Sabbath," ABD 5.850). There were "evil days" each month at approximately seven-day intervals that were determined by the lunar cycle. But there is little similarity of the Babylonian custom with the Hebrew Sabbath. Functionally, there is no indication of a borrowing. The Babylonian days were taboo, unlike the Sabbath, which was a "blessed" day for the Hebrews, and they were determined by the lunar cycle whereas the Sabbath is independent of celestial movements. There is no connection in the Bible between the full moon day on the fifteenth and the Sabbath.

[230] Sarna, *Genesis,* 15.

Hebrews Sabbath takes on cosmic meaning. By the commemoration of "Sabbath," God and his creatures share in the celebration of the good creation, and God's people are enjoined to enter into the rhythm of work and joyful rest. Embracing God's sabbath rest meant experiencing the sense of completeness and well being God had accomplished at creation in behalf of all human life.

Observance of a seventh day among Israel, however, antedates the Sinai injunction. In the wilderness sojourn there is "a Sabbath to the LORD" in which the gathering of manna is suspended for a seventh day (Exod 16:21–30). The passage obviously anticipates the Sinai legislation, but the basis, as in the Fourth Commandment, must be the creation. For the Hebrews, then, the world had always known sabbaths from the beginning. Sabbath existed before man observed it and continues whether or not God's creatures acknowledge it.[231] The practice of a sacred "seventh" was extended beyond the cycle of the week to sacred years, festivals, and days.[232] The Fourth Commandment therefore united the "word" of creation and the regulating "word" of the religious order for the newly created Israel. Israel's Sabbath, like God's sabbath rest, was sanctified and set apart as a special day of worship and celebration. The seventh day then pointed the Hebrew reader to a day of rejoicing over the created work of God. "It is a day on which we are called upon to share what is eternal in time, to turn from the results of creation to the mystery of creation; from the world of creation to the creation of the world."[233]

Also the Sabbath day was tied by Moses to the redemptive purposes of God for Israel. In Genesis the sabbath rest of God did not mean that he was idly distant, for in the garden he is found at work making garments of skin for sinful man and woman (3:21). Deuteronomy's decalogue presents this second reading of sabbath and relates its observance to the historic deliverance of Israel from Egyptian servitude (Deut 5:15). Sabbath released human and beast from the labors of the week, and likewise the Redeemer released Israel from its slavery. Together the two versions of the Fourth Commandment capture the twofold meaning of the seventh day for Israel: a celebration of God as Creator and Redeemer. The redeeming "work" of God continues as expressed through Israel's history and the particular ministry of Jesus Christ (e.g., Ps 111; John 5:17; 9:4; 17:4).

The idea of "rest" was later related to the land of promise that lay before

---

[231] See von Rad, *Genesis,* 62.

[232] These included the sabbath year (Lev 25:1–4) and the "sacred assemblies" (Lev 23:1) known as "a sabbath of rest": Sabbath (Lev 23:3), Feast of Trumpets (Lev 23:24), and the Day of Atonement (Lev 16:31; 23:32). Also the Feast of Weeks (Pentecost) was celebrated seven weeks after the Feast of Unleavened Bread (Lev 23:15–22), and the year of Jubilee occurred at the end of seven cycles of sabbath years (Lev 25).

[233] A. Heschel, *The Earth Is the Lord's and the Sabbath* (New York: Harper Torchbooks, 1966), 10.

Israel. Rest in Canaan was Israel's destiny (Exod 33:14), but the people failed to enter their rest due to disobedience (Num 14:28–30). The second generation awaited its possession (Deut 3:20; 12:10; 25:19) and eventually obtained it with blessing (Josh 1:13–15). The land experienced its sabbaths and jubilees (Lev 25:4,11) as a symbolic recognition of the land as God's provision of rest for Israel. It was God who owned the land of rest, and Israel as aliens entered into that land only at the invitation of God and by the price of redemption (Lev 25:23–24).

Also the theological significance of creation's "seventh day" is eschatological. The seventh day has no closing refrain "evening" and "morning"; the seventh day has no end and therefore is viewed as eternal. Whereas the human workweek recurs after each Sabbath, the sabbath rest of God is eternal since creation's work is finished. Sabbath is taken up by the New Testament and interpreted in the context of the "new Moses." The theology of this perpetual rest was expounded by the writer to the Hebrews, who spoke of a sabbath rest that yet awaits those who are in Christ Jesus (4:3–11). He bound together the two motifs of Canaan's land of rest (3:7–19), drawing on Ps 95:7b–11, and of creation's sabbath rest, quoting Gen 2:2 (4:3–11). Just as Moses' generation had failed to possess their promised rest, the writer forewarned his readers not to commit the same failure through disbelief in Christ.

For the apostle Paul, Sabbath was a foreshadowing of the eternal realities of the Lord and the church (Col 2:16–17). The old signs of circumcision, dietary laws, and sabbath observance were set aside as "boundary markers for the people of the covenant"[234] (cf. Gal 4:10). Christians are circumcised in heart (Rom 2:29), undefiled by foods (John 15:3), and free to treat every day as sacred (Rom 14:5,12; 1 Tim 4:3–5). Sabbath has given way to the realities of the "Lord's day"—the resurrection of Jesus Christ (Acts 2:1; 1 Cor 16:1–2). The church set aside the first day of the week as a special day for worship and proclamation.[235] By the first day the Christian community proclaims the new creation, the era of messianic redemption.

---

[234] F. Thielman, *Paul and the Law: A Contextual Approach* (Downers Grove: IVP, 1993), 213.

[235] See D. A. Carson, ed., *From Sabbath to Lord's Day: A Biblical, Historical, and Theological Investigation* (Grand Rapids: Zondervan, 1982).

SECTION OUTLINE

II. THE HUMAN FAMILY IN AND OUTSIDE THE GARDEN (2:4–4:26)
  1. The Man and Woman in the Garden (2:4–25)
    (1) Creation of the First Man (2:4–7)
    (2) The Man's Life in the Garden (2:8–17)
    (3) The Man's Companion, the First Woman (2:18–25)
  2. The Man and Woman Expelled from the Garden (3:1–24)
    (1) The Serpent and the Woman (3:1–5)
    (2) The Man and Woman Sin (3:6–8)
    (3) God Questions the Man and Woman (3:9–13)
    (4) God's Judgments Pronounced (3:14–21)
    (5) The Man and Woman Expelled (3:22–24)
  3. Adam and Eve's Family outside the Garden (4:1–26)
    (1) Cain and Abel's Birth (4:1–2)
    (2) Cain and Abel's Worship of God (4:3–7)
    (3) Cain's Murder of Abel (4:8–16)
    (4) Cain's Family (4:17–24)
    (5) Seth's Birth and Family (4:25–26)

II. THE HUMAN FAMILY IN AND OUTSIDE THE GARDEN (2:4–4:26)

This second section traces what became of God's "good" creation as depicted in 1:1–2:3, with attention on the pinnacle of creation—human life. "The destiny of the human creation is to live in God's world, with God's other creatures, *on God's terms*."[1] Although 2:4–25 expands on certain points of 1:1–2:3, it is wedded principally to chaps. 3 and 4 as one unit under the first occurrence of the *tōlĕdōt* rubric: "This is the account *[tôlĕdôt]* of the heavens and the earth when they were created" (2:4a). As we discussed in the Introduction, the *tōlĕdōt* heading in Genesis announces the subject matter of the genealogy or narrative that follows. In this passage the formula introduces the narrative, which speaks of beginning events concerning creation, that is, the subsequent history of created human life. Verse 2:4a repeats the same information as 1:1 and therefore ties 1:1–2:3 and 2:4b–4:26 together; both passages recount first things, but the second narrative goes beyond the first by tracking

[1] W. Brueggemann, *Genesis,* IBC (Atlanta: John Knox, 1982), 40.

the story of Adam's family.

LITERARY STRUCTURE AND ORIGINS. Three distinctive literary units make up this section: the Edenic account (2:4–3:24), which describes the first family, their habitat, and their consequent sin and expulsion from Eden; the account of Cain's murder of brother Abel (4:1–16); and last, genealogical records pertaining to Adam's sons, Cain and Seth (4:17–26). There are literary reasons for recognizing in the Edenic account a cohesive narrative produced by an original hand. J. T. Walsh has proposed for it seven scenes, with the central unit at 3:6–8 where the human participants, the man and woman, commit their tragic choice of disobedience.[2]

A Narrative: God sole actor and man passive (2:5–17)
  B Narrative: God main actor, man minor actor, woman and animals passive (2:18–25)
    C Dialogue: snake and woman (3:1–5)
      D Narrative: man and woman (3:6–8)
    C´ Dialogue: God, man and woman (3:9–13)
  B´ Narrative: God main actor, man minor actor, woman and snake passive (3:14–21)
A´ Narrative: God sole actor and man passive (3:22–24)

Also the Cain-Abel narrative (4:1–16) shows interdependence with 2:4–3:24 by structural similarities and language.[3] Although it may be posited that the final narrative unity can be attributed to the skill of a late Hebrew author, there is no compelling reason to supplant the simpler explanation of one hand with a complex and protracted history of source and tradition compilation.

Scholars often look to Mesopotamian myth(s) to explain the origins of the garden episode, but there is no parallel to the garden narrative as a whole in the ancient Near East. Some have proposed that the narrative is made up of two separate sources, a creation myth and a paradise myth (see Introduction, "Genesis 1–11 and Ancient Literature").[4] Others have proposed the broad pattern of varied mythological materials on the creation of man and a "garden of God"

---

[2] See J. T. Walsh's analysis in "Genesis 2:4b–3:24: A Synchronic Approach," *JBL* 96 (1977): 161–77, and its revision, cited in J. Wenham, *Genesis 1–15,* WBC (Waco: Word, 1987), 50. The seven units make up an inverted arrangement, distinguished by the participants and language. Alternatively, the structural analysis of S. Kempf, based on textlinguistics, shows how Genesis 2–3 consists of an introduction (2:4b–7), conclusion (3:22–24), and three interdependent episodes (2:8–25; 3:1–7; 3:8–21) with the penalty oracles of 3:14–19 as their grammatical and rhetorical "peak" (climax). See S. Kempf, "Genesis 3:14–19: Climax of the Discourse?" in *JTT* 6 (1993): 354–77.

[3] Cf. A. J. Hauser ("Linguistic and Thematic Links Between Genesis 4:1–16 and Genesis 2–3," *JETS* 23 [1980]: 297–305), who shows that the two narratives "have been written by one highly-skilled writer who has interwoven all major aspects of the two stories so that structurally, linguistically and thematically they form one unit" (p. 305). Also W. Vogels, "Caïn l'être humain qui devient une non-personne (Gen 4, 1–16)," *NRT* 114 (1992): 341–70.

[4] E.g., C. Westermann, *Genesis 1–11: A Commentary,* trans. J. J. Scullion (Minneapolis: Augsburg, 1984), 190–96.

motif.[5] By yet another approach, Genesis 2–3 is a combination and elaboration of early traditions that had their inception in the Babylonian themes of creation and kingship, as attested, for example, in *Atrahasis.*[6] Such reconstructions, however, do not readily explain the unique features of the Genesis account, such as the tree of knowledge and the emphasis on human sin. Moreover, proposing the author's indebtedness to common mythological materials cuts across the self-conscious historical purposes of the narrative (e.g., *tôlĕdôt,* 2:4). Would it not be incompatible for the Hebrew author to create a myth or modify a fictional account using God as the main character?[7] Rather than myth or an expansion on primal myths, the most that can be said is that Genesis 2–3 "incorporates in its history mythical motifs"[8] in order to address the concerns of the ancient reader.

LIFE IN AND OUTSIDE THE GARDEN. Before we consider the commentary, we will preview the literary and theological scope of the section. The contrast between human life inside and outside the garden depends on the pivotal episode in Eden, where sin makes its first appearance; disobedience impacted three areas of human experience: (1) the relationship of man to God, (2) the relationship of man to the environment, and (3) interpersonal relationships within the human family. Before the ruinous entry of sin, these three relationships were intact. (1) The man and woman enjoy the presence of God without shame, as evidenced by their nakedness (2:25). Eden's garden, graciously provided by God, is the meeting place where God and mankind interact in fellowship and trust. (2) Human life derives sustenance from the garden and exercises dominion over Eden, and the garden flourishes since a man is present to till and care for it. All life benefits mutually from this harmonious relationship. There is no threat and discord between man and nature. All appears in accordance with the blessings of God and his gracious provision (1:28–31). (3) Also the human couple recognize their distinctive identity and enjoy a nourishing harmony. There is no competition or confusion between the man and the woman. Their union is based on an unstated covenant of reciprocal devotion.

Chapter 3, however, surprises the reader by introducing an unforeseen character in the garden. That this serpent will impact the first couple for ill is hinted

[5] H. N. Wallace, *The Eden Narrative,* HSM 32 (Atlanta: Scholars Press, 1985).

[6] See J. van Seters, who posits that the Yahwist author took up the creation motif and expanded on the kingship tradition that he received directly from Ezekiel (28:12–19), who had carried forward and enlarged on the primitive Babylonian myth of the king's creation ("The Creation of Man and The Creation of the King," *ZAW* 101 [1989]: 333–42).

[7] See T. D. Alexander, "Jonah and Genre," *TynBul* 36 (1985): 58, who utilizes this argument for countering Jonah as alleged fiction.

[8] L. Alonso-Schökel, "Sapiential and Covenant Themes in Genesis 2–3," *TD* 13 (1965): 3–10, esp. 5 = "Motivos sapienciales y de alianza en Gn 2–3," *Bib* 43 (1962): 295–315. English reprint in *Studies in Ancient Israelite Wisdom,* ed. J. Crenshaw (New York: Ktav, 1976), 468–80, quote on p. 471.

at from the outset: he is "more crafty" (3:1) than the other beasts. By a play on words, there is a linkage between 2:25 ("naked," *ʿărûmmîm*) and 3:1 ("crafty," *ʿărûm*). The subsequent narration reveals that the harmony once known in the garden is shattered. (1) The garden, which once offered a setting of repose with God for the first couple, now is transformed into a hideout for the inept pair. (2) The subservient Eden suddenly declares war against its caretaker, forcing the man into the toilsome task of controlling his threatening environment. Not only does the ground oppose its human lord, but now there is enmity between the woman and the animal world, as shown by the serpent's guile. (3) Finally, the human family itself experiences the poison of the first sin. The solace of companionship turns to competition and confusion. The bliss and life of paradise in chap. 2 is matched by suffering and threat of death in chap. 3. Yet God reveals his grace in the midst of his judgment by preserving their lives. There is hope in the birth of the woman's seed (3:15), and God takes steps to clothe and protect the couple from the harshness of their new environment (3:21). The promise of blessing (1:28) will continue, but not in the garden. The man and woman no longer dwell in the garden where the "tree of life" is accessible; divine retribution expels them to the wiles of the "east side of the Garden of Eden" (3:24).

Chapter 4 details the moral as well as the familial descent of the human family. The three areas of broken relationship we have traced are continued. (1) Whereas God favors the first couple with children, it is their first child (Cain) who bears the divine "curse," pronounced for the first time upon a human being (4:11). (2) Now the blood-tainted land that had once served Cain's agrarian skills becomes his stranger, and he, in turn, becomes a "restless wanderer on the earth" (4:10–12). (3) Finally, human struggle for preeminence results in fratricide. The death of Abel's sacrificial offerings is joined by the blood of his own death. Death, touching both animal and human life, inaugurates its reign. And like his parents, murderous Cain is expelled "east of Eden" (4:16). But despite the wicked lineage of Cain, embodied in the vicious Lamech, there remains hope for the human family through the birth of Seth, whose descendants began "to call upon the name of the LORD" (4:25–26).

The motif of "blessing" initiated in the creation narrative continues (1:22,28; 2:3) in this section, though the term does not occur. Rather, its antithesis, "curse," appears in this passage three of its eight occasions in Genesis (3:14,17; 4:11). The sole condition for cursing is introduced in 2:17, where God forewarns that human disobedience results in death, but the "curse" is only directed against the soil of which man is made, not the man himself (3:17). The recounting of human sin and its consequences are focal in this section. Yet despite God's judgment, he does not abandon them; he does not curse the man or woman, though he does curse their eldest son for his reprehensible crime of murder (4:11). Rather, it is their adversary, the serpent, and the ground that bear the curses of God (3:14,17). God continues his beneficent provision (1:26–30) for them both spiritually and physically to cope with their new condition (3:15,21–22). Although death awaits them, their lives are mercifully prolonged, and God assures them of ultimate victory over their nemesis, the serpent. Appropriately the means for restoration will be the same vehicle by which they inherit their blessing—propagation; the woman's seed will avenge them. Divine blessing toward the human family is realized through the birth of children; therefore the progeny of the first couple is central to the development of God's blessing and restoration, as it is with the unfolding of God's promises to the later patriarchs. Chapter 4 is pivotal to the plot since now all attention is directed on the children of Eve, the mother of all living (3:20). The narrative turns on the birth and careers of her three sons, but their story has become our story. All human life is in jeopardy because evil resides not just with the tempter but now in the heart of Cain and his kind (4:7). The tempter has his agents. Righteous Abel becomes the first victim of his parents' rebellious deed.

The grace of God shows itself even with the evil Cain, who benefits from the resolve of God to keep his word: human life will flourish. Cain receives protection (4:16) and experiences fruition; his family's genealogy expands (4:17–24), but his influence for bad seems limitless (4:23–24). But there is a reprieve: Eve gives birth to Seth, who offers hope for the human family (4:25). Seth bears still others, and a godly line continues upon the face of the earth. It was by this godly seed of Seth that the Lord is worshiped (4:26b), sounding a renewed prospect for the man and woman.

Although the garden scene presents a universal truth of humanity's condition, for its first readers the message was all too concretely real in their particular experience. Israel knew the threat of disobedience and had witnessed the death of those who rebelled in the desert (e.g., Num 13–17). The just deserts of their obedience or disobedience were spelled out in Deuteronomy's covenant.[9] Nevertheless, God demonstrated the same compassion toward Israel in the wilderness as he did for our first parents; a second generation survives and prepares for entering the land of rest. Whereas Adam and Cain were expelled from the "land," Israel looks toward possessing the promised land. Moses' books conclude with Israel's eyes focused on its "Eden" (Canaan) across the Jordan River. Israel understood the contrast between the godly seed of Seth and that of Cain, whose descendants founded an expanding urban civilization marked by godlessness. Israel saw itself as the godly seed in the earth, chosen by the Lord, but it too faced the "Cains" and "Canaans" of its times who had built up its towers and cities opposing the Hebrews seeking refuge in the land. Nevertheless, they could take solace that God would preserve their number and prosper

[9] The verb "curse" (אָרַר), besides the eight occasions in Genesis, appears twenty-nine times in the Pentateuch, including sixteen times in the "curse" and "blessing" section of Deut 27–28.

them if they too would continue to call upon the name of the Lord as he had instructed Israel at Sinai. The name that is worshiped and proclaimed by Seth and his generation (4:26) takes on fuller meaning at Sinai, where God reveals himself to Moses, explaining that he is the God of their fathers (Exod 3:14–15; 6:2–8). Early Genesis reminded them of God's promise of blessing upon a righteous seed and his full intention of bringing blessing upon Abraham's offspring by prodigious progeny and by establishing them in the land of promise.

1. The Man and Woman in the Garden (2:4–25)

Much has been made of the differences between chaps. 1 and 2 in the history of interpretation. For well over a century critical scholars have attributed these passages to two conjectural sources (P and J) coming from different times and conveying distinct theological perspectives. A line of division is drawn at 2:4a, which is taken as the conclusion of the P(riestly) account of creation in 1:1–2:4a, and the beginning of the Yahwist's story, which consists of 2:4b–4:26. We have described already at chap. 1 the primary reasons for such a division and the problems that a dichotomy at 2:4a and 2:4b creates for this now well-entrenched reconstruction by critical scholars. Although there are some differences between chaps. 1 and 2, which we will address, there is a growing recognition that these differences can be attributed to reasons other than two original, competing creation stories.[10] At 2:4 the author has joined the account of universal creation (1:1–2:3) and the singular story of human history (2:5–4:26).

Studies in the rhetorical features of 1:1–2:3 and 2:4–25 have shown that they are two complementary descriptions that present a congruent narrative, the second picking up on the skeletal telling of the former. They possess a number of similarities in literary structure and content that recommend that they are the product of one hand.[11] Scholars are recognizing that chaps. 1 and 2 are not

---

[10] E.g., see T. Stordalen, who concludes: "Focusing primarily upon Gen 2–3, I hold that the most notable exegetical profit is that according to its native introduction the Story of Eden is not a creation story, but a story of what became of heaven and earth some time after their creation" ("Genesis 2,4: Restudying a *locus classicus*," *ZAW* 104 [1992]: 175).

[11] E.g., J. B. Doukhan has shown that 1:1–2:4a and 2:4b–25 are each built on seven sections (*The Genesis Creation Story: Its Literary Structure* [Berrien Springs, Mich.: Andrews University Press], 1978), 78–79). "God said," occurring nine times in 1:3–31, is matched by the nine occasions of "Yahweh God did/said" in 2:7–22. Also both narratives possess three pairs of inner matching elements: the parallelism of days 1–3 and 4–6 in chap. 1 and chap. 2's parallelism (p. 51):

1. Dust (2:7)	4. Death (2:17)
2. A garden for man (2:8)	5. A companion for man (2:18)
3. Dominion over garden (2:15)	6. Dominion over animals (2:20)

We cannot concur with his analysis at all points, e.g., the division of 2:4, but he does demonstrate that the passages reflect a literary congruity in structure. See the critique of D. Garrett, *Rethinking Genesis: The Sources and Authorship of the First Book of the Pentateuch* (Grand Rapids: Baker, 1991), 194–97.

a repetition of the same matters that in places are at odds with one another, but rather chap. 2 is a thematic elaboration of the key features found in 1:1–2:3. It has long been recognized that the normal use of the formulation "these are the generations of" refers to the progeny that follows as opposed to the progenitor himself. "The generations of Terah" (11:27), for example, does not concern Terah's begetting but his offspring Abraham. Thus "these are the generations of the heavens and the earth" (2:4a) concerns not their own begetting, for this has been seen already in chap. 1; rather, the *tôlědôt* heading introduces what was the aftermath of that creation. Another indication that 2:4–25 is an expansion on chap. 1 is the similarity of 2:4 with Gen 5:1 and Num 3:1 in syntax and narrative function: the heading "this is the account of" *(tōlědōt)* is followed by a temporal clause "when" *(běyôm)*. In Gen 5:1 and Num 3:1 the content of the "when" clause refers to former prominent information, so as to bring it to the attention of the reader for understanding the conditions under which the following *tōlědōt* section occurs.[12]

In chap. 1 the peak days in the progression of creation are days three and six, in which the earth exhibits productivity (vegetation) and population (animal, human). These foci in days three and six are found again in chap. 2, where they are treated not repetitively but in a fuller way so as to give them continuing prominence.[13] Particularly, the sixth day's events regarding the creation of man and woman and their dominion (1:26–28) are taken up in 2:4–25.

Moreover, comparative studies show that the telling of human origins in doublet is a feature observed in Sumerian and Babylonian stories. In *Enki and Ninmah* (ca. 2000 B.C.) the first account of the creation of human life is a general one, with creation by nipping off clay, and the second account covers the same ground in more detail. Babylonian *Atrahasis* has the first creation from the remains of a slain deity mixed with clay, and the second elaborates, showing that the first humans were created in seven pairs by snipping off clay. In both cases the former is general and the second specific.[14]

As with Genesis 1 and 2, a transition from a general account to a specific one also is found in the pairing of the genealogical records in Genesis 4 with 5 and 10 with 11. They exhibit a focusing technique whereby the second genealogy in the pair becomes prominent for the following narrative, that is, Seth (chap. 5) and Shem (chap. 11). The first genealogical record also traces a line of descent; but, unlike the second genealogy, its descendants are excluded from the succeeding narrative, that is, Cain (chap. 4) and Japheth and Ham

---

[12] Noted by Stordalen, "Genesis 2, 4," 171.

[13] See the analysis of W. H. Shea, "The Unity of the Creation Account," *Origins* 5 (1978): 9–38, esp. 17–19; e.g., divisions, land, vegetation, animals, man and woman, food, and dominion.

[14] See I. M. Kikawada, "The Double Creation of Mankind in *Enki and Ninmah, Atrahasis* I 1–351, and *Genesis* 1–2," *Iraq* 45 (1983) 43–45; Kikawada and A. Quinn, *Before Abraham Was: The Unity of Genesis 1–11* (Nashville: Abingdon, 1985), 38–40.

(chap. 10). Creation in 1:1–2:3 is completed without further reference, and the subsequent account (2:4–25) picks up the main aspect of that creation, namely, the man, and focuses on his creation, home, and companion in chaps. 2–4. It is Adam's history that concerns the ongoing narration.[15]

The first indication that the narrative of chaps. 1–2 shifts focus from the broad to the specific is the inversion of "the heavens and the earth" (1:1; 2:4a) to "the earth and the heavens" in 2:4b, which shows a change in attention and prepares for a different narrative arrangement. As we will show, this inversion, "the earth and the heavens," while echoing 1:1, is immediately related to 2:4a. The reversal "the earth and the heavens" also occurs in Ps 148:13 and is found in a chiasmus at Jer 10:11. The allusion to 1:1, "the heavens and the earth," in 2:4a and the inversion "the earth and the heavens" at 2:4b are best explained as a transition in the narrative, carefully integrating the creation account and the narrative of the garden to follow. The genealogical framework, "these are the generations of," in chaps. 1–11 is designed to move the narration forward, indicating the progressive movement of God's program for achieving the promissory blessings despite the setbacks of personal sin and societal wickedness. Chapter 2 picks up the thesis of blessing for mankind already introduced (1:26–28) and carries it thematically forward by recounting the first man's family and environment.

Since both narratives overlap in some points of content but yet are structured for different functions, it is not surprising that dissimilarities result.[16] How their different aims impact the way events are narrated is well illustrated by the creation of the animals (2:19–20; 1:20–25). The different order in the creation of the animals and humanity between 1:1–2:3 and 2:4–25 has been taken as an irreconcilable conflict. Chapter 2, however, presents a topical order in the formation of the man and the animals (2:7,19), giving priority to the man's role as master over Eden (see 2:19 note). Also in chap. 2's narrative hierarchy, the making of the animals is subservient to the larger concern of the woman's creation (vv. 18–25). The animals are paraded before the man to establish the suitability of the woman as his companion.[17] Chapter 1, on the other hand, presents the creation of the birds and beasts before the creation of humanity to indicate a line of ascendancy in creation, from the lesser creatures

---

[15] See the discussion by R. S. Hess, "Genesis 1–2 in its Literary Context," *TynBul* 41 (1990): 143–53.

[16] E.g., 2:4–25 elaborates on what is recounted in only one verse concerning the creation of man and woman (1:26); also the vegetation of "seed-bearing plants" (1:11–12) described on day three is different from the herbage depicted in 2:5 (see discussion at 2:5).

[17] N. H. Sarna comments: "The dominant theme of this section, to which all is subordinate is man and the human condition. . . . Mention of their [animals'] creation is therefore made incidentally, not for its own sake, and is no indication of sequential order in regard to the creation of man" (בראשית *Genesis,* JPST [Philadelphia: Jewish Publication Society, 1989], 21).

to the superior mankind. Such differences can be attributed to the purpose of the present arrangement of chaps. 1 and 2. As a son carries out the purposes of a father, chap. 2 is the offspring (*tôlĕdôt,* 2:4a) of creation (chap. 1), showing that the reason for creation is human history.[18] We conclude that 1:1–2:3 and 2:4–25 are compatible, and the latter is an expansion on the former with special attention on what became of the human family.

(1) Creation of the First Man (2:4–7)

[4]This is the account of the heavens and the earth when they were created.

When the LORD God made the earth and the heavens— [5]and no shrub of the field had yet appeared on the earth and no plant of the field had yet sprung up, for the LORD God had not sent rain on the earth and there was no man to work the ground, [6]but streams came up from the earth and watered the whole surface of the ground— [7]the LORD God formed the man from the dust of the ground and breathed into his nostrils the breath of life, and the man became a living being.

2:4 "This is the account of" is the first occurrence of the popular *tōlĕdōt* phrase that appears in Genesis.[19] The striking difference in 2:4 is that the progenitor is "the heavens and the earth," not a person, as is customary with the expression. This indicates that the subsequent story of human history is viewed as the outcome of the creation narration.

The chiastic parallelism of the verse obstructs the anatomizing that is found in some versions (contra NIV, NRSV but see NASB). Its *ABB'A'* structure evidences a single unit:

A the heavens and the earth
 B when they were created *(bārāʾ)*
 B′ when the LORD God made *(ʿāśâ)*
A′ the earth and the heavens

By using the vocabulary of 1:1, v. 4 echoes the creation narrative's beginning affirmation; it also recalls from 1:1–2:3 the frequent word "made" *(ʿāśâ).* Verse 4 is an independent sentence (as in 1:1), and vv. 5–7 are a distinctive syntactical unit.[20] Verses 5–6 present a series of circumstantial clauses, describing the condition of the land when God formed the first man (2:7). This

---

[18]Noted by B. S. Childs, *Introduction to the Old Testament as Scripture* (Philadelphia: Fortress, 1979), 150.

[19]The formulaic phrase אֵלֶּה תוֹלְדוֹת occurs eleven times in Genesis, with 5:1 having a slight variation (זֶה סֵפֶר תּוֹלְדֹת): 2:4; 5:1; 6:9: 10:1; 11:10; 11:27; 25:12; 25:19; 36:1; 36:9; 37:2. Cf. also Num 3:1. The word תּוֹלְדֹת also appears in 10:32 and 25:13 in Genesis. See Introduction for its role in the structure of Genesis.

[20]The NIV takes 2:4b as a temporal clause with v. 7 as the main clause. Vv. 5–6 then are parenthetical as indicated by NIV's placement of hyphens.

syntactical arrangement is similar to the pattern of 1:2–3,[21] but not exactly the same since 1:2 is a positive description whereas 2:5 is negative.[22] In 1:2 the interest lies with the "earth," but here the sense is uncultivated "land."

Here is the first place in Scripture where the divine name "LORD" (Yahweh) occurs, and it is found in tandem with the name "God" (Elohim). The combination of the divine names is another link between 1:1–2:3 and 2:5–4:26, since the two narratives give priority to different divine names: *Elohim* is exclusively used in the former narrative, and *Yahweh* becomes prominent in the latter.[23] The union Yahweh-Elohim occurs only in Gen 2:4–3:24 and Exod 9:30 in the Pentateuch. The combination of divine names at 2:4b is a favorite evidence cited by source critics for the redactional wedding of the two narrative sources P and J. Problematic for any source reconstruction is why 2:4b as the introduction to the Yahwistic (J) account would have the intrusive name Elohim present. Usually it is assigned to a late priestly editor who added Elohim so as to assert that Yahweh was God, the Creator of the universe.[24] This will hardly do, for we must ask why in late Israel guarding the deity of Yahweh as Creator would have been incumbent upon the conjectural P redactor. Moreover, there are the questions of the aberration of Elohim occurring alone at 3:1–5 in the midst of a Yahwistic source and the oddity of the joined names occurring so infrequently elsewhere if it truly reflects a serious theological concern. The idea that a late scribe whose responsibility was to guard and transmit the sacred text would have improvised with the sacred names of God for his special theological agenda is unlikely.

Rather than a source explanation, the use of the combined names commends a theological explanation that can be attributed to the author. Yahweh-Elohim is transitional in function at 2:4, but the frequency of the unusual merger of names (20x) in chaps. 2–3 indicates there is a special place for the union of names that the subject matter originally elicited.[25] Elohim is appropriate for the majestic portrayal of God as Creator of the universe since it properly indicates omnipotent deity, whereas Yahweh is the name commonly associated

---

[21] 1:2 and 2:5 both begin with the *wāw* disjunctive.

[22] It is wrongly contended that 2:4b–7 has the same syntactical arrangement as 1:1–3 and the opening lines to the Babylonian creation myth *Enuma Elish* (lines 1–9; see Excursus: "Translating Gen 1:1–2). See, e.g., E. A. Speiser, *Genesis,* AB (Garden City: Doubleday, 1964), 19–20. Where 2:5–7 agrees with the Babylonian *Enuma Elish* is its "not yet" pattern: "when [such and such] was not yet . . . then [such and such] happened." See Westermann, *Genesis 1–11,* 97.

[23] Except 3:1–5 and 4:25, where אֱלֹהִים occurs.

[24] E.g., G. von Rad, *Genesis: A Commentary,* rev. ed., trans. J. H. Marks, OTL (Philadelphia: Westminster, 1973), 77; so Westermann (*Genesis 1–11,* 198), who thinks it was an ad hoc addition of the redactor.

[25] Argued, e.g., by U. Cassuto, *A Commentary on the Book of Genesis. Part I. From Adam to Noah, Genesis I–VI:8,* trans. I. Abrahams (Jerusalem: Magnes, 1961), 86–88; J. L'Hour, "Yahweh Elohim," *RB* 81 (1974): 524–56.

with the covenant relationship between deity and his people, Israel (cf. 15:7; Exod 3:14–15). Its combination with Elohim achieves an overlapping of these theological emphases: Yahweh, the Lord of his people, is in fact the all-wise and powerful Elohim-Creator. Hence, the antecedents of Israel's precious communion with its Creator and Covenant Lord had its inception in the garden when man first knew that fellowship. The personal presence of Yahweh-Elohim among his people Israel was not an anomaly but the pattern God inaugurated from the beginning. Conversely, the absence of the name Yahweh in the conversation between the serpent and the woman (3:1–5), where treachery is contemplated, shows that the relationship with God as Covenant Lord is under assault.

2:5–6 Now the author sets about to depict what the land was like before the creation of the first man (2:7): there was (1) "no shrub of the field" (v. 5a); (2) "no plant of the field" (v. 5b); and (3) "streams came up from the earth" (v. 6). The reason for the absence of plant life is specifically stated: "the LORD God had not sent rain," and "there was no man to work the ground" (v. 5cd).[26] There is a subterranean source of water (v. 6), but it by itself is evidently insufficient to support plant life, leading to the critical missing item—the labor of a farmer. All this prepares the reader for the principal clause in v. 7, the creation of the first man, whose occupation will be agriculture.

How 2:5–6 relates to the cosmological account of chap. 1 is perplexing for commentators. Some, assuming two distinct accounts, consider vv. 5–6 a second attempt (J source) to describe the chaos of 1:2. Other scholars see vv. 5–6 as a reference to overall vegetation created on day three (1:11–12); consequently this means the order of creation differs with chap. 1 according to which vegetation antedates the creation of human life on day six. If it is to be harmonized with chap. 1, it is better to relate vv. 5–6 to the formation of the dry land (1:9–10), which preceded both the appearance of vegetation and man.[27] Alternatively, the "not yet" description of v. 5 may describe only what is not living in order to prepare for the goal of the narrative, namely, the creation of the living. The purpose of v. 5 would be to show that the world as we know it did not yet exist when man was created.[28] We will show, however, that 2:5–6 is best related to the judgment oracles of 3:8–24, indicating what the world was like before and after sin.

[26] Alternatively, D. T. Tsumura analyzes it as four clauses. (1) "No shrub" and (2) "no plant" recall the barrenness of the "earth" in 1:2, since God had not sent rain on the "earth." The second half narrows on the "land": (3) "no man" worked the "land" and (4) the subterranean waters watered the "land." In chap. 2 he argues for a narrowing effect: "earth" to "land," "land" to "Eden," and "Eden" to the "garden" (*The Earth and the Waters in Genesis 1 and 2, JSOTSup* 83 [Sheffield: JOT, 1989], 86–90).

[27] So Sarna, *Genesis,* 17.

[28] So Westermann, *Genesis 1–11,* 199.

There is a certain ambiguity in the passage whether it speaks of the entire earth or a portion, since the terms "field" *(śādeh),* "earth/land" *(ʾereṣ),* and "ground" *(ʾădāmâ)* are interchangeable in Old Testament usage. "Field" can refer to the open fields as a wilderness home for the beasts (2:19–20; 3:1,14; 25:29), pasture land (29:2; 30:16), or cultivated ground (37:7; 47:24). Hebrew *ʾereṣ* may be rendered "earth" in its universal sense or "land" in the sense of a tract of land or country, as it commonly is in Genesis. Here it is best taken as "land" since the habitat of the first man is in view. "Ground" often has to do with the soil, which is cultivated by human enterprise,[29] and it is the same material substance of which both man and beast are made (2:7,19). Verse 5 plays on the words "ground" and "man," indicating that the *ʾădāmâ* ("ground") needs *ʾādām* ("man") to produce a robust harvest (also v. 7).[30] Yet ultimately it is God, not man, who provides the garden (2:8) and brings life from the ground (2:9).

The purpose of this *tōlĕdōt* section is its depiction of human life before and after the garden sin; the condition of the "land" after Adam's sin is contrasted with its state before the creation of the man. Genesis 2:5–7 is best understood in light of 3:8–24, which describes the consequences of sin. This is shown by the language of 2:5–6, which anticipates what happens to the land because of Adam's sin (3:18,23). When viewed in this way, we find that the "shrub" and "plant" of 2:5 are not the same as the vegetation of 1:11–12.[31] "Plant *(ʿēśeb)* of the field" describes the diet of man which he eats only after the sweat of his labor (3:18–19) after his garden sin, whereas "seed-bearing plants" *(ʿēśeb mazrîaʿ zeraʿ),* as they are found in the creation narrative, were provided by God for human and animal consumption (1:11–12,29–30; 9:3). These plants reproduce themselves by seed alone, but "plant," spoken of in 2:5, requires human cultivation to produce the grains necessary for edible food; it is by such cultivation that fallen man will eat his "food" (3:19).

The "shrub *[śîaḥ]* of the field" is a desert shrub large enough to shield Hagar's teenage son (Gen 21:15) and those seeking its protection (Job 30:4,7). Since "plant" is best defined by its recurrence in the judgment oracle (Gen 3:18), "shrub" probably parallels Adam's "thorns and thistles," which are the by-product of God's curse on the ground (3:17–18). Thus 2:5–6 does not speak to the creation of overall vegetation but to specific sorts of herbage in the world to follow. The language of cultivation, "work the ground" (2:5), anticipates the labor of Adam, first positively as the caretaker of Eden (2:15) but also negatively in 3:23, which describes the expulsion of the man and woman from the garden. God prepared a land for the man, but in telling of his creation and the

---

[29] E.g., 2:9; 3:17,23; 4:2; 5:29; 8:21.

[30] The etymology of אָדָם is unclear; cf. the Ugaritic epithet for the deity El, *ab adm,* "Father of man." See R. S. Hess, *Studies in the Personal Names of Genesis 1–11,* AOAT 234 (Neukirchen-Vluyn: Neukirchener, 1993), 14–19, 59–65.

[31] So Cassuto, *Genesis,* 102.

land in which he is placed, the text anticipates how the land will suffer from the effects of Adam's sin.[32] Also required for the spreading of such plant life is rainfall. "The LORD God had not sent rain upon the earth" likewise anticipates God's judgment against corrupt man in Noah's day: "I will send rain on the earth" (7:4).[33] Whereas in 2:5–6 rain is perceived as the welcomed welfare of God whereby herbage may survive, in the flood account the rains are the means of divine reparations for a morally depraved earth.

Despite the sin of the garden and the subsequent moral decadence of Noah's age, the grace of God in both accounts is evidenced by his providing the possibility of food and continued life (3:18–19; 9:2). In the later Mosaic community the growth or ruin of cultivated "plants" corresponded to covenant blessing or curse upon the land (e.g., Deut 11:15; 29:22). The Song of Moses draws on this imagery by speaking of God's beneficent teaching as "abundant rain on tender plants" (Deut 32:2d). Although Israel faced a sin-stained world, God blessed Israel with a productive land when it chose to live in covenant faithfulness. Israel also, however, as demonstrated by the author of Kings, will experience expulsion from its good land because of its prolonged apostasy.

Verse 6 defines the subterranean source of water that blanketed the ground. The NIV's "streams" is the rendering of the term *ʾēd*, which has puzzled biblical scholars (AV, NASB's "mist") and hinders a secure interpretation. It occurs but once more in Job 36:27 (AV's "vapour"). The LXX rendering has "spring" at 2:6 but "cloud" in Job.[34] What is at stake exegetically is the condition of the earth's surface: was it dry, lacking rainfall and having only an evaporative mist, or was the land inundated with a flow of water, whether subterranean springs or a river, as modern renderings recommend (e.g., NIV, NRSV, NJPS, NJB, NAB)? In other words, was the absence of plant life due to a lack of water or too much water? Etymologically, *ʾēd* is disputed; it has been attributed to different Semitic, Akkadian, or Sumerian origins.[35] Most are agreed, however, that the term refers to either underground streams that come to the surface or a substantial river. The notion of a faint mist appears foreign to the word itself, but the context may demand it when we consider the following creation of man from the soil (2:7). Such moisture mixed with dirt would provide nicely the necessary consistency for forming man from the "dust"; an excessive watery setting (precluding "dust") would self-evidently present problems for the

---

[32] See J. Sailhamer, "Genesis," EBC (Grand Rapids: Zondervan, 1990), 40.

[33] This does not mean necessarily, as some contend, that there was no rainfall until its first mention in Noah's day, as we would not insist the first sunset happened only when it is cited in the patriarchal period (15:2) (so F. I. Andersen, "On Reading Genesis 1–3," in *Backgrounds for the Bible,* ed. M. P. O'Connor and D. N. Freedman [Winona Lake: Eisenbrauns, 1987], 138).

[34] πηγή (2:6) and νεφέλην (Job).

[35] See the extended discussion in Tsumura, who concludes that אֵד in 2:6 is a loan word from a Sumerian term meaning "high water," and the word אִידוֹ in Job 36:27 is ultimately related to Akk. *edû,* "flood" (*The Earth and the Waters in Genesis 1 and 2,* 94–116).

anthropomorphic description in 2:7. This, however, can be accommodated in the passage by the prior planting of the garden in 2:8, where the Lord routed the water out of Eden by means of four rivers, leaving soil for both the creation of Adam and also arable ground for tilling. It would seem on balance that the explanation of underground streams covering the surface of the ground is the better understanding since it comes closer to etymological speculation and can make sense in the passage.

2:7 God's creative work is highly anthropomorphic in this chapter. He is depicted as an artisan who sculpts the man and beasts (vv. 7–8,19) and a builder who constructs the woman (v. 22). Such personal attention and care in the making of the first human is comparable to the contemplation of God in 1:26, "Let us make man . . ." The word "formed" *(yāṣar)* is used of a potter's activity (e.g., Isa 29:16; Jer 18:4–6) and the making of wooden images (Isa 44:9–10,12; Hab 2:18). It is used also of God "forming" Israel (e.g., Isa 27:11; 45:9,11), the servants of the Lord (Isa 49:5; Jer 1:5), the natural world (e.g., Ps 95:5; Isa 45:18; Amos 4:13), and Leviathan (Ps 104:26).

"Dust *[ʿāpār]*from the ground" is the raw material from which the physical properties of the man and beast had their source. The term may refer to the loose surface dirt of the ground (Exod 8:16–17[12–13]) or the powder of something pulverized (Deut 9:21). Egypt and Mesopotamia also depicted man as made of clay, sometimes mixed with blood derived from a slain god (see "Genesis 1–11 and Ancient Literature"). God is depicted as the potter who forms Israel (Isa 64:8; Jer 18:6; cp. *Sir* 33:13; Rom 9:20). "Dust" as constitutive of human existence anticipates 3:19, where the penalty for the man's sin is his return to "dust" (e.g., Job 34:15). While "dust" may also show that man is fragile physically (e.g., Job 10:8–9; Ps 103:14), the intent of the passage is the association of human life and the basic substance of our making. A second play on the words "man" *(ʾādām)* and "ground" *(ʾădāmâ)* becomes apparent: man is related to the "ground" by his very constitution (3:19), making him perfectly suited for the task of working the "ground," which is required for cultivation (2:5,15). Because of man's sin, however, his origins also became his destiny (3:19; Eccl 3:20); nevertheless, the Bible offers a grand hope for the body.[36] "Human life is embodied life."[37] How the human body is cared for is important to God; both libertine and ascetic views toward the body that demean it are destructive to the whole person.[38]

In the garden man and beast share in the same physical properties and are related to their environment (2:7,19). Unlike the plant world, both animal and human are described as living, possessing the "breath of life" (2:7; 7:22). Thus the animals are declared "living creatures" (*nepeš ḥayyâ*; 1:20–21,24; 9:10), as

---

[36] E. g., Job 19:25–27; Isa 26:19; Dan 12:1–4; 1 Cor 15:35–58; 1 Thess 4:16–17.

[37] D. Atkinson, *The Message of Genesis 1–11,* BST (Downers Grove: IVP, 1990), 57.

[38] Cf. Matt 6:22–25; 1 Cor 6:13–20; 2 Cor 7:1; Phil 1:20; Col 2:23.

man is described identically in the Hebrew of 2:7, "a living being" *(nepeš ḥayyâ)*. Human and animal share in creatureliness, yet a distinction between human and animal is sharply maintained in the narrative. The source of animal life is attributed to the intermediary "ground" (2:19) from which the animals came forth "in a moment." But the man was "gradually formed,"[39] and his fountain of life was the divine breath: God "breathed into his nostrils the breath of life."[40] This description continues the anthropomorphic language of the verse; the man receives his life force from the breath of the Creator himself, hovering over him. "*Breathed* is warmly personal, with the face-to-face intimacy of a kiss and the significance that this was giving as well as making; and self-giving at that."[41] Although both animal (7:22) and human life share in this gift of life (2:7), human life enjoys a unique relationship with God. The correspondence between man and his Maker is expressed both by the language of "image" (1:26–27) and by the metaphor of a shared "breath."

This depiction of "inbreathing" *(nāpaḥ)* has a close parallel in Ezekiel's vision of dry bones (37:9–10), where the reconstituted skeletons of the slain are brought to life again by the inbreathing of the "spirit." Here Ezekiel has "spirit" *(rûaḥ)* for "breath of life" *(nišmat ḥayyim)*, but the two are treated as virtually the same here and at times elsewhere.[42] This inbreathing essentially means that Adam's body came to life, for "breath of life" is the life-sustaining principle embodied in man that comes from God. Job 27:3 reflects this: "As long as I have life *[nišmatî]* within me // the breath *[rûaḥ]* of God in my nostrils." "Breath" is a figure (metonymy), meaning "life," where the breath is put as the cause of life, and "nostril" is associated with the "breath of life" (Isa 2:22) since it is the place of respiration. To possess the "breath of life" or "breath" is to be alive (e.g., Deut 20:16; Josh 10:40; Job 27:3); the absence of it describes the dead (1 Kgs 17:17).

Excursus: The Human Soul

The consequence of this divine inbreathing is that the man became "a living being *(nepeš ḥayyâ)*."[43] The traditional rendering of *nepeš* as "soul" (AV) can

---

[39] Calvin, *Comm.*, 111.

[40] *Atrahasis* describes crudely that the flesh of the slain god is the source of the "spirit" of man, i.e., his life (cp. Lev 17:11; W. G. Lambert and A. R. Millard, *Atraḫasîs: The Babylonian Story of the Flood [Oxford: Clarendon, 1969]*, 22, 59).

[41] D. Kidner, *Genesis,* TOTC (Downers Grove: IVP, 1967), 60.

[42] E.g., Isa 57:16; Job 32:8; 33:4; 34:14; esp. see Gen 7:22. Hebrew חיים ("life") as an abstract formation is plural. Cf. D. Block, "The Prophet of the Spirit: The Use of *rwḥ* in the Book of Ezekiel," *JETS* 32 (1989): 34–41.

[43] For our discussion on this term, see B. K. Waltke, "נָפַשׁ *(nāpash),*" *TWOT,* 587–91; A. Dihle, "ψυχη κτλ.," *TDNT* 9.632–35; E. Lohse, "ψυχη κτλ.," *TDNT* 9.635–36; W. Eichrodt, *Theology of the Old Testament,* OTL, trans. J. A. Baker, 2 vols. (Philadelphia: Westminster, 1967), 2.131–42; G. Harder, "Soul ψυχή," in *The New International Dictionary of New Testament Theology,* trans. and ed. C. Brown, 3 vols. (Grand Rapids: Zondervan, 1978), 3.682–87; W. D. Stacey, *The Pauline View of Man* (London: Macmillan, 1956), esp. 121–27.

mislead the reader since the semantic range of *nepeš* is much broader, including the meanings "life," "person," "self," "appetite," and "mind." Most biblical scholars recognize a difference in the way Hebrew thought understood the soul versus the Platonic and later Hellenistic opinions of the human soul. Early Greek viewed the soul as united with the body; "soul" was also considered the inner person, and there was a dwelling place for the soul. With later Platonic thought, however, the soul was viewed as preexistent and separate from the body; the "soul" *(psychē)* was the immaterial core of the individual that was immortal. Salvation for the soul meant its liberation from the body. The soul in Greek thought gave man meaning and existence beyond physical constitution. In the Hellenistic period Philo stands out as the proponent of Greek speculative thought and the idea of the bodiless soul. This dichotomy shows itself in Jewish apocrypha and pseudepigrapha.[44]

This notion of an abstract, metaphysical sense for "soul" separated from the body is not central to Hebrew thought.[45] *Nepeš* has been etymologically related to the idea "to breathe" or "breath"; Semitic cognates have the meaning "to breathe" or "blow." The term is closely associated, if not synonymous, with *nišmat* in the Old Testament, the particular term for "breath." [46] Thus *nepeš* can be equivalent to "breath": the animals are *nepeš ḥayyâ* ("living creatures")[47] and also are said to possess *nišmat rûaḥ ḥayyim* ("breath of life," 7:22). The *nepeš* is related to that which "breathes" and departs upon death or returns upon life (Jer 15:9). In Akkadian and Ugaritic the word is also broad in meaning and includes "throat." This may be the meaning for *nepeš* at Isa 5:14 and Ps 69:2. *Nepeš* then is related to the life force, the vitality of a person or animal, which is evidenced by the presence or absence of breath at the point of the nasal passage to the throat. However, it is not "life" in the sense of the abstract *ḥayyim* but the concrete vitality of a person. This is clear from how *nepeš* refers to one's appetites and drives (e.g., Deut 24:15) or may refer to a "person" or "self" (sometimes translated with the pronoun "I") as one who has these drives and desires.[48] *Nepeš* as the force of "life" is evidenced in Lev 17:11: "For the life *[nepeš]* of the flesh is the blood."

In our passage man does not possess a *nepeš* but rather *is* a *nepeš* (individual person); "breath," not "soul," comes closest to the idea of a transcendent life force in man. Therefore the breath of God energized the dormant body, which became a "living person"; this is seen in the contrasting expression *nepeš môt,* meaning a "dead person."[49] The Old Testament emphasizes the individual person as a unified whole. In Isa 1:18 *nepeš* occurs with *bāśar* ("body/flesh") as a

---

[44] *4 Macc*, e.g., assumes an antithesis between soul and body (1:20,26–28). Also *2 Macc* 6:30; *Wis* 9:15; 15:8.

[45] J. Barr, *The Garden of Eden and the Hope of Immortality* (Minneapolis: Fortress, 1993), 36–47, argues rather that the OT evidences a dichotomy in man (e.g., Eccl 12:7) that was later developed fully with the aid of Greek influence.

[46] E.g., Deut 20:16; Josh 11:11,14; 1 Kgs 15:29; 17:17.

[47] Gen 1:20–21,24; 2:19; 9:10,12,15; Lev 11:10,46.

[48] E.g., Gen 12:13; 19:20; 27:25.

[49] E.g., Lev 19:28; 21:1,11; Num 5:2; 6:6,11.

merism[50] to express the total person. Hebrew thought does not envision life apart from the body (Job 19:26–27). The breath of God assures life while its absence means death (e.g., Job 34:14; Ps 104:29). Man also possesses a "spirit" *(rûaḥ),* which has its source in God (e.g., Job 33:4; 34:14; Zech 12:1). Unlike the *nepeš,* the *rûaḥ* is not bound up with the body or blood and parallels the mind or inner person (e.g., Ps 77:6[7]). It expresses the inner psychic emotions of the individual (e.g., Gen 41:8; Judg 8:3; 1 Kgs 21:5).

Palestinian Judaism, evidenced by the Qumran writings and rabbinic works, is generally consistent with the Old Testament frame of thought, though not always. New Testament tradition, however, continues the Hebrew sense of "soul" as the vital life force where it means physical life (Mark 8:35 par.). It is also used of the total person (John 10:11) and for the inner person (Matt 26:38 par.; 2 Cor 1:23). Whereas "soul" is more common in the Old Testament than "spirit," in Paul's writings he gave priority to the "spirit" (146x), using "soul" just thirteen times. "Soul" was the human life force, as it is found in Hebrew thought, but for Paul the "spirit" was more important since it was given of God and was the means by which man and God communed. First Thessalonians 5:23 differentiates the soul and body from the spirit; the soul and body constitute the person as living being while the spirit indicates the higher capacities of the person in relation to God. Thus Paul spoke of the natural man *(psychikos)* and the spiritual man *(pneumatikos)* in 1 Cor 2:14–15. Moreover, the New Testament continues the sense of continuity between the soul and body beyond death as it is found in the Old Testament. Matthew 10:28, while providing for some distinction, implies that both the body and soul together constitute a person even in Hades. There are no disembodied souls, for the body and soul as person will experience a new mode of existence. This resurrection of the body and soul for the saints is expressed as a spiritual body; Adam represents the "physical" *(psychikos)* while Christ and the resurrected saints possess the "spiritual" *(pneumatikos)* body (1 Cor 15:44–49). For Paul there was no eternal, preexistent soul as found in Greek thought.

(2) The Man's Life in the Garden (2:8–17)

[8]Now the LORD God had planted a garden in the east, in Eden; and there he put the man he had formed. [9]And the LORD God made all kinds of trees grow out of the ground—trees that were pleasing to the eye and good for food. In the middle of the garden were the tree of life and the tree of the knowledge of good and evil.

**[10]A river watering the garden flowed from Eden; from there it was separated
into four headwaters. [11]The name of the first is the Pishon; it winds through the
entire land of Havilah, where there is gold. [12](The gold of that land is good; aromatic resin and onyx are also there.) [13]The name of the second river is the Gihon;
it winds through the entire land of Cush. [14]The name of the third river is the
Tigris; it runs along the east side of Asshur. And the fourth river is the Euphrates.**

[50] This is a figure by which opposing parts are used to describe the whole.

[15]The LORD God took the man and put him in the Garden of Eden to work it and take care of it. [16]And the LORD God commanded the man, "You are free to eat from any tree in the garden; [17]but you must not eat from the tree of the knowledge of good and evil, for when you eat of it you will surely die."

Following the creation of the first man (2:4–7), the narrative addresses the provision God made for him through the planting of a garden. A constant in this passage is the bounty of God's goodness to his special creation through a beautifully complete environment with luscious verdant herbage and a land rich in water and precious stones. Eden's glittering garden was left to human supervision as his divine charge and partnership in the exercise of earthly dominion. The garden's location in Eden and the trees descriptive of the site are of special interest (2:8–9); details of its contours and possessions are given (2:10–14). Last, the narrative sets the man in the midst of Eden to perform his managerial work, and God sets before him his first opportunity to express his obedient gratitude (2:15–17).

2:8 A garden is divinely prepared for the man as his habitat.[51] The expression here, "a garden *in* Eden," is unique in distinguishing the garden from "Eden" itself.[52] This suggests that "Eden" was a reference to a geographical area of which the garden was a part. For this reason "Eden" is used both of the garden itself and for a larger region.[53] "Garden of the LORD" designates Eden in Gen 13:10 (cp. Isa 51:3) and later "garden of God" in Ezekiel (28:13; 31:9), indicating God as its Owner. In ancient Near Eastern mythology is found a "garden of God" motif that depicts the divine residence on earth; it typically possesses abundant waters, fertile herbage, and beautiful stones.[54] But here "garden of God" or "garden of the LORD" is absent; God does not dwell in the garden; rather it is the place where he meets with man.[55]

---

[51] The NIV (as does the Vg) renders וַיִּטַּע as pluperfect, "had planted"; this rendering maintains the order of chap. 1, where vegetation (third day) appeared before the creation of human life (day six). It is unnecessary, however, since the scope of the context is confined to the garden as a provision for man (cf. 1:29), not as a commentary on the vegetation of day three (1:11–12). The concluding clause, "[which] he had formed" (אֲשֶׁר יָצָר), as a pluperfect, shows that the formation of the man preceded the planting of the garden.

[52] Noted by J. Skinner, *A Critical and Exegetical Commentary on Genesis,* ICC (Edinburgh: T & T Clark, 1910), 57.

[53] With 2:8 the toponym "Eden" occurs by itself in 2:10; "Garden of Eden" is found in 2:15; 3:23–24 (also Ezek 36:35; Joel 2:3); "east of Eden" in 4:16 refers to Cain's expulsion. Outside Genesis, Eden appears in apposition with "garden" (Ezek 28:13).

[54] Such a mythic element is said to be the underlying structure of Gen 2–3, which has been muted by the historical context superimposed by the Yahwist author; thus the garden is a divine dwelling among men (Wallace, *The Eden Narrative,* 79–80, 88; "Eden," *ABD* 2.282). Although God does have access to the garden, there is no sense in chaps. 2–3 that he resided there; his place in the garden does not become important in the narrative until 3:8. Eden was planted for man's abode (2:8,15).

[55] So V. Hamilton, *The Book of Genesis Chapters 1–17,* NICOT (Grand Rapids: Eerdmans, 1990), 161.

Moreover, the uniqueness of the biblical depiction with its original "tree of knowledge" indicates the narrative's independence.

Later the prophets adopted Eden's fertility as a sign of eschatological salvation or, by its reversal, divine judgment (Isa 51:3; Ezek 36:35; Joel 2:3); particularly Ezekiel made extensive use of Eden's incident of fallen pride in his oracles against the king of Tyre (Ezek 28) and Egypt's pharaoh (Ezek 31). Eden's garden has traditionally been termed "paradise," initiated by the Greek rendering and now canonized in Western culture by John Milton's *Paradise Lost*. *Parádeisos*regularly translates "garden" *(gan)* in the LXX version of the garden story.[56] "Paradise" was taken up by Jewish literature (e.g., *T. Levi* 18:10–11) as the eternal home of the righteous and also in the New Testament, designating the presence of the ascended Christ (Luke 23:43; 2 Cor 12:4) and the eternal abode for believers (Rev 2:7).[57]

Hebrew *ʿēden* ("Eden") probably is derived from West Semitic and means "a place of abundant waters." In addition to phonological evidence, this is supported by the allusion to Eden as a well-watered locale in Gen 13:10.[58] Its Hebrew meaning as a common noun is "delight"; whether or not there is an etymological linkage, the sound play of "Eden" suggests even by its name that the garden was luxuriant. However, the Bible does not present the garden as the kind of paradise that is popularly envisioned, where there is only pleasure without work or concerns (cf. 2:15). Although the term "Eden" by itself does not indicate the location of the site, it is used as a geographical designation in Genesis. The account assumes that the Hebrew reader is situated in Canaan since the location of the garden is described directionally in the "east" with respect to Canaan. It is in the general location of the Tigris and Euphrates valley as shown by the naming of these two rivers, which are said to traverse the garden (2:14).

2:9 Eden is characterized by trees yielding fruits that are pleasant in appearance and delightful to the taste: "all kinds," "pleasing," and "good" evidence the extravagance the garden offered. Any charge that God is stingy is unfounded, but the serpent successfully fooled his audience. "The human couple will not be able to plead deprivation as the excuse for eating the forbidden fruit."[59] Ironically, Eve stumbled over the allurement of God's world (3:6) and

---

[56] "Paradise" is a Persian loan word meaning "park" or "enclosed area." It is also adopted by Hebrew and Aramaic, פַּרְדֵּס (e.g., Neh 2:8) and פַּרְדֵּיסָא.

[57] See J. Jeremias, "παράδεισος," *TDNT* 5.765–73, and R. Stein, *Luke*, NAC (Nashville: Broadman, 1992), 593.

[58] See Tsumura, *The Earth and the Waters in Genesis 1 and 2*, 127–37. Among the phonological evidences pointing to a West Semitic derivation is the Aramaic-Akkadian bilingual inscription from Tell Fekheriyeh where the root *ʿdn*, "making abundant in water supply," is attested. See A. R. Millard, "The Etymology of Eden," *VT* 34 (1984): 103–6.

[59] Sarna, *Genesis*, 18.

soiled it with her desire for unlawful gain.

Two trees, which are crucial to the narrative, are especially described: the tree of life and the tree of the knowledge of good and evil. Of the two the "tree of life," though introduced first and noted last in the garden story (2:9; 3:22,24), is second in significance to the tree of knowledge. Both trees are located prominently in the middle of the garden (2:9; 3:3), probably implying that the two stood side by side in the center.[60] Although the significance of their station can only be derived inferentially, D. Bonhoeffer rightly observed that symbolically the middle of Adam's world was not himself but life, the very presence of God; the tree of knowledge as a prohibition signifies that man's limitation as a creature is in the "*middle of his existence,* not on the edge."[61]

"Tree of life" indicates that the tree produces the source of life in the garden. Ultimately the tree's power to convey life was due to its Planter, who alone grants or refuses to give of its fruit. The presence of the tree indicates that the garden enjoys life, and the eating of the fruit will result in continued life—a gift that only God can confer (3:22; cp. Rev 2:7), not an inherent property of the fruit. Common to ancient Near Eastern lore was the story of man's pursuit of eternal life, which only the gods could endow. But the heroic individual in each case falls short, an ancient concession that man cannot obtain the immortality of the gods. The Babylonian *Epic of Gilgamesh,* for example, depicts its hero recovering the "plant" of life, only to lose it to the water serpent.[62]

As we will find, many motifs in the garden story are shared with the biblical Wisdom tradition, and the tree of life is a prominent one among these. "Tree of life" occurs in the Old Testament only in Proverbs outside of Genesis; it was appropriated by the sages to represent what gives man pleasant existence (Prov 3:18; 11:30; 13:12; 15:4).[63] Later John's apocalyptic vision sees its recurrence

---

[60] This is a fair inference drawn from 2:9 and 3:3 when read with 2:17. The former specifically locates the tree of life "in the middle" (בְּתוֹךְ), although it does not say so of the tree of knowledge (cp. NJPS, "with the tree of life in the middle of the garden, and the tree of knowledge of good and evil"). But the unidentified tree "in the middle of the garden" (בְּתוֹךְ־הַגָּן) at 3:3 must be taken as reference to the prohibited tree of 2:17.

[61] D. Bonhoeffer, *Creation and Fall: A Theological Interpretation of Genesis 1–3,* rev. ed., trans. J. C. Fletcher (London: SCM, 1959), 49, and quote p. 51. Elsewhere he comments, "Limit and life, these are the untouchable, inaccessible middle of paradise around which Adam's life revolves" (p. 60).

[62] There are exceptions: Utnapishtim and his wife of the Babylonian myth possess immortality, granted them by the gods, but he is unable to confer it upon Gilgamesh (*ANET,* 95–96). In Sumer's version of the flood story Ziusudra is settled in Dilmun by the gods and receives immortality after escaping the flood. In the Adapa myth the hero, thinking that it will be his death, unwittingly refuses to accept the food and drink divinely offered, which will secure for him immortality (*ANET,* 100).

[63] An exception is the LXX rendering of Isa 65:22 by τοῦ ξύλου τῆς ζωῆς.

where Eden is regained by the saints (Rev 2:7; 22:2,14,19).[64]

The preeminent "tree of knowledge" is commonly referred to in the narrative as simply the "tree" and only twice receives the full appellative "tree of knowledge" (2:9,17). As the "tree of life" indicated the source and presence of life in the garden, which had its origins in its Planter, the "tree of knowledge" thus indicates the presence of the "knowledge of good and evil" in the garden, and the eating of it confers that knowledge (3:5,22). On the basis of 3:22 we may assume that the eating of the tree conferred a kind of knowledge that was an exceptional possession of deity and was attributable only to God, who is the provider of the tree. However, the act of eating the fruit of this tree while granting knowledge resulted concomitantly in death for the transgressors (2:17). One of the striking features of this enigmatic account is that the tree of life, which involves the human concerns of life and death, is overshadowed by the tree of knowledge. This is because the tree of knowledge as the "tree of decision" becomes the touchstone of human destiny on which the narrative turns.

"Tree of knowledge" has been variously understood, but before we speak of the tree, it is sobering to recall that speculation about the tree was in fact Eve's error.[65] After all that might be said, the important feature of the narrative is that the human couple defied God's commandment. This mysterious tree puzzles the interpreter because of the diverse contexts attested in the Old Testament for the phrase "good and evil" where similar expressions are found. In Genesis the exact language is limited to 2:9,17 with similar language in 3:5,22. Important for our purposes is the association of "knowledge" with "good and evil." It occurs in Deut 1:39, where Moses speaks of Israel's children "who do not yet know good from bad." Also Isa 7:15–16 speaks of a child's awareness of good and evil, "when he knows enough to reject the wrong and choose the good." Aged Barzillai exclaims that he has lost this capacity: "Can I tell the difference between what is good and what is not [i.e., evil]?" (2 Sam 19:35[36]). The idea of discernment or judgment is attributed to royal figures, priests, and to God.[66]

Furthermore, the tree of knowledge is a riddle for the interpreter because this "knowledge," we may infer from 3:22, is a feature of deity not inherently possessed by the man and woman but then obtained by them, yet only after their act of disobedience. In some sense this acquisition meant human advancement, even sharing in the divine, but it was a progress that could

[64] "Tree of life" as a feature of future paradise is also found in later Jewish writings, e.g., *4 Macc* 18:16; *2 Esdr* 2:12; 8:52. In *1 Enoch* the tree is described as a fragrant tree, and "not a human being has the authority to touch it until the great judgment. . . . This is for the righteous and the pious. And the elect will be presented with its fruit for life" (25:4–5).

[65] So Kidner, *Genesis,* 60.

[66] Lev 27:12,14; 2 Sam 14:17; 1 Kgs 3:9; Eccl 12:14. Cp. Num 24:13.

hardly be called a reward; it insured only the deserts of the opposite of deity's immortality.

Typically, the acquisition of "good and evil" is related in some way by commentators to human advancement.

1. Argued since the time of Ibn Ezra, it has been proposed that sexual awareness and the consequence of its power for procreation is awakened by the tree. This is suggested by the association of the sin of eating from the tree of knowledge and Adam and Eve's first recognition of their nakedness (3:7). Also the tree's name, "knowledge," is taken as an allusion to "know" *(yādaʿ)* as a sexual inference (e.g., 4:1). The absence of knowing good and evil then is sexual inexperience or incapacity (cf. Deut 1:39; 2 Sam 19:35[36]). Creation is the power of God, and human procreation is man's imitation of deity's immortality.[67] Yet the narrative would lead us to question why sexual experience was prohibited by God (2:17); on the contrary, it is the beneficent empowerment of God, who made the sexes and ordained the institution of marriage (1:27–28; 2:25). There is a connection between the tree of "knowledge" and the awareness of nakedness, but the connection is the disobedience of Adam and Eve at the tree that brought about guilt, illustrated by the shame they experience in nakedness, not a sexual awakening.

2. Another common opinion is that the tree confers the human capacity of moral discrimination.[68] This is supported by the similar language in Deut 1:39 and Isa 7:15–16, where a child lacks such moral judgment; it is a capacity exercised by a wise adjudicator in 2 Sam 14:17 and 1 Kgs 3:9. But this would hardly suit the experience of the aged Barzillai unless we are to consider him in his second childhood (2 Sam 19:35[36]). The difficulty with this view lies in 3:22, which indicates that the knowledge gained is something that is beyond the human experience of the first couple. The story flounders if the couple could not discern already between obedience and disobedience before they ate of the tree; the general tenor of the passage presupposes at least this small measure of knowledge (2:16–17). They are in a state of moral innocence, not moral ignorance. Moreover, there is no apparent reason why God would have prohibited this.

3. As a merism, meaning "everything," the expression "good and evil"

---

[67] R. Gordis, "The Knowledge of Good and Evil in the Old Testament and in the Qumran Scrolls," *JBL* 76 (1957): 123–38: "So long as Adam had access to the tree of life and could eat of the fruit, he would remain immortal. If now sexual awareness were added to him, man would indeed resemble God, for the human procreation of life is the counterpart of the divine attribute of creation" (p. 134).

[68] E.g., Skinner, while taking "good and evil" as reference to a broad knowledge of life and its mature experiences, emphasizes moral discernment: "Man's primitive state was one of childlike innocence and purity; and the knowledge which he obtained by disobedience is the knowledge of life and of the world which distinguishes the grown man from the child" (*Genesis,* 96).

indicates an advanced knowledge, but not necessarily omniscience, which would be true only of deity.[69] This is suggested by David's judicial wisdom exhibited in 2 Sam 14:17,20 and the request for divine insight by Solomon in 1 Kgs 3:9 (cf. 2 Sam 13:22; 1 Kgs 22:18).[70] Deuteronomy 1:39 shows how children are dependent upon their parents for this knowledge of "good and evil" while they remain under parental responsibility; thus the tree of knowledge concerns independent judgment and responsibility (cf. Isa 7:15–16). Yet the significance of the fall is more than the mere transition from adolescence to intellectual or moral responsibility; it involved human autonomy in judgment, an independence of God's supervision.[71]

All three of these viewpoints agree that the "knowledge" gained was in some way related to human maturity, whether in sexual matters or judgment. But in what sense then did the human couple become like God (3:22)? And why would God forbid such maturing experiences?

4. More likely the tree bestowed a divine wisdom.[72] It has long been recognized that features of the garden story bear strong resemblance to wisdom literature and themes.[73] The Wisdom tradition declares that wisdom is possessed by God (Prov 2:6; 8:22) and is humanity's proper goal of attainment (Prov 3:13; 8:10–11). Proverbs indicates, however, that it must be achieved through the "fear of the LORD" and not through grasping it independently.[74] Moreover, there is knowledge that God possesses that man should not seek apart from revelation (Job 15:7–9; 28:12–28; 40:1–5; Prov 30:1–4); to obtain this knowledge is to act with moral autonomy.[75] By obtaining it through dis-

[69] But von Rad takes "good and evil" as omniscience, not a knowledge limited to moral discernment (*Genesis,* 81).

[70] This is argued on the basis of the forensic setting of these passages in W. M. Clark, "A Legal Background to the Yahwist's Use of 'Good and Evil' in Genesis 2–3," *JBL* 88 (1969): 266–78. Cf. also Sarna, *Genesis,* 19. G. W. Buchanan, who takes it as merism, shows that the expression in the Qumran sect referred to those of twenty years old who commenced adult responsibilities ("The Old Testament Meaning of the Knowledge of Good and Evil," *JBL* 75 [1956]: 114–20). Buchanan attempts to apply this age of accountability in the OT where "good and evil" as a phrase occurs.

[71] So Hamilton, *Genesis,* 165–66.

[72] E.g., argued by Wenham, *Genesis 1–15,* 63–64.

[73] E.g., Alonso-Schökel, "Sapiential and Covenant Themes in Genesis 2–3"; G. Mendenhall, "The Shady Side of Wisdom: The Date and Purpose of Genesis 3," in *A Light unto My Path: Old Testament Studies in Honor of Jacob Myers,* ed. H. N. Bream et al. (Philadelphia: Temple University, 1974), 319–34; C. M. Carmichael, "The Paradise Myth: Interpreting without Jewish and Christian Spectacles, in *A Walk in the Garden,* JSOTSup 136, ed. P. Morris and D. Sawyer (Sheffield: JSOT, 1992), 47–63; and L. Perdue, *Wisdom and Creation: The Theology of Wisdom Literature* (Nashville: Abingdon, 1994).

[74] Ps 111:10; Prov 2:1–6; 3:5–6; 9:10; 11:7,29; 15:33; Isa 11:2.

[75] Cassuto, *Genesis,* 113: "He [Adam] was not content with what was given to him, and desired to obtain more. He did not wish to remain in the position of a child who is under the supervision of his father and is constantly dependent on him; he wanted to learn by himself of the world around him; he aspired to become in *knowledge,* too, like God."

obedience, the first couple expressed their independence of God and obtained wisdom possessed by God (3:5,22) through moral autonomy. This autonomous action meant death because this wisdom was obtained unlawfully; transgression against the law of God carried the penalty of death. In the Adapa myth it was possible for the hero to obtain the wisdom of the gods, granted by Ea, but be denied divine immortality.[76] Thus the mortal could obtain one feature of divinity without becoming divine.[77]

The man and woman's usurpation is the analogy drawn by the prophet when he speaks of the proud king of Tyre, who is expelled from Eden for aspiring to have the wisdom of God (Ezek 28:2,6,15–17). The first Adam achieved divine reputation through disobedience; the last Adam obtained exaltation by God through humility and obedience (Phil 2:6–11). Adam seized the prize, but Christ, though uniquely the image of God, refused to promote his rightful position and chose to humble himself, acquiring recognition by obedient humiliation and death.[78] Calvin comments: "We now understand what is meant by abstaining from the tree of the knowledge of good and evil; namely, that Adam might not, in attempting one thing or another, rely upon his own prudence; but that cleaving to God alone, he might become wise only by his obedience."[79]

When the garden setting is read against the backdrop of the Mosaic tradition, there are remarkable similarities to Israel's experience. As has been pointed out by commentators, the two garden trees are comparable to those elements in the tabernacle that represent life and the law of God. The candlestick was shaped like a tree with branches symbolizing life, giving light to the twelve loaves of bread that represented God's provision for Israel. The commands ("law") of God were exemplified by the stone tablets in the ark of the covenant. In the same way the tree of knowledge was indicative of God's commands to be obeyed lest the curse of disobedience fall upon the law breaker. By allusion Ps 19:8–10[7–9] compares the law with the tree of knowledge and shows that it is superior, providing a knowledge obtained only through revelation.[80] As disobedience meant death in the garden, transgressors of God's law in Israel experienced its deathly consequences. The God of the tabernacle was indeed the God of the garden. And, more importantly, as the tabernacle symbolized the presence of God among his people, the descriptive language of the garden's habitat declares that God is present with the first man.[81] The tabernacle for

[76] "To him [Adapa] he [Ea] had given wisdom; eternal life he had not given him" (*ANET,* 101).

[77] Noted by Wallace, *The Eden Narrative,* 104–5.

[78] For the parallelism between the first Adam and Christ as last Adam in Phil 2:6–11, see R. P. Martin, *Carmen Christi,* rev. ed. (Grand Rapids: Eerdmans, 1983), 163–64.

[79] Calvin, *Comm.,* 118.

[80] See D. J. A. Clines, "The Tree of Knowledge and the Law of Yahweh," *VT* 24 (1974): 8–14.

[81] See G. Wenham, "Sanctuary Symbolism in the Garden of Eden Story," in *Proceedings of the Ninth World Congress of Jewish Studies. Division A. The Period of the Bible* (Jerusalem: World Union of Jewish Studies, 1986), 19–25.

Israel indicated the place of communion with God, and, similarly, it was in the garden that God and man first enjoyed that communion.

2:10–14 Eden's garden was rich in minerals and splendidly fertile with flowing waters. Its description is a digression in the text, giving supplementary information about its verdant beauty,[82] but its significance for the narrative's motif of resplendence shows its integral part in the narrative. It is not a foreign accretion as some have proposed. Verse 15 backtracks and picks up the thought of vv. 8–9, indicating that the central concern of the narrative remains the man's place in the garden and the tree of knowledge (vv. 8–9 and 15–17), not so much the garden's appearance per se.

The garden is watered *(šāqâ)* by a second source (cf. *šāqâ,* v. 6), a river that flows out from Eden and becomes four separate tributaries (v. 10).[83] The latter two named, the Tigris and Euphrates rivers, suggest that Eden was in Armenia from where these two rivers have their source (v. 14). The difficulty with this identification lies with the first two rivers, the rhyming "Pishon" and "Gihon" (vv. 11,13), which are unknown. Their etymologies are of no help in locating them geographically. Havilah and Cush as geographical points of identification for Eden are also problematic, though at least we can say they appear to be related (cf. 10:7).[84] Seven Cushite nations are named in the Table of Nations, including Havilah, whose origins are related to the regions of Africa and Arabia (10:6–7; cf. 10:29). There is, however, no necessity in taking this Havilah as the same in the garden story. As a location Cush is Africa's Nubia, south of Egypt; it usually is translated "Ethiopia" *(Aithiopia)* in the LXX, as it is here in v. 13.[85] This has led some to speculate that the two rivers are the Blue and White Niles of Africa. Others have recommended that the Pishon is the Indus or Ganges rivers and the Gihon is the Nile. Cush is later commonly related to Egypt in the prophets.[86] However, in 10:8 Cush is the ancestor of Mesopotamian kingdoms, and some think it should be related to the Kassites (Akk. *Kaššû;* Gk. *Cossaea*), located southeast of the Tigris (modern Luristan). Many have suggested that there are two sites for Cush, an Ethiopian Cush and a Mesopotamian one, but this remains uncertain.[87] Some have taken the Gihon

---

[82] *Waw* disjunctive introduces the section (v. 10), "*Now* a river . . ."

[83] Although this is the traditional understanding of Eden's topography, E. A. Speiser argues that the Hebrew יֹצֵא מֵעֵדֶן does not mean "flows from Eden" but "rises in Eden" and רָאשִׁים indicates the upper courses of the rivers, not the mouth. Thus Eden had four rivers that converged into one *outside* the garden. By identifying Cush with the Kassites, who originated in the region of the Zagros mountains (east of the Tigris), Speiser concludes that the Persian Gulf is the head. See "The Rivers of Paradise," in *Oriental and Biblical Studies,* ed. J. J. Finkelstein and M. Greenberg (Philadelphia: University of Pennsylvania, 1967), 23–24, and his *Genesis,* 17, 20.

[84] For fuller discussion see relevant comments at 10:6–8,29.

[85] R. H. Smith, "Ethiopia," *ABD* 2.665–67.

[86] E.g., Isa 20:3–4; Jer 46:9; Ezek 29:10; 30:4; Amos 9:7.

[87] S. S. Johnson, "Cush," *ABD* 1.1219.

and Pishon as simply river canals related to the Tigris-Euphrates river system of Mesopotamia. Regardless of the identity of Cush, there is no correspondence between the description of Eden, possessing four rivers flowing into or from one central fountain, with the contemporary geography of the Tigris-Euphrates valley and Arabia. This leaves two rivers that are presently identifiable and two that are not.

Although the location remains elusive for the modern cartographer, the point of the description is clear for the reader: the habitat God has prepared is bountiful and beautiful.[88] It has a rich resource of life-giving water and is adorned with precious metals and jewels. Both Ezekiel's temple (Ezek 47:1–12) and Revelation's New Jerusalem (Rev 22:1–2) possess flowing rivers that provide the luscious growth of trees and nurturing power for life and healing. The "good" *(ṭôb)* gold echoes the "good" creation of chap. 1 and testifies to God's excelling provision for the human couple. There was no legitimate place for the cynicism of the serpent's charges (3:5). Gold and onyx are reminiscent of the tabernacle's furnishings and priestly garments (e.g., Exod 25:1–9; and temple, 1 Chr 29:2).[89] Gold overlay finished the sacred furniture of the tabernacle (Exod 25:11,17,24,31). Particularly important was the "onyx" stone of the priestly ephod, upon which were inscribed the names of the twelve tribes (Exod 28:9–14), and the onyx of the high priest's breastplate (Exod 28:20). This language supports what we have already said: the garden is indicative of the presence of God.[90] Moreover, the rivers Euphrates and Tigris, along with the Nile, are future boundaries descriptive of the patriarchal land pledged to Abraham (Gen 15:18).[91] As God had prepared and assigned Eden to Adam's care, the "paradise" of Canaan's land was consigned to Abraham and his future descendants.

2:15 God placed the man in the garden for the stated purpose of supervising it. Verse 15 continues the thought of v. 8 but with a subtle difference in the language. "Put" in v. 15 translates the causative form of the verb *nûaḥ,* "rest," and so could be rendered literally "caused to rest." In v. 8, however, the term is *śîm* ("put, place"). Here the language of v. 15 is essentially equivalent to v. 8 in context, but "rest" bears a special significance for depicting deliverance from

---

[88] Westermann observes that the number four indicates completeness. The object of the description of Eden's four rivers is to show that the rivers that bless the whole world have their origin in the blessing of the garden. In this symbolic sense we can say that the garden for good or for evil impacted the whole of God's earth. Eden is a microcosm of all human and earthly experience (*Genesis 1–11,* 215–17).

[89] See, e.g., Wenham, *Genesis 1–15,* 65.

[90] Eden as prototype for the tabernacle and its practices is reflected in later Jewish folklore. E.g., the author of *Jubilees* (3.8–14) explained the laws of ceremonial uncleanness for women after childbirth (Lev 12) by the events of the garden: Adam was placed in Eden after forty days, and the woman was brought after eighty days; hence the woman was restricted from holy things for forty days after the birth of a male and eighty after a female.

[91] Observed by Sailhamer, "Genesis," 42–44.

Noah's waters (see 5:29 discussion) in Genesis 1–11 and for speaking of the safety that Israel would experience as found in the Pentateuch. God promised to give Israel safety ("rest") in the land from its enemies (e.g., Deut 3:20; 12:10; 25:19). This is illustrated by Lot and his family; visiting angels "led them safely ["gave rest"] out of the city" (19:16). It also is used of dedicating something before the presence of the Lord.[92] God prepares the garden for man's safety, where he can enjoy the divine presence.[93]

In the garden God gives the man a purposeful existence that includes overseeing his environment. Work is a God-given assignment and not a cursed condition.[94] It was sin that spoiled the pristine relationship between the man and his environment, making work a toilsome chore that became a requirement for mere existence (3:17–19,23). Mesopotamian accounts of human creation typically show how human beings were created for the purpose of work, but there human beings work to supply food for the selfish, lazy gods. Divine travail over their incessant labors is relieved by the creation of a human workforce. In contrast the biblical account portrays God as Provider for man's needs, a part of which is the honorable, meaningful labor of tilling the soil. "Life without work would not be worthy of human beings."[95]

The man's principal commission is to "work" and "take care" of his pristine garden home (v. 15). The word translated "work" *(ʿābad)* is the common one for tilling the soil (e.g., 3:23; 4:2,12) or for other labor (e.g., Isa 19:9); it also speaks of "service" to another (e.g., 29:15; 31:6) and is often used of worship (e.g., Exod 3:12).[96] The verb and its noun derivative "service" *(ʿăbōdâ)* frequently describe Levitical duties in tabernacle and temple worship.[97] It also speaks of the completed "work" on the tabernacle (Exod 39:32,42). "Take care" *(šāmar)* probably

[92] E.g., Exod 16:33–34; Num 17:4; Deut 26:4,10; cf. priestly garments, Lev 16:23.

[93] Cf. E. R. Clendenen, "Life in God's Land: An Outline of the Theology of Deuteronomy" in *The Church at the Dawn of the 21st Century* (Dallas: Criswell Publications, 1989), 162–63.

[94] Cassuto argues that tilling the ground was imposed on man for sin (cf. 3:23); however, the punishment is not "working the ground" but laboring outside the garden against the harsh new conditions of the land, which was "cursed" as a result of the fall (3:17–18; *Genesis,* 122).

[95] Westermann, *Genesis 1–11,* 220.

[96] A grammatical problem with the infinitives לְעָבְדָהּ ("to work it") and לְשָׁמְרָהּ ("to take care of it") is the identity of the antecedent for the third feminine suffix (MT's *mappiq*). "Garden" (גַּן) is masculine, and "ground" (אֲדָמָה), though feminine gender, is distant (v. 9). Cassuto reads the final *hē* (without *mappiq*) as the infinitive (with additional *hē*) and renders them "to serve and to guard," indicating the sense of sacrificial worship (*Genesis,* 122–23). Sailhamer agrees and points to how these terms in the Pentateuch indicate worship and obedience to God's commands ("Genesis," 45). We have discovered that the language of the garden has double entendre, but the inferential meaning is always secondary. It is best to interpret our infinitives as referring to "work" but secondarily anticipating the Mosaic context of worship and obedience. The problem of gender is best resolved by taking the gender assignment from the place name "Eden" (absolute) rather than the construct "garden" (*IBHS* § 6.4.1d).

[97] E.g., Exod 38:21; Num 3:10; 18:6; 1 Chr 24:3,19; 2 Chr 8:14.

specifies the nature of Adam's labor. It describes the occupation of Abel (4:9), attending property and flocks (e.g., 30:31), protecting persons (28:15,20), and frequently of "observing" covenant stipulations.[98] For priestly duties it describes the faithful carrying out of God's instructions (e.g., Lev 8:35) and the caretaking of the tabernacle (e.g., Num 1:53; 18:5). Both terms occur together to describe the charge of the Levites for the tabernacle (Num 3:7–8; 18:7), thus again suggesting a relationship between Eden and tabernacle.

We have commented that "work" and "guard" in our passage anticipate 3:23–24, where the man and woman are expelled from the garden. Here there is a play on the word *šāmar* in the narrative: because the man fails through sin to "take care" *(šāmar)* in the garden, he is expelled, and God's cherubim "guarded" *(šāmar)* its access (3:24). Thus the man's assignment was fulfilled in an unexpected way by angels, and, ironically, Adam himself was prohibited from entry.

2:16 As God had given the natural world and all life-forms boundaries, human life too is instructed to live within prescribed boundaries. The verb "commanded" (v. 16) occurs twenty-five times in Genesis, but this first occurrence is the only place in Genesis where the narrative introduces a divine command by this formula: "And the LORD God commanded" (cp. 3:11,17). Elsewhere in Genesis the formula, introducing direct discourse, always has a human subject (e.g., 12:20; 26:11; 28:1). "Commanded" *(ṣāwâ)* is common in the Old Testament and is often found in pentateuchal laws (particularly Deuteronomy) where Israel, "commanded" by God through Moses, received the "commandments" *(miṣwôt)* of the Lord for their way of life. The companion expression found in the Pentateuch, "[all] which the LORD commanded [Moses]," with its slight variations, is especially frequent in the narrative of the tabernacle's construction (chaps. 39–40).[99] At the ark in the tent of meeting, God met with Moses where he gave all "which [the LORD] commanded [Moses] for the Israelites" (Exod 25:22; cf. also 34:32). This same expression for faithful obedience commends Noah's construction of the ark (6:22; 7:5,9,16) and Abraham's circumcision of Isaac (21:4). Unhappily, in the ensuing garden story the same cannot be said for Adam and Eve.

The man is addressed personally as an individual "Thou."[100] Unlike all other created life, the human being is endowed with special significance as a "person" in the eyes of his Creator, enjoying a privileged depth of divine-human communion. This is likewise evidenced in the creation narrative, where God spoke to mankind, unlike the creatures, when bestowing his blessing of procreation (1:28). All human life merits respect and protection by virtue of the esteemed position to which God has exalted it. The prohibition against eating

---

[98] E.g., Gen 17:9–10; 18:19; 26:5; Deut 4:6; 7:12; 29:9.

[99] Exod 39:1,5,7,21,26,29,31–32,42–43; 40:16,19,21,23,25,27,29,32. Also cf. 29:35; 31:6,11; 34:4,18; 35:1,4,10,29; 36:1,5; 38:22.

[100] Noted by Atkinson, *Genesis,* 63.

the fruit of the "tree of knowledge" gave Adam opportunity to worship God through loyal devotion. Luther likened the tree to "Adam's church, altar, and pulpit. Here he was to yield to God the obedience he owed, give recognition to the Word and will of God, give thanks to God, and call upon God for aid against temptation."[101]

The instruction of the Lord is given as a positive expression of God's goodness rather than a harsh restriction (v. 16b). The Hebrew clause is headed by "from any/every tree *[mikkōl ʿēṣ]* of the garden," evidencing God's broad provision. This generosity is heightened by the following Hebrew construction translated "you are free to eat," which could also be translated "you may eat freely" (cf. NRSV).[102] This strong affirmation indicates that the provision of God for the first couple is plentiful and to be enjoyed liberally by them.

2:17 But freedom has no meaning without prohibition; the boundary for Adam is but one tree. This prohibition, however, is stated in the strongest terms, as was the provision. The adversative beginning the clause ("but") establishes the contrast between provision and prohibition. The NIV's rendering reflects the nuance of strong prohibition by "you *must* not eat." The form of the prohibition is the style of command prominent in the Ten Commandments and occurring often in the laws of Moses. The causal clause ("for," *kî*) that follows explains the severity of the prohibition; the consequence of such an action is stated emphatically: "you will surely die." This construction is the same kind as in v. 16, where the emphasis is on the liberality of God's provision.[103] Here its emphatic nuance underscores the forewarning of the Lord. Commonly the expression "you shall surely die" decrees death for a culprit either by God (Gen 20:7; Ezek 33:8,14) or a king.[104] It occurs repeatedly in the legal collections of the Pentateuch, condemning criminals to death (e.g., Exod 21:12; Lev 20:2; Num 35:16–18).

The preemptive warning is necessary because, unlike the other members of the created order, mankind alone has the potential for crossing moral boundaries. Out of God's goodness and mercy he informs the man that the consequence of disobedience is death; what is at stake is whether he will choose to trust God's words. There is no suggestion from the passage, as is assumed by some, that Adam was created immortal but subsequently forfeited immortality by his sin.[105] There is a difference between man's creation, in which he receives life by the divine inbreathing (2:7), and the perpetuation of that life

[101] *LW* 1.95.

[102] אָכֹל תֹּאכֵל with the infinitive absolute.

[103] מוֹת תָּמוּת with the infinitive absolute.

[104] E.g., Gen 26:11; 1 Sam 14:39,44; 22:16; 1 Kgs 2:37,42; 2 Kgs 1:4,6.

[105] Sarna observes that man did not die immediately, and since there is no evidence that God rescinded the penalty, it is best to see the penalty imposed by denying man access to the rejuvenating benefits of the tree of life (*Genesis,* 21). In the *Epic of Gilgamesh* the plant of life is said to restore the youth of its possessor (*ANET,* 96).

gained by appropriating the tree of life (cf. 3:22).[106] Immortality is the trait of deity alone (1 Tim 6:16). Calvin rightly noted that without sin Adam's "earthly life truly would have been temporal; yet he would have passed into heaven without death, and without injury," thereby receiving eternal life.[107] Perpetuating or renewing earthly life was possible through the "tree of life" (v. 9), but once sin was committed, the sanction of disobedience necessarily meant the man and woman's expulsion from the garden and its tree of life (3:22–24).

(3) The Man's Companion, the First Woman (2:18–25)

18The LORD God said, "It is not good for the man to be alone. I will make a helper suitable for him."

19Now the LORD God had formed out of the ground all the beasts of the field and all the birds of the air. He brought them to the man to see what he would name them; and whatever the man called each living creature, that was its name.
20So the man gave names to all the livestock, the birds of the air and all the beasts of the field.

But for Adam no suitable helper was found. 21So the LORD God caused the man to fall into a deep sleep; and while he was sleeping, he took one of the man's ribs and closed up the place with flesh. 22Then the LORD God made a woman from the rib he had taken out of the man, and he brought her to the man.

23The man said,

"This is now bone of my bones
and flesh of my flesh;
she shall be called 'woman,'
for she was taken out of man."

24For this reason a man will leave his father and mother and be united to his wife, and they will become one flesh.

25The man and his wife were both naked, and they felt no shame.

The theme of provision continues in the story as God creates a "helper suitable" for the man (vv. 18,20). Unique to the creation account is God's declaration that the man alone is "not good." The same formula, "then God said," which introduced God's creative word in chap. 1, expresses God's contemplation over what in his otherwise "good" creation requires his special attention. Such observation emphasizes the importance of the woman in the mind of God. Divine initiative is center stage in this passage: "The LORD God said" (v. 18), "the LORD God had formed" (v. 19), "the LORD God caused . . . a deep sleep" (v. 21), and "the LORD God made a woman" (v. 22). This full description of the woman's creation is unique to the cosmogonies of the ancient Near East. The Hebrews' lofty estimation of womanhood and its place in creation was not widely held by ancient civilizations, and Israel itself failed at times to

[106] Observed by Wallace, *The Eden Narrative,* 103.
[107] Calvin, *Comm.,* 127.

give proper recognition and honor to women.[108] The law of Israel, however, was designed to protect those who were commonly subject to abuse by society: the orphan, widow, and alien (e.g., levirate marriage, Deut 25:5–10). Genesis's account of the woman's creation demonstrates that God intended women to be equally important in the purposes of Providence. This was already found in chap. 1, where both "male and female" are said to be image bearers of God and both are commanded to rule the world (1:26–28). The role and relationship of the man and woman is now spelled out in more detail in the garden story.

2:18 The Hebrew construction of v. 18 accentuates the negative phrase "not good" by placing it at the head of the sentence. God has made the man and provided a beautiful environment with honorable work, a setting men may sometimes consider idyllic, but God announces that more is to be done to achieve the ideal for the man. God's concern is that man is "alone." Whether the man felt his aloneness at first is not stated; only the divine viewpoint is given. God has created human life to have fellowship with him but also to be a social entity, building relationships with other human beings. "[Man] will not live until he loves, giving himself away to another on his own level."[109] Isolation is not the divine norm for human beings; community is the creation of God. The commissioning of man and woman to reign over the good land (1:28) involves procreation, and only together can they achieve their destiny. This unity, however, is not merely sexual; it involves sharing spiritual, intellectual, and emotional dimensions as well. Jewish sentiment noted this: "Whoever has no wife exists without goodness, without a helpmate, without joy, without blessing, without atonement . . . without well-being, without a full life; . . . indeed, such a one reduces the representation of the divine image [on earth]."[110]

Moreover, the dignity of the woman is heightened by the monologue of God's creative contemplation. This stands in opposition to the creation of the man and the animals, which are described in the third person. Particularly, the creation of woman gives rise to God's creation of animals in the garden as a pedagogical device for the man's observation. The woman is deemed by the divine mind "a helper suitable for him." "Suitable" (*kĕnegdô,* lit., "like what is in front of him") indicates a *correspondence* between the man and the woman.[111] The focus is on the equality of the two in terms of their essential constitution. Man and woman share in the "human" sameness that cannot be found elsewhere in creation among the beasts. In every way the woman shares in the same features of personhood as does the man. In 1:26–28 this equality of the man and woman as image bearers has priority over their differences in sexual roles, although both were crucial to realizing the intended blessing.

---

[108] E.g., provision for divorce in Deut 24:1–4 is Moses' regulation of the abusive power of the Israelite husband; this may have been in response to the practice of wife swapping.

[109] Kidner, *Genesis,* 65.

[110] *Gen. Rab.* 17.2, quoted by Sarna, *Genesis,* 21.

[111] So BDB, 617.

Here, however, the garden narrative moves beyond that initial assessment by specifying a functional difference that exists between the man and woman. She is called Adam's "helper" *(ʿēzer),* which defines the role that the woman will play. In what way would Eve become a "helper" to the man? The term means "help" in the sense of aid and support[112] and is used of the Lord's aiding his people in the face of enemies (Pss 20:2[3]; 121:1–2; 124:8). Moses spoke of God as his "helper" who delivered him from Pharaoh (Exod 18:4), and it is often associated with "shield" in describing God's protective care of his people.[113]

There is no sense derived from the word linguistically or from the context of the garden narrative that the woman is a lesser person because her role differs (see more at 2:23). In the case of the biblical model, the "helper" is an indispensable "partner" (REB) required to achieve the divine commission. "Helper," as we have seen from its Old Testament usage, means the woman will play an integral part, in this case, in human survival and success. What the man lacks, the woman accomplishes. As Paul said concisely, the man was not made for the woman "but the woman for the man" (cf. 1 Cor 11:9). The woman makes it possible for the man to achieve the blessing that he otherwise could not do "alone." And, obviously, the woman cannot achieve it apart from the man.

Divine "help" *(ʿāzar)* and "blessing" are found in parallel in Jacob's benediction for Joseph (49:25). Similarly, the woman is the provision of divine "help" for the man so that the Lord will bless them as they achieve the mandate. Also *ʿēzer* in 2:18 anticipates in an unexpected way how Eve will be a "helper" to her husband. She will be instrumental in providing salvation for fallen Adam by her "seed," who will defeat the serpent (3:15). Hebrew *zeraʿ* ("seed") may be a wordplay with the similar-sounding *ʿēzer* ("helper"). Since God is said to exercise the role of "helper," the term does not diminish the person who holds that role. If anything, the divine nuance of the term "helper" in the Pentateuch gives special dignity (e.g., Deut 33:7,26,29).

2:19–20 The following narration of the woman's creation explores the similarity and dissimilarity between the woman and man and the animals. It shows the uniqueness of the woman and also the singular relationship shared by man and woman.

First, the descriptive language of the animals' creation echoes the man's creation (v. 7). God "formed" both the man and the creatures out of the same substance ("from the ground"), and both are said to be "living beings/crea-

---

[112] E.g., Deut 33:7; Josh 1:14; Isa 30:5; Dan 11:34.

[113] E.g., Deut 33:29; Pss 33:20; 115:9–11; cf. Ps 70:5[6].

tures" (vv. 7,19).[114] The animal world is a foil for the creation of the woman to distinguish her from the animals; her source is traced to the man himself and not to the "ground." She is the first of creation to come from a living being.[115] God creates the man first and derives the woman from the man to insure that she is his equal in substance and to maintain the unity of the human family. Thus they enjoy a unity despite their sexual difference, and this interdependence is explicit in the expression "one flesh" (v. 24).

Second, animals and birds are paraded before the man by the divine Zookeeper for the man to name them, thereby exercising his authority over them. The creatures are named within three broad categories: domesticated "livestock," "birds," and "beasts of the field" (cf. 3:1). By this the man could observe that there was none among the creatures who matched him in kind. The narration brings out this implication: "For Adam no suitable helper was found" (v. 20).[116] The point is that the man was looking for a human match, but he "found" none. The woman therefore is distinguished from the animals. She is not of the order of the animals over whom the man is to dominate (see 2:23 discussion); she will

[114] The NIV renders "had formed" (v. 19) to indicate that the animals were created prior to the man (as in chap. 1). See v. 8 note. C. J. Collins on syntactic grounds defends the possibility of a pluperfect use of the *wayyiqtōl* verb form; he argues since chaps. 1 and 2 were meant to be read together, logic requires that 2:19 have the pluperfect ("The *Wayyiqtol* as 'Pluperfect': When and Why," *TynBul* 46 [1995]:117–40). Cassuto denies the possibility of reading the pluperfect and accommodates v. 19 to chap. 1 by arguing that the animals of v. 19 were "particular specimens" of the general creation (*Genesis,* 129). Lev 17:13 distinguishes two kinds of animals, "beasts of the field" and "birds of the air," from a third, "the livestock," since the former must be hunted. This distinction occurs in vv. 19–20: the "livestock" presumably was already available with the man in Eden, but the wild beasts and birds required God to bring them to the man for naming. We explained earlier, however, that chap. 2 has a topical order; the intent of the passage is to highlight the man's dominion and the uniqueness of the woman's creation, as opposed to the animals.

[115] Noted by Hamilton, *Genesis 1–17,* 179.

[116] The NIV translates אָדָם as a personal name ("Adam") for the first time. The word occurs with and without the article in chaps. 2–4, making it difficult to determine at what point the personal name is intended. This no doubt is purposeful since the writer conveys by this ambiguity that "Adam" is both a person and also Everyman. This is supported by the occurrences of אָדָם in 5:1–3: in vv. 1 and 3 it is personal "Adam," but in v. 2, though inarticular, אָדָם certainly is generic "mankind" since the verse echoes 1:26–27. Thus 5:1–3 provides the explicit transition from generic human life to the person Adam. Hess proposes that in 1:26 and 2:5 it is generic, and in chaps. 2–4 אָדָם /הָאָדָם serves as a title, "Man." It thus functions like the logographic *lú* ("man, human being") sign in Akk. texts, to designate the office or role of the male as caretaker of the garden ("Splitting the Adam: The Usage of *'Adām* in Genesis I–V," in *Studies in the Pentateuch,* VTSup 41 [Leiden: Brill, 1990], 1–16). This breaks down though at 2:20b; 3:17,21, where the inarticular לְאָדָם must be revocalized as articular לָאָדָם (as BHS notes). This would mean that אָדָם is not a personal name until 4:25, where naming occurs. The LXX begins "Adam" at 2:16; the Vg, at 2:19; modern versions also differ where "Adam" is rendered for the first time (e.g., KJV, NKJV 2:19; NASB, NJPS 2:20; RSV 3:17; and NRSV, REB, NAB, NJB 4:25).

share in the responsibility of dominating the created order (1:26–28). The fact that the man is expressing his rule over the animal world in the search for an appropriate helper caused him to realize his inadequacy to the task if he continues in the impotent condition of "alone." In this way God is preparing the man to value his mate. Just as the man was uniquely made, receiving from God the divine inbreathing of life, the woman's creation in the narrative was unique. Both the man and the woman are mysteriously made by the hands of God.

2:21–22 Third, the narration indicates by the method of making the woman that she is a special creation in the eyes of God (v. 21). She is taken from the man by a "surgical" act of God. The "deep sleep" *(tardēmâ)* that Adam experiences and the procedure that follows is initiated and carried out exclusively by God. The man is not even a conscious spectator. The "sleep" preserves for the man the mystery of her creation and the subsequent surprise at her appearance. "Deep sleep" is commonly used of a night's sleep (Job 4:13; 33:15; Prov 19:15), but here it is the special work of God as with Abraham's slumber (15:12; cf. 1 Sam 26:12 and fig. use Isa 29:10 with Rom 11:8). The verbal root from which this noun is derived *(rādam)* describes Jonah's sleep, which was not disturbed even by the roaring seas battering his Tarshish-bound ship (1:5–6).

The building block for constructing the woman is a portion of the man's essential skeletal frame. As we have already observed, the language of the garden scene is found in the tabernacle description; the term *ṣēlāʿ,* here rendered "ribs," appears frequently in the construction setting of the tabernacle, there translated "side."[117] The woman was taken from the man's side to show that she was of the same substance as the man and to underscore the unity of the human family, having one source. This is made clear by the man's description of her: "Bone of my bones and flesh of my flesh" (v. 23). The verb "took" *(lāqaḥ),* which is given prominence in the narrative (vv. 22–23), may anticipate the marital union of the two since it is the common idiom for marriage.[118]

In Jewish tradition Adam was believed originally androgynous, that is, biologically bisexual (e.g., *Gen. Rab.* 8.1; Rashi), for Gen 5:2 says, "And when they were created, he [God] called them 'man.'" This opinion is not dead. Support for this notion has been advanced by appeal to the rabbinic argument noted above and from 2:22 on the basis that man's "side," not his "rib," was used in the creation of Eve.[119] Whether "side" or "rib," it is transparent from

[117] Of its thirty-nine occurrences, צֵלָע appears nineteen times in delineating the tabernacle construction and its furniture in Exod 25–38 (e.g., 25:12; 26:20,26–27; 27:7; 30:4; 36:31–32; 37:3,5,27; 38:7). It also appears frequently in the construction of Solomon's temple (1 Kgs 6:5,8,15–16,34; 7:3) and Ezekiel's vision of the new temple (Ezek 41:5–9,11,26). There is some dispute regarding the precise sense of צֵלָע in our passage. The NIV text note here indicates the Hebrew can be translated "part of man's side," but אַחַת, meaning "one," suggests that a single "rib" is meant (v. 21).

[118] E.g., Gen 4:19; 6:2; 12:19; 19:14.

[119] A. T. Reisenberger, "The Creation of Adam as Hermaphrodite—and Its Implications for Feminist Theology," *Judaica* 42 (1993): 447–52.

1:27–28, which is the basis of 5:2, that two persons are meant here, not one with two sexes, since 1:27 refers to two persons (plural "them") of differing gender after the singular "him." Moreover, there is no hint elsewhere in the Eden narrative that the first man in 2:7 was bisexual.[120]

Commentators from antiquity to the present have made much of the body image where the woman is derived from the man's side as opposed to some other part of the anatomy. Does it indicate that the woman is the man's equal in position as opposed to his "helper"? In the mind of the modern feminist, "side" may suggest equality, but the rabbis could well take the same "side" and make it suit their patriarchal presumption. *Genesis Rabbah* (18.2) reads, "He [God] thought to himself: 'We should not create her beginning with the head, so that she not be frivolous, nor from the eye, that she not be a starer [at men], nor from the ear, that she not be an eavesdropper, nor from the mouth, that she not talk too much [a gossip], nor from the heart, that she not be jealous, nor from the hand, that she not be light-fingered, nor from the foot, that she not be a gadabout, but from a covered up place on man. For even when a man is standing naked, that spot is covered up." One must beware, then, reading too much into the significance of the "side." Perhaps the best-known explication is Aquinas's *Summa Theologiae* (1a, 92, 3c): "For since the woman should not have 'authority over the man' (1 Tim 2:12) it would not have been fitting for her to have been formed from his head, nor since she is not to be despised by the man, as if she were but his servile subject, would it have been fitting for her to be formed from his feet."

The symbolic significance of the "rib" is that the man and woman are fit for one another as companions sexually and socially. The body metaphor is employed by Paul in his writings to indicate respective roles in community, especially speaking of Christ and the church (1 Cor 12:21–25; Eph 1:22–23; 4:15–16; Col 2:19). In Eph 5:22–31 he draws on the "head-body" imagery in a domestic metaphor where the husband as "head" of the wife parallels Christ as "head" of the church (cp. 1 Cor 11:3). Paul's quotation of Gen 2:24 shows that Eph 5:28–30 is an allusion to Gen 2:22–23.[121] It would seem that Paul had appealed to the woman as man's "rib" to indicate their loving unity, not their domestic equality. This is the significance of the "rib"; they are of the same human "stuff."

---

[120] This traditional interpretation (cf. Paul's opinion, 1 Cor 15:45) has been challenged by feminist theology. See P. Trible in *God and the Rhetoric of Sexuality* (Philadelphia: Fortress, 1978), 80, 98, who renders הָאָדָם ("the man") as "earth-creature," which is taken as a generic expression for human life; this first living human is reckoned as "sexually undifferentiated."

[121] For this discussion see T. O'Loughlin, "Adam's Rib and the Equality of the Sexes: Some Medieval Exegesis of Gen 2:21–22," *ITQ* 59 (1993): 44–54. O'Loughlin's earliest discovery is an eighth-century Irish commentary: "Why was the woman formed from the rib? For if she were formed from his foot or hand or some other part she would stand in shame before him. Another interpretation is that it shows the greatest love, for the rib is, after all, closest to the heart, as it is said: the rib is the guardian of the heart." More important for us, he shows that Augustine's exegesis did not make of the "rib" a metaphor for equality, while otherwise his exegesis is similar to medieval exegesis (e.g., Adam's sleep = Christ's death, Adam's rib = Christ's blood sacrifice and sacrament [John 19:34]).

God is depicted as a "builder" who constructs the woman from the raw resources derived from the man (v. 22). *Bānâ,* translated "made" (NIV, NRSV), "fashioned" (NASB, NJB, NJPS), or "built" (REB, NAB), is a frequent term for the building of edifices, but it occurs only once in early Genesis. Also it is typical in ancient Near Eastern tales where the deity creates human beings.[122] It is used of the Lord elsewhere when he "builds" his sanctuary (Ps 78:69) and is the "Builder" *(bôneh)* of his heavenly residence (Amos 9:6). The anthropomorphic language of God as Potter (v. 7) or Builder shows his special involvement in the creation of the human family. Identifying Adam again in v. 22 as the woman's source reiterates the connectedness of the first couple. Again the "rib" also indicates some discontinuity since it distinguishes her constitution from both the animals and Adam, whose source was the "ground" (2:7,19).

The Lord presents his special "project" to the man, suggesting by this that she is a gift from the man's Maker. The language "brought" is reminiscent of God's presentation of the animals to the man (2:19; cf. 7:9,15). This echo reinforces what the man discovers: the woman is Adam's *human* partner. A significant difference between the two passages is that the first has a stated purpose, the naming of the animals. Here, however, there is no utilitarian purpose prescribed although the man proceeds to name her (v. 23b; 3:20). The garden "Paradise" is now complete with the presence of the woman.

2:23 The narration has steadily progressed toward this pinnacle where the man speaks for the first time, for God alone has spoken up to this point (v. 18). In the man's naming of the animals there was no recorded speech, but with the presentation of the woman, the man exclaims in poetic verse. The embedded poem is peculiar in the narrative flow and by itself draws attention to the importance of this creative event. The exclamation reflects what the narration has sought to show: the unique compatibility of the man and the woman. Adam responds by a shout affirming that he and the woman, indeed, are made up of the same "stuff." The exclamatory nature of his response is indicated by *zōʾt happaʿam,* rendered "This is now" by the NIV but better by the NRSV, "This at last is" (cf. 29:34–35; 30:20; 46:30).[123] The GNB explains the proper sense: "At last, here is one of my own kind." The noun *paʿam* with the definite article is literally "this once" or "this time." The LXX translates the clause with the neuter *touto nun,* "this (is) now," taking the demonstrative ("this," *zōʾt*) as a reference to the event of creation, not in reference to the feminine noun "rib." Another possible reading is to take the demonstrative as a simple deictic and read "this time, bone of my bones."[124]

Adam's response centers on the sameness that he and the woman share as

---

[122] *Banû* occurs in Ug. and Akk. texts (e.g., *Atrahasis*). An epithet for Ug. *ʾIl* (El) is *bny bnwt,* "Creator of creatures" (see citations in *UT* 373).

[123] Other English versions have similarly, "This one at last" (REB, NJB, NJPS, NAB).

[124] *IBHS* § 17.4.2b.

opposed to the creatures. The parallel elements "bone [out] of my bones and flesh [out] of my flesh" have the preposition *min,* indicating source. Although "bone and flesh" are used figuratively in the Old Testament for kinship,[125] this is the one place where it has a literal meaning.[126] Possibly the expression refers to covenant loyalty, in which case Adam is expressing a covenant commitment.[127] "*My* bones" and "*my* flesh" with their pronouns heighten the effect. Also by naming her *ʾiššâ* ("woman"), a sound play on *ʾîš* ("man"), he underscores their attachment. This pun is heard in English "man" and "woman." In naming her the man also names himself *ʾîš,* and in calling her *ʾiššâ* he restates his own name (embedded in hers).[128] The derivations of the two words remain unclear; they are probably used here because of their similar phonetic sound. Adam explains the meaning of the pun in the subsequent clause, again highlighting her source "out of man." Commentators have noted the wordplay between *ʾādām* ("man") and *ʾădāmâ* ("ground") at 2:7 and 3:19 and between *ʾîš* and *ʾiššâ.* The ending *-â* indicates feminine gender, but a double entendre has been suggested for the *-â,* which in Hebrew is sometimes used to indicate direction, "to" or "toward."[129] For the former case the "man" returns to the "ground" *(ʾădāmâ).* In the latter the man moves toward the "woman" *(ʾiššâ)* in 2:24, where by marriage he is "united to his wife" and they "become one flesh."

Genesis 1–3 is the authoritative fountain for the apostle Paul's soteriology and his instruction on home and ecclesiastical order.[130] There is escalating disagreement about the theology and relevancy of the creation-Eden narratives pertaining to the societal and ecclesiastical issues of manhood and womanhood in our culture.[131] What we have in the Eden narrative is the origins of the fun-

---

[125] E.g., Gen 29:14; Judg 9:2; 2 Sam 5:1; 19:12–13[13–14].

[126] The NIV rightly renders the idiom "bone and flesh" with our contemporary idiom for family, "flesh and blood."

[127] See W. Brueggemann, "Of the Same Flesh and Bone (GN 2,23a)," *CBQ* 32 (1970): 532–42. And Hamilton comments: "Thus it would serve as the biblical counterpart to the modern marriage ceremony, 'in weakness [i.e., flesh] and in strength [i.e., bone]'" (*Genesis 1–17,* 180).

[128] So D. Jobling, "The Myth Semantics of Genesis 2:4b–3:24," *Semeia* 18 (1980): 414–49.

[129] I.e., directive *hē*. See S. Meier, "Linguistic Clues on the Date and Canaanite Origin of Genesis 2:23–24," *CBQ* 53 (1991): 19–21.

[130] Rom 5:12–21; 1 Cor 6:16; 11:8–9; 15:21–27,45–49; Eph 5:31; 1 Tim 2:12–15.

[131] See e.g., P. K. Jewett, *Man as Male and Female* (Grand Rapids: Eerdmans, 1975); L. Scanzoni and N. A. Hardesty, *All We're Meant to Be: Biblical Feminism for Today,* 3d rev. ed. (Grand Rapids: Eerdmans, 1992); S. Foh, *Women and the Word of God: A Response to Biblical Feminism* (Phillipsburg, N.J.: Presbyterian & Reformed, 1980); A. B. Spencer, *Beyond the Curse: Women Called to Ministry* (Nashville: Nelson, 1985); S. Adams, *What the Bible Really Says about Women* (Macon: Smyth & Helwys, 1994). For nontraditional evangelical opinions, see A. Mickelsen, ed., *Women, Authority and the Bible* (Downers Grove: IVP, 1986); and for the defense of the traditional view among evangelicals, see J. Piper and W. Grudem, eds., *Recovering Biblical Manhood and Womanhood: A Response to Evangelical Feminism* (Wheaton: Crossway, 1991).

damental institution of ancient Israel's life—the family. This we said is extended beyond the family in some respects by the apostle Paul to ecclesiastical order. Since Israel's chief interest was the family and how chap. 2 presented the prototype family (so 2:24), Genesis cannot be viewed as a paradigm for all man-woman relationships in society. To apply it universally to other social contexts, such as government, education, or commerce, would be unwarranted, for chaps. 2–3 do not address such institutions. Creation and Eden (chaps. 1–3) give a balanced picture of the man and woman in cooperation and companionship. Although they share all in common, Genesis also acknowledges that there are differences. Their sameness does not mean exactness.

Transparently, they are sexually different as "male and female" (1:27) and therefore have different roles in the procreation process. In 1:26–28 the emphasis is on their sexual correlation, but Eden's narrative elucidates and amplifies on their relationship: the man has a leadership role while the woman has a followship position. Before we speak to this, some suppose that the creation account portrays men and women in one way and the Eden narrative presents their relationship differently, even irreconcilably. But the notion of hierarchical role is hardly foreign to 1:1–2:3; there is a certain succession in the creation events from the lesser to the greater. Moreover, there is the notion of "rule" in 1:14–19 regarding the sun and moon where we find the same term as that of 3:16b, "and he shall rule over you." We make only this point: the idea of hierarchy is inferred in 1:1–2:3, and the Eden narrative that ensues is not fundamentally at odds with it. Also some think that submission was unknown until the fall in the punishment oracle of 3:16b (see 3:16 discussion). But leadership-followship is a creation ordinance that is well attested in Genesis 2–3 despite recent protestations. Feminist theology admits this and therefore calls for a new basis for doing theology, freed from what it considers the historically conditioned patriarchy found in Genesis 1–3.[132]

This role relationship of leader and follower is indicated directly and implicitly. First, the participant structure of Genesis 2–3 shows implicitly the hierarchy of creation: God, the man, woman, and animal (serpent). But this was reversed in the fall: the woman listens to the serpent, the man listens to the woman, and no one listens to God. This usurpation of the creation ideal is, however, properly rearranged in the judgment oracles: now the serpent is subject to the "seed" of the woman, the woman subject to the man, and all subject once again under the Lord.[133] Second, 2:18 makes clear that differences are present. The woman is

---

[132] E.g., E. Schüssler Fiorenza, *In Memory of Her: A Feminist Theological Reconstruction of Christian Origins* (New York: Crossroad, 1983); R. R. Reuther, *Sexism and God-Talk* (Boston: Beacon, 1983); D. J. A. Clines, *What Does Eve Do to Help? and Other Readerly Questions to the Old Testament* (Sheffield: JSOT, 1990), 25–48.

[133] See W. Neuer, *Man and Woman in Christian Perspective,* trans. G. Wenham (Wheaton: Crossway, 1991), 75–76.

designated a "helper" in 2:18, which affirms her subordination, for "one could not say in 2:18 that man is created as a helper for the woman."[134] We cannot exchange the roles of the man and woman as though they were equal without undoing the narrative's texture. Also the man names the animals without the assistance of the woman; he expresses dominion over the lower orders, but he cannot complete the task of subduing and thus achieving the blessing by himself. If anything, Eden shows that Eve's attempt to subdue the serpent proved a folly. But this does not mean that the woman was only useful for procreation purposes, for there is no discussion of sexual relations in 2:23–24. The name "Eve," meaning "living," acknowledges her dignity as the source of all human life (3:20); she also is pivotal to the salvation of the fallen family (3:15).

Third, the priority of the man's creation is important for recognizing leadership-followship in the garden (cf. 1 Tim 2:13). It does no good to argue that by this line of reasoning the animals that were created before the woman (2:19) be reckoned as authoritative over Eve, for the sense of the entire narrative makes it indisputable that all human life is superior to the lower orders. It is *within* the human family that leadership-followship is indicated in the garden account. The reference to marriage in 2:24 recognizes the familial structure of authority where parent has priority over son and daughter; that common structure in Israelite life is presupposed in the creation ordinance of marriage (see 2:24). Granted, the reference here is anachronistic, for such parent-child pattern was yet to occur; but we miss the point if we dismiss this too lightly. The supposition of the biblical author is that the familial structure of authority had its inception in the garden, and that pattern is in place before the sin of Adam. For Israel the paradigm for family was that found in the garden narrative, as illustrated in Jesus' instruction on marriage, where he integrates 1:27 and 2:23–24. The rudimentary system was conceptually in place before the fall. Also the man names the woman, indicating a difference in function (2:23; 3:20), in the same way that the naming of the elements in God's creation and the man's naming of the animals indicated a difference in relationship (see 1:5 discussion). Although naming indicates authority in the Old Testament, the narrative of Eve's creation as a whole takes steps to show that the woman is not subject to the man in the same sense that the animals are subject to him. Rather, the text presents them as partners who together exercise rule, fulfilling the mandate of 1:28 by exercising their appropriate sexual functions and respective intrahuman roles.

Fourth, the woman has her source in the man, suggesting that the man is the leader (cf. 1 Cor 11:8). The fact that the woman came from the man, which itself so impressed the man that he exclaimed "bone of my bones," indicates that the two are inherently the same in nature, even as one connectional substance, yet they are distinctive in their person and interpersonal relationship.

[134] Westermann, *Genesis 1–11,* 262.

Ultimately, they have their mutual source in God (cf. 1 Cor 11:12), for neither creates the other. Again the text does not suggest that the man alone has access to God but rather that the man has the greater responsibility as the "firstborn" for the couple's response to God's charge. This is confirmed in chap. 3 by the quizzing of the man first about their collective actions (3:9–12), for the burden lies with the man as the responsible party for the activity of the garden. When God explains man's punishment (3:17), he attributes it to Adam's following the woman in sin. However, the sin of the man is not his listening to the woman per se but his following the woman *in sin.* In other words, it is too much to say that a husband should not listen to the advice of his wife. It was not simply heeding her advice; in this case it was succumbing to the content of the advice that spelled his disaster (cf. 1 Tim 2:14).

2:24 The creation of the first couple leads naturally to their relationship expressed through marriage since it is the couple's charge to procreate and subdue the earth (1:28). This verse is not the continued speech of the man but the commentary of the narrator, which is attributed to God by Jesus (Matt 19:4–5). "For this reason" *(ʿal kēn)* does not indicate an explanation of the foregoing but rather describes the consequence of God's charge for the human family to propagate and rule. Marriage and family are the divine ideal for carrying out the mandate. As we noted, Jesus' appeal to the garden (quoting Gen 2:23) as the basis of his teaching on marriage and divorce (Matt 19:3–9; Mark 10:2–12) indicates that the garden established a paradigm for marital behavior. That Eden was viewed by the Hebrews as the model, authoritative experience can be seen also in Jewish literature of the time but especially by Paul, who appeals to its events in speaking of the most profound theological tenets of Christianity (Rom 5:12–21; 1 Cor 15:45) and in offering instructions concerning the propriety of worship (1 Cor 11:2–16; 1 Tim 2:11–15), moral behavior (1 Cor 6:16), and marriage (Eph 5:31).

As a model for marriage this passage involves three factors: a leaving, a uniting, and a public declaration. The NIV's rendering "*will* leave" is ambiguous (also NASB); it can be taken by the modern reader as a description of future behavior or as an exhortation to marry. Better is the rendering "leaves" and "clings" (NRSV), indicating by the simple present tense that marriage is a universal practice.[135] Marriage is depicted as a covenant relationship shared by man and woman. Monogamy is clearly intended. "Leave" *(ʿāzab)* and "cling" *(dābaq)* are terms commonly used in the context of covenant, indicating covenant breach (e.g., Deut 28:20; Hos 4:10) or fidelity.[136]

---

[135] "Leaves" is the imperfective form יַעֲזָב, and "clings" is the expected corresponding perfective form with the *wāw* consecutive (וְדָבַק).

[136] E.g., Deut 10:20; 11:22; 13:18; 30:20; Josh 23:8,12. At Gen 24:27 and 28:15 "not leave" indicates God's faithful provision for the patriarchs. The figurative use of "cling" occurs in 34:3, where it describes Shechem's love for Dinah.

The significance of the language "leave" is that marriage involves a new pledge to a spouse in which former familial commitments are superseded. Marriage requires a new priority by the marital partners where obligations to one's spouse supplant a person's parental loyalties. Illustrative of this pledge is Ruth's earnest desire to remain with Naomi: "Ruth clung *[dābaq]* to her" (1:14) and "Don't urge me to leave *[ʿāzab]* you" (1:16).

Our passage cannot mean that a man is not married unless he departs his father's house; it was customary in Israel for a man to remain, not leave, his father's household. This is best illustrated by Jacob's family, whose sons remained under their father's influence despite the founding of their own families and wealth. Although the sons are subject to their father's wishes, they also exercise some freedom and maintain their own household identity as shown by Reuben's authority over the life and death of his sons (42:37). Hebrew custom, rather, called for the wife to join the house of her husband (cf. Rebekah [chap. 24] and Tamar [chap. 38]).[137] In fact, the law assumed a woman remained under the auspices of her husband's family even after her husband's death (e.g., Deut 25:5–10). The Eden narrative does not suggest that before the fall in chap. 3 men were ideally to leave their family for the woman's, which subsequently was reversed as a result of the fall.[138] The judgment oracles do not speak to this, and it is best to view the reference to man's "leaving" as due to his priority in the narrative interest. Therefore "leave" here is metaphorical rather than literal since it was the woman who actually left her father's house.

Also marriage involves the two united in commitment; two parties are bound by stipulations, forming a new entity or relationship. The two people, although freed from their parents, are not isolated or independent; they become dependent and responsible toward one another. "One flesh" echoes the language of v. 23, which speaks of the woman's source in the man; here it depicts the consequence of their bonding, which results in one new person. Our human sexuality expresses both our individuality as gender and our oneness with another person through physical union. Sexual union implies community and requires responsible love within that union.[139] The sexual union of the couple is, however, only symbolic of the new kinship that the couple has entered. The sexual act by itself does not exhaust marriage; marriage entails far more.

[137] Laban's response to the departure of Leah and Rachel is not so much their going as the manner in which Jacob secretly departed with them (31:25–28). Another example of this practice is the Levite's wife (Judg 19).

[138] It has been rendered in the modal sense, "should leave," thus depicting the initial divine intention; by sin that unity is broken, and 3:16, where the woman pursues the man, indicates the reversal of 2:24. See R. Lawton, "Genesis 2:24: Trite or Tragic?" *JBL* 105 (1986): 97–98. But rather than the reversal of 2:24, the woman's "desire" in 3:16 continues to be best explained in the light of the foregoing clause regarding childbirth.

[139] So Bonhoeffer, *Creation and Fall,* 62.

Finally, this "leaving" and "uniting" involves a public declaration in the sight of God. Marriage is not a private matter. It involves a declaration of intention and a redefining of obligations and relationships in a familial and social setting. In our contemporary climate of sexual freedom and societal tolerance for moral deviance, we would do well to reconsider the biblical viewpoint toward marriage and sexual behavior. Without question 2:24 serves as the bedrock for Hebrew understanding of the centrality of the nuclear family for the survival of society.[140] Monogamous heterosexual marriage was always viewed as the divine norm from the outset of creation. Mosaic instruction shows considerable efforts to safeguard this ideal against its dissolution by clarifying what is "family." Sexuality was instrumental in defining what a household was in Israel; abrogation of sexual boundaries threatened the identity of this core social institution. Without proper limits "family" ceased, and the consequence was the undoing of Israel as a nation, the same fate suffered by their predecessors (Lev 18:24–30). Strong prohibitions against sexual offenses often prescribed the penalty of death, as in the case of the heinous sins of murder and idolatry.

Adultery and promiscuity encroached upon another's household, and incest within one's own family resulted in confused lines of familial relationships. Since marriage formed a new kinship bond ("nakedness") between the bride and her husband's brothers, making her their sister, and between her and her father-in-law, making her his daughter, sexual relationships and even marriage of in-laws after death or divorce was considered sexual incest. Hebrew marriage expanded legal responsibilities by the family toward the new member even after the death of a spouse (e.g., Deut 25:5–10).[141] Marriage then was viewed as altering familial identity in the eyes of the community. We also find that the Mosaic law reflects the same concern regarding the similarities and distinctions between human and animal that we have found in our Genesis narrative. Sexual relations with animals were abhorrent since that revoked creation's distinctions (e.g., Exod 22:19[18]). Similarly, homosexual behavior was a confusion of sexual identity between men and women (e.g., Lev 18:22; 20:13; cf. Deut 22:5). Christian expectations for sexual behavior were the same and were a given among Jewish converts, but the Gentile world did not follow such norms. It was against the customary practices of the Greco-Roman world that Paul urged sexual restraints (e.g., Rom 1:24–28; 1 Cor 6:9; 1 Thess 4:3–7).

2:25 The final verse is transitional, linking the foregoing narrative of creation and marriage to the subsequent narrative of human sin and the consequences of that disobedience ("naked," 3:7,10–11). Verse 25 explains that

---

[140] For our discussion, see especially T. Frymer-Kensky, "Law and Philosophy: The Case of Sex in the Bible," *Semeia* 45 (1989): 89–102.

[141] Noted by Wenham, *Genesis 1–15,* 71.

nakedness was not always a shameful condition for the human family. The Hebrew verb translated "felt no shame" (NIV) may be taken as a customary use of the verb, indicating that it was their normal condition.[142] The common rendering "felt no shame"[143] may suggest to the modern reader that shame is primarily an emotional response to guilt; in the following narrative, however, it is their knowledge that led to their understanding of personal shame (3:7); thus they "were not ashamed" (NRSV, NASB). True guilt is not manifest primarily in feeling but in knowledge.

Nakedness among the Hebrews was shameful because it was often associated with guilt.[144] The parade example is the discovery of Noah's nakedness by his son, which meant family humiliation (9:22–23). Among the Levitical laws the idioms "nakedness" (e.g., Lev 18:6,10; 20:17) and "make naked" *(heʿĕrâ)* for sexual relations are used of sexual offenses (e.g., Lev 20:18–19). Particularly instructive is Exod 20:26, which prohibits men (i.e., priests) ascending the steps of God's altar, lest they expose their genitals before the Lord (cf. linen underpants, Exod 28:42–43). "*And* they felt no shame" fails to make explicit the adversative sense of "*but* they felt no shame."[145] It would have been remarkable to the Hebrews that the couple could be naked without embarrassment. It was in Greek culture, and not until the early first millennium B.C., that nudity among Greek males was viewed as heroic.[146]

Also v. 25 as transitional anticipates the role of the serpent and associates the viper's trickery with the lost innocence of the first couple. The term "naked" (pl. *ʿărûmmîm*) is a play on the word "crafty" *(ʿārûm),* which describes the nature of the serpent (3:1). As a result of the serpent's "shrewdness," our parents sinned and experienced the embarrassment of their "nakedness" in the presence of God (3:7). Ironically, the first achievement that their newfound wisdom acquired was the realization of their nudity. Luther observed what we suspect the ancient Hebrew audience would have pondered: "Therefore this passage points out admirably how much evil followed after the sin of Adam. For now it would be regarded as the utmost madness if anyone walked about naked."[147]

---

[142] A. B. Davidson renders the nuance of the imperfect יִתְבֹּשָׁשׁוּ "they were not (at any time) ashamed" (*Introductory Hebrew Grammar: Hebrew Syntax,* 3d ed. [Edinburgh: T & T Clark, 1901], #44b).

[143] Cf. NIV, NJPS, NAB, NJB, REB.

[144] Nakedness is related to "shame" (בֹּשֶׁת), particularly public ridicule (e.g., 1 Sam 20:30; Isa 20:4; Mic 1:11). It often occurs as a metaphor for judgment against sin (e.g., Isa 47:3; Ezek 16:7,22,37,39; Lam 1:8). The figure of "shame" at Job 8:22 connects shame and clothing.

[145] Many English versions have "but" or "yet" (REB, NJB, NAB, NJPS) for "and" (NIV, NASB, NRSV).

[146] L. Bonfonte, "The Naked Greek: How Ancient Art and Literature Reflect the Custom of Civic Nudity," *Archaeology* 43 (1990): 28–35.

[147] *LW* 1.140.

2. The Man and Woman Expelled from the Garden (3:1–24)

The events of this chapter disrupt Eden's calm and are central to the purpose of the *tōlĕdōt* segment, which explains what became of the man and woman in their idyllic habitat on earth (2:4–4:26). The Eden narrative in 2:4–4:26 turns on the depiction of the man and woman's sin (3:6–8; see introduction to 2:4–4:26). The narrative 3:6–8 is bracketed by two dialogue exchanges involving the episode's four participants: the serpent and woman (3:1–5) and the Lord's questioning of the man and woman (3:9–13). Divine pronouncement of three judgments against the culprits follows (3:14–19). The reactions of the man, the naming of Eve, and the Lord making skin garments are described in a concise narrative (3:20–21). The garden account ends with an intradivine monologue, determining the couple's expulsion, and the execution of that deliberation (3:22–24).

Genesis 2:4–25 sets the stage for interpreting the snake's challenge to the woman and for recognizing what is at jeopardy for the human couple. If we did not have 2:4–25, we would have no idea how much was lost in Adam's bite of the fruit. Genesis 4:1–26 shows us the aftermath of our first parents' lamentable deed by Cain's murder of Abel and the swelling tide of human wickedness exhibited by his progeny (4:23–24). Yet concomitant with God's three "oracles of destiny" uttered against the criminals (3:14–19), we hear within the judgments themselves the hopeful notes of reconciliation. This too is evidenced in the subsequent account where Eve perpetuates the family through birth (4:1–2), Seth supplants Cain (4:25), and the *tōlĕdōt* section ends with humanity calling upon the name of the Lord (4:26).

LITERARY SOURCE. As we noted in our discussion at 2:4–25, the Eden story is widely thought to owe its origins to a mythological corpus. Many suppose that originally chap. 3's purpose was solely etiological, that is, an explanation of origins, either of evil or of the enmity between humans and snakes, or perhaps how the snake became a legless creature. Since the Eden narrative offers no explanation for the origins of the serpent (other than that it was a created beast—2:19) and does not explicitly call for a change in its anatomy, there is little basis for finding such an etiological purpose.

Moreover, as we have said, Genesis does not explain the origins of evil; rather, the biblical account, if anything, says where evil does *not* have its source. Evil was not inherent in man nor can it be said that sin was the consequence of divine entrapment. The tempter stands outside the human pair and stands opposed to God's word. His career is obscure to the author of Genesis 3, who can only speak of the snake's destiny (3:14–15). As we find elsewhere in Scripture, little is said about the source of evil. Old Testament thought consistently affirms God as the ultimate cause of all things, even the existence of the serpent (3:1), but it never attributes evil to God. He is not morally responsible for the sin of the first couple nor is he culpable for the serpent's deceit.

ADAM'S SIN. John Milton's revered *Paradise Lost* captures in imaginative verse the classical rendition of Adam's sin:

> Earth trembled from her entrails, as again
> In pangs, and nature gave a second groan;
> Sky loured, and muttering thunder, some sad drops
> Wept at completing of the mortal sin
> Original . . .

Until recent times the traditional Christian interpretation of Adam's fall, as the first sin and the origin of all human and earthly travail, has reigned with little challenge among Christian interpreters. The witness of early Jewish interpretation was mixed, attributing the human predicament of sin to the first couple,[148] but elsewhere it is said to be each person's responsibility alone.[149] Augustine hammered out the doctrine of original sin that subsequently was reiterated in the church's councils and refined by the pen of the Reformers, especially Luther's debate with semi-Pelagian Erasmus. The Bishop of Hippo assumed correctly that Genesis told a historical account, as did all interpreters until the ascent of biblical criticism, and thus Eden depicted the first sin, which indelibly marked the whole human family with the misdeed. His touchstone was the view of Paul, who had read Adam's disobedience as the initiation of sin (and human death) in the world, which determined the corrupted condition of people universally (Rom 5:12–21). Paul established the analogy between Adam and Christ, the last Adam, to contrast Christ's achievement of justification and the transgression of Adam (5:15–17). Augustine cut a course that avoided the excesses of the Manichean view that being human was evil and the Pelagian optimism that all were indeterminately free to choose their own destiny, unencumbered by Adam's sin.[150] Luther depicted human will in bondage to sin requiring deliverance, while Erasmus thought man, though fallen, still could obey God but was in need of assisting grace to come to sal-

[148] "For the first Adam, burdened with an evil heart, transgressed and was overcome, as were also all who were descended from him" (*4 Ezra* 3:21), and "O Adam, what have you done? For though it was you who sinned, the fall was not yours alone, but ours also who are your descendants" (*4 Ezra* 7:118). Cf. also *2 Apoc. Bar.* 23:4. Alternatively, sin is attributed to Eve, "From a woman sin had its beginning, and because of her we all die" (*Sir* 25:24), or to the devil, "Through the devil's envy sin entered the world" (*Wis* 2:24).

[149] "For though Adam first sinned and brought untimely death upon all men, yet each one of those who were born from him has either prepared for his own soul its future torment or chosen for himself the glories that are to be. . . . Thus Adam was responsible for himself only; each one of us is his own Adam" (*2 Apoc. Bar.* 54:15–16,19).

[150] See the discussion in S. J. Duffy, "Our Hearts of Darkness: Original Sin Revisited," *TS* 49 (1988): 597–622.

vation.[151] This antithesis has been rehearsed in our century by the debate of Karl Barth and Emil Brunner.[152] Calvin asserted like Luther that man's sin was not merely imitation of Adam's sin as Pelagius had thought, for the sin of Father Adam "proved the destruction of the whole human race." And no part of the human being escaped its calamitous effects.[153]

This time-honored interpretation of an original fall has been wrongly dismissed as a pre-Enlightenment misunderstanding of the garden narrative.[154] According to this modern viewpoint, Eden does not concern itself with the abstract notions of the origin of absolute evil or death. Eden's story explains no more than what happens to men and women when they disobey God, which is true of Everyman.[155] Or it is proposed that Genesis concerns immortality, how Adam and Eve as mortals almost achieved immortality (3:22) and were denied it because of their disobedience or by the trickery of the serpent. Thus there is no sense of rebellion and alienation from God in chap. 3 as later Christian tradition interpreted it.[156] Other proposals are many, including this representative sampling: chaps. 2–3 are polemical against Canaanite worship; a parable from the exilic period chastening the ruling elite that had sought power through wisdom and brought down the nation; the story of struggle between monarchic rule and peasantry; and a parable explaining the human predicament of early Israel's agrarian struggle in the hill country upon entry

[151] In *The Bondage of the Will,* Luther comments: "Furthermore, seeing that through the one transgression of the one man, Adam, we are all under sin and damnation, how can we attempt anything that is not sinful and damnable?" Human sin with Adam is not mere imitation on our part, "since it would be we and not Adam who committed it; but it becomes ours the moment we are born" (*LW* 33.272).

[152] E. Brunner and K. Barth, *Natural Theology,* trans. P. Frankel (London: Centenary, 1946); Brunner, *Man in Revolt: A Christian Anthropology,* trans. O. Wyon (Philadelphia: Westminster, 1947); Barth, *Church Dogmatics* IV/Part One (Edinburgh: T & T Clark, 1958 [Eng. trans.]).

[153] "For all who are not utterly blind, perceive that no part of us is sound; that the mind is smitten with blindness, and infected with innumerable errors; that all the affections of the heart are full of stubbornness and wickedness; that vile lusts, or other diseases equally fatal, reign there; and that all the senses burst forth with many vices," Calvin, *Comm.,* 155. Also *Institutes* 2.1.4–7.

[154] As Carmichael bluntly states: "No sophisticated biblical scholar, standing aside from Jewish or Christian tradition, today interprets the paradise story as a fall into a chasm from a state of innocence and bliss" ("The Paradise Myth: Interpreting without Jewish and Christian Spectacles," 47).

[155] E.g., Westermann understands Gen 2–3 as answering the existential question of why a person is limited by death, suffering, and toil (*Genesis 1–11,* 275–78). The answer lies in primeval time, not history; there is no first sin, no inherited sin, no death as a penalty; rather the narrative speaks to the universal condition of humanity as fallible.

[156] So Barr, *Garden of Eden and Hope of Immortality.* A. S. Kapelrud likens Eden to the myths of Adapa and Gilgamesh, who are tricked into losing their chance at immortality by the gods ("You Shall Surely Die," in *History and Traditions of Early Israel* [Leiden: Brill, 1993], 50–61). Genesis, he says, shows similarly how chthonic forces (i.e., netherworld deities), represented by the serpent, stole away eternal life from the human couple but left them with the knowledge necessary to cope. There is no rebellion against God in Eden, only the couple's inability to stand up to the shrewd serpent.

into Canaan.[157] Thus, they say, mythological Eden has been wrongly read as historical narrative, resulting in centuries of misunderstanding. With myth as its substratum, the story's purpose by universal setting and symbolic features (e.g., trees, serpent) was to depict the universal human experience in the archetypical Humanity. Moreover, there is no explicit connection in Genesis between Adam's sin and his successors. Original sin as inherited sin is foreign to the Genesis narrative.

Regarding the Christian tradition, proponents of this paradigmatic interpretation find support in Paul's use of Adam as a "pattern" ("type," Rom 5:14) of the human condition (Rom 5; 1 Cor 15). Later the apostle's view was misconstrued by Augustinian tradition and perpetuated in the Western church. Alternatively, for others, Paul was following the Jewish tradition of his day and was simply wrong in his interpretation of Genesis 2–3 as the story of sin's origins in the world.[158] Contemporary theologians have reinterpreted the garden story as a depiction of the anxiety of human existence and the self-alienation that results from the exercise of autonomous freedom.[159] R. Niebuhr redefined sin as the outcome between the human capacity to choose and the limitation of human finitude. This anxiety gives opportunity for sin by appealing to prideful autonomy because of the human ability to make choices or by practicing sensuality to escape the realities of our finitude.[160] Alienation from one's ground of being or true self was the essence of sin for P. Tillich.[161]

---

[157] For polemical interpretations see F. Hvidberg, "The Canaanite Background of Gen I–III," *VT* 10 (1960): 285–94; A. Gardner, "Genesis 2:4b–3: A Mythological Paradigm of Sexual Equality or of the Religious History of Pre-Exilic Israel?" *SJT* 43 (1990): 1–18; N. Wyatt, "Interpreting the Creation and Fall Story in Genesis 2–3," *ZAW* 93 (1981): 10–21. As a critique of wisdom see Mendenhall, "The Shady Side of Wisdom." For royal interpretations see Brueggemann, "From Dust to Kingship," 1–18; J. M. Kennedy, "Peasants in Revolt: Political Allegory in Genesis 2–3," *JSOT* 47 (1990): 3–14; K. Holter, "The Serpent in Eden as a Symbol of Israel's Political Enemies: A Yahwistic Criticism of the Solomonic Foreign Policy," in *Scandinavian Journal of the Old Testament* 1 (1990): 106–12. And for labor in early Israel's survival see C. Meyers, "Gender Roles and Genesis 3:16 Revisited," in *The Word of the Lord Shall Go Forth* (Winona Lake: Eisenbrauns/ASOR, 1983), 337–54, and *Discovering Eve: Ancient Israelite Women in Context* (Oxford: Oxford University Press, 1988). For more see the catalogue of interpretations in Hess, "The Roles of the Woman and the Man in Genesis 3," *Themelios* 18 (1993): 15–19.

[158] "Far from it being the case that Paul's thinking is deeply rooted in the thought world of ancient Israel, it is much more precisely formed by the *interpretation* of these ancient texts which took place in Hellenistic times and in a different intellectual atmosphere" (Barr, *Garden of Eden and Hope of Immortality,* 18).

[159] For survey discussion see D. Bloesch, "Sin," *Evangelical Dictionary of Theology* (Grand Rapids: Baker, 1984), 1013–14.

[160] R. Niebuhr, *The Nature and Destiny of Man: A Christian Interpretation* (New York: Scribner, 1941–43); also S. Kierkegaard, *The Concept of Anxiety: A Simple Psychologically Orienting Deliberation on the Dogmatic Issue of Hereditary Sin,* trans. and ed. R. Thomte, with B. Albert (Princeton: Princeton University Press, 1980). Among modern commentators, e.g., "the story is a theological critique of anxiety. It presents a prism through which the root problem of anxiety can be understood" (Brueggemann, *Genesis,* 53).

[161] P. Tillich, *Systematic Theology* (Chicago: University of Chicago Press, 1951–1963).

But Paul's reading of Genesis is not as remote to the narrative as some would contend. Granted, Genesis does not explicitly convey the linkage of Adam's sin and universal guilt as we find it in Paul; but the narrative provides the ideological soil in which Paul cultivated the concepts of universal sin, guilt, and death. What evidence from Genesis points to the idea of original sin, universal guilt, and death? Did Adam's sin irrevocably affect all humanity or only himself? G. Wenham has argued convincingly that the idea of a first sin with universal consequences can be supported from the Genesis narratives.[162] First, Genesis testifies that Adam is an individual, not solely typological, and shows that the world after Adam's sin is forever altered as a consequence of Eden's rebellion. We have already asserted that the intentional *tōlĕdōt* heading (2:4) indicates that the account is to be read as history (see 2:4–25 discussion). Genesis 5:1 echoes creation and also reiterates the *tōlĕdōt* rubric, linking the genealogy of actual people (Adam-Noah) with creation. Certainly the refrain "and he died" is a deliberate association of Adam's sin (2:17; 3:19) with the inevitable experience of Adam's progeny. For the compiler of the Genesis narratives the genealogical strategy unmistakably places Adam on the same historical plane as the individual Abraham (5:1–32; 11:10–26).

Second, Genesis presents real consequences from Adam's sin as noted in chap. 3 itself and the subsequent narrative of chaps. 4–11. Whereas the garden was the perfect and "very good" place of fellowship with God, the human condition was altered forever by their expulsion, and as a consequence the human family lost much. Adam's experience is not repeated by each person, for Abel's and Cain's lives (and all others) begin at a very different point—*outside* the garden. We do not enjoy Eden today, for the expulsion changed the condition of humanity permanently. When we consider the account of Genesis 4, we find in it a number of deliberate structural and lexical echoes of chap. 3's narrative and the dialogue exchange between Adam and God. The questioning (4:9 with 3:9; 4:10 with 3:13), the curses (4:11 with 3:14,17), the beneficent mark of Cain and provision of Adam's clothing (4:15 with 3:21), the divine forewarning of "desire" and "rule" (4:7 with 3:16), and the expulsion (4:14 with 3:24) indicate a linkage. But Cain's sin is not merely a repetition of Adam's failure; the narrative shows a different starting point for Cain's relationship with God. His offering is initially rejected by the Lord (4:5), and the intensity of Cain's rebellion exceeds his father's, culminating in his descendant Lamech (4:23–24). The advance of human wickedness and pride is attested again and again in the narratives that ensue: innate human wickedness is the reason of the catastrophic flood that nonetheless continues (6:5; 8:21); Noah's curse impacts Ham's progeny (9:20–27); and the threatening Babelites seek to enlarge their place (11:1–9).

[162] See Wenham, *Genesis 1–15,* 90–91, who concludes that Gen 3 is both typological and historical. Cf. also his "Original Sin in Genesis 1–11," *Churchman* 104 (1990): 309–28.

Third, the judgment oracles (3:14–19) anticipate actual historical results that exceed the immediate punishment of the guilty. It is presupposed by 3:15 that the serpent as humanity's enemy is a given; each person does not discover this anew. Never again will the creation be deemed "good" because Eden's sin has transfigured creation and the human condition irreparably (Rom 8:19–25). It should not surprise us that Paul, while recognizing the typological value of Adam's act, also spoke of him as the "one man" (Rom 5:12) who committed "one man's trespass" (5:15).[163] Death's reign from Adam to Moses held sway though they "did not sin by breaking a command, as did Adam" (5:14). The terror of Adam's act was both concrete and consequential as was Christ's one deed of life at the cross, which was concrete and had universal consequence.

Has Western tradition distorted Paul? A common remark is that Augustine's notion of inherited sin was due to his unfortunate dependence on the Latin's mistaken rendering of Rom 5:12d, "in whom all sinned."[164] Modern versions rightly read the final clause as causal, "because all sinned." But the matter does not hinge solely on the four Greek words of Rom 5:12d, for most agree that the Greek *eph' hō* ("because") is a conjunction expressing cause or result.[165] Also contended is that Rom 5:12 speaks of both Adam's "sin" *(hamartia)*that entered the world and its power over all individuals who "sinned" *(hamarton)*;[166] but the universality of Adam's sin dominates the passage (Rom 5:12–21), and this demands that we understand humanity as culpable for more than personal sins.[167]

---

[163] For a defense of the traditional view see J. Murray, *The Epistle to the Romans,* NICNT (Grand Rapids: Eerdmans, 1968), 180–210.

[164] Vg's *in quo omnes peccaverunt* ("in whom [Adam] all sinned") for ἐφ' ᾧ πάντες ἥμαρτον in Rom 5:12d. E.g., D. Moody, *The Word of Truth* (Grand Rapids: Eerdmans, 1981), 286–87.

[165] After noting as many as eleven possible translations for ἐφ' ᾧ, J. A. Fitzmyer concludes: "The fate of humanity ultimately rests on what its head, Adam, has done to it. The primary causality for its sinful and mortal condition is ascribed to Adam, no matter what meaning is assigned to *eph' hō*, and a secondary causality to the sins of all human beings" (*Romans,* AB [New York: Doubleday, 1992], 416).

[166] J. D. G. Dunn concludes: "In short, Paul could be said to hold a doctrine of *original sin,* in the sense that from the beginning everyone has been under the power of sin with death as the consequence, but not a doctrine of *original guilt,* since individuals are only held responsible for deliberate acts of defiance against God and his law" (*Romans 1–8,* WBC [Dallas: Word, 1988], 291). Cf. also C. E. B. Cranfield, *The Epistle to the Romans,* ICC (Edinburgh: T & T Clark, 1975), 1.278: "While men do not sin in Adam in Augustine's sense [i.e., participating in Adam's transgression], they certainly do sin in Adam in the sense that they sin in a real solidarity with him [i.e., inheriting his corrupt nature], as a result of the entail of his transgression."

[167] Fitzmyer remarks: "The universality of Adam's sin is presupposed in 15a, 16a, 17a, 18a, 19a. It would then be false to the thrust of the whole paragraph to interpret 5:12 as though it implied that the human condition before Christ's coming were due solely to personal individual sins" (*Romans,* 417). See also S. L. Johnson, Jr., "Romans 5:12—An Exercise in Exegesis and Theology," in *New Dimensions in New Testament Study,* ed. R. N. Longenecker and M. C. Tenney (Grand Rapids: Zondervan, 1974), 298–316, who argues for the Reformed doctrine that Adam sinned as the representative of the race, making his sin our sin, his guilt our guilt.

(1) The Serpent and the Woman (3:1–5)

[1]Now the serpent was more crafty than any of the wild animals the LORD God had made. He said to the woman, "Did God really say, 'You must not eat from any tree in the garden'?"

[2]The woman said to the serpent, "We may eat fruit from the trees in the garden, [3]but God did say, 'You must not eat fruit from the tree that is in the middle of the garden, and you must not touch it, or you will die.'"

[4]"You will not surely die," the serpent said to the woman. [5]"For God knows that when you eat of it your eyes will be opened, and you will be like God, knowing good and evil."

3:1 The serpent is unforeseen in the narrative and appears suddenly. The reader is caught off guard, but not as unsuspecting as Eve. The snake is described by the narrator as "crafty," alerting the reader to weigh the words of the beast carefully. "Crafty" *(ʿārûm)* can be spoken of approvingly or negatively, thereby introducing ambiguity at this stage in the story.[168] Perhaps this also prepares the reader for the serpent as a talking animal, since it is distinguished from all others as "more crafty."[169] Its wordplay with "naked" *(ʿărummîm)* in 2:25, as noted, links the serpent's shrewdness with the woman's deception, finally resulting in the self-consciousness of human nakedness. Also the serpent is identified as an animal that God "had made" among the beasts of the field, referring to 2:19. This dismisses any notion of a competing dualism since the animal owes its existence to God.

Although the origin of the snake is attributed to God, there is no attempt here to explain the origins of evil. The narrative explains only the origin of human sin and guilt. There is no explanation for the serpent's capacity to talk other than possibly that it was "crafty." It is assumed that the animal has this ability, and the fact that the woman did not find this alarming only heightens the suspicion that the serpent is representative of something or someone sinisterly powerful. In any case the substance of what the serpent says is more important than who or what the serpent is.[170] Moreover, the serpent was among the "good" animals God had made (chap. 1), and there was no ostensible reason for the woman to suspect the animal's deceit other than the content of what the animal spoke. Perhaps that the snake was of the wild (see 2:19–20 with 3:1), not as familiar to the domestic couple, explains the woman's gull-

[168]For the negative sense of "crafty," see Job 15:5, where it is used of the "tongue" (cf. Job 5:12–13; Exod 21:14); for the sense of shrewdness see the wisdom of Proverbs (e.g., 12:23; 14:18). Saul deemed David "very crafty," who used his wits to escape danger (1 Sam 23:22).

[169]The preposition מִן is rendered as comparative in the NIV and NRSV, indicating degree; *IBHS* § 14.5d has it comparative superlative "most cunning," but it has also been read as separation, meaning "subtle as none other of the beasts" (GKC § 119w).

[170]von Rad comments, "We are not to be concerned with what the snake is but with what it says" (*Genesis,* 88).

ibility.[171] The reader, on the other hand, has the advantage of the narrator's commentary.

Various explanations for the serpent compete for our understanding. It has been interpreted as a mythological character related to magical powers or taken as a symbol of human curiosity, the fertility cult, or of chaos/evil. Still others have proposed that the voice of the snake is the inner person.[172] Others have found it to be a polemical response to the apostasy of magic or a demythologizing of the serpent deity, which was revered in the ancient Near East. And the traditional opinion among Jewish and Christian interpreters is that the serpent is Satan's instrument.[173] Luther explained: "The devil was permitted to enter beasts, as he here entered the serpent. For there is no doubt that it was a real serpent in which Satan was and in which he conversed with Eve" (*LW* 1.151).

"Serpent" *(nāḥāš)* is the general term for "snake." This reptile had a significant role in the ancient world, where it was both an object of reverence and of disdain. It commonly is found in ancient myths and is represented by religious objects. It conveyed the ambivalent meanings of life/recurring youth, death/chaos, and wisdom.[174] The Bible possesses the same associations for the serpent: the rejuvenating effects of Moses' bronze serpent (Num 21:8; cf. 2 Kgs 18:4), its respected shrewdness (Matt 10:16), its venomous death (e.g., Ps 58:4), and as divine opponent (Isa 27:1). The Babylonian *Epic of Gilgamesh* illustrates how the serpent was perceived in ancient times as man's antagonist. Gilgamesh searches for the immortal Utnapishtim, the famed survivor of the flood, to learn how he too might obtain eternal life. Utnapishtim reveals a secret known only to him and the gods; there is a plant in the depths of the sea that can rejuvenate his life. Gilgamesh obtains it and names it "Man Becomes Young in Old Age." The plant, however, is subsequently stolen away by a serpent which carries it off and when doing so sheds its skin, suggesting the process of rejuvenation.[175]

As we discussed in 2:4–25, the description of the garden scene uses imagery drawn from the tabernacle to convey by double entendre the meeting place for God and man in the garden. This reptile achieves the same purpose, indi-

---

[171] J. Magonet notes that "the snake is described as being more cunning 'than all living creatures of the field,' that is to say, the snake comes from that group defined as living apart from man" ("The Themes of Genesis 2–3," in *A Walk in the Garden,* JSOTSup 136 [Sheffield: JSOT, 1992], 39–46).

[172] Cassuto, e.g., interprets the snake as an allegory for the "man himself"; the serpent's voice is the woman's own thoughts, and therefore it is not surprising that the snake talks (*Genesis,* 142–43).

[173] E.g., *Wis* 2:24; *Sir* 21:2; *4 Macc* 18:8; Rom 16:20 with v.15; Rev 12:9; 14–15; 20:2.

[174] See K. R. Joines, *Serpent Symbolism in the Old Testament: A Linguistic, Archaeological, and Literary Study* (Haddonfield, N.J.: Haddonfield House, 1974).

[175] *ANET,* 96.

cating that opposition to God lurks in the garden. Serpents in the Mosaic community were classified among the unclean animals because of their movement on the ground (Lev 11:41–45) and were associated with the judgment of God for Israel's complaints against God in the wilderness ("venomous snakes," Num 21:6). Furthermore, the snake occurs in ancient Near Eastern imagery as antithetical to creation, representing powerful forces that oppose the creator-god. This imagery occurs in 1:21, where the monsters *(tannîn)* of ancient myth are no more than "sea creatures"—not hostile powers—created by the spoken word of Israel's God. This "monster" *(tannîn)* is the same as the many-headed "Leviathan" or "serpent" *(nāḥāš)*.[176] "Rahab" is identified as the "serpent" *(nāḥāš)* defeated by God's omnipotent hand at creation (Job 26:12–14). This creation imagery is used in the psalter and among the prophets to depict how God, who overcame hostile powers in creation, is the One whose mighty power overcomes Israel's enemies (cf. Ps 74:13–14; Isa 51:9). In the same way, the serpent in the garden symbolized the hostile opposition to the woman and her seed (3:15). This is continued in the Christian tradition as evidenced in John's Apocalypse (Rev 12:9; 20:2).

Many modern interpreters, however, fail to recognize that the serpent's trickery is ultimately the voice of Satan. Although the snake is never identified as Satan in the Old Testament, more than the principle of evil must have been intended by the serpent's presence since 3:15 describes an ongoing war between the serpent and the seed of the woman.[177] "All the days of your life" (3:14) shows that the serpent is treated as a personal being. The role of the serpent is consistent with the adversary *(haśśātan)* depicted in Job 1–2. Although not identified as a serpent, he impugns the character of God and attempts to destroy Job. Jesus' rebuke of the Jews as the children of their "father" (cf. "offspring," 3:15) alludes to the garden scene, where the serpent is the "devil," "a murderer from the beginning" (John 8:44; cf. 1 John 3:12). This interpretation was also found in earlier Jewish wisdom (e.g., *Wis* 2:24) and was shared by Paul (Rom 16:20). In accord with the traditional opinion, the snake is more than a literal snake; rather it is Satan's personal presence in the garden.

We may interpret the role of the serpent in the same vein as Peter's resistance to Jesus' death, where the Lord responded to Peter: "Get behind me, Satan! You are a stumbling block to me. You do not have in mind the things of God, but the things of men" (Matt 16:23). Jesus does not mean Peter is possessed with Satan as Judas was when "Satan entered" him (Luke 22:3), nor was he threatened with possession (Luke 22:31). But Peter unwittingly was an advocate for Satan's cause. Similarly, the snake is a creature speaking against

---

[176] Cf. Isa 27:1, where all three are the same; תַּנִּין occurs at Exod 7:9–10 for "snake" and נָחָשׁ for the rod that turned into a snake at Exod 4:3; 7:15.

[177] Argued by Kidner, *Genesis*, 67.

the "things of God" and whose cause is that of Satan. From the viewpoint of the Mosaic community, the snake's presence in the garden would have been surprisingly incongruent with the pristine character of Eden. The snake was reviled by the Hebrews as a source of uncleanness and a remembered menace.[178] The notion of a slithering snake communicates powerfully that the woman is in grave jeopardy. Job 1–2, where the amorphous "Satan" is named but not described, does not have the same force that the figure of a snake portrays spoiling the garden. By the presence of the snake the Scripture shows that the malevolent Satan was in the garden.

The tactic used by the serpent was to cause doubt in the mind of the woman through interrogation and misrepresentation. First, the opponent does not controvert outright the saying of the Lord (2:16); rather, he questions God's motivation with the subtle addition "really say."[179] Second, the serpent uses the name "God" rather than the covenant name "LORD" that has characterized the narrative of 2:4–25, where "LORD God" appears. Third, the serpent reworks the wording of God's command slightly by (1) adding the negative "not" at the head of the clause, which with "any" expresses an absolute prohibition;[180] (2) omitting the emphatic "freely"; (3) using the plural "you" (hence bypassing the man) rather than the singular as in 2:16; and (4) placing the clause "from any tree" at the end of the sentence rather than at the head as in 2:16, thereby robbing God's command of its nuance of liberality. All of this is to say that the divine injunction in the mouth of the serpent was refashioned for its own interests.

3:2–3 The woman's first mistake was her willingness to talk with the serpent and to respond to the creature's cynicism by rehearsing God's prohibition (2:17). However, she compounded her mistake by misrepresenting God's command as the serpent had done, although definitely without the malicious intent of the snake. The serpent had succeeded in drawing the woman's attention to another possible interpretation of God's command. It would seem that the serpent had heard it all differently! Now the woman changes the tenor of the original command. First, she omits those elements in the command, "any" and "freely," which placed the prohibition in a context of liberality. At this point she still is thinking collectively with her husband, from whom, as the narrator implies, she received the command: "*we* may eat" (v. 2). Second, Eve

---

[178] An exception was the bronze serpent later revered (Num 21:8–9; 2 Kgs 18:4; John 3:14).

[179] אַף כִּי is difficult since there is no exact parallel for it as a question, which is the traditional rendering (as NIV). Speiser comments, "The serpent is not asking a question; he is deliberately distorting a fact" (*Genesis*, 23). BHS recommends the emendation הַאַף (with interrogative). Cassuto retains the sense of question by taking כִּי as the interrogative and אַף as the emphatic (*Genesis*, 144). But intonation is a sufficient explanation since for yes/no questions the interrogative is not required (*IBHS* § 40.3.b).

[180] GKC § 152b.

identifies the tree according to its location rather than its significance; and third, she refers to "God" as the serpent had done, rather than "the LORD" (v. 3). Fourth, she also adds the phrase "you must not touch it" (v. 3), which may make the prohibition more stringent. Yet to her credit the fear of touching the fruit may have been out of deference for God's command. For Israel "touch" was associated with prohibition and death or with consecration to God.[181] Finally, she failed to capture the urgency of certain death, "You will *[surely]* die" (v. 3).

3:4–5 With the woman lured into dialogue on his terms, the serpent directly disputes God's command. The negative "not" *(lōʾ)* at the head of the Hebrew clause contradicts the immediately preceding claim by the woman, "You will die."[182] Any second thought the woman might have had at hearing the serpent's bold statement is answered by the serpent's following explanation (v. 5). The motivation for God's command is impugned by the serpent. In the wisdom tradition the adversary argues the same case in Job (1:9–11; 2:4–5). God is not good and gracious; he is selfish and deceptive, preventing the man and woman from achieving the same position as "Elohim" (v. 5).[183] What are we to say of God's actions? Admittedly, the narrative presents a God who makes a peculiar demand, on the face of it out of "sheer irrationality."[184] When he catches the culprits, he condemns them with all manner of threats and eventually expels them for a motive that could be interpreted as selfish (3:22); yet he does not follow through on his tirade, granting them clothing and assurances. A cynical reader could conclude that the serpent was right. But it may be that this uncertainty about God is used by the author to put his readers in the same place of decision as Eve (and Job). What do we do when presented with the "fruit of temptation"?

Hence the serpent made three counterclaims: First, they will not die. Sec-

---

[181] E.g., Exod 19:12; Num 16:26; Deut 14:8; cf. 2 Sam 6:1–8; and, e.g., Exod 29:37; 30:29.

[182] לֹא־מוֹת תְּמֻתוּן. Unlike here, the negative particle regularly comes between the infinitive absolute and finite verb (GKC § 113v), which is taken as the negation of God's command at 2:17; but Cassuto shows that the plural verb negates the woman's claim, פֶּן תְּמֻתוּן ("lest you die"), which rewords 2:17 (*Genesis,* 145–46). The addition of the infinitive absolute emphasizes the serpent's negation, "will not surely die."

[183] The traditional rendering is "God," but it can be taken as "gods" or "divine beings" as the LXX rendering: καὶ ἔσεσθε ὡς θεοὶ γινώσκοντες καλὸν καὶ πονηρόν. This discussion is complicated by the identity of the plural ("us") in v. 22, where some contend that an angelic host is inferred (see 1:26). The plural participle "knowing" (יֹדְעֵי) argues for the plural "gods" since "Elohim" as "God" normally takes the singular (e.g., Sarna, *Genesis,* 25). "God" can be retained if the participle is predicative, "like God, that is, you shall know good and evil" (e.g., Hamilton, *Genesis 1–17,* 189); but *IBHS* § 37.6a indicates that the subject of the predicative use is usually expressed, unlike here (see also 11.2.9b #3). Ambiguity here may be purposeful since the whole tenor of the serpent's speech is marked with clever devices. Since Elohim as "God" occurs earlier in the verse, it is best to retain the singular sense.

[184] So Barr, *The Garden of Eden and the Hope of Immortality,* 12.

ond, "your eyes will be opened," a metaphor for knowledge, suggesting a newfound awareness not previously possessed. In the Old Testament this awareness sometimes is said to be obtained through divine assistance (e.g., Gen 21:19; 2 Kgs 6:17,20). And finally, they will gain what belongs to God, "knowing good and evil." Essentially he is contending that God is holding her back—a claim that is sometimes echoed today.[185]

When set in the larger context of the story, the serpent's words are shown to be both true and false. They proved true in that the man and woman did not immediately die physically. Their eyes were indeed opened (v. 7), and they obtained knowledge belonging to God as the serpent had promised (v. 22). However, the serpent's half-truths concealed falsehood and led the woman to expect a different result altogether. The serpent spoke only about what she would gain and avoided mentioning what she would lose in the process. Though the man and woman did not die immediately upon eating the fruit, the expectation and assignment to death were soon enough. Furthermore, they experienced expulsion from the garden, which was indicative of death.[186] Later Israel experienced excommunication when any of its members were discovered ceremonially unclean; such victims were counted as dead men in mourning (e.g., Lev 13:45). Expulsion from the garden, which represented the presence of God as did the tabernacle in the camp, meant a symbolic "death" for the excommunicated (cf. 1 Sam 15:35–16:1). Although their eyes were opened, they were rewarded only with seeing their nakedness and were burdened with human guilt and embarrassment (v. 7). Although they became like God in this one way, it was at an unexpected cost. They achieved isolation and fear. The couple was cut off as well from the possibility of life, the one feature of divinity for which otherwise they were destined. They obtained "wisdom" in exchange for death.

(2) The Man and Woman Sin (3:6–8)

[6]When the woman saw that the fruit of the tree was good for food and pleasing to the eye, and also desirable for gaining wisdom, she took some and ate it. She also gave some to her husband, who was with her, and he ate it. [7]Then the eyes of both of them were opened, and they realized they were naked; so they sewed fig leaves together and made coverings for themselves.

[8]Then the man and his wife heard the sound of the LORD God as he was walking in the garden in the cool of the day, and they hid from the LORD God among the trees of the garden.

3:6 At its centerpiece the account moves with a rapid pace: "The woman saw," "she took," "ate," "she gave . . . and he ate." Eve saw what was "good";

[185] Remarked by A. Ross, "Woman after the Fall," *Kindred Spirit* 5 (1981): 11.

[186] See Wenham's discussion, *Genesis 1–15,* 74–75.

the adjective heads the clause accentuating the ironic results of her evaluation. There is a double entendre here: the term for "good" *(ṭôb)* can mean beautiful and also what is moral. In this case what was beautiful proved to be an allurement to disobedience. The term "good" is reminiscent of the created order God declares as "good" (1:4,10,12,18,25,31). But the verbal echo of God's earlier evaluation suggests that she has usurped God's role in determining what is "good." The temptation of the fruit is (1) its substance as food, (2) its appearance, and (3) its potential for making the woman "wise." "Desirable" *(ḥāmad)* is the same word used in the prohibition against covetousness (Exod 20:17). Eve supposes that the tree's fruit would obtain for her "wisdom" *(haskîl),* which she must have equated with the tempter's promise of obtaining divine knowledge (3:5). The term is broad in meaning, indicating sight, insight, and also success. We have commented (2:16) that the transgression is the acquisition of wisdom independently of God. Though the narrative does not specify the fault in this, traditionally since Augustine the sin has been related to human pride. Pride is perceived as the antithesis to prudence in Proverbs (e.g., 11:2). The serpent's guile may be likened to the apostle John's forewarning regarding the enticement of the "world" (1 John 2:16). James likewise warns that illicit desires lead to sin and sin to death (Jas 1:14–15), a course Adam acts out.

The long-standing interpretation of why Eve fails is the deception of the crafty beast (2 Cor 11:3), but no explanation occurs for Adam's decision to eat. If the naming of the animals by Adam shows an awareness of their characteristics (2:19–20), then it is not surprising that the woman is unaware of the serpent's shrewdness, but there is no excuse for the man.[187] Paul was emphatic that Adam was not misled (1 Tim 2:14). This concurs with early Jewish tradition, which placed the blame on Adam's shoulders (e.g., *4 Ezra* 3:21; 7:118). Adam's participation is rather understated in the account, given the attention it receives from God (3:17–19) and in later Jewish and Christian tradition. He simply followed the example of the woman without hesitation. There is no sense that Adam is lured by logic or sexual provocation.[188] "For he would have never dared oppose God's authority unless he had disbelieved in God's Word."[189] Was Adam privy to the conversation between Eve and the snake? Although "with her" does not in itself demand that he is present since the serpent speaks "to the woman," nevertheless, the action of the verse implies that Adam is a witness to the dialogue. "You" at each place in 3:1–5 is plural and thus suggests his presence. However, there is no indication that he too is deceived by the serpent.

---

[187] Noted by Hess, "The Roles of the Man and the Woman in Genesis 3," 16.

[188] *Gen. Rab.* 19.5 attributes to Eve persuasive argument and even tears. Job, who did not yield to his wife's advice, is contrasted with Adam (19.10).

[189] Calvin, *Institutes,* 2.1.4.

3:7 The results are told in the same rapid-fire fashion as the transgression, paralleling the actions of the woman in v. 6: (1) eyes open, (2) realize their nakedness, (3) sew fig leaves, and (4) make coverings. What they "saw" is that they are "naked," what is "pleasing to the eye" causes displeasure with their own nakedness and the need to cover it with "fig leaves," and the "wisdom" gained only enables the making of "coverings." The linkage between act and consequence is found in the wordplay between *ta'ăwâ* ("pleasing") in v. 6 and similar *tĕ'ēnâ* ("fig"). The plural "they" shows that the couple simultaneously experiences the results of eating. The verb "realized," when literally rendered "knew" *(ydʿ)*, echoes the "tree of knowledge" from which they had partaken; the word "naked" is reminiscent again of the "crafty" serpent who tricked the woman into exchanging her innocence for the embarrassing knowledge that they are naked (3:1; 2:25). Their efforts to hide their shame are as puny as their efforts to hide from God since their man-made coverings are ineffective (v. 21). "Made" *(ʿāśâ)* and "coverings" *(ḥăgōrōt)* anticipate v. 21, where God "made" durable "garments" *(kotĕnôt)* from animal skins for their needed apparel.

3:8 The anthropomorphic description of God "walking" *(mithallēk)* in the garden suggests the enjoyment of fellowship between him and our first parents. The adverbial phrase "in the cool of the day" (NIV, NASB, NJB) or "the breezy time of the day" (NJPS, NAB) translates the Hebrew phrase "wind *[rûaḥ]* of the day." The NRSV's rendering makes the time more explicit, "at the time of the evening breeze" (also REB).[190] "Walked with God" is a favorite expression in Genesis, depicting the righteous conduct of Israel's heroes, including Enoch, Noah, and Abraham.[191] Yet now the man and the woman are hiding from God in fear. God's presence is also noted by his "walking" in the camp and sanctuary of Israel. Later Israel recognized that God demanded holiness and obedience if he were to continue to "walk" among his people.[192] It was part of the sad deception that the man and woman who wanted so much to be "like God," rather than obtaining the stature of deity, are afraid even to commune with him. The language of the verse, "the man and his wife," imitates the description of the couple when in their innocence they had lived without shame (2:25). Now they have lost their innocence, their childlike trust in the goodness of God. "Among [i.e., in the midst of] the trees of the garden" echoes v. 3, which describes the forbidden

---

[190] The LXX has τὸ δειλινόν, "afternoon, evening." J. Niehaus ("In the Wind of the Storm: Another Look at Genesis III 8," *VT* 44 [1994]: 263–67) has found in 3:8 the language of theophany and has interpreted it as "the wind of storm," taking *ywm* as "storm" from Akk. *ūmu*; thus the couple hid from the terrible appearance of the Lord. But this argument depends on a doubtful use of *ywm* and is weakened by Adam's confession in 3:10.

[191] Gen 5:22,24; 6:9; 17:1; 24:40; 48:15.

[192] E.g., Lev 26:12; Deut 23:14[15]; 2 Sam 7:6–7.

tree "in the midst of the garden." Their disobedience at the "tree" of knowledge leads to this hiding among the "trees." They are pictured in the narrative like children hiding in fearful shame from their father.

(3) God Questions the Man and Woman (3:9–13)

[9]But the LORD God called to the man, "Where are you?"

[10]He answered, "I heard you in the garden, and I was afraid because I was naked; so I hid."

[11]And he said, "Who told you that you were naked? Have you eaten from the tree that I commanded you not to eat from?"

[12]The man said, "The woman you put here with me—she gave me some fruit from the tree, and I ate it."

[13]Then the LORD God said to the woman, "What is this you have done?"

The woman said, "The serpent deceived me, and I ate."

3:9–11 God is depicted as a gentle father seeking out his own. The means of uncovering their deed (like the serpent's means of entrapment) is interrogation rather than charge and denunciation. The effect is pedagogical and permits the guilty to witness against themselves by their own admissions. These exchanges between God and the couple have no immediate resolution, paving the way to the final word of judgment in vv. 14–19.[193] God first addresses the man, who evidently bears the greater responsibility, then the woman and the serpent. This inverts the order of the participants in the act (serpent, woman, and man) and indicates God's chief interest in the state of the human couple. It is not until the man points to Eve that God addresses her; it is the first time in the Edenic narrative that Eve and God converse.

Verses 9–11 emphasize the second-person singular "you," focusing on the individual liability of Adam. God initiates the dialogue by calling out to the man, "Where are you?" (v. 9). The question is rhetorical and is designed to prompt Adam to consider his wrongdoing. Similarly this question is put to Cain concerning his crime (4:9). There will be no possibility for reconciliation if the guilty are unwilling to confess their deeds.

Adam explains that he hid out of fear because he realized his nakedness (3:10). Actually his fear was his response to the presence of God in the garden; he did not want to appear before God in his nakedness. The NIV's "I heard you" obscures the Hebrew "your sound," which stands at the head of the clause, tying the verse to the language of v. 8.[194] Why did the man fear God because of nakedness? Public nakedness in the ancient Near East and in the

---

[193] Kempf, "Genesis 3:14–19: Climax of the Discourse?" 358–59.

[194] Luther comments: "But had he [Adam] not heard the voice of the LORD before, when He forbade him to eat from the forbidden tree? Why was he not afraid then? . . . But now he is terrified by the rustling of a leaf (Lev 26:36)" (*LW* 1.174).

Bible was a terrible disgrace (see 2:25 discussion; cf. Noah, 9:22–25). Here that shame is explained as the consequence of the guilt of sin. Before human disobedience there was no shame (2:25), but with sin the man's self-consciousness had changed. His sense of humiliation impacts his covering up before the woman as well as before God. By this Adam admits his sense of shame, which has been motivated by his guilt.

Two follow-up questions sharpen the fact of the crime (v. 11). Both questions are rhetorical. The first shows that no one is required to tell the man of his shame because he experiences guilt for his crime. This was not the consequence of false guilt imposed by parent or social convention; it was true guilt arising from a violated conscience. By the second question Adam's nakedness is linked to his transgression concerning the tree. Here "tree" is no longer identified as the tree of knowledge but the tree "that I commanded you not to eat from" (cf. "commanded," 2:16). Together these questions explain to the man that his sense of shame arose from his defiance of God's command.

3:12 Despite his culpability the man points to the woman as the real offender. Unlike the woman, the man was not deceived by the serpent—at least he does not refer to the serpent—so he cites her part in the matter. In particular Adam's punishment is later related to his consent to the woman (3:17). Adam's contention is given force by the emphasis on "she," yielding the sense, "I only took what *she* gave me!"[195] But there could be no exoneration for his crime on this flimsy basis. Not finished with shifting blame, Adam even accuses God for the tragedy by adding, "the woman you put here with me." The NIV's "put" translates the literal "gave," which is repeated in the next clause, "she gave me." By this Adam charges that the Lord "gave" the woman to him and in turn she "gave" him the fruit. The implication is inescapable: God ultimately is responsible for the success of the tempter and Adam's demise.

The woman is depicted as God's gift in 2:22, where Adam initially responds with enthusiastic glee. Now, like the serpent, he charges that God's good gift was malicious, for she has led to his downfall. She is a mistake. This is a line still heard today. Commonly, the Old Testament is not timid in assigning divine responsibility for all manner of human affliction, but nowhere does the Bible acknowledge any divine culpability for this turn of events. The apostle James said that each person is responsible for his own sin (1:13). Sin was the deliberate choice of the man. By shifting the blame, the man hoped to evade accountability for his autonomous actions. Of course, interpretive speculation has

---

[195] The NIV shows this by the insertion of the hyphen, distinguishing the dangling element at the beginning (nominative absolute) from the main clause that follows (also NAB, NJPS). What grammarians have termed nominative absolute or *casus pendens* is a grammatical element that is outside the main clause; it is resumed usually by a pronoun to highlight that element. In this case the nominative absolute is "woman," and the resumptive pronoun is "she," the proper subject of the clause (GKC § 135c; *IBHS* § 4.7.b; 8.3.a).

always reflected on why God would permit the tempter's ploy, but the narrative does not address such theological dilemmas.

3:13 The Lord challenges the woman to explain herself by questioning her actions. The language of the question, "What is *this?*" may point back to the man's exclamation in 2:23, where the pronoun "this" dominates.[196] The woman, who was Adam's delight and was designed by God to be his "helper" in achieving blessing (2:18), becomes a partner in crime. Like the man, she shifts the blame to another party—the serpent. But unlike the man she can rightly claim to be the "victim" of deception. Also she stops short of attributing the snake's wily deed to God as Adam has insinuated (cp. Jer 4:10). The result is that the authority of God has been successfully undermined, first through trickery and then through willful rebellion.

(4) God's Judgments Pronounced (3:14–21)

14So the LORD God said to the serpent, "Because you have done this,
"Cursed are you above all the livestock
and all the wild animals!
You will crawl on your belly
and you will eat dust
all the days of your life.
15And I will put enmity
between you and the woman,
and between your offspring and hers;
he will crush your head,
and you will strike his heel."

16To the woman he said,

"I will greatly increase your pains in childbearing;
with pain you will give birth to children.
Your desire will be for your husband,
and he will rule over you."

17To Adam he said, "Because you listened to your wife and ate from the tree about which I commanded you, 'You must not eat of it,'

"Cursed is the ground because of you;
through painful toil you will eat of it
all the days of your life.
18It will produce thorns and thistles for you,
and you will eat the plants of the field.
19By the sweat of your brow
you will eat your food
until you return to the ground,
since from it you were taken;

---

[196] Jonah was asked similarly by the frightened sailors, "What have you done?" (2:10).

for dust you are
and to dust you will return."

[20]Adam named his wife Eve, because she would become the mother of all the living.

[21]The LORD God made garments of skin for Adam and his wife and clothed them.

Once again the order is inverted, corresponding to the order of the culprits' collusion: the judgment oracles assign punishment to the serpent first (vv. 14–15), then the woman (v. 16), and then the man (vv. 17–19). In each instance the punishment will also correspond to the nature of the crime. Each oracle consists of a divine penalty followed by a description of the consequences—defeat. For the serpent the penalty is humiliation (v. 14a), and the consequence of his sin is his defeat by the woman's "offspring" (v. 15b). For the woman the penalty is painful labor in childbirth (v. 16a), and the consequence of her sin is defeat in her conflict with her husband (v. 16b); and for the man the penalty is painful labor in agriculture (vv. 17–18), and the consequence is defeat in his conflict with the ground (v. 19). Dispute about whether the oracles are prescriptive or descriptive, especially the woman's submission (v. 16b), is overplayed since it is apparent that the whole is shadowed by the tenor of retribution. The passage anticipates judgment for transgression since 2:17; and if 2:5–7 expects the denouement in 3:14–19 (see 2:5–7 discussion), the Eden narrative as a whole is built on this expectation.

God does not inquire further into the calamity by questioning the serpent; the tempter has nothing to learn from the Lord. He only has words of condemnation for the serpent, whereas the man and woman receive God's continued concern and provision in the midst of their punishment. Curses are uttered against the serpent and the ground, but not against the man and woman, implying that the blessing has not been utterly lost. It is not until human murder, a transgression against the *imago Dei,* that a person (Cain) receives the divine curse (see 4:11–12 discussion).

3:14 At the head of the pronouncement against the serpent is the cause for the ensuing judgment.[197] "You have done *this*" echoes the question God put to the woman (v. 13). There is a clear tie between the serpent's actions and the punishment that follows. God does not render judgment arbitrarily or capriciously. Moreover, there is a correspondence between the nature of the judgment and the crime committed. As the cleverness of the serpent distinguishes it from the other animals (3:1), the "curse" for that trickery distinguishes the serpent from them as well.

[197] The NIV has set the first clause, "Because you have done this," outside the poetic structure so as to govern both vv. 14 and 15 (as NJB). Others include it in the poetic stanza (NRSV, NASB, NJPS, NAB). The REB has v. 14a as prose, beginning the poetic stanza at "On your belly" (v. 14b).

In the stream of the narrative's focus on blessing, this pronouncement stands out as the first occurrence of divine "curse." Its root *(ʾārar)* appears fifty-five times in the Old Testament, predominantly in the Pentateuch with eight occurrences in Genesis.[198] It is important particularly to the listed curses and blessings regarding Israel's covenant (Deut 27–28). "Curse" conveys the idea of imprecation where verbal or written utterances invoke misery against a person or thing. The word *ʾālâ* ("curse") commonly is used for such imprecations, whereas *ʾārar* often indicates a decree or pronouncement against someone by an authority. Only God can actually impose this decree, and thus it supposes, even if spoken by a man, that the power carrying out the malediction can come only from deity (as Noah's curse, 9:25). "Cursed" *(ʾārûr),* as found here and in v. 17, is the typical way of introducing a decree of doom (also 4:11; 9:25; cf. 27:29; Deut 27:15–26; 28:16–20).[199]

The serpent's punishment has three aspects: (1) consignment to crawling on its belly, (2) the eating of dust "all the days of your life" (v. 14), and (3) its ultimate destruction by the wounded "seed" of the woman (v. 15). Several elements in the oracle echo the temptation (3:1–5). "Cursed" *(ʾārûr)* is another wordplay on the earlier "crafty" *(ʿārûm;* cf. 3:1). Both verses describe the serpent's distinction within the animal world. Ill-use of his shrewdness resulted in divine censure. "Eating" dust reflects Eve's temptation to "eat" of the tree and the couple's subsequent fall by eating. Also the retaliation of the woman's seed over against the viper's offspring (v. 15) answers the snake's first triumph. His triumph will not be the last word.

These punishments are related to the snake's life of humiliation and subjugation in the natural world. God's condemnation is not directed against the reptile per se but the adversary that it represents. While some Jewish interpreters surmised that the serpent must have originally been four-legged, there is no compelling reason for this conclusion.[200] It is enough to describe the present characteristics of the snake, which indicate by themselves the disgrace of the beast. As mentioned earlier (v. 1), the food laws of the Mosaic covenant declare that animals whose locomotion is on the ground are abhorred as unclean and to be avoided (Lev 11:42).[201]

Eating dust is a common figure for personal humiliation elsewhere in Scripture.[202] Moreover, by "dust" there is an anticipation of God's pronouncement

---

[198] Gen 3:14; 17: 4:11; 5:29; 9:25; 12:3; 27:29; and 49:7.

[199] See H. C. Brichto, *The Problem with "Curse" in the Hebrew Bible,* SBLMS 13 (Philadelphia: SBL, 1963), 114–15; J. Scharbert, "ארר *ʾrr;* מְאֵרָה *mĕʾērāh,*" *TDOT* 1.405–18, esp. 415.

[200] E.g., *Tg. Ps.-J.,* Josephus, *Ant.,* 1.1.50; *Gen. Rab.* 19.1 and 20.5. It is thought to be reflective of an ancient view that the snake was first upright and legged; see e.g., Skinner, *Genesis,* 78–79 and Sarna, *Genesis,* 27.

[201] Heb. גָּחוֹן ("belly") only here and in Lev 11:42.

[202] E.g., esp. Mic 7:17; Ps 72:9; Isa 49:23; cf. Gen 18:27.

of Adam's death (3:19). The reptile is responsible for the demise of the man, who returns to the "dust," and as the serpent's diet it will be a perpetual reminder of its crime. "All the days of your life" speaks to the ultimate end of the serpent and its offspring. "Your life" *(ḥayyêkâ)* may be an allusion to the snake's false promise, "You will surely not die" (v. 4), made to Eve, who ironically is later recognized as the source of "all the living" *(ḥay;* 3:20). Hence, the snake brought about his own death by his treachery, but ultimately Eve through her seed will outlive her adversary.

3:15 The curse upon the serpent includes its final destruction by the descendant of the woman. This animosity is at the instigation of God. The serpent was instrumental in the undoing of the woman, and in turn the woman will ultimately bring down the serpent through her offspring. At one level the hostility between serpent and woman reflects the universal enmity people have for such reptiles and therefore serves as a prototype. However, this is no etiology designed to explain why man abhors snakes since the verse indicates there is a future history for the serpent and the woman. That future history of antagonism is not delineated here, yet the conclusion of the matter is made explicit: the serpent has a limited life expectancy that will come to a violent end.

"Enmity" has the intensity of hostility experienced among nations in warfare (e.g., Ezek 25:15; 35:5) and the level of animosity that results in murder (e.g., Num 35:21). The language of the passage indicates a life-and-death struggle between combatants. "Crush" and "strike" translate the same Hebrew verb *šûp* (AV, "bruise")[203] and describe the combatants' parallel action, but the location of the blow distinguishes the severity and success of the attack. The impact delivered by the offspring of the woman "at the head" is mortal, while the serpent will deliver a blow only "at the heel." Continuing the imagery of the snake, the strike at the human heel is appropriate for a serpent since it slithers along the ground, while the human foot stomps the head of the vile creature.

"Between *you* [serpent]" has the singular pronoun (as elsewhere in the verse), meaning that this hostility begins with the beast and the woman as individuals. Yet their experience is shared by their offspring too; the serpent and woman are distinct from their offspring yet also one and the same with them. Here we have the common case where an individual represents many.[204] Eve and her adversary are the progenitors of a lifelong struggle that will persist until a climactic moment when the woman's offspring will achieve the upper hand.

[203] An alternative interpretation among commentators attributes different meanings to the two occurrences of שׁוּף on the basis of the similar שָׁאַף meaning "crush" (e.g., Amos 2:7) and a homonym meaning "long for, pant after" (e.g., Job 5:5). See, e.g., Cassuto, *Genesis,* 161. "Pant after" is comparable to the notion in 4:7 where sin's "desire" (תְּשׁוּקָה) is to mislead Cain. Thus the serpent "craves" the woman's seed, but her offspring will "crush" the serpent.

[204] In 1 Tim 2:15 Eve's role as childbearer is taken as an archetype in Paul's reference to the Christian women at Ephesus.

This continuum of experience between parent and offspring is seen by the parallelism of the verse (v. 15b//15c): "between you and the woman, and between your offspring and her offspring."[205] Moreover, "offspring" is the rendering of the Hebrew term for "seed" *(zeraʿ),* which may refer to an individual or to a group. It is ambiguous by itself since it may be singular, referring to a specific child (e.g., 4:25), or a singular collective indicating a plural progeny (e.g., 12:7; Isa 41:8). Modern versions show this by their diverse renderings, proposing singular or plural translations for the following pronouns.[206] "Seed" is a resourceful term for speaking of all human history while at the same time permitting a reference to a specific individual descendant. This explains why the individual offspring of the woman ("he," "his heel") can be said to do battle with the progenitor serpent ("your head," "you") in v. 15d and 15e.

"Seed" *(zeraʿ)* is a critical term in the whole of Genesis and the Pentateuch. It first occurs in a literal sense in the creation account (1:11–12,29), but here it is metaphorical and takes on programmatic significance. Of its fifty-nine occurrences in Genesis, the majority are found in the patriarchal narratives (47x), where the focal concern lies with the genealogical lineage of the chosen family.[207] The patriarchal accounts explain what is only introduced in 3:15. The creation blessing (1:28), which was jeopardized by the couple's disobedience, is particularized through the Hebrew fathers, who will be instrumental in its realization. Chapter 3's oracle implies a hope for the human family that despite their sin there will be a fulfillment of the blessing through progeny as foreseen at creation (1:26–28). This hope for the appointed "seed" is unveiled progressively by the offspring of Eve through Seth ("another seed," 4:26; his genealogy, 5:1–32), through Noah's offspring (9:9), and the seed of Abraham first described in 12:7 (with 12:1–3).[208] Moreover, this promise points to the Mosaic community, which defined itself as the offspring promised to Abraham (e.g., Exod 32:11–14; Deut 11:8–12).

Also this hostility finds immediate expression between wicked Cain and his brother Abel (4:8). God's forewarning of Cain that "sin is crouching at your door" (4:7) may be an allusion to the struggle that 3:15 envisions. But the adversary wins the first battle when Cain yields to sin and murders the woman's seed, Abel. This strife between the elect line and the cursed is again envisioned in Noah's curse and blessing (9:24–27). It also foreshadows the tension between the patriarchs and the nations as they experience an uneasy

[205] The English versions' idiom "and hers" omits the Hebrew "seed" (NIV, NJB, NAB, NRSV, NJPS, REB); cp. the NASB's "your seed and her seed."

[206] "It" and "his heel" (AV); "it" and "its heel" (NJB); "he will crush" and "his heel" (NIV, NRSV, NASB; NAB); "they" and "their heel" (REB, NJPS).

[207] See T. D. Alexander, "Genealogies, Seed, and the Compositional Unity of Genesis," *TynBul* 44 (1993): 255–70, esp. 259–60.

[208] Also cf. 13:15–16; 15:3,5,13,18; 16:10; 17:7–12,19; 21:12–13; 22:17–18; 24:7. For the repetition of the promise of descendants, see Isaac (26:3–4) and Jacob (28:4,13–14; 32:12; 35:12; 48:4).

coexistence in Canaan and Egypt (e.g., chap. 38). For later Israel this hostility comes to full fury when Egypt instigates a purge of Hebrew children, from which baby Moses is delivered, and climaxes with God's tenth plague against Pharaoh's firstborn. It also anticipates Moses' wars and the hostility Israel faces as it migrates to the land of Canaan.

Christian tradition has referred to 3:15 as the *protevangelium* since it has been taken as the prototype for the Christian gospel. Historically interpreters have differed about whether "her seed" refers to an individual or is a collective singular indicating all humanity. The LXX version may be the earliest attested interpretation of "seed" as an individual. It translates the Hebrew *zeraʿ* ("seed") with the Greek *sperma,* a neuter noun. The expected antecedent pronoun is "it *[auto]* will crush your head," but the Greek has "he" *(autos),* which suggests that the translators interpreted "seed" as an individual.[209] The Targums, Jewish pseudepigrapha, and later rabbinic commentators, however, generally viewed the "seed" as collective for humankind. Christian interpreters showed a mixed opinion.[210] Justin and Irenaeus interpreted the woman of 3:15 as the virgin Mary by drawing a parallel with Eve. Greek Fathers, such as Chrysostom, viewed 3:15 as a depiction of the struggle between Satan and humanity. Still others interpreted "seed" as the church. Among the Latin Fathers, Augustine with others allegorized or moralized the verse, indicating a collective use. Others saw in it a specific reference to the virgin birth. This was aided by some Old Latin texts and the Vulgate, which had the feminine pronoun "she *[ipsa]* shall crush" rather than the masculine. It was Ambrose who first quoted 3:15 as not "her seed" but "the woman's seed." Among the Reformers, Luther took "her seed" as reference to both humanity in general and Christ in particular;[211] Calvin demurred such a view and applied it as a collective, not to all humanity but rather to the church under the headship of Christ, which would prove victorious (quoting Rom 16:20).[212]

Our passage provides for this mature reflection that points to Christ as the vindicator of the woman (cp. Rom 16:20). There may be an allusion to our passage in Gal 4:4, which speaks of God's Son as "born of a woman."[213] Spe-

---

[209] See R. A. Martin, "The Earliest Messianic Interpretation of Genesis 3:15," *JBL* 84 (1965): 525–27.

[210] For the following survey see J. P. Lewis, "The Woman's Seed (Gen 3:15)," *JETS* 34 (1991): 299–319.

[211] Luther commented on the nature of "the woman's Seed": "This means all individuals in general; and yet he is speaking of only one individual, of the seed of Mary, who is a mother without union with a male" (*LW* 1.195).

[212] Calvin, *Comm.,* 170–71.

[213] T. George, however, notes the expression "man born of woman" in Job 14:1 and considers Paul's point to be that "during his earthly life Jesus experienced all of the finitude and fears, trials and temptations that are the common lot of every human being" (*Galatians,* NAC [Nashville: Broadman & Holman, 1994], 302).

cifically, Paul identified Christ as the "seed" ultimately intended in the promissory blessing to Abraham (Gal 3:16), and Abraham's believing offspring includes the church (Rom 4:13,16–18; Gal 3:8). This is further developed in John's Gospel, where the spiritual dimension is at the forefront. Jesus alluded to our verse when he indicted the Pharisees as children of the "devil" because of their spiritual apostasy (John 8:44), contrary to their claims to be the offspring of righteous Abraham (8:39). John used similar imagery when he contrasted God's "seed" and those who are "of the devil" (1 John 3:7–10). This is heightened by his appeal to Cain's murder of righteous Abel as paradigmatic of one "who belonged to the evil one" (3:11–15). Finally, the Apocalypse describes the "red dragon," who is identified as "that ancient serpent" (Rev 12:9), opposing the believing community (i.e., the woman) and plotting the destruction of her child (i.e., the Messiah). Ultimately, "that ancient serpent" is destroyed by God for its deception of the nations (Rev 20:2,7–10).

3:16 Unlike the penalties announced against the serpent and the man (i.e., "the ground," v. 17), there is no occurrence of "curse" related to the woman's suffering. Moreover, there is no cause specified for her suffering, whereas the serpent is charged with deception (v. 14) and the man with eating disobediently (v. 17). This is due to the woman's culpability through deception, in contrast with the willful rebellion of the serpent and man; also the oracle has a gentler word for the woman since her punishment entails the salvation of the human couple (v. 15). Whereas the man's action condemned the human family, Eve will play the critical role in liberating them from sin's consequences. This is realized in part immediately since the woman gives birth to new life (e.g., 4:1,25), but v. 15 indicates that the final conflict will also be humanity's victory by virtue of the woman's role as childbearer.

Controversial opinion has arisen in recent times regarding the interpretation of the woman's judgment since contemporary feminism has awakened a reconsideration of women's roles in the home, society, and the church.[214] Whereas traditionally the woman's submission to her husband was accepted as an ordinance of creation[215] that was corrupted by the fall and which can only be restored through the Christian gospel, new voices propose that Eve's submission was an altogether new state resulting from sin.[216] Alternatively, it has

---

[214] Five interpretations are noted in R. Davidson, "The Theology of Sexuality in the Beginning: Genesis 3," *AUSS* 26 (1988): 121–31. The first two views agree that hierarchy is a creation ordinance, but (1) it was distorted by sin, or (2) judgment includes a blessing restoring it. The last three views agree that there was no subordination before the fall, but (3) 3:16 is a description, not a permanent prescription for the man-woman relationship, or (4) 3:16 prescribes a new pattern, or (5) "rule" means "like" in 3:16, affirming original equality.

[215] For the traditional view see Calvin, *Comm.,* 172; G. C. Aalders, *Genesis,* BSC, trans. W. Heynen (Grand Rapids: Regency/Zondervan, 1981), 108; Wenham, *Genesis 1–15,* 81.

[216] E.g., Spencer, *Beyond the Curse,* 39–42 and G. Bilezikian, *Beyond Sex Roles: A Guide for the Study of Female Roles in the Bible* (Grand Rapids: Baker, 1985), 56–58. Among commentators, e.g., Sarna, *Genesis,* 28 and Hamilton, *Genesis 1–17,* 175, 201–2.

been proposed that the submissive role of the woman at 3:16b, whether or not viewed originally as a creation ordinance, is read as a "blessing" that insures that salvation will be accomplished by the seed of the woman.[217]

Confusion revolves around the extent to which the penalty in 3:14–19 altered the condition of the participants, many reasoning that the serpent's anatomy was altered and the woman's position as Adam's peer changed. There is no anatomical alteration, however, and no change in the essential position of the serpent and the woman; rather there is added the burden of humiliation. The snake remains the crafty beast that he was, but now he is distinguished from the animals in humiliation as well (cp. vv. 1 and 14). Likewise the woman continues her ordained role as childbearer and, as we contended at 2:23, her followship function, but now she will experience "painful labor" in childbirth, and her submission is insured. Also the man carries on his commission to lead in agricultural pursuits, but now his vocation will be marked by strenuous "labor," and he will return to "dust" in humiliation.

The woman's penalty impacts her two primary roles: childbearing and her relationship with her husband. It is appropriate punishment since procreation was central to her divine commission and because she had been instrumental in her husband's ruin (cf. 3:17a). Just as God initiates the enmity between the woman and serpent, he is responsible ("I will greatly increase") for the pain she will experience in the birth of that "seed," which will ultimately defeat her archenemy (cf. Gal 4:4; 1 Tim 2:15). The verse consists of two parallel lines (literally): "I will greatly increase your painful labor and your conception" // "in painful labor you will bear sons (v. 16a); and to your husband (will be) your desire" // "and he will rule over you" (v. 16b)

First, her penalty stresses the "painful labor" she must endure in childbirth,[218] but the punishment also nurtures hope since it assumes that she will live to bear children.[219] As parallel terms *ʿiṣṣābôn* and *ʿeṣeb* are rendered "painful-labor," which reflects the customary meaning of *ʿiṣṣābôn,* "toil." It occurs just twice more (v. 17; 5:29) and indicates hard labor. Thus the penalty

[217] This has its antecedents among the Reformers too, for Luther read the woman's submission as a consequence of the fall, not a creation ordinance: "Hence it follows that if the woman had not been deceived by the serpent and had not sinned, she would have been the equal of Adam in all respects" (*LW* 1.115). At 3:16 he commented that her submission, however, was a "gladsome punishment," for it insured her salvation (*LW* 1.203).

[218] The rhyming Heb. couplet עִצְּבוֹנֵךְ וְהֵרֹנֵךְ with the traditional rendering "thy sorrow and thy conception" (AV, NKJV) is better taken as a hendiadys, indicating one idea (cf. NIV, NASB, NRSV).

[219] The emphatic construction "I will greatly increase" (הַרְבָּה אַרְבֶּה) with the unusual form of the infinitive absolute, rather than the expected הַרְבֵּה, underscores the intensity of the punishment (A. Reisenberg, "*Harbâ ʾarbeh*," *Beth Mikra* 36 [1990–91]: 80–83 [Heb.]). This construction also anticipates the only other two passages where this unusual infinitival form occurs (16:10; 22:17). In both cases the context is God's promise of blessing through the birth of many children. Therefore the verse includes the hint of blessing as well as the clear decree of pain.

is the attendant labor or hard work that childbearing will now mean for Eve. This matches the "labor" that Adam will undergo as a consequence of the curse against the ground (3:17). By procreation the blessing for the human couple will be realized, and ironically the blessing is assured in the divine pronouncement of the penalty. By this unexpected twist the vehicle of her vindication (i.e., labor) trumpets her need for the deliverance she bears (cp. 1 Cor 11:12). Painful childbirth signals hope but also serves as a perpetual reminder of sin and the woman's part in it.

Second, her sin also tainted her relationship with her husband. "Desire" *(těšûqâ)* occurs but twice more (Gen 4:7; Song 7:10[11]), and its meaning in our passage is highly disputed. It has been explained widely as sexual desire on the basis of Song 7:10[11] and the reference to childbirth in 3:15. If so, the adversative rendering of the following clause, "yet he will rule" (as NASB, NRSV), would mean that despite her painful experience in childbirth she will still have (sexual) desires for her husband.[220] In other words, the promissory blessing of procreation will persist despite any possible reluctance on her part due to the attendant pain of delivery. Others view the woman's desire as broader, including an emotional or economic reliance on her husband. In other words, she acted independently of her husband in eating the fruit, and the consequent penalty is that she will become dependent on him. Her new desire is to be submissive to the man, and, quite naturally, he will oblige by ruling over her.[221] Some have mitigated the idea of penalty by contending that Eve's submission is a penalty only when her husband takes advantage of his position and mistreats her.[222] Others argue that 3:16 is no part of the judgment; it is a description of the inherent consequences of sin wherein the headship of the man has been corrupted by sin.[223]

---

[220] J. J. Schmitt ("Like Eve, Like Adam: *mšl* in Gen 3, 16," *Bib* 72 [1991]: 1–22) proposes for "rule" a Hebrew homonym (מָשַׁל) meaning "to be like," thus "he will be like you." The verse speaks of the mutual sexual desire of the man and woman, making all the more certain that the woman will undergo painful childbirth. This interpretation fits with v. 15 ("childbearing"), but the linguistic support is not strong. The claim that among the numerous usages of "rule" there is no parallel to the persons or context of 3:16 is not convincing since we can hardly expect one to match the unique setting of the garden oracles. מָשַׁל with the meaning "like" is attested in derivative stems, but not in the *qal* as here in 3:16. Also, among the uses of "like," none correspond to 3:16 (cf. Job 30:19; Pss 28:1; 49:12[13],20[21]; 143:7; Isa 14:10; 46:5). Moreover, the reference to marital disharmony in the traditional rendering of 3:16 ("rule") has its match in the subsequent clause, where the judgment against the man makes allusion to the ensuing gender struggle in the indictment, "because you listened to your wife" (3:17).

[221] H. G. Stigers, *A Commentary on Genesis* (Grand Rapids: Zondervan, 1976), 80; for economic dependence see Sarna (*Genesis,* 28), who thinks both penalties in the verse perhaps are a "reflection of social reality" historically for women.

[222] M. Stitzinger, "Genesis 1–3 and the Male/Female Role Relationship," *GTJ* 2 (1981): 23–44.

[223] I. A. Busenitz, "Woman's Desire for Man: Genesis 3:16 Reconsidered," *GTJ* 7 (1986) 203–12.

Although sexual "desire" conforms to v. 15, better is the explanation suggested by Gen 4:7b, where "desire" and "rule" *[māšal]* are found again in tandem: "It desires to have you, but you must master *[māšal]* it."[224] In chap. 4 "sin" is like an animal that when stirred up will assault Cain; it "desires" to overcome Cain, but the challenge God puts to Cain is to exercise "rule" or "mastery" over that unruly desire. If we are to take the lexical and structural similarities as intentional, we must read the verses in concert. This recommends that 3:16b also describes a struggle for mastery between the sexes. The "desire" of the woman is her attempt to control her husband, but she will fail because God has ordained that the man exercise his leadership function. The force of the defeat is obscured somewhat by the rendering "and he will rule"; the conjunction is better understood as "*but* he will rule." The directive for "rule" is not given to the man, for that has already been given and is assumed (2:15,18); rather, the issue of "rule" is found in God's directive toward the woman, who must succumb by divine edict. Thus the Lord affirms in the oracles of judgment the creation order: the serpent is subjected to the woman, the woman to the man, and all to the Lord. "In those moments of life's greatest blessing—marriage and children—the woman would serve most clearly the painful consequences of her rebellion from God."[225]

What is the nature of the man's "rule"? "Rule," as verb or derivative, is found seven additional times in Genesis, where it may indicate governance (1:16[twice],18; cf. Ps 136:7–9) and refers to exercising jurisdiction (24:2; 37:8; 45:8,26). The temperament of "rule" in the Old Testament is dependent on the varying circumstances in which that power is exercised.[226] The term is used too broadly to isolate its meaning in 3:16b lexically as either beneficent or tyrannical.[227] Human jurisdiction over the lower orders, however, is expressed by the different verb "dominate" *(rādâ;* 1:28), suggesting that the man does not "rule" his wife in the sense that he subdues the animals. We cannot understand the divine word "he will rule over you" as a command to impose dominance any more than v. 16a is an exhortation for the woman to suffer as much as possible during childbirth. It is a distortion of the passage to find in it justification for male tyranny. On the contrary, ancient Israel provided safeguards for protecting women from unscrupulous men (e.g., Deut 24:1–4), and the New Testament takes steps to restrain domination. Paul admonished men and women to

[224] S. Foh, "What Is the Woman's Desire?" *WTJ* 37 (1975): 376–83; but 3:16b is more than description, as Foh contends; there is also the prescriptive tenor.

[225] Sailhamer, "Genesis," 56.

[226] See R. Culver, "מָשַׁל *(mashal),*" *TWOT* 1.534.

[227] It is used of royal rule (e.g., Josh 12:2), stewardship (e.g., Prov 17:2), master-slave relations (Exod 21:7–8), despotism (e.g., Prov 22:7; Isa 19:4), and oppression of a subservient people (Judg 14:4). Its metaphorical usage occurs in Gen 4:7b and Prov 16:32, where the context concerns self-control. Also it is used of God's sovereign dominion (e.g., Ps 103:19; Isa 40:10).

practice mutual submission (Eph 5:22–33) and cautioned husbands to exercise love and protection without harshness (Col 3:19). Because of the threat of harsh dominance, Paul commanded Christian charity toward women in the community of the home and the church.

3:17–18 The final word is directed against the man (vv. 17–19). Adam's penalty also fit his crime since his appointed role was intimately related to the ground from which he was made and which he was charged to cultivate (2:7,15). Now the "ground" is decreed under divine "curse" on his account (see 3:14 discussion). The man will suffer (1) lifelong, toilsome labor (vv. 17–18) and finally (2) death, which is described as the reversal of the creation process (v. 19 with 2:7). Although the woman will die too (2:17), the death oracle is not pronounced against her since she is the source of life and therefore living hope for the human couple. It is the man who bears the greater blame for his conduct and is the direct recipient of God's death sentence.

As in the pronouncement against the serpent (v. 14), God pinpoints the reason for the ensuing penalty (v. 17). Adam listened to his wife and ate of the forbidden fruit. Repeating the original prohibition verbatim, "you must not eat of it" (2:17), reinforces the severity of the crime and reminds him of the dire consequences of his rebellion. Emphasis on the second person "you" and "your" sharpens God's focus on the man's individual fault. There is no room for avoidance now; he is caught without a word to say.

Moreover, the punishment reveals that the man's sin is the cause for the "curse" against the ground, resulting in its harvest of thorns and thistles. Ironically, the ground that was under the man's care in the garden as his source of joy and life (2:15) becomes the source of pain for the man's wearisome existence (v. 17). For the woman childbirth was marked with its attendant pain (v. 16), and in the cultivation of the wild and stubborn ground the man will know the toilsome pain of deriving food from the dust. The ground will now be his enemy rather than his servant. The same expression "all the days of your life" occurred in God's judgment against the serpent, where he will eat "dust" as his punishment (v. 14). This punishment also involves the "dust" of the ground, tying together the two crimes and their consequences.

"Thorns and thistles" become the native product of the land (v. 18), but it was not always so (see 2:5–6 discussion). This new condition of the land, "producing" *(ṣmḥ)* its yield of thorns, stands in conspicuous contrast to God's beneficent creative act, where he brought forth *(ṣmḥ)* a gorgeous and nutritious orchard for the man's pleasure (2:9). Adam's sin has spoiled his environment, and it suffers along with him since both are of the "dust." "You will eat the plants of the field" echoes 2:5 and anticipates his expulsion from the garden (3:23), outside where he must battle the elements as a toiling farmer. Now the conditions of land and life are those we are accustomed to, which at one time did not exist (2:5–7) but have come about by the man's sin. The passage has brought us full circle from creation's bliss to sin's burden. Nevertheless, the sentencing itself contains God's gracious provision since the man will still derive sustenance from the ground for survival.

Moreover, there remains hope for a final, full liberation for both Adam and the environment that will occur at the glorious consummation of the age. Paul's commentary on vv. 17–18 in Rom 8:19–22 points to the future hope that the natural (nonrational) creation possesses.[228] The world experienced corruption, not of its own choosing but by the condemnation of God for the sin of Adam; however, creation looks to the prospects of redemption that will be realized by it and the saints at the advent of Christ's glory. Both the creation and the "children of God" groan as with birth pangs (Gen 3:15–16) for the dawning of the new era. Paul's point was that this very groaning confirms the hope of the children of God for their full future adoption and redemption, which presently is assured by the Spirit.

3:19 Here we come to the last word of judgment. Adam's toil will be without relief until his final destiny of death. This explains Lamech's later naming of "Noah," in whom he expresses hope for relief from the drudgery of working the ground that travails under divine curse (see 5:29; 9:20 discussion). Adam is depicted as a broken farmer whose very meals, which are derived from the grain of his agrarian life, are spoiled by the fatigue of his striving. Like the woman's painful childbirth, the man's daily labors with their attendant woes are a perpetual reminder of sin's rewards.

The chiasmus underscores the linkage between the man's creation from "dust" (2:7) and the "return" to the man's beginnings.[229]

A you return
  B to the ground
    C since *(kî)* from it you were taken
    C´ for *(kî)* dust you are
  B´ and to dust
A´ you will return

Adam's death is portrayed by the dreadful wordplay on his creation and essential physical constitution as the "dust" *(ʿāpār)* of the "ground" *(ʾădāmâ)* (2:7; Eccl 3:20; Ps 103:14). His "return" will be from whence he came: *ʾādām* will become once again *ʾădāmâ* ("ground"). Death is exactly what God had forewarned (2:17) and what the serpent had denied (3:4). Death comes by the reversal ("returns") of the man's God-given state, that is, a "living being" (2:7). This reversal is the deterioration of the body that will "return" to the dust from which it was made (cf. Job 10:9; Ps 104:29). The inner elements of the structure are introduced by parallel conjunctions *(kî),* rendered as causal in

---

[228] Murray, *The Epistle to the Romans,* 299–310.

[229] See Kempf, "Genesis 3:14–19: Climax of the Discourse?" 366.

most versions (NIV, NASB, NAB, NJPS, NJB), but the second occurrence has sometimes been taken as emphatic, "indeed dust you are" (REB). "Dust you are" always overcomes the progress of medicine and the ingenuity of cosmetology; every opened casket proves it so.

God did not execute the penalty by taking Adam's life but by banning him from the rejuvenating power of the tree of life (3:22). Though not excommunicated from the divine presence (4:1–2), Adam's expulsion from the garden sealed his doom and that of all who followed. Resounding evidence of the divine penalty is found in Seth's genealogy, where Adam's death is related (5:5) and the unrelenting knell sounded for generation after generation, "and then he died." Paul's interpretation of this passage focuses on physical death brought into this world by the first man (Rom 5:12–21; cf. 6:23). Yet those who are living in the sphere of sin are deemed spiritually dead already (Eph 2:1). Unlike Adam, all his generations are born excluded from the garden; only through the last Adam, who insures the "life-giving spirit," does human mortality take on the garments of immortality (1 Cor 15:35–58).

3:20–21 Following the lengthy pronouncement of judgment, two events signal a continuing hope for the couple—a hope that ironically the ominous verdicts themselves had contained. The first event is Adam's naming of his wife "Eve" (v. 20), and the second is God's provision of animal skins for garments (v. 21). The two events indicate that the couple will survive through the gracious intervention of God.

The name *ḥawwâ,* meaning "living," is traditionally rendered "Eve," following the Greek translation *Zōē* ("Life"; v. 20). Her name occurs sparsely in Scripture (Gen 4:1; 2 Cor 11:3; 1 Tim 2:13; also *Tob* 8:6). Hebrew *ḥawwâ* is phonetically related to the word *ḥay* ("living"); thus by a phonetic play, Adam explains why she is named Eve. She is the "mother of all living," for all human life will have its source in her body. This assumes a prodigious posterity, and it is a tribute to Adam's faith in the prospect that God had revealed (vv. 15–16). Adam had learned, albeit through the most calamitous lesson, to accept God's word in faithful obedience. Another implication of Adam's naming the woman is his exercise of responsible headship (cf. 2:23). Before and after the fall, the man is exercising the same prerogative of naming. In the former case he is her source of life, and by naming her "woman" *(ʾiššâ)* he acknowledges her companionship, but here he admits his indebtedness to her for life's future.

Following Adam's act of faith, the Lord acts immediately in behalf of the vulnerable couple by providing adequate protection to cover their embarrassment and to preserve them in the new hostile environment to which they will be banished (v. 21; cf. vv. 7,18,23). In the same way that the woman's pain at birth is a reminder of their disobedience, their clothing confirms that they have sinned against God and that no longer can they walk before deity in innocence (2:25). The language of the verse alludes to tabernacle setting and worship.

"Garments" *(kūttōnet)* and "clothed" *(lābaš)* are reminiscent of the Pentateuch's description of priestly garments, particularly for Aaron as high priest.[230] This is another lexical link with the symbols of the tabernacle, where the priest must be properly clothed before God in the administration of his service (Exod 20:26; 28:42).[231] But Aaron's priestly garb was woven of colored yarn and fine linen, and his sons wore fine linen garments (e.g., Exod 28:4–5; 28:39; 39:27; Lev 16:4), while the garments of Adam and Eve are made of "skin." In the Mosaic law the skin of an animal offered for sin or guilt atonement was reserved for the officiating priest (Lev 7:8). Here God bestows "garments of skin" upon the guilty in the garden. Although the text does not specify that animals were slain to provide these coverings, it is a fair implication and one that likely would be made in the Mosaic community, where animal sacrifice was pervasive. Since the garden narrative shares in tabernacle imagery, it is not surprising that allusion to animal sacrifice is found in the garden too. Through an oblique reference to animal sacrifice, the garden narrative paints a theological portrait familiar to the recipients of the Sinai revelation who honored the tabernacle as the meeting place with God. Sacrifice renewed and guaranteed that special union of God with his people (e.g., Day of Atonement, Lev 16). This mode of provision then for Adam and Eve affirmed God's abiding goodwill.

Moreover, that God "made" *(ʿāśâ)* these garments stands in striking relief to the seventh day, when God ceased from all that he had "made" *(ʿāśâ)* (2:2–3). "Made" routinely describes God's creative work, occurring eleven times in 1:1–2:4. God has "made" the woman (2:18) and the animals of the fields (3:1) as acts of creation, but now his action in behalf of the couple is salvific in character. The God of the garden as Creator and Savior mirrors the God of tabernacle sacrifice, whom Israel had come to recognize by the voice of Moses and the prophets.

(5) The Man and Woman Expelled (3:22–24)

22And the LORD God said, "The man has now become like one of us, knowing good and evil. He must not be allowed to reach out his hand and take also from the tree of life and eat, and live forever." 23So the LORD God banished him from the Garden of Eden to work the ground from which he had been taken. 24After he drove the man out, he placed on the east side of the Garden of Eden cherubim and a flaming sword flashing back and forth to guard the way to the tree of life.

Initially the trees of life and knowledge were presented together (2:9); in this final scene of the garden account they are focal again. The tree of knowl-

[230] E.g., for "garments," Exod 28:4,39–40; 29:5,8; 39:27; 40:14; Lev 8:7,13; 10:5; 16:4; also Ezra 2:69; Neh 7:70[69],72[71]; for "clothed," e.g., Exod 28:41; 29:8; 40:14; Lev 8:13.

[231] So Wenham, *Genesis 1–15,* 84.

edge represented the command of the Lord to be obeyed; and if the human couple chose to comply, the tree of life would have been theirs to enjoy. But now that possibility is rescinded. Disobedience has doomed them to mortality. To carry out the just deserts of their transgression (2:17; 3:19), the man and woman are denied access to the tree of life. The prediction of the serpent had in its twisted way come to pass after all. The couple shared in the divine privilege of knowledge, but the result was not divine stature but rather the opposite—human death. For the second time we overhear an intradivine conversation; it first was heard in the creation of man, "Let us make man in our image" (see 1:26). Now the conversation deliberates upon the cutting off of that creation from the source of rejuvenating life (v. 22). In this latter case the mood of the divine contemplation (cp. 11:6) is not one of fear of usurpation but rather of sympathy for the misery the first couple must endure and an assurance that their pitiful state is not consigned for eternity.

3:22 As with the elaborate proclamation of punishment (vv. 14–19), the banishment of the couple includes an explanation for the course taken by divine decision. The particle *hēn,* commonly rendered "behold" (AV, NASB) or "see" (NRSV, NAB), is best understood as introducing the logical ground for the expulsion, "Since the man" or "Now that the man" (NJB, NJPS).[232] Hence the reason for the penalty takes first place in the verse;[233] God does not act ruthlessly and arbitrarily toward his creatures. Transcendent moral imperatives are the basis for his chosen action toward the world. The Lord's attention in this decree is focused upon the "man," not the woman, since Adam first received the prohibition and is the responsible party for the sin that requires God's eviction. Although "the man," possessing the definite article *(hāʾādām),* can be taken in its generic sense ("human beings," GNB), it likely refers to Adam, the person, since the narrative specifies the man's assignment as caretaker of the garden (2:15).

The new condition of the man "in knowing good from evil" (NJB) is the reason for God's action against the man. The man has achieved God's wisdom unlawfully, but he will not escape penalty by seizing the tree of life. Eating of the tree would grant him perpetual life, just as the eating of the prohibited tree granted him knowledge. "Take" and "eat" repeats the language of rebellion when the woman "took" and they "ate" from the tree of knowledge (3:6). Though Eve is "the mother of all living *[ḥay],*" they lost their opportunity to possess divinity's "eternal life *[ḥay].*" Life is a divine gift, but it is tied to the stipulation of obedience. Moses offered the same choice of life or death, obedience or disobedience, to Israel on the shores of Moab (Deut 30:11–20). Obedience meant life and prosperity in Canaan, but

[232] *IBHS* § 40.2.1c.

[233] Observed by Speiser (*Genesis,* 24) and Cassuto (*Genesis,* 172).

defiance guaranteed expulsion. Israel's parents chose banishment, and Israel itself chose exile.

3:23–24 Eviction for the man also meant he must work the "ground" (v. 23) in order to sustain life. Whereas before he was the cultivator of a specially prepared habitat, now he must develop his own garden by working the ground, which is under divine curse (v. 17). His sentence of death is echoed by "from which he was taken," reminding the reader of man's temporality (v. 19). The psalmist spoke of the "dust of death" (22:15; cp. Job 7:21) as his end unless the Lord rescues him. His concluding praise (22:22–31) extols God for deliverance *from* his distress, but it is left to the Greater Psalmist to sing of his deliverance *out of* death (cf. Ps 22:1 with Matt 27:46; Mark 15:34).

Adam and Eve's exile is decisive and definitive. "Banished" *(ṣālaḥ)* is the same language used of Abraham's action that "sends away" Ishmael and other possible rivals to Isaac (21:14; 25:6). It is descriptive of the scapegoat that is expelled from the camp of Israel (Lev 16:10). Still stronger is the term "drove" *(gāraš)* in v. 24, which also describes God's exile of Cain (4:14) and Sarah's charge to Abraham to "get rid" of the slave girl Hagar with her son (21:10). It is the language of divorce[234] and dispossession (e.g., Exod 33:2; Deut 33:27). Adam and Eve are "out in the cold," and only by the grace of God does this disowned, homeless pair find refuge.

Our passage continues to share the imagery of Moses' tabernacle by allusion to the "cherubim" at the "east side" of the garden (v. 24). The "east side" of the garden parallels the easterly direction the tabernacle and temple faced, situated west of the altar. This east-west dichotomy indicates that the garden was located to the west of their first habitat outside Eden, and we are told that Cain went eastward "from the LORD's presence" (4:16). This directional motif "east" occurs often in Genesis: the expulsion of Cain (4:14), the locale of the Tower of Babel (11:2), and the dismissal of Keturah's sons by Abraham (25:6).

Another allusion to the "east" signifying withdrawal from God is Lot's departure from Abraham in 13:8–13, where he chose to settle the rich plain of Jordan, which was like the "garden of the LORD" (13:10), and traveled "east" (13:11).[235] Entrance to Eden's garden was guarded by "cherubim," who are known from the Old Testament as winged, composite beings associated with the presence of God (e.g., Ps 18:10; Ezek 10).[236] Their golden images formed the covering of the sacred ark (Exod 25:18–22; 37:7–9) and decorated the curtains of the holy of holies (Exod 26:1,31; 36:8,35). Carved cherubim also adorned Solomon's temple and dominated the most holy place (1 Kgs 6:23–

---

[234] Lev 21:7,14, where it occurs in the *qal* stem, not the *piel* as here.

[235] See J. E. Miller, "Aetiology of the Tabernacle/Temple in Genesis," in *Proceedings of the Eastern Great Lakes Biblical Society* (Grand Rapids: The Society, 1986), 151–60.

[236] C. Meyers, "Cherubim," *ABD* 1.899–900.

29; 7:29,36). Accompanying the cherubim is a "flaming sword flashing back and forth" (cf. Ps 104:4), perhaps indicating the judgment of God (e.g., Deut 32:41–42; Ps 83:14[15]). The cherubim are "placed" *(šākan)* at the east entrance to the garden to "guard/care for" *(šāmar)* it against intruders. What pitiful irony that Adam, who was once put there to "care" *(šāmar,* 2:15) for it, now is "guarded" from it! "Placed," from which "tabernacle" *(miškan)* is derived, frequently depicts the "tabernacling" of God among his people and is used of the erection of the tabernacle in the camp (e.g., Exod 25:8; 29:45; Josh 18:1).

Such imagery effectively depicts the excommunication of the man and woman from the presence of God. Later Israel was all too aware that an audience with God was the exclusive privilege of Aaron's lineage and only at the invitation of God once a year. Our parents squandered what men and women have longed to regain ever since. However, not all is lost since God initiates for Israel a new way into his presence but at the costly price of innocent blood. In spite of man's inability to obtain life through the garden's tree, the tabernacle revealed at Sinai enabled Israel to live with God, though imperfectly. The means and extent of access to God's presence was altered because of sin, but divine mercy overtook the wayward man and woman. For their future generations provision was afforded through Israel. This all, however, only foreshadowed the perfect and final passage into the presence of God by the very body of Jesus Christ, whose blood cleanses us so that we might know life through his death (Heb 9:6–14). John's Apocalypse alludes to the garden's tree of life when it speaks of eternal life granted those who persevere in Christ (Rev 2:7). In the new and eternal city of God, the tree of life will perpetually grant its fruit to those who believe (22:2,14,19). It is then and only then that Adam and Eve may reach for the fruit and enjoy its abiding nectar.

3. Adam and Eve's Family outside the Garden (4:1–26)

Whereas chaps. 2–3 recount the life of Adam and Eve *inside* the garden, chap. 4 will relate a new episode in the ongoing story of the first couple's experience—but now *outside* the garden.[237] The abrupt announcement of Cain and Abel's birth (vv. 1–2) is told so as to show the linkage between chap. 3's intimations of continued life and prosperity (3:15–16,20) and the beginning realization of that hope despite human sin in the garden. Sadly, the optimism of the narrative turns to the sordid account of sin's continuing encroachment by the murder of Abel at the hands of his elder brother (vv. 3–16). Remarkably, however, the grace of God toward Cain enables Adam's firstborn to survive and

[237] Typical of beginning a new episode as in 3:1, the *wāw* disjunctive introduces the chapter and is best rendered, "Now the man . . ." (NASB, NRSV).

later father an impressive lineage whose members are remembered for notable cultural achievements. Unfortunately these achievements were overshadowed by their wicked accomplishments (vv. 17–24). The "*tôlĕdôt* of the heavens and earth" (2:4–4:26) concludes on the high note of another evidence of God's grace toward Adam and Eve. Seth, Adam's third son, replaces the murdered Abel and heads a new lineage that is remembered as the benchmark for "when men began to call on the name of the LORD" (4:25–26).

Eden held for the man and woman a blissful communion with God without mediation. When life outside the garden is first regarded by the narrative, Cain and Abel are depicted at worship presenting offerings before the Lord. This early incident shows what is acceptable worship in the eyes of God. Mosaic custom took the matter of worship seriously, with its emphasis on the time, place, and means; consequently the Cain-Abel narrative held more importance for the ancient reader than it does in the church today, although it was a source of theological reflection in the writings of the New Testament.[238] The initial question in this chapter is why Abel's offering was accepted and not Cain's, but the larger issue is that of what will become of the promised blessing and deliverance (1:26–28; 3:15).

We also learn from this incident in Adam's early heritage how sin has its sway over the human family as we see its expansion from the autonomous choices of Adam and Eve in the garden to the ruthless fratricide outside Eden. God's response of "curse" against Cain underscores the accountability of any person who would dare to tamper with the sacredness of human life, which exclusively bears the *imago Dei* (1:26–27; 9:5–6). The relationship between Cain and brother Abel impacts the relationship Cain has with God: "Gen 4.1–16 makes it clear to sever the tie with one's sibling is to sever one's tie with YHWH and the earth."[239] From the genealogy of Cain (4:17–24), Genesis shows that human ruthlessness pervades a culture that lives outside the "presence of the LORD" (4:16).

LITERARY STRUCTURE AND ORIGINS. Structurally the Cain-Abel narrative (4:3–16) is sandwiched between two sections recounting the birth and genealogy of Adam's eldest, Cain (4:1–2,17–22). The similarity in the naming formula of v. 17 and vv. 1–2 indicates that the two are interdependent sources. Cain's genealogy ends in the "Song of Lamech" ("Song of the Sword"), in which Lamech boasts of his infamous career (4:23–24). This is followed by the announcement of Seth's birth and a brief genealogical statement, concluding the *tôlĕdôt* section (2:4–4:26) with a note about worship of the Lord (4:25–26). Thus the chapter begins and ends with the same subject matter of worship.

---

[238] Cf. Matt 23:35 and parallels; Heb 11:4; 12:24; 1 John 3:4; Jude 11.

[239] E. van Wolde, "The Story of Cain and Abel: A Narrative Study," *JSOT* 52 (1991): 38.

Cynicism concerning the literary unity of the chapter has been fueled by the diverse literary genres constituting the chapter (e.g., narrative, genealogy) and by seeming incongruities in the text. For example, Cain is punished as a wanderer in the narrative, but in the genealogy he is portrayed as a city-builder. Similarities in the genealogies of Cain (4:17–22) and Seth (5:1–32), plus the presence of two genealogies for Seth (also 4:25–26), are attributed by critical scholars to two sources (J and P, respectively); these sources are supposedly the garbled accounts of a prior composite or single genealogy. One tradition critic has described chap. 4 as an original myth of primeval setting that was joined by antiquarian stories about nomadic tribes, all placed in a genealogical framework that included the founders of the civilized arts.[240] This rewriting of the biblical narrative, however, fails to appreciate the pressing evidence for the original unity of the passage that many recent interpreters have come to recognize. New literary studies and more favorable exegetical treatment of troublesome passages encourage confidence in the integrity of the text.

Some believe that the Cainite genealogy (vv. 1–2, 17–24) and narrative (vv. 3–16) originated from an imaginative tradition of the Kenites *(qyny),* according to which their eponymous head (from whom the name is derived) was Cain *(qyn).*[241] The Kenites were a desert tribe which inhabited southern Judah (Gen 15:19; 1 Sam 27:10) and were the tribe of Moses' father-in-law (Judg 4:11). The Kenite connection is based in part on etymological speculation that "Cain" *(qyn)* is related to the word meaning "smith" in Aramaic and Arabic, observing that his descendant Tubal-*Cain* founded metallurgy. Also "Kenite" *(qyny)* and "Kain" *(qyn)* have parallel meaning in Num 24:21–22 (NASB, NRSV; also Judg 4:11). But other etymologies for "Cain" have been proposed,[242] and this uncertainty obstructs the proposal of an original Kenite source. Even if "Cain" were related to the term "smith," there is no convincing connection between the genealogy of 4:17–24 and the Kenites or any other tribe. The interdependence of chap. 4's literary components, such as vv. 17–26, precludes that the genealogy ever circulated independently in its present form.[243]

---

[240] So J. van Seters, *Prologue to History: The Yahwist as Historian in Genesis* (Louisville: Westminster/John Knox, 1992), 146.

[241] See, e.g., von Rad, *Genesis*, 107–9; M. D. Johnson, *The Purpose of the Biblical Genealogies* (Cambridge: Cambridge University Press, 1969), 11–12.

[242] E.g., Arabic *qaynun,* meaning "fashion, shape, give form" (Cassuto, *Genesis,* 197); and Hebrew קִינָה, meaning "song," which has a connection with Cain by the meaning of "Naamah," perhaps related to the Ug. word *(nʿm)* for "song" or "musician" (R. S. Hess, "Cain," *ABD* 1.806–7). Westermann cautions that the meaning of "Cain" is broader than "smith" (e.g., 2 Sam 21:16), and its etymological history must be determined with each specific case (*Genesis 1–11,* 289).

[243] Also tribal genealogies tend to occur in the *segmented* (branched) form of genealogy, and 4:17–26 is in the *linear* form, which would argue against the Cain genealogy as originally tribal in function (Wilson, *Genealogy and History,* 156–58).

Since the Kenite theory rests on the assumption that Cain is the eponymous head and since there is no linkage between the desert Kenites and the city-dwellers of 4:17–24, the theory remains a speculative reconstruction with little merit.

Beyond the supposed Cain-Kenite connection, the notion of a nomadic Cain who in fact fathers urban dwellers would be on the face of it a contradictory effort. This leads to diverse proposals about how this could have happened, including the suggestion that there were two different Cains of folklore: the one who is the farmer-turned-city-father and the other who is the ancestor of the Kenite tribe known for its nomadic life and metal work (cp. Tubal-Cain's metallurgy).[244] If so, it is remarkable that the author of our account would be so unconscious of the problems created by this ill-fated aspiration as to have attempted it. We will speak in more detail of the genealogies and their problems at 4:17, but here we will present in a cursory way the indications of an original literary unity.

Chapter 4 fits harmoniously with the literary strategy of Genesis at large and within the *tôlĕdôt* section (2:4–4:26), especially chap. 3.[245] It is routine in Genesis to include narrative expansions in the genealogies (e.g., Enoch, 5:22–24; Nimrod, 10:8–12), even lengthy ones as we find in 4:3–16 for the Cainite genealogy (cp. Noah's, 5:32–9:29). Also the nonelect line of descent appears first, followed by the elect lineage as we find here with Cain preceding Seth's lineage (e.g., Japheth and Ham before Shem, chap. 10). Chapter 4 can be regarded as a genealogy of Adam's family that would match the genealogical genre of chap. 5.[246] In the former case the genealogy is *branched,* meaning that all three descendants of Adam are specified, whereas in chap. 5 the genealogy presents only the line of one son, Seth.

---

[244] So J. M. Miller, "The Descendants of Cain: Notes on Genesis 4," *ZAW* 86 (1974), 164–74.

[245] For evidence of literary unity see Cassuto, *Genesis,* 185–93; Wenham, *Genesis 1–15,* 96–100; R. R. Wilson (*Genealogy and History in the Biblical World* [New Haven: Yale University Press, 1977], 156–58; Hauser, "Linguistic and Thematic Links Between Gen 4:1–16 and Gen 2–3," 297–305; and C. J. Labuschagne, "The Pattern of the Divine Speech Formulas in the Pentateuch," *VT* 32 (1982): 268–96. Also W. M. Clark, "The Flood and the Structure of the Pre-patriarchal History," *ZAW* 83 (1971): 184–210, esp. 195–203, shows that chaps. 3–4 are unified in structure. But rather than seeing parallelism in origins, he understands their common structure on a form-critical basis as "judgment stories" as also found in 2 Sam 12 and thus as the product of an early monarchic hand, perhaps from prophetic circles.

[246] See J. Blenkinsopp, *The Pentateuch: An Introduction to the First Five Books of the Bible* (New York: Doubleday, 1992), 68.

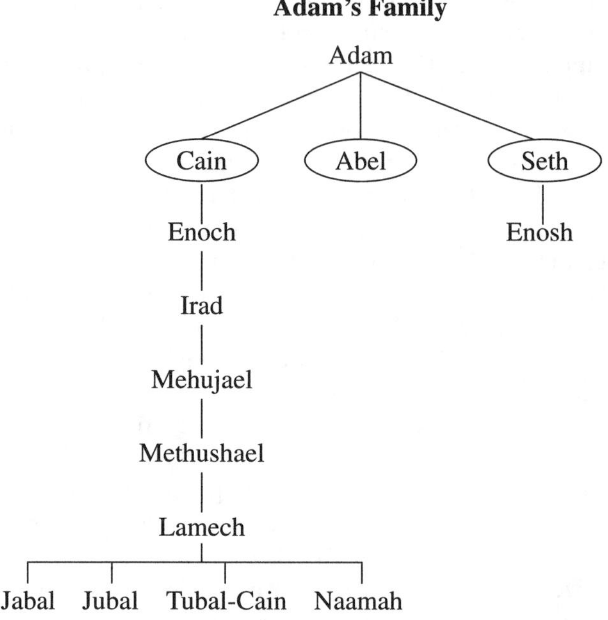

Internally 4:1–26 also possesses evidence of cohesion. (1) The birth announcements at the three seams of the chapter have similar language (e.g., "lay with his wife," vv. 1,17,25). (2) The narrative is built on the numerical congruity of sevens and multiples of seven: the emphatic "seven" for Cain (v. 15) and Lamech (v. 24); "brother" is found seven times, "Cain," fourteen and "Seth," seven; the divine names "God," "LORD God," and "LORD" together in 2:4–4:26 occur thirty-five times (5 x 7), equaling the same number "God" appears in 1:1–2:3, and the seventieth (10 x 7) occasion of deity's name in Genesis is at 4:26b when men called on the "name of the LORD." (3) The same Hebrew construction (participle) identifying the occupations of the participants is found for Cain and Abel (4:2), Cain as builder (v. 17), and Jabal as tent dweller (v. 20). Also the chiasmus of vv. 2–5 overlaps the genealogical notice of 4:1–2 and the narrative vv. 3–5, suggesting an interdependence in genealogy and narrative. F. I. Andersen has noted the alternation between the names "Abel" and "Cain" as well as their profession and acts of worship:

A And became *Abel* a keeper of *flocks*
A′ And *Cain* became a worker of *soil*
B *Cain* brought some of the fruits of the *soil* as an offering to the LORD
B′ But *Abel* brought, also he, some of the firstborn of his *flocks* and their fat portions
C And looked with favor the LORD on Abel and on his offering
C′ And on Cain and on his offering he did not look with favor.

The pairing of the lines and the alternation of the participants create the chiasmus: (1) Abel, Cain, Cain, Abel and (2) flocks, soil, soil, flocks.[247] (4) The narrative in structure and language imitates what is found in chaps. 2–3.[248] Chapters 2–3, and 4 show a chiastic pattern built around the interchange of dialogue and narrative with the central element serving as the dramatic turn in the story. In the Eden narrative 3:6–8 is the turning point, detailing the sin of Adam and Eve, and in the present narrative the centerpiece 4:8 records the murder of Abel:[249]

A 4:2b–5 Narrative: Cain, Abel actors, Lord passive
  B 4:6–7 Dialogue: Lord questions Cain
    C 4:8 (dialogue) Narrative: Cain murders Abel
  B′ 4:9–15a Dialogue: Lord and Cain
A′ 4:15b–16 Narrative: Lord active, Cain passive

There are also many lexical similarities: divine questioning, "Where?" "What?" (4:9 with 3:9; 4:10 with 3:13); Adam's and the LORD's replies, "I heard you [lit., your voice] in the garden" (3:10) and "Listen [lit., "voice"]! Your brother's blood cries out to me from the ground" (4:10); the curse against Cain ("You are cursed from the land *[hāʾădāmâ],*" 4:11) and the curses against the serpent ("You are more cursed," 3:14) and the "ground" *(hāʾădāmâ;* 3:17); the protective "mark" of Cain and the provision of Adam's clothing (4:15 with 3:21); the divine forewarning of "desire" and "rule" (4:7 with 3:16); and the expulsion toward "east of Eden" by "driving" *(gāraš)* out the culprits (4:14 with 3:24). Thematically we find Adam and Cain have the same occupation (2:15; 4:2); both of their sins are related to the "fruit" (3:6; 4:3); their separation from God is brought on by the issue of "knowing" *(yādaʿ;* 3:5–6,22; 4:9); and they are questioned, sentenced, and punished in the same manner.

Clearly chap. 4 must be heard in partnership with chap. 3. We noted there that the theological import of this structural and lexical association is cause-effect. Chapter 4's events are seen as genetically related to the fall of Adam and Eve, and the actions of parent and child are viewed as an organic whole. This attributes the lamentable advances of sin in the Cain-Abel episode to the inception of sin *inside* the garden. Now Cain, Adam's firstborn, acts out the serpent's purposes by murdering the "seed" of the woman Eve (3:15). And, unlike his parents, there is no sense of shame or remorse; if anything, he is incensed that God would censure him. His aggression against Heaven's dictate is surpassed by the vitriolic voice of Lamech, who imitates his ancestor through murdering the vulnerable. Among all these bothersome noises, we

[247] See F. I. Andersen, *The Sentence in Biblical Hebrew* (The Hague: Mouton, 1974), 122.
[248] E.g., noted by Westermann, *Genesis 1–11,* 303.
[249] See Wenham, *Genesis 1–15,* 99, which is modified here slightly.

never hear from poor Abel, except the unnerving sound of the blood-drenched ground that cries out for satisfaction.

(1) Cain and Abel's Birth (4:1–2)

[1]Adam lay with his wife Eve, and she became pregnant and gave birth to Cain. She said, "With the help of the LORD I have brought forth a man." [2]Later she gave birth to his brother Abel.

Now Abel kept flocks, and Cain worked the soil.

4:1 Adam "lay *[yādaʿ]* with his wife" (lit., "knew his wife"), a common idiom for sexual relations in the Old Testament. But "knew" in its conjugal sense is limited to chap. 4 in the early history (chaps. 1–11), where it is found three times (4:1,17,25; cp. 4:9).[250] This recurrence of "knew" in the Cain-Abel narrative probably is an allusion to the "tree of knowledge" and serves as a reminder of Adam's sin and its consequence (2:9,17; 3:5,22), especially the wordplay on the outcome of their eating: "they knew *[yādaʿ]* that they were naked" (3:7). Cain's birth is the first indication that God's beneficent word would come to pass (3:15–16) and that Adam's faith was not misplaced (3:20). Divine superintendence assured for humanity what it could not achieve by itself. Eve acknowledges this when she attributes to the Lord's involvement her giving birth to Cain. The narrator reinforces this indirectly in referring to Adam's wife by the seldom-used "Eve," not found again in the subsequent Old Testament, which echoed Adam's earlier confidence in God's provision for a future family (3:20; cf. 4:25).

The etymological history of the name "Cain" remains disputed (see introduction to this section), but the biblical narrative recounts the popular etymology for the name. Usually the name given to a child in Hebrew narrative conveys an interpretive significance, either explicitly stated in the narrative or by suggestion.[251] By a play on the sound of the verb "brought forth" *(qānîtî),* Eve names her eldest "Cain" *(qayin).* The verb has two different meanings that are reflected in the English versions: (1) the more common meaning of obtain, as "acquired" (NJB), "gotten" (AV, NASB), or "gained" (NJPS); and (2) the infrequent sense of create, as "brought forth" (NIV, REB) or "produced" (NAB, NRSV). When used as "create," God is its subject, but here we have the woman, Eve.[252] Ugaritic *qny,* meaning "create" or "make" as in "procreate,"

---

[250] Cf. also Gen 19:8; 24:16; 38:26.

[251] Wordplay between the name and context may be explicit as with Eve (3:20) and Seth (4:25) (also Jacob = Israel in 32:29), or by the same or similar root of the name used in the context, such as Cain here, and, e.g., Adam (2:7), Noah (5:29), Japheth (9:27), Peleg (10:25), Isaac (21:3–7), Esau and Jacob (25:26,30), and Jacob's sons, such as Joseph (30:24). See R. S. Hess, "A Comparison of the Onomastica in Genealogical and Narrative Texts of Genesis 1–11," in *Proceedings, Tenth World Congress of Jewish Studies* (Jerusalem: World Union of Jewish Studies, 1990), 67–74.

[252] Cf. Gen 14:19,22; Deut 32:6; Ps 139:13; Prov 8:22; also perhaps Exod 15:16; Ps 78:54.

argues for "brought forth." Also the context of creation and procreation supports this understanding. The unexpected use of "man" (*ʾîš*) to identify Cain, which is not used elsewhere for a child, rather than the routine term "son," points up another allusion to chaps. 2–3.[253] Eve is given the childbearing function (3:16,20) in subduing the earth while Adam is ordained to work the "ground" whence he came (2:7,15; 3:17). As the "ground" (*ʾădāmâ*) with the help of the Lord had produced "man" (*ʾādām*), so Eve the woman (*ʾiššâ,* 2:23) with divine help produced the "man" (*ʾîš*), Cain. She sees in creating Cain the realization of her divinely assigned role.

Her commentary on the birth of the child reflects her renewed dependence on the Lord. Eve had a rekindled faith in the goodness of God and the veracity of his word promised in 3:15. Luther (and others), however, attributes too much to Eve by reading the Hebrew "a man of the LORD," as though Cain were the savior foreseen in 3:15.[254] Rather, her exclamation acknowledges that this achievement came only by the assistance of the Lord. This first birth recorded in the Bible is consonant with all of remaining Scripture, which invariably attributes conception and life to the unique work of God and as evidence of his blessing (e.g., Pss 127:3–5; 139:13). From the outset of God's plan for the human family, procreation is the divine-human means whereby the man and woman might achieve the dominion that God has envisioned for them (1:28). This motif of children ("seed") dominates Genesis and was critical to later Israel's understanding of its own destiny as it interpreted the life of the patriarchs (e.g., 12:7).

4:2 From the description of Abel as "his brother," it is apparent that the story is told with Cain in focus. Its language underscores the despicable act of this murderer, who out of envy committed fratricide. "Abel" means "breath" (*hebel*), but since there is no play on his name, as there is with "Cain," it is best to restrain from making more of its significance. At most the name may be an allusion to the brevity of life as a result of the fall.[255] Introducing the two sons in terms of their occupations is more important for the narrator since it establishes the plot for the murder that follows. Abel's vocation is not anticipated in chaps. 2–3, though the garden narrative permits it, while Cain's is the one assigned to Adam (2:15; 3:17–19). Both professions were known in early soci-

---

[253] See van Wolde, "The Story of Cain and Abel," 27.

[254] *LW* 1.242. Heb. אֶת־יְהוָה ("with the help of the LORD") has been the source of textual dispute and divergent interpretations (see P. Zerafa, "I Formed a Man with Yahweh," in *Melita Theologica* 44 [1993]: 29–32). The English versions typically translate the preposition as accompaniment in the sense of helping (as *IBHS* § 11.2.4, cp. Num 14:9; 2 Kgs 9:32). The Heb. "with the LORD" was too anthropomorphic for early Jewish translators. The LXX has διὰ τοῦ θεοῦ ("through God"), avoiding the association of the divine name Yahweh and Eve's sexual relations as well as the infamous "sons of God" in 6:2. *Tgs. Onq.* and *Neof.* read "from before the LORD," as if מֵאֵת יהוה, thus a gift from the Lord (as AV).

[255] הֶבֶל often describes the vanity of human life (e.g., Eccl 1:2; 12:8; Ps 144:4).

ety; sheepherding and agriculture provided an occasion for a natural rivalry. The Sumerian tale of *Dumuzi and Enkimdu* depicts a rivalry between the shepherd god and the farmer god over marriage to a woman, but it ends in a peaceful resolution.[256] Some view this as a parallel motif to the Cain-Abel rivalry or see the substratum of the biblical account as mythological, but the dissimilarities are so great as to render such an analogy or dependence unwarranted. The biblical setting is worship, and the factor that led to Abel's death was Cain's exaggerated pride. Like his parents before him, Cain desired recognition that did not rightly belong to him (4:7). Pride dominates his lineage (Lamech) and is revisited among the "men of renown" in Noah's day (6:4) and the later builders of Babel's tower (11:4).

(2) Cain and Abel's Worship of God (4:3–7)

[3]In the course of time Cain brought some of the fruits of the soil as an offering to the LORD. [4]But Abel brought fat portions from some of the firstborn of his flock. The LORD looked with favor on Abel and his offering, [5]but on Cain and his offering he did not look with favor. So Cain was very angry, and his face was downcast.

[6]Then the LORD said to Cain, "Why are you angry? Why is your face downcast? [7]If you do what is right, will you not be accepted? But if you do not do what is right, sin is crouching at your door; it desires to have you, but you must master it."

After addressing their vocations, their parallel acts of worship are recited as well as the Lord's reaction to their gifts (vv. 3–5). Cain's anger at the rejection of his gift provokes the interrogation and divine counsel that the Lord offers the downcast brother (vv. 6–7). Why God refuses Cain's offering is unspecified in the passage and is the subject of debate among commentators. Some contend that the story reflects a period in Israel's religion when the blood offering was preferred over the grain,[257] but this would not be the case for the period of the Mosaic audience (who we assume would have understood God's disapproval of the offering) when both grain and animal offerings were honorable. Also it is interpreted as divine disapproval of the vocation of farmer versus that of shepherd, but this flatly contradicts the earlier garden narrative, which depicts cultivation as the divinely appointed assignment for Adam (2:15; 3:23). The intentional linkage between Adam and Cain would militate against viewing Cain's profession as dishonorable. If anything, he was carrying out "to the letter" God's exhortation to Adam.

Others suggest that the very absence of a rationale for God's actions shows that divine election is mystery and therefore must be viewed as capricious

---

[256] *ANET,* 41–42.

[257] So Skinner, *Genesis,* 105–6.

(from the human perspective), as "fated by God to be so."[258] This we find too pessimistic toward the text, for we think that the passage entails the reason for Cain's rejection (see below). Another finds the rationale for the rejection in the source of the fruit from the cursed "ground." Cain is not initially condemned; only his offering is rejected. His unwillingness to cope with God's decision leads to murder and the divine curse.[259] But if the problem were the source of the gift ("ground"), it does not square that God directed Adam vocationally to work the "ground," which would inevitably mean the rejection of its food (3:23). The remaining resolutions involve either (1) a deficiency in the matter of the gift or (2) a flaw in the intention of the giver. We will show that the former reveals the latter.

4:3–4 Although this is the first recorded offering in the Bible, there is no indication that the narrative is announcing the first occasion of sacrifice. "In the course of time" (v. 3) is vague and may imply that the practice of giving offerings was customary for the brothers, perhaps learned from Adam. Cain and Abel's offerings were presented to the Lord according to their differing vocations. Cain's "offering" as well as Abel's is described with the same term *minḥâ,* which can be used as a general reference to any kind of "gift," such as that given among brothers (Gen 32:13) or to a king (1 Sam 10:27), or it can be a technical term for the "cereal" offering presented to the Lord (e.g., Lev 2:1–7; 6:12–14; Num 15:1–16).

In addition to the Abel example, *minḥâ* also refers to an animal offering in 1 Sam 2:17.[260] Our passage does not have the common language of the Mosaic sacrificial legislation, neither the general word "sacrifice" *(zebaḥ)* nor reference to the "sin," "burnt," "guilt," or "peace" offerings. However, Cain did not bring the firstfruits *(bikkûrîm;* cp. Lev 2:14); he brought only "some" of his crop (v. 3). This is contrasted with the offering of Abel ("but Abel"), who brought not only "some" of his "firstborn" *(bikkōrôt)* but the best of the animal, the fatty portions (v. 4). Later Israel acknowledged the efficacy of both the grain and blood offerings, but of these particularly the firstfruits (e.g., Exod 23:16) and firstborn (Exod 13:2,15; Lev 27:26; Deut 15:19) were reserved for God. Israel itself was regarded as God's firstfruit (Jer 2:3) and firstborn (Exod

---

[258] Westermann, *Genesis 1–11,* 296; also Brueggemann, *Genesis,* 56. For von Rad (*Genesis,* 104) the blood is preferred by the Lord, but the reason is unknown and must be left to "God's free will." For H. B. Huffmon, Cain's error was his refusal to search out before God why his gift was rejected, but instead he became angry with God's capricious will ("Cain, the Arrogant Sufferer," in *Biblical and Related Studies Presented to Samuel Iwry* [Winona Lake: Eisenbrauns, 1985], 109–13).

[259] F. Spina, "The 'Ground' for Cain's Rejection (Gen 4): *ʾădāmāh* in the Context of Gen 1–11," *ZAW* 104 (1992): 319–32.

[260] See B. K. Waltke, "Cain and His Offering, *WTJ* 48 (1986): 363–72, who adds, "The unusual element in the story from a lexical viewpoint *[minḥâ]* is not that Cain's offering is bloodless but that Abel's is bloody!" (p. 366).

4:22). This imagery shared by the church (e.g., Rom 11:16; Heb 12:23) and Christ (e.g., Rom 8:29; 1 Cor 15:20,23) as the "firstborn" indicates the blessing of God and the veneration of the Lord by his people.[261] It has been suggested that the parallel language "some of the fruits of the soil" and "some of the first-born of his flock" insinuates that Cain also brought the best of his offerings.[262] Yet the passage is intent on showing the contrast between the two men. Also interpreting Cain as stingy conforms with the narrative's depiction of his self-absorbed attitude (4:7) and his absence of conscience (4:13). We think the absence of "firstfruits" for Cain in juxtaposition with Seth's "firstborn" would not have been lost on the Mosaic audience.[263]

God's response toward Cain and Abel, therefore, was not due to the nature of the gift per se, whether it was grain or animal, but the integrity of the giver. The narrative ties together the worshiper and his offering as God considers the merit of their individual worship: "The LORD looked with favor on Abel and his offering, but on Cain and his offering he did not look with favor" (vv. 4–5).[264] Both giver and gift were under the scrutiny of God. Cain's offering did not measure up because he retained the best of his produce for himself. For the writer to the Hebrews (11:4), Abel's offering was accepted because it was offered in faith. As Luther noted, "The faith of the individual was the weight which added value to Abel's offering."[265] Unlike a human observer, God sees the condition of the human heart and weighs the motive of the worshiper (e.g., 1 Sam 16:7). Elsewhere Scripture shows that the Lord requires of the giver an obedient and upright heart (e.g., 1 Sam 15:14; Hos 6:6; Matt 5:24).

4:5 Cain's anger revealed his true attitude, which resulted in his despondency. The characterization "very angry" (lit., "it burned to Cain exceedingly") is similar to the Hebrew construction at Gen 34:7, which describes the "fury" of Jacob's sons upon learning of their sister's abuse (cp. 31:36; Jonah 4:1,4,9). Attempts to define Cain's reaction as "depression" rather than anger smacks of modern distinctions.[266] His "downcast" face indicated a saddened visage (cp. Job 29:24). Approval is described elsewhere in Scripture as acceptance in a person's eyes; acknowledgment of Jacob's "gift" meant favor from brother

---

[261] See L. Walker, "Firstborn," and "Firstfruits," *Holman Bible Dictionary,* 493–94.

[262] E.g., F. Delitzsch, *A New Commentary on Genesis,* vol. 1 (1888; reprint, Edinburgh: T & T Clark, 1978), 181, and Westermann, *Genesis 1–11,* 296.

[263] One rabbinic tradition noted the deficiency of Cain's offering: "It was from the refuse" (*Gen. Rab.* 22.5).

[264] Interestingly, Delitzsch, who saw no difference in the value of their offerings, comes to the same conclusion but on the opposite basis, namely, that the passage distinguishes the giver from the offering (*A New Commentary on Genesis,* 181).

[265] *LW* 1.251.

[266] M. I. Gruber argues that the Heb. idiom חָרָה אַף ("nose burns") indicates anger, whereas חָרָה לוֹ ("burns to him") indicates despondency ("Was Cain Angry or Depressed?" *BAR* 6 [1980]: 35–36).

Esau ("I have seen your face," 33:10; cf. 1 Sam 1:18). For Cain his downward gaze told the whole story.

John's first epistle comments that Cain was of the "evil one" because he hated his brother and murdered him (3:11–12). By appealing to Cain as example, the apostle proved his premise: the one who hates a person is a murderer. In the New Testament, Cain is viewed as the forefather of an unrighteous seed who had drawn first blood in the perpetual struggle between the ungodly and the godly seed first anticipated in 3:15. According to the custom of primogeniture, the firstborn received the bounty of parental inheritance (Deut 21:17), but from the viewpoint of Genesis as a whole, it is not surprising that the firstborn in whom Adam and Eve had so much hope would be refused for another. This rejection of the firstborn for the younger son (in this case Seth) portends the common pattern witnessed among the patriarchs where the custom of primogeniture is superseded by divine election and the outworking of covenant promise. God's gracious dealings with Israel also were initiated by his elective love (Deut 4:37; 7:7–8), but the Mosaic covenant included moral demands. Israel's acceptance was not automatic due to their status as God's "firstborn." Cain and his unrighteous offspring served as a reminder to Israel that its destiny was measured in the scales of ethical behavior.

4:6–7 God questions Cain for the same purpose he queried the man and woman in the garden (3:9,11)—not to scold but to elicit Cain's admission of sin with the view to repentance. The REB's rendering, "Why are you scowling?" (v. 6) captures the visual grimace etched across Cain's face. Cain telegraphed by his facial expression the bitterness of his darkened soul.

Verse 7 presents the translator with a number of problems, so much so that Jewish tradition counted it as one of the indeterminate verses (*b. Yoma* 52a–b), and some modern commentators have given up on discovering its meaning. Proposed solutions, whether ancient or modern, commonly involve emending the text, but there is little agreement, and we can take meager solace in understanding the passage when the understanding is based on rewriting it.[267] Despite the problems, we can achieve a credible understanding of the passage. "Accepted" translates the Hebrew word for "a lifting up" or an "exaltation";[268] this literal rendering is found in the awkward translation of the NJPS: "Surely, if you do right, there is uplift. . . ." The implication is made explicit in the NASB's "If you do well, will not *[your countenance]* be lifted up?" and the REB's emended option, "You hold your head up."[269] In this understanding the

[267] Exemplary of this is the LXX's imaginative reworking: οὐκ, ἐὰν ὀρθῶς προσενέγκῃς, ὀρθῶς δὲ μὴ διέλῃς, ἥμαρτες; ἡσύχασον: "If you have offered correctly but not cut correctly, have you not sinned? Be silent!"

[268] שְׂאֵת is the infinitive form of נָשָׂא, which is broad in use, including forgiveness (50:17) and acceptance (32:21).

[269] Reading תִּשָּׂא ("you lift up") for שְׂאֵת.

expression reverses the earlier imagery of Cain's "downcast" face. When Cain practices what is right, there will be an uplifted face, meaning a good conscience before God without shame.[270] Most versions offer the metaphorical sense "accepted," referring to Cain and his offering (e.g., Vg; NIV, AV, RSV, NRSV). It is best to take the expression "lifting up" as figurative referring to the uplifted face, indicating acceptance from God that comes with a pure heart.

The Lord forewarned Cain that right action would be rewarded but a wrong course meant giving sin an opportunity to destroy him (v. 7a). The rhetorical question put to Cain has the same purpose as the exhortation of the later prophets: "Learn to do right!" (Isa 1:17; cf. Amos 5:14). The rationale of the Lord's question assumes a correspondence between doing "what is right" and receiving divine approval, but the very tenor of the question shows that Cain was not doing "what is right." What is more important here for Cain, however, is what action he will take now that his sin has been found out (v. 7b). The consequences of his reaction to God's correction are more far-reaching than the initial sin itself, for if he pursues sin's anger, it will result in sin's mastery over him. This is his decision. It is possible for Cain to recover from sin quickly if he chooses the right thing.

Here we come to another interpretive obstacle in the verse, how to understand sin as "crouching" and what is meant by "door."[271] "Sin" is likened to an animal "crouching" or "lurking" (NRSV) at the "door," meaning the animal's resting place, ready to stir if incited. "Crouch" (*rābaṣ*) is commonly used of domesticated animals in repose (i.e., 29:2; 49:9; Exod 23:5), including wild animals such as the lion (Gen 49:9). This pictures sin temporarily at bay and subject to its master but coming alive when stirred. Some commentators have compared the Hebrew *rōbēṣ* ("crouch") to the cognate Akkadian term *rābiṣum*, a mythological demon attending the doorways of buildings to guard its inhabitants or conversely to threaten them.[272] The REB thus reads, "Sin is a demon crouching at the door." If there is an allusion to the door demon, then the narrative is personifying sin as a demonic spirit ready to pounce on Cain once he opens the "door" of opportunity. This may well correspond with the

---

[270] Cf. Job 10:15; 11:15; 2 Sam 2:22. The Levitical benediction invokes the approval of God by his uplifted countenance (Num 6:26).

[271] Complicating this is a grammatical incongruity: where Hebrew customarily has gender correspondence, "sin" (חַטָּאת, feminine) disagrees with "crouching" (רֹבֵץ, masculine) as well as the masculine pronouns "its desire" (תְּשׁוּקָתוֹ) and "in it" (בּוֹ). Since it is a predicate, we would expect the feminine form of the participle since its subject "sin" is feminine. A common emendation is based on a haplography of ת, thus לַפֶּתַח חַטָּאת תִּרְבַּץ, "sin lies at the door." Without emendation perhaps רֹבֵץ is a substantive, meaning "lurker, croucher" (GKC § 145u): "Sin is a lurker at the door."

[272] E.g., Speiser, *Genesis,* 33, and Wenham, *Genesis 1–15,* 106. Westermann (*Genesis 1–11,* 299–300) agrees on a connection with *rābiṣum* but offers that the demon is the ghost of Abel, not the personification of sin.

"seed" of the serpent in 3:15, which will do battle with the "seed" of the woman Eve. The imagery is effectively the same and the message clear: sin can be stirred up by wrong choices.

The Lord instructed Cain that though sin "desires" him he can still "master" it (4:7b). This language is a lexical allusion to the judgment oracle against the woman (3:16b), reminding Cain of the earlier consequences of sin's realization.[273] By this divine analysis we learn that sin has a pervasive power that seizes occasion to enslave its victims (cp. Rom 3:9; 1 Cor 15:56; 1 John 5:19). But Cain is urged to repent lest he be consumed; he cannot claim helplessness nor ignorance, for he has divine counsel. The apostle Paul testified to the inner struggle against the power of sin and conceded that the power of Christ alone could liberate him (Rom 7:15–25). Cain's refusal to deal rightly with his sin permitted his anger to fester into murder.[274]

(3) Cain's Murder of Abel (4:8–16)

8Now Cain said to his brother Abel, "Let's go out to the field." And while they were in the field, Cain attacked his brother Abel and killed him.

9Then the LORD said to Cain, "Where is your brother Abel?"

"I don't know," he replied. "Am I my brother's keeper?"

10The LORD said, "What have you done? Listen! Your brother's blood cries out to me from the ground. 11Now you are under a curse and driven from the ground, which opened its mouth to receive your brother's blood from your hand. 12When you work the ground, it will no longer yield its crops for you. You will be a restless wanderer on the earth."

13Cain said to the LORD, "My punishment is more than I can bear. 14Today you are driving me from the land, and I will be hidden from your presence; I will be a restless wanderer on the earth, and whoever finds me will kill me."

15But the LORD said to him, "Not so; if anyone kills Cain, he will suffer vengeance seven times over." Then the LORD put a mark on Cain so that no one who found him would kill him. 16So Cain went out from the LORD's presence and lived in the land of Nod, east of Eden.

This second half of the Cain-Abel narrative turns on the disastrous deed of Abel's murder (v. 8). It is followed by the Lord's interrogation of Cain, the culprit's evasive response, and the judgment of "curse" mitigated by divine mercy (vv. 9–15a). It closes with Cain's expulsion "from the LORD's presence" (vv. 15b–16). The section brings the Cain-Abel narrative full circle but with surprising results. Cain's birth is by the agency of the Lord, and he is a tiller of the soil (vv. 1–2a); but by the end Cain is driven from the Lord's presence and must live apart from the land. He is no longer a farmer enjoying sanctuary, but

---

[273] So Ross, *Creation and Blessing: A Guide to the Study and Exposition of the Book of Genesis* (Grand Rapids: Baker, 1988), 158–59.

[274] Cf. Prov 27:4; Eccl 7:9; Eph 4:26,31; Jas 1:15.

now he is a city-builder ostracized from the land of his birthright (v. 17).

Three recurring words of the section encapsulate what this passage concerns: "brother" (vv. 8[2x],9[2x],10,11), "kill" (vv. 8,14,15), and "ground" (vv. 10,11,12). This chapter is about Cain, not Abel, for Abel is always described as Cain's brother ("his, your brother"). He has no standing other than what the Lord gives him. Moreover, Abel never speaks with God or anyone for that matter; it is only Cain and the Lord who dialogue. But what is at issue is Cain's responsibility for his "brother." His treatment of brother Abel is intrinsically related to his relationship with God and the divine disposition toward Adam's eldest. Cain exchanges that privilege for anger's expression by ambushing the weaker brother. But Cain discovers that as the instigator of the first killing he can be the object of the second and thus protests that he is precariously left without defense. The Lord intervenes by establishing a boundary protecting Cain so that no one exercises a personal vendetta against him. This is bound up with the significance of "ground" in 2:4–4:26, which is integral to understanding Cain's punishment.[275] Cain, as Adam, is a tiller of the "ground," but Cain exceeds the transgression of his father by profaning the ground with spilt blood. Thus the "ground" would no longer give its produce as it had for Adam, and Cain is forced to abandon it for a vagabond life. His destiny is found further "east" of Eden, removed that much more from the blessing of the Lord. Cain is the disowned son.

4:8 Now we come to the fulcrum of the Cain-Abel narrative, but again we come up against a dilemma for the interpreter. In the Hebrew text there is no dialogue where we expect it following the customary introduction to conversation, "Cain said *[wayyōʾmer]* to his brother Abel." The AV's translation "Cain told Abel" (also NASB) is unlikely from the Hebrew,[276] and it implies that the foregoing words of the Lord were reported to Abel, a position held by some commentators but which is inconsistent with Cain's disposition.[277] Ancient versions, followed by many English versions, supply "Let's go out to the field" (SP, LXX, Vg, Syr, *Tg. Neof., Tg. Ps-J.;* NIV, REB, NAB, NJB, NRSV).[278] In this reconstruction Cain lured Abel into the fields, where he assassinated him. This is reminiscent of crimes stipulated in the later Mosaic period that were punishable by death (Deut 19:11–12; 22:25–27).

Throughout chap. 4 change in speaker is marked by the expression "[he]

[275] See Spina, "The 'Ground' for Cain's Rejection (Gen 4)," for its importance for chaps. 1–11.

[276] דִּבֵּר is customary for "spoke, told," not the unusual אָמַר.

[277] Suggested parallels for such a construction in Gen 22:7; Exod 19:25; 2 Chr 2:11[10] are not the same since they contain the object of the speech in subsequent verses (see Sailhamer, "Genesis," 63–64).

[278] The NJPS has an ellipsis, indicating the textual gap. In the Palestinian targums there is a midrashic addition that relates the verbal dispute between the brothers concerning the goodness and justice of God.

said *(wayyō᾿mer)*" followed by dialogue (4:6,8–10,13,15). This argues that some textual problem has arisen in the Hebrew text at 4:8, which the early versions clearly are filling out. Commentators have recommended alternative meanings for the Hebrew term used or have made a variety of proposed emendations.[279] Others have explained the omission on literary grounds, noting that the abrupt account of the murder fits with the parallel brevity in 3:6 and reflects the haste of the author to get to the nefarious deed.[280]

This despicable act is underscored by the repeated phrase "Abel, *his brother*" (also vv. 9–11). Such rivalry is rehearsed time and again among the patriarchs: first with Ishmael, who lived in "hostility toward all his brothers" (16:12; 25:18); Esau's perpetual strife with Jacob, where repeatedly the narrative has the phrase "his brother" yet ends in peaceful separation (36:6); and Jacob's sons, who plot against "brother" Joseph, where again repeatedly "his brothers" is found, but gladly it concludes with a happier resolve (45:15). If the variant "Let's go out to the field" is correct, it makes Cain's action all the more repugnantly calculated and his disobedience all the more rabid.[281] Structurally, as we noted earlier, 4:8 parallels the morbid act of the first disobedience (3:6). The virus of sin has infected the parent's children; Adam and Eve do not have to await their own death to experience the devastating effects of their rebellion in the garden. They witness the murder of their youngest and the exile of their firstborn.

4:9 God's question "Where is your brother Abel?" echoes the inquiry put to Adam in the garden, "Where are you?" (3:9). Both acts of disobedience are thus tied together, indicating that Cain's murderous act had its antecedents in the sin of his father. Unlike his father, who admitted his crime (though reluctantly), Cain adds to his condemnation by lying. He attempts to elude the question and absolve himself of responsibility by his question, "Am I my brother's keeper?" Cain intends it as a rhetorical question requiring a negative reply, but the response from God discloses otherwise. Adam was appointed "keeper" *(šōmēr)* of the garden (2:15), but here the issue involves responsibility for

---

[279] Reading אָמַר (as MT) but from a different root are "to fix a meeting place" from an Arabic cognate (Cassuto, *Genesis,* 215); "to see, watch for" from Ug., Akk. cognates, "Qayin was watching for his brother Abel" (M. Dahood, "Hebrew-Ugaritic Lexicography I," *Bib* 44 (1963): 295–96; "Hebrew *tamrûrîm* and *tîmarôt,*" *Or* Ns 46 (1977): 385, n. 3; "Abraham's Reply in Genesis 20,11," *Bib* 61 [1981]: 90–91, and followed by Hamilton, *Genesis 1–17,* 229–30). Among emendations are וַשְׁמֹר, "and he watched out" (cp. v. 9); וַיֶּמֶר from מָרָה, "and he quarreled, began a struggle"; וַיֵּמַר from מָרַר, "and he was bitter" (see Westermann, *Genesis 1–11,* 302); and וַיֶּאֱרֹב, "and he laid wait" by Sailhamer ("Genesis," 64), who relates 4:8 to Deut 19:10–11 (cities of refuge), which textually shares lexical items and subject matter.

[280] E.g., Delitzsch, *A New Commentary on Genesis,* 183, and Wenham, *Genesis 1–15,* 106. Van Wolde, "The Story of Cain and Abel," 35,39 suggests that it signifies by "empty" speech that Abel, meaning "empty," is worthless in Cain's eyes, not to be looked upon nor talked to.

[281] So Kidner, *Genesis,* 75.

another human being. The definitive reply to Cain's question is found in the later Noahic covenant when the Lord formally sanctions retributive justice against murderers (9:5–6).

The Mosaic law would have given an affirmative answer to Cain's question. His crime would have been recognized as a particularly heinous violation of community solidarity, which was highly esteemed among the Hebrews. Community presupposed mutual responsibility that was foundational to covenant commitment (e.g., Lev 19:18; Gal 5:14). Even death did not obviate family obligations to a deceased family member (e.g., Num 35:19,21; Deut 25:5–10). Community responsibility took priority over individual preferences or rights. Kinship terms such as "brother" characterized those who entered into a mutual covenant agreement. "Brother" is used of fellow Israelites (e.g., Deut 1:16; 15:12) who are protected from exploitation of any kind (e.g., Lev 25:35–43; Deut 23:19); aliens who live within the community are treated as "native-born" (Lev 19:33–34). Human morality assumes an unstated covenant between persons that is grounded in the intrinsic *imago Dei* (9:5–6).[282] The Christian community followed the same pattern of solidarity as in Israel, including corporate guilt (e.g., 1 Cor 11:30; Gal 6:1–2). While individuality was not denied, individualism in the sense of an autonomous person having privilege in opposition to or at the expense of the familial group was not practiced. The church was spoken of and addressed as a collective body or a gathered people in union (e.g., 1 Pet 2:9–10). In describing the relationship of the individual to the whole, it was common to draw on metaphors of the body (e.g., Rom 12:3–8; Eph 4:12) where the particular entity is circumscribed by its contribution to the whole.

Cain abrogates this sacred obligation of kinship loyalty by the appalling crime of fratricide. Because Cain commits this "family scandal," he loses the protection of the family bond and thus fears for his life.[283] Fratricide was so repugnant to Reuben that he opposed his brothers and intervened in behalf of Joseph (37:21). This explains why special treatment was required of Israel toward groups whose family origins were connected with their own, such as Lot's descendants (Moabites and Ammonites, Deut 2:9) and Esau's offspring (Edomites, Deut 23:7). The violence promulgated by Cain and championed by

[282] T. C. Vriezen expresses the implications of covenant community: "The Old Testament might be called the most humanly minded book of the ancient world. . . . The relationship between man and man is dominated by the relationship between man and God . . . ; as Yahweh lives in a community with man, man is also linked with his fellow-man by *chesed* (faithfulness). Men linked together by Yahweh are brothers. Israel is a community of brothers. . . . Within this community men must help each other as much as lies in their power. . . . The background of the words 'faithfulness,' 'righteousness' and 'justice,' without which the Israelite community cannot exist, is the idea of the Covenant" (*An Outline of Old Testament Theology* [Newton, Mass.: Charles T. Branford, 1970], 388).

[283] R. B. Robinson, "Literary Functions of the Genealogies of Genesis," *CBQ* 28 (1986): 602.

Lamech reaches its peak in the days of Noah when God exercises vengeance by the unprecedented destruction of all human society (6:7).

4:10 The second question, "What have you done?" is reminiscent of 3:13 where the Lord asks the same of the woman. As in a criminal trial, God presents condemning testimony against Cain: "your brother's blood" refutes Cain's protestations. Our passage depicts Abel's postmortem call for vindication by this eerie personification: "The *voice* of your brother's blood cries out." Adam also hears the "voice" ("sound") of God and is called to account for his actions (3:8). The source of the disquieting cry is the "ground" that is cursed because of Adam's sin (3:17) and is now polluted by the spilling of innocent blood. Later Israel was forewarned that murder defiled its land, and for such crimes there was no exoneration for the nation except through retribution against the malefactor (e.g., Num 35:33; cf. Gen 9:5). Collective guilt required just and prompt action by the community against the culprit.[284] When a murder victim was found in the open field and the crime could not be solved, the community still made atonement by ritual involving a heifer "so you will purge from yourselves the guilt of shedding innocent blood" (Deut 21:1–9).

Ironically, though Abel never talks in Genesis, his testimony of faith continues to speak, and his voice cries out for revenge against the unrighteous who oppose God's work among the saints (Heb 11:4). Although it is Abel's blood that convicts the sinner, it is the blood of Christ that makes adequate reparations for the sins of the unrighteous, offering forgiveness and not vengeance, speaking a better word (Heb 12:24).

4:11–12 Like the serpent, Cain is placed under a curse; this is the first occasion in Scripture where a human is cursed. This curse indicates the gravity of his crime against God and creation. Cain's culpability is emphasized by the direct accusation "from your [own] hand." The language "you are under a curse" is the same as the oracle delivered against the serpent: "Cursed are you above *[min]* all the livestock" (3:14) is parallel to "cursed are you from *[min]* the ground" (4:11). This linkage shows that like father like "seed," both the serpent and Cain are murderers who receive the same retribution. Because Cain has polluted the ground with innocent blood, he is "driven" from it as his parents were from the garden (3:24).

As a fitting punishment Cain the farmer no longer enjoys the fruit of the ground and is thus by necessity consigned to live as a vagrant.[285] This is a significant departure from God's punishment against Adam; while made difficult

---

[284] E.g., Lev 24:14–16; Num 35:12; Deut 19:13; Josh 7:25. Covenant-law provided for family retaliation against a murderer through the "blood-avenger" (גֹּאֵל הַדָּם), who executed the criminal with societal approval, but for an accidental killing, special societal protections placed limits on the blood-avenger (e.g., Num 35:6–28; Deut 19:1–14; Josh 20:1–9; 2 Sam 14:11).

[285] The NIV's "restless wanderer" translates the rhyming Heb. phrase נָע וָנָד ("wandering and aimless") as a hendiadys.

by the curse, the Lord preserves Adam's agricultural life (3:18–19). But here, by the failure of the land to respond to Cain's cultivation, his sentencing of perpetual exile is much more severe, which explains Cain's complaint. For later Israel a household's tract of land signified its covenant union with God, for the Lord as owner had generously bequeathed it to Israel as his tenants (e.g., Lev 14:34; 25:23; Deut 32:49). Because God owned and occupied the land among his people, it was declared holy in covenant-law, requiring ceremonial provisions; a dead body must be buried by nightfall lest its corpse offend God and defile the land (Deut 21:23). Abel's corpse is left rotting in the open field. Cain's expulsion from the tainted land has its later parallel in Israel's experience of exile as the just deserts for choosing to live immorally (e.g., Lev 18:24–28; 26:33–35; Deut 28:64). Moses' Israel was consigned to a life of wandering because of disobedience at Kadesh (Num 14; Deut 2:14–15). But unlike Cain's family, the subsequent generation emerged from the desert and possessed Canaan (Deut 32:10). Nevertheless the threat of expulsion remained for later Israel all its days, and the desert memory haunted them; for the Mosaic community and generations to come, early Genesis depicted what awaited those who transgressed covenant.

4:13–14 Does Cain lament his condition, or does he ask for forgiveness (v. 13)? Early versions have, "My guilt is too great to forgive" (LXX, *Tg. Onq.*, Vg), which is also followed by Luther and some modern commentators.[286] In this case Cain is expressing remorse over his sin and requesting God's forgiveness. Rabbinic interpretation took the verse in this way but as a question, "Is my guilt too great to be forgiven?" (*b. Sanh.* 101b). This idea of "forgive" reads the opposite of the sense found in most English versions. The problem is the meaning of the two words: Hebrew *ʿăwōnî* may be translated "my iniquity" or "my punishment," and *nāśāʾ* likewise is ambiguous, meaning "forgiveness" or "bear."

The sense of bearing away sins (forgiveness) is found when these terms occur together (e.g., Exod 34:7; Ps 85:2[3]; Isa 33:24), but the expression can also refer to the punishment for those sins (e.g., Exod 28:43; Num 5:31; 14:34–35). In Lev 20:19 "bear their iniquity" (AV) is sufficient alone to indicate "punishment," which is otherwise cited specifically in 20:17–18,20. "Iniquity" and its "punishment" are both indicated by the one term, so the context determines which is in view.[287] The context of v. 14 is more in keeping with complaint than request. Cain protests that his penalty is too harsh; he argues that isolation from God's protective presence effectively results in a death sentence. "Under the weight of this curse, Cain goes to pieces, though not in remorse."[288] There is a decided difference between his response to God's decree and that of Adam (cp. 3:20). Cain

[286] The LXX reads μείζων ἡ αἰτία μου τοῦ ἀφεθῆναί με. *LW* 1.295–98; Cassuto, *Genesis,* 222; and Sailhamer, "Genesis," 65–66.

[287] See B. K. Waltke, "*ʿāwōn,*" *TWOT* 2. 650–51.

[288] von Rad, *Genesis,* 107.

expresses no inkling of remorse, only self-pity and resentment. That Cain does not receive divine forgiveness is shown by his expulsion "from the LORD's presence" (v. 16).

Cain's complaint ("you are driving me") repeats the description in 3:24, where God "drove" (the same verb, *gāraš*) his parents out of the garden, but Cain adds that he will be left to himself and forgotten by God ("hidden"; cf. the psalmist's tormenting fear of lonely abandonment by God in Pss 13:1[2]; 22:1,24[2,25]). Cain's fear for his life presupposes the expansion of civilization over the course of his long life during which there will be many opportunities for retribution by a blood-avenger (e.g., Seth lives 912 years, 5:8). Without God's protection he is left to his own devices to survive. But despite his deserved expulsion, the Lord does not leave him helpless.

4:15–16 How does God respond to Cain's complaint? The Hebrew MT, followed by the AV (also NASB), has "therefore" ("very well," NJB),[289] indicating that God concedes to Cain's objection that his punishment is too severe (vv. 13–14). Thus the Lord promises in a formal declaration to preserve his life.[290] Other versions have the negative "Not so!" which reads with the LXX tradition (Syr, Vg; NIV, NRSV, REB, NAB);[291] thus the Lord's response is a corrective to Cain's fearful outburst, not the expulsion.[292] This makes better sense in the passage because earlier God also corrects Cain (4:6–7,10), and his expulsion "from the presence of the LORD" (v. 16) shows that the sentence is not mitigated. Nothing more than the original sentence (banishment)will occur. To insure this and to diminish Cain's fears, he safeguards the impenitent Cain as though he were his kinsman or protector *(gōʾēl)*.[293] This provision is twofold: (1) God warns that Cain's murder will be avenged seven times over (v. 15a), and (2) he marks Cain with a protective sign (v. 15b).

"Vengeance" *(nāqam)* usually speaks of divine retribution against the Lord's enemies or those of his people (e.g., Deut 32:35,43), though it may describe retaliation by civil authority (e.g., Exod 21:20). Covenant law prohibited personal revenge (Lev 19:18). Reprisal is God's business. Individuals, in exceptional cases, were commissioned to carry out divine sanctions (2 Kgs 9:7). "If anyone kills" (literally, "anyone killing") is forensic language found in the Mosaic law (e.g., Exod 22:19[18], literally, "anyone lying"). "Kills" *(hārag)* frequently describes private violence or warfare. Although it may concern divine judgment (e.g., 20:4; Amos 4:10), it is seldom used for judicial execution with God's authority.[294] Its recurrence five times in chap. 4 under-

[289] לָכֵן. So BDB, 486–87.
[290] E.g., NJPS reads "I promise" for לָכֵן. See Sarna, *Genesis,* 35,355.
[291] The LXX's οὐχ οὕτως reflects לֹא כֵן, "not so."
[292] Westermann, *Genesis 1–11,* 311.
[293] Observed by Kidner, *Genesis,* 76.
[294] BDB, 247.

scores the violence Cain has introduced to the human family (vv. 8,14–15,23,25). "Seven" as a figure of speech meaning completeness or fullness expresses the certainty and severity of God's vengeance against a vigilante. This incident probably motivated Peter's thought when he quizzed Jesus about forgiving "my brother" seven times. Jesus' unexpected response of "seventy-seven times" punctured the contemporary notion (*b. Yoma* 86b, 87a) that three times were all that was required (Matt 18:21–22).[295]

This "mark of Cain," as it is popularly known, has proven to be a seedbed for confusion (v. 15b). "Mark" is the common word for "sign" *(ʾōt);* the exact nature of the sign or its place on the body ("on Cain") is unknown. One Jewish tradition pointed to Cain himself as the "sign" who served to admonish others to repentance (*Gen. Rab.* 22.12). In effect this has become true for later generations, if not his own, for Cain the man has become a token of sin's fruit and divine retribution (1 John 3:12; Jude 11). Although "sign" is used figuratively in several passages (e.g., Exod 13:9; Deut 6:8; 11:18), the only parallel is Ezek 9:4, where certain men receive a mark on the forehead. But even there it is in an extended vision in which it only has symbolic force. What is important here is its purpose: "so that no one who found him would kill him" (v. 15). "Mark" in our passage is not a sign of the "curse"; in fact, it assures Cain's safety rather than acts as a reproach. The mark in Ezekiel's vision had the same effect; it distinguished those who bore the brand and gave them protection.

Why does God preserve the life of this murderer? This is particularly perplexing since Torah requires capital punishment for murder. No substitute for this crime, such as monetary penalty, was acceptable (e.g., Num 35:32). Perhaps the answer is that by the "sign" God prevents the spread of bloodshed that otherwise would escalate. Moreover, God is declaring that life and death are his prerogative, which he does not share with anyone except by divine sanction (cp. 9:5–6). God's judgment against the culprit is restrained by his grace. His promise of procreation is not thwarted even by human murder (1:28; 3:15,20).

Cain will live outside "the LORD's presence," which is another narrative reminder of Adam's crime and penalty (3:22). This same expression also describes Jonah, who fled the Lord's presence (Jonah 1:3,10). In the Mosaic community "the LORD's presence" often referred to the sacred tabernacle (e.g., Lev 9:24; 22:3; Num 20:9; 1 Sam 21:7). Routinely, the garden *tōlĕdōt* (2:4–4:26) has employed the same language and imagery associated with the tabernacle. Here the setting is reminiscent of biblical excommunication, requiring death (e.g., Exod 31:14; Lev 18:29) or quarantine (e.g., Lev 13:46; 15:31). Cain's residing in "the land of Nod, east of Eden," implies that he is further removed from the garden than Adam. "Nod" is a play on the word *nād,* meaning "wanderer," which refers to the sentence against Cain in 4:11–12,14. Scrip-

[295] See C. Blomberg, *Matthew,* NAC (Nashville: Broadman, 1992), 281.

ture does not speak again of "Nod," and no specific locale is known. It may be that Nod is simply meant to say that wherever Cain sojourned could be called the "land of the Wanderer."

(4) Cain's Family (4:17–24)

[17]Cain lay with his wife, and she became pregnant and gave birth to Enoch.
Cain was then building a city, and he named it after his son Enoch. [18]To Enoch
was born Irad, and Irad was the father of Mehujael, and Mehujael was the father of Methushael, and Methushael was the father of Lamech.

[19]Lamech married two women, one named Adah and the other Zillah. [20]Adah
gave birth to Jabal; he was the father of those who live in tents and raise live-
stock. [21]His brother's name was Jubal; he was the father of all who play the harp
and flute. [22]Zillah also had a son, Tubal-Cain, who forged all kinds of tools out of bronze and iron. Tubal-Cain's sister was Naamah.

[23]Lamech said to his wives,
"Adah and Zillah, listen to me;
wives of Lamech, hear my words.
I have killed a man for wounding me,
a young man for injuring me.
[24]If Cain is avenged seven times,
then Lamech seventy-seven times."

By tracing the lineage of Cain immediately following God's promise (vv. 15–16), the mercy and faithfulness of the Lord are aptly demonstrated. Cain survives and founds an impressive posterity. But lest we forget the evil character of Adam's firstborn, his progeny will also testify to the villainy of Cain. This contrasts with the following lineage of Seth, which is presented twice—an abbreviated form (vv. 25–26) and its fuller, formal presentation (chap. 5). In both cases the righteous conduct of the appointed line versus that of Cain's family is accentuated. Whereas Cain's progeny founded the civilized arts, Seth's era is remembered as the time mankind worshiped the Lord (v. 26b). Also chaps. 4 and 5 intentionally contrast the parade examples of each lineage: Lamech, the polygamist and murderer, versus righteous Enoch, who walked with God (5:22).

Cain's genealogy entails an irony that speaks to the personality of this family tree. Genealogies are designed to celebrate life and accomplishment by tracing the continuation of family from one ancestor to the next, but Cain's record involves the cessation of life, as represented by the murderers Cain and Lamech.[296] Whereas Seth's genealogy shows the orderly progress of creation through procreation and the succession of the "image" (5:1b–3), Cain's

[296] So Robinson, "Literary Functions of the Genealogies of Genesis," 600, n. 8.

descendants contradict the order given to creation and history. What has disrupted this orderly progression? As the garden story of Adam and Eve showed, Cain's family likewise attests incipient human sin.

Although the genealogy succeeds in demonstrating how sin disqualified Cain's household as the lineage of blessing, it shows conversely that God's promise of preservation for Cain was honored (vv. 15–16). Generously, the Lord grants even the wicked Cainites the power of propagation, and therefore they too share (partially) in the blessing of all those who bear the "image" of God (1:26–28). This mitigating grace typifies God's dealing with the excluded lineage both in early humanity (e.g., Japheth and Ham's families, chap. 10) and the subsequent history of the patriarchal families (e.g., Ishmael and Esau). It will be left to the Sethite lineage to perpetuate the blessing through Adam's thirdborn (chap. 5).[297]

Another evidence of God's grace may well be the advancements that the Cainite family achieve in the development of three aspects of civilization: animal breeding, music, and metallurgy. Even these elements of human experience, while truly mortal, owe themselves ultimately to Israel's God, who enables human life to discover and "rule" the earth (1:28).[298] Yet just as the blessing of progeny by Cain is shadowed by Abel's murder and the antics of Lamech, the blessing of the learned arts is sullied by the embarrassment of Lamech's polygamy and the weaponry developed by his son Tubal-Cain, who also bears the name of his infamous ancestor.

Beginning with Cain, the lineage consists of ten members (including Naamah) and seven generations (vv. 17–18). It is *linear* in construction, where one descendant alone is named to represent each successive generation. The lineage concludes with the offspring of Lamech, whose four children are presented in a *segmented* form of genealogy (vv. 19–22). Segmented genealogies include more than one descendant and create a family "tree" by branching (e.g., the Table of Nations, chap. 10). This formal presentation of Cain's ancestry is followed by the lyrical "Song of the Sword," as it is sometimes identified (vv. 23–24), in which the descendant Lamech revels in his heinous deeds and intimidates any challengers.

Both form and content in Cain's lineage attract a comparison between his descendants and chap. 5's line of Seth (see following chart). Cain and Seth's lines have identical names twice and several similar-sounding names, and both genealogies are linear, concluding with a segmented branching that gives three

[297] This reversal of the custom of primogeniture becomes a thematic essential in Genesis, especially the patriarchal accounts (Isaac and Ishmael, Jacob and Esau, Ephraim and Manasseh).

[298] Westermann, while taking the passage as a more positive statement on the beginnings of civilization than we have conceded, rightly observes that human discovery is the "blessing God bestows on his creatures" (*Genesis 1–11,* 343).

sons. Also the order of several of the names are close.[299] Moreover, there is the repetition of the names and sequence Adam-Seth-Enosh, which concludes chap. 4 and begins chap. 5, suggesting the same source of information. Some scholars consequently have argued that the two genealogies evidence two parallel literary traditions, both derived from the same, original source.[300]

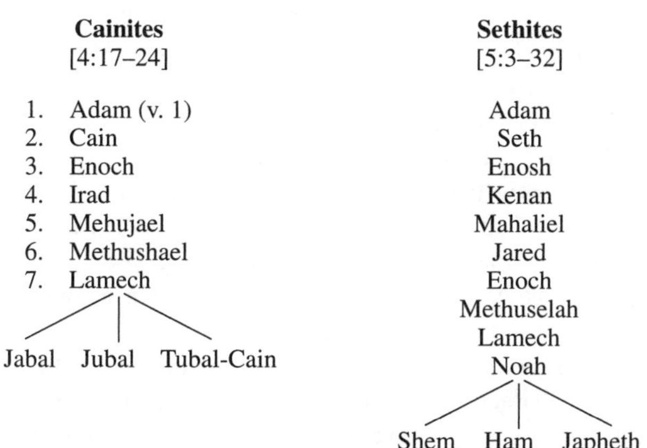

Although their similarities seem to argue for dependency, there are significant distinctions between the two genealogies that manifest originally different sources. Of the names in the lists, only two are actually the same spelling (Enoch and Lamech, excluding Adam). The genealogies show different numbers and sequences of names. More important, however, are those divergences that cannot be attributed to confusion or fluidity between two lists.[301] Chapter 4 does not exhibit knowledge of the flood and stops short of the parade descendant of Adam's line, "Noah." Absent in chap. 5 are the segmented genealogy

[299] "Enoch" and "Lamech" are the same. "Cain/Kenan," "Mehalalel"/"Mehujael," "Irad"/ "Jared," and "Methushael"/"Methuselah" are similar. The names "Enoch, Irad, and Mehujael" (chap. 4) are in reverse order in chap. 5: "Mahalalel, Jared, Enoch." Gen 11:10–26 follows the same pattern, where its linear form ends in a branching of Terah's three sons. In the case of Cain's lineage the segmented branch includes a daughter's name by Lamech ("Naamah").

[300] E.g., Speiser, *Genesis,* 36. Cain's lineage in 4:17–26 is attributed to the J tradition, while Seth's line in chap. 5 is the work of P, but in this view both are dependent on a common source. A variation on this is that P took up the traditions found in J and created a ten-name sequence in chap. 5 (see Westermann, *Genesis 1–11,* 349).

[301] D. T. Bryan contends that the similarities and dissimilarities of the two lists can be attributed to a common feature observed in ancient genealogies and king lists, fluidity in names and order ("A Reevaluation of Gen 4 and 5 in Light of Recent Studies in Genealogical Fluidity," *ZAW* 99 [1987]: 180–88). E.g., the Genealogy of the Hammurapi Dynasty, which duplicates eleven of seventeen names from the earliest kings in the Assyrian King List. See J. J. Finkelstein, "The Genealogy of the Hammurapi Dynasty," *JCS* 20 (1966): 95–118, and Wilson, *Genealogy and History,* 107–14.

of names after Lamech and the woman "Naamah." Also the biographical information clearly distinguishes the "Enoch" and "Lamech" of Seth from that of Cain. Additionally chap. 4 does not use the stereotypical language of Seth's family record in chap. 5, especially the important feature of the patriarchs' ages. Also Seth's genealogy is anchored in the setting of creation (cf. 5:1–3), while the background for Cain's genealogy is the garden expulsion.[302] It is best to explain chaps. 4 and 5 as two independent accounts.

We have seen that the juxtaposition of the two lists in chaps. 4 and 5 attracts a comparison of the two lines of Cain and Seth. When we include Adam as the head of Cain's line (v. 1), "Lamech" occupies the seventh position.[303] Correspondingly, "Enoch" holds the honored position of seventh in the Sethite parentage.[304] Structurally the two genealogies provide a striking contrast by highlighting Lamech and Enoch, and they elaborate on the careers of these two commanding figures. Lamech is a transitional figure who closes out the Cain line and initiates his own genealogy, boasting of his own accomplishments and indelibly marking his heritage by perpetuating the infamous name "Cain" (Tubal-Cain). The rhetorical-theological effect of this parallel is to call attention to the moral character of each line of descent. Lamech is the epitome of Cain's corrupt family. As the seventh name in the genealogy, the number for completeness, Lamech's notorious career attests to the peculiarly wicked life of the Cainites. Chapter 5 shows that Adam was also survived by a righteous line of descendants (Seth) through whom God would choose to preserve and bless the earth's inhabitants (i.e., Seth-Noah).

The advent of urban life with the emergence of Cain's wicked progeny served as a warning against building cities independently of God. Noah's later descendants constructed such a city and its tower (11:1–9) in defiance of God's injunction to settle throughout the world (9:1,7). It was only after God's intervention that the nations "scattered" by necessity (9:19; 11:9; cf. 10:32). Both Cain's antediluvian lineage and the postdiluvian Babel cautioned later Israel

---

[302] Another evidence is the Sumerian King List (ca. 2000 B.C.), which possesses two sets of similar names in which the seven antediluvian *apkallū,* i.e., Mesopotamian mythic sages, are teamed up with their corresponding seven antediluvian kings. Both lists are taken from different sources and had originally different functions. See Hess, "The Genealogies of Genesis 1–11 and Comparative Literature," *Bib* 70 (1989): 246–47 and nn. 19–20.

[303] The wording of 4:17 and 4:1 are near exact: "And PN_1 knew his wife [Eve] and she conceived and bore PN_2" (4:1 has the *waw* disjunctive + perfect versus the preterite form וַיֵּדַע in v. 17). Thus we are to understand Adam as head of the Cainite lineage, although the relationship between Cain and Adam recedes due to the intervening narrative (vv. 3–16).

[304] It is too much to say that there is a *fixed* genealogical convention at work here, but J. Sasson has shown, joining the longstanding tradition of the rabbis, the propensity of the biblical genealogies to give priority to those names whose position occurs as seventh or a multiple of seven ("Generation, Seventh," *IDBSup,* 354–56; "A Genealogical 'Convention' in Biblical Chronology?" *ZAW* 90 [1978]: 171–85).

that cities founded upon arrogance resulted in violence and ultimately destruction. The Israelites of Moses' day faced the ominous cities of the Canaanites with their developed but oppressive culture (e.g., Num 13:26–33; Deut 7:1–6; 20:1–20). These Hebrew descendants of slaves, born and reared in the desert, were admonished by specific injunction (e.g., Deut 7:7–16) to avoid the allurement of Canaan's cultural strongholds. Cities with their highly dense populations are commonly reputed to behave wickedly (as Sodom and Gomorrah). Yet God does not abandon Canaan's cities to evil. He transforms such cities by populating them with his own people. This was the hope of conquest under Joshua, and for the Christian church it is accomplished through the preaching of the gospel (e.g., Matt 9:35). Although the first city was built by evil Cain, the final estate of the redeemed is described in terms of God's city, the "Holy City, the new Jerusalem" (Rev 21:2).

Excursus: The Origin of Civilization in Ane Mythology

Cain built the first city (v. 17), and Lamech's sons contributed to the development of civilized life founded among the earliest cities. The Sumerian flood story (ca. 1600 B.C.) attributes the founding of cities and kingship to the intervention of the mother goddess Nintur for the protection of humanity.[305] In an apology for Sumerian kingship, the story depicts early man suffering primitive living conditions before the rise of kingship, which initiates cultural progress. Genesis does not take such a positive attitude toward the rise of civilization.

In Mesopotamian tradition the arts and sciences were attributed to the seven antediluvian *apkallū* (fish-men) who were mythic sages that advised humanity in how to develop cultural and scientific advances. In one text the names of the seven antediluvian *apkallū* are correlated with the names of the kings. This feature of relating the name of a sage with the contemporary king has been likened to the parallel between the genealogies in chaps. 4 and 5, the list of Cain (i.e., sages) and that of Adam (i.e., kings).[306]

Other ancient Near Eastern traditions also attributed the various aspects of civilization to sages and deities. Striking similarities exist between Mesopotamian and Phoenician traditions and the Cainite genealogy, including the origins of city building and worship.[307] There is no evidence, however, that the biblical

---

[305] For translations and discussion see *ANET*, 42–44; M. Civil, "The Sumerian Flood Story," in *Atra-ḫasīs: The Babylonian Story of the Flood* (Oxford: Clarendon, 1969), 138–47; and T. Jacobsen, "The Eridu Genesis," *JBL* 100 (1981): 513–29.

[306] E.g., Finkelstein, "The Antediluvian Kings," *JCS* 17 (1963) 39–51; W. W. Hallo, "Antediluvian Cities," *JCS* 23 (1971): 57–67.

[307] Wilson notes these: (1) both speak of seven ancestors before the flood who founded the arts and sciences; (2) both place the development of culture in this period along with the founding of worship; (3) the first *apkallū* is connected with the earliest city, according to Mesopotamian tradition, namely, Eridu; this is associated with Cain's descendant Irad for whom the first city was named (cf. v. 17b for discussion); and (d) Phoenician and biblical traditions deal with the same aspects of civilization and couch them in terms of a genealogy (*Genealogy and History*, 154).

writer depended on the Mesopotamian story. If indeed he had knowledge of it, the Genesis account ignores, if not opposes, the pagan notion that civilization derived its highest achievements by divine knowledge. Setting their origins among the wicked Cainite clan would only have brought suspicion toward them, not commendation. Rather, Genesis shows cultural achievements to be solely human inventions in the circle of history, though certainly permitted by God in accord with the charge to subdue the earth (1:28).

4:17–18 The birth of Cain's son is reported in language similar to the account of his own conception and birth (v. 1), except that Cain's wife is not named.[308] We must assume that Cain's wife was one of Adam's "other daughters" (5:4). Later, sibling marriage was unnecessary, and it was soundly denounced in Mosaic tradition (e.g., Lev 18:9).

We have commented that the members of Cain's genealogy are remembered for their cultural advancements, including the building of cities. The NIV's rendering, "*Cain* was then building a city" (also NAB, REB), identifies Cain as the first builder (v. 17b). The Hebrew construction "he was building," however, is ambiguous, permitting Cain or Enoch as the subject. Since the name of the city is "Enoch" (v. 17b), the traditional rendering has attributed the building of the first city to Cain, who names it after his firstborn. If this reading is followed, Cain's action is in direct violation to the injunction of God that has restricted him to the life of a vagabond. However, there are two alternative understandings: (1) although Cain built the city, it is for Enoch to inhabit; or (2) as mentioned, the subject of the verb may be taken as "Enoch," who would then be the first builder. The advantage of this latter interpretation is that "Enoch" is the nearer antecedent for the subject of the verb ("was building," v. 17b).[309] But if Enoch is the builder, the city's name "Enoch" is problematic. To surmount this problem emendations have been suggested, including the excising of "Enoch" at the end of the verse as a secondary gloss.[310] There is, however, no textual warrant for such emendations, and the Hebrew is not so

[308] Verse 25 is also very close to v. 17, thus relating the Sethite line to Cain by virtue of the same father, Adam. On this see Wilson, *Genealogy and History,* 139, 157.

[309] Cassuto, e.g., argues that the construction at 4:2 provides the analogy for reading Enoch as the subject (*Genesis,* 229–31). Eve's children are named (4:1–2a), and then their vocations are cited by a participle (v. 2b). The same pattern explains 4:17. Enoch is meant as the builder, and the participle indicates his lifelong occupation as a city builder. If so, the city was named after Enoch's son, "Irad." The sound plays of *bōneh* ("was building") and *ʿîr* ("city") with *bĕnô* ("his son") and *ʿîrad* ("Irad") further suggest this.

[310] E.g., Wenham views "Enoch" as a secondary copyist's error (*Genesis 1–15,* 111). Westermann, following others, argues that Enoch built the city and named it after himself (*Genesis 1–11,* 327). He reads כִּשְׁמוֹ ("after his own name") for כְּשֵׁם בְּנוֹ ("after his son's name"): "He [Enoch] called it Enoch after his own name" (p. 322). Some OT cities are named after their builders, indicating relationship or ownership (e.g., Deut 3:14; 2 Sam 5:9; 12:28; see Hamilton, *Genesis 1–17,* 237, n. 5).

difficult as to require it. Moreover, Cain's disobedience in this matter is consistent with what we know of his previous behavior.

The etymology of *Enoch* probably is related to Hebrew *ḥānak*, "train up, dedicate," or West Semitic *ḥnk,* meaning "introduce, initiate." Those who interpret Enoch as the first builder understand the name "Enoch" as derived from "dedicator" or "founder" of cities.[311] Alternatively, since we take Cain as the builder, Cain "dedicated" his city to his son "Enoch," after whom he names it. "Enoch" not only is the name of the famous figure in Seth's lineage (5:18–24) but also the name ("Hanoch," NIV) of a grandson of Abraham (25:4) and a grandson of Jacob (46:9).

Verse 18 recounts four successive descendants: *Irad, Mehujael, Methushael,* and *Lamech.*[312] Nothing is said of the initial three other than their names.[313] The attention of the account turns to the infamous Lamech, who holds center stage for the author.

4:19–22 Lamech is the seventh from Adam in his genealogy, and his children, who instigate major advances in urban life, are listed in the seventh position from Cain. The first alarming evidence of Lamech's moral decline is his inauguration of polygamy, a dismal departure from the divine norm (2:23–24). Although Genesis does not condemn the patriarchs for their practice of polygamy, it is transparent from Genesis itself that such practices resulted in painful consequences. In Mosaic legislation it was assumed that polygamy produced troubling home life (Deut 21:15–17).

Lamech's wives (having the names of a rhyming couplet, *Adah* and *Zillah*) appear in both the narrative and the "Song of the Sword," for which they are

---

[311] E.g., Cassuto, *Genesis,* 229, and Westermann, *Genesis 1–11,* 327. See the discussion of Hess, "Enoch," *ABD* 2.508.

[312] We have already mentioned the associative pattern of Cain, Enoch, and Seth's births (4:1,17,25). Two different formulae occur here: (1) the niphal preterite of יָלַד (וַיִּוָּלֵד) for the birthing of Irad (cf. 10:1) and (2) the repetition of the pattern "and PN_1 bore (יָלַד) PN_2" for the last three (cf. 10:8,13,15,24x,26); v. 22 has the same pattern but with the feminine verb for "Zillah," and "Adah" has the preterite construction (v. 20). Still another pattern using the qal passive (יֻלַּד) occurs in 4:26 for the birth of Seth's son Enosh (cf. also 6:1; 10:21,25). Chaps. 5 and 11, however, regularly exhibit the use of the hiphil of יָלַד (6:10 also), distinguishing the Sethite and Shemite genealogies formally from the others (see discussion there).

[313] Little can be learned with confidence from the meaning of their names. "Irad" has been related to Semitic *ʿrd*, meaning "wild ass, onager," or Arabic for "cane huts." "Mehujael" and "Methushael" have the theophoric element *ʾēl* ("El," God). "Mehujael" has the variant "Mehiyyael" in the Hebrew, occurring side by side in our verse (מְחוּיָאֵל and מְחִיָּיאֵל); some suggested meanings are "ecstatic of God," "God has smitten," and "God gives life." "Methushael," beginning with the element *mūtu* ("person"), is widely recognized as "man of God." Other recommendations are "man of request (prayer?)" and "man of Sheol" (see Hess, "A Comparison of the Onomastica in Genealogical and Narrative Texts of Genesis 1–11," 72; "Irad," *ABD* 3.448–49; "Mehujael," *ABD* 4.681; and "Methushael," *ABD* 4.801; also J. Gabriel, "Die Kainitengenealogie. Gn 4, 17–24," *Bib* 40 [1959]: 409–27).

the audience of Lamech's prideful boasts.[314] This probably explains why chap. 4 includes women's names, whereas chap. 5 does not specify a wife or daughter's name ("other sons and daughters," 5:4, etc.). The meaning of their names is uncertain, but "Adah" usually is associated with *ʿădî,* meaning "ornament"; and "Zillah" *(ṣillâ)* with Hebrew *ṣēl,* "shadow, shade," or *ṣll,* "shrill, tinkle." Some have related the latter to the Hebrew word for "cymbal" *(ṣilṣûl),* suggesting that the two are praised for their beauty and sweet voice (as Song 2:14).[315]

Each wife bears two children; Adah has two sons, and Zillah has a son and daughter. The three sons are presented in the same way; each one's birth and name is given, followed by his profession.[316] In the case of Lamech's daughter, *Naamah,* nothing is said of her contribution to social achievement (v. 22).[317] Inclusion of her name gives symmetrical balance to the number of children born to Lamech, with two children from each wife.[318] Jewish imagination explains her inclusion by identifying her as Noah's wife (*Gen. Rab.* 23.3).

Adah births "Jabal," who is the ancestor of pastoral life that involved animal husbandry (v. 20).[319] There is no contradiction with Abel's profession since his occupation was with "sheep" *(ṣōʾn),* and Jabal's trade was broader (*miqneh,* "livestock").[320] Jabel's maternal brother bears the rhyming name "Jubal," who commenced the art and crafts of musicology (v. 21).

Their half-brother, born by Zillah, was Tubal-Cain, who was recognized as the inventor of metalwork (v. 22). He differs from his brothers in the text by his compound name and the absence of "father of" *(ʾăbî),* meaning "progenitor."[321] The

---

[314] The name "Adah" comes into play later in the patriarchal narratives as Esau's wife (Gen 36:2).

[315] See Cassuto, *Genesis,* 234; also U. Hübner, "Adah," *ABD* 1.60, and Hess, "Zillah," *ABD* 6.1093–94. Sarna (*Genesis,* 37) recommends "dawn" and "dusk."

[316] In all three cases the profession is expressed by the participle, as in 4:1–2,17. For discussion of the symmetry see Wilson, *Genealogies and History,* 141–42.

[317] In Heb. her name is "pleasant"; some connect it to the Ug word for "song, singing." Sarna observes that *Tg. Ps.-J.* depicts Naamah as a professional singer (*Genesis,* 38).

[318] So recommends Wilson, *Genealogy and History,* 144. "Naamah" is also the name of Solomon's wife, King Rehoboam's mother (1 Kgs 14:21//2 Chr 12:13).

[319] The construction here is uncertain; "livestock" may be taken as dependent on "father" or "tent-dweller." In the former case he is the ancestor of both bedouin life and herding, and in the latter Jabal is only the first to travel with herds. The NIV's rendering suggests the former meaning (and NAB). Alternatively REB has "the ancestor of tent-dwellers who raise flocks and herds" (also cp. NJB, NASB, NRSV, NJPS).

[320] One might wonder how Jabal's innovation of tent dwelling and cattle rearing can be considered a part of urbanization. All sedentary life in antiquity was dependent upon the domestication of animals. The patriarchs' seminomadic life which involved the close association with cities, such as Hebron, illustrates the relationship of city and herd in a pastoralist society. See E. Firmage, "Zoology," *ABD* 6.1119, and R. Coote and K. Whitelam, *The Emergence of Early Israel in Historical Perspective* (Sheffield: Almond, 1987), 94–95.

context, as with his brothers (vv. 20–21), indicates Tubal-Cain was one of the founders of civilization's technologies. The NIV's rendering "forged" suggests the advanced science of smelting, but *lāṭaš* only means "hammer, sharpen."[322] Although bronze was refined as early as the late fourth millennium, the developed science of iron metallurgy was not widely used until about 1200 B.C. There is some evidence that terrestrial iron was used earlier on a limited basis, but meteoric iron was worked early and probably is intended here.[323] Tubal-Cain's metallurgy probably included weapons as well as agricultural tools. Bearing his ancestor's name, "Cain," and his descent from murderous Lamech suggest that his craft could be used for ill. With the appendage of "Cain" the grim side of his craft comes to mind first. "Cain's family is a microcosm: its pattern of technical prowess and moral failure is that of humanity."[324]

The similarity in the names of Lamech's sons draws attention to their role as founders and to their kinship.[325] "Jabal" and "Jubal" have been related to *yĕbûl*, meaning "produce," and the rhyming "Tubal" is a continuing sound play.[326] Thus the associative sounds imply that they are inventors ("produc-

---

[321] The Heb. construction of v. 22b is challenging: לֹטֵשׁ כָּל־חֹרֵשׁ נְחֹשֶׁת וּבַרְזֶל reads lit. "a hammerer/sharpener of all who work bronze and iron." Two textually related problems impact our understanding of the passage: the absence of "father of" and the difficulty of the two participles. Comparing vv. 20–21, we would expect, as the targums read, אֲבִי כָּל־חֹרֵשׁ נְחֹשֶׁת וּבַרְזֶל ("father of all who work [חֹרֵשׁ] bronze and iron" or אֲבִי כָּל־לֹטֵשׁ נְחֹשֶׁת וּבַרְזֶל ("father of all who hammer [לֹטֵשׁ] bronze and iron"), as the NJB's "ancestor of all who work copper and iron" (cp. NAB). The MT's reading is explained as the result of a secondary omission ("father of") and the conflation of two competing readings of the participle (see Wenham, *Genesis 1–15*, 93, 95). Since the MT's reading is supported by the versions and it is more likely that a reading would be "corrected," the targums are probably secondary. The NIV follows the MT but takes חֹרֵשׁ as "tools" (as does NASB, NRSV, NJPS). This would mean Tubal-Cain invented the metal instruments. The NIV's text variant "who instructed all who work in" is a literal rendering, taking לֹטֵשׁ as "sharpener [i.e., instructor] of" (as Cassuto, *Genesis,* 237), thus the REB's "master of all coppersmiths and blacksmiths." This rendering says more since it would mean he both originated the practice and taught others the craft, as did his brothers in their respective professions.

[322] The term occurs in 1 Sam 13:20; Pss 7:12[13]; 52:2[3]; Job 16:9.The NASB and NAB have "forger," but the NRSV has the better rendering "who *made* all kinds."

[323] There is widespread evidence of iron objects coming from Mesopotamia and Egypt as early as the third millennium, some even nonmeteoric (man-made), showing that the Genesis account reflects a reliable memory of metalwork's beginnings (see G. Hasel, "Iron," *ISBE* 2. 880–81).

[324] Kidner, *Genesis,* 78.

[325] The similarity of their names may also allude to the historic association of their three disciplines. Greek deities, e.g., were revered for their expertise in more than one of these specializations. E.g., Pan, the god of flocks, invented the flute. Sarna (*Genesis,* 37) adds, following W. F. Albright, that the famed rock painting at Beni Hasan (ca. 1900 B.C.) shows Asiatics possessing livestock, a lyre, and bellows (*Archaeology and the Religion of Israel,* 3d ed. [Baltimore: Johns Hopkins, 1956], 98).

[326] In the case of Tubal-Cain, "Tubal" as the offspring of Japhet occurs in 10:2 (and elsewhere), where it refers to a geographical location (see discussion there). It is unnecessary to conclude, as some have proposed, that "Cain" is a later gloss appended to distinguish this Tubal from the son of Japhet.

ers").[327] The name "Jubal," the father of musical instruments, also corresponds closely in sound to the melodic ram's horn *(yôbēl),* which in later Israel announced the Year of Jubilee and other special occasions (e.g., Exod 19:13; Lev 25:9). Specifically, however, the text refers only to the widely known harp (lyre) and flute (pipe).

Moreover, the names of the brothers have a fascinating linkage with both Abel and Cain. All three have a similar sound to "Abel" *(hebel),* but as the father of herding, "Jabal" particularly echoes the name and career of Abel. This surprising juxtaposition of Lamech's sons and Abel may be anticipatory of vv. 25–26, where we learn that Seth takes the place of Eve's slain son. The point is that the progeny of Cain cannot take the place of fallen Abel; it is left to Seth to perpetuate the best of the Adamic line. Also Cain *(qayin)* is subtly referred to in the case of his descendants, Jabal and Jubal, by the repetition of Hebrew sounds *q* and *n* in their professions and, of course, explicitly in the compound Tubal-Cain.[328] Jabal is the father of tending "livestock" *(miqneh),* and Jubal's innovation of harp and flute alludes to Hebrew *qīnâ* ("lament/dirge"). This further cements the union of ancestor and posterity, suggesting that their forefather's wickedness has poisoned their achievements.

4:23–24 In Lamech's poem, the so-called "Song of the Sword," he boasts before his wives his prowess as a combatant, and he revels in the glory of his victims (vv. 23–24). It indicates that violence encircles Cain's lineage since Lamech claims that he is provoked by another who injured him. Although no weapon such as a sword is stated in the poem, Tubal-Cain's industry of forging metal objects implies weaponry that in the hands of evil men resulted in escalating violence. Lamech thinks himself invincible with his newly acquired weapons as he asserts his domination over anyone who might trouble him. The poetic arrangement (displayed in a literal translation) presents parallel members:

Adah and Zillah//wives of Lamech
listen to me//hear my words
a man for wounding//a young man for injuring me
seven times//seventy-seven times

Reference to his wives in this alarming setting probably indicates the worse consequence of the judgment oracle in 3:16b, where the woman suffers under a despotic husband. In this case the women experience the humiliation of polyg-

[327] Another possibility lies with יָבַל, which means "to bring along" *(hiphil)* in the sense of conducting a group. R. North posits that as hypocoristicons of an original compound with theophoric *ʾel* ("God") or *yah* (Yahweh), Jabal-*el/yah* would mean "God heads the procession" and the passive form Jubal-*el/yah,* "Brought in the procession" ("The Cain Music," *JBL* 83 [1964]: 380). Tubal is taken as "procession."

[328] Described by Cassuto, *Genesis,* 235.

amy and the violent spectacle of a savage killing. His repeated exhortation demands their acquiescence: "Listen to me" renders "hear my voice," another possible allusion to Adam's sin (3:10,17) and the murder of Abel (4:10). The demand "hear my words" is captured in the REB's "mark what I say."

It is uncertain whether the boast concerns a specific incident, as most conceive, "I have killed a man" (AV, NIV, NASB NRSV, NJPS, NJB, NAB), or a threat that is generally directed to anyone, "I kill a man" (REB). In this latter case it is not so much a boast of an act already committed but a warning that anyone opposing him does so at his peril. "Kill" *(hārag),* a clear allusion to Cain, is found four more times in our narrative, all in connection with him (vv. 8,14–15,25). Poetic parallelism shows that only one "man," not another "young man," is meant. The term for "young man" *(yeled)* commonly refers to the very young such as the infant Isaac (21:8; cf. 2 Sam 12:15) but also to the teenager Ishmael (21:16) and sometimes to young male adults (e.g., Ruth 1:5; 1 Kgs 12:8). The NASB's rendering "boy" presumes too much ("lad," NJPS). Though we cannot determine the age of the victim, *yeled* probably indicates that the "man" was a younger person and therefore vulnerable, making Lamech's aggression all the more repugnant. The ostensible reason for Lamech's retaliation was his own harm suffered at the hands of the "young man." "Wounding" and "injuring" are likewise in parallel and refer to the same incident, but the circumstances are not forthcoming. Both "wounding" *(peṣaʿ)* and "injuring" *(ḥabbûrâ)* are found in tandem twice more where punishment is inflicted for crime: the classic passage calling for talionic justice, "Eye for eye, tooth for tooth . . . wound for wound, bruise for bruise" (Exod 21:25), and the wisdom saying, "Blows and wounds cleanse away evil" (Prov 20:30). In Lamech's case, his reprisal is excessive since he kills the youth for the cause of a mere wounding.[329]

Lamech's gloating over a reputation more ruthless than infamous Cain's shows the disparagement of human life among Cain's seed that was fostered by his murder of Abel. God's promise to avenge Cain's life "seven times" (v. 15) is interpreted by Lamech as a badge of honor for Cain rather than as a merciful provision by God for a shameful criminal (v. 24). Lamech contends that if Cain's value is reprisal seven times, then his acclaimed deeds merit much more. This also fits the first context, which serves as a warning against any who would seek vengeance against Cain. Lamech's boast therefore has the same concomitant message for any future avenger, but in Cain's case it is the Lord who pronounces vengeance. "Is avenged" *(yuqqam)* renders the same form translated "suffer vengeance" in v. 15 and is one of several references in the poem to Cain's deed and the divine provision promised. Here Lamech in his twisted logic may presume upon divine protection, or he may imply in a sar-

[329] So Stigers, *Genesis,* 92.

castic tone his lack of need for it. This is the first recorded incident in the Bible where crime is venerated by the culprit.

(5) Seth's Birth and Family (4:25–26)

[25]Adam lay with his wife again, and she gave birth to a son and named him Seth, saying, "God has granted me another child in place of Abel, since Cain killed him." [26]Seth also had a son, and he named him Enosh.

At that time men began to call on the name of the LORD.

4:25 The birth of Seth is interpreted by Eve as God's response to the loss of righteous Abel. By bearing "again," the hope of a "another seed" (literally) born to Eve meant a righteous lineage is possible through Adam's son Seth (cf. 3:15). Abel was dead, and Cain was disqualified. As in the case of naming "Cain" (see 4:1), Eve explains theologically the choice of Seth's name. "Seth" *(šēt)* is related by sound (if not etymology) to "granted" *(šāt).* Eve attributes the birth of the child to the mercy of God, who has provided her a third son. It would seem that the first round is won by the serpent in the murder of righteous Abel, but the gift of Seth insures that the promise will stay alive through Eve, who is found after all to be the "mother of all living" (3:20). Although our verse bears remarkable similarities in language with 4:1a, it possesses a significant deviation in having the name *Elohim* rather than the customary *Yahweh.* Quite apart from the problems that Elohim presents to source critics since it occurs in the imagined Yahweh (J) source, the name must be an echo of the dialogue between the serpent and Eve (3:1–5), which is the other place in the garden *tōlĕdōt* where "God" alone occurs. There it is found in the setting of deception and distrust, but now it appears to be Eve's deliberate, though late, rejoinder to the serpent's cynicism toward God's goodness.

4:26 Hope for this "seed" lives with the announcement of Seth's firstborn "son," Enosh (4:26a), who parallels Cain's firstborn "son," Enoch (4:17). Again the narrator returns to the importance of Seth as substitute for deceased Abel (v. 25) by the subtle linkage of language with 4:4: "Abel, he also *[gam hûʾ]* brought . . ." and "Seth also *[gam hûʾ]* had a son." The name "Enosh" *(ʾĕnôš)* in Hebrew can function both as a common noun and as the name of an individual, like the word for "man" or "Adam" *(ʾādām;* 4:26; 5:6–7,9–11; 1 Chr 1:1). As a common noun it may indicate an individual "man" in a general sense (e.g., Job 5:17) or collective "mankind," where it is synonymous with *ʾādām* (e.g., Job 36:25; Ps 8:4[5]). "Enosh" then is the new "Adam" who heads a new line that will receive the blessing and survive the flood (5:1–11,29). Though the etymology of Hebrew *ʾĕnôš* is uncertain, its usage often refers to the frailty and insignificance of "man."[330] Perhaps Seth's naming of Enosh

[330] E.g., Pss 8:4; 10:17–18; 90:3; 103:15–16; Isa 13:7. Cf. Akk. *enēšu,* "to be weak, fragile."

reflects his own sense of mortality and in light of the murder of Abel the tenuous character of human life.

Enosh's birth marks an important point in the development of the righteous lineage of Adam. At this time people "began to call on the name of the LORD" (v. 26b). This concluding remark to the *tōlĕdôt* section (2:4–4:26) serves as a linkage with the following genealogy, which formally presents Adam's lineage through Seth down to the flood survivor, Noah (5:1–32). We have already commented on the contrast between Cain's line (chap. 4) and Seth's family history (chap. 5). This is sharpened by v. 26b. Here Enosh and his descendants contrast with Cain's descendants, who are remembered for their urbanization of society and the vices introduced by Lamech. Moreover, the reference to "calling on the name of the LORD" links 4:25–26a with the succeeding material at 5:2–3, where the "naming" formula reappears, "And she/he called his name . . ." This same formula is reserved for the naming of the final patriarch "Noah" in 5:29. Thus while the Sethite members give birth and name their offspring, they also give homage to the Lord by calling on his name. Sadly this cannot be said of Noah's contemporaries who take up the ways of Cain.

A number of exegetical difficulties are faced in the latter half of this verse (v. 26b), resulting in conflicting translations in the ancient versions. These created a host of varying interpretations of the verse and the man Enosh.[331] First, the Hebrew text has an indefinite construction (literally, "it was begun to call . . ."), resulting in no stated subject. The modern versions rightly supply the subject, such as "men" (NIV, NASB, NJPS) or "people" (NRSV, REB). The LXX and Vg, however, attributed to Enosh himself the innovation of calling on the "name of the LORD." Such a translation does not require too great a change in the Hebrew text and therefore may reflect a real difference in the Hebrew textual history.[332] Yet this reading may have been influenced by the listing of Cain's descendants, who were recognized as founders of the arts and sciences (vv. 20–22), making it secondary. In effect, by attributing to Seth's first genealogical descendant the innovation of public worship, the versions draw an even sharper distinction between Cain's offspring and that of Seth: Cain's firstborn

[331] See S. D. Fraade, *Enosh and His Generation: Pre-Israelite Hero and History in Postbiblical Interpretation,* SBLMS 30 (Chico, Cal.: Scholars Press, 1984); also S. Sandmel, "Genesis 4:26b," *HUCA* 32 (1961): 19–29.

[332] The LXX has οὗτος ἤλπισεν ἐπικαλεῖσθαι τὸ ὄνομα κυρίου τοῦ θεοῦ ("This one [Enosh] hoped [i.e., trusted] to call upon the name of the Lord God"), and the Vg has *iste coepit invocare nomen Domini* ("He [Enoch] began to invoke the name of the Lord"). In both cases the demonstrative "this" indicates a possible variance in the Heb. where זֶה ("this") is read for temporal אָז ("then"). The *aleph* can be explained away as a dittograph arising from the preceding אֱנוֹשׁ ("Enosh"), and the missing *hē* can be accounted for as a haplograph caused by the succeeding הוּחַל ("began"). While the Latin probably reads הֵחֵל from the verbal root חָלַל ("began") as in the MT, the LXX text has ἤλπισεν ("hoped, expected"), which suggests הוֹחִיל, the *hiphil* of יָחַל, "to await, hope."

and successors pioneer cities and the civilized arts, but Seth's firstborn and successors pioneer worship. Is it coincidental that the next utterance of the name "LORD" is Lamech's prayer concerning Noah's birth and role (5:29)?

For the earlier Jews, based on the LXX, Enosh was viewed as a righteous hero, Philo's "ideal man."[333] In the Christian tradition he foreshadowed the church since his hope in the name of the Lord was prophetic of the Christian's faith in Christ.[334] Luther, too, commented that the wording "name of the LORD" referred ultimately to Jesus Christ, and thus Enosh exhorted the people to look toward their redemption.[335] The Jewish targums, however, reflect the opposite opinion of Enosh. They rendered the Hebrew "began" but also took it as the verb "pollute."[336] Thus the verse referred to the defilement of the name Yahweh by the making of an idol and giving it the sacred name. Enosh then was viewed not as the paradigm of antediluvian godliness but the beginning of moral degradation. The infamous "Generation of Enosh" was degenerate and initiated a string of wicked generations that resulted in the flood.[337]

"Called" *(qārā᾽)* can be taken as "invoking" the Lord in prayer and worship (as NRSV, REB)[338] or as "proclaiming " in the sense of declaring the revelation of God (e.g., Exod 33:19; 34:5; Deut 32:3). "Began" *(ḥālal)* appears in Genesis 1–11 to mark strategic new features in the progress of the narrative (6:1; 9:20; 10:8; 11:6). Although worship through offerings was practiced by Cain and Abel (4:1–4), Gen 4:26b announces a new direction in formal worship as in Abram's building of an altar upon arriving in Canaan, where the same descriptive phrase, "called on the name of the LORD," occurs (12:8). By inaugurating altar worship in Canaan, a historic significance for the family of faith occurred. Even so, worship at the birth of Enosh was not new to the Adamic family, and "Yahweh" was already heard from the lips of Eve (4:1); but it was taken up in a decisive way for the Sethite generations.

"Called on the name of the LORD" in 4:26b unites the Lord of the patriarchs

---

[333] E.g., *Jub.* 4:12; 19:23–25; *2 Enoch* 33:10–11; Philo, *On Abraham* 7–15; Josephus, *Ant.* 1.2.3.67–71.

[334] This was encouraged by the passive rendering of the LXX's ἐπικαλεῖσθαι as found in Eusebius of Emesa (A.D. 300–360): "This one hoped to be called by the name of the Lord God." In other words, Enosh was viewed as seeking the epithet of the righteous Sethites, sons of God as in 6:2. Though not following this passive nuance, Augustine emphasized Enosh's hope as a prophecy of the Christ. Seth was the resurrection, and Enosh represents the sons of the resurrection, those who believe in Christ.

[335] *LW* 1.328.

[336] הוּחַל *(hophal)* is derived from חָלַל, which in *qal* and *piel* means "pollute" but "began" in the *hiphil* and *hophal*. The targums translate the term literally "began" and then interpret it as "profane." *Tg. Neof.* reads, "Then the sons of man began to make idols for themselves and to surname them by the name of the Memra of the LORD" (also *Tg. Ps.-J.*). *Tg. Onq.* is not so forbidding; Enosh's generation was derelict in praying.

[337] E.g., *Sifre Deuteronomy; Gen. Rab.* 23.6–7; *3 Enoch* 5.3–13.

[338] E.g., 12:8; Pss 66:17; 99:6; 1 Chr 4:10.

and of Moses with the Lord of the antediluvian line of promise through Seth and shows thereby that the spiritual ancestors of Abraham's family were those descended through Noah, the survivor of the flood's purge. Whereas Cain was alienated from the "LORD's presence" (4:16), the Sethite clan practiced and declared the word of the Lord.[339] The account infers that the Cainite family perished altogether in the catastrophic flood, but the tiny remnant of the Sethite line emerged from the ark to perpetuate its spiritual birthright (9:1–17). This final note in the *tōlĕdōt* section of 2:4–4:26 offers at last a bright spot among the dim accounts of sin and death that have dominated the garden story. There is yet hope for sinful humanity.

EXCURSUS: THE REVELATION OF THE DIVINE NAME

A problem frequently cited in Gen 2:26b is how to correlate what appears to be the introduction of the name "LORD" (Yahweh) here with its use as early as 2:4 and routinely in the garden narrative (2:4–4:26).[340] Moreover, this statement appears to contradict the revelation of the Lord to Moses at Sinai (Exod 3:6,15; 6:2–3). Critical scholars commonly contend that the name Yahweh was unknown until it was first revealed to Moses. If so, what is to be done with the patriarchal narratives that often refer to Yahweh (ca. 90x) in addition to the more common *El/Elohim* and its compounds (e.g., *El Shaddai, El Olam*)?

Source critics have attributed the incongruity between Exodus and Gen 4:26b to conflicting literary sources: the E(lohist) at Exod 3:13–15 and the P(riestly) author at Exod 6:2–3 attributed the first knowledge of Yahweh to the Sinai revelation, while Gen 4:26 reflects the viewpoint of the Yahwist (J) who thought its origin was among early man.[341] Abraham knew God by the name *El Shaddai,* not by the designation Yahweh. Problems arise, however, for such a source reconstruction, for J would on the face of it contradict itself by the recurring use of Yahweh in chap. 4 (also considered part of J). The response to this was the proposal of two J sources. Moreover, it is a predicament for source critics to explain why the P source (Exod 6:2–3), coming from the postexilic era, would have so blatantly contradicted what was surely known at that time from the earlier J source.

Still others believe that the author of 4:26 had no intention in announcing when the name *Yahweh* was first known. Rather, its appearance throughout Genesis is anachronistic. Yahweh, coming from the later religious period of Israel, was imposed on the prepatriarchal and patriarchal eras. The Hebrew theologian's purpose was to pinpoint the inauguration of worship in its general sense (i.e., religion) as he did with the various facets of urban life in vv. 20–22. He used the common name for God known to him, *Yahweh,* which would be connected by the

[339] Noted by Cassuto, *Genesis,* 247.

[340] In 2:4–3:23 יהוה occurs with אֱלֹהִים nineteen times and by itself nine times in chap. 4.

[341] E.g., Skinner, *Genesis,* 127; also Speiser (*Genesis,* 37–38), but he harmonizes the sources by granting J knew of a small group that used *Yahweh,* and E and P focus on this aspect of the faith made known to Moses.

reader with its appearance already in 4:1,6.[342] In regard to the patriarchs, he inserted the name *Yahweh* in the narrative to demonstrate that the God worshiped by Israel's fathers *(El/Elohim)* was the God of covenant at Sinai.[343]

When we consider that *Yahweh* occurs 162 times in Genesis, often in direct discourse (34x), the modification required by the editor exhibits a remarkable license in altering the *theological* content of his sources. Rather than the complicated theories noted, it is methodologically better to consider Exod 6:2–3 on an exegetical basis that is not atomistic. Jewish interpretation, as well as Christian, understood the revelation at Sinai as concerning a special aspect of divine power and character, not the name *Yahweh* itself. Contextually, the issue is not the name of the deity per se (e.g., Exod 7:5) but rather the nature of God.[344] Revelation of the "name" to Moses concerned the content and meaning of *Yahweh* that was not as fully understood by the patriarchs. The Lord's "name" in Moses' experience was related to God's unique self-disclosure of his goodness, mercy, and majesty (cf. Exod 33:19; 34:5; Deut 32:3). Hence to misspeak the "name" was considered an affront to his holy character (Exod 20:7; Deut 5:11) and was punishable by death (Lev 24:15–16). For Israel, bearing the "name of the LORD" indicated covenant identity with God and their distinctive place among the nations (Deut 28:10). Far more than a mere name was at stake in the revelation to Moses.

Neither can we say that Gen 4:26b itself concerns only the appellative *Yahweh*. "Called on the name of the LORD" in Genesis is related to God's self-revelation to Abraham (12:7–8), Hagar (16:13), and Isaac (26:24–25). Also this phrase is commonly connected with the formal worship of altar building,[345] as was also the practice of Moses before the construction of the tabernacle (Exod 17:15; 20:24).

---

[342] So Westermann, *Genesis 1–11,* 339–40.

[343] E.g., G. Wenham, "The Religion of the Patriarchs," in *Essays on the Patriarchal Narratives* (Winona Lake: Eisenbrauns, 1980), 161–95. See also Wenham, *Genesis 1–15,* 116; T. N. D. Mettinger, *In Search of God* (Philadelphia: Fortress, 1988), 50–53.

[344] See W. C. Kaiser, Jr., "Exodus," EBC (Grand Rapids: Zondervan, 1990), 340, 42; also J. A. Motyer, *The Revelation of the Divine Name* (London: Tyndale, 1959). Defense for the traditional view but on linguistic grounds is found in Andersen, *The Sentence in Biblical Hebrew,* 102.

[345] Also 13:4; 16:13; 21:33; 26:25.

SECTION OUTLINE

III. ADAM'S FAMILY LINE (5:1–6:8)

Following the account of human sin and death (2:4–4:26), the author sets out by means of genealogy to show the continuing effects of sin but also the faithfulness of God's promise of procreation and blessing (1:1–2:3). This "written account" (5:1) of Adam's family traces his offspring through Seth, and in effect it is "Seth's" genealogy, the counterpart to Cain's (4:17–24). It has been appropriated by the author to bridge the *tōlĕdōt* of the heavens and the earth (2:4–4:26) and the flood story, which champions Noah (6:9–9:29). It also backtracks to 1:1–2:3 by echoing the creation of humanity in God's "image," showing the realization of the divine command "be fruitful . . . fill the earth" (1:26–28). Moreover, it alludes to the garden scene and the subsequent events that spell out the painful aftermath of sin for the human family (2:4–4:26). Its purpose, like the later Shemite lineage (11:10–26), is to span a gap in the narrative by moving the setting ahead rapidly, from creation to the flood.[1] It both expedites the telling of the early history of humanity and contributes to the author's theological premise that is brought forward.

This *tōlĕdōt* section (5:1–6:8) advances the theological interests of chaps. 1–11 in at least four ways. (1) It presents a convincing case for the intercon-

[1] Cf., e.g., Ruth 4:18–22, which spans two eras, from the patriarchal head Perez (son of Judah) to the time of David's monarchy, but it occurs at the end of the narrative.

nectedness of all mankind and the hope for universal blessing, since the genealogy takes us from the beginnings (Adam) to the diluvian world of Noah (the new Adam). (2) It demonstrates the results of Adam's sin ("death reigned," Rom 5:17) and, despite this harsh reality, the continuation of God's promise of preservation through the gift of procreation. (3) It contributes to the unfolding motif of conflict as anticipated in 3:15, where there is rivalry between an unrighteous offspring and a righteous lineage reflected by the genealogies of chaps. 4 and 5 as well as 6:1–8, which contrasts Noah with his generation. (4) It shows the evolution and universality of human wickedness, which deserves God's angry reprisal (6:1–7), but again, despite this, the hope that rests in God's favor toward Noah (5:29 w/6:8–9).

STRUCTURE AND GENEALOGY. Two different genres are utilized to construct this section. A formal genealogy, consisting of ten members (5:1–32), is followed by a narrative conclusion (6:1–8).[2] The genealogy consists of a title and prologue (5:1–2) followed by ten paragraphs in a fixed pattern, reciting the career of each patriarch from Adam to Noah. Its conclusion, however, is delayed until 9:28–29 (Noah's death) by the narrative epilogue (6:1–8) and the inclusion of the Noah *tōlĕdōt* (6:9–9:27). The epilogue is made up of two paragraphs, describing the intermarriage of the "sons of God" and "daughters of men" (6:1–4) and the spreading sinfulness of man (6:5–8). Genesis 6:1–8 functions as a literary hinge that backtracks to chap. 5 by speaking of marriage and procreation (6:1–4) and also looks ahead by introducing the consequent flood narrative (6:5–8). It conveys the conditions of the world that prevailed when Noah, the tenth and "last" of Adam's sons, lived (5:32). The ominous declaration of worldwide destruction in 6:5–8 creates the same tension that Cain's murder of Abel produced in the previous *tōlĕdōt* section (2:4–4:26). What will become of the human family and the promissory blessings? Seth's birth and genealogy in 4:25–26 answered the former section, and God's favor toward Noah answers the present (6:8). Thus the present *tōlĕdōt* (5:1–6:8) is initiated with creation and ends with the foreboding message that all creation will be destroyed. "The world is going to be reduced to a watery chaos before a new start can be made."[3]

We have already acknowledged the parallels and differences between the Sethite line and Cain's genealogy (see 4:17–24). Although these two lines of descent have superficial similarities, they also present a stark dissimilarity. There is no linkage between Cain and Adam in the formal genealogy (4:17–24). The connection is derived only from the earlier narrative at 4:1. In the Sethite listing the setting of creation is preeminent (5:1b–3) for the purpose of

---

[2] For the unity of 5:1–6:8 see our discussion at 6:1–8. See also, e.g., U. Cassuto, *A Commentary on the Book of Genesis, Part I: From Adam to Noah* (Jerusalem: Magnes/Hebrew University, 1961), 249–50, and G. Wenham, *Genesis 1–15,* WBC (Waco: Word, 1987), 121.

[3] Wenham, *Genesis 1–15,* 145.

cohesion between Noah and first things (Adam). Cain's connections with creation, on the other hand, have been discounted—he is disowned!—and the rite of passage for blessing will be only through Abel's successor, Seth.

Also to capture the meaning of Genesis 5 we must remember the comparison between vile Lamech (4:23–24) and righteous Enoch (5:23–24) inferred from the two genealogies. They highlight the contrast in the moral character between the two lines of descent. Cain's house is typified by the polygamous and murderous Lamech. Conversely, the sons of Seth are righteous, as shown by Enoch, and the hope of blessing lies with Seth's descendant Noah (v. 29). This is all the more startling when we recall that Noah's father is also named "Lamech" (vv. 28–31). The juxtaposition between the "Lamech" of each household underscores the contrast.

Genesis does not again mention by name the generations of Cain; the book narrows its focus by means of the Sethite genealogy to Noah and his sons exclusively. This narrowing effect is the same technique found in 11:10–26, which centers on Noah's son of blessing, "Shem" (9:26–27), who will prepare the way for the birth of the Shemite "Abram" (11:26). We must read chap. 5 and 11:10–26 in concert, recognizing that the flood account is an expanded interlude that details how God's swift response to human sin keeps alive the possibility of future blessing for the Adamic line.

Both chaps. 5 and 11 present *linear* genealogies, which give only one descendant for each successive generation. The purpose of a linear genealogy is to give genealogical depth. By this device twenty generations are sketched expeditiously from Adam to Abram when the Sethite and Shemite genealogies are read together (see chart at 11:10–26). The genealogical arrangements in chaps. 5 and 11 are complementary in having a ten-member lineage.[4] The Shemite genealogy formally includes only nine names, from Seth to Terah, and may therefore point to Abraham as the concluding, tenth figure.

[4] Chaps. 5 (Adam-Noah) and 11 (Shem-Abram) with their ten-name pattern have been related to a practice in Mesopotamia of building a royal genealogy possessing a table of ancestors of ten names (e.g., A. Malamat, "King Lists of the Old Babylonian Period and Biblical Genealogies," in *Essays in Honor of E. A. Speiser* 53 [1968]: 163–73 = *JAOS* 88 [1968]). The Babylonian and Assyrian King Lists show a component of ten generations of ancestors, and the Sumerian King List also has a tradition of ten antediluvian names. This has a striking biblical parallel with David's ten-name lineage (Ruth 4:18–22). However, the number of names in the king lists varies considerably among divergent traditions. This, among other reasons, argues against taking the feature of ten names as a stereotypical feature of royal genealogies (see R. R. Wilson, "The Old Testament Genealogies in Recent Research," *JBL* 94 [1975]: 169–89). At most we can say that the ten-name arrangement appears in diverse traditions but was not a convention. Initially scholars concluded that Gen 5 was dependent upon the Sumerian tradition (e.g., W. G. Lambert, "A New Look at the Babylonian Background of Genesis," *JTS* 16 [1965]: 292–93), but now it is widely contended that they are independent. See, e.g., T. C. Hartman, "Some Thoughts on the Sumerian King List and Genesis 5 and 11b," *JBL* 91 (1972): 25–32.

A *segmented* genealogy, as in chap. 10, gives more than one descendant for each generation. It differs from the linear genealogy by giving a broader range of an ancestor's family descendants (also, e.g., 36:10–14; 1 Chr 1:4–16).[5] In the primeval history the formal structure of the linear genealogical trees, from Adam to Abram, contributes to the narrative account by demarcating the elect family.

Genesis 5 follows a regular pattern, which presents a stereotype for each patriarch. Its scheme is presented here:

> And P(ersonal)N(ame)$_1$ lived *x* years and begot PN$_2$
> And PN$_1$ lived, after he begot PN$_2$, *y* years
> And he (PN$_1$) begot sons and daughters
> And all the days of PN$_1$ were $x + y$ years and he died.[6]

This formulaic device creates the impression of unity across the ten generations of Adam's family. Its uniformity also provides the literary foil for highlighting four members (Adam, Enoch, Lamech, and Noah) where the biographical pattern is altered for a special purpose. Another significant literary diversion is the final entry of the genealogy, which presents a segmented genealogy of Noah's three sons—Shem, Ham, and Japheth (v. 32). Chapter 11 uses the same tactic, ending with the naming of Terah's three sons, Abram, Nahor, and Haran (11:26). In each triad of sons the first listed (Shem, Abram) fathers the chosen line of blessing. Also chap. 4's genealogy concludes with Lamech's three sons but includes the daughter, Naamah. Adam, too, has three named sons (Cain, Abel, Seth).

Thus the matching genealogies of chaps. 5 and 11 isolate the appointed line that spans creation to patriarchal times, giving the patriarchal families a specific historical linkage with the promissory blessing of God upon Adam and Eve (1:26–28). The genealogies are exclusionist in function, indicating by linear descent the one through whom the promissory blessing will be channeled. Although this technique identifies the lineage that will implement the promise, Genesis nevertheless provides for the inclusion of all nations as the beneficiaries of that promise. The Table of Nations depicts the "map" of the world's communities, which are the descendants of Noah's issue—Shem, Ham, and Japheth—who will be blessed through Abraham (12:1–3). This parade figure

---

[5] 1 Chr 2 illustrates the combination of segmented and linear genealogies in giving the descent of the patriarch Judah with emphasis on David's line: sandwiched between the segmented genealogies of vv. 3–9 and 13–17 is the linear (vv. 10–12), citing seven names from Ram to Jesse (father of David).

[6] Chap. 11 differs significantly by the omission of the final line (see 11:10–26 discussion):

> And PN$_1$ lived *x* years and begot PN$_2$
> And PN$_1$ lived, after he begot PN$_2$, *y* years
> And he (PN$_1$) begot sons and daughters.

We are citing the schema in R. S. Hess, "The Genealogies of Genesis 1–11 and Comparative Literature," *Bib* 70 (1989): 243–44.

in the eyes of the Genesis author accomplishes Lamech's hopes for his progeny (5:29) and Noah's invocation for his son Shem (9:27), drawing together under the canopy of blessing the antediluvian and postdiluvian worlds.

Genesis presents history as the course of human events driven by the sovereign dictates of God. Like creation, which has harmony and progression under the authoritative word of God (1:1–2:3), history also has its order, symmetry, and cohesion. Realization of the blessing is not left to happenstance, nor is it subject to the autonomy of human will. Although history is propelled by the hand of God, Genesis does not make human responsibility extraneous. Those through whom God achieves his purposes for the world are godly individuals such as Enoch, Noah, and Abraham. These three are distinctive figures in their times as people of godly character. Genesis appeals to their examples as evidence that human history has a moral factor that impacts its direction for good or ill. The inevitable tension between divine assurances and human culpability is not suppressed by the Genesis narrative; involvement of human choice only enriches the fabric of God's mysterious outworking of his beneficent intention for mankind.

We turn now to the foremost problems of chap. 5, which have confounded ancient and modern interpreters alike. If we include the riddles of 6:1–4, we can safely say that our section presents a preponderance of exegetical conundrums. The immediate difficulty is the long life spans of the patriarchs, which in turn create a host of internal chronological problems of their own.[7] In considering the matter, it is instructive first to see how the textual traditions treated the numbers of Genesis 5.

LIFE SPANS OF THE PATRIARCHS. Textually the Samaritan Pentateuch (SP), Greek (LXX), and Hebrew Bible (MT) have ages for the descendants that are at odds with one another. Variance among the versions occurs also with Shem's line (11:10–26).[8] Charted on the next page are the numbers of the three textual traditions. These general observations regarding the witness of the versions can be made: (1) According to these numbers, the year of the flood varies among the three versions: 1656 (MT), 1307 (SP), and 2242 (LXX).[9] (2) All versions maintain the same total years for Enoch (365). (3) Although the MT's numbers have Methuselah dying the same year of the flood (1656), the SP's reckoning has Jared and Lamech also dying in the same year of Methuselah's

---

[7] Wenham (*Genesis 1–15,* 130–34) includes a helpful excursus on the ages of these antediluvian patriarchs.

[8] See discussion at 11:10–26. For Shem's lineage the versions attempt to deal with the problems posed by the chronological numbers of the MT when they are added together; e.g., Shem outlives Abraham by 35 years! What is at issue among the versions in 11:10–26 is the problem of Abraham's life and the dates of his ancestors.

[9] However, LXX^{A} (Alexandrinus) adjusted the chronology to 2262 for the flood by increasing Methuselah's age at the birth of his first child by 20 years so that he died before the flood (2256). For discussion see D. V. Etz, "The Numbers of Genesis V 3–31: A Suggested Conversion and Its Implications," *VT* 43 (1993): 174.

	TEXTUAL VERSIONS*									Birth and Death From Year of Creation					
	MT			SP			LXX			MT		SP		LXX	
	Age at Firstborn	Remaining Years	Age at Death	Age at Firstborn	Remaining Years	Age at Death	Age at Firstborn	Remaining Years	Age at Death						
Adam	130	800	930	130	800	930	230	700	930	0	930	0	930	0	930
Seth	105	807	912	105	807	912	205	707	912	130	1042	130	1042	230	1142
Enosh	90	815	905	90	815	905	190	715	905	235	1140	235	1140	435	1340
Kenan	70	840	910	70	840	910	170	740	910	325	1235	325	1235	625	1535
Mahalalel	65	830	895	65	830	895	165	730	895	395	1290	395	1290	795	1690
Jared	162	800	962	62	785	847	162	800	962	460	1422	460	1307	960	1922
Enoch	65	300	365	65	300	365	165	200	365	622	987	522	887	1122	1487
Methuselah	187	782	969	67	653	720	617 (187)	802 (782)	969	687	1656	587	1307	1287	2256
Lamech	182	595	777	53	600	653	188	565	753	874	1651	654	1307	1454 (1474)	2207 (2227)
Noah	500	450	950	500	450	950	500	450	950	1056	2006	707	1657	1642 (1662)	2592 (2612)
To Flood	100			100			100								
Flood	1656			1307			2242 (2262)								

* Numbers in parentheses reflect LXX^{A}

death (1307). The LXX strangely has Methuselah surviving the flood (2256), but, recognizing the problem, later Greek tradition adjusted the numbers so as to put his death before the flood.[10]

There is no easy solution for discerning which is the original system of numbers.[11] The LXX has on the whole larger numbers so as to give longer generations and thus a greater period between creation and the flood. This may have been designed to bring the Jewish system of numbers into agreement with Egyptian chronology.[12] The MT's system is preferable since by its reckoning all Noah's ancestors died before the flood (Methuselah dying in the same year). Nevertheless, problems remain, and there is no consensus about how to understand the cluster of numbers. Moreover, the specific numbers themselves are notoriously difficult to preserve in the scribal process. According to the MT chronology, Adam lived some fifty years beyond the birth of Lamech. All Noah's ancestors (except Adam and Seth) lived during his lifetime. Seth died just fourteen years before Noah's birth and thus was a contemporary of Noah's father, Lamech.

This brings us to the second interpretive challenge before us. What is to be made of the lengthy years of these patriarchs? Again there is no totally satisfying answer. Some propose interpreting the numbers on another arithmetic system, but this too has its difficulties.[13] Approaching the figures as symbolic also has its problems since few numbers in the passage appear to have a symbolic

---

[10] For more detail notice the following among the traditions: (1) All three agree on the total years of each patriarch from Adam to Mahalalel, for Enoch (365), and the age of Noah at the birth of his firstborn (500). (2) MT and SP agree on all numbers, except for Jared, Methuselah, and Lamech. (3) LXX, on the other hand, differs considerably from the other versions: (a) From Adam to Mahalalel, adds 100 years to the MT/SP number for each patriarch's age at the time of his firstborn, but then subtracts 100 years from the remaining years of life to equal the total years found in MT/SP. This is the same technique followed in 11:10–26 by SP. (b) Agrees with MT for Jared. (c) Adds and subtracts 100 years for Enoch (see a). (d) For Methuselah, differs from MT and SP but has same total as MT (969 years). (e) For Lamech, differs from both MT and SP.

[11] Some attempts have been made to reconstruct a hypothetical original that lies behind the present versions. The versions are explained as late attempts at solving chronological problems inherent in the original system for the ages of Jared, Methuselah, and Lamech when it was related to the dating of the flood. See R. W. Klein, "Archaic Chronologies and the Textual History of the Old Testament," *HTR* 67 (1974), 255–63, and Etz, "The Numbers of Genesis V:3–31," 171–89. We think G. Larsson appears closer to the right solution, however, when he shows how the LXX (and sometimes SP) altered the numbers in the MT, which he takes as original ("The Chronology of the Pentateuch: A Comparison of the MT and LXX," *JBL* 102 [1983]: 401–9).

[12] Larsson, "Chronology of the Pentateuch," 403.

[13] E.g., the numbers are related to the sexagesimal system (based on sixty); see Cassuto, *Genesis,* 253–62, and J. Walton, "The Antediluvian Section of the Sumerian King List and Genesis 5," *BA* 44 (1981): 207–8. The common complaint against the sexagesimal system is that it does not explain the specific ages of the patriarchs. Also D. W. Young, "On the Application of Numbers to Biblical Life Spans and Epochs," *ZAW* 100 (1988): 331–61, and "The Influences of Babylonian Algebra on Longevity among the Antediluvians," *ZAW* 102 (1990): 321–35.

value.[14] Still others would contend that the genealogy is contrived simply to say that the distant past is so far removed that no present means can account for their antiquity. Moreover, theologically, the remarkable life spans were intended to magnify the breadth of God's blessing.[15]

Traditionally, the genealogy has been understood as a "closed" genealogy, an inclusive listing of descendants, and the numbers have been taken as they stand. Modern proponents of this view maintain that the numbers reflect an uncommon era when agreeable climatic conditions enabled the exceptional duration of the antediluvian patriarchs. Further contended is that sin had not yet achieved its full deleterious effects on human society, shortening human life expectations. This traditional opinion has the advantage of taking the text straightforwardly since there is nothing explicit in the passage to indicate otherwise. But this would leave us with a very short span of time to accommodate all that we know about human history.

Others, however, take Genesis 5 as an "open" genealogy, meaning that there are gaps between the listed ancestors.[16] There is evidence of this practice among ancient Near Eastern peoples; familial terms like "father" and "son of" were used loosely for "ancestor" and "descendant."[17] Attendant to this, some hold that the life spans for the antediluvian patriarchs therefore are not for individuals but cumulative years for several unnamed generations that have been omitted.[18] Still another proposal is that Genesis 5 lists the names of prominent ruling dynasties and the cumulative years of each dynasty's duration.[19] The Sumerian King List (ca. 2000 B.C.) consists of such a listing of regal dynasties;

---

[14] Enoch's 365 years, equaling the days of a solar year, may be taken as indicative of perfection. Lamech's 777 years indicates perfection and may be a veiled repudiation against evil Lamech's oath of vengeance ("seventy-seven times," 4:24).

[15] C. Westermann, *Genesis 1–11* (Minneapolis: Augsburg, 1984), 353–54.

[16] See the classic statement of this view in W. H. Green, "Primeval Chronology," *BSac* (1890): 285–303; this is reprinted in W. C. Kaiser, Jr., ed., *Classical Evangelical Essays in Old Testament Interpretation* (Grand Rapids: Baker, 1972). Green discusses several examples to demonstrate this feature of biblical genealogies.

[17] For examples see K. A. Kitchen, *Ancient Orient and Old Testament* (Chicago: IVP, 1966), 35–39. Kitchen points to the Egyptian ruler Tirhakah (ca. 680 B.C.), who refers to Sesostris III as "his father," though he reigned twelve hundred years earlier (p. 39).

[18] Neither Green nor Kitchen espoused this view per se. Green held that the numbers referred to the individual named. His primary contention was that the genealogies of chaps. 5 and 11 could not be used to establish the chronological date (contra Bishop Ussher) for the antiquity of man since the biblical genealogies were not exhaustive ("Primeval Chronology," 23). Kitchen offers no solution for the uncommon numbers but contends vigorously that extrabiblical data show that the biblical chronologies cannot be used to establish a date for creation. A literal reckoning of the biblical chronologies would put creation at about 4000 B.C. and the flood at about 2300 B.C. Sites in Palestine and Mesopotamia show human settlements and developing civilization as early as 9000 B.C. (*Ancient Orient*, 36–37).

[19] E.g., R. F. Youngblood, *The Book of Genesis: An Introductory Commentary* (Grand Rapids: Baker, 1991), 75.

each dynasty is introduced by the naming of the first king, the length of reign, and then the subsequent rulers and reigns of that given dynasty.[20] After naming the kings for each dynasty, the total number of the kings and the aggregate total of their reigns are listed.[21]

We agree that chap. 5 evidences a selective genealogy by its highly structured conventions of language and its schematic ten-generation depth.[22] We have seen how this parallels the ten-name genealogy of 11:10–26 (when Abram is counted) and David's genealogy in Ruth 4:18–22, which also contains ten names. Such a ten-name scheme telescopes the number of descendants so as to create the effect of a compressed history. This is illustrated by the Davidic genealogy, which is too short to cover adequately the era between the patriarchal and monarchical periods. Its ten-name arrangement also places "Boaz" as the seventh member, highlighting his role, and is similar to Genesis 5's elevation of Enoch in the seventh position.

The Bible contains ample evidence of "open" genealogies that show the same telescoping effect, such as Matthew's report of Jesus' descent, where the Evangelist commits to an artificial symmetry.[23] Ezra's priestly genealogy (Ezra 7:1–5) and its parallel information in 1 Chronicles 6 are exemplary of how the former has omitted names. Ezra 7 has six fewer names, indicating that the Ezra genealogy is not exhaustive but designed to give an abbreviated history.[24]

Of course, it is certain that the beginning and closing of the primeval genealogies show actual descent without gaps. Seth is the third son of Adam (Gen 4:25), and Lamech comments on the naming of Noah, which indicates a literal descent (5:29). Both chaps. 5 and 11 conclude with the listing of Noah's and Terah's actual sons, including the individual Abraham. Moreover, the Sumerian King List is not a perfect analogy; it records reigns and cumulative dynasties, while the biblical genealogy gives the life spans of its members. Yet while it is true that chaps. 5 and 11 show actual descent at sure points, it does not necessarily follow that the same must be so at all points in the listing. Ancient

---

[20] On the Sumerian King List see "Long-lived Patriarchs" in the Introduction.

[21] E.g., for the dynasty at Kish the names of the kings are cited with their reigns, and the totals are, "Twenty-three kings (thus) ruled it [Kish] for 24,510 years, 3 months, and 3 1/2 days" (*ANET,* 265).

[22] Ancient genealogies commonly showed fluidity of names and telescoped generations by omission (Wilson, *Genealogy and History,* 92, 134, 197).

[23] In Matthew's account Jesus' genealogy consists of three units of fourteen names (Matt 1:17; cf. Luke 3:23–28). The basis of this may have been the numerical value of David's name in Heb. (fourteen), a common Jewish interpretive method known as *gematria.* See C. Blomberg, *Matthew,* NAC (Nashville: Broadman, 1992), 52. To achieve this balance three names were omitted from the listing in Matt 1:8 (between "Jehoram" and "Uzziah"), and "Jehoiakim" is excluded after "Josiah" in 1:11. In such cases "father" is fluid in meaning, indicating "grandfather" or "forefather."

[24] See e.g., F. C. Fensham, *The Book of Ezra and Nehemiah,* NICOT (Grand Rapids: Eerdmans, 1982), 98.

sources show the custom of mixing actual descent and linear gapping side by side in genealogies.[25] We agree that we cannot depend naively on ancient sources as parallels, since they are imperfect analogies, yet we do not want to neglect them altogether as some do.

The Sumerian King List helps us view Genesis 5 in its own ancient context when its numbers, in contrast to modern experience, actually are moderate (see "Long-lived Patriarchs," p. 97). The King List attests to a general picture of antediluvian times that is consistent with what the Bible portrays. Yet it presents antediluvian reigns that are fantastically high even if one were to adopt Genesis 5 as a standard. The longest reign cited among the antediluvian kings is 72,000 years, while the least is 6,000 years.[26] Both accounts remember an era of enormous life spans for man, but against the King List the Genesis numbers are reasonably restrained.[27] Indirectly Genesis 5 is a corrective to the fanciful notions of the ancients. More important is that the biblical recollection, although probably not directly polemical, explains what the Sumerian tradition does not. Humanity experienced the abbreviation of life because of sin. Human civilization underwent a deterioration as a result of exceptional sinful conduct (6:1–8). This does not mean, however, that the theological purposes of chaps. 5 and 11, nor for that matter the imposing ages of the patriarchs, require us to assume the individuals are legendary figures. Again, ancient sources such as the Sumerian King List, despite its fantastic numbers, include individuals who are historical figures as shown by collaborative sources.[28]

Later Sumerian tradition in recounting the flood attaches the Sumerian King List for chronological and historical interests. Biblical Genesis has the same broad arrangement where the Sethite lineage connects the stories of creation and the flood, but its purpose was not merely antiquarian. Genesis 5 serves

---

[25] Kitchen observes that the Abydos King List (Egypt) "silently omits three entire groups of kings" (*Ancient Orient,* 38).

[26] Among the various texts of the Sumerian King List there is wide disparity for the length of the kings. See J. J. Finkelstein, "The Antediluvian Kings: A University of California Tablet," *JCS* 17 (1963): 46, where a list of kings and their reigns are provided.

[27] From a text citing the kings of the city Lagash, it reads for the generations after the flood:

In those days a child spent a hundred years
    in diapers (lit. 'in <bits> of the wash')
After he had grown up he spent a hundred years
    without being given any task (to perform)
He was small, he was dull witted
    his mother watched over him,
His straw-bedding was laid down in the cowpen.

Jacobsen ("The Eridu Genesis," *JBL* 100 [1981]: 513–29) observes that not only were the kings long-lived but "took their time about growing up." He observes the same phenomenon for Olympus in Hesiod and that Methuselah was 187 years old before fathering his first child.

[28] Kitchen, *Ancient Orient,* 40–41.

theological purposes by demonstrating the outworking of God's decrees at creation (1:28) and in the garden (3:17–19) as well as points to the chosen line of Adamic descent in terms of antediluvian history. In the Sumerian tale the human condition progresses with the founding of kingship and civilization. Unlike this optimism, Genesis tells how God's perfect world morally deteriorates. It is Genesis's obsession with the moral factor that distinguishes the biblical account of early man from all others.[29] Furthermore, it shows that the peoples of the hoary past were not semidivine beings. The antediluvian patriarchs were decidedly mortal.

By way of summary, the ages of Genesis's patriarchs remain a mystery that will meet with a satisfactory resolution only if new information becomes available. We can assert confidently that the listing concerns actual historical figures. Its appropriation by the author rendered theological purposes: (1) to show the perpetuation of the *imago Dei* and blessing (1:26–28) and (2) to indicate how sin impaired the longevity of human life and that man is mortal, doomed to death because of sin in the garden (3:17–19). Also since Genesis does not offer the ages of the patriarchs as a means of dating creation or the flood,[30] we should avoid using the numbers as a means for establishing an absolute chronology. Genesis 5 is best taken as an "open" genealogy, perhaps spanning several millennia, though we cannot conclusively assert how much time.[31]

1. Introduction: Creation and Blessing (5:1–2)

The opening two verses present a title and prologue to the ten-paragraph genealogy of vv. 3–32. Following the title (v. 1a) the prologue backtracks to 1:26–28 by echoing the motifs of mankind created in the divine image and the blessing of procreation (vv. 1b–2). An inclusio brackets the introduction:

---

[29] Jacobsen comments: "The moral judgment here introduced [in Genesis], and the ensuing pessimistic viewpoint, could not be more different from the tenor of the Sumerian tale; only the assurance that such a flood will not recur is common to both" ("The Eridu Genesis," 529).

[30] The author of Kings, for example, clearly is concerned with chronology in 1 Kgs 6:1. B. B. Warfield concluded that chaps. 5 and 11 were not presented for chronological aims ("On the Antiquity and the Unity of the Human Race," *PTR* 9 [1911]: 1–25). He rightly comments that the issue of the "antiquity of man has of itself no theological significance. It is to theology, as such, a matter of entire indifference how long man has existed on earth" (p. 1). The concern on the part of theologians has been generated by the contrast between science's exaggerated ages of humanity and the illusory appearance of man's recent origins in the early genealogies.

[31] J. A. Boreland rightly observes that any gaps in chap. 5's genealogy could not, on the basis of biblical practice, be sufficient to oblige the hundreds of millennia required by evolutionary paleontology ("Did People Live to Be Hundreds of Years Old Before the Flood?—Yes," in *The Genesis Debate: Persistent Questions about Creation and the Flood* [Grand Rapids: Baker, 1990], 177–78).

"When God created man" (v. 1b) and "when they were created" (v. 2b).[32] Sandwiched between are four comments on human creation: (1) God created mankind in his image; (2) God made mankind "male and female"; (3) God blessed them; and (4) he named them "man" *(ʾādām)*. This last element, naming humanity "man," is novel to the passage and is not found in Genesis 1. As we show at v. 3, this is an adaptation that links chap. 5 with both the language of the creation account (1:1–2:3) and the garden *tōlĕdōt* (2:4–4:26).

(1) Title of the Genealogy (5:1a)

1This is the written account of Adam's line.

The *tōlĕdōt* formula ("account") differs from all others in and outside Genesis by the descriptive word "written" *(sēper),* specifying that the author has used a written source. It is reasonable to surmise that other genealogies occurring in Genesis were also recorded resources available to the author, especially the similar Shemite line (11:10–26). Snippets from similar sources, if not the same source, may be found in 9:28–29 (Noah) and 11:32 (Terah) in Genesis 1–11. It has been posited that there was originally an independent "Toledoth Book," whose title is retained here (5:1a), consisting of genealogies and lists with perhaps some brief theological and biographical comments.[33] The Old Testament elsewhere knows of ancient books as in the "Book of the Wars of the LORD" (Num 21:14) and the "Book of Jashar" (Josh 10:13; 2 Sam 1:18). Although we agree that probably written sources, such as the *tōlĕdōt* materials,[34] were used by the author, the word *sēper* can be taken as any written source without restriction to a "book" in our contemporary sense (e.g., Deut

---

[32] Cf. Westermann, *Genesis 1–11,* 355. The NASB's rendering shows this more readily than the NIV. We have translated so as to show the structure:

In the day God created *ʾādām,*
    In the likeness of God he made him.
    Male and female he created them,
    And he blessed them,
    And named them *ʾādām*
in the day they were created.

[33] G. von Rad proposed that P appropriated information from a Toledoth Book (*Die Priesterschrift im Hexateuch* [1934] and *Genesis,* OTL [Philadelphia: Westminster, 1972], 70). Westermann (*Genesis 1–11,* 355) opposes the idea, arguing that as a title תּוֹלְדֹת must be used only in a general way, whereas here it refers specifically to Adam's line. He concludes that סֵפֶר is best translated "list," referring only to the subsequent list of names generated in chap. 5. Wenham, on the basis that סֵפֶר ("book") indicates a written document, agrees that most likely an independent literary source is being quoted here and at 11:10–26, though we cannot know its contents with certainty (*Genesis 1–15,* 122).

[34] D. Garrett rightly observes that the *tōlĕdōt* sources in Genesis are best viewed as only witnesses to those sources (*Rethinking Genesis: The Sources and Authorship of the First Book of the Pentateuch* [Grand Rapids: Baker, 1991], 103).

24:3; Jer 32:11–12). It is sufficient to say that 5:1a refers to a written document without recommending that it is part of an encompassing book of genealogies. The title probably refers to chap. 5 alone, though 11:10–26 may have been a part. More likely, 11:10–26 was a distinct written literary source available to the author that accounts for significant differences between them.[35]

(2) Creation of Mankind (5:1b–2)

When God created man, he made him in the likeness of God. [2]He created them male and female and blessed them. And when they were created, he called them "man."

5:1b–2 By imitating 1:27–28, the author ties the significance of the genealogy to creation theology, where human life stands in the descent of God (cf. "sons of God," 6:2) and is the preeminent recipient of God's blessing. This linkage is achieved by a number of lexical repetitions, including "man," "created," "likeness," "male and female," and "blessed." The same creation themes of 1:1–2:3 are rehearsed in 5:1b–2 by its appeal to the parade passage of the creation narrative, the making and blessing of mankind (1:26–28). Divine image and blessing are continued among the human family, it would seem, without suspension.

Also the framework of vv. 1b–2 adapts the structure and language introducing the former *tōlĕdōt* (2:4–4:26), which reads: "This is the account *[tōlĕdōt]* of the heavens and the earth when they were created *[bĕhibbārĕʾām],* in the day the LORD God made *[bĕyôm ʿăśôt YHWH ʾĕlōhîm]* earth and heaven" (2:4a, NASB). Verses 1b–2 have similarly, "In the day God created *[bĕyôm bĕrōʾ ʾĕlōhîm]* man . . . in the day they were created *[bĕyôm bĕhibbārĕʾām]*."[36] This sets chap. 5 in the context of the garden events as well.

Moreover, the repetition of *ʾādām,* occurring four times in 5:1–3, enables a transition from the generic sense of "man," as in 1:26–28, to the personal "Adam," as in the garden *tōlĕdōt*. The generic sense in 5:1b–2, "When God created man" and "he called them 'man,'" betrays an ambiguity because more

---

[35] E.g., G. C. Aalders, *Genesis,* BSC, vol. 1 (Grand Rapids: Regency/Zondervan, 1981), 256. Alternatively, 11:10–26 may be a continuation of the original document but which has been altered by the author for a different theological emphasis.

[36] The extended parallelism between the two passages is recognizable:

2:4a בְּהִבָּרְאָם
2:4b בְּיוֹם עֲשׂוֹת יְהוָה אֱלֹהִים
5:1a בְּיוֹם בְּרֹא אֱלֹהִים
5:2b בְּיוֹם הִבָּרְאָם

The inner legs show differences in the verbal infinitives (בְּרֹא/עֲשׂוֹת) and the combination of divine names with *YHWH* (2:4b). For the parallel of the infinitives, see the same verbs (בָּרָא/עָשָׂה) in parallel at 2:4a,b; the rare combination of divine names occurs only in Gen 2–3 and Exod 9:30.

than the generic sense is in view. Individual *ʾādām* ("Adam") in the title that precedes (v. 1a) and the following reference to personal *ʾādām* in v. 3 produces a subtle shift from generic to individual Adam. As a result the double entendre in vv. 1b–2 is resolved in v. 3, which initiates the genealogy of the individual person "Adam."[37]

Both "image" and gender distinction ("male and female") are emphasized as in 1:27–28 because the blessing, as evidenced through procreation (1:28), is realized by the prolific Sethites. By this genealogy creation's order is perpetuated (vv. 1b–3). The recitation of ten names (indicating completeness) in chap. 5 and the common refrain "other sons and daughters" (vv. 4,10,13,16,19,22,26,30) trumpet the mercy and provision of God for the line of Seth. Just as we remember the uniform six days of creation, we hear in chap. 5 the same drumbeat of God's orderly creation by the regular birth of human life.

2. "Image of God" from Adam to Noah (5:3–32)

Following the introduction, the genealogy proper traces the ancestral lineage from Adam, the first to bear the *imago Dei,* to the flood survivor, Noah. The constancy and continuity of the family indicates the uninterrupted succession of the divine image passed down by generation to generation from father to son. Among the passage of its ten members, special theological addenda spotlight Adam, Enoch, Lamech, and Noah. After Adam (vv. 3–5), nine sons are listed, and in each case (except Enoch, Lamech, and Noah) the same formulaic information is followed, assigning (1) the age of the individual patriarch when he fathers his firstborn son, (2) the remaining years of his life, (3) the acknowledgment of "other sons and daughters," (4) the total years of his life, and (5) the notice of his death. Each patriarch's greatest contribution is his role in affecting the promised blessing through the birth of a descendant. This is each patriarch's portion in God's charitable plans for the human family. Nevertheless, no one achieves the full realization of the blessing since death continues its reign. This is true even for righteous Enoch, whose son Methuselah also dies, having inherited the sentence of death.

(1) Adam, the First (5:3–5)

3When Adam had lived 130 years, he had a son in his own likeness, in his own image; and he named him Seth. 4After Seth was born, Adam lived 800 years and had other sons and daughters. 5Altogether, Adam lived 930 years, and then he died.

---

[37] See R. Robinson ("Literary Functions of the Genealogies of Genesis," *CBQ* 48 [1986]: 599–600), who observes that genealogies are for individuals who have life stories.

As we noted earlier, chap. 5 is a new beginning for the human family since it backtracks to 1:26–28; yet this new start does not escape the consequences of the garden. Verses 2–3 also allude to the first *tōlĕdōt* section, 2:4–4:26. There sin had its beginnings, and its defilement was manifested, also in the family of Adam, by the firstborn—Cain the Murderer. This allusion to chaps. 2–4 is achieved by repeating the three names in the concluding verses (4:25–26) of the previous section—Adam, Seth, and Enosh. This overlay of chaps. 4–5 unites the two *tōlĕdōt,* showing that the generations of Adam must be viewed in the context of the former "*tōlĕdōt* of the heavens and the earth" (2:4–4:26).

Further, the two passages show verbal linkage. The naming formula of vv. 2–3 for Adam and Seth echoes the naming formula in 3:20 (Eve) and 4:17 (Enoch), but especially 4:25–26 (Seth, Enosh).[38] The language of 4:25–26 is virtually identical to 5:2–3, and taken together they form a chiasmus.[39] Thus the genealogy of Adam draws together the theological emphases already portrayed in the preceding narratives by the author: (1) the divine image and blessing of humanity at creation (1:1–2:3) and (2) the threat to that promissory blessing through the sinful rebellion of that same humanity, via Adam and Cain (2:4–4:26).

Adam's lineage via Seth presents the renewed optimism of life, "image," and blessing but is sobered by the harrowing refrain "and then he died" (v. 5). This optimism for Seth's line is heard again in Lamech's explanation for naming "Noah" (v. 29), but the sins of the past are not evaded since that hope is shadowed by "the labor and painful toil of our hands" (v. 29; cf. 3:17–19). Such is the double-edged sword of human experience; life produces hope only to see it dashed by the all-too-real finality of death. Nevertheless, Genesis's early genealogies indicate that hope prevails through Adam's successors—namely, in Noah and later Abraham (5:1–32; 11:10–26), both of whom are instrumental in the preservation of the blessing. Carrying on, the Christian message proclaims that those born to the "last Adam" realize that hope, one that transcends even the clutches of Ancient Death (Rom 5:12–21; 1 Cor 15:22,45–49).

Both Testaments show how the message of salvation is anchored in history by presenting genealogies as their prelude.[40] The gospel of Jesus of Nazareth

---

[38] See H. N. Wallace, "The Toledot of Adam," in *Studies in the Pentateuch,* VTSup 41 (Leiden: Brill, 1990), 20–21. Also there is the repetition of קרא שׁם in 4:26b referring to worship ("call on the name") and the naming formula of 5:2–3.

[39] Notice the parallel language and the play of the inner two lines where both "Enosh" and "Adam" mean "man":

4:25 וַתִּקְרָא אֶת־שְׁמוֹ שֵׁת
4:26 וַיִּקְרָא אֶת־שְׁמוֹ אֱנוֹשׁ
5:2 וַיִּקְרָא אֶת־שְׁמָם אָדָם
5:3 וַיִּקְרָא אֶת־שְׁמוֹ שֵׁת

[40] See Westermann, *Genesis 1–11,* 361–62.

is set by the Evangelists in the framework of human history. Luke particularly takes the universal view of the work of Jesus in tracing Jesus' ancestry back to Adam. It shows dependence on Genesis 5 and 11 specifically (3:34–38), where Luke pointed out the unique relationship Adam enjoyed as the "son of God" (3:38). He utilized Jesus' human credentials to contribute to his wider Christological purpose (3:21–38), appealing to Adam as a prototype of Jesus as the Son of God.[41] But Matthew also did not suspend the gospel above history. Although his concerns were no broader than Abraham's headship, he clearly established Jesus' mission in the arena of Jewish history, especially the royal role of David (Matt 1:1,17).

5:3 By referring to Seth as born in the "likeness" and "image" of his father, the genealogy shows the perpetuation of the divine image and blessing, which has its beginnings in the creation of mankind (1:26). The inversion of the order of the two terms from that in 1:26 is a literary device of back reference.[42] The NIV's rendering "own" image and "own" likeness specifies what is reasonably implied by the text: as God bequeathed his image to humanity, Adam has endowed his image to Seth, including human sinfulness and its consequences.

Procreation is the mechanism that assures the passing on of the divine "image." Seth is not "created" (1:27) or "formed" (2:7) as Adam was, but he was "fathered" and thereby is the recipient of Adam's human legacy.[43] Seth perpetuates the blessing bestowed upon humanity, but also he inherits the consequences of his father's sin ("and then he died," v. 8). The ongoing tension between the blessing of the *imago Dei* and the unlawful attempt of humanity to achieve more than God intended is the theological undercurrent of the genealogy. This is well illustrated by the career of Enoch (vv. 21–24) and the special pleading of Lamech (v. 29). Moreover, the *tōlĕdōt*'s conclusion shows the paradox of this Adamic line where corruption by the "sons of God" and the violence of the age (6:1–7) is countered by the favored descendant, Noah (6:8).

5:4 Adam "had other sons and daughters," whose names are not given. This differs from chap. 4's naming of Lamech's three sons and daughter, Naamah. But this is because of the different purposes of the two genealogies. Seth's genealogy wants to show an unbroken line between Adam and Noah by listing only the firstborn sons who represent the inheritance of the divine image and blessing that is enjoyed by all Seth's progeny.

---

[41] For this discussion see R. H. Stein, *Luke*, NAC (Nashville: Broadman, 1992), 142–43.

[42] Note the same device connecting 2:1–3 back to 1:1 (see discussion of literary structure of 1:1–2:3 on p. 114).

[43] "He had a son" renders יוֹלֶד (Heb. gaps "son"), which is traditionally translated "begat a son" (AV). The term יָלַד (in *qal* and *hiphil* stems) is commonly used in genealogical records where it means "to father a child" (e.g., *qal*, 4:18; 10:8,13,15ff. with 1 Chr 1:10–11,13,18ff.; *hiphil*, Ruth 4:18–22; 1 Chr 2:10–11ff.). Genesis's popular rubric תּוֹלְדֹת ("account") is derived from this verb.

"Sons and daughters" is stereotypical of chap. 5 and indicates the prodigious offspring of the Sethite family by the charity of God. It provides a literary foil for the ten descendants noted in the list, since they are distinguished by name as the firstborn and appointed heirs of the blessing. The "daughters" born to Adam and his descendants are included, though not by name, because they, like Eve, played the critical role of procreation in the perpetuation of the blessing and the expansion of the righteous lineage. "Sons and daughters" reflects the introduction's "male and female" (5:1; 1:27–28), showing that both genders benefit, whether named or unnamed. Also "daughters" echoes the programmatic passage of 3:15, which points to the woman's "seed" as the hope of the human family. Lamech's remarks particularly reflect this (v. 29).

The long life spans of each patriarch add to the author's depiction of Seth's line as the lineage of blessing and hope. In the Mosaic law long life was the product of God's blessing for obedience. This was etched in the mind of the community by the Fifth Commandment (Exod 20:12; Deut 5:16), which is distinctive as the first of the commands with a promise (Eph 6:2–3). Long life was commonly tied to the heritage of living in the land (e.g., Deut 4:25; 30:20). Outstanding heroes, such as Abraham, Gideon, and David, were said to have lived to a "good old age" (Gen 25:8; Judg 8:32; 1 Chr 29:28).[44] Strikingly, apart from the patriarchs of Genesis, in the Old Testament only Job (140), Moses (120), Joshua (110), and Jehoiada (130) lived longer than a century of years. Isaiah also points to long life as a feature of blessing in the eschatological age (Isa 65:20).

5:5 The ominous "and then he died" proves the veracity of God's warning (2:17) and the outworking of his punishment imposed for sinful rebellion (3:17–19).[45] This single word in the Hebrew text *(wayyāmōt)* at the close of each patriarch's career becomes a resounding testimony to the inevitable human end. It is literally the last word of each refrain.

As Paul remarks, "sin exercised dominion in death" (Rom 5:21, NRSV). Genesis 5 was for Paul the lamentable evidence of Adam's part in sin's entrance into the world (Rom 5:12–21). That all men and women are as Adam, namely, sinners under the condemnation of death, the apostle demonstrates by appealing to the death knell sounded for each of Adam's generations. Paul shows that all people are condemned by Adam's disobedience since all those who antedated Moses' law suffered the consequences of a lawbreaker, though without the law because all were sinners "in Adam." Christ is Adam's antitype

---

[44] J. G. Harris, "Old Age," *ABD* 5.10–13.

[45] Calvin conceded the edification of this dreadful refrain: "It is useful, in a picture of so many ages, to behold, at one glance, the continual course and tenor of divine vengeance; because, otherwise, we imagine that God is in some way forgetful; and to nothing are we more prone than to dream of immortality on earth, unless death is frequently brought before our eyes" (*Comm.,* 229–30).

and antidote, for what Adam bequeathed, the one man Christ surmounted and surpassed. Unlike the disobedience in Adam's "garden," Christ's Gethsemane triumphed in obedience, and because of his obedience we reap righteousness and life "through Jesus Christ our Lord" (Rom 5:18–21).

(2) Seth through Jared (5:6–20)

6When Seth had lived 105 years, he became the father of Enosh. 7And after he
became the father of Enosh, Seth lived 807 years and had other sons and daugh-
ters. 8Altogether, Seth lived 912 years, and then he died.
9When Enosh had lived 90 years, he became the father of Kenan. 10And after
he became the father of Kenan, Enosh lived 815 years and had other sons and
daughters. 11Altogether, Enosh lived 905 years, and then he died.
12When Kenan had lived 70 years, he became the father of Mahalalel. 13And
after he became the father of Mahalalel, Kenan lived 840 years and had other
sons and daughters. 14Altogether, Kenan lived 910 years, and then he died.
15When Mahalalel had lived 65 years, he became the father of Jared. 16And
after he became the father of Jared, Mahalalel lived 830 years and had other sons
and daughters. 17Altogether, Mahalalel lived 895 years, and then he died.
18When Jared had lived 162 years, he became the father of Enoch. 19And after
he became the father of Enoch, Jared lived 800 years and had other sons and
daughters. 20Altogether, Jared lived 962 years, and then he died.

Of the first half of Adam's noted descendants—Seth, Enosh, Kenan, Mehalalel, and Jared—little is known. Their names as a sequence occur once more in the genealogy of Jesus (Luke 3:37–38). They are presented in Genesis as part of the ongoing chain of human existence. Their obscurity does not dismiss their significance for the progress of the human family.[46] Without them and without each one in the long train of "unknowns," humanity as community would not be complete.

5:6–11 The naming of Seth and Enosh has drawn the narrative of 4:25–26 into the panorama of the genealogy at hand. Seth is the venerated successor to Abel in 4:25. Chapter 5's rhythmic pattern implies that as Adam passed on the image and blessing (v. 3), Seth and his successors do the same. His fathering of Enosh assures that Seth's death, unlike Abel's, will not jeopardize the promise.

We have commented already on the significance of Seth's and Enosh's names (see 4:25–26). Here those notions of "supplant" (Seth) and "man" (Enosh) reflect the perpetuity of the Adamic line. The significance of "Enosh" ("man") as an intentional echo of Father "Adam" ("mankind") has theological implications for Enosh as the head of new stock, for 4:26b indicates that during

---

[46] Compare the opinion of the "Teacher" in Eccl 1:4,11, who observes that the elemental events of life (e.g., birth, marriage, death) are disappointingly the same (see comments in Garrett, *Proverbs, Ecclesiastes, and Song of Songs,* NAC [Nashville: Broadman, 1993], 288). But we see Enoch! Enoch's translation portends a better outcome for people of godly faith.

his times the name of Yahweh becomes paramount on the lips of people. Seth's line therefore accomplishes what is expected for Adam's slain son, Abel.

5:12–20 "Kenan" usually is treated as another form of "Cain," whose etymology is disputed (see introduction to 4:1–26). "Mahalalel" occurs also in Neh 11:4. It is formed by the combination of two words: the verbal root *hālal* ("praise"), probably in the participial form (with *mem* prefix) and the generic divine name *ʾēl* ("El/God"), meaning "Praise of God/El" or "(One who is) Praising God/El." The etymology of Jared is uncertain (cp. "Jered," 1 Chr 4:18). Some relate it to Hebrew *yārad*, "to go down, descend," which is most likely, or Akkadian *wardu*, meaning "servant."

(3) Enoch, Seventh from Adam (5:21–24)

21When Enoch had lived 65 years, he became the father of Methuselah. 22And after he became the father of Methuselah, Enoch walked with God 300 years and had other sons and daughters. 23Altogether, Enoch lived 365 years. 24Enoch walked with God; then he was no more, because God took him away.

5:21–22 As the seventh member of the Sethite clan, Enoch is the highlighted descendant among the ten names.[47] Also by a literary divergence from the highly repetitious schema of the chapter, his career is distinguished from his predecessors. Where the refrain "Enoch lived" would be expected (v. 22), we read "Enoch walked with God."[48] That this feature of Enoch's life was prominent in the mind of the author is evidenced by its recurrence in v. 24. It is his "walk with God" that explains why Enoch did not die.

"Walked with God" is metaphorical and indicates that Enoch had a lifestyle characterized by his devotion to God. The sense of "walk" *(hālak)* in its verbal stem indicates a communion or intimacy with God.[49] It is reminiscent of Adam's initial experience (3:8) and is the same wording that typifies Noah, who is remembered for his godly reputation (6:9). Moreover, the Abraham narrative has similar language where God exhorts Abraham to godly faithfulness (17:1; 24:40; cf. 48:15). In later Israel this nuance of divine Presence describes God's covenantal intimacy with Israel where he "walks" in the camp (e.g., Lev 26:12; Deut 23:14[15]). For the psalmist to "walk before God" means life and prosperity (Pss 56:13[14]; 116:9).

---

[47] See 4:17 for discussion of etymology.

[48] The LXX tradition, probably troubled by the anthropomorphic language of Genesis, interpreted "Enoch walked with God" with the more acceptable "Enoch was well pleasing to God" (vv. 23–24; also 6:9). Verse 24b in the LXX also has "he was not found, because God had taken him" for the enigmatic Heb. "he was no more, because God took him away," quoted directly in Heb 11:6. See F. F. Bruce, *The Epistle to the Hebrews,* NICNT (Grand Rapids: Eerdmans, 1964), 287.

[49] Here and in the following examples הָלַךְ occurs in the *hithpael* stem, which is best taken as iterative in sense, meaning that Enoch walked "back and forth" with God. See *IBHS* § 26.1.2.

5:23–24 Such a distinctive reference is sufficient by itself to honor Enoch, but v. 24 adds a surprising variance; unlike the normative pattern, the phrase "and then he died" is absent. His disappearance is simply but obscurely expressed: "he was not" or "he did not exist" *(ʾêninnû)*. The explanation for Enoch's disappearance is equally veiled by the text, "God took him away" (v. 24). "Took" *(lāqaḥ)* is a common Hebrew term having a variety of meanings, the simplest being "to take, fetch." It may refer to death, where one's life is "taken" (1 Kgs 19:10,14) or the opposite, where one's life is "snatched" from death (Ps 49:15[16]). Yet in some contexts "taking" indicates a reception into the presence of God. The same verb occurs for the assumption of Elijah, whom the Lord "took" in the whirlwind (2 Kgs 2:3,10–11). Also the psalmist (73:24[25]) expected to be "taken" after life "to glory."[50] The writer to the Hebrews clarifies the meaning of "taken" by adding "so that he did not experience death" (Heb 11:5).

Whereas Adam is precluded from the garden and Cain is driven from the presence of God, Enoch experiences that privilege and escapes the sentence of his predecessors—death. "The finality of death caused by sin, and so powerfully demonstrated in the genealogy of Genesis, is in fact not so final. Man was not born to die; he was born to live, and that life comes by walking with God. . . . Walking with God is the key to the chains of the curse."[51] Enoch's transport yet says more for the broader salvific plan of God. It is signal confirmation of God's merciful designs to fulfill his promises of life and blessing. Such favor upon Seth's lineage indicates that his will be the elected vehicle (i.e., Abraham).

Enoch's translation shaped later Jewish and Christian assessment of him as a paragon of righteousness (e.g., *Sir* 49:14; *1 Clem* 9:3).[52] The writer to the Hebrews recognized that such godliness demanded also a person of remarkable faith, and he pointed to Enoch as exemplary of these two interdependent traits, which are required to please God (Heb 11:5).[53] The indisputable evidence of

[50] See Kaiser, "לָקַח *(lāqaḥ)*," *TWOT* 1.482.

[51] T. J. Cole, "Enoch, a Man Who Walked with God," *BSac* 148 (1991): 294.

[52] See, e.g., J. C. VanderKam, *Enoch and the Growth of an Apocalyptic Tradition,* CBQMS 16 (Washington, D.C.: Catholic Biblical Association of America, 1984). He likens Enoch to Enmeduranki of the Sumerian King List, who is often seventh among the antediluvian kings in the various lists and who enjoyed a special relationship with the sun god, Shamash (pp. 33–52). VanderKam concludes that the biblical portrait of Enoch is based on this Mesopotamian figure (p. 50). But there are too many differences to merit such a sweeping assertion. Also J. A. Skinner (*A Critical and Exegetical Commentary on Genesis,* ICC, 2d ed. [Edinburgh: T & T Clark, 1910], 132) recommended this, but he further compared Enoch's translation to the Babylonian figure Utnapishtim (flood hero) who is taken to live with the gods (p. 159). Still others appeal to Enmeduranki's *apkallū* (sage), Utu'abzu, who ascended to heaven, as the mythological base for Enoch's translation. Again there is no evidence other than superficial similarities for concluding that the traditions are related.

[53] Bruce (*Hebrews,* 289) observes that the writer to the Hebrews appropriated the LXX rendering "he had pleased God," for it was consistent with the prophets, who show that it is righteousness that pleases the Lord (Mic 6:8).

Enoch's pleasing God was his translation. Thus the writer could say unequivocally, "And without faith it is impossible to please God" (Heb 11:6).

The comparative brevity of his life among the antediluvians and the symbolic potential of "365 years" also contributed to his reputation in later Jewish thought. Interestingly, he fathered Methuselah (v. 21), who proved to live the longest among the patriarchs (v. 27). The repetition of "Enoch walked with God" may have been designed to dispel any idea that the patriarch's shorter life was a punishment for sin.[54] Enoch's age corresponds to the 365 days in a solar year, suggesting completeness, which has led some to think that his life could be taken early since he had lived a well-rounded life.[55] Certainly the length of a person's life is of negligible value compared to the quality of his relationship with God.

Jewish literature pointed to him as the recipient of special revelations in heaven concerning creation and eschatological events. It was believed that he passed on these mysteries to Methuselah to encourage the righteous during the final days. Of the three books of *Enoch,* particularly important was *1 Enoch,* which consisted of a collection of such speculations among the Jews (fourth to first centuries B.C.; cf. also *Jub.* 4:22–24).[56] The Christian community's knowledge of the book is seen in Jude, where the apostle (v. 14) quotes from the prophecy "Enoch, the seventh from Adam" (*1 Enoch* 1:9) concerning the final judgment of God on the ungodly.

(4) Methuselah (5:25–27)

25When Methuselah had lived 187 years, he became the father of Lamech.
26And after he became the father of Lamech, Methuselah lived 782 years and had other sons and daughters. 27Altogether, Methuselah lived 969 years, and then he died.

Methuselah's 969 years distinguish him as the longest-living person in the Bible.[57] Not only does chap. 5 indicate the longevity of ancient man but it also may reflect a time when human life developed at a slower pace. Methuselah was 187 years old before he fathered Lamech, and Lamech was 182 years when his son Noah was born.[58] The name "Methuselah" is a combination of *mětû*, "man of," and *šelah,* "Shelah." The former is related to West Semitic *mutu* ("person, man, husband"), but "Shelah" is uncertain. Shelah also occurs

[54] N. M. Sarna refers to the medieval commentary Bekhor Shor for this opinion (בראשית *Genesis,* JPST [Philadelphia: Jewish Publication Society, 1989], 43). *Gen. Rab.* 25.1 disputes the conclusion that Enoch did not die. *Tg. Onq.* even adds that the Lord "slew him."

[55] E.g., Westermann, *Genesis 1–11,* 358.

[56] See Hess, "Enoch," and "Enoch, First Book of," *ABD* 2.508.

[57] "As such he is the patron saint of geriatrics" (V. Hamilton, *Genesis 1–17,* NICOT [Grand Rapids: Eerdmans, 1990], 258), but a mere suckling compared to the antediluvian kings of the Sumerians.

[58] See n. 26.

in 10:24 and 11:12–15. “Shelah” is taken either as a weapon (“man of the weapon,” cf. Neh 4:17), a place name, or deity.[59]

(5) Lamech (5:28–31)

[28]When Lamech had lived 182 years, he had a son. [29]He named him Noah and said, “He will comfort us in the labor and painful toil of our hands caused by the ground the LORD has cursed.” [30]After Noah was born, Lamech lived 595 years and had other sons and daughters. [31]Altogether, Lamech lived 777 years, and then he died.

5:28 Lamech is remembered as the father of the flood survivor, Noah, who in explaining the meaning of his son’s name laments the sorry state of man under the burdensome consequences of the cursed ground. “Lamech” is exactly the same in spelling as Cain’s descendant of that name (4:18).[60] At 4:18–24 we commented how the similarity of names and arrangement with chap. 5 invited a contrast between the two genealogies. The contradiction between the piety of Sethite Lamech, reflected by his prayerful hope in the Lord, and the malevolence of Cainite Lamech’s virulent boasts could not be more sharply drawn by the text. Another point of contrast is the association of “seven” with each man’s career. Lamech lives “777 years” (v. 31), which attracts notice to the vengeful “seventy-seven times” uttered by Cain’s Lamech (4:24).

5:29–31 Lamech is the only member of the genealogy to explain the meaning of his son’s name (v. 29). This attendant etymology distinguishes Noah’s place in the ten-member assembly. Verse 28 diverges from the common pattern in chap. 5 by substituting “son” for the name of the firstborn. The paragraph then from the start focuses attention on the naming formula.

Early Jewish commentators recognized the incongruity between the etymology of the name “Noah” and the explanation “comfort” that Lamech gives it (*Gen. Rab.* 25.2). “Noah” *(nōaḥ)* is better related to “rest” *(nûaḥ)* than to “comfort” *(nāḥam)*. For the name “Noah” we expect the interpretation “this one will give us rest *(yĕnîḥēnû)*.” And, conversely, for the explanation “comfort,” a corresponding name such as “Menahem” *(mĕnaḥēm)* or “Nahman” *(naḥmān)* is expected.[61] The LXX tradition “solved” the problem by emending the text with the secondary reading “he will give us rest.”[62]

---

[59] R. S. Hess (“Methuselah,” *ABD* 4.800–1) recommends “man [devotee] of *šalah* [deity]”; the combination of *mutu* and a divine name is attested in second-millennium names. But Hess acknowledges such a deity is not known apart from personal names. Also see Hess, “A Comparison of the Onomastica in Genealogical and Narrative Texts of Genesis 1–11,” in *Proceedings, 10th World Congress of Jewish Studies,* ed. D. Assaf (Jerusalem: World Union of Jewish Studies, 1990), 72–73.

[60] For a discussion of the name’s etymology see chap. 4.

[61] Cp. “Nehemiah” (נְחֶמְיָה), derived from נָחַם.

[62] Assuming יְנִיחֵנוּ, the LXX has οὗτος διαναπαύσει ἡμᾶς.

The ambiguity is best explained as a complex play on the sounds *n* and *ḥ* found both in the name "Noah" and the words "rest" and "comfort." "Noah" *(nōaḥ)* sounds similar to the verb *nāḥam* in "he will *comfort* us" *(yĕnāḥamēnû),* serving as a play on his name, not a true etymology.[63] Also the name "Noah" itself suggests the subtle meaning "rest" *(nûaḥ)* that lies behind the name. This verse anticipates the recurring plays on the name "Noah" in the following flood narrative, where *nûaḥ* and *nāḥam* often arise.[64] Moreover, the terms "rest" and "comfort" are not that distant in meaning; Ezek 5:13 has them in parallel: "Thus My anger will be spent, and I will satisfy [from *nûaḥ*] My wrath on them, and I shall be appeased [from *nāḥam*]" (NASB).[65] For Lamech the name "Noah" suggests "rest/relief" and "comfort" at the same time; "Noah" itself stands for "rest," and thus Lamech appends "comfort."

By naming his son "Noah," then, Lamech expresses hope for the human family through his offspring. His vision for Noah rings with the reverberating sounds of the garden's tragedy. Reference to toilsome labor and the cursed ground reflects the verdict of God's judgment in 3:17–18, where "cursed is the ground," and the man is doomed to beat out his existence by "painful toil." Also the naming formula ("and he/she named him *X*") correlates with what we find in the naming of Seth and Enosh at the close of the former *tōlĕdōt* section (4:25–26) and the naming of Seth in the present chapter (5:3). Noah's naming is set then in the circumstances of the garden's failure and in the earlier framework of creation's promise *(imago Dei)* in 1:26–28; 5:1–3.[66]

Lamech's yearning for a redeemer not only backtracks but also anticipates the iniquity of Noah's day, as described in 6:5–8. The same tandem of terms in 5:29 occurs again in 6:6, where "grieved" (from *nāḥam*) and "filled with pain" appear.[67] Thus Lamech tied the widespread wickedness of human society to man's first act of disobedience in the garden. Yet the naming of Noah is preeminently optimistic. Lamech looks ahead to a future victory (as 3:15) and prays that Noah will be instrumental in achieving it. His sweeping expression "he

---

[63] E.g., Sarna, *Genesis,* 46.

[64] The following allusions to "Noah," in addition to יְנַחֲמֵנוּ in 5:29, are widely recognized: וַיִּנָּחֶם (Yahweh "grieved") 6:6; נִחַמְתִּי ("I am grieved") 6:7; חֵן (Noah found "favor") 6:8; וַתָּנַח (the ark "came to rest") 8:4; מָנוֹחַ (no "resting-place") 8:9; רֵיחַ הַנִּיחֹחַ (Yahweh smelled the "pleasing aroma," better "soothing aroma") 8:21. Also there is the play between "grieved" (נָחַם) and "wipe out" (מָחָה) in 6:6–7 (see 8:21 discussion).

[65] Noted by Hamilton, *Genesis 1–17,* 259.

[66] V. 29 is commonly assigned by source critics to J, since it possesses the divine name Yahweh, and its narrative style diverts from the rhythmic pattern of P's chap. 5. There is no reason to insist on this, however, since 5:3 (P) shows the same diversion; and it is unconvincing, if not disingenuous, when critics attribute 5:3 to a later editor who has combined elements of J and P.

[67] נָחַם in 5:29 is in the *piel* stem, translated "comfort," whereas 6:6 has the *niphal* form, rendered "grieved" (as in 6:7). Also 6:6 possesses the verbal form עָשַׂב ("pained"), while the nominal form occurs in 5:29 and 3:17.

[Noah] will comfort *us"* refers in a general sense to the Sethite ancestral line. Lamech envisions an inclusive vindication. Moreover, the naming of "Noah" anticipates his critical role in the following flood narrative where he, while not achieving his father's highest aspirations, keeps alive the hope of a final deliverer. Lamech's naming of Noah then propels the Sethite line forward to the next *tōlĕdōt* narrative (6:9–9:29).

We have just said that Lamech's plea for "comfort" refers to Noah's future role. What specific "comfort" does Noah actually achieve? Some interpreters have taken the phrase "by the ground" ("from the ground," NASB) as descriptive of "comfort," thus pointing to Noah's discovery of viticulture as "relief" from the curse (see 9:20).[68] If so, Noah's vineyard would evidence a covenant reprieve from the Edenic curse of the ground, interpreting the Lord's promise in 8:21–22 as its repeal. The difficulty with this interpretation lies in the absence of such a respite after the flood. Man does not return to Eden, and the harshness of the ground continues despite the new covenant with Noah and can only be tamed by toilsome work.[69] Rather, the reprieve in 8:21 concerns the flood, not the curse of 3:17–19. The floodwaters are thus another curse that is revoked by God's promise of seasonal regularity (see 8:21 discussion). Such a flood will not "again" be implemented by divine decree, but there is no suspension of the garden's curse. "From the ground" in v. 29 then refers to the *source* of the "pain" (as in 3:17–19), not the *source* of the "comfort."[70] Noah's vineyard is not the answer to the curse of 3:17–18 but part of the new order, which guarantees fruition in the seasonal calendar (8:22).

Lamech's hope then resides with God's blessing on Noah, who, as the flood account shows, perpetuates the Sethite lineage and hence the *imago Dei* promises of creation as the recipient of God's renewed covenant commitment (8:21–9:17). This alleviation ("comfort") does not come about as Lamech wishes, however, for the relief comes only after a calamitous flood. Ironically, it is the Lord, not Noah, who ultimately accomplishes the salvation of the human family (see 6:6 discussion). Because of God's injured heart at the sin of mankind, both the purge of sinful man and the preservation of the divine plan are conse-

---

[68] E.g., Skinner, *Genesis,* 133; von Rad, *Genesis,* 136; Westermann, *Genesis 1–11,* 360; and E. A. Speiser, *Genesis,* AB (Garden City: Doubleday, 1964), 61. It is argued that the flood surely did not bring relief to Lamech's generation but rather death. Production of wine, however, alleviated the misery of the soil's toil and achieved a beneficial commodity for humanity (e.g., Judg 9:13; Ps 104:15; Prov 31:6–7).

[69] P. R. Davies ("Sons of Cain," in *A Word in Season: Essays in Honor of William McKane,* JSOTSup 42, ed. J. Martin and P. R. Davies [Sheffield: JSOT, 1986], 35–36) argues for both: 8:21–22 resolves the problem of the Edenic curse by God's promise of blessing, but it does not revoke the Edenic curse.

[70] See Wallace, "The Toledoth of Adam," 25–27. The NIV's causal rendering of מִן, "caused by the ground," reflects this interpretation of the verse (also REB), rather than the ambiguous "out of the very soil" (i.e., vineyard?) (NJPS, NJB, NAB, NRSV).

quently set in motion. Afterward we find a final play on the motif of "rest" and "Noah" in the acceptance of Noah's offering as a "soothing aroma" *(rêaḥ ḥannîḥōaḥ;* see 8:21 discussion). By the patriarch's worship and propitiatory offering, the Lord's wrath is satisfied. The "comfort," then, is righteous Noah's role in initiating a new era as the "new Adam" who perpetuates the family blessing by virtue of God's covenant mercies (6:8; 8:1,21–22; 9:1–17).

(6) Noah (5:32)

[32]After Noah was 500 years old, he became the father of Shem, Ham and Japheth.

5:32 The linear feature of the genealogy, which has been followed rigorously up to this point, is abandoned for the inclusive listing of Noah's three offspring (cf. Terah's three sons, 11:26). This prepares for the segmented genealogy of chap. 10, the "account of Shem, Ham, and Japheth, Noah's sons" (10:1), which tracks the postdiluvian families who emanate from him. Whereas the genealogy to this juncture has presented the same information for each patriarch (except Adam and Enoch) in its stereotypical way, the presentation of Noah departs considerably. Verse 32 reads "Noah was" rather than the standard "Noah lived." The formulaic "lived" occurs, however, in 9:28, where the genealogy is resumed after the flood. Also the standard conclusion "and then he died" is likewise delayed until 9:29. Genesis 6:9–9:29, then, is a narrative elaboration about Noah, sandwiched between the genealogical linkage of Adam (5:1–32) and the postdiluvian world of Noah's sons (10:1–32). By embedding the narrative in this way, the genealogical stratagem of the account is given priority. The author's theological concerns are the initiation and momentum of the promissory blessings. This the author achieves by establishing the genealogical relationship between Adam and Abraham (1:26–28 with 5:1–32; 11:10–26).

Of Noah's sons, Shem is most likely the eldest, based on the congruity of chap. 5 and 11:10–26, which cite the firstborn son for each generation.[71] The etymology of "Shem" is uncertain; in Hebrew it means "name" *(šēm).* Perhaps the appellation for his firstborn reflects Noah's aspirations for his son to attain a reputation.[72] If so, it is realized in a way that Noah could not have imagined. Shem's lineage dominates the postdiluvian interests of our author, since he is the ancestor of the "Hebrews" by his son "Eber" (10:21) and the forefather of Abraham (10:21–31; 11:10–26). He is also his father's favored son (9:26–27).

Ham, on the other hand, becomes the disgraced son in his father's household (9:26). He is the youngest of the trio (9:24) and the ancestor of many of

[71] Contra NIV at 10:21; see discussion ad loc.

[72] "Name" (שֵׁם) has a sordid nuance at 6:4 and 11:4 (in conjunction with 3:6), but it takes on a redemptive sense in the divine promise to Abraham wherein God freely bestows it (12:2).

Israel's traditional enemies (10:6–20). The etymological derivation of "Ham" is uncertain, but some attribute it to the native term for Egypt, "Keme," which meant "the black land" in reference to the soil of Egypt.[73] "Ham" is synonymous with Egypt in select psalms (78:51; 105:23,27; 106:22). "Japheth" has been related etymologically to Egyptian "Keftiu" (= Crete) or the name of the Greek Titan, "Iapetos," father of Atlas.[74] In the biblical account, however, the name "Japheth" is related to "extend" *(ypt),* at least as the source of a sound play, where Noah prays that God will "enlarge" his territory under the auspices of Shem (9:27).

3. Conclusion: Procreation and Perversion (6:1–8)

At the end of the Sethite genealogy is the narrative epilogue that consists of two literary segments. Verses 1–4 describe intermarriage and procreation by the "sons of God" and the "daughters of men," and vv. 5–8 relate God's angry sorrow over the expanding wickedness of the human populace. Unquestionably, 6:1–4 is the most demanding passage in Genesis for the interpreter. Every verse is a source of exegetical difficulty. Also disconcerting is its trappings of mythological story, which make it, if myth is to be sought, the most likely candidate in the Bible. This requires us to give special attention to it in the following discussion.

Intertwined through chaps. 1–11 is the tension between the progression of God's blessing on mankind and the threat to that blessing. Cain's career and his genealogy point to the unfolding expansion of wickedness among the descendants of Adam (4:1–26). Conversely, the genealogies of Seth showcase Enosh and Enoch, whose reputations were related to worship and godly behavior (4:26; 5:21–24). Though Seth's genealogy shows that the hope for humanity was alive through a righteous offspring of Adam (5:1–32), the power of sin's grip continued ("and then he died"). For Lamech, man endured the ongoing burden of sin's consequences, but there remained a hope in the birth of a son ("Noah") who might deliver them (5:29). That tension continues as the "*tōlĕdōt* of Adam" (5:1) comes to conclusion in the narrative afterword (6:1–8).

Here the end of the *tōlĕdōt* section describes how the corruption of the human population reached an alarming measure (6:1–7), but at the same time it points to the survivor of the flood generation (6:8). Motifs nurtured through chaps. 1–5 are now drawn together in 6:1–8 as the finale to the antediluvian world and in antic-

---

[73] Alternatively, חָמַם, meaning "to be warm, hot"; see E. Isaac, "Ham," *ABD* 3.31–32. Wenham (*Genesis 1–15,* 129) mentions the possible association of "Ham," meaning "hot" in Hebrew (חַם), with the impropriety of his behavior toward Noah (9:22), which in turn is a type of the sensual traits in his descendants' worship, the Canaanites (cf. Isa 57:5). But Ham's offense against his father was not sensual, as Wenham himself agrees, but rather a serious family indiscretion (see 9:20–23 discussion).

[74] See Isaac, "Japheth," *ABD* 3.641.

ipation of the flood: (1) exploding population under God's blessing (6:1; 1:26–28), (2) the vanity of human power (a "name," 6:4 with 3:6), (3) violence and ever-expanding sin (4:1–26; 6:4–7), and (4) hope in a deliverer, namely, Noah as a descendant of Adam's lineage via Seth (3:15; 4:25–26; 5:29; 6:8).

Genesis 6:1–8 backtracks by lexical connections, linking it with chap. 5: (1) *hāʾādām* ("man"), 6:1–7 (7x) with 5:2; (2) *hāʾădāmâ* ("earth," ground"), 6:1,5,7 with 5:29; (3) diverse verbal forms of *yālad* ("born," "became the father," "had children"), 6:1,4 with 5:3–32 (28x) (cf. also 4:1ff. [10x]); (4) the interest in "name" *(šēm),* 6:4 with chap. 5's naming of each descendant, esp. 5:3,29 (cf. also 4:17,25–26); and (5) by recalling "Noah" (6:8), who is the last member cited in the honored Sethite genealogy (5:29–32). Also the language of vv. 1–2 reflects the genealogical table of chap. 5 by reference to increasing population and by the cryptic expressions "sons (of God)" and "daughters (of men)" (v. 2), which recall the formulaic phrase "other sons and daughters" attributed to each patriarch (5:4ff.) (except Noah). Additionally, 6:1–8 has language reminiscent of humanity's first sin and its judgment (e.g., "saw," "beautiful/good," and "married/took," 6:2 with 3:6).

Also vv. 1–8 look ahead to the ensuing narrative (6:9–9:29) by giving the societal conditions in which the protagonist of the flood story and last Sethite descendant lived. Thus it functions as a bridge between the Sethite genealogy (5:1–32) and the next *tōlĕdōt* (6:9–9:29) by linking "Noah" in 5:29 and 6:8, where he is acknowledged as the hope of humanity and the recipient of God's grace, with "Noah" in 6:9, who is further described as "righteous." The withdrawal of God's "spirit" (*rûaḥ,* v. 3), if it can be rightly equated with "the breath of the spirit of life" *(nišmat rûaḥ ḥayyîm)* in 7:22 (cf. 7:15), infers a causal connection between God's judgment and the flood event, where all the living are destroyed.[75]

Genesis 6:1–4 forms an important function in Genesis 1–11 by contributing to its theological motifs. It reflects the author's interests in showing human transgression of divinely established boundaries (3:6,22; 11:1–9),[76] the

[75] This is observed, among others, by D. J. A. Clines, "The Significance of the 'sons of God' Episode (Genesis 6:1–4) in the Context of the 'Primeval History' (Genesis 1–11)," *JSOT* 13 (1979): 33–46. This equation assumes the same meaning of "breath" in 2:7 and "spirit" in 6:3, as in Job 32:8. Our point is complicated, however, by the textual evidence at 7:22, where רוּחַ is absent in the LXX and Vg.

[76] Clines, like many today, takes the "sons of God" as divine beings in origin and relates 6:1–4 to the motif of human mortality in Gen 1–11 and the rebellious endeavors of humanity to transcend divinely ordained barriers (as Eve [3:6,22] and the Babelites [11:1–9]; "The Significance of the 'Sons of God' Episode," 36–41). Yet the sense of the passage is that the "sons of God" are the guilty party, not the "daughters of men"; thus, if they are divine beings (or angels), 6:1–4 describes the heavenly sphere transgressing the terrestrial, while the opposite is true of Eve and the Babelites, who sought heaven's immortality. If the "sons of God" are understood as human, as we will conclude, this notion of infringement is best taken as a breach of the divine ideal for marriage (2:24).

achievement of "name" (3:6; 4:17; 9:18; 11:4), and the multiplication of humanity (1:28; 4:1,17–26; chaps. 5; 10–11). Yet the juxtaposition of 6:1–4 and 6:5–8 creates problems for interpreters since there is no explicit linkage between the two paragraphs. It is common to distinguish 6:1–4 as an independent unit and view 6:5–8 as the prelude to the flood narrative (i.e., 6:5–8:22).[77] Earlier, however, we have shown that 6:1–8 shares in the same language and motifs of 5:1–32 and is best read as the close to the "*tōlĕdōt* of Adam" (5:1–6:8). It is plain that 6:5–8 gives the moral justification for the flood that follows; nevertheless, it is best viewed as the fitting end to the preceding (5:1–6:4) by its allusion to the motif of exploding human population. Paradoxically, 6:5–8 wraps up the motif of human expansion by showing the concomitant development of societal wickedness. The relationship between 6:1–4 and 6:5–8 is intentionally linked by parallel rhetoric: "When men began to increase in number on the earth" (6:1a) and "The LORD saw how great man's wickedness on the earth had become" (6:5a). While 6:1–4 does not explicitly relate how the marriages it describes contributed to human degeneration, the implication is that the actions of the "sons of God" and the presence of the Nephilim contributed to or illustrated the sinfulness condemned in 6:5–8. With this unity of theme in 6:1–8 acknowledged, we turn now to the expositional details.

(1) Sons of God and Daughters of Men (6:1–4)

[1]When men began to increase in number on the earth and daughters were born to them, [2]the sons of God saw that the daughters of men were beautiful, and they married any of them they chose. [3]Then the LORD said, "My Spirit will not contend with man forever, for he is mortal; his days will be a hundred and twenty years."

[4]The Nephilim were on the earth in those days—and also afterward—when the sons of God went to the daughters of men and had children by them. They were the heroes of old, men of renown.

6:1 Although the stated reason for God's judgment against the earth is encroaching moral perversion (6:5), there is an implication in the passage that

[77] As we will mention, commentators often point out how 6:1–4 is unattached to its context, and thus they attribute it to an autonomous source that has been commandeered by the Yahwist (J) to demonstrate his thesis of the sinfulness of man (6:5–8). R. S. Hendel takes a different approach when he argues that 6:1–4 originally introduced the flood account and the Yahwist transposed 6:1–4 to provide a new motive for the flood, a new prelude that was "a more purely ethical motive" ("Of Demigods and the Deluge: Toward an Interpretation of Genesis 6:1–4," *JBL* 106 [1987]: 17), namely, God's anger at wicked man (6:5–8). We can agree that the present arrangement of the passage implies that the events of 6:1–4, by virtue of their connection with vv. 5–8, provide a reason for the flood. Yes, the flood destroyed the children of these marriages, as it did all people, but the absence of any intentional language linking 6:1–4 with the flood makes the suggestion for dislocation untenable.

the marriage between "the sons of God" and "the daughters of men" (v. 2) contributed in some way to this moral decline. This is suggested (1) by the punishment oracle of v. 3, (2) by the parallel use of "saw" in vv. 2 and 5, which describe the behavior of "the sons of God" toward "the daughters of men" (v. 2), and (3) by God's response to sin (v. 5). Essentially v. 1 reports what was depicted in chaps. 4–5 concerning the expansion of human life and achievement, but it also puts to the fore the connection between population growth and the divine pattern for marriage.[78]

The NIV's "men" *(hāʾādām)* should not be taken as a reference to gender but rather as a general reference to mankind at large. Verse 1 then gives the temporal circumstances for the events of v. 2 and reports that marriage and procreation were normative for the times. As the narrative unfolds, this population explosion is linked with an accompanying expansion of human wickedness (vv. 5–8). Babylonian *Atrahasis* (ca. 1600 B.C.) begins in a similar way, telling of rising human population that becomes a threat to humanity's own survival.[79] In the Babylonian myth the noise of expanding humanity angers the god Enlil, who plots their extinction. In Genesis, however, the threat lies in the moral decline of human behavior, which elicits God's retribution. Another significant difference is the absence of marriage as a precursor to the flood in the Babylonian tale.

There is no small irony in 6:1–8, for expanding procreation has been matched by an outbreak of worldwide immorality. Procreation is the realization of God's blessing (1:28) and is venerated in chap. 5, but human survival is not dependent on the mechanism of sexual procreation alone. There must be a concomitant obedience on the part of the human family to God's moral order (e.g., 2:7 with 3:17; 2:24). Human achievement becomes overweening pride if it is obtained independently of God (e.g., 3:6; 6:4; 11:1–9); divine blessing or correction is correlated with human conduct.

6:2 The identity of the "sons of God" and the "daughters of men" is the major interpretive obstacle, though the whole passage is replete with problems that are interdependent. Who are the "sons of God" and "daughters of men"? What was the nature of their actions (v. 2)? What was God's response (v. 3)? Who are the "Nephilim" and "Gibborim" (v. 4)?[80] It is necessary to explore in some depth the meaning of these cryptic appellations if we are to understand how such marriages led to the wickedness antedating the flood and what this means for the author's thesis in chaps. 1–11.

---

[78] E.g., 2:24; 3:15–16,20; 4:1–26; 5:1–32. "Began" (הֵחֵל) in 6:1 introduces new directions in Gen 1–11, but not necessarily innovation (see 4:26; 9:20; 10:8; 11:6).

[79] "The land became wide, the peop[le became n]umerous,/The land *bellowed* like wild oxen./ The god was disturbed by their uproar" (*ANET,* 104).

[80] "Niphilim" and "Gibborim" are transliterations; the NIV agrees with many English Versions by transliterating the former but translating גִּבֹּרִים "heroes" (as English Versions; so NASB's "mighty men").

Many critical scholars view 6:1–4 as a remnant of an old myth, or at least originally mythic in form and function, historicized by the Yahwist (J) or a later editor.[81] "Sons of God" is a common expression for the council of the gods in Canaanite usage *(bn ʾlm)*. This expression and related ones, describing the assembly of the lesser deities under the chief god El, are well attested in Ugaritic texts and in Phoenician and Ammonite inscriptions.[82] Antiquity, it is argued, is full of stories in which deities mate with beautiful women by force or persuasion, giving birth to demigods. Originally, it is contended, the intent of the tale was to explain the beginnings of a race of giants.[83]

If this were the case with 6:1–4, we must fault the enigmatic Yahwist (J) for his poor efforts at camouflaging the mythic element. More likely, as we find in the creation narrative (1:1–2:3) and the Tower of Babel (11:1–9), vv. 1–4 are a refutation of pagan stories that told of a race of superhuman giants. Ancient memory rightly reflected the distant past when fierce tyrants ruled the day, but the author of Genesis by relating the Nephilim to the wickedness of the times and their ensuing judgment showed that they were altogether mortal, not at all superhuman, and subject to the judgment of God.[84] The biblical author not only "set the record straight" but also used it as testimony condemning the

---

[81] E.g., S. R. Driver comments, "As a rule, the Hebrew narrators stripped off the mythological colouring of the pieces of the folk-lore which they record; but in the present instance, it is still discernible" (*The Book of Genesis,* rev. ed. [London: Methuen, 1926], 83). Speiser (*Genesis,* 46) relates it originally to Hurrian myths that tell of bloodthirsty battles among the gods, and E. Kraeling ("The Significance and Origin of Gen 6, 1–4," *JNES* 6 [1947]: 193–208) attributes 6:1–4 to a composite of several non-Israelite myths. Similar method is followed in relating the Nephilim (6:4) to the Mesopotamian sages (fish-men), *apkallū* (A. D. Kilmer, "The Mesopotamian Counterparts of the Biblical *NĔPĪLÎM*," *Perspectives on Language and Text: Essays and Poems in Honor of Francis I. Andersen* [Winona Lake: Eisenbrauns, 1987], 39–44). Westermann (*Genesis 1–11,* 367, 381–82) thinks that it is too simple to attribute to the Yahwist (J) a historicizing of myth; rather, the biblical writer uses the mythological *language* of the tale to speak of primeval events that lie outside history. P. Hanson ("Rebellion in Heaven, Azazel and Euhemeristic Heroes in I Enoch 6–11," *JBL* 96 [1977]: 197–212) and D. L. Petersen ("Genesis 6:1–4, Yahweh and the Organization of the Cosmos," *JSOT* 13 [1979]: 47–64) appeal to a mythic pattern (Hanson) or mythic function (Petersen) for points of comparison.

[82] For the "assembly of the gods," Ug sources have the diverse expressions *pḫr bn ʾilm, pḫr ʾilm, mpḫrt bn ʾil,* and *dr bn ʾil.* El is identified as the "father of the sons of El" (*ʾab bn ʾil*).

[83] E.g., von Rad comments that the original story was "to account aetiologically for the origin of heroes from such marriages" (*Genesis,* 115). But we might raise the objection why, if such an obviously mythic element, it would have been appropriated by the Hebrew author? An etiological explanation does not satisfy the contents of the whole paragraph (6:1–4).

[84] E.g., Cassuto, who considers 6:1–4 the Torah's explanation for the origins of the Nephilim in Canaan (Num 13) and a response to the pagan stories that spoke of giants (*Genesis,* 299–300). Sarna comments that the original story is shaped by the biblical author "to combat polytheistic mythology" (*Genesis,* 45). R. Maars, while accepting its pagan origins, concludes that the story was adapted by the biblical author to demonstrate that Yahweh controlled all creation, including the divine realm, and that the semidivine Nephilim were no threat to his rule ("The Sons of God [Genesis 6:1–4]," *ResQ* 23 [1980]: 220).

wicked generation, which deserved the cataclysmic flood to follow.

Historically, three opinions have won a significant following for identifying the "sons of God": (1) angels, (2) human judges or rulers, and (3) the descendants of Seth. More recently some have suggested that this baffling epithet refers to royal despots, similar to the second view. Others have taken a combination of the angel and human views in which the human despots are demoniacs possessed by fallen angels.[85] Still others, who attribute 6:1–4 to pagan sources, argue that the "sons of God" are the lesser gods of the Canaanite pantheon.[86] These disparate views hold an essential tenet in common: the narrative tells how human conduct transgressed divinely established boundaries.[87] Precisely how this occurred is the problem the expositor faces.

1. As angelic, celestial beings, the "sons of God" *(bĕnê hā'ĕlōhîm)* defied God by moving outside their appointed realm and marrying (molesting?) human "daughters."[88] In this interpretation *'ĕlōhîm* is taken as a proper noun ("God") or as a genitive of attribute (indicating quality), where it refers to a class of beings, giving the sense of "divine beings."[89] In this latter sense it means they are of the realm of the heavenly (angels) in contrast to the "daughters of men," whose realm is terrestrial. As the argument runs, their unnatural sexual union (*contra* 2:24) produced the "Nephilim," whose notorious deeds (v. 4) required the strongest of penalties (v. 5). Proponents of this view can boast that it is the oldest opinion known, since it was advocated among the Jews at least by the second century B.C. as indicated by *1 Enoch* 6–11.[90] Early Christian writers also advocated the angel view. The influence of Enoch is found among Christian authors of the east until

---

[85] E.g., F. Delitzsch, *A New Commentary on Genesis* (Edinburgh: T & T Clark, 1888), 226; A. Ross, *Creation and Blessing: A Guide to the Study and Exposition of the Book of Genesis* (Grand Rapids: Baker, 1988), 182.

[86] E.g., B. S. Childs, *Myth and Reality in the Old Testament* (London: SCM, 1960), 49.

[87] Westermann observes that the purpose of 6:1–4 (and 11:1–9) "is to describe the overpowering force of human passion that brings people to overstep the limits set for them" (*Genesis 1–11,* 381–82).

[88] W. A. van Gemeren presents a detailed exegetical study defending the traditional "angel" view in "The Sons of God in Genesis 6:1–4: (An Example of Evangelical Demythologization?)," *WTJ* 43 (1981): 320–48.

[89] See *IBHS* § 9.5.3b #18. The word בֵּן ("son") can be used in terms of an individual's relationship to a class of beings (e.g., Job 1:6; Ezek 2:1), a feature absent in 6:4.

[90] Cf., e.g., the LXX manuscripts, οἱ ἄγγελοι τοῦ θεοῦ ("the angels of God"); *Jub.* 4.15–22; 5.1–9; Philo (*On the Giants* 2.6); *T. Reub.* 5.6–7; *2 Enoch* 18.3–8; *2 Apoc. Bar.* 56.11–14; 1QapGen 2:1, 16; CD 2.17–19; and Josephus (*Ant.* 1.73). The LXX tradition, however, is not uniform. It may have read originally οἱ υἱοι τοῦ θεοῦ ("the sons of God"). A. Rahlfs' *Septuaginta* and J. W. Wevers' *Septuaginta Genesis* follow the Göttingen tradition, reading "sons of God." Later rabbinic tradition, however, departed from this position and argued for "sons of nobles," i.e., aristocrats, who married women of lower social status, e.g., R. Simeon b. Yohai (ca. A. D. 140) *Gen. Rab.* 26:5; *Tgs. Onq., Neof.,* and *Ps.-J.;* and Symmachus' Greek. *Tg. Ps.-J.* also reflects a confused tradition; its translation infers that the Nephilim are fallen angels. See P. S. Alexander, "The Targumim and Early Exegesis of the 'Sons of God' in Genesis 6," *JSS* 23 (1972): 60–71, and ad loc. in Wevers, *Septuaginta Genesis* (Göttingen: Vandenhoeck & Ruprecht, 1974).

the third century and among Latin authors to Ambrose.[91]

The strength of this traditional opinion lies in the use of this phrase elsewhere in referring to angelic hosts in God's heavenly court.[92] Moreover, since *hāʾādām* ("men") occurs in v. 1 as a reference to collective mankind, we can expect the same meaning in v. 2, where it occurs for the "daughters of men." This indicates, according to this view, that there is a contrast intended between the "daughters of men," which refers to human women, and the "sons of God" who are of the divine sphere, namely, angels. Additionally, as noted earlier, there is evidence of an ancient memory among pagan peoples that celestial beings had cohabited with humans. For example, the *Epic of Gilgamesh* depicts the goddess Ishtar proposing marriage to Gilgamesh (who himself is semidivine).[93] Thus in this view, the Hebrew account corrects the false notion that there was in antiquity a superhuman race of semidivine beings and shows that the culprits were not gods but degenerate angels whose offspring were merely sinful "men [flesh] of renown," subject to the same destruction of God's moral outrage as any mortal human. Christian proponents of the angel interpretation also appeal to the New Testament, where it is contended that the apostles allude to Gen 6:1–4 in referring to fallen angels (1 Pet 3:19–20; 2 Pet 2:4; Jude 6). These "angels" are imprisoned awaiting the day of God's judgment because they "did not keep their positions of authority but abandoned their own home" (Jude 6). If this is the case, then the New Testament writers were in agreement with the Jewish opinion as reflected by *1 Enoch*.

However, taking the "sons of God" as angels has its drawbacks. Contextually, there has been no identification of an angelic host, at least in the sense of a heavenly court, in the account to this point.[94] Moreover, from beginning to

---

[91] E.g., Justin, *Second Apology* 5; Irenaeus, *Against Heresies* 4.36, 4; Ps.-Clem. *Homilies* 7.12–15; 8.11–15; Clement of Alexandria, *The Instructor* 3.2; Tertullian, *On the Veiling of Virgins* 7; Commodianus, *Instructions* I, 3. Those who held to the Sethites were, e.g., Julius Africanus, *Chronicles* 2; Chrysostom, *Homilies in Genesis* 22.2; and Augustine, *City of God* 15.23. Cyril of Alexandria proposed sons of Enoch. See L. R. Wickham, "The Sons of God and the Daughters of Men: Genesis VI 2 in Early Christian Exegesis," in *Language and Meaning, OTS* 19 (Leiden: Brill, 1974), 135–47, and Alexander, "The Targumim and Early Exegesis," 63.

[92] Esp. Job 1:6; 2:1, where the adversary himself ("Satan") is a member (cf. 1 Kgs 22:19–22). Job 38:7b has the same phrase, but it may mean heavenly stars on the basis of its parallel (v. 7a). Also relevant is Dan 3:25, where the equivalent Aramaic בַּר אֱלָהִין indicates "angels" (v. 28). Pss 29:1; 89:6[7] read similarly but not exactly בְּנֵי אֵלִים in their contexts; the phrase is unclear since it may refer to angels, stars, or false deities. Deut 32:8 has בְּנֵי אֵל ("the sons of God") in a Qumran text (4QDeut^{q}), whereas the MT reads בְּנֵי יִשְׂרָאֵל ("the sons of Israel"). The LXX tradition (ἀγγέλων θεοῦ) appears to agree with the Qumran variant and interprets the phrase as "angels." Also similar is בְּנֵי עֶלְיוֹן ("the sons of Elyon") in Ps 82:6b, but here it certainly occurs as a title for human judges.

[93] *ANET,* 83–84.

[94] One could argue that 1:26 and 3:22 indicate a heavenly (angelic) council, but the significance of the plural in these verses is equally problematic. The "cherubim" are given a specific terrestrial assignment, and there is no role of council here. The same problem occurs for the serpent (3:1), especially since it is identified as an animal, avoiding any reference to a heavenly origin.

end 6:1–8 concerns humanity and its outcome, not angels and their punishment. The flood is God's judgment against "man" (vv. 3,5–7), and there is no reference to the culpability of angels. Also it is difficult to reckon this view with procreation as a power bestowed by God upon the terrestrial order of animals and humanity (1:22,28). There is no biblical evidence elsewhere that procreation is a trait of the heavenly hosts, although admittedly angels take on other human properties (cf. 18:1–2,8 with 19:1,5). Yet even here there is significant difference between holy angels who acquire the ability to eat and rebellious angels who acquire sexual properties. By what line of reason does one propose that the fallen condition of angels somehow results in the exercise of corporeal procreation?[95] Angels are spiritual beings, not corporeal (Heb 1:7,14). Also Jesus, when distinguishing earthly life from that of heaven, asserts that angels do not have sexual relations as humans and implies they are not sexual (Matt 22:30 pars.). This differs remarkably from the pagan perception of supernatural beings.

Moreover, the New Testament evidence presented for this interpretation is complicated by its exegetical obscurity and its uncertain relationship to Jewish pseudepigrapha, especially *1 Enoch* (1 Pet 3:19–20; 2 Pet 2:4; Jude 6,14–15). *First Enoch* 1–36 tells of Enoch's journeys following his translation (Gen 5:24). He is commissioned to forewarn the fallen angels who had sinned by cohabitation with human women (Gen 6:1–4); afterward the book recounts his universal travels, including his visit to the abyss, where he sees the imprisoned angels, detained until the final judgment. It is apparent to anyone familiar with Jewish apocryphal literature that this interpretation of Gen 6:1–4 reflected in *1 Enoch* was widespread. Many commentators assume that Peter's readers were familiar with this interpretation and that the apostle either alluded to *1 Enoch* or he himself subscribed to the angel view in showing that the resurrected Christ, not Enoch, was Lord over evil and would triumph over hostile powers, including spiritual forces (1 Pet 3:19–20).[96]

Among several alternatives to this interpretation, however, is the view that Christ "in spirit" preached repentance through Noah (2 Pet 2:5) to the *human* generation of the flood during the building of the ark. This human audience was alive then but now is confined to prison, awaiting judgment.[97] This is likened to 1 Pet 4:6, which says "the gospel was preached even to those who are

---

[95] See C. F. Keil, *Biblical Commentary on the Old Testament. Vol. 1. The Pentateuch* (Grand Rapids: Eerdmans, n.d.), 132.

[96] See E. G. Selwyn, *The First Epistle of Peter,* 2d ed. (London: Macmillan, 1947); R. T. France, "Exegesis in Practice: Two Samples," in *New Testament Interpretation,* ed. I. H. Marshall (Grand Rapids: Eerdmans, 1977), 252–81; J. N. D. Kelly, *A Commentary on the Epistles of Peter and Jude* (Grand Rapids: Baker, 1981 [1969]).

[97] See L. Goppelt, *A Commentary on 1 Peter,* trans. J. Alsup (Grand Rapids: Eerdmans, 1993 [1978]), 256–60; W. Grudem, *The First Epistle of Peter: An Introduction and Commentary* (Leicester: IVP, 1988), 203–39.

now dead," meaning those who heard when alive but now are dead. None of the New Testament passages identifies the sin of the angels ("spirits," 1 Pet 3:19), and there is no detail, such as marriage or bearing children, that ties the passage with 6:1–4. Since the New Testament line of evidence remains unclear, it cannot have undue influence in our reading of the Genesis account.

2. Alternatively, Jewish interpreters have understood the "sons of God" as human judges or rulers (aristocrats).[98] The word *ʾĕlōhîm* has broader usage than the common meanings "God" and "divine." There is ample evidence for taking *ʾĕlōhîm* as human "judges" in the Old Testament.[99] Psalm 82:1,6–7 speaks of human rulers as *ʾĕlōhîm* (82:6a), and, more importantly, the parallel member (82:6b) refers to them as "the sons of the Most High" *(bĕnê ʿelyôn),* a description analogous to *bĕnê hāʾĕlōhîm* in Gen 6:2. The psalmist, as in Gen 6:3, stresses the mortality of the judges despite their lofty assignment. In this view the Nephilim (v. 4) are not regarded the children of their marriages but were their contemporaries.

A variant of this view interprets *bĕnê hāʾĕlōhîm* as a class of polygamous warriors or despotic kings who acquired large royal harems by coercion (rape?).[100] They fathered the "Nephilim" and "the heroes of old" (i.e., "Gibborim," 6:4) who were infamous for their cruel tyranny. "Sons of God," in this view, reflects the ancient Near Eastern conception of sacral kingship in which monarchs were believed to be deities or divine sons who ruled in behalf of the gods. In the Ugaritic myth of King Keret, for example, Keret is identified as "the son of El" *(bn ʾil).*[101] As stated earlier, Hebrew tradition as well understood that divine rule was carried out by appointed (human) magistrates. Related to this is the biblical motif of royal "sonship" in Davidic theology (2 Sam 7:13–16; Pss 2:7; 89:27). Thus it is contended that *bĕnê hāʾĕlōhîm* is best rendered "the sons of the gods," a reference to antediluvian kings whom the ancients believed were divine.[102]

Moreover, it is argued that the account of Cain's dynasty (4:17–24), espe-

---

[98] E.g., בני רברביא ("rulers"), *Tgs. Onq., Ps.-J.;* בני דייניא ("judges"), *Tg. Neof.;* Symmachus, οἱ υἱοὶ τῶν δυναστευόντων, and perhaps Aquila, οἱ υἱοὶ τῶν θεῶν (i.e., judges).

[99] E.g., Exod 21:6; 22:8–9[7–8], where the NIV translates "judges," but at 22:28[27] the NIV has "God." Also אֱלֹהִים can be used in the sense of "great" or "large" and "lofty" (Jonah 3:3).

[100] See M. Kline, "Divine Kingship and Genesis 6:1–4," *WTJ* 24 (1961): 187–204.

[101] *ANET,* 147–48.

[102] Kline clarifies that such a concession by the biblical writer to pagan thought is an *ad hominem* argument, as elsewhere in the OT where the gods of the nations are referred to by the biblical writers as though real (e.g., Ps 97:7; "Divine Kingship," 192, n. 17). Clines offers a different opinion when he argues that the identity of the "sons of God" is not a matter of either human or nonhuman; rather, the biblical author regarded the "sons of God" as antediluvian rulers whose origins traditionally were deemed divine or semidivine ("The Significance of the 'Sons of God,'" 35). This contributes nicely, Clines contends, to the motif of Gen 1–11 regarding the relationship of the human and the divine.

cially Lamech, is the proper background for 6:1. With Cain's lineage we have the origins of city organization, polygamy, and violent tyranny. Thus 6:1–8 describes how this emerging Cainite kingship achieved its evil endeavors and God's judgment. In essence the "sons of God" refers to the Cainites. The Sumero-Akkadian tradition presents a cultural parallel: *Atrahasis* prefaces the flood by describing the origins of divine kingship in association with the founding of urban life. Genesis does the same in 6:1–4, which prepares the reader for the ensuing flood story.

Although this interpretation avoids the obvious problems created by the angel view, it fails to square with the contextual requirements since the larger passage does not speak of kingship. Though individual kings were referred to as "son of god," no evidence can be marshaled for groups of kings in the ancient Near East bearing the name "sons of the gods."[103] The idea of polygamy derived from the phrase "any of them they chose" is only inferential at best. Also there is no sense that coercion is taking place. The NIV rightly renders *lāqaḥ* ("took") as "married" since the term is the common Hebrew expression for wedlock.[104]

3. Church Fathers, such as Augustine, as well as the Reformers (Luther, Calvin) interpreted the "sons of God" as a reference to "godly men," that is, the righteous lineage of Seth.[105] Although this view has its share of difficulties, we find that it is the most attractive.[106] We already have shown how chaps. 4 and

[103] So, e.g., Clines, "The Significance of the 'Sons of God,'" 33; Hamilton, *Genesis 1–17,* 264.

[104] E.g., 4:19; 11:29; 12:19; 20:2–3; 24:4. Note that the term by itself does not discriminate between monogamy and polygamy (cf. Lamech, 4:19). The NASB, NRSV, and NJPS permit either, "they took wives for themselves." The AV suggests polygamy, "wives of all which they chose," and also the NAB, "for their wives as many as they chose"; the REB reads the literal but ambiguous "such women as they chose."

[105] E.g., Calvin comments: "It was, therefore, base ingratitude in the posterity of Seth, to mingle themselves with the children of Cain. . . . Moses, then, does not distinguish the sons of God from the daughters of men, because they were of dissimilar nature, or of different origin; but because they were the sons of God by adoption, whom he had set apart for himself; while the rest remained in their original condition" (*Comm.,* 238). Julius Africanus (ca. A.D. 160–240) was among the first to advocate the Sethite view.

[106] While accepting that the marriages are between the Sethites and Cainites, another opinion proposes that the "daughters of men" are the Sethite women and the "sons of God" are the Cainites. See L. Eslinger, "A Contextual Identification of the *bene ha'elohim* and *benoth ha'adam* in Genesis 6:1–4," *JSOT* 13 (1979): 65–73. Eslinger bases his contention on the analogy between Eve's prideful sin in 3:6, the crime of Cain's hubris (cp. 4:7 w/3:16), and the deeds of the "sons of God" (cp. 6:2 w/3:6). He takes the title "sons of God" as an ironic statement against the Cainites who claim divinity. In all three cases God's punitive reaction is the same: Eve is condemned to death by expulsion (3:22); Cain is expelled from the "land" (4:10–14); and the "sons of God" are condemned to a short life span (6:3). But this viewpoint neglects the linkage between chap. 5's Sethites with their saintly heroes (e.g., Enoch) and the godly appellative "sons of God" (cp. 5:1–3). The analogy between Cain and Eve and the "sons of God" and Eve is that now both the Cainites and the Sethites are imitating the hubris of the garden.

5 contrast the two lines of descent from Adam—the Cainites and Sethites. Genesis 6:1–8 relates how the two lines intermarry, resulting in a community of unprecedented wickedness. The flood account, we have shown, is actually embedded within the Sethite genealogy, which is not completed until the notice of Noah's death (9:29). This provides the appropriate interpretive key for understanding 6:1–8. During this period of amazing Sethite expansion (chap. 5), the Sethite family marries outside its godly heritage, which results in moral decline.

ʾĕlōhîm can be rendered as a genitive of quality, meaning "godly sons," referring to the heritage of the Sethites.[107] We already observed that *bĕnê hāʾĕlōhîm* has analogues pointing to human referents.[108] Also important is the weight of the Pentateuch's testimony, which identifies the Israelites as the children of God (e.g., Deut 14:1; 32:5–6; cf. Exod 4:2; Pss 73:15; 80:15); this resonates well with taking the "sons of God" in 6:2 as an allusion to godly (covenant) offspring (cf. also Isa 43:6; Hos 1:10; 11:1; John 1:12–13). It has been charged that such a reading is inappropriate before the founding of Israel, since there is no designated people of God.[109] However, this disregards the author's efforts at connecting the prepatriarchal fathers (chaps. 1–11) and the founders of Israel (chaps. 12–50). Genesis typically invites Israel to see itself in the events of their parents by employing the language and imagery of institutional life and of events later experienced by Israel. Mosaic law codified the prohibition against marriage outside the covenant community; Genesis illustrates how religious intermarriage resulted in calamity for the righteous (e.g., 28:1; 34:1ff.; 38:1ff.).

Although we have said that the "sons of God" refers to the Sethites, we do not insist that the "daughters of men" *(bĕnôt hāʾādām)* refers exclusively to Cainite women.[110] Verse 1 speaks of human procreation in general by the collective use of "men" *(hāʾādām),* meaning "people," as in 5:1b–2 (cf. 6:5).[111] "Daughters of men," then, in v. 2 again refers to women regardless of parent-

[107] This genitive use attributes a quality or condition to the construct so as to represent or characterize that person. The occurrence of this use is well attested with בֵּן (GKC § 128s–v).

[108] Since בְּנֵי־אֱלֹהִים cannot refer to physical descent, i.e., the angels are not physically generated, then we must take "sons of God" as metaphorical regardless of referent. It follows, then, that the expression can be applied to more than angels, i.e., any who "bear the image of God" (see Keil, *Pentateuch,* 128–29).

[109] Keil counters that "sons of God" has its ideological origins in the divine image, not the theocracy of Israel, and therefore has the potential of universal application (*Pentateuch,* 129).

[110] A common complaint against the Sethite view is its assignment of different meanings to the two occurrences of הָאָדָם ("men") in vv. 1–2. There is no basis for contending that הָאָדָם refers to Sethites in v. 1 and exclusively to Cainite women in v. 2.

[111] The NRSV rightly reads, "When people began to multiply on the face of the ground." Cf. the REB's translation "human race," but the REB wrongly reads "sons of the gods," indicating the distinction between divine and human spheres in 6:1–2.

age, but among these "daughters" are the offspring of Cain.[112] "Any of them they chose" accentuates the Sethites' crime of inclusiveness. Their unrestricted license accelerated the degeneracy of the whole human family. The patriarchs traditionally married within their family (endogamy).[113] Instructions in the Mosaic community prohibited intermarriage with Canaanite neighbors (e.g., Exod 34:16; Deut 7:3), and special regulations carefully governed foreign marriages (e.g., Deut 23:7–8; cf. 25:17–19). Moses' generation had tasted the bitter fruit of foreign entanglements, which resulted in their seduction into sinful practices (e.g., Num 25). Old Testament history illustrates all too well how interreligious unions spelled disaster for Israel. This Sethite incident of intermarriage with the ungodly leads to the deterioration of the godly family; as a forewarning it alerts the holy seed of Israel not to neglect God's prohibition.

The actions of the "sons of God" are described in language reminiscent of Eve's sin (3:6): she "saw" *(rā'â)* that the fruit was "good" (*ṭôb*; here, NIV's "beautiful") and "took" (*lāqaḥ,* NIV's "married"). While no sin or condemnation is specified in the text, the allusion to the garden rebellion suggests that the marriages are in some way tainted. As we already noted, there is no indication of sexual molestation since the common idiom for marriage occurs here. Silence on the part of the "daughters" may well reflect a willing complicity.[114]

"Any of them they chose" does not necessarily mean polygamy. Diversity may be intended here; the "sons of God" selected wives from any family, including Cainite women. If so, the godly lineage exercised a freedom that goes afoul when they embrace the unrighteous. Although not explicitly stated in Genesis as a prohibition, there is much that is embryonic in Genesis but stated explicitly in Mosaic command (e.g., "clean" and "unclean," 7:2). Later Israel could well have read this incident in light of Mosaic restrictions concerning intermarriage with the non-Israelites. Since 6:2 deliberately echoes the garden temptation, perhaps this expression reflects the sinister trap of the serpent in 3:1. There the serpent challenges God's veracity regarding the freedom of the woman to eat from any tree (as in 2:16). As a consequence of believing the snake, she rebels by unlawfully choosing the forbidden fruit.

---

[112] Keil, in arguing for the Sethite view, answers this exegetical difficulty differently (*Pentateuch,* 130). He contends that "men" in v. 1 is generic humanity and that the subsequent "sons of God" and "daughters of men" are "two species of the same genus" (i.e., humanity). There is no necessity for a contrast between the two (celestial vs. terrestrial) when it can be shown that Hebrew permits a general reference followed by a restricted one (e.g., Judg 19:30–20:3; Jer 32:20).

[113] E.g., Abram married his half-sister (20:12); Isaac, his cousin (24:15); and Jacob, his cousins Leah and Rachel (29:12). Such family ties primarily were intended to retain the distinctiveness of the family's religious heritage. Exogamy, marriage outside one's group, was also known (e.g., Esau married Hittite and Canaanite wives, 26:34; 28:6–9). See Hamilton, "Marriage (OT and ANE)," *ABD* 4.564–65.

[114] E.g., *Tg. Ps.-J.* imagines "they painted their eyes and put on rouge and walked about with naked flesh."

Similarly, these "sons of God" stumble by choosing wives from the forbidden lineage.

Although we commend the Sethites as the "sons of God," no view escapes troubling criticism. The mysterious identity of the "sons of God" continues to humble the expositor.[115]

6:3 The consequence of their actions is the divine restriction of human life. As the conclusion to the *tōlĕdôt* of Adam (5:1–6:8), which depicts the antediluvians' lengthy life spans, 6:1–4 recounts the occasion for the shortening of human life to 120 years, which comes closer to the ordinary experience of fallen humanity. In withdrawing his "spirit," the Lord no longer graciously preserves their life span. "The attempt by man to become more than he is results in his becoming less."[116]

Verse 3 is replete with exegetical difficulties, and they are interdependent issues that ideally require us to handle them together. There are four questions we must keep before us in this verse: (1) the identity of *rûḥî,* rendered "My Spirit" (NIV) or "My spirit" (NIV note); (2) the meaning of *yādôn,* translated "contend" (NIV) or "remain" (NIV note); (3) the meaning of *bāśār,* interpreted "man" (NIV) or "corrupt" (NIV note); and (4) the significance of the "hundred and twenty years."

1. Three common meanings for "My Spirit" have been argued by commentators. First, the verse speaks of God's personal presence ("My Spirit"), as in 1:2, where the "Spirit of God" hovers over the darkened waters at creation. In this view God no longer personally "contends" for the human family.[117] Essentially God declares that his longsuffering with sinful humanity has come to an end and he will no longer suspend judgment. Second, God withdraws his "spirit," the principle of life-giving power, which is necessary for survival. The language of "My spirit" *(rûḥî)* anticipates the ensuing destruction of all living things (human and animal) who have the "breath *[rûaḥ]* of life" (6:17; 7:15; cf. Ezek 37:14). But graciously it is the divine delegation of the "wind" *(rûaḥ)* that reverses the floodwaters and enables life to prosper again (8:1). "My spirit" is also an allusion to the making of the man in 2:7, where he experiences life by the inbreathing of God *(nišmat ḥayyîm).* That God refuses to preserve man "forever" again links 6:3 with the garden *tōlĕdōt,* where God expels the man and woman so that they will not "live for-

---

[115] D. Kidner forewarns: "But where Scripture is as reticent as here, both Peter and Jude warn us away. We have our proper place as well. More important than the detail of this episode is its indication that man is beyond self-help, whether the Sethites have betrayed their calling, or demonic powers have gained a stranglehold" (*Genesis,* TOTC [Downers Grove: IVP, 1967], 84).

[116] Eslinger, "Genesis 6:1–4," 72.

[117] For Luther v. 3 describes the cessation of preaching by which people are convicted and instructed; the preaching of Methuselah, Lamech, and Noah was useless in the ears of their corrupt audience.

ever" (3:22–24).[118] In effect these first two opinions are made of the same cloth, for there is little difference in substance since the principle of life is bestowed by God himself. The third perspective emerges from the view that understands the "sons of God" (v. 2) as deities or celestial powers (angels). In this case "spirit" indicates the potential of divine life that man possesses as the consequence of the divine-human marriages. God judges, therefore, that despite the acquisition of this power, mankind will die anyway.

2. Explicitly what God refuses to do "with man forever" is obscured by the meaning of the difficult *yādôn* (NIV, "contend"; AV, NASB, "strive"). It occurs just once, and its derivation is uncertain. The NIV's "contend" probably reflects the root *dîn,* meaning "judge, rule" (as BDB), indicating God will no longer deal with or plead on behalf of man. Thus the NJB reflects this understanding: "My spirit cannot be indefinitely responsible for human beings." Preferable is the traditional understanding "remain" as found in many English versions (REB, NAB, NIV text note; "abide," NRSV, NJPS). Since the philological evidence for the meaning of the word is ambiguous,[119] we are left with context alone to decipher the sense of the passage. The idea of "remain," as suggested by the ancient versions, coalesces well with "My spirit" as an allusion to the "breath of life" (2:7; 6:17; 7:15). Thus God intervenes so that the removal of his empowering, life-giving spirit results in the abbreviation of life. The GNB offers the sense in the paraphrase, "I will not allow people to live forever."

God's punitive action in 6:1–8 is solely directed against humanity, not angels—"My spirit will not remain with *man* forever." The punishment oracle in the garden included the chief culprit, the serpent, as well as his human part-

[118] For those who see a divine-human encounter in 6:2, the allusion to the garden indicates the same rebellious goal—to obtain eternal life ("and live forever," 3:22) but this time through sexual relations (e.g., Wenham, *Genesis 1–15,* 141). J. Sailhamer ("Genesis," EBC [Grand Rapids: Zondervan, 1990], 76–77) understands 6:1–4 differently; there are no negative implications for the intermarriage described here. The expressions "sons of God" and "daughters of men" are allusions to the creation of men and women, as depicted in 2:7 and 2:22. The man came from God; and the woman, from the man's side. Read in the context of God's last speech to humanity (5:2), 6:3 shows that it was the presence of God's Spirit, not their own "flesh," that enabled the antediluvian patriarchs to enjoy such long lives (5:3–32). The ten patriarchs therefore were exceptions to the rule for fallen humanity whose normal life was the much shorter 120 years.

[119] For the root דִּין ("contend") we would expect יָדִין (so לָדִין Eccl 6:10) rather than יָדוֹן. The LXX καταμείνῃ and Vg *permanebit* may reflect Heb. יָדוּר ("dwell") or יָלוּן ("lodge") rather than יָדוֹן (BDB, 192). KB[3] suggests דון and the possible meaning "to stay or simil. by context"; we would expect, however, יָדוּן. Many recommendations have been made by appealing to apparent cognates; e.g., Speiser ("*YDWN,* Gen 6,3" *JBL* 75 (1956): 126–29) proposed Akk. *dinānu*, meaning "substitute, scape-goat," thus God will no longer "shield, protect." Consider Cassuto's defense of Akk. *danānu,* meaning "to remain" (*Genesis,* 295–96; followed by Westermann, *Genesis 1–11,* 375, and Wenham, *Genesis 1–15,* 142). Also consult Hamilton, *Genesis 1–17,* 266–67, for discussion of other proposals.

ners in the first crime (3:15–19), but here the passage speaks only of "man." According to the angel view, the celestial beings are the primary instigators of the decadent deed. Why do they escape God's punitive words? And wherein lies the fault of the women? If angels, it must be maintained that the women's sin was one of omission by their passive acquiescence to the whims of the "sons of God." But it is better to conclude that the recipients of the penalty ("man") are, in fact, the only culprits in the crime (i.e., humans).

3. After God declares his intention, the following clause gives reason for it: "for he [man] is mortal."[120] The interpretive obstacle here is the proper understanding of *bāśār* ("flesh," NRSV, NASB, NJPS, NJB, NAB), which can be rendered "mortal" ("mortal flesh," REB) or construed metaphorically for human sinfulness, "corrupt" (NIV text note). The essential sense of *bāśār* is human helplessness or weakness, whether it is the inherent frailty of corporeal life (e.g., 7:21) or the endemic moral flaws of humanity (e.g., 6:12). If "mortal" is its proper nuance in our verse, we ask how this can be reason for God's reproof (v. 3).[121] Alternatively, moral depravity would fit better contextually, giving reason for the judgment. Yet this ambiguity created by *bāśār* actually bridges the cause-effect sense of both meanings. It is humanity's mortality that is foremost in mind in this passage since the cessation of God's life-giving is tied to the life and death of mankind (cf. 2:7 with 7:22), but the moral failing of human life cannot be dismissed altogether, for standing behind mortality is sinful corruption (3:17–19,22–24). Again we discover in this verse a proleptic reference to the flood catastrophe where all "people" ("flesh") are said to face death (vv. 12–13). We have already found that the motif of unlawful choice in chap. 3 is continued by 6:1–4, and now the punishment also is recalled by the acknowledgment of human frailty (cf. "of dust," 3:17–19).

4. After indicating that humanity will experience a curtailed life span, v. 4

---

[120] The MT has the peculiar בְּשַׁגַּם, which is ambiguous. As it stands, it may be taken as a combination of three elements: preposition בְּ ("in"), relative pronoun שְׁ ("which"), and adverb גַּם ("also"). Hence it is causal, "in as much as he is flesh." The LXX (Syr, *Tgs*. Vg) tradition reflects this by διὰ τὸ εἶναι αὐτοὺς σάρκας ("because they are flesh"). The NIV's "for" (as AV, NASB, NRSV) renders it likewise as causal. Difficulty with this analysis is the odd relative pronoun שְׁ, which occurs nowhere else in the Pentateuch. Also this suggests that the punishment is against man because of his inherent state as "flesh" as opposed to his sinful behavior. Alternatively, having some Heb. textual support, the word can with a small difference read בְּשַׁגָּם, an infinitive from שָׁגַג ("to err") with suffix, meaning "because of their going astray" (BDB, 993). For more see Westermann, *Genesis 1–11,* 375–76, and Hamilton, *Genesis 1–17,* 267–68. D. Christensen ("Janus Parallelism in Genesis 6:3," *HS* 27 [1986]: 20–24) argues that the one word has both meanings: (1) the infinitival form "err" concludes the first half of the verse, explaining the removal of "spirit" and (2) as causal, introducing the second half, "in that he is flesh."

[121] Calvin takes "flesh" in the sense of mankind's carnal nature, his failed reason unable to discern the Spirit (cf. 1 Cor 2:14): "Man ought to have excelled all other creatures, on account of the mind with which he was endued; but now, alienated from right reason, he is almost like the cattle of the field" (*Comm.,* 242–43).

specifies the term limit as "a hundred and twenty years," a greatly diminished number compared to the antediluvians. But, it may be argued, postdiluvian men among the Shemites (11:10–32) live longer than 120 years, as do the patriarchs (e.g., Abraham, 175 years). Therefore some interpret the 120 years as a period of grace before the flood, a kind of "lull before the storm." Jewish tradition understood the 120 years as opportunity for repentance (cf. *Tg. Onq.; Pirke Aboth* 5:2; cf. 1 Pet 3:20). By analogy the Babylonian flood story *Atrahasis* depicts periods of twelve hundred years between the various attempts of the gods to destroy humanity. Since Genesis and the Babylonian story have the same sequence of events (creation, increasing population, flood), this 120 years may be intended as such a break. Furthermore, it is argued, the threat of God's judgment anticipates an approaching event, hence the 120 years as a prologue to the flood correlates well.

Yet the issue of human mortality in 6:1–4, as we have seen it in continuum with the garden *tōlĕdōt* (2:7,17; 3:6,17–24), recommends we take the 120 years as the shortening of life. Since 6:3 concerns God's judgment against all humanity *(ʾādām)* and a period of grace would affect only one generation, it is better to take the 120 years as a reference to human life span.[122] There is no necessary connection between the 120 years and the periods of respite in *Atrahasis* since the 120 years are not an interim between catastrophes in the biblical account. Moreover, Babylonian tradition indicates that the gods set fixed limits on human life following the flood in order to set restrictions on human population.[123] If there is an analogy to be sought, it would lie here where antiquity shows that human life span has been determined by divine edict. The striking difference between the Bible and Babylonian tradition is the divine reason for imposing human limits.

The longer life spans among postdiluvians can be attributed to a gracious delay in the same way that the penalty of death for Adam and Eve was not immediately executed (2:17; 3:16–19). This judicial restriction on human life nevertheless explains and anticipates the drastic decrease in life span among the patriarchs. Because of Moses, who lived 120 years (Deut 31:2; 34:7), this figure may have become enshrined as the ideal achievement—a benchmark of piety. Later, seventy years were recognized as the realistic norm (Ps 90:10).

6:4 The identity of the "Nephilim" and their relationship, if any, to the marriages (v. 2) is perplexing. The word occurs but once more, in Num 13:33, where it refers to an indigenous population inhabiting Canaan. For 6:1–4 the primary question is whether the Nephilim are the offspring of the marriages or merely their contemporaries. The term "Nephilim" *(nĕpilîm)* is of little help

[122] See, e.g., Westermann, *Genesis 1–11,* 376.

[123] W. G. Lambert, "The Theology of Death," in *Death in Mesopotamia,* Mesopotamia 8 (Copenhagen: Akademisk, 1980), 53–66, esp. 54–58.

solving the issue since its etymology is uncertain. "Nephilim" is a transliteration of the Hebrew, not a translation, which indicates a group or class. It is commonly related to *nāpal,* meaning "to fall"; thus the Nephilim are considered "the Fallen Ones." If so, does this refer to their expulsion from heaven, their death as "fallen" in battle, or to their moral degeneracy? Another proposal is the related noun *nēpel*, meaning "miscarriage" (Job 3:16; Ps 58:8[9]; Eccl 6:3), suggesting that they were unusual in appearance since they were born by miscarriage.[124] The terms "fallen" and "warriors" occur repeatedly in Ezekiel's oracles against the nations (Ezek 32:20–27) whose armies fall in battle; this may have alluded to 6:1–4.[125] Ezekiel's use of "fallen," however, is likely a sound play on the word "Nephilim" and not derived from an etymological association.

The traditional English rendering "giants" (AV) follows the LXX (and ancient versions), which translates *gígantes* for Hebrew *nĕpilîm* (Nephilim).[126] We can attribute this most likely to the influence of the later account recorded in Num 13:33. The frightened Israelite spies marveled at the exceptional height of the Nephilim, remarking that the Hebrews were no more than like "grasshoppers" before them. Later Jewish literature interpreted the Nephilim as giants and referred to their infamous pride and wickedness.

Numbers 13:33, however, cannot be used confidently to interpret the meaning of "Nephilim" in 6:4 because of the passage's own problems. From Numbers 13 we learn that the Anakites are said to be descendants of the "Nephilim." If the Nephilim of Num 13:33 and Gen 6:4 are taken as the same group, the verse indicates that the Nephilim and their descendants survived the flood. Related to this is the question of the authenticity of the phrase "the descendants of Anak come from the Nephilim" (13:33). It is absent in the LXX tradition and can be taken as a superficial gloss motivated by a late interpretation of 6:4 as "giants." This is further suggested by the divergent language in v. 33, "sons of Anak" *(bĕnē ʿănāk),* whereas 13:22,28 earlier have "descendants of Anak" *(yĕlidê ʿănāk).*[127] Moreover, the Anakites in Deuteronomy are cataloged with peoples, such as the Rephaites, who resided in Canaan and were known for their size and military prowess (e.g., Deut 1:28; 2:10–23; 9:2). Yet it is significant that the Nephilim are never listed in Deuteronomy where the

[124] KB proposes either נָפַל, "fall," meaning expelled from heaven, or נֵפֶל, "miscarriage."

[125] Note particularly Ezek 32:27, "warriors who have fallen" (גִּבּוֹרִים נֹפְלִים). BHS goes too far by its proposed emendation נְפִלִים ("Nephilim") for נֹפְלִים ("fallen").

[126] *Tg. Ps.-J.* evidently interprets Nephilim as derived from נָפַל ("fall") by identifying them as the leaders of the rebellious angels fallen from heaven (as in *1 Enoch*): "Shamhazai and Azael fell from heaven and were in the earth those days."

[127] "Sons of Anak" occurs once more in Deut 9:2. See G. B. Gray, *A Critical and Exegetical Commentary on Numbers,* ICC (Edinburgh: T & T Clark, 1903), 151. Noted by Sailhamer, "Genesis," 79.

inhabitants of Canaan are given.

Defining the term on the basis of Numbers 13 may be misleading since the spies were certainly exaggerating ("grasshoppers") the opposition they encountered in Canaan. Actually the faithless spies counted all the inhabitants as formidable: "*All* the people we saw there are of great size" (Num 13:32). There is no intention in Numbers to equate the Nephilim of Moses' day directly with the antediluvian Nephilim.[128] When we consider the evidence of Deuteronomy's recollection of these Canaanite peoples, it is better to understand the allusion to the Nephilim therefore in Numbers 13 as figurative, cited by the spies because of the violent reputation attributed to "Nephilim" from ancient times.

Beyond the meaning of the name "Nephilim," the primary exegetical challenge is understanding the logical relationship between v. 4 and the preceding verses, since there is no grammatical connection.[129] Is there a relationship between the marriages of vv. 1–2 and the "Nephilim" (v. 4)? Thus are the "Nephilim" the offspring of these marriages or only contemporaries? Are the "Nephilim" and "heroes" (i.e., "Gibborim") the same? The problem rests with the progression of vv. 1–4. The expected transition from the sexual unions recounted in vv. 1–2 to the acknowledgment of children born to those unions in v. 4 is interrupted by the oracle of judgment in v. 3. Verse 3, however, is logically the end of vv. 1–2, which leads to God's interdiction against the marriages. There is no compelling reason to alter the present arrangement of vv. 3 and 4.

It still remains for us to explain the proper place of the "Nephilim" in the sequence of the passage. Some have recommended that the reference to the Nephilim in v. 4a is either a secondary gloss[130] or a parenthetical aside.[131] Yet recognition of the "Nephilim" who live at this time is integral to the purposes of vv. 1–4, describing what the times were like at the end of the antediluvian age. The presence of the Nephilim, then, was another evidence presented by the author to depict the wickedness that marked antediluvian society.

Sometimes overlooked is the fact that the Nephilim are not specifically said to be the offspring of the marital unions. Rather, for the author, establishing the

---

[128] While understanding Num 13:33 as an allusion to the physical stature of the Nephilim (6:4), Sarna calls its use in Num 13 an "oratorical effect, much as 'Huns' was used to designate Germans during the two world wars" (*Genesis,* 46).

[129] Some, e.g., Skinner, translate הָיוּ "arose" (*Genesis,* 145–46), in which case the Nephilim are the offspring of these cryptic marriages: "The Nephilim arose on the earth." We would expect in this case the *wāw*-consecutive construction וַיִּהְיוּ (cf. Keil, *Pentateuch,* 137).

[130] E.g., Skinner, who sees v. 4 as a series of glosses (*Genesis,* 146). Westermann believes that two originally distinct narratives lie behind 6:1–4, which were later joined and altered, resulting in a significantly disturbed text (*Genesis 1–11,* 365–68, 377–79).

[131] Recommended by Hamilton, who takes v. 4a (Nephilim) as an explanatory supplement, a narrative technique commonly found in Deuteronomy (e.g., 2:10–12; *Genesis 1–17,* 270).

time of the Nephilim's era is prominent: they lived in "those days," a reference to this antediluvian period of human proliferation described in vv. 1–2, and they existed "when" the intermarriages took place and "also afterward."[132] This establishes the period of the Nephilim as being before and after the marriages (v. 2). The verb "went to" *(yābōʾû),* describing the actions of the "sons of God," often is used of sexual relations.[133] Here it has been taken as customary in sense; thus "whenever" the sons of God and daughters of men marry, the result is children born.[134] This fits obviously with the theme of proliferation in vv. 1–4. It may be rendered as ingressive "when [they] began going . . ."; this latter sense focuses on the commencement and continuation of their sexual liaisons.[135] If so, this indicates that the Nephilim are already alive at the beginning of the momentous event of the times, the intermarriage of the "sons of God" and the "daughters of men."

"And also afterward," as rightly shown by the NIV arrangement (also NRSV, NJB, NAB), is a parenthetical note that reflects Num 13:33. We have remarked earlier that "Nephilim" is best taken in Numbers 13 as a scare tactic by the cowardly spies who drew on these shadowy figures of the past to win their case.[136] "*The* Nephilim" *(hannĕpirîm)* with the definite article in 6:4 indicates that a specific or well-known group or class is meant. When the spies appealed to the designation "Nephilim" as imposing adversaries, they drew on the reputation of the Nephilim, probably because of their association with an era infamous for its violence (6:5–8).

This is further insinuated in 6:4 by the presence of the "heroes *[gibbōrîm]* of old" (i.e., Gibborim) who are the "children" born to the sons of God and daughters of men.[137] These are the warrior class, men of ignoble reputation whose violent exploits are remembered (cf. 6:11–13) and whose names strike fear in the hearts of their hearers.[138] They are identified as "*men* of renown" *(ʾanšê haššēm),* not divine or semidivine figures. Despite their notorious

---

[132] "When" (אֲשֶׁר) is the proper rendering, as most modern versions show. If וְגַם אַחֲרֵי־כֵן ("and also afterward") is excised as a late interpolation, Childs takes אֲשֶׁר as causal; thus the giants existed "because" of the unions between the "sons" and "daughters" (*Myth and Reality,* 53).

[133] E.g., 16:2; 30:3; 38:8–9; 39:14, rendered "sleep with" or "lie with" (NIV).

[134] Thus repeated action in the past; see GKC § 107e, 112e.

[135] *IBHS* § 31.2c calls this use of the imperfect verb "incipient past" (6:4 is not listed among its examples; cf., e.g., 2 Sam 15:37; Isa 6:4).

[136] The spies "frightened the sandals off the people" (R. Allen, "Numbers," EBC [Grand Rapids: Zondervan, 1990], 812).

[137] For those who take the Nephilim as the children of the "sons of God" and "daughters of men," they are equated with the "heroes of old" in v. 4b. E.g., the LXX's οἱ γίγαντες οἱ ἀπ' αἰῶνος.

[138] This fear may have been heightened by Nimrod's reputation as גִּבֹּר בָּאָרֶץ ("mighty in the earth") and גִּבֹּור־צַיִד ("a mighty hunter"; 10:8–9). The term is often used of fierce warriors (e.g., Josh 10:2; 2 Sam 17:2; 23:8; Amos 2:16), even of the Lord, who defends his people (e.g., Deut 10:17); but it also can mean simply "a man of standing" (Ruth 2:1).

achievements they are no more than "men," subject to the same judgment as any (v. 3). As warriors of "renown" *(šēm)* they seek reputation by their wicked deeds in the way the people of Babel will seek fame through their building enterprise (cf. 11:4). The allusion in 6:2 to Eve's vain desires (3:6) and the inclusion of "name" here contribute to the motif of prideful autonomy, which characterizes the sins of prepatriarchal times (chaps. 1–11). Not all is lost however. There is in the midst of the wicked generation a favored man, Noah (6:8). God graciously preserves Noah's lineage (8:1) and gives him a "name" *(šēm),* which is his son, "Shem" *(šēm;* 11:10–26); by Shem's family the Lord gives Abraham, upon whom he confers a "name" (12:2; cf. also 2 Sam 7:9).

(2) Worldwide Wickedness (6:5–8)

5The LORD saw how great man's wickedness on the earth had become, and that every inclination of the thoughts of his heart was only evil all the time. 6The LORD was grieved that he had made man on the earth, and his heart was filled with pain. 7So the LORD said, "I will wipe mankind, whom I have created, from the face of the earth—men and animals, and creatures that move along the ground, and birds of the air—for I am grieved that I have made them." 8But Noah found favor in the eyes of the LORD.

This horrid paragraph is an exposé on the degeneracy of the human heart. Collectively, society has decayed beyond recovery in God's estimation. The progression in this small cluster of verses is arresting: "The LORD saw. . . . The LORD grieved. . . . The LORD said."[139] He himself brings sanctions against all humanity, including the most vulnerable (animals). The threat of extinction is not only inclusive of all living things but also is geographically all-encompassing. Repeatedly, "on the earth" highlights the divine intention to obliterate the living world he has created by his own voice and formed with his own hands. Is there any greater pain suffered than parents who witness the loss of a child? Our passage provides a window into the heart of the troubled Creator.

In the flood stories of Israel's neighbors, the Sumerian and Babylonian myths show the gods debating among themselves the justification of a universal flood destroying all mankind. Ea challenges Enlil's drastic actions, "How couldst thou, unreasoning, bring on the flood?"[140] The biblical narrative (6:5–8,11–13) repeatedly sets any question of this sort to rest; so pervasive is human sin that there must be a divine response. God's sorrow is over what has become of his noble creation, not the destruction itself. But God does not act carelessly, for he rightly delivers righteous Noah and extends that grace to his family.

In the *Epic of Gilgamesh* there is recognition that humanity has committed

---

[139] See Westermann, *Genesis 1–11,* 407.

[140] *ANET,* 95.

misdeeds worthy of retribution, but the Babylonian version does not reflect the moral outrage found in Genesis. Also we can turn to another Mesopotamian tale, *Atrahasis,* in which the god Enlil initiates a campaign of terror against the human family because its prodigious growth has created a noise too loud to tolerate. After repeated forays of plague and famine, Enlil undertakes a cataclysmic flood. Genesis, on the other hand, shows that God is not inconvenienced by human achievement; human achievement is, on the contrary, the consequence of his bountiful blessing. Rather, he acts in accord with ethical demands, agitated only by the wicked gains cooperative depravity has mounted.

6:5 Verse 5 records the consequence of vv. 1–4: the Lord "saw" and condemned the unprecedented corruption of the human family. Here is an intentional mimicry of the sons of God, who "saw" that the daughters of men were "beautiful" (*tôb*, "good"; 6:2). The wording in vv. 2 and 5 contrasts this deplorable scene with the pristine setting of creation.[141] God "saw" his creation and evaluated his handiwork as "very good" (*tôb mĕʾōd*, 1:31), but here the sons of God have taken the "good" ("beautiful") and defiled it. This is reinforced by the play between man's "great *(rabbâ)* wickedness" (v. 5) and human "increase in number" *(lārōb*, v. 2). It serves as a sad commentary on the divine command at creation to "increase in number" *(rābû*, 1:28). The blessing of reproduction is realized in v. 2 by the grace of God, but humanity has distorted God's plan and reaped along with their progeny a harvest of sin.

Verse 5 therefore accentuates the decadence of the period: "how *great* man's wickedness," "*every* inclination," and "*only* evil *all* the time."[142] Whereas human society deems these violent *gibbōrîm* as "men of renown," God's response is repulsion at their wickedness. So monstrous becomes the sin of Noah's generation that the gravest of measures is the only proper response from heaven. The recurring phrase "on the earth" (vv. 5–7) anticipates the necessary purging of the now-polluted land by the waters of the flood (v. 13), and it also is reminiscent of the ground stained by Abel's blood, which resulted in Cain's life as a vagabond "on the earth" (4:12). But there would be no mercy for the murdering *gibbōrîm* as there had been for evil Cain.

Wickedness is an inner compulsion that dominates their thoughts and is not just overt action; they plot evil as a matter of lifestyle. Our phrase "inclination of the thoughts of his heart was only evil" is similar to God's utterance after the flood (8:21), where sin is attributed to humanity from his youth.[143] The flood

---

[141] So Cassuto, *Genesis,* 302.

[142] Assonance of the letter ר in the verse exaggerates even more so the terms רַע/רָעַת, rendered "wickedness" and "evil" respectively. "Evil" is used to describe not only sin but its consequences (e.g., 31:29).

[143] See the similar language יֵצֶר מַחְשְׁבֹת לִבּוֹ ("inclination of the thoughts of the heart") at 1 Chr 29:18 (cf. also 1 Chr 28:9).

does not change the essential sinful character of the human heart, but it does exact justice and rescue the lone remnant of a blessed lineage. God recognized the same evil "inclination" toward idolatry in his people Israel (Deut 31:21).[144] "Inclination" *(yēṣer)* probably is a play on 2:7, where God "formed" *(yāṣar)* the first man (also animals, 2:19). The good which God created has been transformed by mankind's evil inclination, over which God greatly anguishes (6:6; cf. Jer 18:11). Such "evil" *(raʿ)* plans are the continuing aftermath of humanity's first partaking of "good *(tôb)* and evil *(raʿ)*" (2:17; 3:5–6,22).

Human machinations are attributed to the "heart" since in Hebrew anthropology the heart is the center of a human's cognitive processes (e.g., Gen 31:20; Ps 33:11; 1 Sam 10:26). This sort of scheming has its parallel in 50:20, where Joseph's brothers "intended to harm" *(ḥăšabtem . . . rāʿâ)* but God "intended it for good" *(ḥăšābāh lĕṭōbâ)*. Such "thoughts" for good, like the artistic skills for decorating Moses' tabernacle, are enabled by the Spirit.[145] Judgment of the human heart is the exclusive domain of the Lord (Jer 9:9–10; cf. 1 Cor 4:3–5).

6:6 Our narrator owes his insight into God's fervent passion to the disclosures lamented by the Lord himself (cf. v. 7). Whereas antediluvian man plots evil in his "heart," God's response to their imaginations is a wounded "heart" filled with pain. In this latter case "heart" conveys the emotional response of God. Our verse, while describing God's reaction to such human depravity, at the same time anticipates the respite God will enjoy at the "sight" of righteous Noah (v. 8). Earlier we acknowledged the debt of v. 6 to the words of Lamech in 5:29; both passages share these three words: "comfort"/"grieved" *(nḥm),* "labor"/"made" *(ʿāśâ),* and "painful toil"/"pain" *(ʿāṣāb).* Thus Lamech's hope for his son as the deliverer from the toils of human sin is realized in part through Noah's survival of the flood and his inauguration of a new world for the blessed seed. As we will see, however, it is accomplished only by the odd intervention of God, who himself is "pained" yet kindly preserves Lamech's lineage through Noah (8:1). It comes about through Noah's offering, which appeases God's wrath and leads to his commitment never again to bring such destruction against the earth (8:21).

"Grieve" *(yinnāḥem),* translated "repent" in the AV, has troubled many expositors since elsewhere Scripture says God does not "repent" (Num 23:19; 1 Sam 15:29; Ps 110:4). We find the same expression *(yinnāḥem YHWH)* only twice more in the Pentateuch (Exod 32:12,14).[146] In the wilderness God changes his harmful intentions against idolatrous Israel because of the inter-

[144] יֵצֶר ("inclination") appears only once more in the Pentateuch (Deut 31:21), where the NIV has "disposed to do" (or NRSV, "inclined to do").

[145] Cf. לַחְשֹׁב מַחֲשָׁבֹת, "to make artistic designs," Exod 31:4; 35:32–35.

[146] Elsewhere יִנָּחֵם יְהוָה in Judg 2:18; 2 Sam 24:16; Jer 26:13,19; see similarly 1 Chr 21:15; Jer 18:8; 26:3; 42:10; Joel 2:13; Jonah 3:10.

cessory prayers of Moses: "Then the LORD relented *[yinnāḥem]* and did not bring on his people the disaster *[rāʿâ]* he had threatened" (Exod 32:14; cf. Ps 78:40–41).

The tension between these characterizations of God partly lies in the diverse contexts in which "grieve/relent" occurs in the Bible.[147] Genesis 6:6–7 is describing the emotional anguish of God; our verse does not present an abstract statement about God's decision making. This would be altogether out of place for the intention of the passage, which depicts God as wronged by the presumptuous sin of humanity. Moreover, the parameters of this verse have been dictated by the author's intention to imitate 5:29 with its distinctive vocabulary and mood. This is shown especially by the subsequent clause, where it describes God's heart as "filled with pain" *(yitʿaṣṣēb).*[148] This further echoes the painful consequences of human sin in the garden, where the cognate nouns narrate the "painful toil" the man and woman will endure (3:16–17; 5:29).

The NIV rightly reflects contextual differences by translating "grieved" ("was sorry," NRSV, NASB) in 6:6–7 but "change his mind" in 1 Sam 15:29 as well as "relent" in Exod 32:12,14 (also Amos 7:3,6). In Samuel's chastening of Saul the concern is the character of God's word, as indicated by the parallel "does not lie" *(šāqar;* 1 Sam 15:29). Close to the sense of 6:6 is God's sorrowful concern over Saul's moral failures, which precipitate rejection of his kingship: "I am grieved that I have made Saul king" (1 Sam 15:11; also v. 35). Similarly, Exodus 32 is speaking of a new course in God's dealing with his people. This too is not a comment on the nature of God's sovereignty or promises. It is told so as to highlight the intercessory position of Moses with God, a reassuring thought for Israel. We have mentioned earlier the common language of our passage and Exodus 32. Now to this we can add "wipe" *(māḥâ)* from Gen 6:7, which is rendered "blot out" in Exod 32:32–33. If the Exodus passage is a veiled remembrance of God's "pain" at antediluvian humanity, Moses is expressing the same remorse over the sins of Israel. In the case of Israel, Moses' mediation delivers his people, but antediluvian man has no intercessor, and the whole world suffers as a result. It is solely by the grace of God that the human family has any chance at all.

---

[147] Traditionally theologians explain divine "repentance" and emotions such as "grief" as uttered in deference to the human reader (a figure called "anthropopathia"; cf. Calvin, *Comm.*, 248–49). Luther explains that the "grief" experienced by God is not in his divine essence but rather a description of the holy men of God (i.e., Noah) who grieved at the wickedness of the age: "When Moses says that God sees and repents, these actions really occur in the hearts of the men who carry on the ministry of the Word" (*LW* 2.44).

[148] As נָחַם is in parallel with עָצַב here, other words expressing emotional pain occur in parallel with נָחַם; e.g., Job 42:6; Jer 31:19. Cf. also the sorrowful context in Judg 21:6,15. See H. Van Dyke Parunak, "A Semantic Survey of *NḤM*," *Bib* 56 (1975): 519.

God's response of grief over the making of humanity, however, is not remorse in the sense of sorrow over a mistaken creation; our verse shows that God's pain has its source in the perversion of human sin. The making of "man" is no error; it is what "man" has made of himself. By recurring reference to mankind *(ʾādām)* in 6:5–7, the passage focuses on the source of his grief. God is grieving because this sinful "man" is not the pristine mankind whom he has made to bear his image. The intensity of the pain is demonstrated by the use of *nāḥam* elsewhere in Genesis, where it describes mourning over the loss of a family member due to death.[149] But his is not regret over destroying humanity; paradoxically, so foul has become mankind that it is the necessary step to salvage him.

This "grief" is explicated by the parallel clause of the sentence, "and his [God's] heart was filled with pain" (v. 6b).[150] By allusion to the "pain" and "painful toil" in God's pronouncement of punishment for the crimes of our first parents (3:16–17; cf. 5:29), God indicates that unbridled human sin has become his source of anguish. Yet this anguish does not reflect impotent remorse; it entails also God's angry response at the injury inflicted by human rebellion. Our earlier verb *nāḥam* may also indicate the execution of God's wrath to relieve his emotional pain.[151] "Lament is always an integral part of the wrath of God."[152] In the only two other passages where the same verb, "pained" *(ʿāṣab),* is used of God's feelings (Ps 78:40–41; Isa 63:10), both motifs of divine grief and anger represent his opposition against rebellious Israel in the desert when they "grieved his Holy Spirit" (Isa 63:10; cf. Eph 4:30). But we hear a mitigated mood in Hos 11:8–11; there the Lord refuses to execute his full wrath against his wayward son, Israel (cf. Deut 21:18–21). The reason is not human repentance; on the contrary, God's repentance is because he is "not man" (Hos 11:9). The motivation for reversal is God's constancy of promise and purpose, unlike capricious mankind (cf. Mal 3:6). Similarly, God's anger is tempered by his favor toward Noah, the ark builder (Heb 11:7),

---

[149] Cf. the *niphal* use "was comforted" in 24:67 and "time of mourning" (38:12, NRSV). The *piel* stem of נָחַם ("console") in Genesis is also associated with mourning (37:35 [also *hithpael*]; 50:21), but not always (5:29); also see, e.g., 2 Sam 13:39; Jer 31:15.

[150] The NIV's "was filled with pain" ("grieved," NRSV, NASB, NJB, NAB; "saddened," NJPS) renders וַיִּתְעַצֵּב *(hithpael),* whose root is related to the nominal form עִצָּבוֹן in 3:16–17 and 5:29. The verbal root עצב occurs elsewhere in the Pentateuch only in Genesis, where Jacob's sons are "filled with grief" over the rape of Dinah, their sister (34:7, *hithpael*) and at Joseph's self-revelation to his brothers, who are "distressed" at their crime (45:5, *niphal*). All three cases express grief in the context of anger at some wrong that deserves redress.

[151] E.g., Isa 1:24, where נקם ("avenge") parallels נחם (notice the assonance and alliteration). נקם occurs in the *hithpael* participle in Gen 27:42, where Esau is "consoling himself" over the loss of his father's blessing as he plots to kill Jacob (Parunak, "*NḤM*," 521–22).

[152] T. E. Fretheim, *The Suffering of God: An Old Testament Perspective* (Philadelphia: Fortress, 1984), 110.

who is the beneficent recipient of God's promise to humanity.

God is no robot. We know him as a personal, living God, not a static principle, who while having transcendent purposes to be sure also engages intimately with his creation. Our God is incomparably affected by, even pained by, the sinner's rebellion. Acknowledging the passibility (emotions) of God does not diminish the immutability of his promissory purposes.[153] Rather, his feelings and actions toward men, such as judgment or forgiveness, are always inherently consistent with his essential person and just and gracious resolve (Jas 1:17). When we consider the metaphor of God as a feeling person who loves, is angry, and grieves, the aim of the figure is to point to a mitigated correspondence between human experience and God. This does not say that the emotions of humans and God are equivalent in their entirety either in intensity or in quality, for God does not grieve in the same way as men and women. Nor is he angry in the same fashion as sinful mortals, but to conclude that such language reveals nothing of God's essential personhood makes all such language pointless.[154] For what purpose is there in describing God in any terms understandable to us other than to reveal something of God's mysterious nature? In Christ we see God so moved by grief and love that he chooses to take upon himself the very suffering of our sins.[155] Do we not appeal to the incarnational role of Christ as our vision of the nature of his Father (cf. Matt 23:37 par.)? God is not a dispassionate accountant overseeing the books of human endeavor; rather he makes a personal decision out of sorrowful loss to judge Noah's wicked generation.

6:7 God's second speech ("so the LORD said") in this narrative epilogue makes explicit what is only intimated in the former utterance (v. 3). God's new policy toward human life is the radical undoing of his creative acts in Genesis 1. The language of our verse is an allusion to 1:26–28, where mankind is created and given dominion over all living things.[156] God declares his

---

[153] For discussion see Fretheim, *The Suffering of God,* 5–8 and 109–13; G. R. Lewis, "God, Attributes of" and "Impassibility of God," in *The Evangelical Dictionary of Theology* (Grand Rapids: Baker, 1984), 453–54, 553–54.

[154] Perhaps we would do better, after all, to adhere to Luther's recommendation concerning this mystery: "I follow this general rule: to avoid as much as possible any questions that carry us to the throne of the Supreme Majesty. It is better and safer to stay at the manger of Christ the Man. For there is very great danger in involving oneself in the mazes of the Divine Being" (*LW* 2.45).

[155] Fundamental to the OT tradition is God's merciful refusal to execute wrath (e.g., Joel 2:13; Jonah 4:2). See Fretheim, "The Repentance of God: A Key to Evaluating Old Testament God-Talk," *HBT* 10 (1988): 47–70, esp. 58–63.

[156] "Man" (אָדָם), first occurring in 1:26, is primary in 6:5–8; "animals" (בְּהֵמָה) in v. 7 occurs in a cluster in the creation account, 1:24–26 (cf. 2:20; 3:14). Otherwise it appears regularly in the flood story (6:7,20; 7:2,8,14,21,23; 8:1,17,20; 9:10). Also vv. 6–7 have the parallel verbs "made" (עָשָׂה) and "created" (בָּרָאתִי), which are standard in 1:1–2:4. V. 7 has additionally "creatures (רֶמֶשׂ) that move along the ground" and "birds [עוֹף] of the air," which appear in 1:26,28. The noun form "creatures" (רֶמֶשׂ) typically occurs in the creation (1:26) and flood narratives (6:7,20; 7:14,23; 8:19; 9:2) as well as the participial form (רֹמֶשֶׂת/רֹמֵשׂ) (1:21,26,28,30; 7:8,14,21; 8:17,19; 9:2). "Birds" also appears often in both (1:26,28,30; 2:20; 6:7,20; 7:3,8,14,21,23; 8:17,20; 9:2,10).

resolve to "wipe [out]" *(māḥâ)* his handiwork. Here "wipe out" is a sound play with the earlier "grieved" *(nāḥam;* 6:6). The word bears the sense of "removal" as in Moses' offer that his name be erased from God's ledger of life (Exod 32:32–33).[157] Here it describes obliteration of all "man"—which means man and animal alike (cf. 7:4,23). The specific means is left unstated until God's later directions for building Noah's ark (6:14–17).

Whereas at the conclusion of creation God declares all is "very good" (1:31), now the created order is distorted by violence beyond repair. All humanity *(ʾādām),* as in 1:26–28, is deserving of God's retribution, but the punishment extends to man's environment as well—just as God had cursed the "ground" for Adam's sin (3:17–19), the living creatures will suffer for human sin. The Lord perceives that the whole "earth" ("ground," *ʾădāmâ*), as in the case of Cain (4:10–12; cf. 3:17–19; 5:29), is polluted by the wickedness of man. Our verse shows a hierarchy in the created order, descending from "man" to "animals" to crawling "creatures" and finally "birds." Omission of "fish," unlike 1:28, is due transparently to their innate properties to survive the imminent waters. This destruction of living things is at odds with God's enabling blessing at creation when he insures that all creaturely life inherently flourishes by his beneficent word (1:20–25). But the last word is not sounded here. He will yet deliver a remnant of the earthly band (8:18–19) and will finally relieve creation's plight (Rom 8:19–21).[158]

The closing words of the divine Judge reiterate those of v. 6, "For I am grieved that I have made them" (v. 7b). It underscores God's sorrow at what his special creation *(imago Dei)* has become. God is not capricious as are the deities that make up the pantheons of pagan invention. His irrevocable action against humanity is the just deserts for so debased a people.

6:8 This divine anguish finds immediate relief, however, when God "eyes" Noah. "But" distinguishes Noah from those who caught God's former attention—because of their corruption (v. 5). The term "favor" *(ḥēn),* also translated "grace," commonly occurs in the formula "found favor in the eyes of."[159] "Favor" *(ḥēn)* functions in our passage as a sound play on the name "Noah" *(nōaḥ)* by the inversion of the Hebrew letters *n/ḥ.*[160] It usually indicates securing approval and provision, often in the context of request, whether

---

[157] This term (מָחָה) is used of erasure from a book (e.g., Num 5:23; Ps 69:28[29]) and obliteration (e.g., Deut 9:14). It describes God's destruction of Jerusalem, where it is likened to "wiping out" a dirty dish, turning it over so that the cleansing is exhaustive (2 Kgs 21:13). Conversely, cf. e.g., the erasure of the sinner's transgressions, Ps 51:2[3].

[158] So observes Kidner, *Genesis,* 86.

[159] E.g., Abraham (Gen 18:3); Lot, whose life is spared (19:19); Laban (30:27); Jacob (32:5[6]; 33:8,10,15; 47:29); Shechem (34:11); Joseph (39:4; 50:4); and Egyptians (47:25). It also has the sense of "disfavor" (with the negative לֹא; Num 11:11; unpleasing wife, Deut 24:1).

[160] J. M. Sasson, "Word-Play in Gen 6:8–9," *CBQ* 37 (1975): 165–66. In the Heb. text "Noah" occurs as the first and last words (inclusio) of vv. 8–9.

of man or God.[161] It is seldom used of God's approval of an individual, as we have it in the case of Noah (cf. Judg 6:17; 2 Sam 15:25). By inference it may be applied to Abraham when we recognize that among his three visitors was the Lord, who complied with the patriarch's request: "If I have found favor in your eyes, do not pass your servant by" (18:3,10,33).

This honor also is known by Moses, who is distinguished as the deliverer of Israel (Exod 33:12–13,16–17; 34:9; cf. Num 11:11,15). Particularly striking is its occurrence in Exodus 33, where the Lord favors the lawgiver by unveiling his "glory"; v. 14 has the name of "Noah" embedded in the sound play "rest" where the letters *n* and *ḥ* occur: "My Presence will go with you, and I will give you rest *[wahănihōtî]*." We commented earlier (see 5:29) that the flood narrative plays on the sound of Noah's name in a way that is reminiscent here. Added to this is the Pentateuch's intentional connection of Moses with his precursor, Noah (cf. 6:14). Just as Noah trusted the Lord and received his "rest" (8:4), so did Moses before the presence of the Lord.

The reason Noah "found favor" is related in the following *tōlĕdōt* section to his "righteous" conduct (v. 9). Later Ezekiel recognized that it was Noah's character that distinguished him from his peers (Ezek 14:14,20). Any attempt to erect a wall between God's sovereign mercies (v. 8) and the merit of Noah's "righteousness" (v. 9) is superficial.[162] No such dichotomy is presented in the text, for the contrast in v. 8 is how Noah looked in God's "eyes" versus how God "saw" his contemporaries (6:5). This infers that Noah's conduct is related in some way to God's bestowal of gracious favor. The same contrast follows in v. 9 between the conduct of Noah, who is "blameless," and the "people of his time." This does not mean that Noah's character automatically secures divine favor, for God is under no obligation to bestow his favor.[163] It presupposes a relationship. The proper emphasis in our passage is God's gracious favor, just as we see his preservation of the human family in chaps. 1–11 despite human sin. For the apostle Paul the promissory favor is realized by faith, hence a gift (grace) that results in righteousness (Rom 4:13–16). Genesis's "grace" and "righteousness" (6:8–9) joined by Noah's "faith" is brought together in the theological reflection of the writer to the Hebrews. He interpreted Noah's obedient "fear" as "faith" that resulted in a saving "righteousness" (Heb 11:7).

[161] E.g., 18:3; Exod 34:9; Num 32:5; Ruth 2:2,10,13. Of its fourteen occasions in Genesis, it only appears in 6:8 for God's approval. Gen 18:3 is also exceptional. For a close parallel at the human level see Potiphar's approval of Joseph, who is rewarded with position (39:4).

[162] E.g., Westermann attributes to v. 8 J's theology of "favor" and to v. 9 P's theology of righteousness (*Genesis 1–11,* 411–12).

[163] This is the mistake in the NEB's rendering "But Noah had won the LORD's favor" (also REB). There is the element of uncertainty, e.g., in Gideon (Judg 6:12,17) and Moses (Exod 34:9), who received God's favor (see A. N. Barnard, "Was Noah a Righteous Man?" *Theology* 74 [1971]: 311–14). "Favor" remains as God's sole discretion.

We already observed that by ironic twist, Noah will prove to be, after all, the consolation of mankind for which Lamech prayed (5:29). Unexpectedly the narrative hints at a double entendre by the appearance of "Noah" in v. 8; it is God too who is "comforted" by Noah. This is implied by the delicate difference in the meaning of *nāḥam* at 6:6–7 and the recurrence of "Noah" in 6:8, both in conjunction with Lamech's lament (5:29). In vv. 6–7 *nāḥam* describes God, who is "grieved," but the word has the hopeful nuance "comfort" for the naming and role of "Noah" (5:29; 6:8).[164] God's grief over the sinfulness of humanity will find a reprieve in the godly Noah (8:21).

[164] "Grieved" is the meaning of the *niphal* form, whereas "comfort" is the *piel.*

SECTION OUTLINE

IV. NOAH AND HIS FAMILY (6:9–9:29)
   1. Righteous Noah (6:9–10)
   2. Corrupt World (6:11–12)
   3. Coming Judgment but the Ark of Promise (6:13–7:10)
      (1) Announcement of the Flood and Instructions for the Ark (6:13–22)
      (2) Entering the Ark (7:1–10)
   4. Waves of Judgment (7:11–24)
      (1) Beginning of the Rains (7:11–16)
      (2) Rising Floodwaters (7:17–24)
   5. God Remembered Noah (8:1a)
   6. Winds of Rescue (8:1b–14)
      (1) Receding Floodwater (8:1b–5)
      (2) Drying Earth (8:6–14)
   7. Exiting the Ark (8:15–19)
   8. Worship and the Word of Promise (8:20–22)
   9. Covenant with the New World (9:1–17)
      (1) Provisions for the New World (9:1–7)
      (2) Covenant and Sign (9:8–17)
   10. Noah's Sons and Future Blessing (9:18–29)
      (1) Sons of Noah (9:18–19)
      (2) Noah's Curse and Blessing (9:20–27)
      (3) Noah's Death (9:28–29)

IV. NOAH AND HIS FAMILY (6:9–9:29)

Noah's *tōlĕdōt* is the centerpiece of early Genesis (chaps. 1–11) and receives the most extensive treatment of the *tōlĕdōt* accounts. This speaks to the popularity of the Noah episode but also its importance for the author's purposes. Noah's experience presents decisively the author's assertion that the Lord judges human sin but provides a means for perpetuating the creation blessing (1:26–28) and the salvation hope for an elect seed (3:15). The recurring theme of blessing, threatened by sin but preserved by divine mercy, is found in the two narratives that make up the Noah *tōlĕdōt*: the flood story (6:9–9:17) and the account of the patriarch's drunkenness (9:20–27). The former is worldwide in scope, and the latter is its microcosm. A genealogical note binds the two (9:18–19), and another concludes it (9:28–29).

The earlier stories about human life in and outside the garden depicted divine blessing, human sin, its penalty, and divine forbearance through an elect lineage. The flood story magnifies these abiding theological foci (6:9–9:17): Noah as the last-named descendant of Seth exhibits the creation blessing by fathering three sons (5:29; 6:9–10); yet the corruption of Noah's generation is full (6:11–12); such corruption merits the severest penalty—the destruction of all living things (6:13–7:24); nevertheless, the Lord favors Seth's seed by preserving Noah and the animals (8:1–9:19). Also these thematic elements are repeated in the family history regarding Noah's drunkenness (9:20–27): Noah enjoys the procreation of the land, which once again yields its bounty (9:20); but Noah becomes drunk, and Ham disgraces the family (9:21–23); the penalty is the patriarch's "curse" against Ham's son Canaan (9:24–25); nevertheless Noah's prayer calls for "blessing" on the elect line of Shem (9:26–27). Noah's two stories are the author's parade examples of his theological proclamation in chaps. 1–11.

Also Noah's *tōlĕdōt* contributes to the broader concerns of early Genesis by preparing the reader for the postdiluvian world. This "new world" is the setting for understanding the perpetuation of the "blessing" by the patriarchs (11:27–50:26), which is the main deliberation of Genesis. Our section provides the interpretive bridge between the shadowy past before the flood and the nearer, more comprehensible era of Israel's fathers following the deluge. It continues the universal interest in man and the world, but at the same time it starts the narrowing process that arrives at the restricted history of the Israelites via Noah's son Shem. After the flood narrative the incident of Noah's drunkenness and the subsequent blessing and curse link the flood survivor to the vast Table of Nations (chaps. 10–11) that depicts the ethnographic world in which Abram hears the call of the Lord to receive and to be a "blessing" (12:1–3). Ham's crime and Noah's blessing and curse convey the moral setting for interpreting the postdiluvian world into which Israel's fathers were born. For the narrator nothing takes place in a moral vacuum. The moral character of the nations and their destiny is foreshadowed in their fathers' behavior. Israel too discovers its history prefigured in the actions of its fathers, the patriarchs.

We have already commented at chap. 5 that the schematic formula in the genealogy of Seth, ending in each case with the death of the individual patriarch cited, is interrupted by the narrative of 6:1–8 and the extensive Noah *tōlĕdōt* (6:9–9:27). The catalog of Sethite names in chap. 5 has Noah as the last antediluvian patriarch (5:32), but the recitation of his career is not completed until 9:28–29 ("and then he died"). This shows that the story of Noah is embedded in the genealogy of Seth begun in 5:1. The effect of this arrangement forces the material to be interpreted in light of the genealogy of Seth. As a genealogical bridge, this encourages a sense of continuity between the antediluvian and postdiluvian eras. The expansive ages between creation and the calling of Abraham are telescoped so that the blessing is passed down through three patriarchs: Adam to Noah to Abraham. Noah is both thematically and genealogically the linchpin in the author's presentation.

CREATION. It is not surprising then that the narrative goes to great lengths to depict Noah as the new Adam. Much of the Noah *tōlĕdōt* is indebted to the language of creation, and Noah's role has remarkable parallels with that of Adam and the first humanity.

The language of destruction in the flood narrative, such as the eruption of the "great deep" and the "floodgates of the heavens" (7:11), shows a reversal of creation days one through three (1:1–13). It is the *uncreation* of Adam's old world. Persistent mention of the animals by creation's categories (e.g., animal, bird, crawlers) and their divine provision point to the air and land creatures created on days five and six (1:20–30). The reemergence of the land and the disembarkation show the *recreation* of the first week (8:1b–19). Shared chronological interests, such as "days," the common use of numeric "seven's," and the recurring "God [Elohim] said" invite reading both stories in concert. The same creation jargon of "blessing," exhortation to "multiply," and the special provisos for the *imago Dei* rehearse the world of Adam (9:1–7).

Noah is depicted as Adam *redivivus* (revived). He is the sole survivor and successor to Adam; both "walk" with God; both are the recipients of the promissory blessing; both are caretakers of the lower creatures; both father three sons; both are workers of the soil; both sin through the fruit of a tree; and both father a wicked son who is under a curse. Also there is a wordplay between Adam in the garden and the "rest" motif recurring in the Noah story (see 5:29; 8:21). The Lord "put" *(nûaḥ)* Adam in Eden as the divine ideal for man (2:15), but because of sin the soil is man's new opponent (3:17). Lamech's prayer is that "Noah" *(nōaḥ)* alleviate the toil and achieve "comfort" (*nḥm;* 5:29), but it comes about in an unexpected way when Noah preserves the human family by the "resting" ark (8:4) and the "resting-inducing odor"[1] (8:21) of sacrifice, which appeases God and leads the way for a new promise. We can only view Noah through the template of Adam, both the promise and the garden sin.

That Noah was also a prototype for Moses and the practices of later Israel is widely recognized. Both share in the language of ceremonial matters, such as "clean" and "unclean" animals, the practice of "burnt offering," restrictions on "lifeblood," the language of covenant-law ("whoever," 9:6), attention to numeric "seven's" and "forty's," and a covenant "sign" (rainbow, Sabbath). Noah and Moses both were delivered by means of a *tēbâ,* the word for Noah's "ark" and also for Moses' "basket." Both did their assigned tasks (Noah's

---

[1] So rendered by V. Hamilton, *The Book of Genesis Chapters 1–17,* NICOT (Grand Rapids: Eerdmans, 1990), 308.

building the ark and Moses' building the tabernacle) according to "all that the LORD commanded" (e.g., 6:22; 7:5; Exod 40:16). Noah then is the ideal patriarch who founds the new world, fathers the ancestral heritage of Israel, and, as Moses' precursor, establishes the core institutions of law and sacrifice that gave order and life to the nation Israel. This establishes an organic unity between the patriarchal world of promise and the Mosaic world of fulfillment.

STRUCTURE. Several studies following different methodologies have shown that the flood narrative (6:9–9:19) follows the pattern of an extended chiasmus. In a chiasmus each element is matched by a corresponding part in reverse order. Thus the first half has its mirror image in the second. Also the chiasmus highlights the center "leg" (8:1a) that is the structural and theological "hinge" on which the flood narrative turns. B. W. Anderson's study has presented the following analysis:[2]

Transitional introduction (6:9–10)
1. Violence in God's creation (6:11–12)
2. First divine address: resolution to destroy (6:13–22)
3. Second divine address: command to enter the ark (7:1–10)
4. Beginning of the flood (7:11–16)
5. The rising flood waters (7:17–24)
God's Remembrance of Noah (8:1a)
6. The receding flood waters (8:1b–5)
7. The drying of the earth (8:6–14)
8. Third divine address: command to leave the ark (8:15–19)
9. God's resolution to preserve order (8:20–22)
10. Fourth divine address: covenant blessing and peace (9:1–17)
Transitional conclusion (9:18–19)

R. Longacre's structural display of the flood narrative graphically depicts how the structure accentuates the thematic material of the rising and falling waters (see chart, "General Profile of the Flood Narrative," p. 354).[3] His analysis, based on discourse type and linguistic features, concludes that the "peak" (climax) of the account is 7:17–24, where the floodwaters reach their crest. It agrees that the "decisive turn of events" is marked at 8:1–5. His analysis explains on a firm linguistic basis the rhetorical purposes of duplications in the narrative that have been attributed by critical scholars to two documentary sources. Longacre delineates three "prepeak" and five "postpeak" episodes. His study recognizes a secondary or "thematic" peak in the narrative at 9:1–17, which is the renewal of creation's divine blessing and the offering of the Noahic covenant.

As these two analyses show, the flood account exhibits a literary cohesion

[2] B. W. Anderson, "From Analysis to Synthesis: The Interpretation of Genesis 1–11," *JBL* 97 (1978): 23–29, chart on p. 28.

[3] R. Longacre, "The Discourse Structure of the Flood Narrative," *JAARSup* 47 (1979): 89–133; our reproduction has modified slightly his original chart (p. 95).

that can best be explained as the product of one hand.[4] This consciously confirms what readers have assumed intuitively, namely, that the story hangs together as a whole and makes sense. G. Wenham presents a case for the consonance of the narrative and shows how the troubling chronological spans can be accounted for on literary grounds. In his study the palistrophic structure (i.e., correspondence) for 6:10–9:19 was detected for embedded sections (e.g., 6:9–10), especially the chiasmus of the time spans.[5]

7 days of waiting for flood (7:4)
  7 days of waiting for flood (7:10)
    40 days of flood (7:17a)
      150 days of water triumphing (7:24)
      150 days of water waning (8:3)
    40 days' wait (8:6)
  7 days' wait (8:10)
7 days' wait (8:12)

Viewing the story as an original unity is at odds with the standard explanation for the narrative's composition, which has been attributed by critical scholars to two putative sources J and P.[6] Genesis 6:5–9:17 has been championed as the parade example of the classic source method of analysis. Essentially the alleged P source entails the two blocks 6:9–22 and 9:1–17, and the intervening chaps. 7–8 are mixed between J and P materials. The evidence presented for two different flood stories is twofold: (1) supposed inconsistencies in the narrative and (2) twice-told content in the passage.[7] Contradictions are

---

[4] Cf. also G. Wenham, "The Coherence of the Flood Narrative," *VT* 28 (1978): 336–48, and *Genesis 1–15,* WBC (Waco: Word, 1987), 156–57; and R. T. Radday, "Chiasmus in Hebrew Biblical Narrative," in *Chiasmus in Antiquity,* ed. J. Welch (Hildesheim: Gerstenberg, 1981), 99–100.

[5] Wenham shows how the chronology is arranged so as to give primacy to the structure; i.e., the waiting for the flood is actually seven days, but the repetition of the information (7:4,10) matches the two concluding seven days of waiting (8:10,12). In this last case there is "another" seven-day period (8:10) left unstated that maintains the harmony of two "sevens" before and after the flood.

[6] For a defense of the source position and a critique of narrative unity, see J. A. Emerton, "An Examination of Some Attempts to Defend the Unity of the Flood Narrative in Genesis, Part I," *VT* 37 (1987): 401–20, and "Part II," *VT* 38 (1988): 1–21. For counterresponse arguing for literary unity see G. Wenham, "Method in Pentateuchal Source Criticism," *VT* 41 (1991): 84–109.

[7] E.g., difference of divine names in parallel verses, Yahweh (7:5[J]) and Elohim (6:22[P]); the animals on board with seven pairs of "clean" and one pair of "unclean" (7:2–3[J]) versus two pairs of animals (6:19–20[P]); duration of forty days with seven-day intervals (7:4,12; 8:6[J]) versus a year's time including 150 days of rising waters (7:6,11,13–14,24; 8:3[P]); and the flood by rainfall (גֶּשֶׁם) (7:12[J]) versus a collapse of the celestial flood (מַבּוּל) and underground "deep" (תְּהוֹם) (7:11; 8:3[P]). Duplicate information is found for command and report of entrance (7:1–3,7–9[J]; 7:13–16a,18–21 [P]); coming flood (7:10[J]; 7:11[P]); flood's end (8:2b–3a[J]; 8:3b–5[P]); the swelling waters (7:17b[J]; 7:18–20[P]; and destruction of life (7:22–23[J]; 7:21[P]). For more see J. Skinner, *A Critical and Exegetical Commentary on Genesis,* ICC (Edinburgh: T & T Clark, 1910), 148–49.

General Profile of the Flood Narrative (Gen 6:5–9:17)

Surface features	Profile	Content	Text
(Character introduced before his *tōlĕdōt*) (rundown of previous paragraph)	Preview	Yhwh as thematic	6:5–8
tōlĕdōt (goes with whole unit 9:20)	STAGE	Noah and world conditions	6:9–12
(God said Noah did) And God said to Noah	Ep(P-3)	Command to build the ark; further instructions to Noah	6:13–22
(Yhwh said Noah did) And Yhwh said to Noah	Ep(P-2)	Noah enters ark. Yhwh and Noah thematic in 7:1–5; Noah in 7:6–10	7:1–10
Yhwh shuts the door long date	Ep(P-1)	Flood begins. Flood; animals are thematic	7:11–16
terminus (time span) *wayĕhî hammabbûl*	Peak CLIMAX	The flood (thematic) prevails. Remorseless mechanism of judgment. God is not mentioned. Noah mentioned only at the end	7:17–24
terminus (date) But God remembered Noah	Ep(P+1)	Receding waters	8:1–5
(dove doesn't return) *wayĕhî* and date	Ep(P+2)	Noah sends birds (assumes active role)	8:6–12
wayĕhî and long setting (double dating)	Ep(P+3)	Leaving the ark	8:13–19
poetic climax (Noah Yhwh Yhwh Noah) weak onset, but distinct section	Ep(P+4)	Yhwh receives sacrifices. Yhwh is thematic	8:20–22
ends with quote And God said to Noah And God said to Noah And God said to Noah	Secondary Peak Ep(P+5) WRAP-UP	God's discourse to Noah: blessing, covenant, covenant sign	9:1–17

claimed for the inhabitants of the ark, the duration of the flood, and the nature of the flood. Twice we are told of the command and entrance into the ark, coming of the flood, mounting waters, destruction of all life, and the end of the flood. Although critical scholars debate how the composition came together,[8] there is a consensus that the present form is a combination of two flood stories. Even B. W. Anderson, for example, believes that the unified passage is the consequence of the priestly editor (P) integrating the older epic source (J).

These textual features could point to a composite text, but the symmetry of the narrative we have demonstrated recommends one originally unified text. Although symmetry cannot rule out the work of a final editor in achieving this artful arrangement from the assemblage of two stories, there are problems with the source reconstruction of chaps. 6–9 when we consider that the proposed sources have significant gaps and the source division violates the inner cohesion of sentence and paragraph structures.[9]

Also the widely recognized extrabiblical parallels to the Genesis flood, *Gilgamesh* and the Sumerian flood story (see "Genesis 1–11 and Ancient Literature," p. 86), are closer to the existing passage in chaps. 6–9 than to either the J or P account as reconstructed by source critics. Added to this is the biblical parallel of the Sodom and Gomorrah account in chaps. 18–19, which shares similar structure and many of the same lexical items with chaps. 6–9 as a unit.[10]

We discover evidence, then, that could point to two opposite conclusions. But since it can be shown that the supposed incongruities that have troubled scholars can be explained on the basis of the story's literary and discourse features, it is unnecessary to posit a complex source history and later redac-

---

[8] E.g., the widely accepted opinion is that P was retained essentially intact by the redactor while the J source was added, though not in its entirety; e.g., it lacks an account of building the ark (cf. C. Westermann, *Genesis 1–11: A Commentary* [Minneapolis: Augsburg, 1984], 396; J. Blenkinsopp, *The Pentateuch: An Introduction to the First Five Books of the Bible* [New York: Doubleday, 1994], 78). By another reconstruction the J source is found complete in chaps. 6–8, and it was the primary document that was embellished by P (see J. van Seters, *Prologue to History: The Yahwist as Historian in Genesis* [Louisville: Westminster/John Knox, 1992], 160–65).

[9] E.g., if P were the basic source, it had no sending out of the birds and no sacrifice by Noah. Also the Yahwist source, as the narrative now stands, has no instructions for the ark's building or exit from the ark. Some contend the Yahwist's account has been trimmed to coalesce with the fuller P, but why in the redacted form is some information duplicated from the sources, whereas other elements, which are at points even more essential, are not repeated? Duplicates are better attributed to rhetorical effect than different literary sources. Repetition retards the action so as to highlight the passage and build tension in the narrative plot. Also the documentary reconstruction at places cuts across chiastic sentences and paragraph patterns. See F. I. Andersen, *The Sentence in Biblical Hebrew* (Mouton: The Hague, 1974), 39–41, 123–26.

[10] G. Wenham, "Method in Pentateuchal Source Criticism," 103–6.

tional effort.[11] Of course, all are agreed that the author made use of antecedent material in the composition of Genesis, but those materials cannot be recovered or defined as source critics have proposed and are unnecessary to explain the text's features.

1. Righteous Noah (6:9–10)

[9]This is the account of Noah.

Noah was a righteous man, blameless among the people of his time, and he walked with God. [10]Noah had three sons: Shem, Ham and Japheth.

6:9 Noah is distinguished from the "people of his time" by his upright character (i.e., "the only good man," GNB). His piety and righteous courage became renowned in later times (Ezek 14:14,20; Isa 54:9–10), and he was commonly associated with the virtue of godliness (Heb 11:7; 1 Pet 3:20), receiving the unique appellation "preacher of righteousness" (2 Pet 2:5). Jewish literature celebrated Noah's place in history as the paragon of righteousness (e.g., *Sir* 44:17; *Jub.* 5:19; *Wis* 10:4; *1 Enoch* 67:1) and added to his reputation by fanciful stories about his birth (e.g., 1QapGen 2; *1 Enoch* 106).[12]

Unlike the Mesopotamian flood stories (see "Genesis 1–11 and Ancient Literature"), there is no antecedent act of righteousness by Noah that would explain his favored place before God.[13] This points theologically to the elective purposes

---

[11] See, e.g., Longacre, who shows that the overall integrity of the macrostructure argues that the repetitions are best explained as structural "overlays." Overlays are paragraphs giving the same approximate information again and again so as to highlight the information ("The Discourse Structure of the Flood Narrative," 108–12). E.g., the three "entry" narratives reiterate the information of Noah and the animals' embarkation for emphasis, but each has a different aspect: the general plan of construction and entry (6:13–22); the focus on Noah's entry (7:1–10); and attention to the animals' entry (7:11–16). Longacre also shows that commonly in the flood narrative *Elohim* occurs rather than *Yahweh* when the thematic participant of the paragraph is not God (pp. 128–29). Wenham shows that the chronologies in 7:17–24 and 8:1–5 are to be read as overlapping, telling the same events, not chronologically consecutive ("Method in Pentateuchal Source Criticism," 91–93). Gen 7:17–24 describes the human perspective on the rains and flood, while 8:1–5 gives the divine vantage point of the same events by describing what could not be known by the human occupants. There is the forty-day rain (7:17) followed by a second phase of a 110-day abatement, constituting a 150-day flood (7:24). The same two-phase description is implied in 8:1–5: the cessation of the forty-day rain is in 8:2, when compared with 7:11's description of its beginning, and 8:3–5 depicts the progressive abatement for 110 days, arriving at the same 150-day period for the flood. This reconstruction shows how 7:4,12,17 speaks of a forty-day "rain" and 7:24; 8:3 refer to a 150-day "flood" without contradiction.

[12] In *1 Enoch* Noah is said at birth to have "opened his eyes and made the whole house bright" and "opened his mouth and blessed the LORD of Heaven."

[13] For our discussion of Jewish and Christian interpretation see J. C. VanderKam, "The Righteousness of Noah," in *Ideal Figures in Ancient Judaism: Profiles and Paradigms* (Chico, Cal.: SBL, 1980), 13–32; J. P. Lewis, *A Study of the Interpretation of Noah and the Flood in Jewish and Christian Literature* (Leiden: Brill, 1968); E. G. Selwyn, *The First Epistle of Peter,* 2d ed. (Grand Rapids: Baker, 1981); J. N. D. Kelly, *A Commentary on the Epistles of Peter and Jude* (Grand Rapids: Baker, 1981); F. F. Bruce, *The Epistle to the Hebrews,* NICNT (Grand Rapids: Eerdmans, 1964).

of God for Noah, showing that the patriarch already enjoyed a relationship with the Lord before his recorded acts of obedience. Noah was perceived in *Jubilees* and *1 Enoch* as a priest who made atonement for the corrupted earth and maintained the laws of cultic purity. Moreover, he was a prototype for the eschatological judgment of God, which we also see reflected in the New Testament (Matt 24:37–38 pars.; 2 Pet 3:3–7).[14] In early Christian tradition Noah's water and ark were deemed a type of the Lord's cross whereby we are saved through "water, faith, and wood . . . just as the wood of Noe" (Justin, *Dialogue* 138.2) and a type of the church at baptism (Tertullian, *On Baptism* 8.4). Noah's story serves as an exhortation to righteousness and enduring faith in the face of degenerate times.

Genesis is silent about Noah's relationship with his contemporaries; thus later Jewish and Christian imagination attempted to fill in the lacuna.[15] Noah forewarned and urged repentance, but the people would have nothing of it and opposed his preaching. Noah is depicted as the stalwart preacher forewarning doom, but the people "sneered at him, each one, calling him demented, a man gone mad" (*Sib. Or.* 1.171–73).[16] Josephus's account envisions that the patriarch felt threatened for his life and fled the country with his family (*Ant.* 1.3.1). Luther supposed, "More than one miracle was necessary to prevent the ungodly from surrounding and killing him."[17] Noah as "preacher of righteousness" (2 Pet 2:5) reflects Gen 6:9 and may refer to his preaching of repentance to his disobedient generation during the building of the ark (1 Pet 3:19–20; see 6:2 comments). Peter asserted that just as judgment against the wicked and mercy for the godly (i.e., Noah) were certain in the past, it would be so in his day for the false teachers and those who remained faithful to the gospel. Need for such a firm reminder still exists. For the author of Hebrews, however, it was not Noah's preaching but his faith by which he "condemned the world" (Heb 11:7).

Noah is described by three phrases: "a righteous man," "blameless," and "walked with God." Each has its emphasis, but they collectively tell the same story about Noah's life. He stands out from his contemporaries as a man of right conduct who enjoys a right relationship with God during a day of unrestrained evil (6:5). "Righteous" *(ṣaddîq)* occurs here for the first time in the Bible.[18] Its significance for our narrative is conveyed in 7:1, where "righteous" occurs again; the Lord explains that Noah's moral conduct is the reason he and his family are preserved. The word group "righteous" *(ṣādaq)* often conveys a

---

[14]Common early Christian motifs of Noah include Noah's righteousness, his preaching, his typifying Christ, the flood typifying baptism and final judgment, and Noah's blessing as the gospel for the Gentiles (Lewis, *A Study of the Interpretation of Noah and the Flood,* 120).

[15]E.g., *Gen. Rab.* 30.7; *Sib. Or.* 1.128–29; 147–98; *1 Clem.* 7.6.

[16]J. J. Collins, "Sibylline Oracles," *OTP* 1.213.

[17]*LW* 2.56–57.

[18]צַדִּיק appears only seventeen times in the Pentateuch, seven of these in chap. 18, where Abraham intercedes for Lot, whose life is spared. Cp. also Gen 15:6: "Abram believed the LORD and he credited it to him as righteousness [צְדָקָה]."

forensic nuance in which the "righteous" person or "just one" meets a standard of right conduct (e.g., 15:6). In the Mosaic law that standard is the character of God and his holy law (e.g., Deut 32:4). The person who meets the righteous standard of the law does not suffer death (Exod 23:7), but the transgressor experiences God's retribution (as with Pharaoh, Exod 9:27). Noah's conduct exonerates him, and he survives the ordeal because he has not committed the "violence" practiced by his generation.

"Blameless" *(tāmîm)* means "complete, sound" and indicates moral uprightness and integrity in a person's behavior (e.g., Deut 18:13; Prov 11:5; cf. *tōm,* Gen 20:5–6). This same term is used of God's work where it is coupled with "righteous" to characterize his person (e.g., Deut 32:4; cf. Pss 18:30[31]; 19:7[8]). "Righteous" and "blameless" appear together in Job's protestations that he is innocent of wrongdoing (Job 12:4); the story describes Job by the related noun "integrity" (*tōm;* e.g., 1:1,8; 2:3; 9:21–22). This is also cultic terminology describing the healthy animal "without blemish" *(tāmîm),* which is required for sacrifices offered to the Lord (e.g., Exod 12:5; Lev 1:3). This approval of Noah is not saying that he is sinless but that he does not behave as the wicked of his day. This antithesis between the godly and wicked, first anticipated in the antagonism between the "seed" of the serpent and the woman (3:15), is continued by distinguishing Noah from his generation. The REB captures this by its rendering "the one blameless man of his time." Noah is a reproach to the believer who surrenders to the allurement of a sinful generation. He maintains his fidelity and purity when all others have followed the pack. But his singleness of heart, though without apparent reward, "at the proper time" (Gal 6:9) is acclaimed by the only One whose opinion counted for life.

Further, Noah "walked with God," as did Enoch (see 5:22,24), indicating that Noah is of the same righteous lineage as Seth both by physical descent and moral conduct. Here, however, the construction differs from 5:22,24 by "God" *(ʾĕlōhîm)* appearing at the head of the Hebrew clause, emphasizing Noah's dependence on the Lord. This arrangement forms an envelope structure for 6:8, which begins with "Noah," and 6:9, which in the Hebrew verse ends with "Noah." In v. 9 "Noah" occurs three times, and we find another inclusio embedded in the verse: "Noah was a righteous man . . . and with God walked Noah."[19] There is no other person besides these ancient patriarchs, Enoch and Noah, who have this distinction, "walked *with* God" (cp. Mic 6:8). This is reinforced by the similarity of sound in their names by the inversion of *ḥ* and *n*: *ḥănôk* ("Enoch") and *nōaḥ* ("Noah"). Similar language describes the later patriarchs, who are said to have walked "before" the Lord (24:40; 48:15). In issuing the covenant sign of circumcision, the Lord exhorts Abraham in prepa-

[19] See J. Sasson, "Word-Play in Gen 6:8–9," *CBQ* 37 (1975): 165–66.

triarchal terms, "Walk before me and be blameless" (17:1). Noah's life not only mirrors the stellar example of Enoch (5:22,24) but reflects the experience of Adam, with whom God walked in the garden (3:8). With the genealogies of chaps. 5 and 11 we find an uninterrupted line of descent from Adam to Noah to Abraham, and the ethical language of "walking with God" shows the continuing piety of those whom God favors in the antediluvian to postdiluvian worlds: Adam-Noah-Abraham.

6:10 "Shem, Ham, and Japheth" reverberates the final genealogical note in 5:32, which resumes the author's persistent attention to the development of the chosen lineage of blessing. Prominent patriarchs tend to father three sons: Adam, Lamech, and Terah. Particularly instructive is the genealogical parallel between the Sethite (5:32) and Shemite lines (11:26), which both end naming three offspring. The sons' names anticipate the Table of Nations, which shows God's continued mercy upon the human family (9:18; 10:1). Elsewhere in the flood narrative, excepting 7:13, they are noted only by the anonymous term "sons" (6:18; 7:7; 8:16,18: 9;1,8). Since Noah is the apparent heir of God's promises, the postdiluvian population could take heart that the Lord would perpetuate the promise through Noah's appointed offspring. Genesis looks to these three descendants as the fountainhead of all peoples. Yet it will become clear that the sons do not all imitate their father's godly behavior, as shown by Ham's sin (9:22). It remains to be seen who of these will carry on the elect line of Noah (9:26–27; 11:10–26).

2. Corrupt World (6:11–12)

[11]Now the earth was corrupt in God's sight and was full of violence. [12]God saw how corrupt the earth had become, for all the people on earth had corrupted their ways.

6:11 The justification for the calamity is the complete moral corruption of the human family and the defilement of the earth (cf. 6:6–7). The repetition of "corrupt," occurring three times in vv. 11–12, underscores God's appraisal of the human condition (6:5) and proves the legitimacy of the extreme penalty he will invoke. "Earth" also occurs three times in the passage, indicating that the fortunes of humanity and the earth are intertwined. This "corruption" is further defined by the term "violence" (*ḥāmās,* v. 11), which is used of severe treatment against another person (e.g., 16:5; Exod 23:1; Mic 6:12) and may involve physical harm (e.g., 49:5; Judg 9:24). Whereas God has blessed the human family with the power of procreation to fill the earth (1:28; 9:1), these culprits have "filled the earth" by procreating "violence" (cf. v. 13; Ezek 8:17; 28:16). In the Pentateuch the perverted practices of the land's inhabitants defile it, making it impossible for God to dwell there (e.g., Lev 18:25–28; cf. Jer 2:7).

Murder is abhorred, for innocent blood pollutes the land and prevents atonement unless the murderer's blood is shed (Num 35:33–34; cp.9:6). This explains the divine determination to purge the "earth" *(ʾereṣ),* which is echoed time and again in the narrative (6:13,17; 7:23; cf. *ʾădāmâ,* 7:4). But the Lord does not abandon his "earth," for covenant blessing is ultimately God's answer to this condemnation. Following its cleansing by waters, the Lord restores the "earth" (8:22), and it is secured and replenished by covenant decree (e.g., 8:16–17; 9:1–17).

6:12 Verse 12 intentionally recalls v. 5, where "the LORD saw" the intensity of human evil ("every," "all"), and 1:31, where "the LORD saw" the "good" earth he had made. Here "God saw" that the "good" earth was now corrupt, and the corruption was all-inclusive ("all people"), excepting Noah. For this reason "only Noah was left" from the earth (7:23). The burden of guilt rests with man, although the earth and all its creatures suffer with him. "Their ways" reiterates that sin is not an isolated event here or there: corruption pervades the lifestyle of the antediluvian population. They are corrupt to the cultural core.

The NIV's "all the people" is the proper rendering for Hebrew "all flesh," though elsewhere the phrase is broader, referring to the lower orders that will perish with humanity (7:21) but which also are the recipients of divine preservation and covenant (e.g., 6:19; 7:16; 8:17; 9:11,15–17). Here, however, the focus concerns the culpability of humanity, as we find in 6:5–6, while in both passages the whole created order bears the consequences (6:7,13). "Flesh" first occurs in the Eden story, which describes the unity of the first couple as "one flesh" (2:21,23–24). Now the unity of the human family is sealed by their despicable acts of sin, which are related in part to unlawful marriage (6:1–4). "Flesh" also reflects the mortality of the human family (cf. 6:3), which cannot stand up to the raging waters (6:13,17).[20]

3. Coming Judgment but the Ark of Promise (6:13–7:10)

God's response to the "corruption" and "violence" of the human family is a worldwide cataclysm but also the provision of a safe haven for one of its number. We have two divine speeches in this section, each entailing a divine command and Noah's execution of the directive (6:13–22; 7:1–10). The first speech gives instructions for building the ark and recruiting the occupants (6:13–22). It consists of two parts, each arranged with an announcement of destruction followed by instruction. At the end is the acknowledgment of their execution.

---

[20] The NAB has accordingly "all mortals on earth."

First Speech

6:13–16

Announcement: "I am surely *(hinnî)* going to destroy both them and the earth" (v. 13)
Instruction: "Make yourself an ark" (v. 14)

6:17–21

Announcement: "I am *(ʾănî hinnî)* going to bring floodwaters on the earth to destroy" (v. 17)
Instruction: "You will enter the ark . . . you are to bring into the ark" (vv. 18–19)
"take every kind of food" (v. 21)

6:22

Execution: "Noah did everything just as God commanded him" (v. 22)

Although the announcement of God is impending doom (vv. 13,17), the focus of the divine decree turns immediately in each case to the detailed instructions for building and equipping the ark for Noah's safety and the deliverance of the creatures.

The second address consists of instruction (7:1–5) and then a narrative report of its execution (7:6–10). It concerns the further directive to take on board "clean" and "unclean" animals, a seven-day hiatus, and the compliance of Noah. Noah's age is supplementary information that will be taken up in the following paragraph (v. 11). Execution of the divine word stands out in this section with statements of Noah's compliance (vv. 5,9) and the Lord carrying out his threat (v. 10). Verses 6–10 are an elaboration of the execution statement found in v. 5.

Second Speech

7:1–5

Instruction: "Go into the ark, you and your whole family" (v. 1)
"Take with you seven [pairs] of every kind of clean animal" (v. 2)
Announcement: "Seven days from now I will send rain . . . and I will wipe from the face of the earth" (v. 4)
Execution: "Noah did all that the LORD commanded him" (v. 5)

7:6–10

Execution: "Noah and his sons and his wife and his sons' wives entered the ark" (v. 7)
"Pairs of clean and unclean animals . . . came to Noah and entered the ark" (vv. 8–9)
"As God had commanded Noah" (v. 9)
"After the seven days the floodwaters came on the earth" (v. 10)

Both 6:13 and 7:1, which initiate each speech, include an explanation for the Lord's actions: "For *[kî]* the earth is filled with violence" (6:13) and "because *[kî]* I have found you righteous" (7:1).

(1) Announcement of the Flood and Instructions for the Ark (6:13–22)

[13]So God said to Noah, "I am going to put an end to all people, for the earth is filled with violence because of them. I am surely going to destroy both them and the earth. [14]So make yourself an ark of cypress wood; make rooms in it and coat it with pitch inside and out. [15]This is how you are to build it: The ark is to be 450 feet long, 75 feet wide and 45 feet high. [16]Make a roof for it and finish the ark to within 18 inches of the top. Put a door in the side of the ark and make lower, middle and upper decks. [17]I am going to bring floodwaters on the earth to destroy all life under the heavens, every creature that has the breath of life in it. Everything on earth will perish. [18]But I will establish my covenant with you, and you will enter the ark—you and your sons and your wife and your sons' wives with you. [19]You are to bring into the ark two of all living creatures, male and female, to keep them alive with you. [20]Two of every kind of bird, of every kind of animal and of every kind of creature that moves along the ground will come to you to be kept alive. [21]You are to take every kind of food that is to be eaten and store it away as food for you and for them."

[22]Noah did everything just as God commanded him.

6:13 God's intentions are certain, and the destruction will be inclusive: "all people" and "both them and the earth." Echoing vv. 11–12, the narrative attributes moral reasons for the coming flood. This is implied by the wordplay of "destroy" *(mašḥît)* in v. 13 with "corrupted" *(hišḥît)* in v. 12. Explicitly stated, judgment is imminent "because of them" (humanity), and yet the whole earth also will undergo the penalty (v. 17). There is a correspondence between human morality and the state of the animal and natural worlds. Nature suffers because of human sin (3:17–19; e.g., Rom 8:20–21); ironically, however, it is enlisted by God to penalize human disobedience (6:17; e.g., Deut 28:21–24).

The Lord takes the patriarch into his confidence, forewarning him of the disaster to come. In the Mesopotamian flood stories the deity also apprises the flood hero, but here Noah receives an explanation for God's actions. The Lord is not acting impulsively or selfishly but in moral outrage against the reprehensible conduct of that generation. We have a similar setting for Abraham, remembered as God's "friend" (2 Chr 20:7; Isa 41:8; Jas 2:23), to whom the Lord confides Sodom and Gomorrah's demise (Gen 18:17–21) and whom God permits to intercede in behalf of the righteous. Jesus too confides in his disciples as "friends" (John 15:13–15).

Although Noah does not experience the translation of Enoch, he holds in the prepatriarchal narratives the honored place of confidant to the Lord's plans. There are a number of similarities between the flood narrative and the Lot episode, which also tells of a lone family escaping a calamitous judgment.[21] But here there is no mediation to avert the anger of God. It is only after the cleansing floodwaters and the priesthood of Noah's sacrifice that the Lord is satisfied (8:20). Noah is silent throughout the flood episode. How he feels and what he thinks we do not know.

6:14 God follows his announcement of judgment with a plan for rescue. Noah is instructed to construct a special vessel designed to ride out the ensuing flood. Peter speaks of the longsuffering God who "waited patiently" for repentance as the patriarch carried out the building enterprise (1 Pet 3:20). Jewish *Pirqe Aboth* (5.2) comments that God waited ten generations, from Adam to Noah, to unleash his judgment. Clemency outweighs his just fury against the fomenting earth, whose evil thoughts and violent cries ascend on high. But at last divine patience reaches its end.

The vessel is identified as an "ark" (*tēbâ;* v. 14); it occurs five times in these three verses and is their focus. Outside of chaps. 6–9, this term is found only in Exod 2:3–5, where it describes the "basket" *(tēbâ)* in which the baby Moses was placed. There are remarkable similarities between Noah's deliverance and that of Moses as recounted in Exodus 1–2. The accounts of how the ark/basket are constructed are parallel. Moreover, both tell of a removal of people by water (cf. Exod 1:22), but Noah and Moses are delivered from the waters by the grace of God to introduce a new era in the Lord's work among his people. This linkage is also suggested by the floodwaters of the Red Sea that swallow up the Egyptians and enable the preservation of Moses' people (Exod 14–15). Moses, like Noah, receives detailed instructions in the building of the tabernacle that are revealed exclusively to Moses. Moses, then, is another Noah whose career inaugurates a new epoch.[22]

Unlike the vessel described in *Gilgamesh,* the dimensions and construction of the Noahic vessel make it seaworthy. Utnapishtim, the Babylonian "Noah," is instructed by the deity Ea to build a vessel quadrangular in shape to escape the flood planned by the angry god Enlil. It is a perfect cube of 120 cubits in dimension.[23] With its cubical construction, it would inevitably sink. It has been

[21] E.g., both concern sexual improprieties as reason for the disaster (6:1–4; 19:1–11) and there is drunkenness by the survivor which results in family shame (Ham's sin, 9:22–23; Lot's incest, 19:30–38). There are divine forewarning and instructions for escape (6:13–22; 19:15–22), and one family alone is preserved (7:21–23; 19:15,25–29). Also there are many shared lexical items: "destroy" (מַשְׁחִית; 6:13; 19:13); "going in" (בָּאוּ) and "shut" (וַיִּסְגֹּר) the door (7:16) and "brought in" (וַיָּבִיאוּ) and "shut" (סָגָרוּ) the door (19:10); "God remembered" (וַיִּזְכֹּר; 8:1a; 19:29); "rained" (מַמְטִיר) floodwaters (7:4) and "rained" (הִמְטִיר) brimstone (19:24). See W. M. Clark, "The Flood and the Structure of the Pre-patriarchal History," *ZAW* 83 (1971): 184–211, esp. 194–95, and I. M. Kikawada, "Noah and the Ark," *ABD* 4.1129–30.

[22] So Kikawada, "Noah and the Ark," 1126–27.

[23] Mesopotamian penchant for the sexagesimal system (numbers of sixty) may be reflected here in an idealized number of 60 x 2 for each side. See L. R. Bailey, "Noah's Ark," *ABD* 4.1131. Bailey recognizes that the fifty cubits for the width of Noah's ark is not a multiple of sixty but observes that the cubical volume of Noah's ark is $(60^3 \times 2) + (60^2 \times 5)$.

proposed that the ship's geometrical shape is symbolic for an idealized ziggurat.[24] This brick staircase tower held central religious significance for the Mesopotamians, indicating a stairway between heaven and earth, which at the pinnacle was believed to be the residence of the gods (see discussion at 11:1–9). The Hebrew account describes the ark as an actual vessel, having no stylized features and no cultic significance. While the Mesopotamian vessel has points of contact with Noah's, the latter's only religious significance lies in how Noah foreshadows Moses and his faithful carrying out of the Lord's tabernacle plans (Exod 26:30; 40:16).

The building material in the construction of the ark is "gopher" *(gōper)* wood, an obscure term occurring only here, probably meaning pine or cypress wood. It is sealed watertight inside and out with "pitch" as is Moses' basket of safety (Exod 2:3), and it possesses an unspecified number of "rooms" (*qinnîm,* "nests") or "compartments" (NAB, NJPS). Some have taken the term as "reeds" *(qānîm),* referring to another item of building material.[25] Utnapishtim's hut is made of reeds, which perhaps are used in the construction of his vessel, but "reeds" are not used for building material among the Hebrews in the Old Testament, though there is reference to a "reed" (but *ʾēbeh*) boat in Job 9:26. If "reed" is correct, it may be an allusion to the tabernacle *menorah* since *qānîm* is used of the shaft and branches (Exod 25:31–32; 37:17–18).

6:15–16 Assuming a "cubit" of about eighteen inches, the vessel was approximately 450 feet long, 75 feet wide, and 45 feet high (v. 15).[26] Although this craft is impressively large for antiquity, its volume is about five times less than the unrealistic *Gilgamesh* version. "Ark" is related to an Egyptian term meaning "box," chest," "coffin." As the LXX rendered "ark" by the word "wooden box" *(kibōtos),* it would appear that the vessel was envisioned as rectangular in shape, probably flat bottomed, and square at the ends. Essentially the vessel is a floating barge that is designed to ride out the storm without

---

[24] See S. Holloway, "What Ship Goes There: The Flood Narratives in the Gilgamesh Epic and Genesis Considered in Light of Ancient Near Eastern Temple Ideology," *ZAW* 103 (1991): 328–55. Holloway's assessment that Noah's ark is likewise a religious symbol for Solomon's temple is based on the general similarity of the temple, rectangular and three-story in shape; but it falters since the dimensions are not the same, especially if the ark story dates after the Solomonic temple, as he contends, and there is no allusion to the ark as temple or palace in the OT as he finds for the Babylonian vessel *(ekallu)* in *Gilgamesh.*

[25] E.g., NJB, REB; also Wenham, *Genesis 1–15,* 173.

[26] "Cubit" was a measurement derived from the length of the elbow to the tip of the fingers. It varied in length among the peoples of the Near East, including the Hebrews (e.g., Deut 3:11; Ezek 40:5; 43:13). Most scholars work with cubits measuring fifty cm. per cubit, but this cannot be verified since it is a modern approximation based on circumstantial evidence. For general purposes the number of cubits can be converted into the modern system by halving the number of cubits and multiplying it by three for the number of feet (see M. Powell, "Weights and Measures," *ABD* 6.899–900).

direction. Noah trusts the hand of God as its rudder. Although there are a host of unanswered questions about the ark and its cargo, the biblical version is much more plausible than the Babylonian parallel.

The relationship of the "roof" to the vessel is difficult to understand (v. 16) since the Hebrew word *(ṣōhar)* occurs only here. Some commentators take it as a reference to the "window" *(ḥallôn),* which is important for the later dispatching of the birds (8:6–7).[27] If taken as an opening, it would be best understood as a space of one cubit high (eighteen inches) extended around the ark and interrupted only by the supporting posts of the roof. If a "roof," it is constructed so as to overhang the sides of the vessel by one cubit (eighteen inches) or so that there is a gap of one cubit between the walls and the roof.[28] Also the vessel possesses a side "door," which is prominent in the later narrative (7:16). The purpose of this description is to point up the commendation of Noah's careful obedience (v. 22; cf. 7:5,9,16). This sort of detail is given, though not as elaborate, for the construction of the Mosaic tabernacle and the prescriptions for proper cultic practices. Noah's compliance is matched by the Pentateuch's praise for Moses and Israel's obedience to the Lord's directions (e.g., Exod 39:42–43; Lev 8:36; Num 27:22; Deut 34:9). God must be obeyed in all his instructions if his people expect to enjoy the fruit of life and blessing (e.g., Deut 26:16–19; 28:1–14).

6:17 Verse 17 parallels v. 13 as another divine pronouncement, reiterating God's determination to destroy "all," "every creature," and "everything"; there is no escape for human life or any living thing that possesses the "breath of life" (cf. 1:30; 2:7). Much of the same language as v. 13 recurs here: "all people" in v. 13 and "all life" in v. 17 both translate *kol bāśār;* "come" in v. 13 and "bringing" in v. 17 are from the same verb *(bôʾ);* "destroy" in both verses translate forms of the root *šḥt;* and "earth" *(ʾereṣ)* occurs twice in each verse. Our verse elaborates on the earlier announcement of v. 13; it gives attention to human culpability, but v. 17 is inclusive, "all life under the heavens" and "everything" with the "breath of life." This inclusive language as elsewhere in the account suggests that the cataclysm was worldwide in scope.[29] An alternative understanding is that the comprehensive language of the text is hyperbolic or a phenomenological description (from Noah's limited viewpoint), thus permitting a regional flood (see 7:17–20 discussion). And "earth" can be rightly rendered "land," again allowing a limited venue. This kind of inclusive language for local events is attested elsewhere in Genesis (e.g., 41:54–57), but the insistence of the narrative on the encompassing character of the flood favors the literal understanding of the universal view. Its massive destruction shows

---

[27] Thus translated "opening" in NAB, NJPS.

[28] See Wenham, *Genesis 1–15,* 173–74.

[29] See 6:7,12–13; 7:4,19,21–23; 8:21; 9:11,15; cf. 2 Pet 3:6.

God's wrath in the face of unbridled sin and the utter dependence of life on the grace and pity of God.

The means of God's wrath ("floodwaters") is an image familiar to Israel's national experience. We have already mentioned at vv. 14–16 the similarity between Moses and Noah and how the Red Sea event (Exod 14–15) parallels the salvation of the righteous Noah. Threatening waters is a common motif in the ancient Near East and occurs in the Bible as subservient powers to God's rule over creation or as metaphorical for Israel's national enemies.[30] "Flood" *(mabbûl)* is a technical term for Noah's waters, occurring only in chaps. 6–9, with the exception of Ps 29:10 where it speaks metaphorically of God's sovereignty as One "enthroned over the flood." The LXX reflects this technical meaning of "flood" by its terminology *(kataklusmós),* which is limited to describe Noah's flood (and Ps 29:10[28:10]). Jewish writings and the New Testament *(kataklusmós)* have the same practice for reference to the famous deluge (Matt 24:38–39; Luke 17:27; 2 Pet 2:5).[31]

"Breath of life" *(rûaḥ ḥayyîm)* pertains foremostly to the animal world as in 7:15 *(rûaḥ ḥayyîm),* but not exclusively (7:22); both passages are intimations of creation though the language there differs somewhat *(nepeš ḥayyâ)* (1:30). "Breath of life" is inclusive for all living things in 7:22, as shown by the additional language "breath" *(nišmat)* and "nostrils," which reflect the creation of the first man (2:7). This life made by God's creative word "will perish." "Perish" appears again in 7:21, which describes the realization of this pronouncement ("everything . . . perished"). "Perish" *(gāwaʿ)* is essentially equivalent in meaning to the common word "die" (*mût,* Num 20:29), but it often is associated with the departure of a person's vital "breath" (e.g., Gen 25:8,17; 35:29), hence translated at times "expire."[32] In Elihu's discourse he acknowledges that it is the presence of the creative breath that sustains life, but if withdrawn by God each "perishes" and returns to "dust" (Job 34:14–15). The psalmist acknowledges the same: "When you [LORD] take away their breath, they die and return to the dust" (Ps 104:29). By the floodwaters the Creator God takes back his life-giving breath so that all die (see 6:3 comments). This is another evidence that the flood is anticreation; God now is the earth's adversary. He must destroy it to renew it.

6:18 "But" despite the vast destruction announced, God has a plan for the deliverance of a remnant, which includes representatives of all his creatures (cf. 9:9–10). Up to this point, Noah is informed of coming disaster, but it is left to the instructions for building the ark to suggest that he will escape. Now the Lord gives specific assurance to Noah in announcing a forthcoming "cove-

[30] E.g., Job 26:12; Pss 29:3; 74:13–14; 89:9–10; 93:4; Isa 27:1; 51:9–10.

[31] BAGD, 412.

[32] See H. Ringgren, "גָּוַע *gāvaʿ,*" *TDOT* 2.438–39.

nant." "God remembered" is the turning point in the floodwaters (8:1a; cf. 9:15; Exod 2:24), and as covenant language it alludes to this prior commitment in 6:18. The formal expression of the "covenant" and the giving of its "sign" (rainbow) are "established" in 9:8–17 following the deluge, but its early mention here explains why Noah and his family will survive. It is the consequence of God's gracious decision. Unquestionably, it is a word of security that the fearful band needs for the disaster unfolding before them.

The common language for entering a covenant is "to cut a covenant" (e.g., 15:18; 26:28), which is believed associated with the rite of animal sacrifice. In the Noahic covenant, however, the expression is "establish my covenant" (*hēqîm bĕrîtî;* 6:18; 9:9,11,17), and the word "give" appears once (9:12). "Establish" usually is taken to mean the "inauguration of a new covenant,"[33] but *hēqîm* commonly means to "confirm a preexisting commitment."[34] If that is the sense here, God is confirming his prior commitment to creation (1:1–2:3).[35] The difficulty with this view is that *hēqîm* can mean "inaugurate" (see Exod 6:4), and the word "give" is an adequate synonym at 9:12 (cf. 17:2). Also the language of "covenant" or "oath" is not found in the creation and garden narratives (2:4–4:26). Thus it is best to take 6:18 as anticipatory of the formal initiation of a new covenant in chap. 9 rather than the confirmation of a former covenant. Nevertheless, the Noahic covenant includes the renewal of the creation promises to Noah and the surviving animals (1:22,26–28; 9:1,7,9–10).

This is the first occurrence in the Bible of *bĕrît,* commonly rendered "covenant" or "pact." Its importance for biblical theology is indicated by our traditional parlance, Old "Testament" and New "Testament," meaning "covenant." For Genesis it is theologically significant, occurring twenty-seven times, eight of those in the flood narrative and sixteen times in the Abraham narratives, especially pertaining to the rite of circumcision as a sign.[36] This is also true of the flood account, since the majority of its uses appear in conjunction with the rainbow (9:12–17). The etymology and development of the term "covenant" remain uncertain. Although the word may be used of mutual agreement among peers (e.g., 26:28), it often is found in the context of unequal parties where obligations are imposed on both or one. This is true of the international treaties in the second millennium B.C. that have their analogy in the Mosaic covenant,

---

[33] See M. Weinfeld, "בְּרִית b^{e}*rîth,*" *TDOT* 2.253–79, esp. 260, and G. Mendenhall and G. Herion, "Covenant," *ABD* 1.1179–1202.

[34] הֵקִים בְּרִיתִי also occurs in Gen 17:7,19,21; Exod 6:4; Lev 26:9; Deut 8:18; 2 Kgs 23:3.

[35] So W. J. Dumbrell, "The Covenant with Noah," in *RTR* 38 (1979): 1–9, and *Covenant and Creation: A Theology of the Old Testament Covenants* (1984; reprint, Grand Rapids: Baker, 1993), 15–26.

[36] Gen 6:18; 9:9,11,12,13,15,16,17. Of the uses in Genesis, one use of בְּרִית is "allies" (14:13). For the Lord's covenant with Abraham see 15:18; 17:2,4,7(2 x),9,10,11,13(2 x),14,19(2 x),21; for his pact with Abimelech, 21:27,32; also Isaac-Abimelech (26:28) and Jacob-Laban (31:44).

where obligations are undertaken both by God and Israel (e.g., Exod 20–24).

The Noahic covenant is closer to the royal grant known from the ancient Near East where a deity bestows a benefit or gift upon a king. It has its closest parallels to the Abrahamic and Davidic covenants (Gen 15; 17; 2 Sam 7), which are promissory charters made by God with the individuals and their offspring, characteristically forever. Unlike the Mosaic covenant, in the royal grant form of covenant God alone is under compulsion by oath to uphold his promise to the favored party. Divine charter is a proclamation made by the Lord and is not an agreement. We find this in the Noahic covenant where the Lord obligates himself ("my covenant") to save the Noahic family and preserve the new world, also forever, without specific demands placed upon the patriarch (see 9:8–17). The narrative, however, while acknowledging that the initiative and burden of the covenant are with the Lord, shows that it is offered in conjunction with Noah's righteous conduct (7:1). No one else receives the gracious attention of the Lord in Noah's generation because of their failure to live uprightly. The narrative assumes that Noah already enjoys a relationship with God (6:9) and hence the Lord rewards his servant for his fidelity. Abraham and David, who serve the Lord faithfully (22:16–18; 26:4–5; 1 Kgs 3:6; 9:4–5), also accrue the benefits of their integrity.

As a royal grant this covenant is made with Noah personally; the singular "you" is highlighted throughout vv. 18–21 so as to make prominent Noah's role. But Noah also is representative of the new humanity and the new world; in the formal presentation the covenant is specifically extended to his family and all the surviving creatures (9:9–10). This already is implied by the command to take on board his family, identified by their familial relationship to Noah—"*your* sons," "*your* wife," and "the wives of *your* sons, with you." This is similar to the family description of 8:16 when their exit from the ark is commanded. The Hebrew tradition of family solidarity explains why Noah's righteousness benefitted his whole family. The same may be said of Lot's family, which escapes because of his relationship to Abraham, but Lot cannot guarantee his wife's survival when she disobeys the Lord (19:26). This is not foreign to Christian expectation, for the household is blessed by the presence of a godly witness in the home (e.g., Acts 16:31; 1 Cor 7:14; 1 Pet 3:1–2). Ezekiel notes in his days that none of the righteous heroes, such as Noah, Daniel, or Job, would be able to deliver any one other than himself from coming judgment (Ezek 14:14,20; 18:5–13).

6:19–21 Noah is instructed to include a representative group from the animal world, "two of all living creatures," which will serve to replenish the earth (v. 19). Our passage twice says that the ark is designed "to keep them alive" (vv. 19–20) in the face of the certain death that awaits them. The language of vv. 19–21 reflects the creation account of chap. 1, indicating the continuity in the created order before and after the flood: "male and female" (1:27), "bird," "beast," crawling "creature" (1:25), "kind" (1:11, etc.), and "food" (1:30). God is saving that which was declared "very good" at creation (1:31). Reference to "male and female" (v. 19) indicates the power of procreation that was God's blessing upon the animal population (1:22) as well as mankind (1:27–28). This provision signaled God's intention of carrying out his promised blessing at creation despite the wickedness of humanity. Once on board, all of earth's future hope will be huddled under a single roof.

As the Lord brought the animals to Adam to be named (2:18–19), this second Adam will "bring" the animal kingdom "with you" on the vessel, having the greater responsibility of their preservation. But also they are said to "come" to Noah (v. 20), indicating that God directs their way to the ark (cf. 7:15). "Kind," like its occurrence in chap. 1, cannot be defined with zoological precision; it is enough to say that the "kinds" are related to three major groups: land animals, birds, and crawlers. Transparently, the water creatures have no need for safety. The inclusive language "every" (3x) shows that no group is excepted, including the "unclean" (7:2–3), for all the creatures are God's making and his unique possession (Ps 104:24). This was a lesson the apostle Peter and others learned regarding God's inclusion of the Gentiles (i.e., unclean) in the church by Christian baptism (Acts 10:34; 1 Pet 3:21). Among the preparations are the gathering up of "food" for both man and beast that matches the creation provision for the first Adam and the animals (1:29–30). But it also brings to mind the "food" that leads to Adam's demise (3:6,17) and ultimately to the deplorable condition of humanity in Noah's day.

6:22 We have commented earlier that Noah's obedience is a recurring feature in Noah's *tōlĕdōt* (v. 22; cf. 7:5,9,16). Here, like the encompassing destruction to come, we are told that his obedience to God's instructions is inclusive—"everything" (v. 22). The verse begins and concludes with the verb "did," emphasizing the patriarch's part: "Noah did *(wayyaʿaś)* . . . so he did" *(kēn ʿāśâ,* NASB). "So" *(kēn)* is reminiscent of creation's first obedience to the divine word, "and it was so" *(wayhî kēn;* 1:7,9,11,15,24). The failure of the first Adam and the succeeding patriarchs does not obviate God's commitment to bless the human family. However, disobedience has its painful consequences of toil, sorrow, and death, which they cannot escape. This execution statement is heard again at Moses' completion of the tabernacle: "Moses did everything just as the LORD commanded him" (Exod 40:16). Israel could look to Noah as a model of covenant fidelity as they drew the parallel between God's "command" for that ancient patriarch and the divine directives by the voice of Moses for their own times (cp. Exod 39:32,42; Num 1:54; 2:34; 9:5).

Noah's actions model for later generations the obedience and the efficacy of faith when it is placed in the veracity of God's word (e.g., Heb 11:7). Noah's venture to build his vessel upon dry land while awaiting the impending floodwaters is exemplary of a person trusting in what cannot be seen or proven (Heb

10:38; 11:1–2). As is the case for many of the saints, God is calling upon Noah to accomplish a task that has no precedent, for an experience that had no counterpart. Ironically, the destruction by water that dooms all the living is the vindication of Noah's faith and credits him with righteousness. Such persevering faith in the word of promise motivated Peter to challenge the scoffers of his day who disputed the eschatological conflagration heralded by the prophets and apostles. The divine word declaring the "day of judgment" (2 Pet 3:6–7; cf. 2:5,9–10) is just as certain as the cataclysmic waters of Noah's generation.

(2) Entering the Ark (7:1–10)

**1The LORD then said to Noah, "Go into the ark, you and your whole family,
because I have found you righteous in this generation. 2Take with you seven of
every kind of clean animal, a male and its mate, and two of every kind of unclean
animal, a male and its mate, 3and also seven of every kind of bird, male and
female, to keep their various kinds alive throughout the earth. 4Seven days from
now I will send rain on the earth for forty days and forty nights, and I will wipe
from the face of the earth every living creature I have made."**

5And Noah did all that the LORD commanded him.

**6Noah was six hundred years old when the floodwaters came on the earth.
7And Noah and his sons and his wife and his sons' wives entered the ark to escape
the waters of the flood. 8Pairs of clean and unclean animals, of birds and of all
creatures that move along the ground, 9male and female, came to Noah and
entered the ark, as God had commanded Noah. 10And after the seven days the
floodwaters came on the earth.**

This passage entails two parts: the divine directive, which is the second divine speech of the narrative (vv. 1–5), and the narrative's description of Noah's compliance (vv. 6–10). The clause "floodwaters came upon the earth" repeated in vv. 6,10 enclose the second half (an inclusio), stressing that the waters come precisely as God foretold. Our verses expand on the earlier divine speech (esp. 6:17–22) and reiterate Noah's conformity to the divine word (7:5,9). We are told for the first time explicitly that the salvation of Noah and his family is due to his virtuous character (7:1). Further, the animals taken on board are distinguished by their ritual status, "clean" and "unclean," with numeric priority ("seven pair") given to the clean (7:2–3). The destruction by "floodwaters" (6:17) we learn will be accomplished by a forty-day and forty-night rain (7:4). Also there is a seven-day period involved in the preparations for entry (7:4,10), and the first of many dates in the story marks the progress of the flood (7:6). This protracted retelling of the gathering and entry into the ark points to the special interest the author has for the embarking parade, which enters in obedience to the divine command. This is the salvation of creation's fifth and sixth days.

7:1 After the completion of the ark (6:22), God commands Noah and his family to enter the vessel (v. 1a). This exhortation is matched by the postdiluvian command, "Come out of the ark" (8:16), but there the family is delineated as in 6:18. Twice more in the flood story we are told that the small band "entered the ark" (7:13) and their animal companions "entered the ark" (7:15). The salvation of the Noahic family is specifically attributed ("because") to the "righteous" character of the patriarch (see 6:8–9 discussion). Later references to Noah's family identify them in terms of familial relationship or personal names (7:7,13), but here it is the anonymous "your whole family." The family is secondary at this point, for it is Noah's righteousness that means salvation for his dependents. This will become clearer when we consider the coarse impudence of Ham, who "saw" his father's nakedness (9:22). Both in our verse and at 6:8–9, Noah is distinguished by his conduct in the context of his contemporaries ("in this generation"). It is not that Noah's works of righteousness gains him salvation, for none is cited. Rather, his upright character is noted to condemn his generation, which merits death.[37]

"You" (Noah) stands at the head of the Hebrew clause for emphasis: "For you alone in this generation" (REB). "Found" is a metaphorical translation of the Hebrew word "saw" (NRSV, "I have seen"), which obscures the contrast to 6:5 and 6:12, where God "saw" the corruption of Noah's generation. The Lord is depicted as the Overseer of all creation, which is subject to his ethical evaluation.

7:2–3 Beyond bringing on board the ark two of each animal group (6:19–20), Noah is given further instructions to bring "seven," or "seven pairs" (most English versions), of "clean" and "unclean" animals.[38] In *Gilgamesh* the vessel's cargo beyond family and animals includes valuable metals and also the craftsmen who construct the vessel.[39] Our passage's distinction between "clean" versus "unclean" reflects the practice of the Mosaic economy, where specific animal life is labeled with respect to the dietary habits of the people (Lev 11:1–47; Deut 14:3–21), but here the concern probably is with the appropriateness of sacrifice (cf. 8:20). This distinction also includes the "birds" as 8:20 indicates. Thus the greater number of "clean" animals for sacrifice and population would be expected in light of the Mosaic instruction.

The pairings of clean and unclean animals are described in terms of gender ("male and female"), anticipating the postdiluvian command to multiply and thereby replenish the earth's animal population (1:22; 8:17). The specifics of the animals here are not intended to be inclusive since the creeping things are not mentioned until later (vv. 8,14,21,23). Its omission in this discussion of the

---

[37] So Calvin, *Comm.*, 265.

[38] שִׁבְעָה שִׁבְעָה, "seven seven," which is best rendered "seven pairs" ("seven by seven," *IBHS* § 16.6c; 39.3.2a). If "seven" animals per kind are intended, then three pairs were taken aboard for preservation with the "seventh" animal reserved for sacrifice after the flood (8:20).

[39] *ANET,* 94.

"clean" and "unclean" may be because all crawlers were considered ritually unclean (Lev 11:44). How could such ritual distinctions be important to Noah's times? By these later cultic distinctions Israel is distinguished from other nations as God's special possession and deemed "holy," but this cultic instruction is not isolated from Israel's historic deliverance from Egypt (e.g., Lev 11:45). It is not the Mosaic laws that introduce such distinctions in the life of the righteous. Genesis tells us that this was practiced before the time of Moses because such rites reflect the same understanding of God and his relationship to the righteous (e.g., Sabbath, Exod 16:23–29). It is consistent with what we have found in Genesis that the later Israelites recognize themselves and their own experiences in the primeval events of the world.

"Seven" indicates that the animals and birds are considered a full complement, adequately representing the whole created order. The foremost purpose of their recruitment is to preserve the life of their "kind" (*zeraʿ*, "seed"). Here "seed" is surprising since "kind" *(min)* is regular in the creation and flood narratives for animal reproduction as well as the Mosaic dietary laws.[40] "Kind" *(min)* is never used of the human family; rather "seed" is customary for human procreation (e.g., 4:25) and is the common term in the promissory blessing for the patriarchal family (e.g., 13:16; 15:3; 17:7). Yet both the serpent and the woman are said to have a future "seed" (3:15). "Seed" in our verse then is an allusion to the creation ordinance of blessing on humanity and the lower orders (1:26–28; 9:1–2) that has its realization in the patriarchal promises. God commits to preserving the animal world as he does the human family.

7:4–5 Verse 4, best rendered "*For* seven days from now," explains why steps must be taken by Noah to go aboard. The Lord discloses that the deluge is imminent and the way of escape will be sealed off in a week's time.[41] As in the earlier *tōlĕdōt* (e.g., 2:2; 4:15), the flood story commonly uses the number "seven" (vv. 2,3,4,10,11; 8:4,10,12,14). Seven-day intervals are found in the later dispersing of the birds from the ark (8:10,12). The narrative also has the recurring number "forty" (vv. 4,12,17; 8:6). Although the number "seven" is a constituent feature of the sacred calendar in ancient Israel, "forty" also is an important figure marking events in Israel's experience under the patriarchs and Moses. Both Isaac and Esau are forty years of age when they marry (25:20; 26:34). Moses remains on the mountain forty days and nights in receiving the law and in witnessing the glory of the Lord (e.g., Exod 24:18; 34:28; Deut 9:11,18–25). Moses' life is divided into periods of forty years in Stephen's rehearsal of his career (Acts 7:23,30,36; cf. Matt 4:2). Israel's spies are in the land for forty days and upon their disobedience God sentences them to forty

[40] E.g., Gen 1:21,24–25; 6:20; 7:14; Lev 11:11; Deut 14:13.

[41] The participle מַמְטִיר has the sense of imminent future, "I am about to send rain."

years in the wilderness.[42] The forty-day deluge that the patriarch escapes, therefore, is matched by the forty-year wilderness survived by the lawgiver (e.g., Num 14:33–34; Deut 2:7). Also the forty days have been explained as a period of atonement.[43] Moses' fast is forty days of contrition because of the idolatry of Israel, and as we noted, the forty-year wandering requites their rebellion. Yet if so, the forty days are not sufficient, for it is not until the sacrifice Noah offers that the Lord's anger is fully pacified (8:20–21).

God does not shrink from the responsibility of the impending cataclysm. The Hebrew construction of v. 4 emphasizes the first-person ("I") role of God as the responsible agent for the destruction. What he destroys, however, is what he has "made" (*ʿāśâ*), another inference linking the creation account (e.g., 1:31; 2:4). It echoes 6:6–7, where the Lord is remorseful that he has "made" man and the creatures, pledging to "wipe" away all that lives (see 6:7; 7:23). "Earth" ("ground," *ʾădāmâ*) is a reference to the cursed "ground" as a result of human sin (e.g., 3:17–19; 5:29; 8:21). God's retributive judgment is motivated by the expansion of that first sin, which now threatens the possibility of blessing.

Our verse elaborates on 6:17 when the Lord first announces a "flood." He will "send" a forty-day rain that will destroy "every living creature," that is, all that exists (*kōl hayqûm,* also 7:23; Deut 11:6). The term rendered "send rain" (*mamṭir*) occurs first in 2:5 (*himṭîr*), where the earth exists without the benefit of rainfall. It frequently describes the judgment of God, as in 19:24, where God "rained down" (*himṭîr*) fire upon Sodom and Gomorrah (e.g., Exod 9:23; Ps 11:6; Ezek 38:22).[44] Pharaoh's challenge to the rule of God is answered by the "raining" (*mamṭîr*) of hail, which destroys man and beast as well as plant (Exod 9:18,33–34). Thus, for later Israel, from heaven "rained" either death or life (cf. manna, Exod 16:4).

In v. 5 the narration repeats the commendation of Noah for his careful attention to God's explicit orders. We commented at 6:22 on the importance of this theme to the flood story and how obedience is critical to the success of later Israel. These two longer citations (cf. the shorter 7:9,16), however, are not arbitrarily placed in the text. They occur at points in the developing story line where the ensuing stage of the flood will only take place upon Noah's faithful completion of the assigned tasks.

7:6–7 The initiation and duration of the flood is measured by the age of Noah himself, who is six hundred years old at its inception and six hundred and one at its completion, a course of one year and eleven days (vv. 6,11; 8:14).

[42] *Gen. Rab.* 32.5 explains the forty days as retribution for violation of the Torah, which was given in forty days.

[43] So N. H. Sarna, בראשית *Genesis,* JPST (Philadelphia: Jewish Publication Society, 1989), 54, 356.

[44] מַמְטִיר (*hiphil* participle) occurs also in Exod 9:18; 16:4.

Much of these verses repeat 6:18–20, which entails the first directive to "enter the ark" and describes its human and animal occupants. Here we find that the divine word is precisely carried out by Noah and his family, who "entered the ark" as the Lord commanded (6:18; 7:1), and they are joined by the chosen animals and birds who "came to Noah" (v. 9). Verse 7 reads as though they scramble on board just "before the waters of the flood."[45]

7:8–10 This description is reminiscent of when God "brought" (2:19) the creatures to the first Adam to be named (see 7:15). Adam names the creatures, and Noah as the second Adam preserves them. The description of the animals as "pairs" and "clean" and "unclean" unites the two earlier divine mandates at 6:18–19 and 7:2–3 to show Noah's compliance. In the former the dictate is primarily interested in their inclusiveness and propagation, thus requiring "two" and of "every kind" of bird, animal, and crawler. The second charge focuses on the ritual status of "clean" and "unclean." These two foci are echoed in our present passage without the necessity of mentioning the "seven pairs" in 7:2.

Why a seven-day pause? According to Jewish midrash, the seven-day interval is a period of mourning for the death of Methuselah (as *Tgs.*), who dies in the year of the flood (see 5:27–28), or a period for God's own grief for the world (e.g., *Gen. Rab.* 32.7); *Tg. Ps.-J.* adds that the respite is a final opportunity for repentance. The passage does not give any indication of the week's purpose. Verse 10 can be misread to indicate that the ark's occupants reside in the ark for a week until the rains begin, but this is illusory because v. 13 clarifies that it is on the same day that the family enters the ark that the rains commence. Rather, v. 10 indicates that the rains fall precisely on the day that God had forewarned one week earlier (v. 4). Noah's confidence is not misplaced. His devoted obedience exemplifies the later psalmist's exhortation, "Commit your way to the Lord; trust in him and he will do this" (37:5).

4. Waves of Judgment (7:11–24)

This section details the beginning of the flood, the entrance of the ark's occupants, and the mounting effects of the waters. The first half focuses on the "day" of the flood's commencement and delineates the human and animal membership in the divine rescue operation (vv. 11–16). It ends with a thud when the Lord "shut" in Noah (v. 16). "All" and "every" *(kōl)* occur seven times, six in the short stretch of two verses to insure that "all creatures" are brought on board (vv. 14–15). These have the "breath of life" *(rûaḥ ḥayyîm;* v. 15), representing the living, but all those outside the ark with the "breath of life" *(nišmat rûaḥ ḥayyîm)* will succumb to the watery grave (v. 22). The second half of the narrative begins with the "forty days" of rain and ends with the

---

[45] מִפְּנֵי מֵי הַמַּבּוּל is rendered metaphorically in English versions as "escape" (e.g., NIV, NRSV, NJB, GNB) or as causal, "because of the waters" (AV, NASB, NJPS, NAB).

inclusive "hundred and fifty days" (vv. 17–24). It is packed with repetition: "on the earth" (*ʿal hāʾāreṣ* 8x),[46] "all" and synonyms *(kōl;* 7x),[47] and "the waters increased" (*rābâ*; 2x) and "the waters rose" (*gābar*; 3x). By this the narrative confirms that "*every* living thing" is destroyed "on the *earth*," and in all this destruction "*only* Noah" is preserved (v. 23).

(1) Beginning of the Rains (7:11–16)

11In the six hundredth year of Noah's life, on the seventeenth day of the sec-
ond month—on that day all the springs of the great deep burst forth, and the
floodgates of the heavens were opened. 12And rain fell on the earth forty days and
forty nights.

13On that very day Noah and his sons, Shem, Ham and Japheth, together with
his wife and the wives of his three sons, entered the ark. 14They had with them
every wild animal according to its kind, all livestock according to their kinds,
every creature that moves along the ground according to its kind and every bird
according to its kind, everything with wings. 15Pairs of all creatures that have the
breath of life in them came to Noah and entered the ark. 16The animals going in
were male and female of every living thing, as God had commanded Noah. Then
the LORD shut him in.

7:11–12 The day of eruption is marked by a specific date, the "seventeenth day of the second month" of Noah's six hundredth year (v. 11).[48] So momentous is the event that the narration underscores its commencement, "on that day" (v. 11) and "on that very day" (v. 13). Such phrases designate significant events in the life of later Israel. "On that day" distinguishes the entrance of Israel into Sinai, and "on that very day" acclaims Abraham's circumcision (17:23,26), the Passover exodus (Exod 12:41,51), and Moses' death (Deut 32:48). Some one year and eleven days later the earth returns to its former state (see 8:14).

Typically, the Bible marks significant events by citing the year of the reigning monarch, as we find in the prophets, or by catastrophic events (e.g., Ezek 40:1; Amos 1:1). The means for dating the flood is the life of its chief survivor. By Noah's lifetime the life spans of the antediluvian and postdiluvian patriarchs can be coordinated (Gen 5; 11). "Second month" assumes a New Year, but two calendars were used by the Hebrews in their history, one with the New Year in the autumn (Exod 23:16; 34:22), and another beginning the New Year in the spring (Exod 12:2,18; Deut 16:1,6). Which is meant here remains uncertain, but the mention of "seedtime" in 8:22 may suggest the flood begins in the

---

[46] Also עַל־פְּנֵי הָאֲדָמָה ("on the face of the ground,") and מִן־הָאָרֶץ ("from the earth," v. 23).

[47] The NIV has "entire," "every," and "everything."

[48] The LXX has the "twenty-seventh day," making the flood last one solar year to the day (8:14).

autumnal New Year with its heavy rains.[49] Unlike the Mesopotamian flood stories, the biblical account sets the event in a historical framework. For the author of Genesis the flood event is as real as the birth of Abraham.

What was the day like for the people of Noah's generation? It was like any new morning—no alarm and no thought for their doom. Jesus makes this point in portraying his own sudden coming. That generation will be like Noah's, "eating and drinking, marrying and giving in marriage" (Matt 24:37–39). They are carrying on with the normal affairs of their lives, indifferent to the gathering clouds above. In Peter's day the detractors had not yet learned the lesson of Noah's waters (2 Pet 3:5–7), and likewise today many regard it as no more than a children's tale.

The commencement of the deluge is described in creation language, drawing on the imagery of creation's second day when the waters are harnessed and divided (1:6–10), enabling the surface ground to produce vegetation (1:11–13). Now the Lord sets in motion the un-creation of the world by releasing the powers that always stand ready to overwhelm life. The waters once separated will now be rejoined for the purpose of destruction.[50] Earth's disruption is comprehensive; "all" the waters of the "great deep" came forth. The immense floodwaters involve the flow of waters from below and from above, a merism indicating the complete transformation of the terrestrial structures. The prophets also appeal to the imagery of creation's reversal to depict the day of the Lord's judgment (e.g., Isa 24:18b; Jer 4:23–26; Amos 7:4). The "deep" echoes 1:2, and the added description "*great* deep" is reminiscent of 6:5, which speaks of how "great" human wickedness has become. The tidal waves of destruction, therefore, are not excessive; they match the exceeding wickedness of man and are required for the purging of the thoroughly corrupted earth. The "great deep" also is the tool whereby God brings destruction against the armies of Egypt at Israel's escape (Isa 51:10). But the language is redeemed by the psalmist, who describes the vastness of God's power to save, reaching up to the heavens and below as far as the "great deep" (cp. Ps 36:5–6[6–7]).

Subterranean waters "burst forth," and the cloudbursts are overwhelming so that they are like the "floodgates of the heavens" (i.e., sky) flung open. The word for "burst forth" *(bāqaʿ)* is used of Israel's experience that witnesses the "divided" waters at the Red Sea (Exod 14:16,21; Ps 78:13; Isa 63:12) and the earthquake that "split apart" and swallows the members of Korah's rebellion (Num 16:31).[51] It occurs with "deep" *(tĕhôm)* once more at Ps 78:15, which alludes to God's "splitting" the rock in the wilderness (Exod 17:6). But here the divine "divide" means death for Noah's generation. "Floodgates" (i.e., "win-

---

[49] So Sarna, *Genesis,* 54.

[50] Noted by G. von Rad, *Genesis: A Commentary,* OTL, rev. ed. (Philadelphia: Westminster, 1973), 128.

[51] בָּקַע also occurs in Genesis, where the wood for Isaac's sacrifice is "cut" (22:3).

dows") may either depict God's judgment, as here, or his blessings (2 Kgs 7:2,19; Mal 3:10). Isaiah alludes to our verse (and 8:2) as he likens the universal and cataclysmic events of the flood to the great day of the Lord's eschatological appearance when the nations of the earth are overturned at the coming of God's kingdom (Isa 24:18–20). Noah's waters are not just a memorable rain but an unparalleled event in human memory that is brought about by the unique work of God. In the Babylonian *Gilgamesh* the gods were terrified at the flood and "cowered like dogs."[52] The polytheism of *Atrahasis* is reflected in its description of the flood: "Adad [i.e., thunder] was roaring in the clouds." But it is Israel's Lord of creation who rends the heavens and the earth in judgment.

The rain's outpouring occurs for "forty days and forty nights" (v. 12) in accordance with God's prediction (7:4). Our passage shows not only Noah's exemplary faith but also the good reason for such faith; God is proving himself trustworthy at every point. Elsewhere overflowing "rain" *(gešem)* is found as a metaphor for the Lord's judgment (e.g., Ezek 13:11,13). Forty days' duration for the "rain" appears to conflict with the "hundred and fifty days" stated for the "flood" in v. 24 and 8:2–3. The rains begin with the eruption of the deep and the opening of heaven's floodgates (7:11–12), and they are said to close at 8:2, it would seem, after the hundred and fifty days of 7:24. It is standard fare to cite the two periods of "forty" and "hundred and fifty" as irreconcilable differences between conflicting chronological systems arising from the two underlying sources of the flood narrative.[53] But the forty days are "rains" while the hundred-and-forty-day period defines the "flood." It is best to explain the forty days as counted among the one hundred and fifty; thus forty days of rain were followed by a hundred and ten days of abatement until the first signs of land emerge. The NIV's translation at 8:2 and 8:3 accommodates this by its pluperfect renderings, "had been closed," "had stopped," and "had gone down" (see 8:3 discussion). This translation is possible, but not necessary. The abatement of waters ("receded steadily") and the grounding of the ark in 8:3–4 show that the waters already started their descent within the hundred-and-fifty-day period.[54] The landing of the ark on the specific date, "seventeenth day of the seventh month," rhetorically matches the date of the first rains on the "seven-

---

[52] *ANET,* 94.

[53] Recent attempts to reconstruct the chronologies are N. P. Lemche, "The Chronology in the Story of the Flood," *JSOT* 18 (1980): 52–62, who finds evidence of three chronological systems in Gen 6–8: J, P, and a Redactor. F. H. Cryer, "The Interrelationships of Gen 5,32; 11,10–11 and the Chronology of the Flood (Gen 6–9)," *Bib* 66 (1985): 241–61, posits that chaps. 6–8 possess two complete, parallel chronologies, one involving a 360-day scheme and the other a 370-day chronology which when added together constitute two solar years (730 days) and thus account for P's perplexing reference to "two years after the flood" in 11:10. L. M. Barré also finds two complete chronologies but each based on a 360-day year, which originally were independent systems ("The Riddle of the Flood Chronology," *JSOT* 41 [1988]: 3–20).

[54] So, e.g., T. E. Fretheim, "Genesis," NIB (Nashville: Abingdon, 1994), 392; Hamilton, *Genesis 1–17,* 298.

teenth day of the second month" (7:11), that is, five months (= 150 days), indicating thereby that the hundred-and-fifty-day period includes the forty-day rain (7:11) and the duration of abatement (8:3) necessary for the ark to take hold.

7:13–16 These verses detail, by resuming and expanding, what is generally related in 7:6–10, thereby providing two accounts of entry.[55] The narrative shows an alternation of the flood and entry notices: flood (v. 6) and entry (vv. 7–9), flood (vv. 10–12) and entry (vv. 13–16), and finally flood (v. 17).[56] This second entrance narrative is not contradictory to vv. 6–10 but supplementary, giving additional specifics so as to reinforce the critical act of faith by this small band of eight trusting souls who do not turn back. Twice in vv. 13–16 we are told the occupants "entered the ark," which prepares for the all-important shutting of the door after them (v. 16b). In the first occasion it refers to the human residents who "entered" (v. 13); and the second, to the animals (v. 15). Here we find the only place in the entry narratives where the sons are noted by name. Citing the names "Shem, Ham, and Japheth" at this juncture in the account ties the genealogical notice of 6:10 to the exit statement in 9:18, "who came out of the ark." For the compiler of Genesis the whole world rests with these three sons who become the progenitors of the nations (chaps. 10–11).

We have already discovered that the narrative as a whole repeatedly reaches back for the language of the first creation. Here again much of vv. 13–16 draws on the creation imagery of chap. 1: the same animal groups cataloged in 1:21–25, "kinds" (1:11, etc.), and "male and female" (1:27). Special reference to the "birds" as "everything with wings" becomes important to Noah's discovery of the withdrawing waters when raven and dove are released (8:7–12). "Pairs" ("two by two") anticipates the divine charge at their debarkation to "multiply" in accord with the creation ordinance (8:17; cp. 1:22). The animals "came" to Noah at the ark (also 7:9), suggesting that they volitionally arrive, an interpretation found in early Jewish midrash.[57] But 6:19 has the command to "bring" the animals, indicating that Noah plays some part in their recruitment.

The concluding remark, "the LORD shut him in," initiates his protective care over the vessel and finally ends the anxious moment of the narrative as the occupants hasten within the walls of safety (v. 16b). Closing the ark's door signals the divine protection that kept out the raging seas. Noah and his companions did their part "as God had commanded." Now the covenant Lord does his part, sealing the door, which could result in either their doom or their salvation. But God would "remember" (8:1a) Noah's righteousness, who exemplified the

---

[55] So Anderson, "The Interpretation of Genesis 1–11," 35.

[56] Observed by Andersen, *The Sentence in Biblical Hebrew,* 124–25.

[57] "They came on their own" (*Gen. Rab.* 32.8).

wisdom of the later sage, "The name of the Lord is a strong tower; the righteous run to it and are safe" (Prov 18:10).

(2) Rising Floodwaters (7:17–24)

**17For forty days the flood kept coming on the earth, and as the waters
increased they lifted the ark high above the earth. 18The waters rose and
increased greatly on the earth, and the ark floated on the surface of the water.
19They rose greatly on the earth, and all the high mountains under the entire
heavens were covered. 20The waters rose and covered the mountains to a depth of
more than twenty feet. 21Every living thing that moved on the earth perished—
birds, livestock, wild animals, all the creatures that swarm over the earth, and all
mankind. 22Everything on dry land that had the breath of life in its nostrils died.
23Every living thing on the face of the earth was wiped out; men and animals and
the creatures that move along the ground and the birds of the air were wiped
from the earth. Only Noah was left, and those with him in the ark.**

24The waters flooded the earth for a hundred and fifty days.

7:17–20 With Noah and crew safely "shut in," the flood commences. The brief description in v. 12 is protracted in vv. 17–20 by means of structural overlay and numerous repetitions so as to give the literary effect of increasingly rising waters.[58] "The tautologies of the account . . . portray the fearful monotony of the unbounded expanse of waters."[59] "Waters" (5x), "increased" (2x), "rose" (3x), and "greatly" (3x in Heb.) dominate the short span of forty-seven Hebrew words (vv. 17–20) to underscore the sense of the escalating waters. Exemplary of this highlighting is vv. 18–19, where in v. 18 the adverb "greatly" is followed in v. 19 by its occurrence twice, "very greatly" *(mĕʾōd mĕʾōd)*.[60] Verse 17 corresponds to v. 12 in structure and content, with the parallel descriptions "rain" and "flood."[61] The former features the downpouring rains while "flood" in v. 17 concerns the accumulating waters they produce.

The language of our passage, including vv. 21–24, backtracks to 6:1–8, which tells of humanity's increasing sin and God's response to destroy the earth: "increased" (*rābah*, vv. 17–18) is reminiscent of how "great" *(rabbâ)* man's wickedness is (6:5); "rose" (*gābar*, vv. 18,20,24), rendered "prevailed"

---

58 NRSV, NJPS have this effect by "swelled" (גָּבַר) in vv. 18–20; others have "higher and higher" at v. 19 (NJB, NAB), while GNB has the waters "became deep" (v. 17), "became deeper" (v. 18), and "became so deep" (v. 19).

59 F. Delitzsch, *A New Commentary on Genesis,* trans. S. Taylor (1888; reprint, Edinburgh: T & T Clark, 1978), 269.

60 The NASB has captured the repetition by "prevailed more and more upon the earth" (v. 19).

61 "The rain came upon the earth forty days and forty nights" (v. 12)

"The flood continued forty days on the earth" (v. 17)

וַיְהִי הַגֶּשֶׁם עַל־הָאָרֶץ אַרְבָּעִים יוֹם וְאַרְבָּעִים לָיְלָה (v. 12)

וַיְהִי הַמַּבּוּל אַרְבָּעִים יוֹם עַל־הָאָרֶץ (v. 17)

The LXX adds "forty nights" in v. 17 to perfect the parallel.

(AV, NASB), echoes its noun derivative "heroes" or "strong ones" (*gibbōrîm;* 6:4); and "wiped out" (*māḥâ;* v. 23) repeats the first condemnation in 6:7. The inclusive language, "all," "every" and "everything" *(kōl),* imitates the universality and pervasiveness of humanity's wickedness (6:5). By this linkage the narrative shows the causal relationship between the sin of humanity and the consequent flood that came upon the perverse world.

The "waters" (vv. 17–18,20) in the context of "earth" and "heavens" (v. 19) is a reminder of 1:1–2, God's good creation. Now the waters are released "upon the earth" for destruction rather than curbed by God in creation (1:6–9). They ascend, covering the mountains "under the entire heavens" (v. 19), whereas at creation these waters are gathered into seas "under the heavens/sky" so as to uncover the "dry ground" (1:9). But what appears amidst these escalating waters is only the "ark high above the earth" (v. 17).

The inclusive language "all"/"every" occurs eight times (in Hebrew) in vv. 19–23, leaving no doubt about the all-encompassing nature of the destructive floods and the death left behind. There can be no dispute that the narrative depicts the flood in the language of a universal deluge ("entire heavens"), even the "high mountains" are "covered" (2x; vv. 19–20).[62] Some believe, however, that the passage is using hyperbole as elsewhere in the Pentateuch (see also comments at 6:17).[63] Yet if the report is a phenomenological depiction, permitting the possibility of a local flood, the meaning is not substantially altered: all that Noah and his generation know is swallowed up by the waters so that none survives. The details of the floodwaters rising fifteen cubits ("twenty feet") above the peaks and the duration of the waters at one hundred and fifty days show that the destruction is certain. "Covered" is another shared term in the narrative of the Mosaic deluge that drowns the Egyptian chariotry (Exod 14:28; 15:5,10; Josh 24:7).

7:21–24 "Every living thing that moved," . . . "Everything on dry land," . . . and "Every living thing on the face of the earth" (vv. 21–23) emphatically declare that no one escaped the purging of the floodwaters. Verses 21–23 reiterate in detail what has already been stated succinctly in 6:17. A close reading shows that there are significant variations among vv. 21–23 that contribute to the already-graphic depiction of the swirling waters and the doom they hold for the earth's inhabitants. To the modern reader these verses appear redundant, but when taken together, they build toward the climactic contrast, "Only Noah was left" (v. 23b). This steady building up of the narrative commemorates all

---

[62] For discussion see "Did Noah's Flood Cover the Entire World?" S. Austin, "Yes," and D. Boardman, "No," *The Genesis Debate,* ed. R. Youngblood (Nashville: Nelson, 1986), 210–29.

[63] תַּחַת כָּל־הַשָּׁמָיִם ("under the entire heavens"), e.g., Deut 2:25 ("everywhere under heaven," NRSV); cf. also Deut 4:19; Job 37:3; Acts 2:5; Rom 1:8; Col 1:23. See "all the world," Gen 41:57. Yet the same Hebrew may also have the literal universal sense ("everything under heaven," e.g., Job 41:11[3]; cf. Dan 7:27[Aramaic]).

the more Noah's survival.

Again the earlier motifs of creation, sin, and the penalty of death, now common to the flood story, are restated in this culminating conclusion to the rising torrents. Verse 21 catalogs the creatures of chap. 1 and includes in this listing "creatures that swarm" (1:20–21,24–25), absent in the earlier summaries (6:20; 7:8–9,14–15). "All mankind" not only reaches back to the creation account (1:26) but also recalls God's first declaration that he has condemned all sinful humanity (6:3,5,7). The comprehensive rhetoric, all "that had the breath of life in its nostrils," builds on the similar statement in 6:17 by the addition of "nostrils" *(ʾap)*. This points to humanity both to its origins, "and breathed into his nostrils *(ʾap)* the breath of life" (2:7), and its toil as punishment, "by the sweat of your brow" (*ʾap;* 3:19).

"Perished" and "wiped out" (vv. 21,23) occur earlier in the flood narrative (e.g., 6:7,17), but "died" is new to the story and only occurs here (cf. 9:29). This deliberate reflection of the garden scene (2:17; 3:3–4), where human death is forewarned, and the genealogy of Seth (5:5 etc.), where death reigns, brings forward to culmination the forceful response unmitigated sin requires. Also the weakness of humanity as a product of the earth's dust (2:7) is accented in the Hebrew text by the juxtaposition of the words "earth"/ "ground" *(ʾădāmâ)* and "men" *(ʾādām)* in v. 23, which form a pun (cf. also 6:7).[64] And should the purge not begin with humanity? On their account the ground suffers divine curse twice (3:17; see 8:21 discussion). Against the invincible waters and the God who has released them, neither puny humanity nor vulnerable creature can resist.

"Only Noah was left" points to the righteous remnant of the former world that the patriarch embodies. "Remnant" is derived from the verb "remain, left over" *(šāʾar)*,[65] and theologically the idea of remnant depicts the future hope of God's people as a holy, regathered people (e.g., Jer 23:3; Isa 4:3; 10:20–23; Rom 9:27–28). This idea was associated with Noah by the Jews: "A remnant was left to the earth when the flood came" (*Sir* 44:17). In Genesis "remnant" refers to those escaping danger (14:10; 32:8[9]) or the survival of the patriarchal heritage (45:7). Among the Egyptian armies not one "survived" *(nišʾar)* at the Red Sea (Exod 14:28).

We have shown earlier that the flood narrative points ahead to Moses and the escape of the Hebrews through the Red Sea. This is evidenced again by the term "dry land" *(ḥārābâ)*in our passage (v. 22) rather than the customary "dry ground" *(yābāšâ)*. This infrequent term occurs eight times, only once more in the Pentateuch at Exod 14:21, where it describes the transformation of the sea

---

[64] עַל־פְּנֵי הָאֲדָמָה מֵאָדָם: "on the face of the ground, human beings" (v. 23, NRSV).

[65] שָׁאַר in the *niphal* stem parallels יָתַר ("remain"); "remnant" commonly is the participle נִשְׁאָר (e.g., Gen 32:9) or nouns שְׁאָר (e.g., Isa 10:20) and שְׁאֵרִית (e.g., Gen 45:7), comparable to the noun יֶתֶר.

into "dry land" by a "strong east wind."[66] This exodus parallel is confirmed by 8:1b, which speaks of God's sending a "wind" upon the waters. Later Israel identified itself with Noah and the tiny group of survivors who escaped the wicked by the awesome deeds of God.

Verse 24 concludes the narrative's report of the raging floodwaters of "a hundred and fifty days" (see 7:12 discussion). It ties the former half of the story, where the "waters flooded the earth" (chap. 7), and the following narration of their withdrawal from the earth "one hundred and fifty days" (8:3). According to the lunar calendar, one hundred and fifty days would constitute five months for the period from the commencement of the rains to the resting of the ark (see 8:3).

5. God Remembered Noah (8:1a)

1 But God remembered Noah and all the wild animals and the livestock that were with him in the ark,

Just two words, "God remembered," explain the reversal in the flow of the waters and thus the flow of the narrative. "*But* God" contrasts the destruction brought by the Lord and the deliverance of Noah and the ark's occupants that will ensue. As the Lord had promised (6:18; 7:1), the floodwater's cessation and recession begin, but only because "God" (*ʾĕlōhîm*) took the initiative to save the eight souls in the ark (1 Pet 3:20). Receding waters became testimony to God's faithfulness to Noah and "all" the animals in the ark. Is it any surprise that the delivered soul upon disembarking straightway offered up sacrifice of thanksgiving to his God (8:20)? God's mercy is extended to all that he has made, including the animals (cf. Ps 145:9). If the Lord had pity on the least of these dumb creatures, we dare not withhold mercy toward humanity made in his "likeness" (Jas 3:9).

The expression "remembered" *(zākar)* does not mean "calling to mind" here; it is covenant language, designating covenant fidelity (e.g., the Fourth Commandment, Exod 20:8; cf. Luke 1:72). God is acting in accordance with his earlier promise to Noah (6:18). We find the same expression in the Noahic covenant, where the Lord commits to carrying out his promises (8:21) and establishes the covenant sign of the rainbow (9:14–15). "Remembered" often is found in the circumstance of deliverance, based on God's prior covenant commitments, as in Israel's exodus and occupation of Canaan (e.g., Exod 2:24; 6:5; Num 10:9). It describes the Lord's response to the requests of his people, as when he delivers Lot from the destruction of Sodom and Gomorrah on account of Abraham's mediation (19:29) and when he hearkens to barren Rachel, who gives birth to Joseph (30:22). Divine "remembrance" was the

---

[66] Also the "dry land" at the Jordan crossing (Josh 3:17[2x]; 4:18); also 2 Kgs 2:8; Ezek 30:12; Hag 2:6. Verbal חָרַב ("to dry") occurs twice in 8:13.

appeal of Moses' intervention on behalf of apostate Israel (Exod 32:13), and it was reason for God's return to a contrite people (Lev 26:42,45). "Remember" speaks of the future as well as the past and present, for the psalmist declares that for the sake of covenant the Lord will bring about a future "blessing" on his people (Ps 115:12).[67] People of the covenant, whether yesterday or today, are expected to exercise covenant allegiance by "remembering" the Lord (e.g., Deut 8:18; Ps 103:18). Israel's God had remembered Noah, and by this Israel too was incited to remember the Lord of Sinai.

6. Winds of Rescue (8:1b–14)

Blowing wind, retreating waters, and the emergence of drying land dominate the telling of the deluge's reversal. The language of the passage echoes the description of Genesis 1, showing that God has set about making a new creation. There is a general correspondence between the progression of creation's six days and chap. 8's delineation of the new creation.

First Day	1:2	"earth," "deep," "Spirit" *(rûaḥ),* "waters"
	8:1b–2a	"wind" *(rûaḥ),* "earth," "waters," "deep"
Second Day	1:7–8	"waters," "sky"
	8:2b	"sky"
Third Day	1:9	"water," "dry ground," "appear"
	8:3–5	"water," "tops of the mountains," "appear" (NIV, "visible")
(Fourth Day	No need for the re-creation of the luminaries)	
Fifth Day	1:20	"birds," "above the earth," "across *(ʿal pĕnê)* the expanse"
	8:7–8	"raven," "from the earth," "from the surface *[ʿal pĕnē]* of the ground"
Sixth Day	1:24	"creatures," "livestock," "creatures that move along the ground," "wild animals"
	8:17	"creature," "birds," "animals," "creatures that move along the ground"
	1:26	"man," "image"
	[9:6	"image," "man"]

The summary of the disembarking people and animals in 8:17–19, with its divine exhortation to "multiply . . . be fruitful and increase" is reminiscent of creation's fifth and sixth days (1:20–22,24–25,28–30). Noah's ark and the animal world is Adam's world resumed (see 9:1–7). Both are set in a chronological framework. Chapter 1 has its seven "days," and chap. 8's narrative marks out the strategic points of the ebbing waters by dating the progression by "year," "month," and "day" until its completion (8:13–14). We remarked ear-

[67] So A. Verhey, "Remember, Remembrance," *ABD* 5.667.

lier that the repeated use of sevens and tens in chap. 8 imitates the same numeric occupation in 1:1–2:3.

The three movements of the Lord's salvation include (1) the receding floodwater (8:1b–5), (2) the drying earth (8:6–14), and (3) the disembarkation (8:15–19). Each stage logically leads to the next as we find in the story a methodic inversion of the earlier embarkation, rains, and cresting floodwater, annihilating all that had the "breath of life" (7:22). Description of retreating floodwater dominates the first phase (8:1b–5), where four times in the Hebrew we are told that the waters "receded" (*šākak,* v. 1b), "receded steadily" (*wayyāšūbû . . .hālôk wāšôb,* v. 3a), "had gone down" (*wayyaḥsĕrû,* v. 3b), and "continued to recede" (*hālôk wāḥsôr,* v. 5). The centerpiece of the narrative (8:6–14) reiterates the "earth dried up" (vv. 7,13–14), forming an inclusio by the repetition of "dried up" *(yĕbōšet)* at v. 7 and the concluding "was dry" *(yābĕšâ)* at v. 14. Sandwiched between is the twice repeated "dried up" (*ḥārab*, v. 13). This recessional culminates in the last movement (8:15–19), containing the third divine speech, "Come out" (v. 16) and "Bring out" (v. 17), followed by the corresponding, "Noah came out" (v. 18), and "all the animals . . . came out of the ark" (v. 19), all derived from the same Hebrew word *(yāṣāʾ).* God commanded the wind, the waters, and the inhabitants of the ark, and all obeyed.

(1) Receding Floodwater (8:1b–5)

and he sent a wind over the earth, and the waters receded. 2Now the springs of the deep and the floodgates of the heavens had been closed, and the rain had stopped falling from the sky. 3The water receded steadily from the earth. At the end of the hundred and fifty days the water had gone down, 4and on the seventeenth day of the seventh month the ark came to rest on the mountains of Ararat. 5The waters continued to recede until the tenth month, and on the first day of the tenth month the tops of the mountains became visible.

8:1b–2 "Wind" *(rûaḥ)* echoes the description of God's "Spirit" *(rûaḥ)* hovering over the "waters" at creation (1:2c). *Elohim,* as in Genesis 1, brings this to pass, indicating that the wind is the renewed work of the Creator. "Remembered" in the previous sentence reflects the covenant name *Yahweh,* who is faithful to his promise, and by *Elohim* we find that the divine power of creation is unleashed anew to the ends of accomplishing that covenant pledge. As he had superintended the conditions of the "earth" at the beginning, the divine mind plots a destiny for the second beginning of the earth, which will be delivered from the clutches of deathly waters. As *Tg. Neof.* translated, it was a "spirit of mercy."

Moses witnessed the might of God's "wind" to induce and chase away a locust plague (Exod 10:13,19) and deliver his people from Egyptian armies at the sea on "dry ground" (*ḥārābâ*, Exod 14:21; 15:10). It was with the same "wind" that the Lord provided quail for the vagabond people of the desert (Num 11:31). The Lord of Israel delivered and sustained his people by his omnipotent "wind," enlisting nature's forces to do his bidding in their behalf (e.g., Josh 10:11; Pss 18:7–19; 148:8). He was celebrated as the One who "rides on the wings of the wind" and makes them "his messengers" (Ps 104:3–4).

Using the same imagery, v. 2 describes the reversal of 7:11–12, which told of the earth's bursting "springs of the great deep," the opened "floodgates of the heavens," and the falling "rain." Now the deep is no longer "great"; it and the floodgates are "closed," and the rain was "stopped" (i.e., "restrained").

8:3–5 "Little by little" (NJB) the diminishing waters safely "receded" (*šûb*, v. 3), unlike the torrent of water that "returned" *(šûb)*, drowning the Egyptian armies (Exod 14:26–28). This idea of "returned" is continued in the subsequent paragraph by reference to the "returning" *(šûb)* of birds to the ark (vv. 7,9,12).

Significant time periods and dates are often cited in chap. 8, acting like milestones in tracing the water's steady regression. The flood's inversion of mounting waters to receding waters is perfectly paralleled by the number "a hundred and fifty days" (see 7:12 discussion).[68] The ark at last comes to rest on the "seventeenth day of the seventh month" (v. 4), giving a five-month period from first rains (7:11) to the ark's grounding. The same five-month period extends from the first sighting of the mountains (8:5) to the completely dried earth (v. 14). The seventh month in the religious calendar of the Hebrews was Tishri, the most important month of the sacred convocations; it included the Day of Atonement as well as the Feasts of Trumpets, Tabernacles, and Sacred Assembly (Lev 23:23–36). It was appropriate, therefore, that the ark should find refuge in the cultic month celebrating atonement and God's provision. By the ark coming to "rest" (*nûaḥ*, v. 4), the passage is reminiscent of Noah's naming (see 5:29). In a play on "Noah" *(nōaḥ)* the author indicates that the patriarch achieved, in a most unexpected way, the hopes of his father Lamech.

"Ararat," known as ancient Urartu in Assyrian records, was an extensive territory and bordered the northern Mesopotamian region. It reached its political zenith in the ninth to sixth centuries B.C. Urartu surrounded Lake Van with boundaries taking in southeast Turkey, southern Russia, and northwest Iran. Among the mountains of modern Armenia is the impressive peak known today as Mount Ararat, some seventeen thousand feet in elevation, which the Turks

[68] The NIV's "had gone down" renders וַיַּחְסְרוּ as a pluperfect (cp. "had abated," NRSV, REB), permitting the period of abatement to have begun already within the 150-day period. The same pluperfect sense has been suggested for 8:1–2, "God had remembered" and "had sent" the wind, and the springs and gates "had been closed" and rains "had stopped." For the pluperfect use of *wāw* + imperfect, see *IBHS* § 33.2.3a. For discussion see Wenham, "Method in Pentateuchal Source Criticism," 89–91.

call Byk Ari Da.[69] "Mount Ararat" as a geographical designation comes from later tradition. During the eleventh to twelfth centuries A.D., it became the traditional site known as the place of Noah's landing.[70] Verse 4, however, does not specify a peak and refers generally to its location as the "mountains of Ararat." "Urartu" (Ararat) is mentioned seldom in Scripture (2 Kgs 19:37; Isa 37:38; Jer 51:27), and it had no special significance in the history of Israel's religious or national life. The search for the ark's artifacts has been both a medieval and a modern occupation; but to the skeptic such evidence is not convincing, and to the believer, while not irrelevant, it is not necessary to faith.

Some seventy-two or seventy-three days (counting the first day) after the vessel landed, the waters had sufficiently retreated so that the peaks of the Ararat mountains became "visible" to Noah (v. 5). It was the first sign of land, no doubt a solace for the weary sailor. Whereas it took but forty days for the rains to submerge the earth, it would be five lingering months before the waters would completely subside. So Noah befriended patience and "waited" (vv. 10,12). When troubles come, they advance swiftly but retreat slowly. Our verse alludes to creation's gathering of waters on the third day when the "dry land appeared" for the first time (1:9–10). Both verses have the verb "appeared/ visible" (*rʾh*), and creation's "dry land" *(yabbāšâ)* is echoed later in our narrative by its verbal forms "dried up" (v. 7) and "was dry" (v. 14, *yābaš*). The emerging "earth" would once again support life as it had at the beginning. With each new stage of its drying, the heart of the captive inmates could leap with the hope that their deliverance was nearing.

(2) Drying Earth (8:6–14)

6After forty days Noah opened the window he had made in the ark 7and sent out a raven, and it kept flying back and forth until the water had dried up from the earth. 8Then he sent out a dove to see if the water had receded from the surface of the ground. 9But the dove could find no place to set its feet because there was water over all the surface of the earth; so it returned to Noah in the ark. He reached out his hand and took the dove and brought it back to himself in the ark. 10He waited seven more days and again sent out the dove from the ark. 11When the dove returned to him in the evening, there in its beak was a freshly plucked olive leaf! Then Noah knew that the water had receded from the earth. 12He waited seven more days and sent the dove out again, but this time it did not return to him.

13By the first day of the first month of Noah's six hundred and first year, the water had dried up from the earth. Noah then removed the covering from the ark

[69] In the Babylonian version it is on Mount Nisir, identified as Pir-Omar-Gudrun in Kurdistan, that the boat comes to land (*ANET,* 94). *Jub.* and 1QapGen identify Mount Lubar as the landing point.

[70] L. R. Bailey, "Ararat," *ABD* 1.352–53.

and saw that the surface of the ground was dry. [14]By the twenty-seventh day of the second month the earth was completely dry.

8:6–12 Following the first appearance of land, the drying of the earth continues, taking five more months to complete (vv. 5,14). A raven and a dove, the latter three times, are released by Noah to measure the water's retreat, apparently in intervals of seven days.[71] Forty days following the disclosure of the mountain peaks, Noah releases first a "raven." "At the end *(qēṣ)* of forty days" echoes God's intent to put an "end" *(qēṣ)* to all peoples (6:13) by "forty days" of rains (7:4,11,17).[72] This the Lord had accomplished, and the period of vengeance had come to its "end" with the release of first life from the ark. The allusion to "forty" was also the period of Israel's captivity in the wilderness until God's wrath was satisfied (e.g., Num 14:33–34; see 7:4 discussion).

There is no reason stated for the raven's release, as we find with the dove, but we may assume the raven was commissioned for the same purpose.[73] As the stronger bird and a consumer of carrion, the raven could remain in flight longer, going back and forth while deriving its food from floating carcasses (v. 7).[74] The foremost significance of the raven is its symbolic value as an "unclean" bird, unfit for consumption (Lev 11:15; Deut 14:14). According to rabbinic tradition, the raven was released first as expendable since it was neither good for food nor sacrifice. Also Isaiah, in predicting Edom's desolation, drew on the symbolic raven and on the creation language of 1:2, *tōhû* ("wasteland") and *bōhû* ("empty"), to depict its demise (34:11). Its departure from the ark signified that the impurities of the past had been removed and the creation of the new world had a fresh start.

Second, a "dove" is released, probably seven days later, but it cannot find a place to alight (vv. 8–9). Noah commissions the dove to "see" as the eyes of the patriarch in order to discover if the water "had receded" further (v. 8). Noah is imprisoned in the ark and must depend on his animal shipmates until later he "saw" the dry land firsthand (v. 13). The bird conveys for the ark's inhabitants the opposite meaning to the raven.[75] It was commonly found in

---

[71] Babylonian *Gilgamesh* also has Utnapishtim after seven days aground dispatching three successive birds for the same purpose, first a dove, then a swallow, each returning, and last a raven (*ANET,* 94–95).

[72] Noted by Sarna, *Genesis,* 57.

[73] The LXX gives it a purpose by the addition "to see if the waters had ceased" as in v. 8.

[74] The LXX's καὶ ἐξελθὼν οὐχ ὑπέστρεψεν ("and it went forth and did not return"), followed by Syr and Vg, misconstrued the Heb. and clarified that the raven did not return to the vessel. The expression וַיֵּצֵא יָצוֹא וָשׁוֹב means that the raven flew back and forth repeatedly (*IBHS* § 35.3.2c), but whether it reentered the ark is uncertain. The absence of a specific statement in contrast to the dove (vv. 9,11–12) suggests that it found a place to perch on the mountains and did not rejoin Noah.

[75] Thus one *Tg. Ps.-J.* text adds "clean" dove.

the sacrificial legislation for rites of purification (e.g., Lev 12:6,8; cf. Num 6:10; Luke 2:24) and was appropriated for the "burnt offering" and "sin offering" among the poor (e.g., Lev 1:14; 5:7; 14:22). "Dove" was used as a word of endearment (e.g., Song 2:14); it was noted for the beauty of its eyes (e.g., Song 1:15) and remembered for its wings of flight, perching peacefully among the cliffs (e.g., Ps 55:6; Jer 48:28). It was numbered among the ritual offerings in the confirmation of the Abrahamic covenant (15:9).[76] From among the "clean" animals the dove would be sacrificed in Noah's postdiluvian "burnt offering" (8:20).

The bird failed to find a resting "place" because the waters still claimed the "whole earth" (v. 9). In 7:3 animal life from the "whole earth" was fetched to the ark, but here there is still no possibility for the renewal of that life. "Place" *(mānôaḥ)* is derived from the Hebrew word for "rest" *(nûaḥ)* and is a second play on the name "Noah," continuing the idea of "Noahic rest" (see 5:29). Whereas the ark found "rest," the dove does not and is rescued from the waters by Noah's personal retrieval ("to himself"). Noah with the dove in hand reflects the religious interests of the passage: the raven, an unclean bird, departs from the ark, but the dove, indicative of purity (cf. Matt 10:16), is a welcomed resident upon the vessel.

After waiting another seven days, the second release of the dove proves promising because it returns with the first testimony to life, "a freshly plucked olive leaf" (8:10–11). As a fresh leaf, it was newly born and thus was confirmation that the earth again was yielding its herbage (as 1:11–12 30). The detail of an "olive" leaf too may have caused early readers to reflect on connections with the tabernacle, where olive oil fueled the menorah in the tabernacle (Exod 27:20; Lev 24:2–4) and was added to the mixture of perfumed oil for anointing tabernacle and furnishings (Exod 30:24–29). It was obviously something that pleased God.

By this sign Noah "knew" that the waters had receded; this emblem of life and prosperity gave this second Adam reassurance of continued life and safety. Both anointing oil and dove had symbolic value in Israel for the empowering presence of the Spirit, especially the ministry of the messianic figure (e.g., 1 Sam 16:13; Ps 89:20; Isa 61:1). Jesus of Nazareth took up that ministry (Luke 4:18; Acts 10:38), and at his public baptism all four Evangelists note that the Spirit came upon him in the form of a descending "dove" (Matt 3:16 pars.). After yet another seven days, the bird is released a third time, and at last the dove does not return (v. 12). "By not returning it proclaims this freedom to those who are still shut up in the ark."[77]

---

[76] But 15:9 has גּוֹזָל for "young pigeon" rather than the usual word יוֹנָה ("pigeon").
[77] Westermann, *Genesis 1–11*, 449.

8:13–14 Special attention to the exact dates of the earth's drying indicates the importance attributed to the events they detail. "First day of the first month . . . six hundred and first year" (v. 13) with its emphasis on "first" ("one") signaled a new "year," that is, the beginning of the new creation that God had accomplished through Noah's survival. Only by hoisting the "covering" ("hatch," REB) was Noah able to see the land below; he viewed the "surface of the ground" *(pĕnê hāʾădāmâ)* for the first time. The NJB captures the excitement of the moment with the exclamation, "The surface of the ground was dry!" Evidently puddles of water still remained, and on the "twenty-seventh day of the second month" the whole "earth" *(ʾereṣ)* was dry for disembarking (v. 14).[78] One year and eleven days since the initial outpouring (7:11), the last vestiges of the waters disappeared.[79] "Dried" *(ḥārab)*, occurring twice in v. 13, was found in 7:22 and is the language describing Israel's trek under Joshua across the "dry" Jordan River (Josh 3:17; 4:18). It spoke of God's intent to destroy in 7:22, but here it testifies to God's salvation for the flood's survivors. Yet another term for "dry" is in v. 14 (also 8:6). It is the language of creation when the dry land appeared (1:9–10) and also the dry ground at the Red Sea and Jordan River crossings (Exod 14:16; 15:19; Josh 4:22).

Again the narration ties the flood deliverance to the worship activity of Israel by drawing on tabernacle jargon for the "cover" *(mikseh)* of the ark (v. 13). It was not the side "door" noted in 6:16 but another opening. With the exception of Noah's ark, the term designates exclusively the "covering" (tanned animal hides) for the "tent of meeting" (e.g., Exod 26:14; 36:19; Num 3:25). Even as God was with Israel in the wilderness sojourn, he was with Noah in the midst of his watery voyage.

7. Exiting the Ark (8:15–19)

[15]Then God said to Noah, [16]"Come out of the ark, you and your wife and your sons and their wives. [17]Bring out every kind of living creature that is with you—the birds, the animals, and all the creatures that move along the ground—so they can multiply on the earth and be fruitful and increase in number upon it."

[18]So Noah came out, together with his sons and his wife and his sons' wives. [19]All the animals and all the creatures that move along the ground and all the

[78] Both dates claim the "drying" of the "ground" (פְּנֵי הָאֲדָמָה) and of the "earth" (הָאָרֶץ); some versions answer this by rendering v. 13 "the waters began drying out" (e.g., NJB, NAB, NJPS) or the NIV's addition in v. 14 "completely" dry. The resolution is the difference in "ground" and the inclusive reference "earth."

[79] U. Cassuto counts one lunar year (354 days) and eleven days, totaling a solar year of 365 days; he comments: "The cycle was complete: the sun returned to the point at which it was on the day the Deluge began, and the earth returned to the state in which it then found itself" (*A Commentary on the Book of Genesis. Part II. From Noah to Abraham, Genesis VI:9–XI 32,* trans. I. Abrahams [Jerusalem: Magnes, 1964], 114).

birds—everything that moves on the earth—came out of the ark, one kind after another.

8:15–17 The third divine speech instructs Noah to disembark from the ark. It parallels the command to enter the ark (7:1), except the configuration of the family is cited specifically here. These eight are the new humanity, and the future of the blessing remains with them. Those who entered the ark successfully rode out the storms and were delivered intact by the mercies of God. For the long year of rising and receding waters, Noah received no word from the Lord. He had waited and waited yet did not anxiously exit until given the heavenly word to disembark. As Calvin remarked, Noah "did not move a foot out of his sepulchre, without the command of God."[80] As the second creation, God instructs Noah to bring out the animals so that they might "multiply," "be fruitful," and "increase" on the earth. This instruction is also reminiscent of God's blessing upon the initial creation, where he enabled the lower orders to propagate (1:22). Reference to Noah's "wife" and the sons' "wives" infers that the human family too in accord with 1:28 will increase. This charge is formally reissued to Noah and his sons in 9:1.

8:18–19 These may be taken by the Western reader as tedious repetition, but the report style of Hebrew narrative shows Noah's obedience, a feature repeatedly ascribed to him throughout the flood account. In contrast to his generation, Noah as a "righteous man" believed God and obeyed his command both in entering the ark (7:1) and in departing. As one midrash observed, "The righteous comes out of trouble" (Prov 12:13; *Gen. Rab.* 34.3). Noah's animal menagerie exited the ark "one kind after another" (v. 19). Although this reminds us of the creation refrain "after its kind" *(mîn),* the different Hebrew word in v. 19 for "kind" *(mišpāḥâ)* points ahead rather than to the past. It is the typical term for human "families" and anticipates the genealogies of Shem, Ham, and Japheth, which delineate their descendants by "families" (10:5,20,31; also 24:38,40; 36:40).[81] The same term is found in God's blessing on Abraham by which "all peoples" ("families") will be affected (12:3; also 28:14).

8. Worship and the Word of Promise (8:20–22)

[20]Then Noah built an altar to the LORD and, taking some of all the clean animals and clean birds, he sacrificed burnt offerings on it. [21]The LORD smelled the pleasing aroma and said in his heart: "Never again will I curse the ground because of man, even though every inclination of his heart is evil from childhood. And never again will I destroy all living creatures, as I have done.

[80] Calvin, *Comm.*, 280.

[81] Verse 19 is also rendered in English versions "by (their) families" (see NRSV, NASB, NJPS).

22"As long as the earth endures,
seedtime and harvest,
cold and heat,
summer and winter,
day and night
will never cease."

Contrasting God's former resolve to destroy the earth (6:13–22), this section exhibits God's determination to preserve the second creation. In response to the Lord's deliverance, Noah built an altar for sacrifice.[82] By this, Genesis testifies at its start to the human duty to acknowledge the Lord as Creator and Savior in sacrifice and worship. We have in Noah's sacrifice a reminder that sinful humanity always required a mediation with God, as shown by the shadows of the past (Col 2:17; Heb 8:5; 9:9; 10:1). "Now, however, the manifestation of Christ has taken away these ancient shadows."[83]

8:20 Although worship was known from the days of Cain and Abel (4:3–4; also 4:26), this incident is the first account of an "altar" erected for that purpose. Here worship is specifically directed "to the LORD." This same language describes the patriarchal custom of building an altar for worship wherever the fathers resided in their sojournings, especially Abraham, who constructed his altar "to the LORD" (12:7–8; 13:18).[84] Noah then was the pious forerunner of Israel's fathers both in terms of physical ancestry and in veneration of Israel's God, Yahweh. Moses perpetuated this practice even before the tabernacle construction, following his victory over the Amalekites and, more importantly, later in the ceremony ratifying the Sinai covenant (Exod 17:15; 24:4; cf. 20:24–25). Moreover, the Sinai directives for constructing the tabernacle's bronze "altar of burnt offering" *(mizbēaḥ hāʿōlâ)* and for levitical sacrifice share the language of our passage: "altar" (e.g., Exod 27:1–8; 38:1–7), "clean animals" and "clean birds" (e.g., Lev 20:25), and "sacrificed burnt offerings" (e.g., Exod 24:5; 32:6; Lev 17:8; Deut 12:13–14). As already noted, the horned altar of the tabernacle was commonly described as "the altar of burnt offering,"[85] making Noah a prototype of Moses, who made sacrifice in the wilderness. Although Noah's altar is not described, the first audience would have assumed it conformed to the Mosaic

[82] According to some Jewish authorities, the altar was that of Adam, used by Cain and Abel (4:3–4) but later destroyed in the flood; it thus was rebuilt by Noah. It was also identified as the altar of Jerusalem, showing a linkage between the antediluvian fathers and Israel's worship (*Tg. Ps.-J.; Gen. Rab.* 34.9). In *Tg. Ps–J.* at Gen 22:9, Abraham is said to have rebuilt Noah's altar. The point is that worship of Yahweh was viewed as an organic unity.

[83] Calvin, *Comm.*, 281.

[84] Also 22:9; 26:25; 33:20; 35:1,3,7. There is no occasion where an altar was built in the Joseph cycle.

[85] E.g., Exod 30:28; 31:9; 35:16; 38:1; 40:6,10,29.

legislation requiring all temporary altars be constructed of "earth" or "unhewn stones" (e.g., Exod 20:24–26; Deut 27:5–6).

The sacrifice of "burnt offerings" *(ʿōlōt)* is specifically "clean animals" and "clean birds," foreshadowing the practice of later Israel. The "burnt offering" was a blood offering given in the Mosaic community as a voluntary offering for sin (Lev 1:4; 5:10; 9:7) and as an act of thanksgiving in worship, where it usually is joined with peace offerings.[86] It was the continual, daily offering presented each morning and evening in the tabernacle (Exod 29:38–42; Lev 6:8–13; Num 28:3–8). The "burnt offering" was totally consumed upon the altar with no part left for priest or offerer. "Burnt offering" usually occurs, as here, with the cognate verb "offered" (*haʿăleh;* "sacrifice"), which means "ascent," referring to the smoke and its scent rising toward heaven.[87] "Burnt offering" is found again in Genesis, where God tests Abraham's devotion by commanding him to offer up Isaac (22:2,3,6,7,8,13). Since this offering was wholly burned, it indicated the person's complete devotion to the Lord. Thus for the Mosaic community it would be viewed as the appropriate sacrifice for Noah, who presented it freely out of thanksgiving to God for sparing his life. "A spontaneous celebration, the result of salvation experienced, is just as much a part of the necessary life of worship as the permanent, regularly organized service."[88] Noah sacrificed "some of *all"* the clean animals, evidencing his overflowing gratefulness toward the Lord.

8:21 The favorable response of the Lord shows his pleasure at Noah's offering. Verse 21 echoes 6:5, where the Lord determined to destroy the earth as a result of human wickedness; now God resolves to spare the earth such further calamity. The mitigation of God's former policy is plain when read against his antediluvian charges (6:5–7). Both 6:5 and 8:21 have the words "inclination," "his heart," and "evil," but 6:5 has the inclusive "every," "only," and "all." In 6:5 the emphasis is on the unprecedented pervasiveness of sin, which deserved divine retribution, and in 8:21 God acknowledges that sin is a given with humanity and has ruled the human heart from the outset (i.e., Adam's sin).

The description "The LORD smelled the pleasing aroma" is typical in the Pentateuch for expressing God's favor toward sacrifice and worshiper (e.g., Exod 29:18; Lev 1:9; 3:16; Num 15:3).[89] Refusal to "smell" meant God's rejection of Israel's worship (Lev 26:31; cf. Amos 5:21). Noah's worship

---

[86] E.g., Lev 22:17–25; 23:18; Num 10:10; 15:1–11.

[87] See G. A. Anderson, "Sacrifice and Sacrificial Offerings (OT)," *ABD* 5.877–78.

[88] Westermann, *Genesis 1–11*, 453.

[89] In the *Gilgamesh* tale the flood hero offers sacrifice and libations after the flood, and the hungry gods, having been denied food during the deluge, smell the "sweet savor" and "crowded like flies around the sacrificer" (*ANET,* 95). The similarity is only superficial, for the biblical record consistently understands God's dealings with Noah as rooted in moral demands. Sarna observes that the absence of a libation by Noah shows that the offering did not feed a hungry deity (*Genesis,* 59).

soothed the broken "heart" (v. 21) of God, which had been injured by man's wickedness (6:6). "Pleasing aroma" *(rêaḥ hannîḥōaḥ)* is another sound allusion to the narrative's motif of "rest" *(nûaḥ)* and "Noah" (*nōaḥ;* cf. 5:29 discussion).[90] The translation "soothing aroma" (NASB, REB) best reflects the idea of "rest" or "appeasement."[91] Here we have the several sound plays on the name "Noah" brought together.[92] Through the "soothing" offering *(nîḥōaḥ),* God is brought to "rest" *(nûaḥ)* by "Noah" *(nōaḥ).* Thus by "Noah" *(nōaḥ)* the divine "grief/regret" *(nḥm)* over human creation (6:6) and his decision to "wipe out" *(mḥh;* 6:7) all humanity is transformed into his "compassion" *(nḥm)* for postdiluvian humanity.[93] As a result of Noah's offering, God determines in "his heart" ("within himself," REB) to stay any future curse and destruction. By this the author invites us to hear the inner thoughts of the Lord (cp. 1:26; 3:22; 11:7), whose former meditations had called for destruction (6:7). Although his promises are not declared to Noah, they find their promissory character explicitly in 9:1–17. In an allusion to the "waters of Noah" and the "mountains," Isaiah takes it as a divine oath that has a correspondence in God's loving commitment to the Hebrew exiles (Isa 54:9–10).

We have found that Noah's sacrifice was an offering of thanksgiving, but was it also a propitiation for sin? From the example of the patriarch Job, "burnt offering" was presented in earliest times as atonement for sin (1:5; cf. Lev 1:4). Noah's sacrifice too was an appeasement in behalf of all postdiluvian humanity as well as an offering of thanksgiving.[94] As Job mediated for his family, Noah was priest for the postdiluvian world. The role of Noah as the second Adam is coupled with the imagery of Moses, who mediates for the people of God (cf. Exod 32:32).[95] From the narrative it was Noah's offering for atonement that prompted God to declare his new intentions toward the sinful earth, despite human propensity toward sin. But this was not a persuasion elicited solely by ritual, for it is a constant in Genesis 1–11 that the LORD'S favor overcomes and supersedes human wickedness (cf. Rom 5:15,20–21). Moreover, Noah already had a faith relationship with God, for "he walked with God" (6:9; 7:1; 8:1a; cf. Heb 11:7), and it was also out of this devotion that his sacrifice pleased God.[96] Here we see God's grace at work in accepting Noah's sacrifice and establishing a new basis for the Lord's relationship with the world.

---

[90] Luther's etymological rendering "odor of rest" makes his point, "at that time God rested from wrath" (*LW* 2.116).

[91] BDB (629) has "soothing, tranquilizing odour," and KB (614) reads "smell of appeasement."

[92] These include וַיַּנִּחֵהוּ, "put" (2:15); יְנַחֲמֵנוּ, "comfort" (5:29); וַיִּנָּחֶם, "grieved" (6:6); נִחַמְתִּי, "grieved" (6:7); חֵן, "favor" (6:8); וַתָּנַח, "came to rest" (8:4); and מָנוֹחַ, "resting place" (8:9).

[93] See E. van Wolde, *Words Become Worlds: Semantic Studies in Genesis 1–11* (Leiden: Brill, 1994), 82–83.

[94] *Jub.* 6.1–2 has Noah offering atonement for the "guilt of the earth."

[95] So Wenham, *Genesis 1–15,* 189.

[96] So T. Fretheim, "Genesis," NIB (Nashville: Abingdon, 1994), 393.

The Lord makes two related vows: not to "curse the ground" (v. 21b) and not to "destroy" its inhabitants (v. 21c).[97] The divine reassurance "never again" (v. 21), repeated twice in this short pronouncement, is heard further in the formal covenant that follows (9:11,15), where the Lord has this same compassion for impotent humanity. There is, however, by this promissory intention no alleviation of the "curse" brought on by Adam's sin as some have thought.[98] There is no new age of blessing following an age of curse. The language of 8:21 is tied to 6:5b, not the Edenic curse in 3:17, showing that God's vow reflects on the punishment of the deluge.[99] The troubling aftermath of the Edenic curse with its toil and pain continues in the new world. Here God pledges only to desist from imposing any further affliction on the already-burdened ground. The flood is viewed as another curse upon the "ground/earth" that was the result of human disobedience as in the garden, where the earth suffered its first judgment (3:17–19). Yet it is because of Noah as mediating priest that the world experiences some "comfort" from the pain of the cursed ground (see discussion at 5:29; 9:20).

In the first vow "curse" *(qālēl)* is different from the common term used for "curse" *(ʾārar)*in Genesis and can mean to "despise" or "show contempt."[100] It is found for derision of parents (e.g., Exod 21:17) or blasphemies against God (e.g., Exod 22:28[27]). For this reason some translations have "doom," meaning "to mistreat or disparage."[101] In the basic verb stem *(qal)* the word has the

---

[97] The clauses are parallel:

לֹא־אֹסִף לְקַלֵּל עוֹד אֶת־הָאֲדָמָה

לֹא־אֹסִף עוֹד לְהַכּוֹת אֶת־כָּל־חַי

"I will not add to curse again the ground . . .

I will not add again to destroy all living creatures."

Note the inverted repetition (chiasmus) of infinitive and adverb that stitches the two promises together. Cassuto notes that the placement of עוֹד ("again") after the verb "curse" indicates "I will not curse any more," while its occurrence in the second clause before the verb "destroy" means "never again" (*Genesis,* 120). See Andersen, *The Sentence in Biblical Hebrew,* 113. The chiasmus is secondary and does not suspend the syntactical significance of their placement.

[98] R. Rendtorff argues that the curse in 3:17 is rescinded by God's promise in 8:21 ("Genesis 8,21 und die Ur-geschichte des Jahwisten," *KD* 7 [1961]: 69–78). Also, e.g., von Rad, *Genesis,* 122; Fretheim, "Genesis," 393.

[99] E.g., 8:21 has קַלֵּל ("curse") rather than אָרַר ("curse") as in 3:17. See the arguments by H. N. Wallace, "The Toledot of Adam," in *Studies in the Pentateuch,* VTSup 41, ed. J. A. Emerton (Leiden: Brill, 1990), 26–27; also Westermann, *Genesis 1–11,* 456.

[100] אָרַר occurs at 3:14,17; 4:11; 5:29; 9:25; 12:3; 27:29. Verbal קִלֵּל *(piel)* is found at 8:21 and 12:3 and nominal קְלָלָה at 27:12–13; קָלַל also appears in the *qal* stem at 8:8,11; 16:4–5 but with the meaning "light, trifle."

[101] E.g., E. A. Speiser, *Genesis,* AB (Garden City: Doubleday, 1964), 53; also NJPS, NAB; yet they translate מְקַלֶּל "curse" at 12:3. H. C. Brichto (*The Problem of "Curse" in the Hebrew Bible,* JBLM (=SBLMS) 13 [Philadelphia: SBL, 1963], 118–20, 176) shows that קִלֵּל is broad in meaning, "from verbal abuse to material injury," but does not have the force of verbal imprecation as found in אָלָה or אָרַר. The weakness of his study is in the four passages where imprecation seems certain (1 Sam 17:43; 2 Kgs 2:24; Deut 23:5; Josh 24:9), which he explains away as secondary accretions to the verse, not in the original text (pp. 172–76).

sense of “swift, slight, light,” as in Gen 8:8,11, where it means “abatement” of the floodwater. Hagar treats Sarah “lightly,” that is, with contempt (16:4–5). The word *ʾārar;* often occurring in the passive form “cursed,”[102] is used by an authority to achieve his demands.[103] While some suggest that “curse” in 8:21 is a softer term, we should not insist on too rigid a distinction since the terms appear in parallel at Exod 22:28[27].

Also the same word for “curse,” as found in 8:21, occurs in Genesis once more in the provision of God’s covenant blessing upon Abraham, where it is in parallel with the common term “whoever curses *[qallēl]* you I will curse *[ʾōrār]*” (12:3).[104] The verbs appear to have the same force, especially when we consider that this covenant is essentially repeated for Jacob with the sole use of *ʾārar:* “May those who curse you *[ʾōrĕrêka]*be cursed *[ʾārûr]*and those who bless you be blessed” (27:29). Whatever is the force of “curse” in our passage, we know from elsewhere that the term conveys the opposite of “blessing” (e.g., Ps 109:28). The noun “curse” *(qĕlālâ)* appears twice in the narrative of young Jacob, who expresses apprehension that his trickery might result in Isaac’s “curse” rather than favor (27:12–13). What Jacob fears is the consequence of a paternal curse, meaning his repudiation. In our passage “curse” is also a metonymy where the cause (“to curse”) is put for the effect (“to destroy”). This is borne out by the parallel verb “destroy” in 8:21b. By refraining from “curse,” God promises that he will not utter a malediction that will bring about destruction. Rather, his words will be reserved for blessing, namely, upon Noah’s descendant, Abraham.

What follows the vow is God’s commentary on the sinful state of the human condition, which acknowledges that there has been no change in the wicked predilections of postdiluvian people. How is it then that God pledged not to bring another disaster “because of man”?[105] There are two opposing ways to understand the passage, depending on how the following clause is explained. It has been translated as causal, “because *[kî]* their heart contrives evil from their infancy” (NJB; also NJPS, NAB). In this interpretation the *reason* God will not mount curse upon curse is the human disposition toward transgression. From this it might be taken that God deemed the flood a failure and conceded man’s condition as irrevocable.[106] This does not square, however, with 6:5, which explains that the wickedness of man was the propelling basis for God’s judgment in the first place. Better is reading the clause as concession “even though” or explanatory “for” (AV, NASB, NRSV), meaning that despite warrant for another judgment God will exercise clemency.[107]

---

[102] אָרוּר, e.g., 3:14,17; 4:11; 9:25; 27:29.

[103] So J. Scharbert, “ארר,” *TDOT* 1.405–18, esp. 412–15. E.g., consider the divine curse in Deut 27:16: “Cursed [אָרוּר] is the man who dishonors [מַקְלֶה] his father or his mother.”

[104] Gen 8:21 (infin.) and 12:3 (ptc.) have the *piel* form (קִלֵּל).

[105] The LXX explains, “because of the works of men.”

[106] So D. L. Petersen, “The Yahwist on the Flood,” *VT* 26 (1976): 438–46.

[107] The REB has “however evil their inclination may be from their youth upwards.”

Humanity is said to be evil from its infancy ("childhood"),[108] referring to humanity collectively or the individual person.[109] In the final analysis both are true. This does not mean that Adam and Eve were sinful at their creation, for all that God made was "good" (1:31). It was in Eden that mankind initiated its pilgrimage with sin, and since that time each person has been born already on that journey. The progressive character of collective human sin, following the rationale of 6:5–7, should require more punishment in the postdiluvian world, a "daily deluge" as Calvin put it,[110] but here the Lord commits to forgiveness as a new beginning. Later Israel also failed to abide by the covenant law, which resulted in its annulment and the penalty of exile. But by etching in the human heart the "new covenant," the Lord creates for himself an obedient people (Jer 31:31–34), which is accomplished by the transforming power of Christ Jesus (Eph 3:16–17).

God's second vow to postdiluvian humanity is his refusal to "destroy" the earth's inhabitants. "Destroy" *(nākâ),* also translated "strike down" (NJB, NAB), is not the same term uttered in the divine threats before the flood (6:7, *māḥâ;* 6:13,17, *šāḥat*). It is the common term for slaying a person or beast (e.g., 37:21), subjugating a people (e.g., 14:5), or bringing on plague (e.g., 19:11). It occurs once more in Genesis 1–11, also spoken by the Lord, when he promises to avenge any person who "kills" Cain (4:15). Both vows are sealed with a sign, Cain's "mark" and the Noahic "rainbow" (9:12–13).

8:22 Instead of destruction, the earth will be blessed with the regularity of predictable environmental patterns that are undergirded by the directive hand of God (v. 22). This promise is dependent upon the goodness of God and not the righteousness of humanity, for humanity will always languish in sin. The only condition established is temporal, "as long as the earth endures" (v. 22). The survivors of the flood had known storm and wind as their adversaries and had witnessed their power. By this promise, the Lord restored their confidence in a subdued world, subjected to the divine promise, where they could once again thrive. "However irregular the human heart may be (8:21b), there will be regularity in God's world and its cycles."[111] Our passage shows God's persistent allegiance to the earth and earth's inhabitants with the intent of blessing.

Verse 22 also echoes the language of creation: "as long as" (lit., "all the days of"; "day," 1:5ff.); "seed" ("seedtime," 1:11–12,29); "day" and "night" (1:5); and "cease/rest" (*šābat,* 2:2–3). The Lord in recreating the earth reestablishes its order and boundaries as at the beginning (1:14) and "as long as the

[108] מִנְּעֻרָיו indicates "youth" (e.g., 1 Sam 17:33; 1 Kgs 18:12; Jer 3:24; Zech 13:5) and "infancy" at Job 31:18.

[109] Speiser considers the phrase neutral, appealing to "youth" in Gen 46:34, where it appears to refer to both the individual and the ancestor (*Genesis,* 53).

[110] Calvin, *Comm.*, 284.

[111] Hamilton, *Genesis 1–17,* 310.

world exists" (GNB). This shows a permanency for the world, but it also infers that the present heavens and earth will someday cease. Countering those who scoffed at the anticipation of a coming Christ, Peter pointed to Noah's flood as evidence that God had already shown the will and capacity to bring about a worldwide cataclysm. The apostle forewarns there is yet a great conflagration that at the Lord's command will close the final chapter of Noah's new world (2 Pet 3:3–7). Ours is not a "world without end" (AV, Eph 3:21).

The NIV's rendering (as most English versions) arranges v. 22 in poetic stanza. The figure of merismus (opposites) dominates, indicating the inclusiveness of all seasons and times. The agrarian seasons, necessary for the sustenance of life, are represented by "seedtime and harvest." The fertility religions of the ancient Near East, with their dying and rising deities, attributed the seasons to the actions of the gods. Canaanite religion, for example, depicted the fruition of spring as the result of Baal's liberation from the underworld ruled by Mot (Death). Biblical religion explained that the seasonal cycle was the consequence of Yahweh's pronouncement and, moreover, evidence of a divine dominion that transcends the elements of the earth. There is no place for Mother-earth in biblical ideology. Earth owes *its* powers (not her powers!) to the divine command.

"Cold and heat" with "summer and winter" are chiastic and essentially parallel to the seasons of seed and harvest, which are marked by these changes in climatic conditions. "Day and night" is the concluding pair and show that they too are at the command of the Lord, who here guarantees their punctual arrival (cf. 1:3–5). Nature will not act capriciously but will be timely and predictable ("will never cease"), giving security to the world and its inhabitants. For Moses' audience this made the marshaling of such forces for Israel's exodus and sojourn all the more impressive, as the plague of darkness showed (Exod 10:21–23). More important for later Israel the seasons of plenty were tied to God's covenant blessing for a faithful people, but the opposite was true as well (e.g., Deut 27–28). Israel rightly expressed its homage to the Governor of the seasons through its annual ritual of firstfruits (e.g., Lev 23:9–14).

9. Covenant with the New World (9:1–17)

The fourth divine speech answers the description of the corrupt and violent creation before the flood (6:11–12). It consists of two divine utterances: (1) the renewal of promissory blessing with the inauguration of postdiluvian laws (9:1–7) and (2) the Noahic covenant and sign (9:8–17). "Increase" occurs in vv. 1 and 7, forming an inclusio and setting the literary boundaries of the blessing, which give focus to renewed procreation for human and animal. This blessing involves new dietary provisions, and within the passage are two prohibitions, each introduced by the same Hebrew term *ʾak* ("but," "surely"), pertaining to the eating and killing of animals (v. 4) and to the killing of human life by animal or human (vv. 5–6).

The "blessing" of procreation and dominion conferred upon the postdiluvian world is a restatement of God's creation promise for the human family and the creatures (1:22–25,28–30), but now its provisions are modified in light of encroaching societal wickedness. "Primarily, therefore, God's word to the new aeon is a word of divine return . . . divine forbearance (Rom 3:25)."[112] The Lord, however, must institute safeguards whereby human society in its new environment can persevere and prosper. Now that the Lord has insured that never again such devastation will occur on the earth, laws are established that will curb the violence among humanity that had brought about the necessity of the flood (6:11–12). Neither Adam nor Noah can preserve creation from sin, as both Adam's tree and Noah's vine show (3:6,17; 9:20–27).[113] Regulations insure the continuation of the earth until its final, future redemption.

Following the announcement of blessing is the formal declaration of God's covenant commitment to Noah and family as first promised before the floodwaters (9:8–17; 6:18). This promissory covenant has universal and eternal application that is marked by the universal "sign" of the "rainbow." "Establish" and "covenant" repeat in vv. 9 and 17 to fashion a second inclusio that accentuates the message of the pericope. Covenant takes center place in the narrative (vv. 9–11), and the "sign" of the Noahic agreement is explained theologically as a prompting to God's continued covenant loyalty (vv. 12–16).

The Noahic covenant's common allusions to 1:1–2:3 show that Noah is the second Adam who heads the new family of humanity, indicating that the blessing continues through the progeny of the Sethite line. Also 8:20–9:17 possesses lexical and thematic connections with the ratification of the Sinai covenant by Moses and the elders (Exod 24:4–18). Both have the building of altar and sacrifice followed by "covenant" (*bĕrît,* 9:9; Exod 24:7); divine "blessing" (*bārak,* 9:1; Exod 23:25); provision for protection from beasts (*ḥayyat*, 9:2; Exod 23:29); divine preservation of the "land" (*ʾereṣ*, 9:11; Exod 23:29); and the "cloud" for rainbow and the descent of the glory of God (*bĕʿānān,* 9:13–17; Exod 24:15).[114] If our author has joined Noah's covenant with that of Moses' Israel, we have another association of early Genesis with later Moses by which the author establishes the thematic linkage of God's

[112] von Rad, *Genesis,* 133.

[113] See T. Frymer-Kensky, "The *Atrahasis* Epic and Its Significance for Our Understanding of Genesis 1–9," *BA* 40 (1977): 147–55, and R. W. E. Forrest, "Paradise Lost Again: Violence and Obedience in the Flood Narrative," *JSOT* 62 (1994): 3–18.

[114] Discussed by J. Sailhamer ("Genesis," EBC [Grand Rapids: Zondervan, 1990], 93–94), who finds another tie between creation, Moses, and Noah through the repetition of the "ten words" in 1:1–31 ("And God said"), Moses' "Ten Words," and the tenfold "God/the LORD said" in the flood narrative (6:7a,13a; 7:1a; 8:15(2x),21a; 9:1a,8a,12a,17).

blessing—Adam (1:26–28; 5:1–2), Noah as the new Adam (9:1–2), and Moses' Israel. By this means the author shows how God achieved the universal blessing through Noah's descendant Abraham, who is the covenant progenitor of all Israel.

(1) Provisions for the New World (9:1–7)

[1]Then God blessed Noah and his sons, saying to them, "Be fruitful and increase in number and fill the earth. [2]The fear and dread of you will fall upon all the beasts of the earth and all the birds of the air, upon every creature that moves along the ground, and upon all the fish of the sea; they are given into your hands. [3]Everything that lives and moves will be food for you. Just as I gave you the green plants, I now give you everything.

[4]"But you must not eat meat that has its lifeblood still in it. [5]And for your lifeblood I will surely demand an accounting. I will demand an accounting from every animal. And from each man, too, I will demand an accounting for the life of his fellow man.

[6]"Whoever sheds the blood of man,
by man shall his blood be shed;
for in the image of God
has God made man.

[7]As for you, be fruitful and increase in number; multiply on the earth and increase upon it."

9:1 The blessing and its provisions for Noah antedate the Sinaitic covenant and thus are universal in scope, pertaining to all men and women in any era. Despite human sin and the corruption of the earth, God graciously presents anew to fallen humanity the same task of exercising dominion over the terrestrial world, primarily through procreation. This is the consequence of being "human" ("image of God"), and the sin of the garden did not erase the humanness of Adam's progeny. Children are the universal evidence of the Lord's creation "blessing," who are not to be disparaged nor exploited but celebrated by responsible parenting and societal protection. Dominion also involves accountability before God for the stewardship of the "good" earth. Though it is tainted by sin, it still possesses valued life in his eyes. Humanity is the recipient of this second chance, "even though they have spoiled it all once, and can spoil it again."[115] It is by this second human beginning that ultimately Abraham's promised offspring, Jesus Christ, will bring fallen creation under subjection and thereby its redemption (Rom 8:19–22; Heb 2:8–9).

The simple language of this verse, "Then God blessed *[bārak]* Noah," reaches back to the old world before the flood when all creation had received the first herald of blessing (1:22,28; 2:3; 5:2). Now it is reissued to the new

[115] D. Atkinson, *The Message of Genesis 1–11,* BST (Downers Grove: IVP, 1990), 155.

Adam and his offspring. Just as Adam fathered a righteous seed through Seth (5:3), Noah would likewise propagate a privileged lineage of blessing. As we have come to expect, much of what early Genesis portrays has its reflex in the life of the patriarchs. As here, the narrator declares the same state of blessing for Abraham (24:1), Isaac (25:11; 26:12; cp. 26:24), and Jacob (32:29[30]; 35:9). But also the assurance of blessing for the patriarchs (and others, such as Sarah, 17:16) is heard from the mouth of God himself (e.g., 12:2), the testimony of the recipients themselves (e.g., 48:3), or for that matter from an indirect beneficiary of the promise (such as Laban, 30:27).

The recipients of the renewed blessing, specifically stated to include Noah's "sons," underlines the corresponding term "descendants" ("seed") in the covenant that follows (v. 9). No longer can we view Noah apart from his sons. They, even more so than Noah, will provide the linkage between the antediluvian world and the new world. They become central to the progression of the book by the genealogical record of chap. 10 (cf. 5:32 with 9:18–19; 10:1,32), especially Shem, who heads the all-important genealogical table that ends with Terah's son "Abram" (11:10–26). The imperatives of procreation ("be fruitful, increase, fill"), which must be achieved for the realization of the blessing, are precisely those of 1:28a. But they are also the command of creation's blessing for the lower orders (1:22a). Hence the effects of sin and the flood had not altogether robbed the new world of the old hope.

9:2–3 Since 1:28 forms the background to the blessing (9:1), it is striking that the charge to "subdue" and "rule" (1:28b) is absent.[116] This admits that the new circumstances of the sin-burdened world have altered this aspect of the Adamic blessing, which now will be difficult to accomplish in the hostile environs of the new world. The language of "beasts," "birds," creeping "creature," and "fish" mirrors the first divine command as well as the original commissioning on dietary practices (vv. 2–3; 1:28–30).[117] The advent of human sin and the flood did not obviate the initial provision to domesticate and utilize the animal world for the advantage of man, but new concerns required proscriptions. Noah's world included killing, a feature of life that has become regrettably "old hat" to us, and this demanded safeguards. Reverence for life in general and the inviolability of human life in particular, coupled with the threat of divine retribution, would impede indiscriminate killing that otherwise would be routine.

To insure that animal life will not be a threat to the human family, the Lord endows the animal population with a "fear and dread" of human beings,

[116] The LXX has the secondary καὶ κατακυριεύσατε αὐτῆς ("and rule over it"), which is found in 1:28, rendering וְכִבְשֻׁהָ ("and subdue it").

[117] Some Greek texts have καὶ ἐπὶ πᾶσι τοῖς κτήνεσι ("and upon all creatures") after "all the beasts of the earth," thus including domesticated as well as wild animals. Although the reading probably is secondary, its interpretation reflects the inclusive character of the verse.

enabling mankind to exercise a limited authority over them. As noted by Calvin, "The providence of God is a secret bridle to restrain their violence."[118] This appears remarkably different from the relationship that the first man and woman enjoyed in the garden with their animal residents (2:19–20). This would also be true of Noah's animal companions on board the ark, where evidently there was a docile relationship. It is saying too much of the narrative to suppose that before the Noahic covenant there were no carnivorous animals. Rather, the Lord is formally announcing that this new enmity against humans cannot win out because the animal order is "given in your hands" (v. 2). This expression describes the divine provision of Israel's victory over its enemies (e.g., Exod 23:31) and the handing over of a murderer to the blood-avenger (Deut 19:12). God has now put the life and death of the animal under the power of the human arbiter.[119] As we learn from vv. 3–4, this refers to the killing of animals for food.

This "fear and dread of you" is heard again in the life of the patriarchs and later Israel. Our passage's "dread" *(ḥat)* is echoed in the Jacob narrative in the related noun *(ḥittâ),* where the "*terror* of God" impedes any opposition to the patriarch's return to Bethel from Haran (35:5). "Fear" was the response of the nations to the approaching Israelites, a fear engendered by God (Deut 2:25; 11:25). In contrast the Israelites are exhorted not to "fear" and "dread" their enemies (e.g., Deut 1:21). As God had created a safer haven for Noah's descendants, he softened the way for his appointed people to dispossess Israel's enemies.

Also God reissues the provision of food for both humanity and all the lower orders (v. 3), hearkening back to the "green plants" at creation that were food for human and animal alike, "everything that has the breath of life" (1:29–30). This allusion comes after the devastating destruction of all that had "the breath of life" (6:17; cp. 7:22), but the provision is graciously reinstituted for all its survivors. The inclusive character of the directive ("everything," occurring twice) includes meat as a dietary feature, as shown in v. 4. God did not expressly prohibit the eating of meat in the initial stipulation at creation, but by inference 9:3's provision for flesh is used as a dividing mark between the antediluvian and postdiluvian periods. Whether or not early man could eat meat by permission from the beginning, now it is stated formally in the Noahic covenant. Meat eating was an important part of the human diet in the new world, and specific instructions were required since such practice impinged on the question of human survival and the subservience of animal life. Moreover, for the Mosaic community such instructions had serious cultic implications (e.g., Lev 7:26–27; 17:10–14). The significance for the immediate narrative, however, was answering the question of what the taking of life, animal or human,

[118] Calvin, *Comm.,* 290.

[119] Westermann, *Genesis 1–11,* 462.

might mean. It was "not a license for human savagery."[120]

9:4 With the development of new dietary provisions, the concession of killing is mitigated by strict boundaries established by God for the taking of life. First, the strong adversative "but" *(ʾak)* introduces the prohibition against eating raw meat that still possessed the animal's "lifeblood" (v. 4). "You must not eat" is the same kind of direct prohibition found at 2:17 restricting the tree of knowledge. Ironically, it was the failure of the man and woman to observe the first prohibition that initiated the sad road of human degeneracy and made the Noahic stipulations necessary. The same law formula is found in the Ten Commandments, as "You shall not murder" (Exod 20:13). Restricting the "lifeblood" meant forbidding the eating of an animal while yet alive and, what logically follows, draining the blood from a slain animal as later required in the Mosaic proscription (e.g., Deut 12:24).

This restriction was not a matter of decorum but a recognition that the blood was representative of the life force. In Hebrew "blood" is in apposition to "life," which the NIV has rendered "lifeblood."[121] This is the stated basis for the cultic prohibition of eating blood in later Israel: "For the life of every creature is its blood" (Lev 17:11a). The rationale for sacrificial atonement was the substitution of the animal's life, represented by the shed blood, in place of the offerer's life, who thereby averted divine reparations (Lev 17:11b). Thus as indicative of life, "blood" required special treatment in the Mosaic tradition (e.g., Lev 7:27; 17:10–14; Deut 12:23–24; cp. Acts 15:29). Animal life, though given to humanity for sustenance, remained valuable in the eyes of God as a living creature and therefore merited proper care, not wanton abuse. This privilege of killing animals for food assumed the responsibility of caring for animal life as it was first formulated in Eden (cf. 2:15). Disregard for the gift of life was an affront to the Giver of that life, for life was deemed "good" as a creation edict. For benevolent reasons animal as well as human in later Israel enjoyed the sabbath rest for refreshment (Exod 20:10; 23:12; Deut 5:14). At the tabernacle the sacrificial animal was regarded by God and was costly to the offerer, testimony to the enormity of human sin.

9:5 Verse 5's beginning repetition of *ʾak* (NIV's "surely") parallels v. 4 and marks another divine directive—this time regarding human life. As reflected in the NIV's rendering, "your lifeblood" heads the Hebrew clause, tying it to the previous prohibition regarding the value of life ("blood") whether animal or human. Human life must be treated with special caution, however, because it is of singular value as life created in the "image of God" (v. 6). Whereas the former prohibition concerning meat eating did not state a

---

[120] Sarna, *Genesis,* 60.

[121] The REB has, "But you must never eat flesh with its life still in it, that is the blood" (also NRSV).

specific sanction against the offender (v. 4), here we have a wordy (and somewhat cumbersome) sanction drawing attention to itself, stressing the grave consequences for taking human "lifeblood" (rendered literally):

5a And indeed for your lifeblood I will demand an accounting *(dāraš)*;
5b From the hand of every animal I will demand an accounting *(dāraš)*,
5c And from the hand of "man" *[ʾādām]*,
From the hand of each person *[ʾîš]* his brother,
I will demand an accounting *[dāraš]*for human *[ʾādām]* life.

Human death requires an "accounting" *(dāraš)*, an admission Reuben will make for his brother Joseph, presumed dead (42:22). "Accounting" occurs three times in the verse: first it designates the general principle (v. 5a) and then specifies that animal and fellow human both are under divine sanction (v. 5b–c). Hebrew *dāraš* in this construction indicates an exacting or calculation and is found in the sense of vengeance (e.g., Deut 18:19; cp. REB's "satisfaction").[122] It is the accounting, for example, required of a shepherd for the owner's sheep (Ezek 34:10). The general rule is that human life when violated, either by animal or fellow human, required the life of the offender. Exemplary of this in later Israel is the requirement of death by stoning for both ox and owner as responsible agents in the case where an ox's goring results in a person's death (Exod 21:28–32). Israelite tradition deemed monetary compensation as an unacceptable penalty where malicious murder was involved (e.g., Lev 24:17; Num 35:31–34).[123]

Our verse emphasizes God's place as plaintiff against the culprit—"*I* will demand" (3x). First and foremost, the taking of human life is offense against God; the "accounting" is a divine initiative and requirement (cp. Exod 23:7). As v. 6 implies, killing a person who is made in the "image of God" is a blow against God himself. Verse 6 shows that the burden of carrying out recompense is on society ("by man"), but the offense itself is not against the murdered, nor his family, nor society at large (obviously it impacts them as well). Jewish tradition ascribed to the final judgment divine recompense against any who escaped societal adjudication (e.g., *Tg. Ps.-J.; Gen. Rab.* 34.14). The basis of the prohibition against taking human life is rooted in the transcendent value of human life conferred at creation. Twice our Hebrew verse says that God will exact recompense from "the hand of man"; the first occurrence is generic "mankind" *[ʾādām]* versus the animal, and second is the individual person, "each *[ʾîš]* his brother." There is no exemption regardless of the victim's status (slave or free) or the culprit's; each offender will pay.[124] Israel's covenant law

[122] Usually followed by the preposition מִן.

[123] An obvious exclusion is involuntary homicide; in such cases a "ransom," if accepted by the injured family, was permitted for the manslayer to save his life (e.g., Exod 21:30; Num 35:22–25).

[124] The NJPS has the more literal translation: "I will require it of every beast; of man, too, will I require a reckoning for human life, of every man for that of his fellow man!"

prohibited a double standard for Hebrew and alien in the administering of justice (Lev 24:22). With respect to human life, whether criminal or victim, God is no respecter of persons.

Obscured by the modern rendering "fellow man" (e.g., NIV) is the Hebrew idiom "his brother," which possesses a double entendre. Here it echoes the first human murder, the fratricide of Cain and Abel, "his brother" (4:2,8). "Am I my *brother's* keeper?" argues Cain (4:9). Our passage answers explicitly yes. Moreover, there are other allusions in our passage to that early fratricide, such as Abel's "*blood* which cries out" (4:10) and Cain's concern that "whoever will find me will kill me" (4:14). The popular notion that retributive justice is canonized in the Noahic covenant may be true, but it is only a reflection of antecedent practice as indicated by the fearful Cain and the boastful Lamech (cf. 4:14–15; 4:24). As we noted at chap. 4, murder is fratricide by virtue of the inherent covenant all people have with God as created in his "image." We are to that fundamental degree all brothers and sisters in that we are all human.

9:6 The poetic stanza (quatrain) of v. 6 has the first two lines arranged so that the emphasis is on "man" as both victim and avenging agency. The NIV has successfully retained this feature and thereby shows the intentional correspondence between the act and the punishment. The severity of the punishment is required because of the heinous nature of the crime. This long-standing principle of jurisprudence, known as *lex talionis* (i.e., "an eye for an eye"), insures that the punishment is commensurate with the weight of the crime. "Shedding blood" is used of premeditated murder (e.g., 37:22; 1 Kgs 2:31; Ezek 22:4) and also killing in battle (1 Chr 28:3). Here it refers to the former and shows that the Ten Words of the Mosaic covenant were not innovative but reflective of existing moral belief (e.g., Exod 20:13).

How we are to read the prepositional phrase *bāʾādām* ("by man") speaks to whether our passage approves the practice of capital punishment.[125] Is God the avenger, as we find in v. 5, or is vengeance the function of human institutions? Most English versions have "by man," indicating that humanity itself is the instrument of God's recompense against the criminal.[126] The preposition can be taken (though less commonly) as substitution: "*for* man shall his blood be shed" (cf. REB; cp. "a tooth *for* a tooth," Deut 19:21). Thus the criminal's life is substituted as compensation for the victim's life. In the former case the passage's intent is to establish the means for dealing with the murderer, whereas in the latter reading the passage is underscoring the price the murderer must

[125] *Tgs. Onq.* and *Ps.-J.* add "before witnesses," assuming a judicial setting as found in Num 35:30; Deut 17:6–7; 19:15.

[126] Also *IBHS* § 11.2.5d.

render for his sordid deed.[127] Since the value of the victim's life already is presented in v. 5, v. 6a is best taken as building on this by adding that the divine means of God's "accounting" includes human agency.[128] The appointed instrument is society's enforcement agency, a restraint on threatening behavior. No details here are given, but for later Israel restrictive prescriptions govern how society, especially the "blood avenger" in the case of a family member's death, responds to homicide (e.g., Exod 21:12–14; Deut 19; Num 35). Exacting retribution is not a personal matter but a societal obligation. In Paul's Roman correspondence he acknowledges the effectiveness and legitimacy of civil retribution for crime but decries personal vengeance (cf. 12:19; 13:1–5).

The last two lines (v. 6b) explain ("for") why execution is the appropriate measure against the malefactor. The language appropriated for this is "creation language" derived from 1:26–28 (e.g., "God," "image," and "made"), which gives another explicit linkage between the first Adam, that is the old order, and the new world of Noah. Justification for penal execution is the value of the victim, the "image of God." God alone may make or dispose of a person as he sees fit (cf. Deut 32:35 with Rom 12:19; Job 1:21). This we saw in the case of Cain, whose life is spared by the "mark" because the Lord reserves for himself the authority to avenge the violation. To take human life unlawfully therefore is to usurp God's sovereignty over life and death. But without the possibility of divine purging by flood, societal conditions jeopardizing human life would escalate to intolerable proportions. For just reprisal God delegates the authority to carry out his vengeance ("by man"). As we noted earlier with regard to Israel's practice, even then only great care can be given to executing God's vengeance. In accordance with the principle of *lex talionis,* Israelite law recognizes, as did ancient law in general, that particular circumstances, such as involuntary manslaughter (Exod 21:20–21; Deut 19; Num 35), mitigate the consequences of lesser degrees of homicide.

Mosaic law emulated this Noahic provision by protecting human life: "You shall not murder" (Exod 20:13). Hebrew *rāṣaḥ* ("murder") is commonly used for premeditated killing, and death by execution is prescribed for those who transgress this prohibition (e.g., Exod 21:12–14; Num 35:16–32). This high premium placed on human life is indicated elsewhere in the Torah. We have already mentioned that animals who kill men are executed in the same way as the human murderer is punished—by stoning (Exod 21:28–32). The value of human life is extended even to the unborn child, who in the case of injury mer-

[127] This may be the interpretation in the LXX: ἀντὶ τοῦ αἵματος αὐτοῦ ἐκχυθήσεται ("for his blood, it [i.e., blood of the murderer] will be shed"). See J. Lust, "'For Man Shall His Blood Be Shed' Gen 9:6 in Hebrew and in Greek," in *Tradition of the Text: Studies Offered to Dominique Barthélemy in Celebration of His Seventieth Birthday,* OBO 109, ed. G. Norton and S. Pisano (Göttingen: Vandenhoeck & Ruprecht, 1991), 91–102.

[128] Otherwise vv. 5–6 exhibit a "tautology" (Hamilton, *Genesis 1–17,* 315).

its reparations (Exod 21:22–25).[129]

After establishing the inviolability of human life, how can the divine directive at the same time exact killing the criminal who also is the divine "image"? Capital punishment is not interpreted as a threat to the value of human life but rather is society's expression of God's wrath upon anyone who would profane the sanctity of human life. New Testament writings interpreted capital punishment as a necessary function of society, where the state is defined as the divinely designated "servant" *(diakonos)* that administers retribution (Rom 13:1–5; 1 Pet 2:13–14). Genesis removed personal vengeance and restricted blood feuding that led to reckless killing. In our contemporary judicial system this is expressed by the prosecutor who represents the "people" of the State, not the victim per se. Mosaic law limited the excesses of personal and family vengeance as attested in the ancient Near East by the imposition of *lex talionis* (Lev 24:17–21) and the restrictions placed upon the "blood-avenger." In the case of murder the elders of the city where the offense occurred adjudicated the case and only then gave up the convicted criminal to the "blood-avenger."

9:7 After establishing the stipulations regarding animal and human life, the exhortation to Noah and his sons, "be fruitful and increase," is repeated (vv. 1,7).[130] Here it serves as an inclusio with v. 1, closing this unit.[131] Society can thrive, and the blessing of procreation can be achieved but only if human life is protected from the kind of unbridled wickedness that pervaded society in the days of the Nephilim (6:4). In contrast to the murderer who terminates life (vv. 5–6), Noah's family is commissioned to propagate and celebrate life. The plural "As for *you*" showcases Noah's sons because they will

---

[129] Our point here is that life, even in the womb of the mother, has value and merits covenant protection. This passage has been swept up in the abortion debate and as a result has been marshaled by both sides to show biblical justification for their position. It is unfortunate since the passage concerns accidental injury rather than deliberate abortion. Even if one were to conclude that the fetus has only relative value to the life of the mother, on the grounds that the recompense for the fetus is monetary (not "life for life"), it would be gratuitous to conclude on the basis of this incident that Israelite law did not recognize the fetus as alive. The preceding case (Exod 21:20–21), concerning a slave beaten by his owner, did not require *lex talionis* for his injuries, and one cannot conclude that the absence of the *talionic* formula meant that the slave was not alive or not a person (see this argument by B. K. Waltke, "Reflections from the Old Testament on Abortion," *JETS* 19 [1976]: 3–13, esp. note 3). See also J. W. Cottrell, "Abortion and the Mosaic Law, *Christianity Today* 17 (1972–73): 602–5, and M. Kline, "*Lex Talionis* and the Human Fetus," *JETS* 20 (1977): 193–201.

[130] The MT has v. 7 as part of the poetic stanza begun in v. 6 (as NASB, NJB). The NIV has rightly rendered it as prose and distinguished it from the quatrain of v. 6 (also NRSV, REB, NAB, NJPS). The verse is prose, reflecting the language and structure of 9:1.

[131] The repetition of רְבוּ ("increase") at the end of the verse has been emended by some (BHS) to רְדוּ ("rule") in conformity with 1:28, but the verb pattern with its repetition of "increase" is closer to that found in 1:22. For a defense of the MT, see B. Porten and U. Rappaport, "Poetic Structure in Genesis IX 7," *VT* 21 (1971): 363–69.

realize God's blessing in the earth by fathering the nations (v. 9b), as achieved in the subsequent Table of Nations (10:1–32). The GNB shows the sense, "You must have many children, so that your descendants will live all over the earth."

"Multiply" *(širṣû),* also rendered "teem" (NJB) or "abound" (NAB, NJPS, NRSV), occurs only here in Genesis for human, whereas elsewhere it describes the procreation of water and land creatures (1:20–21; 7:21; 8:17). It also refers to human population in the Exodus narrative when Israel "multiplied *[yišrēṣû]* greatly" in Egypt (Exod 1:7). Our verse brings together the dual recipients of God's creation blessings, both the lower orders and the human family. The new world has the same commission as the first, and it resonates the divine benediction at the start for the "good" earth. This blessing is tied to later Israel in Exod 1:7 by the rehearsal of creation's vocabulary; four of its five verbs are derived from the command to animal (1:22; 8:17) and human (1:28; 9:1) to proliferate. Moses' Israel thrived under God's creation blessing as the recipient of the divine promises for humanity (1:28) and the new humanity in Noah and his "seed" (cf. 9:9).

(2) Covenant and Sign (9:8–17)

8Then God said to Noah and to his sons with him: 9"I now establish my cove-
nant with you and with your descendants after you 10and with every living crea-
ture that was with you—the birds, the livestock and all the wild animals, all those that came out of the ark with you—every living creature on earth. 11I establish
my covenant with you: Never again will all life be cut off by the waters of a flood; never again will there be a flood to destroy the earth."

12And God said, "This is the sign of the covenant I am making between me and you and every living creature with you, a covenant for all generations to
come: 13I have set my rainbow in the clouds, and it will be the sign of the cove-
nant between me and the earth. 14Whenever I bring clouds over the earth and the
rainbow appears in the clouds, 15I will remember my covenant between me and you and all living creatures of every kind. Never again will the waters become a
flood to destroy all life. 16Whenever the rainbow appears in the clouds, I will see it and remember the everlasting covenant between God and all living creatures of every kind on the earth."

17So God said to Noah, "This is the sign of the covenant I have established between me and all life on the earth."

The narrative recounts three divine speeches in which the covenant is formally instituted and the "sign," marking the event, is adopted. The announcement is found in vv. 8–11, followed by the sign (vv. 12–16), and then a précis concludes (v. 17). The repetition of the terms "establish" (*qûm,* vv. 9,11,17) and "covenant" (*bĕrît,* vv. 9,11–17) marks off the unit (an inclusio) and binds the three speeches.[132] Particularly instructive are the variant tenses for the verb "establish," showing the divine initiative and realization of the covenant: "I now establish" (imminent future, v. 9); "I establish" (present, v. 11); and "I have established" (present perfect, v. 17).[133] God initiates, sustains, and completes the covenant (cp. Heb 12:2). Although the "sign" was primarily for God (vv. 15–16), it was also reassurance to the earth's families that they would not again experience the horrors of a devastating flood. Luther comments: "We, too, need this comfort today, in order that despite a great variety of stormy weather we may have no doubt that the sluice gates of the heavens and the fountains of the deep have been closed by the Word of God."[134] The sign of the "rainbow" should elicit in us both awe and thanksgiving, considering the "kindness and sternness of God" (Rom 11:22).

9:8–11 Verses 8–11 formally state the promissory covenant of 6:18, where God promised Noah and the ark's inhabitants safety from the deluge. Much of the language reflects this earlier anticipation of God's covenant with the flood's survivors. "I establish my covenant" in v. 11 (cp. vv. 9,17) is the same Hebrew at 6:18 ("I will establish my covenant"). In the first case it is for those who "enter the ark" (6:18), whereas here it is addressed to the party that "comes out of the ark" (v. 10). Specific family relationships are cited in 6:18, but in our passage it is enough to say "you" (pl., vv. 9,11) and "your descendants after you" (v. 9). Similar "creature language" in 6:19–20, "bird" and "animal" ("livestock"), occurs in 9:10. The same inclusive language of man and animal is found: "all life" will perish in 6:17, but now "all life" is protected under the provisions of the covenant (v. 11; also v. 17). Our passage in v. 11, with its twice-repeated "never again," echoes the divine promise issued after Noah's disembarkation and offering (8:21–22).[135] Moreover, he promises not to "destroy" the earth ever again, the same term "destroy" as he had forewarned in 6:17. Our passage then is a clarification and amplification of the covenant anticipated before.

God's declaration is emphatic in the Hebrew construction: "Now I—behold—I am establishing my covenant" (v. 9). The covenant obligation rests with the Lord alone, who has determined not to devastate repeatedly the earth's inhabitants ("all life") with floodwaters, despite man's continued sinfulness (cf. 8:21). Both the covenant and its sign have their origins in the Lord: they are "my covenant" (6:18; 9:9,11,15) and "my bow" (9:13). Gathering storm clouds, lightning bolts, and torrents of driven rainwaters no longer meant imminent disaster for the earth. The Lord's commitment to the new world is

[132] בְּרִית ("covenant") appears seven times in the passage (9:9,11,12,13,15,16,17; also 6:18).

[133] מֵקִים (*hiphil* participle, v. 9); וַהֲקִמֹתִי (perfect with *waw* consecutive, v. 11); הֲקִמֹתִי (perfect) (v. 17). Observed by Hamilton, *Genesis 1–17,* 319.

[134] *LW* 2.146.

[135] Also v. 15; in each instance the Heb. has וְלֹא . . . עוֹד.

irreversible: twice he promises never again to "cut off" and "destroy" the earth with waters (v. 11; cf. 6:17). "Cut off" occurs once more in Genesis, where it describes excommunication for anyone who refuses to enter Abraham's covenant by circumcision. Noah's covenant is continually presented as universal and inclusive, involving all the animal life that emerged from the ark "with you" (pl.; v. 10). "Every living creature" appears both at the beginning and end of v. 10, producing an inclusio and thus emphasizing at the start the promise's comprehensiveness. Verse 11 has the language of covenant making (or confirming) found in the Pentateuch (see 6:18 discussion). "I establish my covenant" occurs first in 6:18 but again in the making of the Abrahamic covenant (17:7,19) and the Mosaic covenant at Sinai in Exod 6:4.[136] Our author has fashioned these covenants with the same language so as to show how they are interrelated. God, who commits to all humanity (and animals) in the time of Noah, will achieve the blessing through the narrow particulars of patriarchal promise and the creation of Israel.

9:12 The eternal nature of the covenant promise is stressed in the second speech (vv. 12–16), where the giving of the "sign" guarantees the parties of its perpetual validity. This is the first occasion in the Bible where "sign" *(ʾôt)* appears as "covenant sign" (*ʾôt bĕrît;* cf. 1:14; 4:15). It bears a familiar pattern in the Hebrew tradition, most notably circumcision and Sabbath as covenant signs (cf. Gen 17:11; Exod 31:16–17). As a "sign" the bow functioned as a visible token of God's invisible word of grace. "Stretched between heaven and earth, it is a bond of peace between both, and, spanning the horizon, it points to the all-embracing universality of the Divine mercy."[137] The sign of the heavenly bow is seen in the "clouds," which is language commonly associated with the Lord's majestic presence and self-revelation (theophany).[138] Outside Genesis 9 "rainbow" is noted but once more in the Old Testament, where Ezekiel sees the radiant glory of God as the brightness of the rainbow (Ezek 1:28). Similarly, John's vision of the "one seated on the throne" entailed a rainbow of emerald adorning the throne (Rev 4:3; cf. 10:1). Thus the appearance of the rainbow, while principally a reminder to God of his promises (v. 15), is also a testimony to the presence of the Lord, who has revealed himself through both destruction and preservation of all that has life on the earth.

Three things are said of "sign" and "covenant" in v. 12. First, the "sign" is attached to the "covenant" promise; its purpose is to confirm "ritually" what has been committed by word. Second, this is the Lord's doing, "I am making." Third, the "sign" marks a universal covenant "between me and you [pl.]" and for "every living creature with you [pl.]." Whereas the patriarchal promise has

---

[136] Cp. also the similar construction at 9:17.

[137] Delitzsch, *A New Commentary on Genesis,* 290.

[138] E.g., Exod 19:9; Deut 31:15; 1 Kgs 8:10–11; Ps 99:7.

the same language, "between me and you and your descendants after you" (17:7), it does not have the universal feature. Repeatedly we find this rhetoric in the pericope:

"Every living creature" *(kol nepeš haḥayyâ,* v. 10a)
"Every living creature" *(kol haḥayyâ,* v. 10b)
"All life" *(kol bāśār,* v. 11b)
"Every living creature" *(kol nepeš haḥayyâ,* v. 12b)
"All living creatures of every kind" *(kol nepeš ḥayyâ bĕkol bāśār,* v. 15a)
"All life" *(kol bāśār,* v. 15b)
"All living creatures of every kind" *(kol nepeš ḥayyâ bĕkol bāśār,* v. 16b)
"All life" *(kol bāśār,* v. 17b)

"Between" is also accentuated in the divine speech (vv. 12–13,15–17) and is itself ironic, pointing up the absence of any response from the recipients—no assent, no action, no ratification. Any attempt to read the foregoing demands (9:5–7) as covenant obligations has failed to understand how 9:1–7 is a restatement of creation promise (1:26–31) and that 9:8–17 is a new word. To what degree then is this covenant really "between" God and the families of the earth? The recurring word "between" underscores the unilateral character of this covenant as divine self-obligation and hence declaration.[139]

The "sign" affects "all generations to come *[dōrōt ʿôlām]*." In v. 16 the covenant is identified as "the everlasting covenant *[bĕrît ʿôlām]*." All peoples of every era, including our own, enjoy the benefits of God's good grace. While the Abrahamic covenant was not inclusive, limited to the offspring of the patriarchal family, it too was an "everlasting covenant *[bĕrît ʿôlām]*" for all the patriarch's generations (13:15; 17:7,13,19), and it entailed the "eternal" possession of land (17:8; 48:4). The Lord also entered a "perpetual covenant" with Moses' Israel, observed by "sabbath" as pledge for all generations (Exod 31:16; cf. Lev 24:8), the priesthood of Aaron's Phineas (Num 25:13; cf. Exod 40:15; Num 18:19), David's royal dynasty (2 Sam 23:5; cf. 2 Sam 7:13–16, 24–26), and a restored, redeemed Israel (Jer 32:40). For the Christian these ancient benefits are ultimately realized through Christ "by the blood of the eternal covenant" (Heb 13:20; cf. 9:15).

9:13 "My bow" is positioned prominently in the Hebrew sentence since this is the primary subject of the speech (vv. 12–16). It occurs three times in the passage and always in connection with the thrice-repeated "clouds" (vv. 13,14,16).[140] The brightly colored bow, as viewed from the earth, dispels the ominous darkness of the storm clouds. The covenant is between the Lord and "earth," which God had sworn to destroy (6:13,17) but now has pledged never again (9:11), fixing the "rainbow" as testimony to his promise. The NIV's

[139] See Westermann, *Genesis 1–11,* 473.
[140] Noted by Cassuto, *Genesis,* 134.

"rainbow" is simply "bow" *(qešet),* which is the term for the bow used in war and hunting.[141] It may also refer anthropomorphically to the Lord, who defeats his foes with weaponry, including flashes of lightning bolts as arrows flung by his bow.[142] Ancient mythology frequently has such imagery where a deity employs the bow and arrows of the skies (i.e., lightning bolts).[143] The Lord in Hebrew tradition is depicted as a Divine Warrior who subjugates his foes (e.g., Exod 15:3; Isa 42:13; Zeph 3:17). Some commentators interpret the celestial bow as a symbol for peace, indicating the cessation of divine hostilities against the earth.[144] There is no reason to speculate beyond what the covenant declaration tells us of its purpose—not a symbol for victory but a reminder for God to honor his promise (v. 15).[145] We have no obligation to conclude that the "rainbow" was unknown before, even as circumcision was not unique to Abraham nor was Sabbath to Israel before its designation as the covenant sign (cf. Exod 16:23–29). Rather, the rainbow was newly appropriated and accorded special significance by the Lord for future generations.[146]

9:14–16 What follows elaborates on the function of the "sign," explaining how it secures the covenant and tying it to the specifics of the covenant itself. A "sign" points to something beyond itself and therefore requires interpretation, which we find here. Its importance lies in what it communicates and evokes, not the wonder itself.[147] Verse 14 connects the sign's appearance with the forbidding clouds brought about by the Lord. With the coming of the storm clouds, the bow would prompt his assent to the vow. "Remember" (*zākar*) is the language of covenant promise, as God "remembered" his oath to Abraham in behalf of Lot (19:29) and his promise for Israel (e.g., Exod 6:5; Ps 106:45; cf. Mal 3:16). Here it recalls the turning point of the flood narrative, "God remembered *[zākar]*Noah" (8:1a). Thus the assurance of future security for the earth's families has its root in the character of God himself and the precedent

---

[141] E.g., Gen 27:3; 48:22; 49:24; 1 Sam 31:3. "My bow" in 9:13–16 is the usual English rendering (e.g., AV, NASB, NJPS, NAB, NJB, REB, NRSV).

[142] E.g., Hab 3:9–11; Ps 7:12[13]; Lam 2:4; 3:12; cf. Deut 32:23,42. Also in later Jewish tradition, e.g., *Wis* 5:21, *4 Esd* 16:13.

[143] E.g., in *Enuma Elish,* Marduk's victorious bow defeating Tiamat is placed in the sky *(ANET,* 69).

[144] E.g., Skinner, *Genesis,* 173; von Rad, *Genesis,* 134; Sarna, *Genesis,* 63. As early as rabbinic discussion, the sign was thought by some to be the war bow.

[145] G. E. Mendenhall ties the bow of Gen 9 to the iconography of the ancient Near East, where the undrawn bow of a victorious king symbolized peace by subjugation. But for Gen 9 Mendenhall observes that the bow motif is not God's victory over the vanquished earth but God's commitment to his enemies never to bring another such display of powerful destruction (*The Tenth Generation: The Origins of the Biblical Tradition* [Baltimore: Johns Hopkins University, 1973]: 44–48).

[146] This is a long-disputed issue; the Reformers, e.g., differed here, Luther holding to the rainbow as a "new creature" (*LW* 2.149) and Calvin contending that a new "mark was engraven" upon the existing arc (*Comm.,* 299).

[147] F. J. Helfmeyer, "אוֹת (*ʾōth*)," *TDOT* 1.170–71.

of Noah's salvation. The Passover event for later Israel was also marked by a "sign," the smearing of blood above the doorposts of the Hebrew homes (Exod 12:13). For both Noah and the Hebrews, God "saw" the "sign," which averted disaster and resulted in his salvific favor.

Verse 15 rehearses all that has gone before of the promissory prohibition, once more reversing the language of the antediluvian threat to "destroy all life" (cf. 6:17). Verse 16, concluding this speech, is highly repetitive of the former verses, though not stereotyped. Here God as speaker refers to himself in the third person, "between God *[Elohim]* and all living creatures," thus indicating a formal declaration of his unilateral obligation. The promise as "everlasting" (cf. 8:22) reinforces the unconditional and certain commitment of God. The recurring covenant terminology of "remember" is sprinkled throughout the narrative to describe God's fidelity. The NJB's rendering, "I will call to mind," captures the anthropomorphic intention of the language.

9:17 In a recapitulation of the foregoing, God concludes the formal establishment of the agreement. The elements of the prior statements are gathered here: "sign of the covenant," as evidence of God's abiding promise; "I have established," echoing the divine initiation and now completion of the covenant; and "all flesh," showing the inclusive character of the agreement.

10. Noah's Sons and Future Blessing (9:18–29)

The final section of the flood *tōlĕdōt* (6:9–9:29) concerns the sons of Noah with respect to their populating the earth. The Noahic blessing is realized through human procreation and its subjugation of the earth (9:1; 1:28). With the covenant in place (9:8–17) the focus turns properly toward what will become of the survivors of the flood and their progeny. Do the postdiluvian successors fare better? The answer is soon found in the deflating debacle of Noah's drunkenness, but even there we will discover afresh how God will transform that sordid incident into a hope for future generations by the preeminence given to Shem, who fathers the Abrahamic ancestry (11:10–26). Transition verses at 9:18–19 open the section and bridge the covenant narrative (9:8–17) and the subsequent story, ending in patriarchal curse and blessing for the sons (9:20–27). This prepares the reader for the Table of Nations, where the offspring of each son is presented in detail. The shadow of Noah's drunken affair, which precipitated the invocation of blessing and curse, appears to shape the future relations of the nations that are reflected in the extensive genealogies that follow. Even before the onset of future generations, however, the narrative shows that the sons have stumbled (i.e., Ham). The reality of sin's "curse" is heard again, but this time on the lips of the patriarch rather than God, jeopardizing the promissory blessing and dividing the human family as in the antediluvian days of Cain and Abel (4:11). On the heels of this is the concluding note of Noah's death (9:28–29), which brings to an end the Sethite genealogy begun in 5:1 and suspended at 5:29 by the intervening account of the flood.

(1) Sons of Noah (9:18–19)

[18]The sons of Noah who came out of the ark were Shem, Ham and Japheth. (Ham was the father of Canaan.) [19]These were the three sons of Noah, and from them came the people who were scattered over the earth.

9:18–19 These two verses subtly shift the narrative's eye from Noah to the sons and their role in the future progression of God's blessing for humanity. Verses 18–19 bring to an end the flood account and prepare the way for the Table of Nations that will dominate the remainder of the universal history. Verses 18–19 could function as an introduction at 10:1, but it is not redundant by virtue of the allusion to the "ark" and their anticipation of Noah's curse against Ham-Canaan. The naming of the sons in the stock formula "Shem, Ham and Japheth" occurs five times in proximity.[148] Repeating the names of the sons backtracks to 7:13, which speaks of them by name entering the "ark" with their wives, and also looks ahead to chaps. 10–11, which recall how their descendants (nations) are "scattered over the earth" (9:19).[149] Noah's sons, either listed by name or simply as "sons," are a constant feature of the narrative.[150] In this concluding element of the flood account, it is appropriate that they should occupy the reader's attention once more because the focus of the salvific act as well as the covenant has been ultimately toward future generations.

Of the sons, only Ham's filial successor is given in the passage (vv. 18,22). He is the "father of Canaan" who becomes the object of the patriarch's curse (v. 25) and is of special interest to the compiler of the Table of Nations (10:6,15). The importance of this connection for the patriarchal stories and Moses' Israel cannot be overstated. The expression "land of Canaan" dominates the patriarchal accounts (35x), beginning with Terah's sojourn (11:31) and concluding with the anticipated burial of Joseph (50:5,13). For later Israel the Table of Nations oriented the Hebrews to their neighbors geographically and, inferentially, forewarns them of those peoples whose moral history and inclinations are suspect, especially the people of Canaan, where they will reside (e.g., Exod 6:4). Canaan was first and foremost associated in the Hebrew mind with a corrupt ancestry.

---

[148] Gen 5:32; 6:10; 7:13; 9:18; 10:1; cf. 1 Chr 1:4.

[149] Two related Heb. roots are found: נָפַץ ("scattered") in 9:19 and פוּץ ("scattered") in 10:18; 11:4,8–9. "Divided" in 10:25 is yet another, פָּלַג, for the wordplay "Peleg."

[150] Gen 6:10; 7:7,13; 8:18; 9:1,8,18–19; 10:1,32; also the inclusive "household," 7:1.

(2) *Noah's Curse and Blessing (9:20–27)*

[20]Noah, a man of the soil, proceeded to plant a vineyard. [21]When he drank some of its wine, he became drunk and lay uncovered inside his tent. [22]Ham, the father of Canaan, saw his father's nakedness and told his two brothers outside. [23]But Shem and Japheth took a garment and laid it across their shoulders; then they walked in backward and covered their father's nakedness. Their faces were turned the other way so that they would not see their father's nakedness.

[24]When Noah awoke from his wine and found out what his youngest son had done to him, [25]he said,

"Cursed be Canaan!
The lowest of slaves
will he be to his brothers."

[26]He also said,
"Blessed be the LORD, the God of Shem!
May Canaan be the slave of Shem.
[27]May God extend the territory of Japheth;
may Japheth live in the tents of Shem,
and may Canaan be his slave."

The telling of Noah's drunkenness, which results in the patriarch's invocation for curse and blessing, recalls the language of the world before the flood, especially Adam's story, but also Cain's rivalry with brother Abel.[151] We have seen in the flood story that the creation and garden accounts (1:1–2:3; 2:4–4:26) are re-presented, especially 9:1–7, so as to picture Noah as the second Adam, the father of the postdiluvian world. In this concluding episode, the parallels are also unmistakable: Noah and Adam share in the same profession (2:15; 9:20); the language of "curse" (3:14,17; 4:11; 5:29; 9:25) and "blessing" (1:28; 5:2; 9:26) are heard again; both experience the shame of "nakedness" (3:7,10–11; 9:22–23); and, like Adam, Noah's transgression results in familial strife among his descendants, resulting in fratricide for Adam's sons (4:8) and slavery for Noah's youngest (9:25–26). There are many allusions to the garden sin: the tree of knowledge "in the middle of *[bĕtôk]* the garden" (2:9; 3:3,8) and Noah "inside *[bĕtôk]* the tent" (9:21); the woman "saw" (*rā'â*, 3:6), and Ham "saw" (*rā'â*, 9:22), though the brothers did not "see" (*rā'â*, 9:23); Adam and Eve "knew *[yādaʿ]* they were naked" (3:7), and Noah "knew *[yādaʿ]* what his youngest son had done to" him (9:24); and God asked, "Who told *[nāgad]* you that you were naked?" (3:11), and Ham "told" *(nāgad)* his brothers. Indeed, Noah is the second Adam both

[151] See A. J. Tomasino, "History Repeats Itself: The 'Fall' and Noah's Drunkenness," *VT* 42 (1992): 128–30, and D. Steinmetz, "Vineyard, Farm, and Garden: The Drunkenness of Noah in the Context of Primeval History," *JBL* 113 (1994): 193–207.

as recipient of divine blessing and as father of a corrupt seed.[152]

When we consider the post-Eden episode of Cain's birth and subsequent murder of brother Abel (4:1–16), we find that Cain's story also shares a number of similarities with Adam's and Noah's accounts. All three worked the ground (2:15; 4:2; 9:20); each narrative involves fruit that gives occasion for human transgression in the story (2:17; 4:3; 9:20–21); "knowledge" *(yādaʿ)* is a common motif (2:17; 3:1–7,22; 4:1,9,17; 9:24); and each story's sin involves a curse (3:14,17; 4:11; 9:25). There are significant dissimilarities, such as the absence of expulsion in Noah's story[153] and the absence of nakedness in the Cain-Abel narrative, but taken together the postdiluvian drunkenness of Noah shows what God had already conceded about the human "heart," as sinful from its youth (8:21). There were new relationships, new assurances, and a new order to things in the world; but there remained the same old human heart.

Verses 20–24 tell of Noah's inebriation and Ham's transgression against his father. As a consequence Noah utters an invocation, which is rendered in poetic verse, calling for curse and blessing (vv. 25–27). These are the only words heard from the mouth of the flood survivor in the whole of the narrative. They are in effect his last will and testament, for the subsequent verses report his death, bringing an end to the ancient Sethite lineage (5:3–32) with the same fateful refrain, "Then he died" (9:28–29). Conversely, in the flood narrative the Lord forewarns, instructs, assures, blesses, and makes covenant with Noah; but in the final episode we do not hear a divine word. Although the passage does not condemn Noah's intoxication, the abrupt silence of God suggests that all is not well between heaven and earth. We will see this played out decisively in the Tower of Babel episode (11:1–9), where heaven has the last word for Noah's offspring.

9:20–21 Noah is introduced by his postdiluvian vocation; he is a cultivator of the soil (v. 20). Unlike the myths of the ancients, which attributed wine to the gods (e.g., Egypt's Osiris; Greek's Dionysus), the biblical record shows that viniculture was the result of human achievement as with the arts and sciences of Cain's genealogy (4:20–22). Adam's role in his world was caretaker of the "Garden of Eden" (2:15), and Noah's task in his new world is similar. God "planted *[wayyiṭaʿ]* a garden" (2:8), where Adam worked (2:15), and Noah "planted *[wayyiṭaʿ]* a vineyard." The particular Hebrew expression for Noah, "a man of the ground" ("soil"), is thematically juxtaposed with Adam, who was made "from the ground" (2:7). "Adam" is *ʾādām,* who was derived from the *ʾădāmâ* ("ground"), and Noah is *ʾîš* ("a man") who toils the *ʾădāmâ*

[152] Another interesting association with Adam is imagined in *Tg. Ps.-J.,* which connects Noah's vineyard to a vine recovered from Eden's garden. Tractate *b. Sanh.* 70b believed that Adam's tree was a vine.

[153] Yet Jewish midrash took from the word "uncover" the same consonants as "exile" (גָּלָה) and concluded that the result of Noah's sin was the exile of future generations (*Gen. Rab.* 36.4).

("ground"). "Ground" is reminiscent of Adam's life and punishment (2:7; 3:17–19). It also reverberates the blood-stained "ground" of Abel's murder (4:10), the subsequent "curse" of Cain "from the ground" (4:11), and Lamech's hope in Noah, who will console humanity's "painful toil" because of the "ground the LORD has cursed" (5:29). This linkage with the sin of the antediluvian family is further insinuated by the opening word of our narrative (in Hebrew), "began" (*ḥālal,* NIV's "proceeded"), which echoes 6:1, "When men began *(ḥālal)* to increase in number on the earth." It also is associated with the later career of the infamous Nimrod in the Table of Nations, who "grew *[ḥālal]* to be a mighty warrior" and founded empires (10:8), and the sinful ambitions of Babel's builders, who had "begun" *(ḥālal)* their prideful deed (11:6).[154]

Many commentators have interpreted Noah's vineyard as fulfillment of the "comfort" for which Lamech longed (5:29). Noah's wine provided a pleasant relief for man (e.g., Ps 104:15) from the toilsome work of the crop. But the request of Lamech cries out for relief from the pain of the "cursed" ground, and that is not alleviated by flood or vineyard (see discussion at 5:29; 8:21). Noah's vineyard is only the backdrop for the story of Noah's curse and blessing, and it bears no allusion to Lamech's invocation as we would expect if viewed by our author as the postdiluvian fulfillment.

Was Noah the innovator of farming? Or was he the discoverer of viticulture and thus unaware of wine's effects? If so, can we absolve Noah of his behavior? The Hebrew construction is difficult, and the proper translation is disputed.[155] Modern renderings interpret that he was "the first tiller of the soil" (REB, RSV) or "the first to plant a vineyard" (NAB, NJPS, NRSV; also NJB, GNB), but the NIV's "proceeded to plant a vineyard" says nothing of an innovation (also NASB). In the first case it is difficult to square Noah as the initiator of agriculture because Cain was a tiller of the soil (4:2). For Noah as "first" viticulturalist, the verb *(ḥālal)* can refer to a "first" (cf. 10:8; 1 Sam 14:35), but it does not require the sense of innovation at most places, rather the beginning ("began") of an activity or series (cf. Gen 11:6; 41:54; 44:12). The closest construction to 9:20 is at Ezra 3:8, which describes Zerubbabel, who "began the work" on the temple by appointing Levites. It is mistaken to ascribe the idea of novelty to "began" for worship under the name *Yahweh* (Gen 4:26) or the practice of marriage (6:1). We cannot determine from the syntax whether Noah was the first viticulturalist or merely began his vocation anew following the flood.

[154] וַיָּחֶל (9:20), הֵחֵל (6:1; 10:8), הַחִלָּם (11:6) are all *hiphil* stem derived from חָלַל, meaning "begin." But cp. the positive context of הוּחַל at 4:26, "began to call on the name of the LORD." Also in Genesis *hiphil* חָלַל occurs at 41:54 and 44:12.

[155] We would expect the verb וַיָּחֶל to have a complement such as an infinitive construct as its object (e.g., Gen 4:26; 6:1; 10:8; 11:6; 41:54; Num 25:7; Deut 2:25; 3:24), "began to plant," but here the noun phrase "man of the soil" occurs. Thus GKC § 120b has "and Noah began to be a husbandman." But the phrase is best taken as apposition, as in the NIV and most English versions.

The meaning of *ḥālal* is best seen as it is found elsewhere in Genesis 1–11 to suggest a strategic point in the direction of the narrative (see 4:26).

Verse 21 tersely recounts Noah's inebriation and its consequence, nakedness. "He who kept his ground against the waters of the great Flood succumbs to wine."[156] The potential harm from drunkenness for the drinker and his family is aptly demonstrated by this incident for which Noah and his progeny pay dearly. To what degree Noah was to blame in the matter cannot be answered confidently. His drinking "some" of the wine may suggest a mitigating factor, perhaps even an allusion to 3:12, where Adam feebly excuses himself ("some of the fruit"). Or, more likely, his culpability is irrelevant and was passed over by the author since Noah's drunkenness is only incidental to the narrative's focus, the curse and blessing.

Noah's drunkenness was reason for shame by itself,[157] but his nakedness required action on the part of his sons. Even as Adam disgraced himself through sin and thereby "knew" his nakedness (3:7,10–11), Noah degraded himself by drunken stupor and concomitant nakedness. "Lay uncovered" *(yitgal)* describes his state in the tent; he is visibly naked. The verb occurs in the same Hebrew stem *(hithpael)* once more and is clearly reflexive (Prov 18:2), thus "uncovered himself" (NJPS) is meant. The GNB has the explicit "took off his clothes." There is no indication here that Ham disrobed his father. Noah was so inebriated that he stripped himself and probably passed out in the tent unclothed. Noah's reproach was not in the drinking of the wine per se but in his excess, which led to his immodesty.

9:22–23 The verses are cryptic that report Ham's offense and his brothers' assistance to their father. How the sons reacted to Noah's indecency is the basis for the curse and blessing they will bear in the invocation of their father that follows (vv. 25–27). It is not Noah's drunkenness and misdeed per se that are the goals of the story; it is the consequence of the infraction. Noah's curse and blessing foreshadow the relationship of the nations that the three brothers originate.

Our passage pauses, therefore, at the start to identify Ham again as "the father of Canaan" (v. 22; cf. v. 18) in anticipation of the curse against Canaan (v. 25). As indicated previously, because the descendants of Canaan coexisted with Israel, the patrimony of Canaan was of special relevance to Moses' Israel. Also we will find that the recurring emphasis in this pericope on the relationship of father and son, with Ham as "father" and Noah as "father," hints at where the sin of Ham lies and why his son Canaan will suffer. The disrespect Ham showed toward his father led to Noah's curse against Ham's son Canaan, a *talionic* penalty for Ham's familial transgression. This interpretation is fur-

[156] Delitzsch, *A New Commentary on Genesis,* 292.
[157] See 19:30–35; Lev 10:9; Deut 21:20; Prov 20:1; 23:29–35.

ther supported by v. 24, where Ham is identified as the "youngest" of the three. Canaan also was possibly the youngest of Ham, judging from 10:6, where Canaan's name occurs last. Rabbinic midrash reckoned him the fourth and last son of Ham.

Without supposing a covert meaning, the episode is plain on the face of it. Ham "saw his father's nakedness" and told his brothers outside the tent (v. 22). The role of Ham has been compared to the serpent who was instrumental in the discovery of Adam's nakedness (3:6,11–13) and who was cursed for the deed (3:14). Since the Cain-Abel event was a consequent replay of the garden enmity (see 4:1–17 discussion), we find that Ham also revives Cain's place as an opponent to the elect line of blessing. Whereas Adam was "clothed" by God (3:21), Ham left his father bare. Unwilling to desert him, Shem and Japheth "covered the nakedness" of Noah and carefully avoided seeing his nakedness by covering themselves (so as to blind their peripheral vision) and by walking backward (v. 23). Verse 23b elaborates with particulars showing how the two sons took precautions to do the opposite of their brother. It reads literally, "Their father's nakedness not they saw." "Saw" as the last word of the Hebrew verse forms an inclusio with "saw," which heads the section at v. 22. This provides an even stronger contrast between "Ham saw" and the refusal of the brothers, who "saw not." Thus the brothers countered the reproach of Noah by covering the "uncovered" and the reproach of Ham by not seeing what Ham "saw."[158] They, in effect, imitated God in the garden when he covered Adam and Eve (3:21).

What was Ham's sin? Why did Noah invoke curses against Canaan instead of the culprit, Ham (v. 25)? The meaning of the phrase "saw his father's nakedness" has been variously interpreted. Both Jewish and Christian interpretation speculated that Ham's deed was a sexual offense since the same language is found in the Pentateuch describing sexual transgressions. Further support was garnered from v. 25, which refers to what Ham "had done to him." Many suppose that the original story contained the sordid details but that they were excised for reasons of propriety when later placed in the Torah. Castration was thought to have been the crime by some Jewish and Christian interpreters, and others argued for a homosexual act. Jewish midrash explained that physical abuse by Ham answered why the curse was directed against Canaan; this act prevented Noah from having a fourth son, and thus Canaan as Ham's fourth son should suffer (*Gen. Rab.* 36.7).[159] This may have been fueled by the absence of any notice that additional

---

[158] Observed by Steinmetz, "Vineyard, Farm, and Garden," 200.

[159] Theophilus of Antioch (second century A.D.), while not the source of the view, is the earliest known reference for the castration interpretation; among the Jews it is found in *Tg. Ps.-J.* and assumed in *Gen. Rab.* 36.7. Homosexuality and castration are found debated in *b. San.* 70a. That the rabbis created the story of castration to answer why Canaan was cursed, see A. I. Baumgarten, "Myth and Midrash: Genesis 9:20–29," in *Christianity, Judaism and Other Greco-Roman Cults, Part Three, Judaism before 70,* SJLA 12, ed. J. Neusner (Leiden: Brill, 1975), 55–70.

children were born to Noah, since all the other patriarchs are said to have had "other sons and daughters" (5:3–32; 11:10–25). This lack of reference to other children, however, may be due to the author's desire to parallel the Sethite and Shemite lines, which both end with three sons (5:32; 11:26).[160]

Concerning a homosexual desire or act, there is no indication that a sexual indiscretion occurred when Ham viewed his father or that Ham desired his father in an illicit way.[161] Levitical language for the homosexual act is "to lie with a male," which we do not find here. "Saw" *(rāʾâ)*is the common term for observing and does not convey necessarily the idea of sexual lust; the term can be used in this way (cf. 6:2; 34:2), but such meaning must be derived from the context and not the term by itself. On the contrary, the expressions "to see *(rāʾâ)*nakedness" (Lev 20:17) and "to uncover *(gālâ)* nakedness"[162] are used of heterosexual actions, not homosexual encounters.[163] The expression in our passage is not a figurative statement since the two sons actually cover up the exposed nakedness of their father, who was in a drunken stupor in the tent. This is reinforced by the description "their faces were turned." If in fact some lecherous deed occurred inside the tent, it is inexplicable why the covering of their father is in juxtaposition to Ham's act. On other occasions Genesis is straightforward in its description of sexual misconduct (e.g., 19:5,30–35; 34:2). There is no reason to assume that homosexuality or, for that matter, heterosexual misconduct would be described euphemistically by the author.

Ham's reproach was not in seeing his father unclothed, though this was a shameful thing (cp. Hab 2:15), but in his outspoken delight at his father's disgraceful condition. The penalty against Ham's son may be thought too severe for mere sibling gossip, but this is because we fail to understand the gravity of Ham's offense. We have commented elsewhere (see 2:25; 3:7) that nakedness was shameful in Hebrew culture.[164] In later Israel specific prohibitions

---

[160] Another proposal argues that the suppressed story concerned Ham's incestuous relationship with Noah's wife (stepmother?). The language "see his father's nakedness" is found in the Levitical litany of sexual taboos where "nakedness" is a euphemism for sexual relations. To "see" and to "uncover the nakedness of your father" (NASB) have the same force in Lev 20:17. A parallel is found in Reuben's affair with his father's concubine, Bilhah, which results in his loss of privilege as firstborn (35:22; 44:3–4). Noah's curse against Canaan, the child of this incest, would be explained. See F. W. Bassett, "Noah's Nakedness and the Curse of Canaan. A Case of Incest?" *VT* 21 (1971): 232–37. The problem here is that Noah uncovers himself and is not "uncovered" by his son. See the critique by G. Rice, "The Curse That Never Was," *JRT* 29 (1972): 5–27, esp. 11–13.

[161] E.g., H. C. Leupold thought Ham's transgression was a prurient voyeurism (*Exposition of Genesis,* vol. 1 [Grand Rapids: Baker, 1942], 346).

[162] Euphemism for sexual relations, often incestuous; e.g., Lev 18:6–19; 20:10–21; also metaphorical for Jerusalem's (e.g., Lam 1:8; Ezek 16:37; 23:10,29) and Babylon's shame (Isa 47:3). Cp. Nah 3:5.

[163] Both Hebrew expressions are translated "have sexual relations" in the NIV.

[164] E.g., the public mistreatment of David's envoy (2 Sam 10:4) and the public ridicule of the nations (Isa 20:4; 47:3; Mic 1:11).

guarded against the public exposure of the genitals and buttocks (e.g., Exod 20:26; 28:42), and nakedness was commonly associated with public misconduct (e.g., Exod 32:25). It is not surprising then that the euphemism "nakedness" was used for the shameful travesty of incest. Ham ridiculed the "old man's" downfall. In the ancient world insulting one's parents was a serious matter that warranted the extreme penalty of death. Mosaic legislation reflected this sentiment.[165] This patriarchal incident illustrated the abrogation of the Fifth Commandment, "Honor your father and mother." To do so means divine retaliation, for the crime is not against parent alone but is viewed as contempt for God's hierarchical order in creation. Shem and Japheth, unlike Ham, treated Noah with proper respect. They refused to take advantage of him despite his vulnerable condition.[166]

9:24 When Noah sobered up, he learned of Ham's misbehavior (v. 24). How he came to know "what his youngest son had done to him" is left unstated. "Had done" may be another allusion to the garden crime, where God asked Eve, "What have you done?" (3:13) and reprimanded the serpent, "Because you have done this" (3:14). Reference to Ham as "youngest" bespeaks the custom of primogeniture, where the eldest receives the "double portion" of family inheritance (Deut 21:17).[167] Usually in Genesis the expected line of descent is disregarded, and the youngest receives the patriarchal blessing (e.g., Seth, Isaac, Jacob, Ephraim). Ham's case, however, does not fit the pattern because his sin assailed the principal underpinning of family stability by defaming the father. Ham disqualified himself as Cain had done with his murderous treason. The severity of Ham's sin is pointed up by the later trickster Jacob, who, though he deceived his father to obtain the blessing (27:19–30), retained the favored place in the eyes of Isaac. Ham, on the other hand, received Noah's strongest contempt.

Answering the question of Canaan's accountability is left to speculation since the text is not troubled to explain the circumstances of Canaan's involve-

---

[165] E.g., Exod 20:12; 21:15,17; Deut 21:18–21; 27:16; cf. Eph 6:1–2.

[166] Luther reminds us of Paul's admonition against gloating, "He who stands should take heed lest he fall" (1 Cor 10:12, *LW* 2.171).

[167] בְּנוֹ הַקָּטָן ("his small son") as comparative or superlative must be derived from the context here. The chronological ages of the three sons are disputed by ancient and modern commentators, though the traditional order, Shem, Ham, and Japheth, sometimes is assumed to be the chronological order of their births. Related to this is the question of who is elder between Shem and Japheth in 10:21. Most English versions take Ham as the last born, translating "his youngest son," but the AV has the unlikely "his younger son," following the LXX and Vg. The chronological arrangement of Shem, Japheth, and Ham is the correct one. See discussion at 10:21. The biblical arrangement of Shem, Ham, and Japheth is best attributed to the importance the Hamitic families (e.g., Canaan, Egypt) had for Israel's history. Cassuto (*Genesis,* 165) explains it differently as a Hebrew preference for the short word before the longer, while taking the actual chronological order as Japheth, Shem, and Ham (reading Japheth as the elder at 10:21).

ment, if any. Theologically, we are challenged to explain how God can punish Canaan for the sin of his father. Mosaic law makes clear that a person received punishment for his own crimes, not another's (Deut 24:16; cf. Ezek 18). This tension is resolved in part when we recognize that Noah's curse and blessing do not impose judgment but are an invocation to the Lord. Jewish midrash reflects varying rabbinic opinions in answering this question (*Gen. Rab.* 36.7). One attributed blame to Canaan, who it was believed committed the violation and told others. Another contended that Noah could not curse one whom God had blessed (9:1), choosing rather Canaan. Yet another explained it as Noah's retaliation against Ham's fourth son (10:6) for the castration that prevented Noah from a fourth son. Medieval Jewish commentators resolved the problem by the proposed reading, "Cursed be *the father of* Canaan," following the earlier expression found in vv. 18,22.[168]

Some modern interpreters find in the story two parallel but conflicting traditions of Noah's sons: Shem, Ham, and Japheth and Shem, Japheth, and Canaan. The original story supposedly had Canaan as its villain and was altered with the insertion of "Ham" in the story (vv. 18,22) by a later editor so as to bring the story into alignment with chap. 10's Table of Nations, which attributed to Ham a primary role as progenitor of nations.[169] This is not satisfactory unless we accept an impossibly inept editor who left the contradiction, but did not achieve his goal. Others suppose that the original story, which was later shortened, explained how Canaan was involved in the deed.[170]

A better explanation is afforded by noting the purpose of 9:20–27 in its theological context. Its perspective concerns the life of later Israel as it anticipates entry into the land of Canaan. As the patriarchs' actions may foreshadow the national life of Israel, for example Abraham's descent into Egypt (12:10–20), the lives of the antediluvian fathers modeled in a sense the future nations derived from Noah's sons. Shem, the father of Abraham, is the paradigm of later Israel; and Ham of their archenemies, Egypt and Canaan (10:6). Lying behind this is the ancient concept of corporate personality. Because of this unity of father-son, the character of the father is anticipated in the deeds of the sons. Hebrew theology recognized that due to parental influence future generations usually committed the same acts as their fathers whether for ill or good.[171] In this case the curse is directed at Ham's son as Ham's just deserts for the disrespect he had toward his own father, Noah. Yet the imprecation was

---

[168] Saadia Gaon and Ibn Jana, noted by Sarna, *Genesis,* 66.

[169] E.g., von Rad, *Genesis,* 136.

[170] Sarna, *Genesis,* 66.

[171] E.g., "punishing the children for the sin of the fathers to the third and fourth generation who hate me but showing love to thousands of those who love me and keep my commandments" (e.g., Exod 20:5–6; 34:7; Deut 7:9–10). As the prophets note, however, this was never accepted as a defense against personal accountability (e.g., Jer 31:29–30; Ezek 18:2–4).

spoken against future generations of Canaanites who would suffer subjugation "not because of the sins of Ham, but because they themselves acted like Ham, because of their own transgressions."[172] Those deplorable acts by the Egyptians and Canaanites are sexual aberrations that merited their dispossession by Israel and thus were forbidden by Moses as obscene offenses against the Lord (Lev 18:3–30).

9:25–27 Noah's invocation in vv. 25–27 is expressed in three triplets of Hebrew poetry, one in each verse.[173] The beginning of each triplet is parallel: "Cursed" (v. 25) and "Blessed" (v. 26) and "May [God] extend" (v. 27). "He said" introduces the curse at v. 25, and "he also said" distinguishes the blessing in vv. 26–27. The curse and blessing are best taken as an invocation rather than a prophecy.[174] This is shown by the Hebrew verbal mood, expressing a wish, in the last triplet, "May God extend" *(yapt)*.[175] Thus its parallel words in the former lines, "cursed" and "blessed," while imperatives in form, have the force of request. This is supported by the same verbal mood in "May [Canaan] be" *(wîhî),* occurring twice in vv. 26 and 27. This recommends that all the verbal forms should be rendered as prayers of invocation.[176] Noah's words held no magical powers that destined the fates of future generations. His appeal was to God, whose will alone counted for what would become of the nations.

The first and last triplets concern Canaan and Japhet, while the center triplet focuses on the favored lineage of Shem. All three remark on Canaan's future status by the parallel recurrences of the term "slave" *(ʿebed).* The first triplet (v. 25) gives special attention to this as it defines the "curse" Canaan must endure: "the lowest of slaves."[177] The theme of sibling servanthood is found in the blessing of Isaac on Jacob (27:29–30,39–40) and in the Joseph story (37:6–9; 44:10,17,33). The NIV's "slave of Shem" (v. 26c) and "his slave" (v. 27c) obscure the parallel Hebrew at the end of the second and third triplets, which is exactly the same: "May Canaan be a slave to him [or them]" (vv. 26c and 27c).[178] Singular "his slave" (i.e., Shem) is found in a number of translations (AV, NASB, NRSV, NJB, NAB, REB), but the plural "their slave," referring to both brothers, as in the NIV text note, is supported by the earlier "his brothers"

---

[172] Cassuto, *Genesis,* 155.

[173] The NIV translates v. 26 as a doublet.

[174] See Sailhamer, "Genesis," 97, who takes v. 25 as prophecy and vv. 26–27 as invocation.

[175] יַפְתְּ from פָּתָה is a *hiphil* jussive, indicating prayer or request.

[176] Problematic for this is the imperfect יִהְיֶה (indicative), which suggests a prophecy, "Will he [Canaan] be" (as NIV). The imperfective form, however, is used with jussive force (e.g., Gen 1:9; 2 Kgs 6:17; GKC § 109a, n. 2; *IBHS* § 34.2.1a).

[177] Heb. עֶבֶד עֲבָדִים has been rendered lit., "a slave of slaves" (RSV) or "servant of servants" (AV, NASB), which expresses the superlative, "most servile of slaves" (REB).

[178] Heb. וִיהִי כְנַעַן עֶבֶד לָמוֹ. The NIV's translation "slave of Shem" (v. 26c) is an interpretive plus (also GNB). לָמוֹ may be a rare form of לוֹ, "to him" (cf. Isa 44:15; GKC § 103g, n. 3; *IBHS* § 11.1.2d).

at v. 25 (also *Tgs. Onq.* and *Neof.;* NJPS). There is a hierarchical pattern with Japheth second to Shem, but Canaan is subject to both.

"Cursed" *(ʾārûr)*heads the invocation (v. 25) and echoes the "curses" of the antediluvian era: against the serpent (3:14), the "ground" because of Adam's transgression (3:17), against Cain (4:11–12), and the earth again (8:21).[179] The curse against Canaan, therefore, is the second curse against a human, following the curse upon Cain, but it is the first spoken by a human. When the Lord cursed Cain, he drove him from the "ground." Cain had "served" *(ʿābad)* the land as his father Adam had, but because he profaned the land with his brother's blood, he was prevented from enjoying its fruit (4:11–12). Canaan's punishment also would determine his occupation: he would become his brothers' slave. For those who see here a prophecy, or historical reflex, most look to a historical fulfillment in David's time.

There are no grounds in our passage for an ethnic reading of the "curse" as some have done, supposing that some peoples are inferior to others. Here Genesis looks only to the social and religious life of Israel's ancient rival Canaan, whose immorality defiled their land and threatened Israel's religious fidelity (cf. Lev 18:28; Josh 23). It was not an issue of ethnicity but of the wicked practices that characterized Canaanite culture. The biblical revelation made it clear that if Israel took up the customs of the Canaanites, they too would suffer expulsion. It is transparent from Genesis 1–11, especially the Table of Nations (10:1–32), that all peoples are of the same parentage (i.e., Noah) and thus are related by ancestry. This we find at the outset by creation's *imago Dei,* which is reaffirmed in God's covenant with Noah and his sons, including Ham (9:1,5–6). The blessing that befalls all peoples is carried forward by the Abrahamic promises, which counter the old curses by the blessing received by all peoples in any era who acknowledge the Lord. "Any attempt to grade the branches of mankind by an appeal to 25–27 is therefore a re-erecting of what God has demolished"[180] (cf. Col 3:11; Gal 2:18; 3:28).

"Blessed" is spoken by Noah to the Lord and only indirectly to Shem (v. 26). It is the patriarch's recognition that what blessing comes to Shem is the Lord's doing. This first shows that the elect line of promise will be Shem's offspring, which is spelled out in the genealogy of 11:10–26, ending in the appointed "Abram" (12:1–3). Here particularly it is difficult to read Noah's prayer apart from the vista of later Israel's struggle against the Canaanites. In this sense the invocation is that Israel might subjugate the inhabitants of Canaan. This was the promise to Abraham (15:18–21), the abiding belief of Joseph (50:24–25), and the charge the Lord gives Moses to achieve (e.g., Deut

[179] In this last instance the evidence of the "curse" is recited in the oath of God after the fact (8:21).

[180] D. Kidner, *Genesis,* TOTC (Downers Grove: IVP, 1967), 103.

7:1–2; Exod 3:8). It is clear from v. 27 that Shem receives the blessing of primogeniture and that Japheth will live under his shadow. Shem is identified in terms of his relationship to God, "the God of Shem," which contrasts remarkably with the previous line, where Canaan is identified as "the lowest of slaves" (v. 25). Although Shem is master over Canaan, Japheth's supremacy to Canaan is derived from his favorable position with Shem. He will be protected by Shem and will live in peace with Shem. How this will happen is left to God's providential outworking.

Canaan, however, will languish as servant to both (v. 27). Noah's prayer for Japheth involves a play on the sound of his name: *yapt* ("extend") is similar in sound to *yepet* or *yāpet,* "Japheth" (v. 27a).[181] The NJB has "may God make space for Japheth." The second line of v. 27 describes the protective relationship Japheth enjoys under the auspices of Shem's blessing ("the tents of Shem"). "Live" or "dwell" *(yiškōn)* is associated with the Lord's presence in the camp of Israel (e.g., Exod 25:8; Lev 16:16), being semantically related to "tabernacle" *(miškan).* Some Jewish interpreters understood the subject as God, who will reside with Shem: "And God shall dwell in the dwelling of Shem."[182] The NIV's rendering, "may Japheth live," makes explicit what most versions subtly state by "let him [Japheth] dwell/live" (e.g., NASB, NRSV, NJPS). It is best taken as a blessing upon Japheth, and thus he is the proper subject. The Hebrew "tents of Shem" forms a wordplay with the parallel "God of Shem" in v. 26, where a transposition of letters alone distinguishes "tents of" *(ʾhly)* and "God of" *(ʾlhy).* To reside in the "tents" of Shem is tantamount to declaring that his "God" is Japheth's as well. Japheth will be welcomed in the camp of Israel and privileged to benefit from the tent of meeting, but the Canaanites will be driven from the land (e.g., Exod 3:8,17; Deut 7:1; 20:17), accepted only as servants (cf. Gibeonites, Josh 9:27).

As the Table of Nations points to the descendants of Japheth in Asia Minor and Europe (10:2–5), Israel's history actually shows little contact with the Japhethites. How then do the Japhethites share in the land of Israel? Commentators are uncertain where to look for a historical fulfillment. *Targum Pseudo-Jonathan* interpreted this as the conversion of Greek proselytes. Isaiah envisioned a day when the descendants of Japheth (10:2–5) would be gathered to a restored Israel (Isa 66:19–20). The Church Fathers as well as the Reformers interpreted the reference to Shem as messianic.[183] It would not be

[181] Heb. יָפֶת is the pausal form.

[182] *Jub.* 7:12, 19; also *Gen. Rab.* 36.8 and *Tgs. Onq., Neof.*

[183] Luther, *LW* 2.178–85; Calvin comments that Shem and Japheth are gathered under the "same tabernacle." "This is done by the sweet and gentle voice of God, which he has uttered in the gospel; and this prophecy is still daily receiving its fulfillment, since God invites the scattered sheep to join his flock, and collects, on every side, those who shall sit down with Abraham, Isaac, and Jacob, in the kingdom of heaven" (*Comm.,* 309).

until the time of the Gentile church that Japheth could be said to reside under the shelter of the "God of Shem," for the church's apostolic writings themselves (i.e., New Testament) bear the language of Japheth's descendant, Javan [Greece].[184] The presence of Canaanites in the land, however, was a continuing concern in the patriarch narratives (e.g., 12:6; cf. 34:30), and intermarriage was disapproved (e.g., 24:3; 28:1; 38:2). The questionable character of Ham (thus Canaan) presented in the Genesis narrative anticipates the wickedness that will characterize his Canaanite descendants (e.g., Lev 18:3,24–30). Yet the prophet Isaiah (Isa 19:23–25) envisioned a glorious day when Ham's descendants (Egypt and Assyria) would be reconciled to Shem's future progeny, Israel.

(3) Noah's Death (9:28–29)

[28]After the flood Noah lived 350 years. [29]Altogether, Noah lived 950 years, and then he died.

9:28–29 These concluding verses of our pericope backtrack to the genealogy of Seth presented in 5:3–32. Noah's obituary completes the record of Seth's descendants, which traces the Sethite lineage down to Noah, by concluding with the formulaic death notice "and then he died" (9:29). The patriarch then holds the final, tenth position in the record. Noah was the vital genealogical link between the old world and what followed "after the flood" (v. 28). Now the memory of the antediluvian era will be perpetuated by his sons and their descendants.

[184] Noted by Delitzsch, *A New Commentary on Genesis,* 298.

SECTION OUTLINE

V. THE NATIONS AND THE TOWER OF BABEL (10:1–11:9)
   1. Table of Nations (10:1–32)
      (1) Introduction (10:1)
      (2) Sons of Japheth (10:2–5)
      (3) Sons of Ham (10:6–20)
      (4) Sons of Shem (10:21–31)
      (5) Conclusion (10:32)
   2. Tower of Babel (11:1–9)
      (1) United People (11:1–2)
      (2) Building Babel (11:3–4)
      (3) Divine Inspection (11:5)
      (4) Stopping Babel (11:6–7)
      (5) Scattered Peoples (11:8–9)

V. THE NATIONS AND THE TOWER OF BABEL (10:1–11:9)

This section recounts what became of Noah's sons "after the flood" (10:1,32). Much of what we hear from these chapters is squandered by the Christian reader because we have lost sight of the theological intent of the "map." From this section we learn that the "blessing" is for all peoples because all nations have their source in the one man, Noah, whom God favored. Moreover, the disunity among Noah's offspring that resulted from the tower event did not prevent the blessing God had envisioned for humanity. That blessing would be achieved through Abraham's seed, which as the apostles assert was accomplished in behalf of Israel through Christ and the church (e.g., Matt 28:18–19; Rom 4:16–18; Gal 3:6–9).

The increasing population of the world, as suggested by the numerous nations listed, shows that the "blessing" of procreation and rule continues through Noah's offspring (cf. 1:28; 9:1). From three sons of the one person, Noah, emerged the many nations of the world, fulfilling the divine exhortation to subjugate the earth (9:1,19). Yet this did not occur until *after* their descendants had sinned through their autonomous efforts to make a "name" (11:4) for themselves. The tower story explained what led to the nations' remarkable diversity and dispersion, as shown in the table. Their achievement of "spread[ing] out over the earth" (10:32), therefore, was tainted since it was only as a consequence of divine intervention: "The LORD *scattered* them over the face of the whole earth" (11:9).

LITERARY STRUCTURE. The genealogical table (10:1–32) and the narrative of the tower (11:1–9) are intended to be read together.[1] This is indicated by the lexical and literary connections they share, particularly the vocabulary of the refrain after each genealogical segment (10:5,20,31–32) and the biographical particulars concerning Nimrod as the founder of Babylon (10:8–12). Both the genealogy and tower narratives speak of "territories/earth" (*ʾereṣ,* 10:5,20,31–32; 11:1,8–9); "language" (*lēšôn*, 10:5,20–21; *śāpâ,* 11:6–7,9); dispersion of peoples ("spread" [*pārad,* 10:5,32], "scattered" [*pûṣ*, 10:18; 11:4,8–9], and "divided" [*pālag,* 10:25]); "Babylon" and "Shinar" (10:10; 11:1,9); an "eastern/eastward" location (*qedem*, 10:30; 11:1); and the building of cities (10:11–12; 11:4–5,8). Also both include a wordplay: "Peleg" with "divided" (10:25) and "Babylon" with "confused" (11:9). The literary linkage of 11:1–9 with the table's chief figure, Nimrod, the father of the great Mesopotamian cities (10:8–12), is heightened by the same role of God as Overseer: Nimrod's deeds were "before the LORD" (10:9), and the "LORD came down to see the city [Babylon]" (11:5).

The Tower of Babel incident (11:1–9), though following the table in the present literary arrangement, actually precedes chronologically the dispersal of the nations. This interspersal of narrative (11:1–9) separates the two genealogies of Shem (10:21–31; 11:10–26), paving the way for the particular linkage between the Terah (Abraham) clan and the Shemite lineage (11:27). The story of the tower also looks ahead by anticipating the role that Abram (12:1–3) will play in restoring the blessing to the dispersed nations.

Elsewhere in Genesis the nonelect lineage is dispensed with first before the detailing of the chosen family of blessing (e.g., Cain and Seth, Ishmael and Isaac). In the table the families of Japheth (10:2–5) and Ham (10:6–20) are cited first, and then the elect line of Shem is given (10:21–31). But also the line of Shem itself takes two different roads. In chap. 10 the nonelect line of Joktan is followed, and in chap. 11 the chosen line of Peleg is traced down to Terah's sons. The tower account then is sandwiched between the two genealogies of Shem, the first completing the table (10:21–31) and leading to the Babylon account (11:1–9): Shem → Joktan → Babel. The second continues the lineal descent as Shem → Peleg → Abram (11:10–26), followed by the Abraham narrative. This arrangement highlights the end of each line of descent from Shem. Structurally, the nonelect tribes of Joktan's line end up with the sordid story of the Babel builders, while conversely the privileged genealogy of the Peleg branch aims for the Abram clan and the subsequent narrative.[2]

THEOLOGICAL MESSAGE. Our author has appropriated ancient records to

[1] See the argument of G. Wenham, *Genesis 1–15,* WBC (Waco: Word, 1987), 209–10.
[2] Observed by J. Sailhamer, "Genesis," EBC (Grand Rapids: Zondervan, 1990), 102–3.

show how the covenant "blessing" with Noah (9:1,17), that is, the new Adam, gained momentum "after the flood" (10:1,32), but also how it was threatened by the sin of pride (11:4; cf. 3:5–6; 4:23–24; 6:4). The emergence of nations is depicted as meeting the goal of God's blessing in chap. 10, but the tower episode shows how divine intervention achieved it. It was God's imposition that hindered the collusion of humanity, whose unity attempted wicked aims. As long as sin reigns, diversity among nations is required to restrain the wickedness that a unified *sinful* humanity might achieve (11:6).

There was a time when humanity enjoyed a solidarity based on its common parentage, rooted in the creation itself (1:26–28). This table highlights the essential interconnectedness of the human family despite the present diversity of genealogical descent, language, geography, and political alignment. The essential oneness of man is his descent from our common source in Noah, the reflex of Adam. The covenant with Noah was universal in scope (9:8–17), providing the blessing for all peoples. Harmony among peoples was not primarily centered in the sameness of language, geography, and culture, but in the innate dignity of human beings as the *imago Dei* under the blessing of God (1:26–28). Genesis 10–11 shows that a disproportionate consideration on "races," as in our modern world, forfeits our inherent unity and may lead to a primitive tribalism that fosters war.

The presence of Israel's traditional enemies (e.g., Canaanites, Assyrians, Egyptians) in the table as part of the human family shows them also to be beneficiaries of the promissory blessing. But Genesis shows how this blessing is realized only through Israel (e.g., 12:3; Isa 42:1–4).[3] The Old Testament consistently portrays God as a universal God who rules the affairs of all nations, but this does not suggest that God is an international deity worshiped by many names. The distinctive Sinai covenant Israel enjoyed was not shared by others, and it was the necessary vehicle by which the Gentiles must recognize the Lord for salvation. Yahweh was not the God of Moab or Egypt, for instance.[4] Only through God's revelation of himself to Israel would the world of nations have access to salvation. Thus, because of the unity and sole rule of God (cf. Israel's *shema,* Deut 6:4), Paul could speak of God as the "God of the Gentiles" too, who holds all people accountable for their sins. Salvation comes to us, whether Jew or Gentile, by the one means of faith in the atoning sacrifice of Israel's Greater David, Jesus Christ (Rom 3:27–31; cf. 1 John 2:2).[5]

---

[3] C. Westermann, *Genesis 1–11,* trans. J. J. Scullion (Minneapolis: Augsburg, 1984), 529–30.

[4] H. Orlinsky shows the difference between the nationality and universality of God versus the mistaken notion of an international deity ("Nationalism-Universalism and Internationalism in Ancient Israel," in *Translating and Understanding the Old Testament: Essays in Honor of Herbert Gordon Mays,* ed. H. T. Frank and W. L. Reed [Nashville: Abingdon, 1970], 206–36).

[5] For discussion of the principle of faith in Paul, see J. Murray, *The Epistle to the Romans,* NICNT (Grand Rapids: Eerdmans, 1959), 122–24.

The table indicates that God is the Creator of all peoples. Supportive of this is the numerical structure of the map's nations, totaling seventy members in all. This multiple of "seven" and "ten," numerical figures indicating "completeness," indicates that the whole of the world's families are under the eye of God. The striking absence of "Israel" in the table as well as the use of the term *gôy* ("nation") rather than the covenant term *ʿam* ("people") shows a God whose purposes transcend the particularism of Israel.[6] "People" *(ʿam),* as opposed to "nation" *(gôy),* is typically used in expressing the Lord's personal relationship with Israel. "Nation" is related to land and state, therefore commonly indicating a geopolitical entity as in Genesis 10.[7] God regards the actions of all nations as evidenced by his attention to Nimrod ("before the LORD") and the Babel builders (10:9; 11:5; cf. Ps 67:4). There was a world of peoples before the call of Abram, and it is that map of peoples that concerns the God of Abram ultimately. Out of concern for the salvation of the nations, God calls Abraham and his posterity.

Nevertheless, the possibility of a yet-future, unified mankind rests upon Abraham alone, who as the recipient of God's blessing will be instrumental in accomplishing this for the "families" of the earth (12:3). The table's common use of "lands" *(ʾarṣîm),* "families" *(mišpěḥōt),* and "nations" *(gôyim)* in its structural refrain (vv. 5,20,31–32) is heard again in the call to Abraham (12:1–3). Moreover, there is the derivative *môledet* ("people") from *yālad* ("was the father of"/"were born"), frequent in the table (10:8,13,15,21,24,25,26). "Abram" will become "Abraham," for he will be the "father of many nations *[gôyim]*" (e.g., 17:5). The apostle Paul acknowledges this in terms of appropriating the promise through faith in Christ; the ancient patriarch is the "father of us all"—both Jew and Gentile (Rom 4:16–18; cf. Gal 3:6–8). By the offspring of Abraham, namely Christ, there is the one new humanity (e.g., Eph 2:14–18).

Implicit in the table's distribution of the nations is the sovereign outworking of God's designs. In the Pauline address at Athens we hear the ring of our table's theology, "[God] determined the times set for them [nations] and the exact places where they should live" (Acts 17:26). This imitates Moses' sentiment, "[God] gave the nations their inheritance, when he divided all mankind" (Deut 32:8; cf. also Amos 9:7).

---

[6] D. E. Gowan observes: "Without referring to ch. 11 one would not have a clue where Israel will belong in the Table of Nations. Here we have expressed an interest in all people, in their own right. The chapter is thus a significant anticipation of 12:3, 'By you all the families of the earth shall bless themselves'" (*Genesis 1–11: From Eden to Babel,* ITC [Grand Rapids: Eerdmans, 1988], 114).

[7] Evidence of this is the frequent use of a possessive pronoun with עַם (e.g., עַמִּי, "My people") where divine relationship is meant, whereas such possessives occur only seven times with גּוֹי. See E. A. Speiser, "'People' and 'Nation' of Israel," *JBL* 79 (1960): 157–63.

The theological paradigm for that sovereign design is the relationship of the nations as foreshadowed by the blessing and curse invoked by Noah concerning his sons (9:25–27). This is well-illustrated by the character of the table with its tripartite arrangement and attendant emphases. Shem, of course, is the central character in the invocation of Noah and therefore is the most important in the table. The introduction to Shem's family (10:21) acknowledges the fraternal relationship between Shem and "Japheth," which suits the guardianship that the prayer of Noah envisions for Shem toward his brother ("in the tents of Shem," 9:27). A peaceful coexistence between their offspring prevailed because of the distance that separated the Japhethites who were in the far north and west. Israel's history had little contact with these peoples. Thus the least attention of the three sons is given to Japheth's dependencies (10:2–5). Conversely, the servitude of Ham that Noah's curse petitioned required more notice in the table (10:6–20). The perpetual tussle between the Israelites and the inhabitants of Canaan as well as the great empires of the Nile and Tigris-Euphrates justifies the obsession of the table with the biographical, genealogical, and geographical details presented in Ham's lineage.

The genealogies of Noah's sons also give its readers an orientation to the various sociopolitical groups that made up the ancient Near East. Such a distribution of the nations would have been significant for Moses' Israel as it surveyed the various groups that occupied Canaan and the Levant. It is not coincidental that the nation "Israel" is absent in this catalog. It may be that the existence of Israel is assumed and the genealogies are told from the perspective of an Israelite. Some would explain this omission as evidence that at the time of its composition Israel was not yet a nation. Certainly in its extant arrangement the table depicts the situation *before* the emergence of Israel's patriarchs. Thus the author shows us the ethnolinguistic and geopolitical terrain of the nations at the time of the call of Abram, though his roots are well represented by the table's prominent figure "Eber" (10:24–25; 11:16). The nation Abram fathers, therefore, is understood as the divine antidote for the sinful calamity that befell the postdiluvian offspring of Noah's sons.

1. Table of Nations (10:1–32)

The story of Noah's sons is reported by the use of genealogy rather than narrative. The same technique was employed for the recounting of the Cainite and Sethite families (4:17–24; 5:1–32). Like these genealogies, the table contains embedded narratives that reflect the special interests of the author. Prominent are the interludes concerning "Nimrod" (10:8–12), "Peleg" (10:25), and the supplemental summaries of the geographical distribution of the entities cited (10:5a,18b–19,30).

GENEALOGICAL FORM. The Table of Nations occurs in the segmented form of genealogy, giving the full complement of each patriarch's offspring. A notable exception to this is the offspring of Eber, whose sons Peleg and Joktan are treated differently (vv. 25–29). Joktan's families are fully traced while Peleg's line is absent, yet "Peleg" is listed in Shem's second genealogy, which as a linear genealogy gives the members of the exclusive chosen line (11:18). The segmented feature distinguishes the Table of Nations from the linear form of genealogy for the ancestors of the chosen Abram, that is, the Sethites and Shemites (5:1–32; 11:10–26).

The Table of Nations in Genesis remains unique among ancient peoples and enigmatic in many ways to the modern reader. The Chronicler adapted this chapter (1 Chr 1:4–23) in recounting the genealogy from Adam to Jacob (1:1–2:1). Otherwise there is no parallel to the table in antiquity. This alone should sober any hasty judgment questioning its value.

In antiquity there are, of course, lists of persons as founders of cities and peoples who were regarded as their ancestors. This trait of a fictitious "eponymous ancestor" is commonly attributed to the table.[8] The difficulty in assuming this for Genesis's catalog of nations is that it fundamentally undercuts the carefully crafted genre of Genesis 1–11 as historical narrative. The author of Genesis goes to great lengths, even to the point of polemic, to distance its materials from the common ancient Near Eastern fare of legend or the sort. To incorporate such a piece of legendary material under the rubric of *tōlĕdōt* (10:1) would be at serious odds with the framework of the entire composition of Genesis. Another point of contact with ancient Near Eastern genre is the use of narrative embedded in the genealogical framework. This is well illustrated by the Sumerian King List, which registers kings, places, and length of rule. Occasionally biographical notes are supplied regarding these ancient kings.[9] The table presents the same feature by the occasional inclusion of special information about the entries (e.g., Nimrod).

The geographical breadth of the table is remarkable. It ranges to the north as far as the Caucasus mountains, south into the Arabian peninsula, east as far as the Iranian plateau, and west at least as far as the Aegean, if not Spain (Tarshish?). So diverse are the locations within a given branch that it is difficult to assign a branch to a locale, except in the broadest sense. The ancient cartographer

---

[8] The term "eponymous" does not itself mean a fictitious person, but it is commonly used in this way in reference to Gen 10. E.g., J. Skinner defines the eponymous ancestor of each nation as an "imaginary personage bearing its name, who is called into existence for the purpose of expressing its unity, but at the same time is conceived as its real progenitor" (*Genesis,* ICC [Edinburgh: T & T Clark, 1910], 189). Etiological narratives explain present circumstances and are not necessarily contrived. Each must be weighed on its own merits and not assumed fictitious. See A. R. Millard, "Story, History, and Theology," in *Faith, Tradition, and History: Old Testament Historiography in Its Near Eastern Context,* ed. A. R. Millard et al. (Winona Lake, Ind.: Eisenbrauns, 1994), 37–64.

[9] E.g., the reference to the noted figure Gilgamesh: "The divine Gilgamesh, his father was a *lillû* [demon], a high priest of Kullab, ruled 126 years" (*ANET,* 266).

arranged the "map" of peoples from the perspective of Israel's Canaan (later "Palestine") as the point of departure. The three geographical arcs of the branches intersect at the center—that is, Canaan, Israel's future homeland.[10] The Japhethites are primarily associated with northern and western sites (Asia Minor and Europe); the Hamites with Egypt, Mesopotamia, and some of Arabia; and the Shemites with the areas of northern Mesopotamia, Syria, and Arabia.

STRUCTURE AND SOURCES. The macrostructure of the table indicates a carefully unified work, though it probably draws on differing kinds of sources such as tribal and city lists and biographical accounts. Verses 1 and 32 enclose (i.e., an inclusio) the table by referring to "Noah's sons" and the time "after the flood." The table has a tripartite structure with each section recounting the line of one of Noah's sons. The tripartite arrangement of the table is characteristic of Genesis 1–11. Cain's genealogy concludes with the three sons of Lamech (Jabal, Jubal, Tubal-Cain; 4:20–22) as do the final members of Seth's genealogy (Noah: Shem, Ham, Japheth; 5:32) and Shem's lineage (Terah: Abram, Nahor, Haran; 11:26).[11]

The sons' genealogies are given in the reverse order (Japheth, Ham, and Shem) of their initial listing in the introduction (v. 1; cf. also 5:32; 6:10; 9:18). A concluding refrain, similar in language, marks the end of each son's descendants (vv. 5,20,31).[12] The refrain shows that the table considers each one's "territories" *(ʾereṣ),* "clans" *(mišpĕḥâ),* "nations" *(gôyim),* and "languages" *(lāšôn).* The concluding verse (v. 32) echoes the formulaic language of the refrain ("clans" and "nations").

"This is the account of *[tōlĕdōt]* . . . Noah's sons . . . after the flood" (v. 1)

- "The sons of Japheth . . ." (v. 2)
  "territories" "language" "clans" "nations" (v. 5)[13]
- "The sons of Ham . . ." (v. 6)
  "clans" "languages" "territories" "nations" (v. 20)
- "Sons were also born to Shem . . ." (v. 21)[14]
  "clans" "languages" "territories" "nations" (v. 31)

---

[10] For depiction of the three geographical arcs, see Y. Aharoni and M. Avi-Yonah, *The Macmillan Bible Atlas,* rev. ed. (New York: Macmillan, 1977), 15.

[11] Adam also fathered three sons, named in chap. 4: Cain, Abel, and Seth.

[12] The refrains for the sections of Ham and Shem are the same, whereas the refrain for Japheth differs slightly in detail (v. 5). In the former two the name of each patriarch occurs, whereas "Japheth" is absent in v. 5. Also Ham and Shem have the same order of the recurring four terms, "territories," etc., while Japheth differs. This same formulaic order in the refrains shared by Ham and Shem shows again the table's intention to depict the closer contact that their dependencies experienced.

[13] We are following the Heb. order of the formulaic elements in v. 5.

[14] The construction here for Shem's introduction differs considerably, drawing attention to the relationships Shem had with Japheth and the all-important "Eber," ancestor of the Hebrews (see discussion at v. 21).

"These are the clans of Noah's sons . . . according to their lines of descent *(tōlĕdōt)* . . . after the flood" (v. 32).

By the colophon (concluding notation) "territories," and so on (10:32), the table suggests the criteria by which the names were grouped. Some of the perplexities regarding the makeup of the table can be explained in part by recognizing that the genealogies contain differing sorts of information. (1) The table presents individuals' names (e.g., Nimrod, Peleg, Eber).[15] A name such as "Canaan" may indicate both an individual (as in 9:18) and a geopolitical entity (10:6).[16] (2) It includes people groups, such as tribal names and nations. They bear the distinctive plural suffix *-îm* (e.g., Kittim, v. 4) or possess the gentilic suffix *(-î)* indicating native affiliation (e.g., Jebusites, v. 16).[17] (3) Finally, the table possesses place names (e.g., Babylon, Nineveh). In some cases it is uncertain if a place or an individual is meant (e.g., "Sidon his firstborn," v. 15). With such a mixture of criteria for determining relationships, it is not surprising that the table at points makes it difficult for the modern reader to recognize the relationship as presented by the author since the table depicts ancestral connections that later became obscure.

Yet even when we allow for such diverse criteria, there remain challenging problems. For example, we are surprised that "Cush" (Africa), as a descendant of Ham, is the "father of Nimrod," who is the ancestor of the great Mesopotamian cities (vv. 6–8). "Elam" was a non-Semitic people yet is said to be a son of Shem (v. 22). Moreover, Canaanite languages are Semitic linguistically, but "Canaan" is counted among the Hamites. Also we encounter duplicates: "Havilah" and "Sheba," for example, occur both in the Hamite and Shemite divisions (vv. 7 and 28–29). We will address these specific issues in the following exposition. Alternative recommendations have been offered, but not widely received.[18] Let it suffice to say at this point that the focus of the table

[15] As in the case of chap. 5 the lineal genealogy of 11:10–26 presents individuals, tracing the progeny of Shem down to Abraham; therefore the overlap of names here with Gen 10 would suggest personal names, e.g., Shem, Arphaxad, Shelah, Eber, Peleg (11:10–17).

[16] Here "Canaan" is parallel with the names of nations, such as "Mizraim" (Egypt).

[17] The plural names are Kittim, Rodanim (v. 4), Mizraim, Ludim, Anamim, Lehabim, Naphtuhim, Pathrusim, Casluhim, and Caphtorim (v. 13). The NIV's rendering of the nations (vv. 13–14) uses the ending "ites," which obscures the distinctive *-îm* ending (see Eng. versions). Names with the gentilic suffix *-î* are Jebusites, Amorites, Girgashites, Hivites, Arkites, Sinites, Arvadites, Zemarites, and Hamathites (vv. 16–18). NIV "Hittites" (חֵת, "Heth") in v. 15 does not have the gentilic ending.

[18] B. Oded proposes that the three divisions originally represented types of communities: mariners (Japheth), nomadic peoples (Shem), and agricultural-urban societies (Ham); but later changes occurred that "do not fit into the author's original intention, thus obscuring the basic pattern and hampering our correct interpretation of the text" ("The Table of Nations (Genesis 10)—A Sociocultural Approach," *ZAW* 98 [1986]: 31). The weakness here is that wherever discrepancies appear with Oded's thesis, he explains them away as late, mistaken accretions (e.g., Arabian tribes listed with Ham [v. 7]).

is ethnogeographic,[19] as shown by the recurring emphasis on the boundaries of each division's "nations" (vv. 5,19,30,32), not languages or ethnicity.

This is not to say that we are left with a hodgepodge of incongruous, disparate sources that have gradually accrued around an original core list.[20] Such is the suggestion of some who attempt to reconstruct an original document that once possessed rhyme and reason in its contents but that suffered later, sometimes mistaken additions, thus obscuring and distorting the primal source.[21] This reflects the classic source reconstruction that explains the extant table as a composite picture of two different accounts.[22] C. Westermann recommends that the table underwent two stages of formation where the final compositor took from both sources to present a history of the nations.[23] It is commonly dated to the seventh century,[24] but others have recommended the earlier period of David-Solomon (ca. 1000 B.C.).[25] D. J. Wise-

[19] Wiseman, "Introduction," xviii.

[20] Oded, for instance, comments, "The Table is an artificial composition in a genealogical pattern reflecting no reality in any historical period" ("The Table of Nations (Genesis 10)," 16).

[21] E.g., J. Simons, "The 'Table of Nations' (Gen. X): Its General Structure and Meaning," *OTS* 10 (1954): 155–84.

[22] The framework is the P source, which is built around the simple enumeration of nations introduced by the בְּנֵי ("sons of") formulae. Evidence in the table for the narrative account of J is distinguished by the *yālad* supplements, i.e., Nimrod (vv. 8–12), Mizraim (vv. 13–14), Canaanites (vv. 15–19), and Shemites (vv. 21,24–30). E.g., Speiser, *Genesis,* AB (Garden City: Doubleday, 1964), 64–65. Lying behind this line of argument is the use of יָלַד, the occurrence of which in the different stems of *qal* and *hiphil* is cited as evidence of two disparate genealogies. The regular use of P's *hiphil* stem (וַיּוֹלֶד/הוֹלִיד) in Seth's and Shem's lineages (chaps. 5 and 11) and J's use of *qal* (יָלַד) elsewhere, such as in Cain's line (4:17–26), distinguishes two literary strata. U. Cassuto, however, shows that this is not a dependable criterion for distinguishing sources since the use of *qal* and *hiphil* is not limited to any particular linguistic genre (i.e., they occur outside the Pentateuch's strata) and, more important, is dependent upon linguistic habits, not authorial preferences (*The Documentary Hypothesis and the Composition of the Pentateuch,* trans. I. Abrams [1941; reprint, Jerusalem: Hebrew University, 1983], 45–47).

[23] For Westermann the P source presented only a list of names (genealogy), and therefore when the editor added J's narrative contributions of historical and biographical details, it enabled the table to offer a history of the emerging nations after the flood (*Genesis,* 498–503).

[24] E.g., G. von Rad, *Genesis: A Commentary,* OTL, rev. ed., trans., J. H. Marks (Philadelphia: Westminster, 1973), 144.

[25] The seventh-century date is suggested by the presence of some people groups in the list that did not impact the ancient Near East until the Assyrian period (e.g., Cimmerians, Scythians). The earlier date of ca. 1000 B.C. is the result of the table's emphasis on Arabian peoples, known during Solomon's internationalism, and the mention of the "Philistines," who were not a significant presence in Canaan until ca. 1200 B.C. F. V. Winnett, however, attributes the Arabian genealogies in Genesis (10:6–7; 10:26–30; 25:1–4; 25:12–26) to a late sixth-century editor (his "J2"; "The Arabian Genealogies in the Book of Genesis," in *Translating and Understanding the Old Testament: Essays in Honor of Herbert Gordon May,* ed. H. T. Frank and W. L. Reed (Nashville: Abingdon, 1970, 206–36). He nevertheless concludes that "they [genealogies] preserve ancient traditions of undoubtedly Arabian origin" (p. 195), though he expresses less confidence in the sources for the south Arabian tribes than in the table's knowledge of the north Arabian inhabitants (p. 196).

man, however, has shown that the list could be the product of fourteenth-century Egypt.[26]

We have already shown that the table, while incorporating different genealogical formulae, evidences a unified whole that is best taken as the creation of one mind drawing on a number of ancient lists and accounts. The proposal of an editor working off two alleged sources proves unproductive for resolving the problems the table creates for the modern reader anyway. Such a suggestion only amounts to shifting the burden of culpability for its difficulties upon the editor.[27] Moreover, there is no reason to presume that a Hebrew author was restricted to one formulaic presentation of a genealogical history. Using E. A. Speiser's commentary as representative of the multiple source theory, we observe that elsewhere in Genesis where a genealogy shows a composite use of differing formulae, he attributes these to one hand.[28] We can accept the table as essentially one composition, of an early period, and permit some updating by a later hand as we have evidence of elsewhere in Genesis (e.g., the derivation of the "Philistines," v. 14).

Also the table enjoys the use of the number "seven" and its multiples. As a whole there are seventy nations named: Japheth lists fourteen; Ham lists thirty (omitting Nimrod as an individual), and Shem has twenty-six descendants.[29] The table's favorite term "sons of" *(bĕnê)* occurs fourteen times (seven twice). Japheth's section shows two groups of seven (sons and grandsons). The Hamites also have arrangements of seven: seven descendants of Cush (vv. 6–7) and seven offspring of Mizraim (if "Philistines" is omitted; v. 13). Earlier we saw the importance of marking sevens for early Genesis

---

[26] D. J. Wiseman, "Genesis 10: Some Archaeological Considerations," in *Journal of the Transactions of the Victoria Institute* 87 (1954): 25). The notion of later updates is not necessary but plausible since we know of intensive scribal activity during the reigns of Solomon and Hezekiah. G. C. Aalders, e.g., while holding to an early date for table authorship, acknowledges this possibility for the inclusion of the Cimmerians, who migrated in the eighth and seventh centuries from the region of the Black Sea to Asia Minor (*Genesis,* BSC, vol. 1, trans. W. Heynen [Grand Rapids: Regency Reference/Zondervan, 1981], 241). The symmetry of "seventy" nations in the list indicates that little, if any, updating occurred.

[27] At points source critics see the hand of the redactor attempting to reconcile his sources (e.g., v. 24 with v. 21 and 11:10–14), but at other places, according to the same critics, the redactor lets apparent contradictions stand (e.g., vv. 7 and 28–29). See Aalders, *Genesis,* 215.

[28] E.g., 25:1–4 has more than one formula, including "sons of," but Speiser attributes the passage to J alone; 36:1–37:2a is attributed to P^{a} but possesses both "sons of" and, more important, the יָלַד formulae (36:4–5,12,14). The same can be said of P's passage 46:6–27, where the יָלַד formulae also appear (46:15,18–19,22,25). The linear Sethite account (chap. 5), attributed to P, possesses the embedded narrative concerning Enoch (vv. 22–24). Speiser takes chap. 5 as P and defers to J only at v. 29, where *Yahweh* occurs, but even there he admits that the clause must have been a part of P as well.

[29] The number seventy can also be achieved by retaining Nimrod but omitting the "Philistines," who are mentioned in a parenthetical appendage (v. 14).

(e.g., seven days, 1:3–2:3). The intentional total of seventy nations, a multiple of seven and ten, symbolizes the "whole" world of nations. It is obvious that the table does not attempt to include every nation (Babylonia itself is omitted, though well represented by Nimrod's "Babylon" and "Shinar").[30] Rather, the symmetry of the count "seventy," collected in three branches, shows that the table is representative of the totality of all peoples. This may well foreshadow the number of Jacob's offspring, whose seventy members descended into Egypt (46:27; Exod 1:5; Deut 10:22).[31] Moreover, Israel in the wilderness was represented by a complement of seventy elders (Exod 24:9; Num 11:24). In this way Israel is representative of the world of the Gentiles. According to Moses' Song, God established the nations corresponding to the number of the Israelites (Deut 32:8).[32] Not only will Israel be instrumental in God's designs for blessing the nations, but the blessing that Israel experiences is a foretaste of that eventually received by all.

The table's figure of "seventy" for the world's nations is alluded to by Jesus in the sending forth of the seventy disciples, as recounted by Luke (10:1–16). Here the evangelist emphasizes the mission of the church in its worldwide evangelistic endeavors.[33] The Christian tradition recognized that the church had taken up the charge of bringing the promissory blessing to the nations. In the Lukan narrative the form of the blessing was the proclamation of the imminent coming of the kingdom of God. Luke's ascension narrative in Acts (1:8) contributes to the universality of the Lord's commission for the church. This motif of inclusion is reflected in the telling of the Spirit's coming at Pentecost upon the gathered Jews and Gentile proselytes (cf. "from every nation under heaven," Acts 2:5–11).

Another characteristic of the table is its recurring formulaic expressions

---

[30] The table itself admits its limitations by summarizing unnamed descendants of Japheth, "from these the maritime peoples spread out" (v. 5).

[31] See Cassuto, *A Commentary on the Book of Genesis. Part II. From Noah to Abraham, Genesis VI:9–XI 32,* trans. I. Abrahams (Jerusalem: Magnes, 1964), 175–180. "[Israel] is a small-scale world, a microcosm similar in form to the macrocosm" (p. 180).

[32] The MT reads בְּנֵי יִשְׂרָאֵל ("sons of Israel") whereas the LXX, supported by the Heb. text of 4QDeut^q, has ἀγγέλων θεοῦ (= בְּנֵי אֱלֹהִים, "sons of God," i.e., angels). Whichever reading is adopted, the basis of Deut 32 is the Table of Nations as the presence of פֶּרֶד in both texts shows. If the LXX reading is followed, the sense of Deuteronomy is that God as Sovereign appointed the number of the nations according to the number of his heavenly court, which provided a patron angel over each people. This, however, was not the case for Israel since God reserved the role of overseer for himself. Each nation received from God a specific geographical territory for occupation. For this discussion see D. I. Block, *The Gods of the Nations: Studies in Ancient Near Eastern National Theology* (Jackson, Miss.: Evangelical Theological Society, 1988), 7–23.

[33] The textual problem in the Lukan passage regarding the number "seventy" or "seventy-two" disciples does not jeopardize the passage's intimation of the Table of Nations. See R. Stein, *Luke,* NAC (Nashville: Broadman, 1992), 304.

"sons of" *(běnê)*[34] and "was father of" *(yālad).*[35] Here these favorite terms of the table are elastic in meaning: at times they reflect biological descent, and at other places in the table they are metaphorical, indicating geographical, commercial, and political dependencies.[36] Familial terminology, such as "daughters" *(bānôt),* is used metaphorically of such geographical relationships (e.g., Num 21:25; Josh 17:11, NIV's "settlements"). "Father," "son," and "brother" are used of covenant parties (e.g., 2 Sam 7:13–16; 2 Kgs 16:7; Ps 2:7), and "born" may speak of general citizenship (e.g., Ps 87:4–6). "Salma," for instance, is said to be the "father" *('āb)* of the city of Bethlehem (1 Chr 2:51). The formulaic "sons of" *(běnê)* in the table focuses on the ancestor, such as the heading "sons of Noah" (v. 1), which indicates from whom the families descended.[37] On the other hand, "was the father of" *(yālad)* emphasizes the developing nations of the branch. Exemplary of this is the case of Nimrod, whose ancestry of "Cush" is of less importance than the consequence of Nimrod's role (vv. 8–12). The distribution of the "descendants" then may be gathered around geographical and political associations.[38] This does not necessarily permit us to conclude that there was no ancestral connection at all, since the familial terms employed suggest actual origins. The nature of the table's purpose and Genesis's genealogical-historical emphases *(tōlědōt)* presuppose the real descent of these peoples, states, and cities from individual founders. Ancient Near Eastern sources attest to such practices where lists of persons and places give genealogical information.[39]

---

[34] בֵּן is the prevalent term, occurring twelve times in chap. 10 (vv. 2,3,4,6,7 [2x], 20,21, 23,29,31).

[35] יָלַד occurs six times in the *qal* stem (vv. 8,13,15,24 [2x], 26) and three times in the passive voice (*niphal* וַיִּוָּלְדוּ, v. 1, and *pual* יֻלַּד, "were born," vv. 21,25). The verb is traditionally translated "bore" or "beget." There are actually three different formulae in the table: (1) "the sons of *A* were *X, Y, Z*"; (2) "*A* was the father of *X, Y, Z*"; and (3) the seldom used "To *A* were born *X* and *Y*" (vv. 21, 25). See Block, "The Table of Nations," *ISBE* 4.711.

[36] For this discussion see A. Ross, "The Table of Nations in Genesis 10—Its Structure," *BSac* 137 (1980): 340–53.

[37] We can point to the Japheth section as illustrative of this point. It uses only the formula "sons of," thereby emphasizing Japheth as founder rather than detailing the developing families that emerged. This concurs with what we find as the general approach of the table toward the nations. It elaborates on those peoples who came into contact with Israel, whereas the handling of peoples in the remote regions, such as Japheth's posterity, is condensed.

[38] N. H. Sarna (בראשית, *Genesis,* JPST [Philadelphia: JPS, 1989], 68) recommends, therefore, that the twelve "sons"/"tribes" of Ishmael (17:20; 25:16) are a confederation of Arab tribes rather than "sons" of actual descent. The difficulty of this view for Genesis is that the relatives of Abraham number twelve (22:22–24) and thus are clearly to be taken as individuals and as a conscious parallel with Ishmael's posterity of twelve. Jacob too had twelve sons who founded a confederation of twelve tribes, and the author presents them as of actual descent. Often in Genesis the terms בֵּן and יָלַד are intended as literal familial descriptions.

[39] E.g., Hammurapi's genealogical ancestry (ca. 1750 B.C.; see Wiseman, "Introduction," xvi–xvii).

The date of the table remains disputed, but it may be argued that it points to the second millennium. Block has summarized the primary grounds for dating it to this early period.[40] (1) The absence of Israel's neighbors, such as the Moabites, Ammonites, and Edomites, rules out the early first millennium.[41] (2) Sidon is listed, representing all of Phoenicia. This is consistent with the primacy of Sidon in the second millennium, which was surpassed later by its sister city, Tyre. (3) The description of Canaan's geography gives attention to the cities of the plain. (4) The affiliation of the Philistines with the Casluhim rather than the Caphtorim (Jer 47:4; Amos 9:7) may reflect an earlier memory of their origins (see discussion at v. 14). (5) And attention is given to Eber, the ancestor of the Hebrews, who is not identified in this way after the time of David.

(1) Introduction (10:1)

[1]This is the account of Shem, Ham and Japheth, Noah's sons, who themselves had sons after the flood.

"This is the account" translates the recurring *tōlĕdōt* rubric that introduces the genealogies of Noah's sons and includes the Tower of Babel account (see discussion at 2:4). The tripartite formula "Shem, Ham and Japheth" is the familiar order (5:32; 6:10; 9:18), but here the genealogies reverse the order by beginning with Japheth. This rearrangement sandwiches the tower incident between the two accounts of the Shem genealogy (10:21–31; 11:10–26). It also shows that the tower debacle resulted in the dispersion of the nations, of which Shem's descendants were a part, but also that Shem's lineage (via Peleg → Terah → Abram) will be instrumental in perpetuating the tenuous blessing for all the nations despite their sin.

(2) Sons of Japheth (10:2–5)[42]

[2]The sons of Japheth:
Gomer, Magog, Madai, Javan, Tubal, Meshech and Tiras.
[3]The sons of Gomer:
Ashkenaz, Riphath and Togarmah.
[4]The sons of Javan:
Elishah, Tarshish, the Kittim and the Rodanim. [5](From these the maritime peoples spread out into their territories by their clans within their nations, each with its own language.)

Japheth was the second son born to Noah; Ham was the youngest (9:24)

[40] Block, "The Table of Nations," 712.

[41] Likewise the glaring omission of Persia defies any late date of the postexilic period.

[42] 1 Chr 1:5–7 parallels 10:2–5 and shows its dependence on this section.

and Shem the eldest (see v. 21, *contra* NIV [see NIV text note]). By dispensing with Japheth's offspring first, the author focused on the Hamites and Shemites, who played a larger role in the life of the Israelites. This pattern is characteristic of Genesis in which the nonelect lineage is issued first and the chosen seed recounted last (e.g., Cain and Seth, Joktan and Peleg, Ishmael and Isaac). We have observed that the number "seven" and its multiples are the numerical key for interpreting the significance of the whole. The fourteen names of Japheth's division (seven sons and seven grandsons) begin the table of seventy names.

JAPHETH'S DESCENDANTS

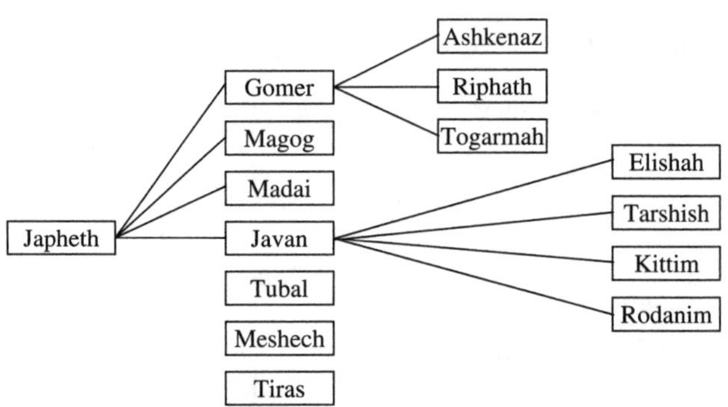

10:2 After Japheth himself the first tier of descendants in Japheth's group consists of seven names. *Gomer* probably refers to the Cimmerians, also known from Assyrian and Greek texts, who originally inhabited the area north of the Black Sea (southern Russia/Ukraine). In the late second millennium B.C. they were pushed into the Caucasus mountains and beyond by invading Scythians. "Gomer" also occurs in Ezekiel's (38:1–6) description of Israel's northern enemies, along with "Gog" and "Magog," and is related to the armies of "Beth Togarmah"—the name of Gomer's son (10:3). *Magog,* because of its geographical depiction in Ezekiel (38:2; 39:6), has been assigned to the regions of the far north (cf. Rev 20:8). Yet it is also associated with the peoples of Asia Minor, such as Tubal and Meshech, in the table.[43] *Madai,* a common term in the Old Testament, refers to the Medes, who inhabited the region northeast of the Tigris River (modern northwest Iran). "Javan" refers to Ionian

[43] Some have taken "Magog" in Ezekiel's prophecy as equivalent to "the land of Gog," on the analogy of Akk. *mā(t) gugu*, "land of Gyges" (= "Gog"), who was the Lydian king of the seventh century. This too would point to an Asia Minor location. See D. Baker's discussion in "Magog," *ABD* 4.471.

Greeks who settled southern Greece and western Asia Minor. The name occurs with *Tubal* and *Meshech* in the prophets (Isa 66:19; Ezek 27:13).[44] "Tubal" and "Meshech" usually occur in tandem in the Old Testament (e.g., Ezek 27:13; 32:26; 38:2; 39:1). They inhabited central and eastern Asia Minor. "Tubal" is associated with Akkadian *Tabali,* and "Meshech" is commonly identified with the *Muški* or *Mušku* named in Assyrian texts. According to 1 Chr 1:17 and the LXX version at 10:23, "Meshech" also occurs in the Shemite lineage, but the Hebrew is *maš* ("Mash") at 10:23.[45] If "Meshech" is read in 10:23 (as NIV), its appearance in both families probably reflects an intermingling of two different peoples. *Tiras* is mentioned only here and is unknown. Some have related it to ancient Thrace.

10:3 The second tier of Japhethites, the sons of Gomer, consists of three peoples. The descendants of *Ashkenaz* (= Akk. *Ishkuza*) are usually identified with the "Scythians" (= Gk. *Skythēs*), as they were known by Herodotus. The term occurs in Jer 51:27, where it is associated with northern sites.[46] The Scythians were tribes from the Russian steppes that occupied areas north and east of the Black Sea. *Riphath* (= "Diphath" in 1 Chr 1:6) remains unidentified. Last, *Togarmah* is known from Ezekiel as "Beth Togarmah" (27:14; 38:6), where it is associated with sites in the far north and also Asia Minor (e.g., Javan, Tubal, Meshech, and Gomer). On the basis of Hittite and Assyrian texts, some have identified the location as modern Gurun in Asia Minor.[47]

10:4 The parallel tier of descendants, the sons of Javan, possesses four names in two pairs. Javan and his sons are Mediterranean peoples. The first pair refers to place names, and the last two names are in the plural form referring to peoples. *Elishah* is also mentioned in Ezekiel (27:7) and probably refers to Cyprus (known as *Alashia* in Akk. sources).

The identity of *Tarshish* is problematic, although it occurs often in the Old Testament. Its etymology has been related to Akkadian *rašāšu* meaning "to heat, smelt," but this is uncertain. Tarshish is best known in connection with its maritime activities, "the ships of Tarshish" (e.g., 1 Kgs 10:22 and NIV note). Also various metals were exported from Tarshish (e.g., Ezek 27:12). Biblical references suggest that the ships of Tarshish operated in both the Red Sea at

---

[44] Cf. also Dan 8:21; 10:20; 11:2; Joel 3:6; Zech 9:13.

[45] מַשׁ ("Mash") at 10:23 has been taken as a scribal error and emended to "Meshech" (as LXX); thus the NIV at 10:23 follows 1 Chr 1:17, which reads מֶשֶׁךְ, and the LXX tradition, which has Μοσοχ. However, this emendation is not required since Mash at 10:23 may refer to another people altogether (see 10:23 discussion).

[46] Also it appears in Col 3:11 (and *2 Macc* 4:47; *3 Macc* 7:5; *4 Macc* 10:7; Josephus, *Ag. Ap.* 2.269), where Paul alludes to the ferocious character of the barbaric Scythians, who nevertheless were subject to the grace of Jesus Christ (see E. Yamauchi, *Foes from the Northern Frontier* [Grand Rapids: Baker, 1982], and "The Scythians: Invading Hordes from the Russian Steppes," *BA* [1983]: 90–99; K. S. Rubinson, "Scythians," *ABD* 5.1056–57).

[47] Baker, "Togarmah," *ABD* 6.594–95.

Ezion Geber and the Mediterranean (e.g., 2 Chr 20:36–37; Ezek 27:35). Among the sites advocated for Tarshish are Tarsus in southeast Asia Minor, Tartessus in southwest Spain, and Tharros in Sardinia of Asia Minor—all west of Israel. The westward direction of Jonah's flight (1:3; 4:2) and the association of the site with "islands" (10:5), usually identified as Mediterranean ports, would suggest a western site. Yet the association of Tarshish with other places, such as Arabia (e.g., Ps 72:10; Ezek 38:13), recommends that "Tarshish" may describe a particular activity (such as smelting) rather than a locale. This would explain how "Tarshish" could speak of different sites.[48]

The *Kittim* are the people of Greek "Kition," which is on the island of Cyprus. "Kittim" is used often in the Old Testament for the western extremities of the world and is associated with maritime activities (e.g., Num 24:24; Isa 23:1,12; Jer 2:10; Ezek 27:6). Its companion term in the table, if it is read as *Rodanim* with 1 Chronicles (1:7) and the LXX *(Rhodioi),*[49] is taken as a reference to the Greek isle of Rhodes, southwest of Asia minor, thus placing both peoples in the region of the Aegean as we would expect. If the MT's *Dodanim* is retained, its identity remains uncertain.

10:5 Japheth's colophon indicates that "from these" came the "maritime peoples" who "spread out," settling the coastal regions and isles of the Mediterranean.[50] The antecedent of "these," whether the Mediterranean "sons of Javan" in v. 4 or all the sons of Japheth, amounts to attributing the inhabitants of the Mediterranean ultimately to Japhethite stock. "From these" may refer to the whole Japhethite group, including those of Asia Minor and the far north, since *ʾî* (commonly rendered "isle") can point to territories reached by sea, not just isles (e.g., Isa 23:2,6; Jer 25:22).[51]

This refrain is echoed in v. 32, where as a closing colophon for the whole table it indicates that the dissemination ("spread out," *pārad*) of all nations came from those cataloged. The table and tower pericope uses several terms to emphasize its theme of dispersal.[52] The term *pārad*, meaning "divide," anticipates the divine action taken against the Babel builders. Significantly, the term also occurs in the Song of Moses ("when he *divided* all mankind,"

---

[48] For a summary of current opinion see D. Baker, "Tarshish (Place)," *ABD* 6.331–32.

[49] The MT reads דֹּדָנִים ("Dodanim," e.g., NASB) but has רוֹדָנִים in the parallel passage at 1 Chr 1:7; the latter probably is correct for 10:4 too, with דֹּדָנִים as the result of scribal confusion of the letters ד and ר. The LXX reads Ῥόδιοι (רוֹדָנִים) at both places.

[50] "Maritime peoples" is the rendering of אִיֵּי הַגּוֹיִם, indicating the distant "isle" or "coastal" peoples.

[51] W. Horowitz shows that the nations of Asia Minor, such as Meshech and Tubal, are considered maritime nations too (e.g., Homer's *Odyssey* XI 13–15; Ezek 27:12–15; 39:6; Isa 66:19; "The Isles of the Nations: Genesis X and Babylonian Geography," in *Studies in the Pentateuch,* VTSup 41, ed. J. A. Emerton [Leiden: Brill, 1990], 35–44).

[52] In the order of their appearance they are the roots נָפַץ (9:19), פָּרַד (10:5,32), פּוּץ (10:18; 11:4,8–9), and פָּלַג (10:25).

Deut 32:8), which shows the intended linkage between the sovereign pattern for the nations (seventy in number) and the descendants of Israel (seventy sons of Jacob; cf. 46:27; Exod 1:5; Deut 10:22).[53]

(3) Sons of Ham (10:6–20)[54]

6The sons of Ham:
Cush, Mizraim, Put and Canaan.
7The sons of Cush:
Seba, Havilah, Sabtah, Raamah and Sabteca.
The sons of Raamah:
Sheba and Dedan.
8Cush was the father of Nimrod, who grew to be a mighty warrior on the
earth. 9He was a mighty hunter before the Lord; that is why it is said, "Like Nim-
rod, a mighty hunter before the Lord." 10The first centers of his kingdom were
Babylon, Erech, Akkad and Calneh, in Shinar. 11From that land he went to
Assyria, where he built Nineveh, Rehoboth Ir, Calah 12and Resen, which is
between Nineveh and Calah; that is the great city.

13Mizraim was the father of
the Ludites, Anamites, Lehabites, Naphtuhites, 14Pathrusites, Casluhites
(from whom the Philistines came) and Caphtorites.
15Canaan was the father of
Sidon his firstborn, and of the Hittites, 16Jebusites, Amorites, Girgashites,
17Hivites, Arkites, Sinites, 18Arvadites, Zemarites and Hamathites.

Later the Canaanite clans scattered 19and the borders of Canaan reached from Sidon toward Gerar as far as Gaza, and then toward Sodom, Gomorrah, Admah and Zeboiim, as far as Lasha.

20These are the sons of Ham by their clans and languages, in their territories and nations.

With the listing of the youngest son, Ham (9:24), we come to those peoples who significantly impacted the history of the Israelites. Among these were the traditional enemies of Abraham's descendants, such as Egypt, Canaan, Assyria, and Babylon. Included in the names listed are clans, individuals, and cities. There are four groups: Cush, Mizraim (= Egypt), Put, and Canaan.[55] Seven peoples are named as descendants of Cush (v. 7) and seven

---

[53] At both passages the LXX reads "seventy-five" descendants as echoed in Stephen's sermon (Acts 7:14). The MT's Deut 10:22 has "seventy," and there is no variant reading tradition. Whether exactly seventy or nearly so (if the LXX is preferred), the connection between the number of nations and Israel is probable.

[54] 1 Chr 1:8–16 parallels 10:6–20 but with extensive modifications.

[55] Sarna observes that three are of north Africa, and the fourth is the land bridge (Canaan) connecting Africa with Asia (*Genesis,* 72).

from Mizraim (vv. 13–14, excluding the "Philistines"). The dominant interest of the author, however, is the Hamite "Nimrod," who receives special attention as the progenitor of Mesopotamia's urban centers that later are prominent adversaries to ancient Israel (vv. 8–12).

HAM'S DESCENDANTS

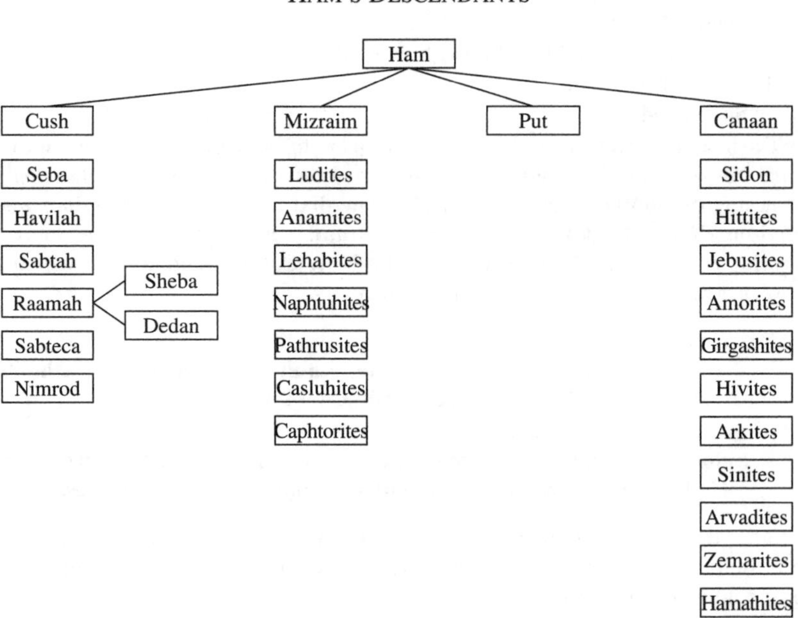

10:6 The first tier of Ham's lineage consists of four offspring. *Cush* is Africa's Nubia (the LXX's "Ethiopia,"[56] not modern Ethiopia), located south of Egypt. Both Hebrew and Akkadian names for Cush are derived from the Egyptian *Kš* ("Kush"), which originally referred to the region between the second and third cataracts of the Nile and which later among the Egyptians became a term for general Nubia,[57] a practice followed by the Hebrews and others. "Cush" often occurs elsewhere in the Old Testament (e.g., Isa 37:9; Jer 13:23 [NIV note]) and appears in the garden description (2:13). Some have posited that the term "Cush" in the Old Testament also can refer to two other

[56] Here the LXX transliterates Χους ("Chous") but usually as with the classical authors translates Ἀιθιοπίας (as at 2:13).

[57] See K. A. Kitchen, "Cush," *NBD* 284.

countries, a Kassite "Cush" and an Arabian "Cush."[58] This remains disputed (see 10:8 discussion).

The NIV's *Mizraim* is a transliteration of the Hebrew word for "Egypt." It is a dual form, meaning "two Egypts," in reference to Upper and Lower Egypt. It is later remembered as the "tents of Ham" (e.g., Ps 78:51). *Put* is disputed, although the LXX usually translates it as "Libya,"[59] which is west of Egypt on the northern coast. Others have recommended Egypt's "Punt" (modern Somalia) south of Ethiopia because Nah 3:9 distinguishes Put from the Libyans (Lubim). Libya is preferred on linguistic grounds and because of the geographical progression in our verse from south to north in the listing of Ham's offspring.[60] The term occurs among the prophets and is associated with "Cush" (Jer 46:9; Ezek 30:5; 38:5) and with "Tyre" (Ezek 27:10).

Canaan is critical to understanding the table as 9:24 shows. It occupies the author's attention, as its lengthy space in the Hamite lineage (vv. 15–18) and its territorial elaboration indicate (v. 19). The term "Canaan" has a complex history of use in and outside the Bible. It exhibits a fluidity in usage, varying between geographical locations and peoples. Its etymological history remains ambiguous as well.[61] As a geographical reference it speaks generally of the strip of land that lies west of the Jordan River (modern Israel) and includes modern Lebanon and portions of Syria. By associating the name with Egypt, the table reflects an early period when the "land of Canaan" was subject to Egyptian control. "Canaanite" occurs in a cuneiform text from Mari (eighteenth century), and the name "Canaan" appears in Egyptian and Mesopotamian texts in the fifteenth century and is often cited as an administrative district governed by Egypt during the Amarna period (fourteenth century).[62] The boundaries of Canaan reported in v. 19 (see discussion) are especially sig-

[58] The association of the name "Cush" with the Tigris-Euphrates in the garden (2:13) has led some to identify it with the Kassites (Akk. *Kaššu*) who lived northeast of Babylonia. For additional support they point to 10:8, where "Cush" is the father of Nimrod, who founded the great Babylonian cities (see 10:8). Another proposed Mesopotamian connection for Cush is the famed city Kish. A third "Cush" is identified with northwestern Arabia on the basis of the parallel "Cushan" and "Median" in Hab 3:7 (cf. also Num 12:1; Judg 3:8–10; 2 Chr 14:9–15[8–14]) as well as extrabiblical evidence. See, e.g., M. C. Astour, "Sabtah and Sabteca: Ethiopian Pharaoh Names in Genesis 10," *JBL* 84 (1965): 422.

[59] Here, however, the LXX transliterates the Heb. as Φουδ.

[60] See Westermann, *Genesis 1–11,* 511; for the linguistic argument see Kitchen, "Put," *NBD* 1066.

[61] The once-popular association of "Canaan" with dyed cloth from Phoenicia on the basis of Akk. *kinaḫḫu* in Nuzi texts, meaning "red purple" (e.g., B. Maisler, "Canaan and the Canaanites," *BASOR* 102 [1946]: 7–12), has been seriously challenged. More recently west Semitic derivations have been sought, but no consensus has been achieved. See M. C. Astour, "Toponomy of Ebla and Ethnohistory of Northern Syria," *JAOS* 108 (1988): 545–55.

[62] P. Schmitz summarizes the history of the term and also reviews its etymological possibilities (see "Canaan," *ABD* 1.828–29).

nificant for later Israel since it is the "land of Canaan" that is the inheritance of Abraham (e.g., 15:18–21; 17:8).[63]

At times in the biblical record, as is found among external sources as well,[64] "Canaan" was used specifically of a people. At other places the term overlaps with many diverse peoples who inhabited Syro-Palestine. Canaan, for example, refers to the peoples inhabiting the plains and the Jordan Valley (e.g., Num 13:29; Deut 1:7; Josh 11:3). And it may also specifically distinguish them from their immediate neighbors (e.g., 15:21; 34:30; Exod 3:17). On the other hand, "Canaan" can refer to a variety of peoples living in proximity. This is the case of Esau's wives, who are said to be from the "women of Canaan," which include a Hittite, Hivite, and Ishmaelite (36:2–3). This fluidity is reflected by Ezekiel's commentary on Israel's beginnings, "Your ancestry and birth were in the land of the Canaanites; your father was an Amorite and your mother was a Hittite" (16:3).[65] Canaan as a people or location also commonly fluctuates with the term "Amorites" (cf. e.g., 15:16; Josh 24:15–18; Judg 6:10; 1 Sam 7:14; Amos 2:10), though elsewhere "Amorite" can be used of specific residents of Cisjordan's hill country and the Transjordan kings Sihon and Og (e.g., Num 13:29; 21:21; Deut 3:8; Josh 10:5). The table shows by genealogy the intermingling of the inhabitants of Syro-Palestine (10:16). In later usage among the Greeks, "Canaan" was used of Phoenicia.

10:7 The second and third tiers of names, the sons (five, not counting Nimrod) and grandsons (two) of Cush, number seven descendants. The locations of his sons are largely unknown though clearly associated with African and Arabian locations. The identity of *Seba* (v. 7a) and its relationship to other tribes in the Hamitic and Shemitic families is obscure. "Seba" *(sĕbāʾ)* is similar in spelling to another descendant of Cush (by Raamah), "Sheba" (*šĕbāʾ;* v. 7b).[66] According to Genesis 10, the tribes therefore were distinct but both descendants of Ham. Yet a second "Sheba" is later noted in the table as a descendant of Shem (v. 28). What is striking is that *both* the Hamitic and Semitic lines share in the names "Sheba" and "Havilah" (vv. 7,28–29), which in turn are closely related tribal families within each line. Moreover, the duo

---

[63] "Land of Canaan" by far occurs most often in the Book of Genesis (34x), all in the patriarchal narratives (including 11:31).

[64] For such citations see Kitchen, "Canaan, Canaanites," *NBD* 183.

[65] C. G. Libot offers this illustration in "Canaan," *ISBE* 1.586.

[66] This points up recurring problems for modern scholars in locating ancient toponyms. Similarity in the spelling of place names can be taken in one of two ways: as orthographic variants of the same locale or as evidence of two related but different groups. Additionally, there is the problem of identical names (homonymy) for different places. In his work on the place names cited in the Ebla (north Syria) tablets from the latter half of the third millennium, Astour commented on such hindrances in his study of ancient Ebla's empire ("Toponymy of Ebla and Ethnohistory of Northern Syria: A Preliminary Survey," *JAOS* 108 [1988]: 545–55, esp. 549). This should caution those who conclude that similarities in the names of the Table of Nations are mistaken duplicates.

of names "Sheba and Dedan" in the Hamitic lineage (10:7b) occur again for the grandsons of the Shemite Abraham (25:3). This means Genesis presents (1) Sheba and Dedan as sons of Raamah (10:7b), (2) Sheba as son of Joktan (10:28), and (3) Sheba and Dedan as by Jokshan (of Abraham-Keturah, 25:3).

Traditionally the Sabeans of southwest Arabia (Yemen) have been identified with Sheba. As we noted, some have thought that Seba and Sheba are the same tribe with the spelling "Seba," an Ethiopic variant of the original "Sheba" pronunciation. There is ample evidence that there were migrations between southwest Arabia and Ethiopia.[67] Yet the biblical evidence shows Seba and Sheba occur as separate peoples in Ps 72:10, indicating that they are best taken as two different groups though closely related as the table indicates. Seba is grouped with Egypt and Cush in the Old Testament (Isa 43:3; 45:14), thus probably it refers to an African people. Herodotus (vii. 70) and Josephus (*Ant.* 2.10.2[249]) report that Seba was believed to be the ancient capital of Ethiopia, which Cambyses had named Meroe.

Havilah is part of the garden description, though it need not be the same location intended here (see discussion at 2:11). The name also occurs in 10:29, where it designates a son of the Shemite Joktan. Both Ham's and Shem's "Havilahs" are related to Arabia, and therefore the genealogies may indicate the intermingling of two peoples. Later the name as a geographical designation is related to the lineage of Ishmael (25:18; cf. 1 Sam 15:7), which again reflects a possible blending of peoples.[68]

Sabtah has been identified with ancient Shabwat, capital of Hadramaut in south Arabia. Another proposal has Sabtah as the name of the Ethiopian Pharaoh Shabaka of the late eighth century B.C.[69] Related to this proposal the unknown *Sabteca* of our verse is also identified as a personal name, Pharaoh Shabataka who succeeded Shabaka. However, to achieve the first equation it is assumed that the original Hebrew was *sbkh* (= Sabkah), which was miscopied *sbth* (= Sabtah). Both Sabtah and Sabteca are best taken as unknown south

[67] W. W. Müller ("Seba," *ABD* 5.1064) concludes that the two names are the same and that the association of Seba with north African sites is best explained as the result of migrations by Arabian Sabeans to Ethiopia. W. W. LaSor, while acknowledging the migrations of Arabian and Ethiopian peoples, argues on phonetic grounds (as well as the biblical evidence) that the two should be considered originally separate peoples though closely related (see his "Sabeans," *ISBE* 4.253). Also S. D. Ricks prefers to cite the appearance of Seba among the topographical names of east Africa as evidence of a distinctive people ("Sheba," *ABD* 5.1169–70).

[68] F. V. Winnett argues that "Havilah" in the OT refers to two different locations: (1) northeast Africa (2:11; 10:7) and (2) the Arabian desert ([25:18] "The Arabian Genealogies in the Book of Genesis," in *Translating and Understanding the Old Testament: Essays in Honor of Herbert Gordon May,* ed. H. T. Frank and W. L. Reed [Nashville: Abingdon, 1970], 177–79).

[69] Astour, "Sabtah and Sabteca," 422–25, and F. J. Yurko, "Sennacherib's Third Campaign and the Coregency of Shabaka and Shebitku," *Serapis* 6 (1980): 221–40. Also see Müller, "Sabtah," *ABD* 5.861–82, and "Sabteca," *ABD* 5.862.

Arabian sites. *Raamah* is commonly associated with south Arabia. It is named with Sheba in Ezek 27:22 as partners in trade with Phoenicia's Tyre. One recommendation for its location is ancient Ragmatum, the capital of the oasis of Nagran, located in then north Yemen but southwest Saudi Arabia today.[70]

The next tier of names, *Sheba* and *Dedan,* lists the two grandsons of Cush by Raamah (v. 7b). Both names are Arabian tribes that are known for their commercial trade (e.g., 1 Kgs 10:1–13; Ps 72:10; Ezek 27:15) and are associated together (e.g., Ezek 38:13). Sheba is best remembered because of its Sabaean queen, who visited Solomon's courts (1 Kgs 10:1; 2 Chr 9:1). Also, as noted, the grandsons of Abraham and Keturah bear the names Sheba and Dedan (Gen 25:3; 1 Chr 1:32). These we may take as individuals who were related to Abraham but not considered descendants of the Arabian tribes.[71] Dedan may be related to north Arabia since it appears to have a connection with Edom (Jer 49:8) and with Tema, a city in northern Arabia (cf. Gen 25:15; Job 6:19).[72] As for the appearance of "Sheba" in both the Hamite and Shemite lines (vv. 7,28), it is reasonable that two different peoples are intended, perhaps inhabiting the same region of southwest Arabia. Or two different locations may be in view with Hamitic "Sheba" in the north, where Dedan's location is probable, and the "Sheba" of Shem in southwest Arabia (modern Yemen).[73]

10:8–12 Another son of "Cush," if we are to take this as the same "Cush" of v. 6, is *Nimrod.* This narrative digression recounts the career of Nimrod, since he is the founder of prominent cities that impacted the history of the Hebrews (e.g., Babylon, Nineveh). Moreover, the means by which Nimrod achieves his ascendancy suggests that his distinction came by aggressive force rather than the gradual diffusion of peoples as shown elsewhere by the table. Nimrod in that sense was typological of how ancient Near Eastern empires came into existence.

Ancestral descent is recounted for the first time in the table by the expression "Cush was the father of Nimrod." "Was the father of" *(yālad)* introduces

---

[70] Müller argues this in "Raamah," *ABD* 5.597.

[71] Winnett surmises that the reason for positioning the Arab genealogies at different points in Genesis was the nature of the narrative materials; thus the Arab families which are not related to Abraham occur in Gen 10, while those people considered of Abraham were positioned in Gen 25 ("Arabian Genealogies," 195). We may add that the narrative scheme of Genesis has the repeated sequence of narrative and genealogy that advocates the placing of his genealogy at the end of the Abraham narratives.

[72] See LaSor's discussion, "Sabeans," 255.

[73] Sarna commends two Sheba's in Arabia (*Genesis,* 73). Winnett proposes that Dedan and Sheba had a common source (Raamah = Ragran of north Yemen) and migrated north and south, respectively ("Arabian Genealogies," 180). The second appearance of "Sheba" in 10:28, he explains, is from another source, which attributed all south Arabian tribes to the same ancestor, Joktan (p. 189).

three such sections in this Hamite genealogy (cf. vv. 13,15; on the use of this term see earlier discussion). The identity of "Cush" has been disputed since it is difficult to reconcile how the Semitic kingdoms, such as Babylon and Akkad (via Nimrod), could be attributed to the Hamites. As mentioned earlier, some have argued that the "Cush" of this passage is not the Hamite "Cush" (vv. 6–7) but is the ancestor of the Kassites (Cossaeans), perhaps an Indo-Aryan tribe that supplanted the Babylonians in the northeast region of Mesopotamia in the sixteenth century B.C. Since there is no indication in the text to take "Cush" differently from the same name of the immediate verses, it is best to interpret Nimrod's father as the Hamitic Cush. A better resolution lies in the observation that the predecessors of the Semite kingdoms of Mesopotamia were non-Semitic, which is consistent with the table's depiction.[74]

The identity of Nimrod is the subject of much discussion. Most suggestions arise from vague Mesopotamian or Egyptian connections and the reputation of Nimrod as warrior and hunter. The question revolves around whether Nimrod is understood as a god or a historical figure. Among the chief candidates for a mythological prototype are (1) Marduk, the patron deity of Babylon, (2) Ninurta, the Babylonian god of war and the hunt, and (3) the divine-human hero Gilgamesh of Erech. Ninurta has received stronger support. One proposal has interpreted Nimrod as the Israelite author's historicized version of the cult figure Ninurta.[75] Since we have seen already the Babylonian background of Genesis 10–11 in general, it is not remarkable that Nimrod's role as founder of Babylonian cities would create special interest. The commitment of the biblical author to history, however, would militate against a mere adoption of the Ninurta figure, even if "historicized." Although present scholars may imagine traces of Mesopotamian religious qualities lying behind the enigmatic Nimrod, it would be hazardous for an Israelite to risk such linkage among his ancient audience between his account and Mesopotamian ideology. Rather, at most, the career of Nimrod might serve as a polemic against Babylonian lore, as we will see in the case of the tower parody (11:1–9).

Proposals of historical figures include (1) Sargon of Akkad, (2) Naram-Sin, king of Akkad and grandson of the great Sargon, (3) the Egyptian ruler Amenhotep III, and (4) the Assyrian king Tukulti-Ninurta I (1243–1207). This last

---

[74] Wiseman, "Genesis 10," 21.

[75] See K. van der Toorn and P. W. van der Horst, "Nimrod before and after the Bible," *HTR* 83 (1990): 1–29, esp. 1–16. Van der Toorn's argument is based on the similarities between 10:8–12 and the chronology of the Ninurta cult, first prominent in southern Mesopotamia and later Assyria, and the exploits of the deity as hunter and city builder with the achievements of Nimrod. He admits the troublesome evidence opposing his proposal but dismisses it as not prohibitive, though in our view it is condemning: (1) "Ninurta" and "Nimrod" have no philological connection; (2) "Nisroch" in 2 Kgs 19:37//Isa 37:38 probably refers to Ninurta; and (3) Ninurta did not actually build "cities," though Mesopotamian urbanization is attributed to him.

suggestion has received some attention since he was the first Assyrian king to control Babylonia, and he was noted in antiquity for his building enterprises.[76] But we have seen that the table as a whole reflects a much earlier period than the thirteenth century. Moreover, the chronological and geographical progression shown in 10:8–12, from Babylonia to the northern cities of Assyria, does not correspond with the career of Tukulti-Ninurta.

The Nimrod pericope tells that he was (1) the first noted potentate and champion hunter (vv. 9–10), (2) whose exploits occasioned a proverb on later Israel (v. 9), and (3) who founded significant cities in Upper and Lower Mesopotamia (vv. 10–12). The recurrence of *hēḥēl,* translated "began"[77] in previous occasions (4:26; 6:1; 9:20 and 11:6), indicates a significant point in the narrative's progression (see 4:26; 9:20 discussion). The association of "mighty warrior" (v. 8) with the prowess of the hunt ("mighty hunter," v. 9) reflects the early traditions of Egyptian and Mesopotamian kings famous for this practice. In both expressions *gibbōr* ("mighty") refers to the strength of Nimrod as a champion warrior. It is reminiscent of 6:4, which describes the infamous heroes of the past. Usually the term occurs in the context of military achievements (e.g., Josh 10:2; Amos 2:14,16).

The proverb "Like Nimrod, a mighty hunter before the LORD" is unclear about how the author interprets the expression. "Before the LORD" has been taken as God's favor toward Nimrod or, conversely, suggesting sinful rebellion as in the thought of Ps 66:7: "He [God] rules forever by his power, his eyes watch the nations—let not the rebellious rise up against him." Some conclude alternatively that the phrase is neutral, only expressing a superlative, thereby indicating that Nimrod's activities stood out especially. Lexical connections between the Nimrod narrative and the tower event (11:1–9), however, encourage the reader to interpret Nimrod's activities, as the founder of Babel, in the same negative light the Lord "saw" the efforts of the tower builders.[78]

Following the description of Nimrod as warrior, the extent of his kingdom is reported (10:10–12). There appear to be two stages, first the cities "in Shinar" (v. 10) and then the founding of the Assyrian sites (vv. 11–12). Hebrew *rēʾšît,* translated "*first* centers," can also be rendered "chief centers," showing prominence, not just chronological order. The cities that are said to be "in the

[76] Speiser is the primary proponent of this suggestion; see his "In Search of Nimrod," in *Eretz-Israel* 5 (Jerusalem: Israel Exploration Society/Hebrew University, 1958), 32–36, and his commentary, *Genesis,* 72.

[77] The NIV translates "grew to be" for הֵחֵל לִהְיוֹת ("began to be," AV); REB has "began to be known." English versions also take it as "first": "Nimrod, who was the first potentate on earth" (NAB, NJB; also NRSV).

[78] Among the shared vocabulary are references to Babel, Shinar, the building of cities, and "began."

land of Shinar" are listed together (v. 10). "Shinar," or "the land of Shinar" (11:2; NIV "Babylonia," Dan 1:2; Zech 5:11), includes at least the region of Babylonia known in antiquity as "Sumer and Akkad" (see 11:2 discussion). The name appears again in Genesis for the site of the Babel builders (11:2) and also for one of the eastern kings defeated by Abraham (14:1,9). It occurs elsewhere in the Old Testament and refers to Babylon (NIV "Babylonia," e.g., Josh 7:21; Isa 11:11; Dan 1:2; Zech 5:11). Among the cities of Shinar listed, Babylon is given priority due to the tower incident (11:1–9). "Erech" refers to the important city Uruk of the Babylonians (modern Warka). "Akkad" was the ancient center of Sargon's empire (2350 B.C.), which later became associated with the whole Upper Mesopotamian region. The specific site has not been located. "Calneh" is problematic since the site is unknown from Akkadian inscriptions. Most agree that this place differs from the Calneh of Syria named in the prophets (Amos 6:2; NIV "Calno," Isa 10:9). A popular emendation to alleviate the difficulty is reading *wĕkullānâ,* "and all of them,"[79] but there is no parallel in the table for such a reading.

Verse 11 describes the expansion of Nimrod's influence into the region of *Assyria* (Heb. *ʾaššûr;* Akk. *aššûr*).[80] The expected syntax would read Asshur as the subject; thus, "Asshur went out and built," but the syntax permits Nimrod as the subject ("he," as NIV, NRSV), which best fits the flow of the narrative description where Nimrod moves "from that land," namely, Shinar, to the new region of Assyria. This tradition is reflected in the eighth century prophet Micah, who speaks of Assyria as "the land of Nimrod" (5:6[5]), the only passage other than Genesis and Chronicles where "Nimrod" is mentioned. It is often observed that the description of Nimrod's geographical expansion is consistent with what we know of the migration of Sumerian culture from the south to the northern regions of the Tigris-Euphrates Valley.

There Nimrod "built" a number of prominent cities, reminding the reader of wicked Cain, who constructed cities (4:17), and of the Babel builders (11:4,5,8). But righteous Noah and Abraham are remembered for "building" altars of worship to the Lord (e.g., 8:20; 12:7–8). *Nineveh* is listed first as the prominent city of the region. It is located on the east bank of the upper Tigris River opposite the city Mosul (northern Iraq) and had a history reaching back to earliest times. Much later it became central to the neo-Assyrian Empire of the eighth and seventh centuries that so grievously impacted the political history of Israel and Judah and was the focus of the prophetic ministries of Jonah and Nahum. Also noted are *Rehoboth Ir, Calah,* and *Resen*. Calah (Akk. *Kalkhu*) is well known to us as modern Nimrud, located about twenty miles south of Nineveh. Resen, however, is known only from the present descrip-

[79] Suggested by W. F. Albright, "The End of 'Calneh in Shinar,'" *JNES* 3 (1944): 254–55.

[80] See the discussion of "Asshur" at 10:22.

tion "between Nineveh and Calah."

Rehoboth Ir poses another problem for translators since, if taken as a place name, the city is unexplained.[81] This has prompted alternative readings of the Hebrew *(rĕḥōbōt ʿîr).* It can be translated "open places [plazas] of the city," referring to Nineveh's public squares (see NIV text note). The plazas would refer to various districts in the environs of the city (cf. the circuitous travels of the prophet Jonah). Or the phrase, if taken as a parallel usage to the Akkadian expression "open spaces in a city" *(rēbît ali),* can be understood as unbuilt areas around Nineveh. A related option is taking the phrase as a superlative, rendered "broadest among individual cities," which would correlate well with the final phrase, descriptive of Calah, "that is the great city."[82] Another recommendation is taking Rehoboth Ir as an interpretation of the Sumerian name *(AŠ.UR)* for the famous ancient city "Asshur," which one would expect in this catalog of Assyrian cities.[83] It would seem best to take the Hebrew as the place name, as we find in the LXX tradition *(Roōbōth polin),* since it occurs in a sequence of sites and all are introduced by the direct object marker *ʾet,* which in the case of Rehoboth Ir should not be explained away as some have.

"That is the great city" concludes the verse, but its antecedent is uncertain since it may refer to the immediate Calah or to the earlier Nineveh. Many prefer Nineveh due to the same report in Jonah (1:2; 3:2–3; 4:11), yet the expression is used of other citadels (e.g., Gibeon, Josh 10:2).

10:13–14 The second occurrence of *yālad* ("was the father of"; cf. vv. 8 and 15) introduces the offspring of Mizraim (Egypt). This tier of names, consisting of seven offspring if "Philistines" is parenthetical, parallels the tier of Cush's sons (v. 7). These names are in the Hebrew plural *(-îm),* referring to people groups. The first named are the *Ludites*, who have been commonly identified as the Lydians in western Asia Minor, although this is uncertain.[84] The name "Lud" in the singular occurs in the Shemite lineage (10:22).[85] Two different peoples are most likely intended. The Ludites of the Mizraim line formed one group and are mentioned in association with African peoples in the prophets (Jer 46:9; Ezek 30:5). The second group is of the Shemite lineage, noted with peoples from Asia Minor (Isa 66:19).[86]

Anamites, the second people listed, remain unknown, though some sugges-

[81] An unrelated "Rehoboth" occurs in Genesis as a site in Canaan (26:22; 36:37).

[82] J. M. Sasson, "*Reḥōvōt ʿîr*," *RB* 90 (1983): 94–96.

[83] See Wiseman, "Rehoboth-Ir," *NBD* 1083, for the philological description.

[84] The NIV translates "Lydia" or "Lydians," whereas the NRSV, e.g., has the transliterated Heb. לוּד ("Lud") and לוּדִים ("Ludim").

[85] The singular form "Lud" occurs in 10:22 (= 1 Chr 1:17); Isa 66:19; Ezek 27:10; 30:5.

[86] See D. R. Bratcher, "Lud," *HBD* 582. Yet this is not entirely satisfactory since the north African "Put" occurs in Isa 66:19 and Ezek 27:10 to complicate the matter. Nevertheless, the different forms of the two names "Lud" and "Ludites" probably show that two different peoples are in view.

tions have been made, including (1) Egyptian *knmt* in the Libyan desert (by reading the LXX *enemetiem* = *knmtym*) and (2) *mrywt'y*, as in *Tg. Ps.–J.*, which refers to a site west of Alexandria.[87] The third group is the *Lehabites*, who are commonly identified with the "Lubim," referring to the Lybians as in the LXX rendering *(Labiim)*. The Lybians resided west of Egypt (e.g., Dan 11:43; Nah 3:9). Fourth, the identification of the *Naphtuhites* is also unresolved, though their association with the Lehabites (= Lybians) and the Pathrusites (Upper Egypt) would argue for placing the Naphtuhites in Egypt, perhaps the Delta region. Various possible Egyptian etymologies for "Naphtuhites" recommend the site in Lower Egypt (i.e., northern delta) or perhaps near Memphis in Middle Egypt.[88]

Pathrusites (v. 14) are the people of Pathros (Upper Egypt, i.e., the southern region), which is regularly connected with Egypt by the prophets (Isa 11:11; Jer 44:1,15; Ezek 29:14; 30:14). The sixth and seventh peoples, the *Casluhites* and *Caphtorites*, must be treated together since our understanding of these peoples is related to the phrase "from whom the Philistines came" (v. 14). We do not know the location of the Casluhites, but there is wide agreement that Caphtor is the Aegean isle Crete. The association of Cretan culture with Egypt has long been established. Amos 9:7 and Jer 47:4, as well as extrabiblical sources, indicate that the Philistines were from Caphtor (Crete). In the table, however, the origins of the Philistines are attributed to the unknown Casluhites. Commonly, interpreters emend the reading of the text by taking the last clause with "Caphtorites" rather than Casluhites, thereby resolving the apparent tension between the sources.[89] Alternatively, the addendum "Philistines," as it stands, is recognized as a necessary explanation of Philistine origins that was based on an authentic early memory, namely, that the Philistines originally descended from the Casluhites.

To complicate the problem is the troublesome issue of early references in the patriarchal narratives to the "Philistines" (21:32,34; 26:1,8,14–18), whose presence in Canaan would antedate by centuries the arrival of the Philistines as indicated by Egyptian sources (ca. 1300–1200 B.C.). The "Philistines" are not known from extrabiblical sources by name *(prst)* until the early twelfth century B.C. during the reign of Rameses III (1198–1166 B.C.). They were part of the Mediterranean peoples, known from Egyptian sources as the "Sea Peoples," who invaded Syria, Palestine, and Egypt during the latter half of the thirteenth century. They

---

[87] For this discussion see R. S. Hess, "Anamim," *ABD* 1.222–23.

[88] C. G. Rasmussen, "Naphtuhim," *ISBE,* 490. On the option of Middle Egypt, see G. A. Rendsburg, "Gen 10:13–14: An Authentic Hebrew Tradition Concerning the Origins of the Philistines," *JNSL* 13 (1987): 89–96, esp. 91. He argues *Naptûḥîm* is a Hebraized form of Egyptian "those of Ptah," referring to the Memphites (Middle Egypt) since Ptah was the deity of Memphis.

[89] E.g., NAB, NRSV, NEB, NJPS, and among commentators, e.g., Westermann, *Genesis 1–11,* 496, 519; von Rad, *Genesis,* 147.

were successfully repelled by Rameses and settled along the Mediterranean coast in southwestern Canaan.[90] The association then of the Philistines with Caphtor (= Crete) as reflected by Amos and Jeremiah (cf. Ezek 25:16), it is widely thought, refers to the migration of the Sea Peoples. Generally, commentators have explained the early appearance of the Philistines in the patriarchal accounts as anachronistic. Others, as we will see next, argue that there are two migrations in view, an earlier group that Abraham and Isaac encountered in Canaan and a subsequent migration among the Sea Peoples (ca. 1200 B.C.).

How can Genesis 10 be squared with biblical and Egyptian sources that attribute Philistine origins to the Aegean Caphtorim? One answer observes that according to Amos 9:7 Israel came from Egypt, though the people did not originally have their source there; likewise the "Philistines" came from Caphtor, though originally they were of the Casluhites (as 10:14). In this opinion the term "Philistine" had reference to an early settlement of Caphtorites in southern Canaan (as Deut 2:23 illustrates) whom the patriarchs knew. "Philistine" was an elastic term and could refer to a number of Aegean groups that migrated to Canaan, including those cited in Egyptian sources.[91] This would accommodate the use of "Philistine" in both passages.

Another explanation points to evidence of Egyptian migration into southern Canaan in the early third millennium (3000–2800 B.C.). Some contend that among the migrants were the Casluhim, later known as "Philistines," who settled near Beersheba. These were the "Philistines" of the early period known to the patriarchs (e.g., Gen 20:2; 26:1; Exod 13:17; 23:31; Josh 13:3). Later the invasions of the Sea Peoples included the Caphtorites, who adopted the name "Philistines." This later migration is the subject of the prophets (Amos 9:7; Jer 47:4; cf. Deut 2:23). Thus two different but once-related peoples migrated to Canaan at separate times.[92] Another recent proposal has claimed the identity of the Casluhites as peoples of Lower Egypt (i.e., Delta region) who migrated to Crete before going to Canaan. It is contended, on the basis of linguistic analysis, that the Pathrusites are of Upper Egypt, the Naphtuhites of Middle Egypt, and the Casluhites therefore of Lower Egypt.[93] Such recommendations

[90] See T. Dothan, *The Philistines and Their Material Culture* (Jerusalem: Israel Exploration Society, 1982), 1–23. Even the association of the Philistines with Crete has been disputed; some recommend Caphtor is Cappadocia, located in southeast Asia Minor (pp. 21–23).

[91] So Kitchen, "The Philistines," in *Peoples of Old Testament Times,* ed. D. J. Wiseman (Oxford: Clarendon, 1973), 56–57. Kitchen observes that the Philistines of the patriarchal period appear to differ from the later groups; the former are ruled by a king whereas the later Philistines live under the pentapolis of five lords.

[92] R. K. Harrison, "Philistine Origins: A Reappraisal," in *Ascribe to the Lord: Biblical & Other Studies in Memory of Peter C. Craigie,* JSOTSup 67, ed. L. Eslinger and G. Taylor (Sheffield: JSOT, 1988), 11–19.

[93] Rendsburg shows that during the Bronze Age a general migration occurred from Egypt to Crete to Canaan as Gen 10:13–14 reflects ("Gen 10:13–14: An Authentic Hebrew Tradition," 89–96).

are reasonable and give priority to the witness of the biblical text, but none can be confirmed until more is learned about the obscure Casluhites.

10:15–19 The third elaboration in the table, introduced again by the use of *yālad* (also vv. 8,13), is the description of Canaan's descendants. Of Ham's four sons there is no tracing of the lineage of Put. Eleven groups descended from Canaan, by far the majority among the Hamite clans. They make up the tier of names corresponding to the five sons of Cush (excluding Nimrod) and the seven of Egypt. Only Joktan among the Shemite line lists more groups (thirteen; vv. 26–29). Beginning with the Jebusites, the last nine names of the Canaanite clans have the distinctive Hebrew gentilic suffix *-î,* designating ethnicity. The importance of Canaan for the author is shown by the detail of the passage, particularly its territorial boundaries (v. 19), and the impressive number of descendants listed.

First, *Sidon* is distinguished from the others as Canaan's "firstborn" (v. 15). This ancient city was the earliest among the great urban centers of Phoenicia. This attribution "firstborn" and the absence of Tyre, which later supplanted Sidon in importance, suggests that the table reflects an early second millennium understanding of the nations. The second name is the *Hittites* (= *ḥēt/ ḥittî,* Akk. *ḫattû*), which may be confused with the Hittites of Asia Minor (modern Turkey), that is, the Hittite Empire (ca. 1800–1200 B.C.), or the neo-Hittite kingdoms of northern Syria that survived the dissolution of the empire.[94] The "Hittites" in Genesis 10 and elsewhere in Genesis were inhabitants of Canaan who antedated the arrival of the patriarchs and later Israel (15:20). According to Ezekiel, the city of Jerusalem owed its existence to the Amorites and Hittites (16:3; see Jebusites in the following paragraph). The Hittites during the patriarchal period resided in Judah's territory, especially in the Hebron area. They play an important role in the life of the patriarchs. The cave of Machpelah purchased from Ephron the Hittite is the family tomb of the patriarchs (23:3ff.; 25:10; 49:29–32; 50:13), and Esau married Hittite wives (26:34; 36:2).[95] Specific Hittites named in the Old Testament (e.g., Ephron, Zohar, and Uriah) have Semitic names, as we would expect since they are part of Canaanite culture.

The listing continues to cite Canaan's peoples whom the later Hebrews will encounter in the land. *Jebusites* (v. 16) were the inhabitants of "Jebus," that is, Jerusalem, antedating the patriarchs (15:21) and entrance of Israel into Canaan (e.g., Josh 15:8). Their ethnic origins are disputed, though most agree that they were non-Semitic, as the table shows. Some recommend that "Jebus"

[94] The Hittites of the old Empire were an Indo-European people who migrated to Asia Minor about 2000 B.C., where they assimilated the native inhabitants of the region known as the Hattians and adopted their name, calling themselves the "men of Hatti." For this discussion see H. A. Hoffner, "The Hittites and Hurrians," in *Peoples of the Old Testament Times,* ed. D. J. Wiseman (Oxford: Clarendon, 1973), 197–228.

[95] Cf. Rebekah's disgust over the Hittite women (27:46).

(Yebus) is related to Amorite *Yabusum,* which correlates with Ezekiel's attribution of Jerusalem to the Amorites (16:3). The Jebusites make a significant impact on later Israel, successfully defending their citadel until the time of David (e.g., Exod 3:8; Josh 12:8; Judg 1:21; 2 Sam 5:6–9).

The fourth name is the *Amorites*, who are best known in the Old Testament as a member of the list of nations whose residence in Canaan preceded the patriarchs and later Israel (e.g., 15:16). Abraham enjoyed a peaceful coexistence with the Amorites, who joined him in defeating a coalition of eastern kings (14:5–7,13). The Akkadian word *amurru* first referred to the "west" and later designated the peoples and kingdoms northwest of Mesopotamia.[96] On the basis of Akkadian and Egyptian sources, it is generally thought that the "Amorites," whose rulers bore Semitic names, migrated from the west and subjugated the old Mesopotamian cities. Among these were Babylon's famed King Hammurapi and the people of Mari, in the early half of the second millennium. The influx of the Amorites in Canaan is disputed. It does not necessarily follow that the original Amorites, attributed to Hamite descent in Genesis 10, were a Semitic people since the term "Amorite" in ancient Near Eastern documents does not serve as a definitive source for designating ethnicity. Moreover, linguistic evidence does not always assure true ethnic derivation.[97] In the Old Testament the name is used broadly of the land (e.g., 15:16; Deut 1:7) and is associated with the specific Transjordan kings Sihon and Og (e.g., Num 21:25,32–34). The Amorites and Hittites were instrumental in the origins of Jerusalem (Ezek 16:3; see previous comments on "Jebusites").

Next, *Girgashites* refers to another Canaanite populace the Israelites confronted (e.g., 15:21; Deut 7:1; Josh 3:10; 24:11), but little is known about them. The sixth name is the *Hivites* (v. 17), about whom we know little except their early occupation of Canaan and their opposition to the Israelites (e.g., Exod 3:8; Deut 7:1). Shechem, responsible for the rape of Jacob's daughter Dinah, is identified as the "son of Hamor the Hivite" (Gen 34:2). Other "Hivites" mentioned in the Old Testament lived in Lebanon (Judg 3:3), Gibeon (Josh 9:1,7), and near Mount Hermon (Josh 11:3; 2 Sam 24:7) as well as Transjordan (Gen 36:2). Some associate the Hivites with another obscure people, the Horites, who dwelt at Mount Seir, on the basis of Zibeon the Hivite (Gen 36:2), who is included among the Horites (36:20,29). Also the LXX has "Horite" rather than "Hivite" in Gen 34:2 and Josh 9:7. This textual difference can be attributed to the confusion of spellings (*ḥwt* and *ḥrt,* where the Hebrew letters *w* and *r* are similar in appearance). The matter is complicated, however, by the suggestion

[96] See G. Mendenhall, "Amorites," *ABD* 1.199–202; H. B. Huffmon, "Amorites," *HBD* 27.

[97] A. R. Millard, "Amorites," *NBD* 31–32; M. Liverani, "The Amorites," in *Peoples of the Old Testament Times,* ed. D. J. Wiseman (Oxford: Clarendon, 1973), 101.

of some that the Horites are the ancient non-Semitic Hurrians, known from extrabiblical texts, though this is seriously questioned. In short, the table shows that the Hivites were an originally non-Semitic people, and perhaps later the association of the Hivites and Horites came about as a result of migration and displacement where "Horite" came to refer to different ethnic groups.[98]

The *Arkites* resided on the Lebanon coast (city Irqata), and the *Sinites*, though their identity is uncertain, probably were located nearby. Some have identified the Sinites with the north Phoenician city of Siyanu, which is known from Akkadian texts.[99] The ninth name, the *Arvadites*, is well attested in ancient Near Eastern texts, including Ezek 27:8,11. It is modern Ruad, located on an island off the north Phoenician coast. The home of the *Zemarites* is commonly mentioned in texts outside the Bible as Akkadian *Simirra* and in the Amarna correspondence as *Sumur*. It is identified by many as modern Sumra, which lies on the Mediterranean coast of Syria between Tripoli and Arvad.[100] Finally, the *Hamathites* are the inhabitants of the well-known Hamath (= modern Hama), the ancient Syrian city located on the River Orontes. It marked the northernmost boundary of the land of Canaan (e.g., Num 34:8; Josh 13:5) and was the northern marker for the realm of Solomon and the state of Israel under Jeroboam II (1 Kgs 8:65; 2 Kgs 14:25–28).

From these the various families of the Canaanites "scattered" (*pûṣ*, v. 18b). We observed earlier (cf. v. 5) the repetition of the dispersal motif that runs throughout this section (10:1–11:9). This first use of the term *pûṣ* anticipates the punishment of the tower builders (11:4,8–9). This implied association of the Canaanites and the disapproved Babelites echoes Noah's invocation against Canaan (see 9:25 discussion). Here it prepares the reader for the geographical dimensions of the land that follow (v. 19).

The description of Canaan's territories points to Sidon as the northernmost boundary and the southwestern perimeter toward Gerar "as far as Gaza," which sits on the main north-south highway, connecting Egypt and the Fertile Crescent along the Mediterranean coast. The southeastern line runs through the southern region of the Dead Sea marked by the cities Sodom and Gomorrah and the lesser known Admah and Zeboiim (cf. Hos 11:8) to "as far as Lasha," whose locale is unknown. The location of the infamous pentapolis (including Zoar) in the Dead Sea region remains a puzzle.[101] "Lasha" occurs

[98] For proposed solutions see further discussion in Baker, "Hivites," *ABD* 3.234; J. J. M. Roberts, "Horites," *HBD,* 404–5; and A. van Selms, "Hivites," *ISBE* 2.724.

[99] For this proposal see the summary of J. M. Wiebe, "Sinites," *ISBE* 4.529, and for others see Baker, "Sinites," *ABD* 6.50–51.

[100] B. J. Beitel, "Zemarite," *ISBE* 4.1188.

[101] The cities Sodom, Gomorrah, Admah, Zeboiim, and Zoar are identified as a pentapolis in *Wis* 10:6 (cf. Gen 14:2,8). For a discussion of the location of Sodom and Gomorrah, see D. M. Howard, "Sodom and Gomorrah Revisited," *JETS* 27 (1984): 385–400.

only once in the Old Testament and is regarded as a southern site only because of its association with the pentapolis here. The table's description of Canaan's land is not like the detailed assessments found elsewhere (e.g., 15:18; Num 34:2–12; Ezek 47:15–20; 48:1–28) and focuses only on the Cisjordan area.[102] The description of Canaan's boundaries here correspond to the Egyptian province of Canaan during the reign of Ramsses II (ca. 1280 B.C.).[103]

Gerar, Sodom, and Gomorrah become important to the patriarchal narratives, especially Abraham's travels.[104] This probably explains why northern sites that were of less importance to the patriarchs are ignored by the table. "Gaza" is included probably since it was well known for its strategic place in international matters and was important to later Israel's understanding of Canaan's geopolitical history (e.g., Deut 2:23).

10:20 This is the second of three colophons in the table (also vv. 5,31), differing somewhat from that of Japheth (v. 5) but sharing in the same observation that these peoples were members of the general dispersal of nations across the face of the earth.

(4) Sons of Shem (10:21-31)[105]

[21]Sons were also born to Shem, whose older brother was Japheth; Shem was the ancestor of all the sons of Eber.

[22]The sons of Shem:
Elam, Asshur, Arphaxad, Lud and Aram.
[23]The sons of Aram:
Uz, Hul, Gether and Meshech.
[24]Arphaxad was the father of Shelah,
and Shelah the father of Eber.
[25]Two sons were born to Eber:
One was named Peleg, because in his time the earth was divided; his
brother was named Joktan. [26]Joktan was the father of Almodad, Sheleph,
Hazarmaveth, Jerah, [27]Hadoram, Uzal, Diklah, [28]Obal, Abimael, Sheba,
[29]Ophir, Havilah and Jobab. All these were sons of Joktan.

[30]The region where they lived stretched from Mesha toward Sephar, in the eastern hill country.

[31]These are the sons of Shem by their clans and languages, in their territories and nations.

---

[102] Gen 15:18–21 and Deut 1:7 describe the land as far east as the Euphrates.

[103] So Sarna, *Genesis,* 77.

[104] E.g., Abraham's battle against the vassal kings of the east in chaps. 13–14, the destruction of the cities of the plain in chaps. 18–19, and the sojourn of the patriarch (and later Isaac) in the Negev, where he meets Abimelech of Gerar (chaps. 20–21; 26).

[105] 1 Chr 1:17–23 parallels the Shemite lineage of 10:21–31.

SHEM'S DESCENDANTS

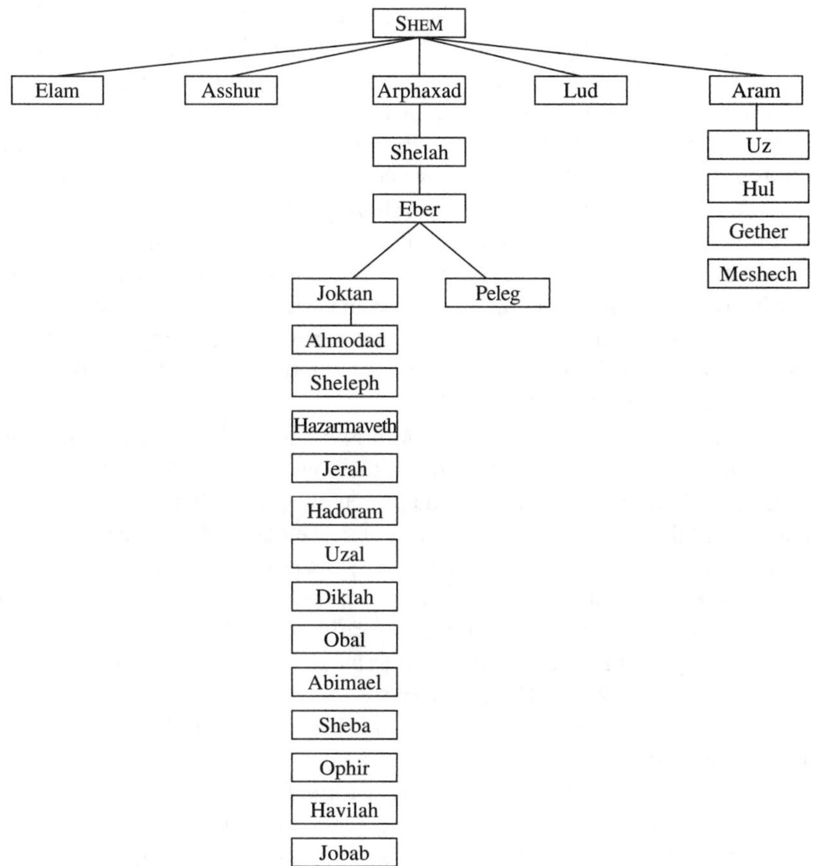

Now the author turns attention to the chosen lineage of the Shemites, from whom will come Eber, the ancestor of Abraham's father, Terah. We have said it is the practice of Genesis to give the lines of the nonelect families before the lineage of the chosen descent. When the two lines of Shem are compared (10:21–31; 11:10–26), there is a striking divergence at the point of Eber's descendants, Peleg and Joktan. In chap. 10 Peleg is dropped altogether after his mention, while the nonelect line of Joktan is detailed. It is left to the second lineage in chap. 11 to trace out Peleg's role as ancestral father of Abraham (see 11:10 discussion).

Included in this catalog are the names of individuals, clans, and regions. There are four tiers of names, twenty-six in all, with most detail given to the offspring of Joktan, who has thirteen descendants.

10:21 This introductory statement highlights the Shem line, which differs from the prologues of the previous two branches by its additional phrase, "[Sons] were born also to Shem." The verb *yālad* occurs again (cf. vv. 8,13,15) but here in the passive ("were born"), as in the preamble of 10:1,[106] yet without an expressed subject. The versions must supply the subject (NIV's "sons"), but the ellipsis of *bĕnê* in the Hebrew text draws even more attention to the heading. This is clear from 4:26, where the same construction occurs with the stated subject "son" *(bēn)*. We commented earlier that the author has used *yālad* in the Hamite branch to highlight particular members (Cush, Mizraim, and Canaan). Now the Shemite lineage has a preponderance of the verb, occurring five times in all, four of which appear in the short stretch of vv. 24–26. This is striking since the same verbal root is standard in the construction of the elect lines of Seth (chap. 5) and Shem (chap. 11). By appropriating the same term, our author has highlighted the line of Shem in the midst of the nonelect families named (Ham, Japheth).

Also the heading accents the descent of Shem through *Eber* by the description of the patriarch as "the father of all the sons of Eber." Because he is the ancestor of Abram (11:16–26), his name receives immediate attention in the table, although Eber is a fourth-generation descendant. In the Hebrew syntax of our verse this clause takes precedence over the subsequent addendum that reports Shem's filial relationship with Japheth (contra NIV; see NASB, NRSV). Inferred from the gentilic form of the term "Hebrew" *(ʿibrî)* is that Eber *(ʿēber)* gave his name to the patriarchs and later Israelites (e.g., 14:13; 39:14; 41:12; Exod 2:11). The etymology of "Hebrew," however, remains disputed.[107] "Hebrew" does not occur in the genealogies of chaps. 10 and 11. The term is seldom used in the Old Testament compared to "Israelite(s)" and occurs usually to distinguish the Hebrew people from foreigners (e.g., 43:32; Exod 2:6; 1 Sam 4:6–9). Joseph describes Canaan as the "land of the Hebrews" (40:15), and later at the burning bush God identifies himself to Moses as the "God of the Hebrews" (Exod 3:18).

---

[106] At 10:1 it is in the *niphal* rather than the *pual* as here.

[107] Another recommendation is Heb. עֵבֶר, meaning "across" or "beyond," thus "one who is from beyond the other side" (see BDB, 719–20). The LXX adopts this in its rendering of Gen 14:13, where "Abram the Hebrew" is Αβραμ τῷ περάτῃ ("Abram the wanderer"; see LSJ, 1179). Others attribute it to Akk. *abiru/apiru* (Sumerian *SA.GAZ;* WSemitic *ʿabiru*/*ʿapiru*), which referred to a social class of outcasts or fugitives who were of many different ethnic groups and served as mercenaries known throughout the ancient Near East in the second millennium B.C. For a brief treatment see A. F. Rainey, "Hebrews," *HBD,* 378–80, and "Khapiru," *HBD,* 525; also N. P. Lemche, "Habiru, Hapiru," *ABD* 3.6–10. Also M. Greenberg, *The Hab/piru,* AOS 39 (New Haven: Yale University Press, 1955), and O. Loretz, *Habiru-Hebräer. Eine sozio-linguistische Studie über die Herkunft des Gentiliziums ʿibrî vom Appellativum habiru,* BZAW 160 (Berlin: de Gruyter, 1984).

In 9:24 the reference to Ham as the youngest brother leaves it to our verse to sort out who is the older between Shem and Japheth (see 9:24 discussion). Jewish tradition and some modern commentators interpret the Hebrew of 10:21 so as to make Japheth the elder brother to Shem (so NIV, AV).[108] Most English versions, however, interpret Shem as "Japheth's older brother."[109] Thus our author has shown in yet another way that Shem has priority among the three sons, despite coming third in the table, with the actual chronological order of birth Shem, Japheth, and Ham.[110]

10:22 After Shem the first tier of names includes five descendants (v. 22). *Elam* is located in the mountainous region east of the Tigris-Euphrates Valley (modern southwest Iran). Its ancient capital was Susa (e.g., Esth 1:2–5; Dan 8:2). Among the coalition of eastern kings whom Abraham routed was the king of Elam (14:1,9). Problematic for modern readers is the presence of Elam in the Shemite lineage since the language is non-Semitic. Its placement in the Shemite branch cannot be solely for cultural or geographical reasons since on this basis we would expect such Hamitic peoples as Babylon, Assyria, and Canaan under Shem, not Ham. More reasonably, it may be posited that the earliest settlers of Elam were Semites who never became the dominant group in the region.[111] *Asshur* (= Akk. *aššur*) is located on the upper Tigris River in northern Mesopotamia (modern Iraq). Its name was appropriated for the region and inhabitants (i.e., Assyria). It also appears in the Ham lineage, where the NIV translates "Assyria" (10:11). The appearance of "Asshur" in each list probably refers to two different people groups possessing the same name. The earliest settlers of Asshur were of Sumerian culture (i.e., Hamitic), and they were supplanted by the Semitic culture that spread throughout Mesopotamia.[112]

Arphaxad remains a mystery, though some attempt to relate it to Arrapha, modern Kirkuk in Iraq. Others relate it to Babylonia on the basis that the last three letters of Arphaxad *(kšd)* may refer to the Chaldeans (*kaśdîm,* 11:28) who inhabited the southern region of Babylonia (cf. "Kesed," 22:22). His name also occurs in 11:10. We have mentioned already the puzzle of *Lud* in 10:13, where the plural form "Ludites" occurs.

The final name in this tier is the important *Aram*, which the Greeks called

[108] E.g., the LXX, *Gen. Rab.* 27:6, Rashi; also *Vg* and perhaps MT. The identity of the elder son bears on a problematic chronological notice in 11:10 (see *ad loc.*).

[109] Among English versions, e.g., the NIV text note, NASB, NRSV, REB, NAB, NJB, NJPS. The Heb. has אֲחִי יֶפֶת הַגָּדוֹל. Usually an adjective (הַגָּדוֹל) does not modify a proper name (i.e., "the elder Japhet") in Hebrew (so Sarna, *Genesis,* 78).

[110] In the formulaic expression "Shem, Ham and Japheth," the disqualified son takes the second place (e.g., 5:32; 6:10; 7:13; 9:18; 10:1; 1 Chr 1:4).

[111] So Wiseman, "Genesis 10," 22; also see A. R. Millard, "Elam, Elamites," *NBD,* 355.

[112] See Wiseman, "Genesis 10," 20, 22.

"Syria." However, the terms Aram and Arameans are fluid, sometimes referring to the whole Aramean kingdoms (e.g., 1 Kgs 10:29) and at other times tied to specific areas and cities (e.g., Aram-Naharaim, Paddan-Aram, Aram-Zobah).[113] The Arameans settled diverse sites in Syria and Mesopotamia during the second millennium. The table's early association of Aram with Mesopotamian areas (Assyria and Elam) is also indicated by the later prophet Amos (9:7), who attributes their origins to Kir, perhaps located in Elam or Assyria (cf. Isa 22:6). The notion of a proto-Aramean settlement in Mesopotamia has been recommended but cannot be confirmed.[114]

Aram plays an important role in the patriarchal narratives where family connections with Aramean stock in the district of Haran are maintained (e.g., 11:28–32; 25:20; 28:5; 31:18,20–24). This explains the identification of Jacob as a "wandering Aramean" in Deut 26:5. The name "Aram" also occurs in the genealogy of Nahor, brother of Abraham (22:21). Moreover, "Uz," which follows Aram in Genesis 10, is the same name in chap. 22 listed as Aram's uncle. Since the genealogies are vastly different in form and function, it is best to view each "Aram" as a different entity. The "Aram" of the table refers to an eastern ancestor whose name was given to the Arameans. This is supported by Amos 9:7, which places Aram as a Shemite neighbor of Elam. In the patriarchal narratives Aram refers to an individual named after his Aramean heritage.[115]

10:23 Of the five sons of Shem, only the offspring of Arphaxad and Aram are given. The inclusion of Aram with his descendants probably is because of the Arameans' importance in the history of the Hebrews. In this second tier of names there are four descendants of Aram (v. 23).[116] *Uz,* probably head of an Aramean tribe, has already been mentioned in his connection with Aram in the genealogy of Nahor, Abraham's brother (22:21). Here the name refers to an Aramean tribe. Uz is best known as the home of Job (1:1), situated in the "east" (1:3), perhaps Edom or in the Arabian desert (cf. 1:15,17,19; 2:11; 32:2 w/Jer 25:21,24).[117] The Edomite Uz appears as the son of a Horite chieftain dwelling at Seir (36:28–29), and Uz and Edom are depicted as interdependent (Lam 4:21; cf. also Jer 25:20–21). Most likely Job's "Uz" is not the same since the Arameans were located in Syria and northern Mesopotamia.[118] *Hul* and *Gether* are unidentified. "Meshech," as it is rendered in the NIV, appears

[113] W. T. Pitard, "Aram (Place)," *ABD* 1.338.

[114] Proposed, among others, by K. Kitchen, "Aram," *NBD,* 56.

[115] Suggested by Block, "Table of Nations," 710.

[116] In 1 Chr 1:17 these four names are listed as the sons of Shem also; this probably is the result of a simple haplography.

[117] See R. Alden, *Job,* NAC (Nashville: Broadman, 1993), 46–47, who argues for the "northernmost part of Saudi Arabia."

[118] This is the conclusion of W. S. LaSor, "Uz," *ISBE* 4.959.

to duplicate the *Meshech* of the Japhethite lineage (see 10:2 discussion). Yet the Hebrew text at 10:23 reads "Mash" *(maš)* and may well refer to another people. Its identity remains undetermined. Possibilities are "Masa," located in central Asia Minor and known from Hittite texts, the mountains of Lebanon, which are called *mâšu* in the *Gilgamesh Epic,* or Mount Masius of northern Mesopotamia.[119]

10:24 As noted earlier, the line of descent through Arphaxad is another elaboration in the table, indicated at each place by the use of *yālad* (v. 24; cf. vv. 8,13,15). This tier parallels the four sons of Aram but consists of one name only, *Shelah,* who is the son of Arphaxad and father of Eber (cf. 11:12–15). The identity of Shelah is uncertain, but the name occurs again among the families of Judah (38:5,11,14,26; 46:12; Num 26:20; 1 Chr 2:3; 4:21–23).[120]

10:25 Eber is said to father two sons, *Peleg* and *Joktan* (v. 25). While Joktan occupies the genealogical attention of our author, tracing thirteen descendants (vv. 26–29), it is Peleg's mention that elicits the etymological comment "because in his time the earth was divided" (v. 25). The play between the name "Peleg" *(peleg)* and "divided" *(niplĕgâ)* is created by their homonymity, both of which have the letters *p-l-g*. This explication on the name "Peleg" ties the genealogy to a specific event known to the original readers.[121] The problem for us is the identity of the event to which the table alludes.

The verb "divide" occurs only twice more, though its related noun "channel" or "stream" is well attested (e.g., Ps 1:3); it is used of digging a channel for rainwater (Job 38:25) and the "confounding" of language (Ps 55:9[10]). Supported by this latter passage, the traditional opinion has been to take it as a reference to the tower episode, where the "scattering" (vv. 5,8–9) of the Babelites is the result of God's "confusing their language" (v. 7). This is the more likely viewpoint, but this linkage cannot be dogmatically held since there is no clear allusion to 11:1–9 because "scattered" *(pûṣ)* and "divided" *(niplĕgâ)* are different words. Other possibilities have been proposed. "Earth" can be rendered as "land," in which case it could indicate an earthquake or a significant water works development for agricultural irrigation. If we take "land" as a metonymy for "people," it can be taken as a political schism. If the traditional opinion is declined, more attractive is the "division" of the "land" (i.e., people) as a reference to the split between the

---

[119] See these and other proposals in D. W. Baker, "Mash," *ABD,* 4.587–88.

[120] Also Shelah occurs in Luke 3:35–36, where he is a son of "Cainen," who is the son of Arphaxad, according to the LXX tradition of 11:12 (see 11:10–26).

[121] The obscurity of "Peleg" became a source of later rabbinic discussion, by which the rabbis referred to the Babel generation as the "Generation of Separation" *(dwr hplgh),* and also a subject alluded to in the Dead Sea Scrolls, where the "House of Peleg" *(bêt peleg)* may have been an appellative for the Covenanters themselves or a group that split from the original community. See R. T. White, "The House of Peleg in the Dead Sea Scrolls," in *A Tribute to Geza Vermes: Essays on Jewish and Christian Literature and History,* JSOTSup 100, ed. P. Davies and R. T. White (Sheffield: JSOT, 1990), 67–98.

two families of Eber, the Pelegites and the Joktanites.

A geographical identification for "Peleg" is unknown, but the name is clearly intended as an individual in chap. 11. "Joktan" on the face of it can be related to the word for "small" or "young" *(qāṭān)*, perhaps suggesting "younger brother," but there is no attempt in the text to derive a play with the appellative as it does with "Peleg." As for Joktan, no location can be ascertained except for the general region of Arabia as recommended by the subsequent descendants, which can be pinpointed as Arabian sites and tribes.

10:26–29 This final tier of names dominates the Shemite group, consisting of half (thirteen) of the total names cataloged under Shem. Those that can be identified are in the south Arabian peninsula.[122] *Almodad* is unknown. If the LXX's rendering *elmōdad* is followed, Almodad may be related to Hebrew *dôd* or *mōdad* ("beloved"), thus meaning "God [El] is a friend." If Arabic *ʾāl*, meaning "clan" or "family," is taken as the first part of the name, the second part may refer to a specific tribe, *mawdad*. A proposal for a South Yemen location has been made.[123] *Sheleph* has been related to Yemenite tribes on the basis of its association with *Hazarmaveth*, that is, modern Hadramaut in southwest Arabia, east of Yemen. *Jerah's* location is unknown, but it probably refers to another tribe in the south Arabian peninsula. Some relate it to Warah in Yemen. In Hebrew and South Arabic, *yeraḥ* means "month" and is closely related to the word for "moon" *(yārēaḥ)*, which was the primary deity of the south Arabian pantheon.[124]

Hadoram also remains a mystery (v. 27). Literally it means "Had[ad] is exalted," referring to the storm deity of Mesopotamia (and Baal of Ugarit). The name occurs later for the son of Tou, king of Hamath (1 Chr 18:10) and Solomon's overseer (= "Adoram," 1 Kgs 12:18; "Adoniram," 2 Chr 10:18). Some associate it with the modern site Dauram in Yemen. *Uzal* has been identified with modern Sanaa, capital of Yemen, though this has been brought into serious dispute. It appears also in Ezek 27:19, but there it probably refers to a northern Syria location.[125] Its identity is unsolved. "Diklah" (Heb. *diqlâ*) is thought to be an oasis in south Arabia but only because of its name, which is related to *deqel*, meaning "date palm."[126]

Obal also is unknown (v. 28; "Ebal," 1 Chr 1:22), although some have suggested modern Ubal or other Yemenite highland locations.[127] The name is

[122] Winnett concludes that 10:26–29 offers south Arabian groups while Ishmael's descent (25:13–16) gives north Arabian inhabitants ("Arabian Genealogies," 195).

[123] For the connection with Yemen, see W. W. Müller, "Almodad," *ABD* 1.160–61.

[124] See W. W. Müller, "Jerah," *ABD* 3.683.

[125] So W. S. LaSor, "Uzal," *ISBE* 4.960.

[126] W. W. Müller recommends the districts Sirwāh or Mārib because of their reputation for date groves ("Diklah," *ABD* 2.198–99).

[127] Ibid., "Obal," 4.4–5.

absent in the LXX at 10:23, which means twelve sons are listed.[128] "Abimael," meaning "my father is truly God,"[129] remains unidentified. One proposal has Abimael in the region of the ancient town Haram in the Yemenite Jawf.[130] *Sheba* has already been discussed at v. 7, where the name occurs in the Hamite lineage.

Ophir (v. 29) is best known in the Old Testament as a distant land noted for its gold (e.g., 1 Kgs 9:28; 10:11; 1 Chr 29:4; Job 22:24; Ps 45:9[10]). Recommendations for its location have varied from Africa to India. If the Joktanite name refers to the same "Ophir," it may be in southwest Arabia, as the other names of the Joktanite line have indicated. Another name already mentioned is *Havilah* (see v. 7). The final name of the Shemite branch is *Jobab,* which was the name of an Edomite king (36:33–34) as well as other individuals (e.g., Josh 11:1; 1 Chr 8:9,18). Some have proposed various Arabian connections, such as the Sabean tribe Yuhaybab,[131] but the identification eludes us.

10:30 As in the case with the Canaanites (v. 19), a summary of the Joktanite territory follows the naming of the Arabian tribes. This supplementary detail serves as another indication of the importance attributed to the Shemite line by the author. The Joktanite branch deserved special distinction as a descendant of the Hebrew ancestor "Eber" (v. 25). The particular boundary sites of Mesha and Sephar are a dilemma, though possibly the further depiction "in the eastern hill country" suggests that the perimeters are given in terms of the east-west boundaries of the Arabian locale. Mesha has been associated with north Arabia, perhaps a branch of the Ishmaelites (= "Massa," 25:14), though most of the Joktanite names are in the southwest. On this basis too it has been ventured that Sephar is located in south Arabia.[132] The identity of Mesha and Sephar remains an enigma.

10:31 We have already discussed the importance of this concluding colophon for the Shemite line in the table (see vv. 5,20).

(5) Conclusion (10:32)

[32]These are the clans of Noah's sons, according to their lines of descent, within their nations. From these the nations spread out over the earth after the flood.

---

[128] The configuration of twelve sons matches that of Esau and Jacob.

[129] This assumes the *mêm* element in אֲבִימָאֵל is the enclitic *mā,* which indicates emphasis; thus אֲבִי ("my father") + מָ ("truly") + אֵל ("El" or "God").

[130] This association is based on Sabaean epigraphic evidence; it is argued that proper names from Haram have the linguistic peculiarity of an enclitic *m,* which distinguishes the names coming from this site (W. W. Müller, "Abimael," *ABD* 1.20).

[131] See W. W. Müller's citation of E. Glazer (1890) in "Jobab," *ABD* 3.871.

[132] For proposals see the summary of G. H. Oller, "Mesha," *ABD* 4.708, and "Sephar," *ABD* 5.1089.

10:32 The final summary statement for the whole catalog of Noah's offspring draws together the themes already heard in the presentation of the table. The summary forms the closing inclusio with the introduction of v. 1 by repeating its contents, but it also exceeds it by adding the key idea of dispersal. Verse 1 spoke of "Noah's sons, who themselves had sons," and v. 32 shows the consequence: "From these the *nations* spread out."

"These are the clans of Noah's sons" returns to the thesis that all peoples *(mišpĕḥōt)* have a solidarity by virtue of their union in the one source, Noah. Yet their "lines of descent" inevitably led to the multiplicity of "nations" *(gôyim)* that "spread out" (*pārad*, cf. v. 5) over the earth. It will be left to the Babel story to explain that the dissemination of the peoples was the repercussion of God's impediment against the rebellious Babelites. The temporal reference "after the flood" imitates v. 1 and recalls that the antediluvian world was different. That paves the way for the Babel narrative that tells how the new world of "nations" came into existence.

2. Tower of Babel (11:1–9)

After portraying the postdiluvian world as made up of related but "scattered" nations (10:5,18b,32), the Babel story explains the reason for the dispersed setting (11:4,8–9). The initial breakup of the postdiluvian people was achieved by the muddling of their language, which foiled the ambitions of the human family. The story provides a striking contrast between human opinion of its self-achievements and God's viewpoint of such endeavors. Human cooperation, when it is fueled by autonomy and directed toward self-interest, is shown by the story to be shallow, impotent hubris.[133]

PRIMEVAL HISTORY. Genesis 11:1–9 is the final narrative of the primeval events that prepare the way for the introduction of Father Abraham by means of Shem's genealogy (11:10–26). It echoes much of what has been portrayed in chaps. 1–10; the tower event must be viewed against the backdrop of the primeval events collectively. For the thematic purposes of the author we have reached a pivotal passage in the development of his thesis for understanding the antecedent events of Abraham's call and the founding of Israel as a nation. Both 1:1–2:3 and 11:1–9 share in a number of verbal and thematic associations; thus 11:1–9 brings to culmination the events of chaps. 1–11. Generic "man" (*ʾādām*, 1:26–28 *passim;* 11:5), "heavens" (*šamayim*, NIV "sky," "air," 1:8,26; 11:4), "one" (*ʾeḥad*, 1:5,9; 11:1,6), and

[133] We do not speak of hubris in the classic sense of Greek religion where the deity's anger (nemesis) is roused by the success of human achievement (see D. E. Gowan, *When Man Becomes God: Humanism and Hybris in the Old Testament,* PTMS 6 [Pittsburgh: Pickwick, 1975], 14–15). In 11:1–9 God is not angry but disturbed, and it is not related to the achievement of human industry per se but rather the goal of unity apart from God.

"all the earth" (*kol hāʾāreṣ*, 1:26,29 *passim;* 11:1,8–9) are among the verbal allusions. Particularly significant is the relationship of 11:1–9 with 1:26–28, which presents the motif of blessing through "filling the earth." Both passages have the divine plural: "Let us make man" (1:26) and "Come, let us go down" (11:7). The consequence of the tower event (when coupled with chap. 10) led to the "scattering" that ultimately will accomplish the promised blessing of God upon all humanity.

Genesis 11:1–9 also mirrors the attempt of humanity in the garden to achieve power independently of God. The attempt of the Babelites to transgress human limits is reminiscent of Eve's ambition (3:5–6).[134] As in the tower story, the divine plural also appears in the garden account (3:22), and both indicate the divine distress over the potential havoc that the new knowledge achieved by mankind may bring about (3:22; 11:6).[135] Broadly speaking, the setting is the same since the garden's Tigris and Euphrates Rivers (2:14) are in the same region as the "plain of Shinar" (11:2). Following the Ararat departure, the people migrated southeast to the lower Euphrates valley. Genesis 1–11 then has come full circle from "Eden" to "Babel," both remembered for the expulsion of their residents.

Also the Babel account reflects the Cain narrative, where both involve the motif of migration and the building of cities (4:12–18).[136] In the first case Cain's family inaugurates sedentary life that develops the "civilized" arts and metallurgy. The Babel story also has as its setting urban life that further boasts the architectural and engineering advances of tower building. Moreover, the theme of pride is common to both, as the Lamech taunt shows (4:23–24).

Less so, but nonetheless apparent, are the ties of 11:1–9 and the events concerning the flood (chaps. 6–9). The minor allusions of "heaven" (6:11), "see/saw" (6:2,5,12; 9:22), generic "man" (6:5–6 *passim*), and "find/found" (6:8; 8:9) are bolstered by the highly repetitive references to "all the earth/on the earth" (6:5,12 *passim*), which also is highlighted in the Babel story (11:4,8–9).[137] Critically important is the reissuing of the divine command to Noah's progeny to "fill the earth" (9:1; 1:28). This is the background for interpreting the necessity of the Babelites to disband. Also the theme of pride occurs again in the Noah narrative, where the Nephilim are memorialized for their physical

---

[134] There are a number of verbal similarities between 11:1–9 and the garden events of chaps. 2–3: מָצָא, "find" (2:20; 11:2); קֶדֶם, "east" (2:8; 3:24; 11:2); רָאָה, "see/saw" (3:6; 11:5); רֹאשׁ, "head" (3:15; 11:4); בָּנָה, "build" (2:22; 11:4–5); עָשָׂה, "make/made" (1:26; 2:4; *passim*; 11:6); and קָרָא שֵׁם, "named" (2:19; 3:20; 11:9) are among them.

[135] See Westermann, *Genesis 1–11,* 555.

[136] For verbal associations with the Cain-Abel narrative, see 11:2 discussion.

[137] This is observed, among others, by I. M. Kikawada, "The Shape of Genesis 11:1–9," in *Rhetorical Criticism: Essays in Honor of James Muilenburg,* PTMS 1, ed. J. J. Jackson and M. Kessler (Pittsburgh: Pickwick, 1974), 31.

"renown" ("name," 6:4; 11:4). The relationship of the Babel story with chap. 10's Table of Nations has been described at length already (see chap. 10 discussion).

LITERARY STRUCTURE AND ORIGIN. The literary structure itself contributes to the motif of "reversal" and thereby unveils the theological message of the composition. The salient features of the story are structurally inverted.[138] An inclusio (bracketing) formed by the repetition of language in vv. 1 and 9 mark the boundaries of the pericope: "The whole world had one language" (v. 1) and "the language of the whole world . . . whole earth" (v. 9).[139]

A "the whole world had one language" (v. 1)
B "there" (v. 2)
C "each other" (v. 3)
D "Come, let's make bricks" (v. 3)
E "Come, let us build ourselves" (v. 4)
F "a city, with a tower" (v. 4)
G "the LORD came down . . ." (v. 5)
F´ "the city and the tower" (v. 5)
E´ "that the men were building" (v. 5)
D´ "Come, let us . . . confuse" (v. 7)
C´ "each other" (v. 7)
B´ "from there" (v. 8)
A´ "the language of the whole world" (v. 9)

The story evidences a balance in which the human endeavor (vv. 1–4) is matched by the divine deed (vv. 6–9). The center element (v. 5) is the midpoint of the composition.[140] This results in a pattern that shows the inversion of the story's events, moving from the human deed of construction to the divine deed that triggered the city's *de*construction. The "mirrored" image of the narrative heightens the focal event of God's descent (v. 5). It is the fulcrum upon which the fortunes of the people turn, and it functions at the same time as the preeminent irony of the story. Despite the monumental efforts of the Babelites to reach "to the heavens" (v. 4), the Lord "came down" from heaven to witness their puny efforts (v. 5). The overarching message is that human pride resulted in the Lord's punishment of dispersal.

The narrative marshals numerous wordplays to highlight the "reversal" and judgment motifs of the account.[141] Chief among these are (1) the inversion of the Hebrew phonetic sounds *lbn* (*nilbĕnâ*; "let's make bricks," v. 3) and *nbl*

[138] See J. P. Fokkelman, *Narrative Art in Genesis* (Assen: Van Gorcum, 1975), 19–32.

[139] כָל־הָאָרֶץ שָׂפָה (v. 1) and שְׂפַת כָּל־הָאָרֶץ . . . כָּל־הָאָרֶץ (v. 9).

[140] See Kikawada, "The Shape of Genesis 11:1–9," 20.

[141] These will be referred to in the exposition as they occur in the text. For a convenient listing of the wordplays and assonance in Hebrew and their English equivalents in the NIV, see Sailhamer, "Genesis," 106.

(*nābĕlâ*; "let us go down," v. 7) and (2) the sound play between *bābel* ("Babel," v. 9) and *bālal* ("confused," v. 9). In the first case the wordplay shows that what men build up, the Lord tears down. Second, the play of the debasing appellation "Babel" and the judgment of "babble" conveys *lex talionis* ("eye for an eye") between the crime and its punishment.

Added to such phonetic plays is the wide use of irony and sarcasm in the story. Exemplary of this is the misspent efforts of the Babelites. First, while their unity enabled an ambitious project, it was this very partnership that ultimately brought about their dissolution. What they most feared, namely, the loss of security and power by "scattering" (v. 4), came to pass as a result of their own doing (vv. 8–9). Second, their architectural goal of reaching the "heavens" (v. 4), symbolizing their grasp for autonomous power, was frustrated by God, who "came down" to earth (v. 5); yet they themselves stopped building because of their own incompetence (v. 8). What appeared to be an unstoppable plan proved to be a dismal failure. Third, though they sought a "name" (v. 4), they received the humiliating name "Babel" (= "babble," v. 9). This is all the more derisive when we recall that the Akkadian name for the colossal city "Babylon" meant "gate of the god(s)" (Akk. *bāb-ili, bāb-ilāni*). Finally, it was this very onus of dispersal that enabled them to fulfill the divine dictate to "fill the earth" (9:1,7; 1:28), which chap. 10 shows occurred (vv. 5,18,20,30–32).

The source of this story has puzzled commentators because it is unique in ancient Near Eastern literature.[142] Granted, some aspects of the account have superficial parallels, such as the Sumerian tradition of one universal language, but there is no parallel that captures the story in its entirety. Usually commentators have contended that originally separate motifs (oral) have been joined in this Israelite telling. The exquisite artistry of the pericope, however, would argue strongly for an original literary unity.[143]

Some hold that the account originally was an aetiological legend, contrived to explain the existence of many nations and the diverse languages of cosmopolitan Babylon. It was supposedly integrated by the Israelite author into his story of diverse languages and peoples presented in chap. 10.[144] Others regard it an Israelite version of *Enuma Elish*'s tale of Babylon's origins that was

---

[142] See the overview in F. A. Spina, "Babel," *ABD* 1.561–2.

[143] Cassuto details the literary features which show that the work is best viewed as a literary unity, not one based on two literary sources (*Genesis,* 231–38). Westermann acknowledges the literary unity of the work but argues that the preliterary history of the story consisted of three once-distinct motifs: (1) confusion of languages, (2) dispersion of peoples, and (3) the building of cities (*Genesis 1–11,* 553–57). The aetiological explanation of "Babel" (11:9), according to Westermann, is deemed a late accretion.

[144] E.g., von Rad speaks of it as "aetiological saga" that was not Babylonian in origin but Israelite, and whose author had knowledge of Babylon's building achievements, in particular the ziggurat Etemenanki (*Genesis,* 150–51).

appropriated as a polemic against human folly while also employing it as the reason for the variety of human language.[145] In both cases, however, it is difficult to square how an original Babylonian story could be so easily adopted by an Israelite in light of its bitterly strong anti-Babylon sarcasm. Moreover, the antimythical character of Genesis 1–11 questions the notion that the biblical author would depend on such sagas. Rather, Genesis recounts a unique historical event in which God confounded human speech.

Although describing a historical event, the account cannot be confidently assigned to a specific historical period. Those who attempt to specify the historical period point to the collapse of the Third Dynasty of Ur, when Sumerian rule was displaced by Elamites and Amorites of the early second millennium B.C. Sumerian cities boasted of ziggurats, and Ur-Nammu (2062–2046 B.C.), founder of the Third Dynasty, began the construction of Ur's immense ziggurat tower. The ruins of their ziggurat towers, which some contend were the background for Genesis, came with the end of Sumerian dominance in Mesopotamia.[146] The account is too vague to determine the historical setting, even generally. Genesis, however, does not suggest political tumult as the cause of dispersion since it conveys only the theological perspective. We do not know by what processes the confusion of tongues occurred.

As we have seen earlier, Genesis 1–11 shows a knowledge of Mesopotamian ideology, and undoubtedly the tower episode is the most telling example of the author's awareness of Babylonian tradition. The Genesis author, however, is not writing in the shadow of any specific literary tradition, but rather he is aware of Mesopotamian religion in general. There is no requirement that biblical allusions to the ideas portrayed in the Babylonian *Enuma Elish,* for example, mean that Genesis was dependent on it. It is sufficient that the biblical author was generally aware of Babylonian mythic lore and chose to couch his historical account in a way that spoke against their misguided beliefs.[147] As a mockery the story lampoons the pride of human autonomy, which sought after the power of the divine. Our narrative's sarcasm, if not polemic, sets Gentile pomposity in its paltry place.

Mesopotamian religion claimed that their cities were of divine parentage. A symbol of this obsession with divinity among the Mesopotamians was the ziggurat (Akk. *ziqqurratu*) that was erected as early as the third millennium

---

[145] E.g., Speiser, who argues that the similarities of Genesis and the Babylonian story show the former's dependence on the Mesopotamian tradition (*Genesis,* 75).

[146] See D. S. DeWitt, "The Historical Background of Genesis 11:1–9: Babel or Ur?" *JETS* 22 (1979): 15–26. D. F. Payne acknowledges that a specific historical occasion cannot be known, if one were intended at all by the author, and recommends generally the incursion of Semites among the Sumerian city-states of the third millennium B.C. ("Babel," *ISBE* 1.382–83).

[147] Sarna (*Genesis,* 81) remarks that the story is told in conscious opposition "to some cherished notions of ancient Mesopotamia."

B.C.[148] The ziggurat was a step-ladder edifice, made up of mud bricks, whose bottom was square or rectangular. The precise meaning of the structure is unknown, though it is widely agreed that it formed a stairway between the gods and earth (cf. Gen 28:12).[149] At the foot of the ziggurat as well as the pinnacle was a temple area serving as a habitation for the god. Ziggurats may have been considered an earthly imitation of the heavenly residence of the gods. *Enuma Elish* shows that the Babylonians touted a correspondence between the heavenly citadel and their earthly sanctuary: "Make a likeness on earth of what he [Marduk] has wrought in heaven."

Such is the description of the city Babylon in the creation myth *Enuma Elish*. It relates how thankful gods, the Anunnaki, vow to build a shrine of residence to honor King Marduk for his defeat of vicious Tiamat and the slaying of her captain, Kingu.

> When Marduk heard this,
> Brightly glowed his features, like the day:
> "Construct Babylon, whose building you have requested,
> Let its brickwork be fashioned. You shall name it 'The Sanctuary.'"
> The Anunnaki applied the implement;
> For one whole year they molded bricks.
> When the second year arrived,
> They raised high the head of Esagila equaling Apsu.
> Having built a stage-tower as high as Apsu,
> They set up in it an abode for Marduk, Enlil, (and) Ea.
> In their presence he was seated in grandeur.[150]

The similarities of Genesis and the Babylonian story are striking. The Babylonian edifice, like the Genesis story, has a particularly conspicuous pinnacle: "They raised high the head of Esagila equaling Apsu. Having built a stage-tower as high as Apsu." "Esagila" was the sacred precinct of Marduk's residence in Babylon and beside it stood the impressive temple-tower Etemenanki, both of which were restored by the Babylonian ruler Nabopolassar (626–605 B.C.).[151] In the Babylonian text the name "Esagila" *(E-sag-ila)*, meaning "the structure which raises the head," is a wordplay with the preced-

---

[148] For a site distribution of the ziggurat, see A. Parrot, *The Tower of Babel,* trans. E. Hudson (London: SCM, 1955), fig. 3, p. 31, or M. Beek, *Atlas of Mesopotamia,* trans. D. R. Welsh (London: Nelson, 1962), map 21.

[149] Some have suggested that the shape of the ziggurat as a mountain was a religious symbol for the cosmic mountain in Sumerian myth which signified the source of life and the place of divine activity (P. R. S. Moorey, *Ur "Of the Chaldees": A Revised and Updated Edition of Sir Leonard Woolley's Excavations at Ur* [Ithaca: Cornell University Press, 1982], 139).

[150] *ANET,* 68–69.

[151] During the neo-Babylonian period the ziggurat was also called *ziggurrat Babilī,* "the tower of Babel."

ing clause, "they raised its head" *(ullū rēšīšu)*. "Apsu" here refers to the heavenly realm. Hence the myth describes Esagila as reaching "toward heaven."[152] The biblical account reads similarly, "a city, with a tower that reaches (lit., "and its head") to the heavens" (v. 4). Also the construction of Babylon's tower, made up of "brickwork" and "molded brick," corresponds to the materials for the Genesis city-tower. It consists of brick and tar rather than Palestinian stones. Archaeological remains show that mud bricks and bitumen were used for the assembling of the sacred ziggurats. The remarkable ziggurat at Ur, the best preserved one in Iraq, has a solid inner core of mud bricks with an outer covering of baked ones that were placed in bitumen for mortar.[153]

Taken together the similarities of the Genesis story and the literary tradition of *Enuma Elish* and/or the architectural witness of the ancient ziggurat have encouraged scholars to connect the biblical and Mesopotamian traditions.[154] We have already said that the traditions of Mesopotamia were at best only the general backdrop for the Genesis tower. There is no clear architectural connection between the *migdāl* ("tower") and the ziggurat, nor do we see a compelling reason for attributing the biblical account to Mesopotamian literary parentage. Genesis 11:1–9 concerns itself foremostly with the building of the "city" and the "scattering" of peoples. Genesis's tower is an appendage to the city and is by no means a temple, and the Babylonian *Enuma Elish* lacks the features of universal language and worldwide dispersal found in Genesis. The detailed reference to the making of bricks shared by both traditions does not argue for the blind dependence of Genesis on Babylonian tradition but speaks to the authenticity of the account by the author's knowledge of Mesopotamian engineering and technology.

There is yet another proposed connection of our tower story with Sumero-Babylonian culture. Among Sumerian literary works is a text that speaks of a united people who enjoy a universal language. In the epic tale "Enmerkar and the Lord of Aratta," there is a conflict between Enmerkar, king of the Sumerian city Erech,[155] and the ruler of Aratta, an unidentified city in western Iran. Enmerkar attempts to intimidate the Lord of Aratta into submission by incan-

---

[152] See Speiser, "Word Plays on the Creation Epic's Version of the Founding of Babylon," *Or* 25 (1956): 317–23, esp. 319–20, and his commentary, *Genesis,* 75–76.

[153] C. L. Woolley, *Excavations at Ur* (New York: Thomas Y. Crowell, 1954), 130, and Moorey, *Ur Of the 'Chaldees,'* 144. For photos and drawings see Woolley's *Ur Excavations Volume V: The Ziggurat and Its Surroundings* (New York: Joint Expedition of the British Museum and The University Museum, University of Pennsylvania, 1939), and Moorey, *Ur 'Of the Chaldees,'* 143, 148, and 234.

[154] Parrot, e.g., expresses certainty: "At all events it is recognized and admitted by all biblical scholars that the narrative in Genesis 11 had its 'starting-point' in the ruins of one of those huge towers which archaeologists call *ziggurats,* and that the 'Tower of Babel' could only be the *ziggurat* erected at Babylon, in the very heart of the land of Shinar" (*The Tower of Babel,* 17).

[155] Akk. "Uruk" (modern Warka).

tation. With the help of Enki, the god of incantation, Enmerkar's envoy delivers the spell. The poem tells of a time when there is no fear or rivalry among men and describes how with "one tongue" (language) all the countries worship the high god Enlil. S. N. Kramer, who first published the Sumerian myth, concluded that the *nam-shub* (magical speech) described a "golden age" in the idealized past.[156] Conversely, the Sumerian tale has also been interpreted as a prophecy of future peace when, because of the wisdom of Enki, all countries will organize into one superior civilization, speak the same Sumerian language, and unite in worship to the god Enlil.[157]

In either case the approach taken by Genesis toward a universal language is remarkably different. Sumerian tradition applauds the solidarity of language as indicative of an era of peace (past or future) and a period of undivided worship to Sumer's gods. The epic of the Sumerian hero Enmerkar, as well as other Sumerian tales, present Sumer's society as the ideal and superior to all others.[158] Yet Genesis views one language for the human family as a threat to the ideal because of human sinfulness. A diverse humanity is for the better according to Genesis since God thwarts the sinful intent of the collective human will. This moral factor is also absent in the Sumerian "confusion of tongues" but is vital in the biblical understanding.

THEOLOGICAL MESSAGE. The story presents a number of interpretive problems. Why was the tower an offense against God? What was it about the people's unity that God rejected? Also, how are we to understand "scattering" as a motif of judgment (vv. 4,8–9) when dispersal was presented positively as God's blessing in the creation and flood accounts (1:28; 9:1–3)? In the preceding Table of Nations the author's opinion of the division of peoples can be taken as neutral, if not positive, as a normal course of emerging nations (9:18–19; 10:5,18,32). But 11:1–9 shows that the antecedent to that development of peoples was a dispersal instigated by God's punitive intervention. There was a time when humanity enjoyed a unity of purpose, enterprise, and language. Was this not an admirable accomplishment?

Indeed, there was a unity desired by God, but it was one bestowed by God, not one founded on a social state. The postdiluvian community resisted the

---

[156] S. N. Kramer, "The Babel of Tongues: A Sumerian Version," *JAOS* 88 (1968): 108–111; for translation see Kramer and J. Maier, *Myths of Enki, the Crafty God* (New York: Oxford University Press, 1989), 88–89. Also J. Van Dijk, "La 'confusion des langues,' Note sur le lexique et sur la morphologie d'Ermerkar, 147–155" *OrNs* 39 (1970): 302–10.

[157] B. Alster, "An Aspect of 'Enmerkar and the Lord of Aratta,'" *RA* 67 (1973): 101–9; "Enki and Ninhursag," *UF* 10 (1978): 15–27; and "Dilmun, Bahrain, and the Alleged Paradise in Sumerian Myth and Literature," in *Dilmun: New Studies in the Early Archaeology and History of Bahrain,* ed. D. Potts (Berlin: Dietrich Reimer, 1983), 39–74, esp. 52–60. Alster argues that the passage is a prophecy on the basis of the epic's context. See also H. Schmökel, in *Near Eastern Texts Related to the Old Testament,* OTL, ed. W. Beyerlin (Philadelphia: Westminster, 1978), 86–87.

[158] Alster, "An Aspect of 'Enmerkar and the Lord of Aratta,'" 106–9.

divine command to "increase" and "fill the earth" (1:28; 9:1). In their eyes their security rested on their homogeneity, and thus they set about to preserve their union by building the city as a haven with its symbolic tower of corporate achievement. This act of arrogant defiance resulted in disbandment. By their own measure the Babelites would have reckoned their dissolution as punishment, but in the larger scheme of God's purposes it was an act of gracious intervention to insure that humanity would eventually attain the promissory "blessing." In this case God opposed unity and favored disunity, the very thing the Babelites feared. God's purposes included the diversity that a dispersal of Noah's family would have ultimately meant, but the wicked aims of the Noahic offspring required God to intervene to save them, so to speak, from themselves. This has its parallel in the garden *tōlĕdōt* where the couple are driven from the tree of life, which not only meant their punishment but ironically also their rescue from perpetual life in shameful misery. We may remember that the same irony occurs in the scattering of the church in Acts 8, where, in that case, persecution propelled the church into the diaspora, so that by taking the gospel they accomplished the charge of the resurrected Lord (1:8).[159]

Also the Bible envisions a single people of God without suppressing the national entities that make up that spiritual citizenry. The prophets speak of diverse ethnic personalities when they depict the future universal kingdom of God (e.g., Isa 2:1–4). At Pentecost the outpouring of the Spirit upon the representative nations gathered in Jerusalem results in the spiritual union of the new church but does not create a homogeneous language, ethnicity, or statehood. John's vision of the heavenly family includes diverse peoples from "every nation, tribe, people and language, standing before the throne and in front of the Lamb" (Rev 7:9).[160]

The nations to this day languish under the afflictions of disparate language and culture. Yet Genesis tells how God graciously responded to the dispersed nations through the creation of a particular *gôy* ("nation") in the call of Abraham (12:2). With the "scattering" at the tower of Babel, the end of God's blessing appears to have closed the "gates to the future," but the Lord "opens them again and in a unique way"[161] through the commissioning of Abraham and later Israel. Abraham is both the recipient of God's promissory blessings and also the facilitator of that blessing for the nations (12:3). Moreover, the patriarchal lineage will establish new nations *(gôyim),*[162] and Israel will be

[159] I. H. Marshall comments, "The scattering of the Christians led to the most significant step forward in the mission of the church. One might say that it required persecution to make them fulfil the implicit command in 1:8" (*The Acts of the Apostles,* TNTC [Grand Rapids: Eerdmans, 1980], 152).

[160] See B. W. Anderson, "Unity and Diversity in God's Creation: A Study of the Babel Story," *CurTM* (1976): 69–81.

[161] See J. Muilenburg, "Abraham and the Nations," *Int* 19 (1965): 387–98, quote on p. 393.

[162] E.g., Gen 17:4–6; 18:18; 21:13,18; 35:11; 46:3; 48:19.

the Lord's possession as a "holy nation" (*gôy*; Exod 19:6; cf. 32:10; 34:10). Yet early Israel recognized too that as a people they were parented by prior nations and thus part and parcel of the world's communities (Deut 26:5). Therefore the particularism of the Abrahamic call and the genesis of Israel did not by any means derail the universality of the promissory blessing intended for all humanity (1:28; 9:1). Rather, the particularism achieved the universal possibilities. This we find discharged by the psalmists, who summoned the nations to join in the worship of the Lord: "Clap your hands, all you nations; shout to God with cries of joy" (Ps 47:1).[163]

The prophetic tradition denounced the nations who cast themselves against the Lord (and Israel),[164] but the prophets also regularly envisioned a kingdom of universal proportions in the eschatological "day of the LORD" when all peoples would convene in Jerusalem and recognize the rule of God. Zephaniah 3:9 may be an allusion to 11:1–9, where the prophet anticipates the future purging of the nations so that they might enjoy a redeemed speech: "At that time I will change the speech *[śāpâ]* of the peoples to a pure speech, that all of them may call on the name of the Lord and serve him with one accord *[ʾeḥad]*" (NRSV). Israel would become that instrument of "blessing" among the nations, which results in the cessation of international rivalry and conflict.[165] Anointed Israel was charged with becoming a "light for the Gentiles" (Isa 49:6; cf. Luke 2:32; John 8:12), and through Israel's salvation "the nations will be blessed by him [God]" (Jer 4:2).

This was taken up by the apostolic tradition in preaching the gospel to the nations (Acts 13:47), for the efficacy of Christ's crucifixion reached far beyond the boundaries of Israel (John 11:52). The character of God's kingdom as inclusive is echoed time and again in the New Testament where Abraham is said to father the faith of all believers through his "seed" the Messiah, and the Gentile church is cited as the chosen people of God (e.g., Rom 4:16–17; 9:24–26; Gal 3:6–9; 1 Pet 2:9–10).

Luke's report of the founding of the church at Pentecost has been interpreted by some commentators as an intentional echo of Genesis 10–11. If so, by the outpouring of the Spirit the human family again becomes one people, and language no longer is an impossible barrier (Acts 2:5–13). The Spirit does not give one language but numerous dialects by which the gospel is heard.[166] Pentecost shows that national distinctions are secondary to the union of a single people by the baptism of the Spirit in Christ. The gospel therefore is the

---

[163] E.g., Pss 2:10–12; 47:1–9; 67:4; 72:17; 117:1.

[164] Cf. the oracles against the nations, e.g., Isa 13–23; Jer 46–51; Ezek 25–32; Amos 1–2; Obadiah; and Nahum.

[165] E.g., Isa 2:1–4//Mic 4:1–5; 11:9; 19:23–25; 51:2–3; 66:20; Jer 3:17; Amos 9:12; Zeph 2:11; Zech 2:11; 8:13,20–23; 14:16. Cf. also 1 Kgs 8:41–43; Pss 66:3–8; 67; 86:9.

[166] J. B. Polhill, *Acts,* NAC (Nashville: Broadman, 1992), 106.

reconciling antidote to the plurality of nations as it is preached among the world's peoples. It is Jews (and proselytes) of the diaspora who as the facilitators of the gospel first hear, believe, and evangelize the Gentiles (Acts 2:9–11a). This is consistent with the Genesis paradigm, which has the spread of the "blessing" through Abraham among "all peoples on earth" (12:3).

Babylon became the biblical paradigm for depicting Gentile pride and wickedness. It is for this reason, as we saw earlier, that Nimrod's achievements as the founder of Babel often have been interpreted negatively as ungodly arrogance (10:8–12). "Babylon" and its king are castigated by the prophets for their pride, idolatry, and wickedness, which God will judge "like Sodom and Gomorrah" (Isa 13:19). The city was the object of prophetic scorn for its infamous commercial and military tyranny.[167] Because of Babylon's historic affliction of Judah (exile), the city became a symbol in Jewish writings and the early church for corrupt Rome, which also had subjugated the Jews.[168] "Babylon" could represent any anti-God power, whether past or future, that persecuted the righteous community.[169]

We do not hear of Babylon again in the Pentateuch (only 10:10; NIV "Babel," 11:9). It is actually "Ur of the Chaldeans," a site considerably south of Babylon, that is the home of Terah's family (11:28,31; cf. 15:7; Neh 9:7). Although some have attributed this site to northern Mesopotamia, it is widely held that Ur is in the southern region of Babylonia (modern Tell el-Muqayyar). Strikingly, Ur, not Babylon, gives us the best existing example of the ancient ziggurat.[170] Abram's association with "Ur" as a leading center of Sumerian and Babylonian culture contributes to the linkage provided by the Shem genealogy (11:10–26) between the tower event and the origins of Abraham's family.

---

[167] E.g., Isa 13:19–14:27; 43:14; 47:1–15; Jer 50:1–51:64; Dan 4:30; Hab 2:6–20.

[168] E.g., among Jewish works, *2 Apoc. Bar* 11:1–2; 67:7; *2 Esdr* 3:1–2, 28; *Sib. Or.* 5.143, 155–61, and for the early church, e.g., Tertullian *Against Marcion* 3.13; Augustine, *City of God* 18.22; 1 Pet 5:13 identifies Peter's place of writing as "Babylon," which until the Reformation period was taken popularly as Rome (e.g., Eusebius, *Ecclesiastical History* 2.15.2).

[169] In the Apocalypse the city is designated "Babylon the Great" (cf. Dan 4:30) and depicted as a bloodthirsty harlot reveling in licentious luxury (Rev 14:8; 16:19; 17:5; 18:2,10,21).

[170] Babylon's ziggurat is known primarily from late literary sources, including the testimony of Herodotus (ca. 460 B.C.) and a third century B.C. Babylonian text ("Esagila text"). Its archaeological remains are only the bare outline of the foundation, due primarily to the robbery of its bricks. Its early construction is disputed, though the site's archaeologist, R. Koldewey, dated the foundation to the Old Babylonian period (ca. 1800 B.C.). Many reconstructions of the ziggurat were carried out by Assyrian and Babylonian kings. Best known is the famed work of Nabopolassar (626–605 B.C.) and his son Nebuchadnezzar (605–562 B.C.). The ziggurat *Etemenanki* was located near the Marduk temple *Esagila*. Together they dominated the city's architecture. The ziggurat's demise occurred at the hands of Xerxes in 472 B.C. Alexander the Great planned a renovation, but it was never undertaken except for clearing the rubble. See Parrot, *The Tower of Babel;* R. Koldewey, *The Excavations at Babylon,* trans. A. S. Johns (London: Macmillan, 1914); Wiseman, *Nebuchadrezzar and Babylon* (Oxford: British Academy, 1985), 68–73.

(1) United People (11:1–2)

[1]Now the whole world had one language and a common speech. [2]As men moved eastward, they found a plain in Shinar and settled there.

11:1 The opening verses establish the unity of mankind, both in its language and its habitation. This will be reversed by the story's end in which there is neither one language nor one settlement. Verse 1 particularly captures this motif of inclusiveness ("oneness") by the phrases "*whole* world" and "*one* language and a *common* ("one") speech" (italics added). "Whole world" renders the Hebrew "all the earth" *(kol hāʾāreṣ),* meaning the inhabitants of the earth collectively.[171] Its importance in the story is indicated by the literary role of our phrase, forming an inclusio with the same wording at the end of the unit in v. 9. This nuance of inclusiveness dominates the narrative as shown by the comparable phrase "over the face of the whole earth" in vv. 4,8–9. Moreover, the solidarity of the people is highlighted by the recurring use of "one" in reference to their "one language" and "common ["one"] speech."[172] The repetition of the adjective "one" creates a morphological equivalency and emphasizes the adjective in the construction.[173] Here "one" in both phrases means a "particular" (but nonspecified) language they held in common.[174]

Commentators are divided on the geographical extent meant by "whole world." If it is taken at face value, our passage speaks comprehensively of the world's populations. Others view it as a figure of speech (hyperbole) or better translated "all the land," limiting it to the Mesopotamian region. The Hebrew

[171] The LXX tradition clarifies the text by the additional πᾶσιν (lit., "and [there was] one voice *to all* [of them]").

[172] "Language" (שָׂפָה) and "speech" (דְּבָרִים) have been taken by some as characterizing two different linguistic phenomena. E.g., C. H. Gordon, *Before Columbus: Links Between the Old Testament and Ancient America* (New York: Crown, 1971), 107, 165–66, and "Ebla as Background for the Old Testament," in *Congress Volume: Jerusalem, 1986,* VTSup 40 (Leiden: Brill, 1988), 295, cited in V. Hamilton, *The Book of Genesis Chapters 1–17,* NICOT (Grand Rapids: Eerdmans, 1990), 350, n. 7. "Language" occurs in the singular and is interpreted as the official language *(lingua franca)* for communication. "Speech," on the other hand, is in the plural and refers to the local dialects for family and ethnic communication, as shown by the various "languages" (לְשֹׁנוֹת) noted in the preceding Table of Nations (10:5,20,31). In this view the "confusion of tongues" would be the disruption of the diplomatic language that assured the breakdown of cooperative efforts among the differing families. This dissection of the verse is unwarranted, however, for the difference in number between the two phrases has no more bearing on their respective meanings than the difference in their gender (the former feminine and the latter masculine).

[173] See A. Berlin's observation in *The Dynamics of Biblical Parallelism* (Bloomington: Indiana University, 1985), 43, 48; she proposes "the same language and the same words."

[174] The plural form of "one" as an attributive adjective occurs three more times in the OT and always designates an indefinite span of time, meaning "a few (days)." *IBHS* 15.2.1d renders 11:1 as "a certain language and *certain* vocabulary." Here and in Berlin's rendering the plural use of the adjective stresses the unity of language.

phrase may be used in Genesis and the Old Testament both to designate a limited region and also the whole earth.[175] Since the author has tied the Babel event to the Table of Nations, which exceeds the boundaries of a given region, it would be best to understand the expression in its broader application—at least in the sense of the world known to the author.

11:2 The location of their settlement is identified as "eastward" *(miqqedem).*[176] This is reminiscent of the garden, where its location is described as "east in Eden" (2:8); the language "east(ward)" marks events of *separation* in Genesis. By this spatial term the narrative also conveys a metaphorical sphere, meaning the Babelites are outside God's blessing. At the expulsion of Adam and Eve, cherubim guarded the entryway to the garden, facing the "east side" (as the tabernacle, Exod 27:13; 38:13). Lot departs Abraham and journeys eastward (13:10–12), where he ultimately meets with disaster in the cities of Sodom and Gomorrah.[177] Also Abraham's sons by Keturah are dispersed "to the land of the east" to detach them from the elect Isaac (25:6), and deceitful Jacob flees his homeland to live among the "eastern peoples" of Aram (29:1). In the tower story the migratory pattern was a portent of the Babelites' defiance. They have moved outside the place of blessing.

Verse 2 may well be an intentional echo of Cain's expulsion and punishment, resulting in a vagabond life (4:12–16). Cain, like the Babelites, settled for urban life (4:17). Both passages share several lexical references, including Cain's migration toward "Nod, east of *[qidmat]* Eden" (4:16).[178] As Cain feared insecurity as a "restless wanderer on the earth [ground]" (4:14), the people of Babel feared the wanderings of a dispersed people (v. 4). Cain rightly viewed his wanderings "from the LORD's presence" as a punishment, but the punishment resulted in the guarantee of divine protection and the propagation of his offspring (4:17–24). The dispersal of the people in 11:1–9 resulted equally in the increase of the nations as the Lord had so commanded (9:1).

We have spoken of "Shinar" in 10:10 for its importance in casting Nim-

---

[175] E.g., כָּל־הָאָרֶץ ("the whole land") is used of a specific, limited territory in 13:9,15. "Canaan" is so designated in Deut 11:25; 19:8; 34:1. The phrase also may be used with a specific designation, e.g., "all the land of Egypt" (כָּל־אֶרֶץ מִצְרָיִם), in Gen 41:41,43,54; 45:20; Exod 9:9; 10:14. The inclusive phrase עַל־פְּנֵי כָל־הָאָרֶץ ("over the face of the whole earth/land," v. 9) can also indicate a distinctive location, e.g., Deut 11:25; 1 Sam 30:16. But the universal meaning is attested for both phrases as well (e.g., Gen 1:29; 19:31; Exod 19:5; Num 14:21). Of course, the meaning of its occurrence in the flood account (7:3; 8:9) is disputed, but the additional descriptions would argue for a universal meaning (e.g., 6:17; 7:11,19).

[176] It may also be rendered "from the east" (NIV text notes; NRSV). Here, however, מִקֶּדֶם indicates direction, "toward the east," as in 13:11 (BDB, 869).

[177] מִקֶּדֶם traces Abraham's and Lot's movements but all within the land of promise (12:8 twice; 13:11 with Josh 7:2).

[178] Also מָצָה ("find") in 4:14–15; יָשַׁב ("dwell/live") in 4:16, and the parallel constructions "in the land of Shinar" and "in the land of Nod" (4:16).

rod's career in the shadow of the infamous Tower of Babel. At 10:10 the cities located "in the land of Shinar" are Babylon, Erech, Akkad, and Calneh. Shinar refers to the region "Babylonia." It sometimes is translated "Babylon" or "Babylonia" in the LXX tradition (cf. Isa 11:11; Zech 5:11).[179] It was the area known in antiquity as the Mesopotamian region "Sumer and Akkad."[180] One of the eastern kings Abraham defeated was "Amraphel king of Shinar" (14:1,9). Elsewhere in the Old Testament it refers to the Babylon/Babylonia area (e.g., Josh 7:21; Isa 11:11; Dan 1:2; Zech 5:11). The topography of a "plain" for their settlement prepares the reader for the erection of the tower that follows. This is consistent with what we know of the southern Babylonian region that is subject to seasonal inundations by the Tigris and Euphrates Rivers.

The introduction concludes "and [they] settled there." This is not incidental to the account since "settled" is an antonym of the narrative's key idea "scattered" and opposes the divine command directed to Noah and his offspring, "fill the earth" (9:1).[181] Moreover, "settled" *(yāšab)* shows that the Noahic descendants had taken up permanent residence.[182] This same phrase occurs once more in Genesis, in this same chapter, where Abram's family makes its home in Haran after migrating from Ur (v. 31). This parallel is further evidence that the two accounts are integrally linked and shows that the calling of Abraham (12:1–3) must be read against the backdrop of the Babel event. Abraham's obedience to God's command to "leave" his family residence and to "go" to an undesignated land sharply contrasts with the Babelites' resolution to "sit tight." It was thereby Abraham's willingness to depart the "land of Shinar," so to speak, that resulted in the salvation of the stubborn peoples who had refused.

Hebrew *šām* ("there"), occurring five times in the narrative, creates a phonetic play with *šēm* ("name") and *šāmayim* ("heavens").[183] "There" indicates the geographical center where the human family collected; the antithesis

---

[179] See J. R. Davila, "Shinar," *ABD* 5.1220.

[180] "Sumer" in its restricted sense indicated the Babylonian area south of ancient Nippur and "Akkad" the Babylonian region north of Nippur. Today, this area corresponds roughly to Iraq, south of Baghdad (J. S. Cooper, "Sumer, Sumerians," *ABD* 6.231–34). Ur-Nammu, founder of Ur's Third Dynasty (ca. 2000 B.C.), claimed the title "king of Sumer and Akkad" (S. J. Schwantes, *A Short History of the Ancient Near East* [Grand Rapids: Baker, 1965], 29).

[181] Plural verbs in 9:1 indicate that the command includes, if not stresses, Noah's sons.

[182] This is well illustrated in Genesis, where migratory movements result in more-or-less permanent settlement (e.g., 4:16; 13:7; 19:29; 24:3,37; cf. Deut 1:4; Ruth 1:4). The participle יוֹשֵׁב ("dweller," "resident") commonly describes inhabitants of a particular land (e.g., 34:30; 50:11). The same expression as 11:2 but in the singular, "and he dwelt there," describes Isaac's settled encampment (26:17).

[183] These Hebrew terms are distributed as follows: "there" in vv. 2,7,8,9, and 9(2x); "name" in vv. 4 and 9; "heavens" in v. 4.

"from there" *(miššām),* occurring twice, announces and reports the breakup of that center (vv. 8–9). But "there" also indicates the ideological core of the Babelites as well as their location, for the alliterative words "name" and "heavens" reveal the motives for centering at Shinar and the building enterprise they initiated to secure their ideology.[184] By ironic twist, their efforts at obtaining a "name" through their "heavenward" tower results in the antithesis of their intentions since they succeed only in starting over where they began. "There" leads to "from there" (vv. 2,8).

(2) Building Babel (11:3–4)

3They said to each other, "Come, let's make bricks and bake them thoroughly." They used brick instead of stone, and tar for mortar. 4Then they said, "Come, let us build ourselves a city, with a tower that reaches to the heavens, so that we may make a name for ourselves and not be scattered over the face of the whole earth."

Now the human enterprise becomes the focus of the narrative story. Verses 3–4 report the dialogue of the Babel family. They enjoy at this point a cooperative spirit, "Come, let's make bricks" (v. 3). This expression of community collaboration occurs twice in parallel (vv. 3–4) and is imitated afterward, with sarcasm, by the deliberations of God, "Come, let us go down" (v. 7). The phonetic play among these successive speeches, with their preponderance of the sounds *l, b,* and *n,* show their interdependency: *hābâ nilbĕnâ lĕbēnîm . . . hābâ nibneh lānû . . . hābâ nērĕdâ wĕnābĕlâ*("Come, let's make bricks . . . Come, let us build ourselves . . . "Come, let us go down and confuse"). This repetitive structure exhibits the ironic consequences of their undertaking. The cause-effect relationship among the clauses, that is, making bricks leads to building the city, which in turn evokes the divine word, shows that God's action was charted paradoxically by the deluded plan of the human family itself.

11:3 The speech of the people is punctuated with wordplay and verbal alliteration and assonance. "Make bricks" and "bake them thoroughly" is the idiomatic rendering of the ponderous Hebrew "let us brick bricks *[nilbĕnâ lĕbēnîm]*" and "bake [them] baking *[niśrĕpâ liśrēpâ]*" If this were not enough, the verse closes with yet another verbal tautology, "tar *[ḥēmar]* for mortar *[ḥōmer]*."[185] The parade wordplay, which was mentioned earlier, is the inversion of the letters *l-b-n* in the word *nilbĕnā* ("let us make bricks") to *n-b-l* in the parallel term *nābĕlâ* ("let us confuse") uttered by God (v. 7). "Brick" *(hallĕbēnâ)* and "stone" *(lĕʾāben)* also strengthen the assonance of

[184] Discussed by Fokkelman, *Narrative Art,* 16–18; Anderson, "Unity and Diversity," 72–73.
[185] The NIV's "*tar* for mor*tar*" approximates the sound play.

the sounds *l-b-n* in the verse.

The narrator provides his Hebrew audience an explanation for the building practices of the Babelites. Unlike Mesopotamian structures, Israelite and Canaanite buildings were constructed of Palestine's rocks that were ubiquitous to the region. Production of brickware for construction was a common feature in early Mesopotamia.[186] Its technology was invented in Babylonia during the fourth millennium and later exported to other countries. Both conventional mud bricks and baked (fired) bricks were used in monumental structures, as in the ancient ziggurat. Bricks for foundation walls and courts were set in asphalt. A representative group usually was inscribed with the name of the royal benefactor of the edifice. Akkadian *lābinu,* meaning "brickworker," is cognate with Hebrew *lāban,* "to brick." As we have seen, this aspect of the tower's construction was a persistent source of wordplay for the author of 11:1–9. He seized Mesopotamia's prized accomplishment as a target for ridiculing its religious polytheism and cultural pride.

11:4 The aim of preparing the brickwork was to erect a "city and a tower" (v. 4). Whereas "city" is repeated (vv. 5,8), v. 4 is the only appearance of "tower." Some have rendered the nouns as a hendiadys, "city-tower." Even if not a hendiadys, the point is well taken that the tower and city were not to be distinguished, for it was the "tower" that symbolized the purpose of the "city's" construction.

The description of the tower "that reaches to the heavens" has been taken as the builders' ambition of autonomy. This does not mean that they intended to depose God. A similar expression describes Jacob's ladder with "its top reaching to heaven" (28:12). In recognizing the sacredness of "Bethel" ("house of God"), the patriarch exclaimed, "This is none other than the house of God; this is the gate of heaven" (28:17). Taken in this sense the tower at Babel was conceived as a stairway that would give them access to the realm of the divine. Others have regarded the phrase as saying no more than that the tower was especially tall, as in our modern term "skyscraper." This is the sense of the same language that portrays Canaan's city-walls as tall as the "skies" (Deut 1:28; 9:1). Yet this verbal association with the despotic Canaanite cities would for later Israel cast even greater suspicion upon the motives of the Babelites.

Since the purpose of the city and tower is that the builders will "make a name for themselves," it is best to understand the reference to "heaven" in concert with Babel's prideful autonomy. In Genesis the Lord speaks from heaven, which is understood as his dwelling place (e.g., 19:24; 21:17; 22:11,15; cf. Deut 26:15). He established his "throne" of dominion in heaven

[186] For this discussion see W. von Soden, *The Ancient Orient: An Introduction to the Study of the Ancient Near East,* trans. D. Schley (Grand Rapids: Eerdmans, 1994 [1985]), 112–13.

(e.g., Pss 103:19; 123:1), and it is the privileged place of God open only to his heavenly council (e.g., Ps 82:1), while the earth alone is the appropriate domain of humanity (Ps 115:16). The motives of the tower builders therefore are as sinister as their predecessors who desired power (3:6; 6:1–4).

The builders confess their intentions as twofold: (1) to make for themselves a "name" and (2) thereby to avoid being "scattered." They want to "empower" themselves, as we moderns say. These are interdependent goals, though the latter expresses their root fear, which has incited them to build. "Name" *(šēm)* and "scattering" *(pûṣ),* as we have seen, are integral ideas in the narrative.[187] They appear for the first time in the mouths of the builders themselves, echoing the antediluvian "men of renown *[name]*" in 6:4 and countering the postdiluvian command of 9:1 ("fill the earth"). "Make" and "name" are also proleptic of God's promise to "make" of Abraham a great nation and to magnify his "name" (12:2–3). The striking difference between the two examples lies in how the "name" is achieved. Reflexive "ourselves" and "for themselves" highlight the self-interested and independent efforts of the Babelites,[188] but for Abraham the Lord bestows the blessing of reputation as a gracious gift. As the Babel narrative unveils, the "name" they achieve, however, is only "Babel" ("muddle"!). "Man certainly did not expect his project to take such a turn. He did not anticipate that the name he wanted to make for himself would refer to a place of noncommunication."[189]

(3) Divine Inspection (11:5)

[5]But the LORD came down to see the city and the tower that the men were building.

Upon man's misdirected efforts at establishing his self-sufficiency (vv. 3–4), the narrative describes the reaction of God (vv. 5–8). Here the literary structure and concomitantly the mood of the discourse turns. The contrast "*but* the LORD . . ." highlights the divine interference in their efforts and the redirection that God will impose. Unlike the flood event, where God's anger is stirred and the measures taken are extreme, here we encounter a God who responds to human frailty as he did in the garden fiasco (3:22). With a gentler

[187] Although the Heb. word for "name" occurs but twice in the narrative (vv. 4,9), here we are speaking of the familiar sound play of שֵׁם ("name") with שָׁם ("there") and שָׁמַיִם ("heaven"). The term פּוּץ occurs twice more in v. 9 (cf. 10:18), and the idea of dispersal (using different vocabulary) appears already in 9:19; 10:5,25,32.

[188] Note also the use of reflexive לָהֶם twice in v. 4.

[189] J. Ellul, *The Meaning of the City,* trans. D. Pardee (Grand Rapids: Eerdmans, 1970), 18. Babel would also be a fitting name for our "postmodern" world of pluralism, deconstructionism, and therefore "noncommunication," which declares the autonomy of text and reader and sets meaning afloat in a sea of uncertainty. Revolt against divine and absolute truth has fated lost humanity to wander aimlessly and alone in a silent, chaotic world.

hand and a concern for the consequences of human folly, the divine will sets in motion the circumstances that will stop the venture.

The narrative's penchant for irony is nowhere any stronger than in this verse, whose sad message is told in an entertaining style. The necessary descent of God and the humanness of the enterprise, "that the men were building," shows the escapade for what it was—a tiny tower, conceived by a puny plan and attempted by a pint-sized people. God's lofty viewpoint ("see") must be related to the previous reference to the tower's reach for the "heavens," where the divine abides. Psalm 2 is explicit about God's attitude toward such mortal schemes, "The One enthroned in heaven laughs; the LORD scoffs at them" (2:4). There the rebuke regards the Gentile conspiracy to overthrow Israel's king; here the aspiration is more ambitious. God's tempered remarks only point up the childish character of their lark.

The frailty of their engineering is marked by the description of the builders; they are *bĕnê hāʾādām*—"the sons of mankind" ("men"). The generic term *ʾādām* and the idiomatic use of *bēn* ("son") particularizes the *human* condition of the builders.[190] The alliteration of the *b* sound in the full clause *bānû bĕnê hāʾādām* ("the men were building") shows their enterprise to be equally mortal, that is, perishable. The edifice can hardly outlast the mortals who build it, for such is the perpetual condition of man's endeavors at sovereignty. The language here repeats 6:1–4, where the cohabitation of the "sons of God" and the "daughters of men" results only in the abbreviation of human life (6:3).

(4) Stopping Babel (11:6–7)

[6]The LORD said, "If as one people speaking the same language they have begun to do this, then nothing they plan to do will be impossible for them. [7]Come, let us go down and confuse their language so they will not understand each other."

11:6 Now the Lord speaks his mind on the matter. The divine commentary echoes largely what the reader has already learned. The narration (v. 1) has taken its cue from the divine contemplation, which observes that humanity has the "same [one] language, all of them" (v. 6).[191] But the heavenly commentary brings out what only was inferred before; by virtue of their common language they are also "one people" *(ʿam ʾeḥad)*. This is the first occurrence of "people" *(ʿam)* in Genesis rather than "nation" *(gôy)*, which dominates the Table of Nations. "People" commonly emphasizes kinship ties (e.g., 14:16; 23:7,11–13), whereas "nation" tends to indicate geographic and political rela-

---

[190] *IBHS* § 9.5.3b.

[191] וְשָׂפָה אַחַת לְכֻלָּם, rendered by the NRSV "they have all one language."

tions.[192] By this word alone the narrative has strongly contrasted the situation at Shinar with the plurality of nations the table exhibits. The "one people" is the concern of God. Communication with its comforts has become their entanglement, for it has left them as a single people rather than the diversity of peoples the blessing had portended.

"Nothing they plan to do will be impossible for them" places the divine foreboding openly before the reader. The weight of the issue lies beyond the present failure to what may yet come of it (v. 6). "Nothing" is inclusive as was the case in 6:5, which detailed the depravity of the antediluvian heart.[193] The infrequent terms "plan" and "impossible" (NIV "thwarted") occur in tandem just once more in Job 42:2. The patriarch there admits that the Lord's blueprint for life is preeminent. This lesson discovered through the hard experience of Job was one the Shinarites were about to apprehend.

That something different is happening or about to happen at Shinar is indicated by the divine opposition to their innovation ("begun to do," v. 6).[194] There is a shared lexical item (*ʿāśâ*, "make, do") between the stated intention of the builders (v. 4) and the apprehensions heard in the Lord's dialogue (v. 6), pointing up the relationship of the two. "Let us make *[naʿăśeh]*a name for ourselves" as to their undertaking is imitated by the appearance twice of "to do" *(laʿăśôt)* regarding their potential. The intervention of the Lord was a preventive measure as well as a penalty.

This is reminiscent of the garden, where the first couple's expulsion is designed to hinder what may happen if given access to the tree of life (3:22). The mutual occurrence of intradivine dialogue ("one of us"/"let us") encourages the reading of Genesis 11 in light of the garden events (3:22; cf. 1:28). In the garden the alarm was the newly acquired knowledge of the disobedient couple ("knowing good and evil"), whereas here the prospects of the Babelites' ingenuity and collective will forecast trouble. In both instances it can hardly be that the heavens trembled because the "advancement" of mankind in any way threatened celestial rule. But, on the contrary, God was troubled over the injurious consequences that would fall upon the human family if left unchecked.

11:7 Verse 7 presents God's ultimate mimicry of the towerites: "Come, let us go down and confuse their language" (cf. vv. 3–4). We have spoken

[192] This is not always the case since "people" and "nation" can be used interchangeably in parallel constructions (e.g., 17:16), but the customary use of the possessive suffix with "people" (e.g., "my people") versus the seldom-used possessive with "nation" shows the prevalent difference in the terms. See Speiser, "'People' and 'Nation' of Israel," 157–63.

[193] We refer to כֹּל ("every, all") in both passages.

[194] The previous occasions of חלל ("begin") in Gen 1–11 suggest a new direction (4:26; 6:1; 9:20; 10:8).

already of the inversion of the Hebrew letters in the words "let us build" (v. 3) and "let us confuse" (v. 7), indicating the divine reversal of their lot. Here "confuse" *(bālal)* sets up the following pun concerning the name of the site ("Babel"). Confusion of language results in an absence of "understanding" that in turn condemns their project.

(5) Scattered Peoples (11:8–9)

8So the LORD scattered them from there over all the earth, and they stopped building the city. 9That is why it was called Babel—because there the LORD confused the language of the whole world. From there the LORD scattered them over the face of the whole earth.

11:8 Babel's culture of "power" was now fragmented, permitting the diverse groups to realize their blessed potential, though admittedly by God's initiative alone. The building enterprise spontaneously dissipated as a result of the builders' dispersal. When read later as a commentary on Mesopotamian empires, the Babel story showed that the will of God superseded the designs of Gentile rule. They had not a heavenly directive, but rather a heavenly disgust.

Once "scattered," the people of the plain can regain only through submission the security that Adam and Eve once enjoyed in the garden. That resignation to the command of God can come about only through the appointed patriarch Abram, who is called from among their own: Shem → Peleg → Abram. It was true of later Israel as well that the Gentiles must submit to the rule of God through an appointed vessel—Israel and its king.[195]

11:9 The narrative comes full circle with this verse, which presents the consequences of the tower event ("Therefore"). Now the people of Shinar are depicted in disarray. The parade indication of their changed situation is the new appellation "Babel." This verse brings together the key interpretive elements we have discovered in the account. "Confused," "name," "whole world/earth," "language," "there/from there," and "scattered" occur again as a crowning crescendo. The author's symmetrical story has contributed to the reader's sense that the tower awaits only to topple.

Naming a place or person based on popular etymology is common in the Bible and in Genesis in particular.[196] Here we have the familiar naming formula where "call" *(qārā')*and "name" *(šēm)* appear jointly, often preceded by "therefore/that is why" *('al kēn)*. Thus the formula reads, "That is why he/she/

---

[195] E.g., Gen 49:10; Exod 19:5–6; Deut 2:25; 4:6; 15:6; 20:10–12; 32:43; Ps 2:10–12; Isa 11:10.

[196] BDB (896) has nineteen times for the naming of places in Genesis.

they called his/her/its name X."[197] Usually the occasion for the naming is an incident at birth or a momentous event at a specific location. The etymology is not linguistic but derived by the similarity in sound between the name and the incident in view. In the case of "Babel" *(babel)* the name is phonologically related to the verb "confused" *(bālal),* which occurs twice in the story (vv. 7,9). We remarked earlier that the Babylonians themselves understood their city to mean "gate of the gods" *(bāb-ili).* Our author's sarcasm bites at the Babelites' deluded aim of obtaining a "name" through the erection of the city (v. 4). We also point out the intriguing coincidence of *Enuma Elish,* where following the building of Babylon for the hero Marduk the assembly of the deities proclaims the fifty names of the god. Biblical Genesis shows that the appropriate name of Babylon—Babble—is no commendation!

The significance of the Babel story for the Mosaic community would speak to the critical role its father Abraham played in the world of nations. Israel, as his successor, must take up the same role, serving as the appointed vehicle of God's salvation among the Gentiles. Moreover, Babel exemplified the threat that the indigenous Canaanite cities presented for Israel. These cities were perceived as overwhelming fortresses (Num 13:28; Deut 1:28; 3:5; 9:1); nevertheless they would fall before the judgment of God. Any culture, such as Babel, that defied the moral will of God would meet with the same end as the tower.

Canaan's cities no doubt were attractive to the Israelite sons of Egypt's slaves. It was the temptation of idolatry, a blatant rejection of the Ten Words, that especially spelled disaster for the Israelites. They were forewarned that their adoption of idolatry meant the "scattering" of the populace among the nations and the ruin of their cities.[198] Just as the scattering meant ultimately the purging of the Babelites and their fulfillment of God's will to "fill the earth," the diaspora of Israel resulted in their final cleansing from idolatry. It was the exile that would pave the way for the ultimate restoration of the people whose affections once more would be turned toward their Sovereign Lord (Deut 30:3).

---

[197] The exact formula used in 11:9 occurs with "Abel Mizraim," 50:11. Variations on the formula are many. See similar language for others, e.g., "Zoar," 19:22; "Edom," 25:30; "Levi," 29:34; "Galeed," 31:48; and "Succoth," 33:17. In Gen 1–11 cf. the naming of "Eve," 3:20; "Enoch," 4:17, "Seth," 4:25; "Enosh," 4:26; "Seth," 5:3; "Noah," 5:29; and "Nimrod," 10:9.

[198] Deut 4:27; 28:64; 30:3 use the same term פּוּץ (= "scatter") as Gen 11; cf. Num 10:35. Also see Lev 26:33 ("scatter" = זרה) for the same warning.

SECTION OUTLINE

VI. SHEM'S FAMILY LINE (11:10–26)
1. Shem "After the Flood" (11:10–11)
2. Shem's Sons (11:12–26)
   (1) Arphaxad through Eber (11:12–17)
   (2) Peleg through Nahor (11:18–25)
   (3) Terah's Sons (11:26)

VI. SHEM'S FAMILY LINE (11:10–26)

The Babel account (11:1–9) is not the end of early Genesis. If it were, the story would conclude on the sad note of human failure. But as with earlier events in Genesis 1–11, God's grace once again supersedes human sin, insuring the continued possibilities of the promissory blessings (1:28; 9:1). The genealogical record of Shem is presented a second time (10:21–31; 11:10–26; also 1 Chr 1:17–27), though in a different form, to show that the orderly creation of God, reaching back to Adam/Seth (chap. 5), continues despite the sin at Shinar (11:1–9). The scaffolding of human pride would be dismantled by the erection of the Shemite line that culminates in obedient Abraham, who likewise is found in the region of Shinar. Abraham would prove to be the nations' deliverance.

The genealogy is headed by the *tōlĕdōt* rubric, tying this section into the larger framework of the book by linking it to the preceding occasions of the formula that highlight the primary figures of Adam and Noah (5:1; 6:9; 10:1). Shem's line forms an important bridge between the antediluvian and postdiluvian worlds, for it was "two years after the flood" that the genealogy begins (11:10b). The genealogy of 11:10–26 imitates the pattern of Genesis 5 in several ways, indicating its continuum with the antediluvian world.[1] By this means Genesis 1–11 showed the unity and purposeful aim of God's salvific enterprise for humanity.

1. Both Genesis 5 and 11 have the linear form of genealogical descent. We have commented elsewhere that the linear pattern distinguishes the elect offspring of the human family, which narrows the text upon the key descendant, Abraham. By linkage with the Sethite line in chap. 5, which reaches back to creation with the beginnings of Adam (vv. 3–32), the Shemite genealogy provides a coherence as well as progression in the appointed lineage of blessing: Adam → Noah → Terah (Abram). When considered together, Abraham is tenth

[1] For a discussion of a proposed "Toledoth Book" and its relationship to 11:10–26, see 5:1a. Also for the issues of genealogy and chronology, see chap. 5 discussion.

from Shem and twentieth from Adam. This means that Shem is at the midpoint of the antediluvian generations. Abraham is also in the seventh position from "Eber," the celebrated ancestor of the Hebrews.[2] Eber himself is fourteenth (7 x 2), counting from Adam.

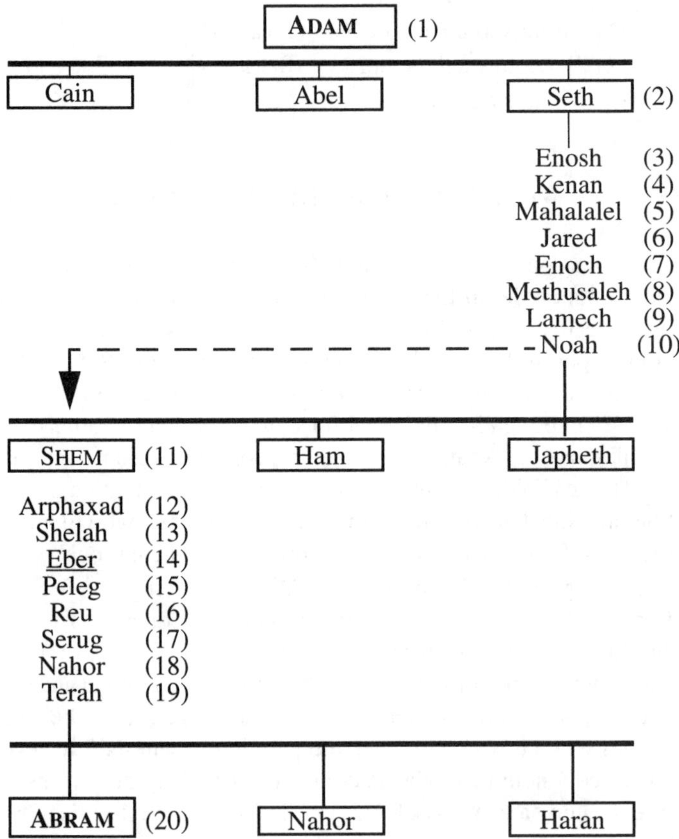

2. Both Genesis 5 and 11 possess the same vocabulary and literary pattern in naming each patriarch and announcing the birth of his descendant.[3] Also

[2] See J. M. Sasson for importance of the number seven for biblical genealogies, esp. Genesis ("A Genealogical 'Convention' in Biblical Chronology?" *ZAW* 90 [1978]: 171–85, esp 176). The Greek tradition has the additional name Kainan (Cainan) after Arphaxad, which if followed would alter this by one. This would mean that Terah holds the tenth position, matching Noah in chap. 5; and Abraham, twenty-first (7x3) from creation while retaining Abraham as seventh from Eber.

[3] Some commentators observe that the Sethite and Shemite genealogies both possess ten names, but it is achieved only by counting Noah at the head or Abram at the end in the Shemite line. The actual count is nine names in 11:10–26, from Shem to Terah (see more at 11:12–26).

they share the refrain "sons and daughters," reflecting the blessing of procreation (1:28; 9:1). In each case the linear march, naming one descendant only for each generation, ends with the naming of three sons (5:32; 11:26). Moreover, in each listing the chosen person of the three offspring is cited first: Shem and Abram.[4] It is apparent that the author has arranged the genealogical materials of chaps. 5 and 11 to be considered in concert so as to produce a sense of constancy and permanency. The flood's intrusion as a disruptive threat to the promissory blessing is punctuated by the apparent unity of the Seth–Shem line.

This literary order of genealogy-flood-genealogy has a parallel in the Sumerian King List, where the event of the flood interrupts its listing of the kings.[5] In the case of the biblical arrangement, the flood story actually occurs as an extended parenthesis within the overarching genealogy of chap. 5, since Seth's genealogy finishes only after the flood with the formulaic death notice of Noah at 9:29. Hence, while the threats of the flood and Babel are alarming, the return to the predictable pattern of genealogical descent after each (9:29; 11:10–26) shows that God's purposes for humanity are back on course. Human sin, despite its damaging severity, cannot undermine the determined progress of God's salvation for his people. This is notably true for 11:10–26 since it points to Abraham, whereas chap. 5 is followed by the cataclysmic event of the flood.

Yet remarkable variations in pattern exist between Shem's genealogy and Seth's that contribute to the author's theological interests. (1) Genesis 11 does not give the total years of the patriarch's life, and (2) more important, it omits the death formula that is a constant in chap. 5 ("and then he died").[6] The genealogies in Genesis have the effect of looking ahead by pushing forward the narrative stories. Chapter 11's omissions make for a swifter sequence of names, which propels the reader quickly down the line to "Abram." This is all

---

[4] Noah: Shem, Ham, and Japheth (5:32)//Terah: Abram, Nahor, Haran (11:26). Adam also fathered three sons: Cain, Abel, and Seth. G. Wenham observes that the fathering of three sons ties together the critical genealogical figures of the primeval history: Adam//Noah//Terah (*Genesis 1–15,* WBC [Waco: Word, 1987], 248).

[5] See "Genesis 1–11 and Ancient Literature" in the Introduction.

[6] See R. S. Hess, "The Genealogies of Genesis 1–11 and Comparative Literature," *Bib* 70 (1989): 243–44:

Gen 5 And PN_1 lived *x* years and begot PN_2
And PN_1 lived, after he begot PN_2, *y* years
And he (PN_1) begot sons and daughters
And all the days of PN_1 were $x + y$ years, and he died.

Gen 11 And PN_1 lived *x* years and begot PN_2
And PN_1 lived, after he begot PN_2, *y* years
And he (PN_1) begot sons and daughters.

Among the versions the SP fills out the pattern in chap. 11 by including the total years of the patriarch's life span; also both the SP and the LXX regularly have the death notice ("and he died").

the more so in comparison to the sluggish account of Shem's line in chap. 10 that is arrested at the naming of Joktan's descendants, where thirteen tribes are listed. This "streamlined" approach to the postdiluvian world brings the patriarchal family closer to the flood and tower events. It projects the continuity that the framework of Genesis 1–11 seeks to convey.

This startling omission of the death notice, however, does more than push the narrative ahead. It also is consistent with the optimism that the new era of Abraham brought. The absence of "death" is the author's reflection on God's patience toward sinful man.[7] The promise of God's new dealings with postdiluvian humanity (8:21–22) encouraged such hope. There is no catastrophe following the Babel calamity as with the flood; rather there is the appearance of Abraham's family. Despite this exception to death in chap. 11, the apostle Paul assumed death had its way from "Adam to Moses" (Rom 5:14), an allusion to Genesis 5 and 11. The Genesis author's optimism was founded on the arrival of Abraham, but for Paul the reign of death's terror was finally undone by the arrival of the last Adam, Jesus Christ.

We have said that the Shemite line of 11:10–26 looks back to the antediluvian world by the linkage with chap. 5. We can also add that it fits nicely into the postdiluvian world by anticipating the patriarchal history to come. The *tōlědōt* mirrors the introduction to the genealogies of Noah's three sons in the Table of Nations, who fathered sons "after the flood" (10:1; 11:10b).

More important, "Shem" is the chosen recipient of Noah's invocation for blessing (9:26) and therefore receives special recognition by the offering of two complementary genealogies (10:21–31; 11:10–26). For the immediate context the Shemite line of 11:10–26 reaches back to 10:21–31, which speaks of the enigmatic event of Peleg's time when "the earth was divided" (10:25). Peleg is the dividing point in the two recensions of Shem's lineage. Chapter 10 follows Joktan's branch and leaves off Peleg's family. As discussed earlier, the nonelect family of Joktan is dispensed with first (segmented genealogy), and chap. 11 omits Joktan altogether and traces the Peleg line down to the key character Abraham (11:26). As we observed in our remarks at chap. 10, the Joktan line is followed by the Babel failure, while chap. 11's giving of the Shemite family by Peleg results in the hero Abraham. This highlights the difference in the two inner branches of the Shemite family—one leading to disgrace and the other to grace.

There is more. The very name "Shem" *(šem)* creates an irony in the narrative, a genealogical link, following as it does on the heels of the Babel foolishness. At 11:1–9 we observed that the Babel story is replete with paronomasia and verbal irony. We heard this in the sound play of the letters *šm* for "name" *(šēm),* "there/from there" *(šām/miššām),* and "heavens" *(šāmayim).* The gen-

[7] See H. G. Stigers, *A Commentary on Genesis* (Grand Rapids: Zondervan, 1976), 132.

ealogical record of "Shem" in the opening words picks up and exaggerates this play by the repetition and juxtaposition of "Shem" *(šem)* in the Hebrew text (11:10a).[8]

And further the irony of the name points up the faithfulness of God's intentions for creation. God already had a *šm* ("Shem"/name) for the human family.[9] There was no need for the misguided efforts of the Babelites to secure a "name" for themselves. Their security would rest in the offspring of the Shemite family as Noah had anticipated (9:26). Shem's genealogical tree demonstrates this by tracing his descendants to the name "Abram," who becomes the appointed recipient of the ancient blessing by which he obtains a "name" (12:1–3). The disruption at Babel is a significant setback to be sure, but not one that escapes the forethought of God. After God disperses the peoples, the Shemite genealogy reinstates the continuum of God's blessing by bringing to the forefront the elect family announced in chap. 5 (via Seth).

We are told of Noah's death (9:29), but we do not hear of the death of Shem or his brothers. Not until the notice of Terah's passing does the text repeat chap. 5's requiem for the patriarchs ("and he [Terah] died in Haran," 11:32). This verse most likely comes, as did the announcement of Noah's death, from the same or similar source(s) as those of 5:3–32 and 11:10–26, but the author has chosen to announce Terah's death at 11:32 just prior to Abraham's call (12:1–3). From a literary perspective the notice of Terah's death under the Terah *tōlĕdōt* (11:27–25:11) established the new era of Abraham just as Noah's passing marked the beginnings of the postdiluvian world. It transitions the primeval history ending with Terah to the patriarchal period beginning with Abraham.

1. Shem "After the Flood" (11:10–11)

10This is the account of Shem.

Two years after the flood, when Shem was 100 years old, he became the father of Arphaxad. 11And after he became the father of Arphaxad, Shem lived 500 years and had other sons and daughters.

In the Table of Nations the author distinguished the Shem line from his brothers by placing it last, the common technique of Genesis for marking out the elect line (see 10:21 discussion). He is identified in the table as the progen-

[8] The NASB shows this: "These are the records of the generations of *Shem. Shem* was . . ." (italics added).

[9] R. Robinson, "Literary Functions of the Genealogies of Genesis," *CBQ* 48 (1986): 603.

itor of those descended from "Eber" (10:21), the ancestor of the Hebrews.[10] In the case of chap. 11 no such special steps are taken to distinguish the role of Shem. The linear format of its genealogy is sufficient. What appears uppermost for the role of Shem is the announcement that his line commences the era "after the flood."

11:10 Shem fathers Arphaxad "two years" following the flood. This chronological notice presents a problem with 5:32, where Noah begets Shem at 500 years of age and the flood occurs at Noah's age of 600 years (7:6,11), which would make Shem 100 years old at the time of the flood. Here, however, v. 10 indicates that Shem was 100 years old "two years" beyond the deluge. This would mean that Shem was born at Noah's age of 502, and Shem fathered Arphaxad at Noah's 602d year. A number of proposed resolutions have been presented.[11] The NIV (and NRSV) reads at 5:32, "*After* Noah was 500 years old, he became the father of Shem, Ham and Japheth" [italics added].[12] This resolves the tension by permitting Shem's birth at Noah's 502d year; thus Shem was 100 years old (Noah's 602nd year) two years after the flood.[13] The difficulty here is that the rendering of the Hebrew most naturally in the context of chap. 5 reads "Noah was 500 years old when he fathered Shem, Ham, and

[10] Although the term "Hebrew" (and Israel) does not occur in the genealogies of chaps. 10–11, "Eber" may be said to represent the Hebrews (cf. 11:16). "Eber" (עֵבֶר) essentially is a proxy for the name "Hebrew" (עִבְרִי), from which it was formed with the gentilic ending *-î* (see 10:21). The etymologies of both Eber and Hebrew are disputed. For a discussion see our comments at 10:21.

[11] E.g., C. F. Keil (*Biblical Commentary on the Old Testament. Vol. 1. The Pentateuch,* trans. J. Martin [Edinburgh: T & T Clark, 1866; reprint, Grand Rapids: Eerdmans, n.d.], 177) has the "two years" included rather than added to the sum of the chronological number. J. Skinner argues that the troublesome phrase is a late gloss intended to make Arphaxad's birth the beginning of a new era rather than the flood (*A Critical and Exegetical Commentary on Genesis,* ICC [Edinburgh: T & T Clark, 1910], 232).

[12] U. Cassuto takes Noah's age of 500 years (5:32) as a reference to the birth of Japheth, whom he takes as the firstborn (*A Commentary on the Book of Genesis. Part II. From Noah to Abraham, Genesis VI:9–XI 32,* trans. I. Abrahams [Jerusalem: Magnes, 1964], 260–61). Shem then was born two years later (Noah 502), making Shem 98 years old when the flood began. "After the flood" (cf. 9:28) Cassuto takes as a technical reference to the cessation of the forty-day rain, not the entire event, which would include the drying period. Thus, by this reckoning Shem was 100 years old two years after the rains ceased falling. This viewpoint hinges, however, on taking Shem as the second born, which we do not believe can stand up (see our discussion at 10:21).

[13] F. H. Cryer presents the novel view that the flood narrative (chaps. 6–8) possesses actually two separate but parallel chronologies, involving a 360-day scheme and a 370-day chronology, which when added together constitute two solar years (i.e., 730 days; "The Interrelationships of Gen 5,32; 11,10–11 and the Chronology of the Flood (Gen 6–9)," *Bib* 66 [1985]: 241–61). These "two years" explain the cryptic reference in 11:10 and the birth of Shem at Noah's 502d year in 5:32. This reconstruction depends on the conjecture that there are two parallel chronologies in chaps. 6–8, which cannot be satisfactorily demonstrated, and that we are to suppose that Shem was born at Noah's 502d year (5:32).

Japheth" (REB, NKJV, NASB; see discussion at 5:32).[14] The recommendation that the figures are rounded numbers for approximation is reasonable, but not altogether satisfying.[15]

11:11 Shem fathers Arphaxad at 100 years old and lives 500 more years, giving him a shorter life span than that of Noah (950 years, 9:29). Abraham was also 100 years when he fathered the appointed son, Isaac (21:5); Ishmael was born at the age of 86 years (16:16). What we learn from the relative ages of the patriarchs is the dwindling life spans of the patriarchs following the flood. Arphaxad's life (438) is only two-thirds of his father Shem (600), and Peleg's life (239) is about half of his father Eber (464).

The same phenomenon occurs in the Sumerian King List, where the reigns after the flood, though still enormous compared to the biblical numbers, are dramatically shorter. Chapter 11 then depicts a shorter stretch of time from Shem to Abram than the Sethite line from Adam to Noah. The numbers of the concluding members in the Shemite line are like those of the patriarchs. Abraham's grandfather Nahor lives only 138 years (11:24–25), significantly less than Abraham's 175 years. By this means the transition from the antediluvian period to the focal concern of Genesis, namely, the patriarchal period, is completed. Theologically, the difference in life span between chaps. 5 and 11 shows the realization of 6:3, which speaks of 120 years as humanity's allotment. This the author implies is the consequence of encroaching human sin. Granted, sin has not altogether derailed creation's promise of procreation, but it has altered the power of life so as to diminish its longevity.

Related to the numbers of 11:10–26 are the problems they create for the chronology of the patriarchs, particularly Abraham, and their ancestors. As the numbers stand in the Hebrew text (MT), Abraham was born 292 years after the flood.[16] This would mean that Noah and Abraham were contemporaries as were Shem and Eber with Jacob.[17] Since Shem's life span was 600

---

[14] Or, "When Noah was 500 years old . . ." (NAB, NJB, NJPS).

[15] E.g., G. C. Aalders, *Genesis,* BSC, vol. 1, trans. W. Heynen (Grand Rapids: Regency Reference/Zondervan, 1981), 144, and N. H. Sarna, בראשית *Genesis,* JPST (Philadelphia: Jewish Publication Society, 1989), 85.

[16] This is figured by adding all the numbers of the ages of the patriarchs, from Shem to Terah, when their first son was born. This and the following calculations are derived from the tables provided in D. V. Etz, "The Numbers of Genesis V 3–31: A Suggested Conversion and Its Implications," *VT* 43 (1993): 171–89, esp. 188–89.

[17] Noah was 600 years old at the time of the flood (7:6), and Abraham was born 292 years after the flood, meaning that Abraham was born 892 years after Noah's birth. Since Noah died at 950 years of age (9:29), Abraham would be his young contemporary. According to Jacob's calculations he was born 452 years from the year of the flood, when Shem was 98 years old. Since Shem lived to 600 years of age, he was 550 years old at the birth of Jacob. Eber, too, was his contemporary. Jacob was born 385 years after Eber, and Eber lived 464 years.

years, and his son Arphaxad was born at 100 years and Abraham was born 290 years after Arphaxad (= 390), given that Abraham died at 175 years (= 565), Shem's life span would actually exceed the death of Abraham by thirty-five years.[18]

Although some may not consider this situation problematic, most think that such overlaps are contrary to the progression of time implied in the text. A period of 292 years from the flood to the birth of Terah's first son would appear too short.[19] Apparently to ease such tensions the Samaritan Pentateuch (SP) and Greek (LXX) traditions present different calculations.[20] The SP (unlike the MT, LXX) gives the total life span of each patriarch, as in chap. 5, and the Greek (unlike the MT, SP) has the additional generation "Kainan" after Arphaxad. More important, the SP and the LXX add a hundred years to the age of each patriarch (i.e., Arphaxad-Serug) at the time of his first son's birth.[21] By making each patriarch older when his first son is born, the aggregate effect is the distancing of Abraham's birth from Shem's birth by 1,040 (SP) or 1,170 (LXX) years rather than the 390 years of the MT. This then leaves only Abraham's near ancestors alive at the time of his birth, and none outlives him.

---

[18] This is true also of Shelah and Eber, who respectively would outlive Abraham by three and sixty-four years.

[19] See Aalders, *Genesis,* 258.

[20] For discussion of the divergencies see R. W. Klein, "Archaic Chronologies and the Textual History of the Old Testament," *HTR* 67 (1974): 255–63, and Etz, "The Numbers of Genesis V 3–31: A Suggested Conversion and Its Implications," 171–89; also C. Westermann, *Genesis 1–11: A Commentary,* trans. J. J. Scullion (Minneapolis: Augsburg, 1984), 560, and Wenham, *Genesis 1–15,* 251. Both Klein and Etz propose that neither MT nor the versions (SP, LXX) is the "original" chronology (see chap. 5 discussion).

[21] Thus, e.g., Arphaxad fathers a son at 35 years in the MT but 135 in the SP and LXX. Exceptions to this are (1) Shem and Terah, whose ages at the birth of their first son are not changed, and (2) Nahor, whose age is increased by 50 years in the SP and LXX. The SP compensates for the increase by subtracting years from the remaining years of the patriarch. So Arphaxad lived 403 years after the birth of his son according to the MT but only 303 in the SP. This results in the MT and SP having the same number of total years (SP's 438 years). The Greek tradition, however, generally has higher numbers all the way around.

Patriarch	MT		SP			LXX	
	A	B	A	B	C	A	B
Shem	100	500	100	500	600	100	500
Arphaxad	35	403	135	303	438	135	430
Kainan	—	—	—	—	—	130	330
Shelah	30	403	130	303	433	130	330
Eber	34	430	134	270	404	134	370
Peleg	30	209	130	109	239	130	209
Reu	32	207	132	107	239	132	207
Serug	30	200	130	100	230	130	200
Nahor	29	119	79	69	149	79	129
Terah	70	135*	70	75	145	70	135

*Derived from 11:32

A: Age of patriarch at first son's birth

B: Remaining years of patriarch's life

C: Total number of years (only in SP)

The MT shows itself to be the more reliable text because of its difficulties. The SP and the LXX reflect attempts to harmonize the ages of the patriarchs and perhaps to correlate the span of 11:10–26 with the longer period of Adam to Noah in 5:3–32. The LXX has lengthened the total era between Adam and Abraham by fourteen hundred years, perhaps trying to bring Jewish and Egyptian chronologies closer together. In the Greek system the patriarchs die in about the same order as their births, and their ages at the birth of the first son gradually diminish from Adam down to Terah. It would seem that the LXX is giving the system a firmer "rationale" for the Genesis chronologies.[22] This still

[22] So G. Larsson, "The Chronology of the Pentateuch: A Comparison of the MT and LXX," *JBL* 102 (1983): 401–9.

leaves us with the difficulties of the MT just cited, and there is no simple solution. If the genealogies in chaps. 5 and 11 are not exhaustive (see chap. 5 discussion), the genealogies may give the appearance of a compressed period. Perhaps other undetectable factors are at work that have created the problematic circumstances noted by both ancient and modern interpreters.

2. Shem's Sons (11:12–26)

Including "Shem," the list gives the names of nine generations, whereas Genesis 5 presents ten generations from Adam to Noah. The LXX compensates for this by the additional name "Kainan" between Arphaxad and Shelah, but this is clearly secondary.[23] More likely the absence of the tenth generation points the reader to "Abram," who follows Terah as the anticipated "tenth" member.[24] By accomplishing the configuration of "ten," the birth of Abraham indicates a completed line of descent, reaching from the flood down to the call of the patriarch. Whereas the Shemite line in the Table of Nations gave special attention to such notable figures as Eber and Peleg (10:21,25), this second genealogy does not. Moreover, whereas the Sethite genealogy paused to comment on the career of Enoch (5:24) and the naming of Noah (5:29), there is no such diversion in 11:10–26. There is no interruption in this compacted line from Shem to Terah.

(1) Arphaxad through Eber (11:12–17)

12When Arphaxad had lived 35 years, he became the father of Shelah. 13And after he became the father of Shelah, Arphaxad lived 403 years and had other sons and daughters.

14When Shelah had lived 30 years, he became the father of Eber. 15And after he became the father of Eber, Shelah lived 403 years and had other sons and daughters.

16When Eber had lived 34 years, he became the father of Peleg. 17And after he became the father of Peleg, Eber lived 430 years and had other sons and daughters.

11:12–13 In the first listing of the Shemite line (10:21–31), "Arphaxad" was treated as the name of a place or tribe (see 10:22). Here the genealogy encourages the reader to view the names *also* as persons, since individuals such as Terah are included. This points up the fluidity of the names among the genealogies of chaps. 10 and 11. An individual and/or the tribe that is derived from that individual can be represented by the one name of the progenitor. In chap. 10 Arphaxad is the third of five sons named (10:22), but here he takes the role of prominence. This shows that either chap. 10 or 11 (or both) has not listed the descendants in

---

[23] "Kainan" may be derived from chap. 4; in any case his numbers are taken from those for the following "Shelah" (11:14–15).

[24] Another way of achieving "ten" names in chap. 11 is by including "Noah" as the head of the Shemite line. Cf. A. Ross, *Creation and Blessing* (Grand Rapids: Baker, 1988), 250.

the order of the firstborn.[25] This we found true of Ham, who regularly occupies the second position though identified as the youngest (9:24). As here, there is but one descendant named in chap. 10 from Arphaxad, that is, Shelah (10:24).

11:14–17 "Shelah" (v. 14) is a common name among the families of Judah (38:5,11,14,26; 46:12; Num 26:20; 1 Chr 2:3; 4:21–23), but there is no site associated with the name, and as a place it remains uncertain. "Eber" (v. 16) strikingly is named without fanfare, although he is the ancestor of the "Hebrews." He has a prominent mention in the Table of Nations (10:21,25) and occupies a significant place as fourteenth from Adam.

(2) Peleg through Nahor (11:18–25)

18When Peleg had lived 30 years, he became the father of Reu. 19And after he became the father of Reu, Peleg lived 209 years and had other sons and daughters.

20When Reu had lived 32 years, he became the father of Serug. 21And after he became the father of Serug, Reu lived 207 years and had other sons and daughters.

22When Serug had lived 30 years, he became the father of Nahor. 23And after he became the father of Nahor, Serug lived 200 years and had other sons and daughters.

24When Nahor had lived 29 years, he became the father of Terah. 25And after he became the father of Terah, Nahor lived 119 years and had other sons and daughters.

11:18–19 With "Peleg" comes the departure point between the two branches of Shem in chaps. 10 and 11. Here the genealogy traces the family of Peleg rather than his brother Joktan (10:25–26). Joktan was the father of Arabian tribes while Peleg is the progenitor of northwest Mesopotamian families. In the Table of Nations the name "Peleg" generates a pun that associates his era with a momentous but now cryptic event: "Because in his time the earth was divided" (see 10:25). When we count Abraham as the tenth member of the Shem line, Peleg occupies the halfway mark (fifth) in the line of Shem. We cannot be certain, but if the folk etymology of 10:25 ties his generation to the tower event, then the dispersion is situated at the midpoint between Shem and the era of Abraham. Another striking feature of Peleg's role is the sudden reduction in the years of his life span (239) compared to his father (464) and grandfather (433). This may underscore that the Peleg era, if it were contemporaneous with the Babel generation, was particularly impacted by the sin of the age.

11:20–25 By tracing the line of Peleg, the author presents Shemite descendants not previously cited. "Reu" (v. 20) cannot be identified with a specific site. The name appears only once in the Old Testament and in Luke's genealogy of Jesus (Luke 3:35). It may be related to "Ruel," meaning "friend of

---

[25] Skinner (*Genesis,* 231), while accepting Arphaxad as the firstborn in 11:10, sees no contradiction since 10:22 mainly concerns geographical matters.

God" or "God is friend," which appears again as the son of Esau (36:4,10–17).[26] Personal names having the element "Reu" are widely attested in the second and first millennia B.C. in Aramaic and Akkadian texts.[27]

"Serug" (v. 22) also occurs only once more, in Luke 3:35. Serug and other relatives of Abraham have names that are also names of Mesopotamian cities. Serug has been related to the neo-Assyrian site *sa-ru-gi,* which is just west of Haran in Upper Mesopotamia. The name possibly is found in a personal name attested during the Sumerian Ur III period (ca. 2000 B.C.).[28]

"Nahor" (v. 24) is the grandfather of Abraham, whose brother bears his name (v. 27). Nahor lived 138 years, a much shorter span than his father Serug (230) or his son Terah (205).[29] The grandson Nahor will play an important role in the life of the patriarchs (22:20–24; 31:53). The city Nahur, located near Haran in northwest Mesopotamia, occurs in a number of ancient Near Eastern texts, including Mari of the early second millennium B.C. Also the personal name Nahurum is attested as early as the Ur III period. Rebekah, the wife of Isaac and mother of Esau and Jacob, is from the "town of Nahor" (24:10) and the granddaughter of Nahor (22:23).

The last name in the listing is "Terah," the patriarch of the Abraham clan. His name heads the Abraham story (11:27–25:11) and therefore is the critical link in the transition from early Genesis to the era of Israel's patriarchs. Terah fathers children at a much later age (seventy years) than his predecessors, who became fathers in their early thirties. This becomes a portent that will haunt the Abraham-Sarah family. The transitional paragraph 11:27–32 makes it explicit that Sarah was barren (11:30), preparing the reader for the tension that dominates the Abraham account (e.g., 15:3). Abraham persisted in his faith and was declared right with God (Rom 4:3,20–23 with Gen 15:5–6). Terah's "seventy" years, as a product of seven and ten, is reminiscent of the seventy nations of chap. 10 and the common use of numeric sevens and tens in chaps. 1–11. If there is any special meaning attached to "seventy," it may be that it distinguishes the propitious moment that Father Abraham comes into the world.

"Terah," as with the names of his ancestors, has also occurred as a place name, Til *(ša)* Turahi, known from neo-Assyrian texts of the ninth century B.C. It was located on the Balikh River near Haran and in the area of the already-mentioned cities Nahur and Sarugi.[30] This northwest region of Upper Mesopotamia became the home of Terah's family, which had migrated from Ur en route to Canaan (11:31) and is the background for the patriarchal narratives. Terah dies in Haran

[26] Also it is the name of Moses' father-in-law (Jethro) in Exod 2:18; Num 10:29. At Gen 25:3 the LXX adds his name to the offspring of Abraham's wife Keturah (see E. A. Knauf, "Ruel," *ABD* 5.693–94).

[27] R. S. Hess, "Reu," *ABD* 5.692.

[28] Hess, "Serug," *ABD* 5.117–18.

[29] The SP, however, has 145 years for Terah (see 11:26 discussion).

[30] P. K. McCarter, Jr., "Terah," *ISBE* 4.792–93.

at 205 years (v. 32). The word "Terah" has been related to *trḥ*, perhaps meaning "ibex, mountain goat," and also *yārēaḥ*, meaning "moon." At Ur and Haran the moon deity was prominent, but recently the association of Terah with the moon god *Têr* of Haran has been rejected.[31] Nevertheless the biblical tradition clearly associates Terah's household with idolatry. Abram's worship of the Lord God is distinguished from Terah's polytheistic life at Ur ("beyond the River") in Josh 24:2. It was out of such a household that Abraham answered the call of God.[32]

(3) Terah's Sons (11:26)

[26]After Terah had lived 70 years, he became the father of Abram, Nahor and Haran.

11:26 Appropriately the final verse of early Genesis concerns the procreation of three children. From the outset God's promissory blessing for the human family (1:28; 9:1,7) has been the ongoing concern of the author. Despite the remarkable threats and detours of eleven chapters, the promise has been kept alive by the forbearance of God. Terah's fathering of three sons at the close of the genealogical record trumpets the hope that awaits the human family through the appointed "seed," Abraham.[33]

As noted earlier, with the Shemite line climaxing in the naming of three, we have the parallel structure of Genesis 5 with Noah fathering Shem, Ham, and Japheth (v. 32). Shem is the eldest son (see 10:21), but Abram, his counterpart, is never said to be the firstborn.[34] If he is the firstborn, then Shem heads the elect lineage, and Abraham as his parallel concludes it. At least, it is safe to say that Shem and Abraham are the prominent figures of their respective households for God's elective purposes and thus are named first in each one's respective trilogy.

---

[31] R. S. Hess, "Terah," *ABD* 6.387–88.

[32] In the fanciful *Book of Jubilees,* Abram chastises his father Terah for his manufacture and worship of false gods: "Why do you worship things that have no spirit in them, for they are the work of *men's* hands?" (*Jub.* 12.5).

[33] E.g., Gen 3:15; 12:7; 13:16; 15:5 (Rom 4:18); 17:7; 21:12,18 (Acts 3:25); 26:24; Rom 4:16; 9:8; Gal 3:16–19; Heb 11:11.

[34] Some reckon that Haran was the eldest and that Abraham as the youngest was not born until sixty years later. This answers the chronological problem of 11:26,32; 12:4 and Stephen's sermon in Acts 7:4. According to the MT, if Abraham is the eldest, Abraham departed from Haran some sixty years before Terah's death, but Stephen indicates that it was not until after his death. The SP has Terah die at 145 years (11:32), suggesting rather that Abraham left Haran upon his father's death. Stephen's sermon in Acts 7:4 and Philo's *On the Migration of Abraham* (177) show that this tradition was wider than the Samaritans. Yet if a Greek variant agreeing with the SP existed, which could be the basis for the comments in Acts and Philo, there is no surviving evidence of it. If the MT is correct, Stephen's statement can still be accounted for by positing that Abraham was born when Terah was 130 years of age: 70 (birth of Haran) + 60 (birth of Abraham) + 75 (Abraham's departure) = 205 years (Terah's death). For textual discussion see J. A. Emerton, "When Did Terah Die (Genesis 11: 32)?" in *Language, Theology, and the Bible: Essays in Honour of James Barr,* ed. S. Ballentine and J. Barton (Oxford: Clarendon, 1994), 170–81.

Abram's name later becomes the source of an important wordplay when his name is changed to "Abraham" (17:5) in connection with the covenant promise of offspring for the patriarch and Sarah.[35] "Abram" is generally interpreted as a combination of "father" *(ʾab)* and "exalted/exaltation" *(rām<rûm)*. The possibilities are many for understanding the name: "he is exalted as to his father," "exalted father," "the father is exalted," and combinations of "my father" understood on the analogy of "Abiram" (*ʾăbîrām; ʾăbî*= "my father," Num 16:1). In the first case the name would refer to the distinction of the person's parentage. "Father" also can be taken as an allusion to God, thus "my father [God] is exalted" would be the sense. "Abarama" (and variants) as a personal name occurs in cuneiform texts from as early as the early second millennium. If the name is derived from Akkadian *ramu,* then the meaning is "he loves the father" or "the father loves him."[36]

"Abraham" is explained in Genesis 17 to mean "father of many nations" (17:5). This name may be taken merely as a phonological variant of "Abram" formed by the inclusion of *h*, a practice attested in Semitic elsewhere. Following the analogy of Abram, we would expect a combination of *ʾab* ("father") and *raham* ("many, multitude"). There is, however, no such root *raham* attested in the Hebrew Bible, though Arabic has *ruhām,* meaning "multitude." Some posit that either Hebrew *raham* or a similar root existed as the basis for the name.[37] "Abraham" is similar in sound to the word "multitude" *(hămôn)* in 17:4–5 and may be the result of a popular etymology.[38] In any case the point of the new name is clear. By another benevolent gesture God affirms his commitment to Abra(ha)m and insures his future.

Abraham's brothers are "Nahor," named after his grandfather (papponymy), and "Haran." Nahor will father twelve sons, nephews of Abraham (22:20–24; see 11:24).[39] Haran should not be confused with the place name Haran *(ḥārān)*. The personal name is derived probably from the compound of *har,* "mountain," and the suffixal element *n.* Though Haran died before the family departed Ur (v. 28), his progeny was important to the life of Terah's family. His son was Lot, who migrated with Terah and later accompanied Abraham in his travels to Canaan (v. 27; 12:4). Haran's daughter Milcah married his brother (her uncle) Nahor (v. 29) and bore eight sons, one of which was Bethuel, who fathered Laban and Rebekah, the wife of Isaac (22:23).[40]

---

[35] "Abram" occurs through 17:5, whereupon "Abraham" becomes standard (except 1 Chr 1:27; Neh 9:7).

[36] Suggested by Sarna, *Genesis,* 86, n. 4.

[37] D. J. Wiseman, "Abraham," *NBD* 5; Wenham, *Genesis 1–15,* 252.

[38] V. Hamilton, *The Book of Genesis Chapters 1–17,* NICOT (Grand Rapids: Eerdmans, 1990), 464, observes that "father of a multitude" would be *ʾab hāmôn* ("Abhamon").

[39] Twelve plays an important role in Abraham's family: twelve rulers are the offspring of Ishmael, Abraham's son, and Jacob fathers the twelve tribes of Israel (25:16; 35:22b–26).

[40] Since 11:27 begins the *tôlĕdôt* of Terah that includes chap. 12, 11:27–32 is treated in vol. 2.

Selected Subject Index

Person Index

Scripture Index